COMPUTER FUNDAMENTALS
AND
PROGRAMMING IN C

Second Edition

Pradip Dey

RCC Institute of Information Technology

Manas Ghosh

RCC Institute of Information Technology

OXFORD

UNIVERSITY PRESS

OXFORD
UNIVERSITY PRESS

Oxford University Press is a department of the University of Oxford.
It furthers the University's objective of excellence in research, scholarship,
and education by publishing worldwide. Oxford is a registered trade mark of
Oxford University Press in the UK and in certain other countries.

Published in India by
Oxford University Press
YMCA Library Building, 1 Jai Singh Road, New Delhi 110001, India

© Oxford University Press 2006, 2013

The moral rights of the author/s have been asserted.

First Edition published in 2006
Second Edition published in 2013
Second impression 2013

All rights reserved. No part of this publication may be reproduced, stored in
a retrieval system, or transmitted, in any form or by any means, without the
prior permission in writing of Oxford University Press, or as expressly permitted
by law, by licence, or under terms agreed with the appropriate reprographics
rights organization. Enquiries concerning reproduction outside the scope of the
above should be sent to the Rights Department, Oxford University Press, at the
address above.

You must not circulate this work in any other form
and you must impose this same condition on any acquirer.

ISBN-13: 978-0-19-808456-3
ISBN-10: 0-19-808456-0

Typeset in Times New Roman
by Pee-Gee Graphics, New Delhi
Printed in India by India Binding House, Noida 201301

Preface to the Second Edition

Evolution of ideas is a never-ending process. New technology and changing needs have a profound influence on computing requirements, which in turn lead to continuous enhancements of the power and scope of computers as well as programming languages.

One of the latest technologies soon to be launched is the 32-core CPUs from Intel and AMD. Intel has named this 32-core processor 'Kelifer', which is a combination of 32 brains that can work for the user at one time. These CPUs will be built around a paradigm that will allow them to have plug-in and add-on abilities. Then there are other possibilities such as gesture-based remote controls and smartphone applications to open car doors.

Another computing application that has had a profound impact on every aspect of our lives is the Internet. Today, more than 2.4 billion people use the Internet, according to Internet World statistics, and the numbers are still growing. Some industries, such as music and newspapers, have been all but destroyed, even as it has created whole new lines of business, such as search engines and social media. The Boston Consulting Group estimated recently that if the Internet were a country, it would rank as the world's fifth-largest economy.

Naturally, then, programming languages are also being updated to keep pace with these technological leaps. C is one of the most widely used programming languages of all time. Its modern standard C99 (an informal name for ISO/IEC 9899:1999) extends the previous version (C90) with new language and library features, and helps programmers make better use of available computer hardware and compiler technology. The new features include inline functions, several new data types, and new header files. Hence, with the new features suggested by the C99 committee, C has expanded its scope and range of applications. With the development of embedded systems, the frontiers of C have moved further, to evolve as a very effective programming language for programming embedded systems.

ABOUT THE BOOK

Computer fundamentals and programming in C is an introductory course at most universities offering engineering and science degrees, and aims to introduce the basic computing and programming concepts to students. The general course objectives are to enable the student to learn the major components of a computer system, know the correct and efficient ways of solving problems, and learn to program in C.

This second edition of *Computer Fundamentals and Programming in C*, designed as a textbook for students of engineering (BE/BTech), computer applications (BCA/MCA), and computer science (BSc), offers an improved coverage of the fundamental concepts of computing and programming. It offers several new topics and chapters, programming updates based on the recommendations proposed by the C99 committee in relevant chapters, and many other useful pedagogical features.

A special effort has been made to simplify existing treatments and better explain concepts with the help of improved illustrations and examples containing appropriate comments. Further, most chapters now include notes, check your progress sections, key terms with brief definitions, frequently asked questions with answers, and project questions. These will aid the reader in understanding the concepts and their practical implementations.

NEW TO THE SECOND EDITION

- C99 features highlighted wherever relevant in the text
- 2 New chapters: Introduction to Software; Internet and the World Wide Web
- Extensive reorganization of the computer fundamentals and functions chapters
- Note, Check Your Progress sections, Key Terms, Frequently Asked Questions, and Project Questions in most of the chapters
- Improved explanation of algorithms and codes, and new in-text examples
- New sections such as working with complex numbers, variable length arrays, searching and sorting algorithms, pointer and const qualifier, and applications of linked lists

EXTENDED CHAPTER MATERIAL

Chapter 1 Extensively rewritten sections on classification of computers, anatomy of a computer, memory revisited, introduction to operating systems, and operational overview of a CPU

Chapter 8 New sections on

- Compilation model of a C program
- Philosophy of main() function
- The concept of Type qualifiers
- How integers are stored in memory

Chapter 10 New sections on different forms of loop and moving out from a nested loop

Chapter 12 News sections on

- Scope, storage class and linkages
- Inline function
- Different sorting and searching methods along with the analysis of time and space complexity

Chapter 13 New sections on

- Pointer and const Qualifier
- Constant parameter
- Returning pointer from a function

COVERAGE

Chapter-wise details of content coverage are as follows:

Chapter 1 traces the history of development of computers. The chapter also identifies the different generations and the various categories of computers. It briefly describes the basic hardware units and software modules in a computer, with particular reference to the personal computer. A brief description on the start-up process of a personal computer is also included.

Chapter 2 presents the concept of number systems. The rules and methods applied in number system conversions are explained and demonstrated with appropriate examples. It then deals with arithmetic operations of addition, subtraction, multiplication, and division of binary numbers with examples. It also describes the various binary codes used in computers.

Chapter 3 introduces Boolean algebra. It defines Boolean variables and the various laws and theorems of Boolean algebra. The formation of Boolean expressions, Boolean functions, and truth tables along with the methods of simplifying Boolean expressions are also demonstrated. It presents the different forms in which Boolean expressions can be expressed and represented.

Finally, the chapter discusses logic gates and explains how these are realized using electronic devices. It also demonstrates how Boolean expressions can be realized using logic gates.

Chapter 4 identifies the different types of software and the various categories of programming languages available. The roles played by the compiler, linker, and loader in the development of programs are highlighted.

Chapter 5 explains the concept of programs and programming. The chapter also defines and explains the key features of algorithms. The significance of an algorithm in developing a program for solving a problem has also been explained. The chapter then discusses some convenient tools and techniques for building and representing algorithms. It also discusses the strategy of problem solving.

Chapter 6 begins with the history of evolution of the Internet and the world wide web. It briefly discusses the nature of information transported and the protocols used within the Internet. It introduces the concept of web page, web browser, web server, IP address, and search engines. The chapter concludes by describing the different types of Internet connections followed by the various applications of the Internet.

Chapter 7 introduces operating systems. It briefly traces the history of development of operating systems. It explains the functions of an operating system and identifies the component of operating systems in general. The chapter discusses the different types of operating systems that exist. Some popular operating systems such as UNIX and MSDOS have been discussed.

Chapter 8 introduces the basic components of C. The keywords and standard data types available in C and the type conversion rules have been discussed. The use of basic operators in C and expressions involving variables and operators has been explained. The basic structure of a standard C program has also been explained. Some common commands used in MSDOS and UNIX to compile and run programs in C have been discussed in this chapter.

Chapter 9 discusses the input and output statements in C that are commonly used for the console. It presents the single character non-formatted input/output functions and the formatted input/output functions scanf() and printf().

Chapter 10 presents the decision and loop constructs available in C as also the special constructs that are mostly used with them. It throws light on the reasons behind the choice of control constructs for problem solving. Several examples have been given to illustrate the use of these constructs.

Chapter 11 discusses arrays and strings. It explains how arrays of different dimensions are initialized, referred to, used, and printed. The available string arrays and string library functions have been dealt in detail with an adequate number of illustrations. The chapter also illustrates how the input and output functions available in C accept and print strings and arrays.

Chapter 12 deals with functions in C. It explains the need of functions in a program. It explains the different components of a function and the method of passing and returning variables in functions. Scope rules and different storage classes have been discussed with examples.

Chapter 13 deals with the concept of pointers. The various features of pointers, including the method of passing pointer variables in functions and other advanced features, have been explained with examples. Multidimensional array handling with pointers has also been discussed.

Chapter 14 presents the user-defined data types: structures, unions, enumerators, and bit fields. These have been explained in detail with the help of examples.

Chapter 15 discusses the file system used in C. The various functions involving input to and output from a file have been discussed with illustrations. Sequential as well as random access methods adopted in writing to and reading from files have been explained in detail.

Chapter 16 highlights some of the advanced features of C such as command-line arguments, bitwise operators, different memory models, and type qualifiers. These features have been discussed with several illustrations. Memory models and special pointers have also been explained.

The appendices contain case studies where the problem is first defined and then the algorithm is developed, based on which the C program is coded. Some sample run results have

been provided for the reader to verify the programs. I contains tables for ASCII codes, number system conversions, escape sequences, operators, data types and data conversion rules, commonly used conversion characters, and format tags. In addition, it provides an exhaustive listing of library functions of C along with programs that depict their use. There is also a section on common problems encountered while writing programs in C.

ACKNOWLEDGEMENTS

We are grateful to a host of readers, who have encouraged us in improving this book by their useful suggestions from time to time. There are no words to express our gratitude to Oxford University Press for their continuous support, suggestions, and assistance while preparing this edition.

Despite our best endeavour to make this edition error free, some may have crept in inadvertently. Comments and suggestions for the improvement of the book are welcome. Please send them to the publisher by logging on to their website www.oup.com or to the authors at pdey.mghosh@gmail.com.

MANAS GHOSH
PRADIP DEY

Preface to the First Edition

C stands out among general-purpose programming languages for its unrivaled mix of portability, power, flexibility, and elegance. The language has block structures, stand-alone functions, a compact set of keywords, and very few restrictions. Like any low-level language, C allows the programmer to manipulate bits, bytes, and memory addresses, among other features. Like any high-level language, C also supports various data types to provide a higher level of abstraction to programmers, thereby making coding easier. C provides features for writing and separately compiling, shorter programs that can be linked together to form a large program. For all these reasons, it is a versatile language suited for projects of various sizes in both systems as well as applications programming.

ABOUT THE BOOK

This book is intended for a one-semester introductory course on computers and programming in C. The first few chapters of the book impart adequate knowledge of number systems, Boolean logic, hardware, and software of computer systems with particular emphasis on the personal computer. The book assumes no prior programming experience in C or any other language. Once the readers grasp the preliminary topics, it then becomes easier for them to delve into the process of creating algorithms for solving problems and implementing them using C.

Throughout the text it has been our endeavor to keep the level of explanations and definitions as lucid as possible. Figures have been included in the text to clarify the discussions on the features of C. Almost all the features of C have been illustrated with examples. Though every attempt has been made to avoid and check errors, we will be grateful to readers if they can point out any that may have crept in inadvertently.

ACKNOWLEDGEMENTS

We express our gratitude to Dr J. Debroy, Principal, RCC Institute of Information Technology, Kolkata, for encouraging us to write this book. We are also grateful to the staff of Oxford University Press for the cooperation, interest, and assistance extended to us for this book. We thank our colleague Mr Manas Sinharoy for assisting us in preparing the manuscript in time. We are also thankful to Mr Tapas Kumar Tunga and Mr P.N. Pathak for extending their services to us during the preparation of the manuscript. We wish to thank Vijay Kumar R. Zanvar and Jayasimha Ananth for the article on pointers and arrays as also Thomas Jenkins for the article on recursion, both of which have served as a guide during the development of this manuscript.

MANAS GHOSH
PRADIP DEY

Features of the Book

Learning Objectives at the beginning of each chapter to focus attention on the major learning outcomes of the chapter

After studying this chapter, the readers will be able to

- analyse the basic structure of a C program
- discuss the commands used in UNIX/Linux and MS-DOS for compiling and running a program in C
- enumerate the various keywords in C

Fig. 14.4 Three members of a union sharing a memory location for a 16-bit machine

Text interspersed with well-illustrated and labelled figures to enable easy understanding of concepts

Updated programming concepts recommended by the C 99 Committee highlighted in the relevant chapters

According to C99, a comment also begins with // and extends up to the next line break. So the above comment line can be written as follows:

```
// A Simple C Program
```

// comments were added for C99 due to their utility and widespread existing practice, especially in dual C and C++ translators.

```
#include <stdio.h>
```

Note

- C uses a semicolon as a statement terminator; the semicolon is required as a signal to the compiler to indicate that a statement is complete.
- All program instructions, which are also called statements, have to be written in lower-case characters.

Note provided after few sections to help impart better understanding of the key points discussed

Check Your Progress modules
to test understanding of
concepts mid-way through
chapters

Check Your Progress

1. What will be the output of the following program?

(a)
```
#include <stdio.h>
int main()
{
    int a=010;
    printf("\n a=%d",a);
```

Numerous examples
interspersed in the
text to illustrate the
use of constructs
and presentation of
programming formats

Example

```
3. int i = 42;
   i++; /* increment contents of i, same as i = i + 1; */
                                 /* i is now 43 */
   i--; /* decrement contents of i, same as i = i - 1; */
                                 /* i is now 42 */
   ++i; /* increment contents of i, same as i = i + 1; */
                                 /* i is now 43 */
   --i; /* decrement contents of i, same as i = i - 1; */
                                 /* i is now 42 */
```

Key Terms with definitions
help to recapitulate the
important concepts learnt
in the chapter

ASCII   It is a standard code for representing characters as numbers and is used on most microcomputers, computer terminals, and printers. In addition to printable characters, the ASCII code includes control characters to indicate carriage return, backspace, etc.

Assembler   It creates the object code.

Associativity   The *associativity* of operators determines the order in which operators of equal precedence are evaluated when they occur in

1. What is the difference between compiling and linking?

Compiler converts each source file into an object file. Linker takes all generated object files, as well as the system libraries that are relevant, and builds an executable file that is stored on disk.

2. What is a bug?

Any type of error in a program is known as *bug*. There are three types of errors that may occur:

Frequently Asked Questions
to address common queries
about programming
concepts and reinforce the
learning

Project Questions to
encourage readers to
learn the application of
concepts

1. Write a program that performs the following. The user inputs a number and then enters a series of numbers from 1 to that number. Your program should determine which number (or numbers) is missing or duplicated in the series, if any. For example, if the user entered 5 as the initial number and then entered the following sequences, the results should be as shown.

```
Input Sequence          Output
------------------      ----------------
1 2 3 4 5               Nothing bad
```

Brief Contents

Contents

Computer Fundamentals

LEARNING **O**BJECTIVES

After studying this chapter, the readers will be able to

- trace the evolution of computers—generations and classification of computers
- explain the basic units of a computer system

- explain the hardware and software of a personal computer
- load an operating system (OS) in a personal computer

1.1 INTRODUCTION—WHAT IS A COMPUTER?

The *Oxford Dictionary* defines a computer as 'an automatic electronic apparatus for making calculations or controlling operations that are expressible in numerical or logical terms'.

The definition clearly categorizes the computer as an electronic apparatus although the first computers were mechanical and electro-mechanical apparatuses. The definition also points towards the two major areas of computer application: data processing and computer-assisted controls or operations. Another important conclusion of the definition is the fact that the computer can perform only those operations or calculations that can be expressed in logical or numerical terms.

A computer is a data processor. It can accept input, which may be either data or instructions or both. The computer remembers the input by storing it in memory cells. It then processes the stored input by performing calculations or by making logical comparisons or both. It gives out the result of the arithmetic or logical computations as output information. The computer accepts input and outputs data in an alphanumeric form. Internally it converts the input data to meaningful binary digits, performs the instructed operations on the binary data, and transforms the data from binary digit form to understandable alphanumeric form.

1.2 EVOLUTION OF COMPUTERS—A BRIEF HISTORY

Computing in the mechanical era

The concept of calculating machines evolved long before the invention of electrical and electronic devices. The first mechanical calculating apparatus was the **abacus**, which was invented in 500 BC in Babylon. It was used extensively without any improvement until 1642 when Blaise Pascal designed a calculator that employed gears and wheels. But it was not until the early 1800s that a practical, geared, mechanical computing calculator became available. This machine could calculate facts but was not able to use a program to compute numerical facts.

In 1823, Charles Babbage, aided by Augusta Ada Byron, the Countess of Lovelace, started an ambitious project of producing a programmable calculating machine for the Royal Navy of Great Britain. Input to this mechanical machine, named the **Analytical Engine**, was given through punched cards. This engine stored 1,000, 20-digit decimal numbers and a modifiable program, which could vary the operation of the machine so that it could execute different computing jobs. But even after several years of effort, the machine that had more than 50,000 mechanical parts could not operate reliably because the parts could not be machined to precision.

Computing in the electrical era

With the availability of electric motors in 1800, a host of motor-operated calculating machines based on Pascal's calculator was developed. A mechanical machine, driven by a single electric motor, was developed in 1889 by Herman Hollerith to count, sort, and collate data stored on punched cards. Hollerith formed the Tabulating Machine Company in 1896. This company soon merged into International Business Machines (IBM) and the mechanical computing machine business thrived.

In 1941, Konrad Zuse developed the first electronic calculating computer, **Z3.** It was used by the Germans in World War II. However, Alan Turing is credited with developing the first electronic computer in 1943. This computer system, named the **Colossus**, was a fixed-program computer; it was not programmable.

J.W. Mauchly and S.P. Eckert of the University of Pennsylvania completed the first general-purpose electronic digital computer in 1946. It was called the **ENIAC**, Electronic Numerical Integrator and Calculator. It used 17,000 vacuum tubes, over 500 miles of wires, weighed 30 tons, and performed around 100,000 operations per second. The **IAS** computer system, under development till 1952 by John von Neumann and others at the Princeton Institute, laid the foundation of the general structure of subsequent general-purpose computers. In the early 1950s, Sperry-Rand Corporation launched the UNIVAC I, UNIVAC II, UNIVAC 1103 series while IBM brought out Mark I and 701 series. All these machines used vacuum tubes.

The transistor was invented at Bell Labs in 1948. In 1958, IBM, International Computers Limited (ICL), Digital Equipment Corporation (DEC), and others brought out general-purpose computers using transistors that were faster, smaller in size, weighed less, needed less power, and were more reliable.

Meanwhile, at Texas Instruments, Jack Kilby invented the integrated circuit in 1958 that led to the development of digital integrated circuits in the 1960s. This led to the development of IBM 360/370, PDP 8/1, and HP 9810 in 1966. These computers used medium- and small-scale integrated circuits (MSI and SSI).

Thereafter, in 1971, Intel Corporation announced the development of the single-chip microprocessor 4004, a very large-scale integrated circuit. In 1972, the 8008 8-bit microprocessor was introduced. Subsequently, the 8080 and MC 6800 appeared in 1973, which were improved 8-bit microprocessors. The last of the 8-bit microprocessor family from Intel, 8085, was introduced as a general-purpose processor in 1974. In 1978, the 8086, and in 1979, the 8088 microprocessors were released.

Though desktop computers were available from 1975 onwards, none could gain as much popularity as the IBM PC. In 1981, IBM used the 8088 microprocessor in the personal computer. The 80286 16-bit microprocessor came in 1983 as an updated version of 8086. The 32-bit microprocessor 80386 arrived in 1986 and the 80486 arrived in 1989. With the introduction of the Pentium in 1993, a highly improved personal computer was available at an affordable price.

With the development of the desktop computers, in the form of personal computers, and networking, the whole scenario of computing has undergone a sea change. Now, portable computers such as the laptop and palmtop are available, which can execute programs, store data, and output information at speeds higher than that possible with all the earlier computers. Efforts are now being made to integrate a palmtop computer with a mobile phone unit.

Along with the development of computer hardware, programming languages were devised and perfected. In the 1950s, Assembly language was developed for UNIVAC computers. In 1957, IBM developed FORTRAN language. Then in the years that followed came programming languages such as ALGOL, COBOL, BASIC, PASCAL, C/C++, ADA, and JAVA.

Further, with the creation of the operating system (OS), a supervisor program for managing computer resources and controlling the CPU to perform various jobs, the computer's operational capability touched a new dimension. There are a variety of operating systems today. Some which gained popularity are UNIX for large and mini-computers and MSDOS and MS-WINDOWS for personal computers. However, with the availability of LINUX, a trend to change over to this operating system is on.

1.3 GENERATIONS OF COMPUTERS

What generation a computer belongs to is determined by the technology it uses. Table 1.1 shows the technology used in the different generations of computers. With advancement in the generation, the performance of computers improved not only due to the implementation of better hardware technology but also superior operating systems and other software utilities.

Table 1.1 Technology used in different generations of computers

Generation number	Technology	Operating system	Year of introduction	Specific computers
1	Vacuum Tube	None	1945	Mark 1
2	Transistor	None	1956	IBM 1401, ICL 1901, B5000, MINSK-2
3	SSI and MSI	Yes	1964	IBM S/360/370, UNIVAC 1100, HP 2100A, HP 9810
4	LSI and VLSI	Yes	1971	ICL 2900, HP 9845A, VAX 11/780, ALTAIR 8800, IBM PC
5	HAL	Yes	Present and beyond	–

1.4 CLASSIFICATION OF COMPUTERS

Most designs of computers today are based on concepts developed by John von Neumann and are referred to as the von Neumann architecture. Computers can be classified in variety of ways on the basis of various parameters such as usage, cost, size, processing power, and so on. The classification of computers is presented below based on their power and their use.

Supercomputer

Supercomputer is the most expensive and fastest type of computer that performs at or near the currently highest operational rate for computers. A Cray supercomputer is a typical example. These are employed for specialized applications that require immense amounts of mathematical calculations such as weather forecasting, nuclear energy research, and petroleum exploration etc.

Mainframe

A mainframe computer supports a vast number of users to work simultaneously and remotely. Apart from providing multi-user facility, it can process large amounts of data at very high speeds and support many input, output and auxiliary storage devices. These computers are very large in size, and expensive. The main difference between a supercomputer and a mainframe is that a supercomputer can execute a single program faster than a mainframe, whereas a mainframe uses its power to execute many programs concurrently. The IBM 370 and IBM 3090 are examples of mainframe computers.

Minicomputers

A minicomputer is powerful enough to be used by multiple users (between 10 to 100) but is smaller in size and memory capacity and cheaper than mainframes. Two classic examples were the Digital Equipment Corporation VAX and the IBM AS/400.

Microcomputers

The microcomputer has been intended to meet the personal computing needs of an individual. It typically consists of a microprocessor chip, a memory system, interface units and various I/O ports, typically resided in a motherboard. There are many types of microcomputers available.

Desktop computer   A micro computer sufficient to fit on a desk.

Laptop computer   A portable microcomputer with an integrated screen and keyboard.

Palmtop computer/Digital diary/Notebook/PDAs   A hand-sized microcomputer having no keyboard. The screen serves both as an input and output device.

1.5 ANATOMY OF A COMPUTER

A computer can accept input, process or store data, and produce output according to a set of instructions which are fed into it. A computer system can be divided into two components which are responsible for providing the mechanisms to input and output data, to manipulate and process data, and to electronically control the various input, output, and their storage. They are known as hardware and software. The *hardware* is the tangible parts of the computer. Whereas, the *software* is the intangible set of instructions that control the hardware and make it perform specific tasks. Without software, a computer is effectively useless.

1.5.1 Hardware

Hardware is the physical components of a computer that includes all mechanical, electrical, electronic and magnetic parts attached to it. A computer consists of the following major hardware components:

- Input and output devices
- Central processing unit (CPU)
- Memory unit and storage devices
- Interface unit

A brief description of the most common hardware found in a personal computer is given in the next few sections.

Input devices

The data and instructions are typed, submitted, or transmitted to a computer through input devices. Input devices are electronic or electro-mechanical equipment that provide a means of communicating with the computer system for feeding input data and instructions. Most common input devices are briefly described below.

Keyboard Keyboard is like a type-writer. A keyboard, normally, consists of 104 keys. These keys are classified into different categories which are briefly described below.

Character keys These keys include letters, numbers, and punctuation marks. On pressing any character key, the corresponding character is displayed on the screen.

Function keys There are 12 functional keys above the key board which are used to perform certain functions depending on the operating system or the software currently being executed. These keys are placed at the top of the key board and can easily be identified with the letter F followed by a number ranging from 1 to 12.

Control keys Alt, Ctrl, Shift, Insert, Delete, Home, End, PgUp, PgDn, Esc and Arrow keys are control keys.

Navigation keys These include four arrows, Page Up and Page Down, Home and End. These keys are normally used to navigate around a document or screen.

Toggle keys Scroll Lock, Num lock, Caps Lock are three toggle keys. The toggle state is indicated by three LEDs at the right-top side of the keyboard. For example, on pressing caps lock, letters typed by the user will appear in upper case. On pressing again, letters are typed on the screen in lower case.

Miscellaneous keys These keys include Insert, delete, escape, print Screen etc.

The keys on the keyboard are placed in a series of rows and columns called the *key matrix*. Each key holds a position with respect to a row and column. When a key is pressed, the key switch in that position closes a circuit, sending a signal to the circuit board inside the keyboard. The keyboard controller uses the x and y coordinates of the matrix position to determine which key was pressed, thereby determining what code is transmitted to the computer by the keyboard.

Mouse A mouse is the pointing device attached to a computer. It is used to move the cursor around the screen and to point to an object (such as icon, menu, command button etc.) on the computer video screen for the purpose of selecting or activating objects on graphical interface provided by the operating system or the software currently being executed and executing various tasks. It has two or three buttons for clicking. The mouse tracks the motion of the mouse pointer and senses the clicks and sends them to the computer so it can respond appropriately.

The mouse can be connected to the system either through a USB connector or wirelessly through infrared radiation. A wireless mouse needs to be powered through batteries.

Scanner A scanner is a device that captures pictures or documents so that they can be stored in storage devices, seen on the video screen, modified suitably, transported to other computers, or printed on a printer. A personal computer with a scanner and printer can function as a photocopier.

Output devices

Output devices mirror the input data, or show the output results of the operations on the input data or print the data. The most common output device is monitor or visual display unit. The printer is used to print the result. A hard copy refers to a printout showing the information. On the other hand soft copy means information stored on a storage device.

Monitor Computer display devices are commonly known as Visual Display Unit (VDU) or monitor. It operates on a principle similar to that of a normal television set. Various technologies have been used for computer monitors. They are also of different sizes. CRT (Cathode-ray tube) and LCD (liquid crystal display) monitors are the two common types which are widely used.

The CRT is composed of a vacuum glass tube which is narrower at one end. One electron gun is placed at this end which fires electrons. The electron gun is made up of cathode (negatively charged) and one anode (positively charged). On the other side it has a wide screen, coded with phosphor. The beam of electron strikes on the surface of screen and produces an image by photo luminance process. There is some vertical and horizontal coil to deflect the electron beam in any position of the screen. An image is formed by constantly scanning the screen. To send an image to the screen, the computer first assembles it in a memory area called a video buffer. The graphics are stored as an array of memory locations that represent the colors of the individual screen dots, or pixels. The video card then sends this data through a Digital To Analog Converter (DAC), which converts the data to a series of voltage levels that are fed to the monitor.

CRT monitors are too bulky and consume high power. Apart from these, users are very much concerned about potentially damaging non-ionizing radiation from CRT monitor.

Nowadays, LCD monitors are replacing CRTs and becoming the de-facto choice to the users because of its size, display clarity, low radiation emission and power consumption.

An LCD display produces an image by filtering light from a series of cold cathode fluorescent lamps (CCFLs).through a layer of liquid crystal cells. Gradually, CCFL backlighting technology is being replaced by low-power light-emitting diodes (LEDs). A computer screen that uses this technology is sometimes referred to as an LED display.

Printer   The printer is a device that prints any data, report, document, picture, diagrams, etc. Printers are categorized based on the physical

contact of the print head with the paper to produce a text or an image. An *impact printer* is one where the print head will be in physical contact with the paper. In a *non–impact printer*, on the other hand the print head will have no physical contact with the paper. The

Wide-carriage dot matrix printer. Courtesy: **Dale Mahalko** (This file is licensed under the Creative Commons Attribution-Share Alike 3.0 Unported license; http://creativecommons.org/licenses/by-sa/3.0/deed.en)

Dot matrix printer is considered as an Impact printer and Laser printer is considered as Non-impact printer.

In a *dot matrix printer*, the printer head physically 'hits' the paper through the ribbon which makes the speed of the printer relatively slow. The printer head consist of some two dimensional array of dot called 'dot matrix'. Every time when it strikes the paper through ribbon its dots are arranged according to the character which is going to be printed. The ink in the ribbon falls on the surface of the paper and thus the character get printed. In *inkjet printer*, instead of a ribbon one ink

cartridge holds the ink in it. They are placed above the inkjet head. The printing head takes some ink from the cartridge and spreads it on the surface of the paper by the jet head. This ink is electrically charged. An electric field is created near the paper surface. Thus the small drops of ink are arranged in the surface according to the character it prints. These printers are fast and capable of printing good quality graphics. The *laser printer* uses a laser beam to create the image.

Central processing unit (CPU)

Central Processing Unit or CPU can be thought of as the brain of the computer. Most of the processing takes place in CPU. During processing, it locates and executes the program instructions. It also fetches data from memory and input/output devices and sends data back.

Physically, it is an integrated circuit (IC) silicon chip, mounted on a small square plastic slab, surrounded by metal pins. In the world of personal computers, the term microprocessor and CPU are used interchangeably. It is more accurate to describe it as a CPU on a chip because it contains the circuitry that performs processing.

The CPU itself can be divided into different functional units which are described below-

Registers   These are high-speed storage devices. In most CPUs, some registers are reserved for special purposes. For example, the Instruction Register (IR) holds the current instruction being executed. The Program Counter (PC) is a register that holds the address of the next instruction to be executed. In addition to such and other special-purpose registers, it also contains a set of general-purpose registers that are used for temporary storage of data values as needed during processing.

Arithmetic logic unit (ALU)   It is the part of the CPU that performs arithmetic operations, such as addition and subtraction as well as logical operations, such as comparing two numbers to see if they are the equal or greater or less.

Control unit (CU)   The control unit coordinates the processing by controlling the transfer of data and instructions between main memory and the registers in the CPU. It also coordinates the execution of the arithmetic logic unit (ALU) to perform operations on data stored in particular registers. It consists of

- an *instruction decoding circuit* that interprets what action should be performed.
- a *control and timing circuit* directs all the other parts of the computer by producing the respective control signals.

Nowadays, a high-speed memory, called *cache memory*, is embedded with the CPU chip. This improves the computer performance by minimizing the processor need to read data from the slow main memory.

The CPU's processing power is measured in terms of the number of instructions that it can execute per unit time. Every computer comprises of an internal clock, which emits electronic pulses at a constant rate. These pulses are used to control and synchronize the pace of operations. Each pulse is called a *clock cycle* which resembles a rectangular wave with a rising half of the signal and a falling half. In other words, a full clock cycle is the amount of time that elapses between pulses of the oscillating signal. Each instruction takes one or more clock cycles to execute. The higher the clock speed, the more instructions are executed in a given period of time. Hertz (Hz) is the basic unit of computer clock frequency which is equal to one cycle per second. CPU speed has been improved continuously. It is typically measured in megahertz (MHz) or gigahertz (GHz). One megahertz is equal to one million cycles per second, while one gigahertz equals one billion cycles per second.

Nowadays, multiple processors are embedded together on a single integrated-circuit chip, known as multi-core processor e.g. a *dual-core processor* has two CPUs and a *quad core processor* has four CPUs.

> **Note**
>
> - An integrated circuit, or IC, is a matrix of transistors and other electrical components embedded in a small slice of silicon.
> - A microprocessor is a digital electronic component with miniaturized transistors on a single semiconductor integrated circuit (IC). One or more microprocessors typically serve as a central processing unit (CPU) in a computer system or handheld device allocating space to hold the data object.

Memory unit

Components such as the input device, output device, and CPU are not sufficient for the working of a computer. A storage area is needed in a computer to store instructions and data, either temporarily or permanently, so that subsequent retrieval of the instructions and data can be possible on demand. Data are stored in memory as binary digits, called *bits*. Data of various types, such as numbers, characters, are encoded as series of bits and stored in consecutive memory locations. Each memory location comprises of a single byte which is equal to eight bits and has a unique address so that the contents of the desired memory locations can be accessed independently by referring to its' address. A single data item is stored in one or more consecutive bytes of memory. The address of the first byte is used as the address of the entire memory location.

CPU uses registers exclusively to store and manipulate data and instructions during the processing. Apart from registers, there are mainly two types of memory that are used in a computer system. One is called *primary memory* and the other *secondary memory*.

Primary memory   Primary memory is the area where data and programs are stored while the program is being executed along with the data. This memory space, also known as *main memory*, forms the working area of the program. This memory is accessed directly by the processor.

A memory module consists of a large bank of flip-flops arranged together with data traffic control circuitry such that data can be stored or read out on or from a set of flip-flops. A flip-flop can store a binary digit. These flip-flops are grouped to form a unit memory of fixed length and each of which is identified by a sequence number known as a memory address. These type are called Random Access Memory, or RAM, where any location can be accessed directly, and its stored contents get destroyed the moment power to this module is switched off. Hence, these are volatile in nature. Primary memory devices are expensive. They are limited in size, consume very low power, and are faster as compared to secondary memory devices.

There is another kind of primary memory increasingly being used in modern computers. It is called *cache memory* (pronounced as "cash"). It is a type of high-speed memory that allows the processor to access data more rapidly than from memory located elsewhere on the system. It stores or caches some of the contents of the main memory that is currently in use by the processor. It takes a fraction of the time, compared to main memory, to access cache memory. The management of data stored in the cache memory ensures that for 20 per cent of the total time, during which the cache is searched, the data needed is found to be stored in cache. As a result the performance of the computer improves in terms of speed of processing.

Secondary memory   Secondary memory provides large, non-volatile, and inexpensive storage for programs and data. However, the access time in secondary memory is much larger than in primary memory. Secondary storage permits the storage of computer instructions and data for long periods of time. Moreover, secondary memory, which is also known as *auxiliary memory*, stores a huge number of data bytes at a lesser cost than primary memory devices.

> **Note**
>
> - The memory unit is composed of an ordered sequence of storage cells, each capable of storing one byte of data. Each memory cell has a distinct address which is used to refer while storing data into it or retrieving data from it.
> - Both RAM and cache memory are referred to as primary memory. Primary memory is comparatively expensive, and loses all its data when the power is turned off. Secondary memory provides less expensive storage that is used to store data and instructions on a permanent basis.

Memory operations There are some operations common to both primary and secondary memory devices. These are as follows.

Read During this operation, data is retrieved from memory.

Write In this operation, data is stored in the memory.

Using read and write operations, many other memory-related functions such as copy and delete are carried out.

Unit of memory The memory's interface circuit is designed to logically access a byte or a multiple of a byte of data from the memory during each access. The smallest block of memory is considered to be a byte, which comprises eight bits. The total memory space is measured in terms of bytes. Thus, the unit of memory is a byte. The capacity of memory is the maximum amount of information it is capable of storing. Since the unit of memory is a byte, the memory's capacity is expressed in number of bytes. Some units used to express the memory capacity are as follows:

- Kilobyte (KB)   = 1024 bytes
- Megabyte (MB) = 1024 Kilobytes
- Gigabyte (GB)   = 1024 Megabytes
- Terabyte (TB)   = 1024 Gigabytes
- Petabyte (PB)   = 1024 Terabytes
- Exabyte (EB)   = 1024 Petabytes
- Zettabyte (ZB) = 1024 Exabytes
- Yottabyte (YB) = 1024 Zettabytes

The size of the register is one of the important considerations in determining the processing capabilities of the CPU. *Word size* refers to the number of bits that a CPU can manipulate at one time. Word size is based on the size of registers in the ALU and the capacity of circuits that lead to those registers. A processor with a 32-bit word size, for example, has 32-bit registers, processes 32 bits at a time, and is referred to as a 32-bit processor. Processor's word size is a factor that leads to increased computer performance. Today's personal computers typically contain 32-bit or 64-bit processors.

Memory hierarchy The various types of memory used in a computer system differ in speed, cost, size, and volatility (permanence of storage). They can be organized in a hierarchy. The memory hierarchy in the computer system is depicted in Fig. 1.1.

Figure 1.1 shows that on moving down the hierarchy, the cost per bit of storage decreases but access times increases (i.e., devices are slow). In other words, from top to bottom, the speed decreases while the capacity increases and the prices become much lower.

Of the various memories specified in the hierarchy, those above the secondary memory are volatile and the rest are non-volatile. While designing a computer system, there must always be a balance on all of the above factors, namely speed, cost, volatility, etc. at each level in the hierarchy.

Fig. 1.1 Memory hierarchy

The devices in a computer system other than the CPU and main memory are called **peripherals.** Popular peripheral devices include printers, digital cameras, scanners, joysticks, and speakers.

Interface unit

The interface unit interconnects the CPU with memory and also with the various input/output (I/O) devices. The instructions and data move between the CPU and other hardware components through interface unit.

It is a set of parallel wires or lines which connects all the internal computer components to the CPU and main memory. Depending on the type of data transmitted, a bus can be classified into the following three types:

Data bus The bus used to carry actual data.

Address bus memory or Input/output device Addresses travel via the address bus.

Control bus This bus carries control information between the CPU and other devices within the computer. The control information entails signals that report the status of various devices, or ask devices to take specific actions.

A model of the bus-based computer organization is shown in Fig. 1.2.

Most of the computer devices are not directly connected to the computer's internal bus. Since every device has its own particular way of formatting and communicating data, a device, termed *controller*, coordinates the activities of specific peripherals. The processor reads from the input devices or writes on the output devices with the help of the device controllers. Each input device or output device has a specific address. Using these addresses, the processor selects a particular I/O device through the associated device controller for either transferring data or any control commands.

Fig. 1.2   Bus-based computer organization

Motherboard

All the components in the computer system are mounted and connected together by an electronic circuit board called motherboard or main board.

To make all these things work together the motherboard provides some kind of physical connection among them. (See Fig. 1.3).

Fig. 1.3   Motherboard

In general, a motherboard consists of the following.

CPU socket   This holds the central processor which is an integrated chip along with the system clock, cache, cooling fan, etc.

Memory sockets   These sockets hold the RAM card that contains RAMs.

Interface module   This is for the hard disk, floppy disk, and CD-ROM drives.

ROM integrated chip   This is embedded with the basic input/output system software.

Ports and expansion slots   A port is used to connect a device with the bus. Physical ports include serial and parallel ports, to which peripheral devices such as printers, scanners, and external storage devices can be attached. The slots are used to attach accessories such as graphics (video) cards, disk controllers, and network cards. There are two different standards for expansion slots: ISA (Industry Standard Architecture) and PCI (Peripheral Component Interconnect). Most common types of ports and slots are briefly described below.

ISA slots   These are for connecting ISA compatible cards.

PCI slots   These are for connecting I/O devices.

Advanced graphics port (AGP)   Video card is inserted into this slot.

Parallel port   The parallel port is also known as the printer port, or LPT1. It is capable of sending eight bits of information at a time.

Serial ports   these are sometimes called communication ports or COM ports. There are two COM ports, COM1 and COM2. size of COM1 is larger than that of COM2. COM1 has 25 pins and used for connecting Modems. COM2 is 9 pin port used for interfacing serial mouse. D-type connectors are used to with there ports.

USB (universal serial bus)   This is also a serial port but data rate is more than the serial port. USB is used as a general-purpose communication channel in Personal Computers. Many different devices, such as mouse, keyboards, hard disk drives, portable CD-ROM/DVD drives, pen-drives, scanners, cameras, modems and even printers are usually connected to these ports.

CMOS   The CMOS in a Personal Computer stands for Complementary Metal Oxide Semiconductor memory. It is a type of RAM that stores the necessary attributes of system components, such as the size of the hard disk, the amount of RAM, and the resources used by the serial and parallel ports etc. Since RAM loses its content when the power is switched off, a small battery, on the motherboard, powers the CMOS RAM even when the computer power is switched off thereby retaining its stored data.

System unit

The System Unit holds all the system components in it. It is sometimes called cabinet. The main components like motherboard, processor, memory unit, power supply unit, and all the ports to interface computer's peripherals. Inside the unit all the components work together to give the service that the user needs. Based on its use, cabinets are of two types.

   (i) AT cabinets (or mini-tower)
   (ii) ATX cabinets

AT cabinets are smaller and cheaper than ATX cabinets and are popularly called mini-tower cabinets. They are used for older processors and smaller motherboards. ATX cabinets, on the other hand, are marginally larger in size than AT cabinets and are more expensive as they come with more features such as powered sliding front panels and extra disk storage compartments.

Note

- The motherboard is a printed circuit board which contains the circuitry and connections that allow the various components of the computer system to communicate with each other. In most computer systems, the CPU, memory, and other major components are mounted to wiring on the motherboard.

- The input, output, and storage equipment that might be added to a computer system to enhance its functionality are known as *peripheral devices*. Popular peripheral devices include printers, digital cameras, scanners, joysticks, and speakers.

1.5.2 Software

Software provides the instructions that tell the hardware exactly what is to be performed and in what order. This set of instructions is sequenced and organized in a computer program. Therefore, a program is a series of instructions which is intended to direct a computer to perform certain functions and is executed by the processor. In a broader sense, software can be described as a set of related programs. But software is more than a collection of programs. It refers to a set of computer programs, which provide desired functions and performance, the data which the programs use, data structures that facilitate the programs to efficiently manipulate data and documents that describe the operation and use of the programs.

A comparison between computer program and software is listed below (Table 1.2).

Table 1.2 Comparison between computer program and software

Computer program	Software
Programs are developed by individuals. A single developer is involved.	A large number of developers are involved.
Small in size and have limited functionality	Extremely large in size and has enormous functionality.
The user interface may not be very important, because the programmer is the sole user.	For a software product, user interface must be carefully designed and implemented because developers of that product and users of that product are totally different.

Nowadays, most of the software must be installed prior to their use. Installation involves copying several files to computer memory or requires a series of steps and configurations depending on the operating system and the software itself so that it can be run or executed when required.

Software is generally categorized as system software or application software or utility software.

System software

System software is designed to facilitate and coordinate the use of the computer by making hardware operational. It interacts with the computer system at low level. Examples of such software include language translator, operating system, loader, linker, etc. However, the most important system software is the *operating system* which is a set of programs designed to control the input and output operations of the computer, provide communication interface to the user, and manage the resources of the computer system, such as memory, processor, input/output devices etc. and schedule their operations with minimum manual intervention. Other programs (system and application) rely on facilities provided by the operating system to gain access to computer system resources. The *loader* is the system software which copies a executable program from secondary storage device into main memory and prepares this program for execution and initializes the execution.

Hardware devices, other than the CPU and main memory, have to be registered with the operating system by providing a software, known as *device driver*, for communication between the device and other parts of the computer. This type of system software is used by printers, monitors, graphics cards, sound cards, network cards, modems, storage devices, mouse, scanners, etc. Once installed, a device driver automatically responds when it is needed or may run in the background.

Modern operating system recognizes almost all connected hardware devices and immediately begins the installation process. Such a device, for which the operating system automatically starts the installation process, is called a *plug-and-play* device. However, there are few hardware devices for which the user has to manually initiate the installation process.

Application software

Application software is designed to perform specific usages of the users. Microsoft Word, Microsoft Excel, Microsoft Power Point, Microsoft Access, Page Maker, Coral Draw, Photoshop, Tally, AutoCAD, Acrobat, WinAmp, Micro Media Flash, iLeap, Xing MP3 Player etc. are some of the examples of application software.

There are two categories of application software, *custom software* and *pre-written software packages*. Software that is developed for a specific user or organization in accordance with the user's needs is known as *custom software*.

A pre-written software package is bought off the shelf and has predefined generic specifications that may or may not cater to any specific user's requirements. The most important categories of software packages available are as follows:

- Database management software, e.g. Oracle, DB2, Microsoft SQL server, etc.
- Spreadsheet software, e.g. Microsoft Excel.
- Word processing, e.g. Microsoft Word, Corel Wordperfect and desktop publishing (DTP), e.g. Pagemaker.
- Graphics software, e.g. Corel Draw.
- Statistical, e.g. SPSS and operation research software, e.g. Tora.

Note

- Without any software, the computer is called a bare machine, having the potential to perform many functions but no ability to do so on its own.

1.6 MEMORY REVISITED

The different types of memories available for a computer are shown in Fig. 1.4.

1.6.1 Primary Memory

All modern computers use semiconductor memory as primary memory. One of the important semiconductor memories used in desktop computers is *Random Access Memory (RAM)*. Here "random access" means that any storage location can be accessed (both read and write) directly. This memory is faster, cheaper, and provides more storage space in lesser physical area. These very large-scale integrated semiconductor memory chips are mounted on pluggable printed circuit boards (PCBs). Enhancement or replacement of memory with such PCB memory modules is easy. These characteristics have made semiconductor memory more popular and attractive. The only drawback of semiconductor memory is that it is volatile, i.e., it loses its contents whenever power is switched off. RAM holds the data and instructions waiting to be processed by the processor. In addition to data and program's instructions, RAM also holds operating system instructions that control the basic functions of a computer system. These instructions are loaded into RAM every time the computer is turned on, and they remain there until the computer is turned off. There are two types of RAM used in computer systems– *dynamic* and *static*.

Dynamic RAM (DRAM) is a type of RAM that employs refresh circuits to retain its content in its logic circuits. Each memory cell in DRAM consists of a single transistor. The junction capacitor of the transistor is responsible for holding the electrical charge that designates a single bit as logical 1. The absence of a charge designates a bit as logical 0. Capacitors lose their charge over time and therefore need to be recharged or refreshed at pre-determined intervals by a refreshing circuitry.

A more expensive and faster type of RAM, *Static RAM (SRAM)*, does not require such type of refreshing circuitry. It uses between four to six transistors in a special 'flip-flop' circuit that holds a 1 or 0 while the computer system is in operation. SRAM in computer systems is usually used as processor caches and as I/O buffers. Printers and liquid crystal displays (LCDs) often use SRAM to buffer images.

SRAM is also widely used in networking devices, such as routers, switches, and cable modems, to buffer transmission information.

Both dynamic and static RAM are volatile in nature and can be read or written to. The basic differences between SRAM and DRAM are listed in Table 1.3.

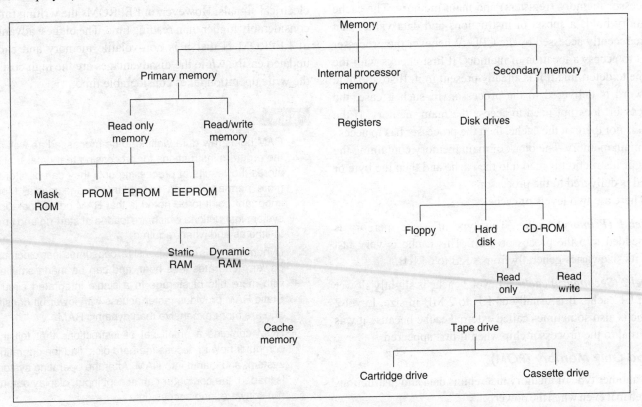

Fig. 1.4 Types of memory

Table 1.3 Static RAM versus dynamic RAM

Static RAM	Dynamic RAM
• It does not require refreshing.	• It requires extra electronic circuitry that "refreshes" memory periodically; otherwise its content will be lost.
• It is more expensive than dynamic RAM.	• It is less expensive than static RAM.
• It is lower in bit density.	• It holds more bits of storage in a single integrated circuit.
• It is faster than dynamic RAM.	• It is slower than SRAM, due to refreshing.

There are several popular types of dynamic RAM used in computers. They are SDRAM (Synchronous Dynamic RAM), RDRAM (Rambus Dynamic RAM) and DDR RAM (Double Data Rate RAM).

The SDRAM used to be the most common type of RAM for personal computers. It was reasonably fast and

inexpensive. It is no more used in the present day for personal computers as much improved RAMs are available now.

The RDRAM was developed by Rambus Corporation and is its proprietary technology. It is also the most expensive RAM and is used mostly in video interface cards and high-end computers that require fast computation speed and data transfer. RDRAMs are preferred for high-performance personal computers.

The DDR RAM is a refinement of SDRAM. DDR stands for *Double Data Rate*. It gives faster performance by transmitting data on both the rising and the falling edges of each clock pulse. DDR 2, DDR3 are other higher-speed versions of DDR RAM.

Another type of RAM, termed Video RAM (VRAM), is used to store image data for the visual display monitor. All types of video RAM are special arrangements of dynamic RAM (DRAM). Its purpose is to act as a data storage buffer between the processor and the visual display unit.

There is a persistent mismatch between processor and main memory speeds. The processor executes an instruction faster than the time it takes to read from or write to memory. In order to improve the average memory access speed or rather to optimize the fetching of instructions or data so that these can be accessed faster when the CPU needs it, cache memory is logically positioned between the internal processor memory (registers) and main memory. The cache memory holds a subset of instructions and data values that were recently accessed by the CPU. Whenever the processer tries to access a location of memory, it first checks with the cache to determine if it is already present in it. If so, the byte or word is delivered to the processor. In such a case, the processor does not need to access the main memory. If the data is not there in the cache, then the processer has to access the main memory. The block of main memory containing the data or instruction is read into the cache and then the byte or word is delivered to the processor.

There are two levels of cache.

Level 1 (Primary) cache This type of cache memory is embedded into the processor itself. This cache is very fast and its size varies generally from 8 KB to 64 KB.

Level 2 (Secondary) cache Level 2 cache is slightly slower than L1 cache. It is usually 64 KB to 2 MB in size. Level 2 cache is also sometimes called external cache because it was external to the processor chip when it first appeared.

Read Only Memory (ROM)

It is another type of memory that retains data and instructions stored in it even when the power is turned off. ROM is used in personal computers for storing start-up instructions provided by the manufacturer for carrying out basic operations such as bootstrapping in a PC, and is programmed for specific purposes during their fabrication. ROMs can be written only at the time of manufacture. Another similar memory, Programmable ROM (PROM), is also non-volatile and can be programmed only once by a special device.

But there are instances where the read operation is performed several times and the write operation is performed more than once though less than the number of read operations and the stored data must be retained even when power is switched off. This led to the development of EPROMs (Erasable Programmable Read Only Memories). In the EPROM or Erasable Programmable Read Only Memory, data can be written electrically. The write operation, however, is not simple. It requires the storage cells to be erased by exposing the chip to ultraviolet light, thus bringing each cell to the same initial state. This process of erasing is time consuming. Once

all the cells have been brought to the same initial state, the write operation on the EPROM can be performed electrically.

There is another type of Erasable PROM known as Electrically Erasable Programmable Read Only Memory (EEPROM). Like the EPROM, data can be written onto the EEPROM by electrical signals and retained even when power is switched off. The data stored can be erased by electrical signals. However, in EEPROMs the writing time is considerably higher than reading time. The biggest advantage of EEPROM is that it is non-volatile memory and can be updated easily, while the disadvantages are the high cost and the write operation takes considerable time.

> **Note**
>
> - RAM holds raw data waiting to be processed as well as the program instructions for processing that data. It also stores the results of processing until they can be stored more permanently on secondary storage media. Most important point to be noted is that RAM holds operating system instructions which are loaded at start-up and time to time as and when required.
> - Dynamic RAM is less expensive, consumes less electrical power, generates less heat, and can be made smaller, with more bits of storage in a single integrated circuit. Static RAM provides faster access with lower bit density and are more expensive than dynamic RAM.
> - ROM contains a small set of instructions that tell the computer how to access the hard disk, find the operating system, and load it into RAM. After the operating system is loaded, the computer can accept input, display output, run software, and access data.
> - The programmable read-only memory (PROM) is non-volatile and can be reprogrammed only once by a special write device after fabrication. An erasable programmable ROM (EPROM) can be erased by ultraviolet (UV) light or by high-voltage pulses.

1.6.2 Secondary Memory

There are four main types of secondary storage devices available in a computer system:

- Disk drives
- CD drives (CD-R, CD-RW, and DVD)
- Tape drives
- USB flash drives

Hard disk, floppy disk, compact disk (CD), Digital Versatile Disk (DVD) and magnetic tapes are the most common secondary storage mediums. Hard disks provide much faster performance and have larger capacity, but are normally not removable; that is, a single hard disk is permanently attached to a disk drive. Floppy disks, on the other hand, are removable, but their performance is far slower and their capacity far smaller than those of hard disks. A CD-ROM or DVD-ROM is another portable secondary memory device. CD stands for Compact Disc. It is called ROM because information is stored permanently when the CD is created. Devices for operating storage mediums are known as *drives*. Most of the drives used for secondary memory are based on electro-mechanical technology. Mechanical components move much more slowly than do electrical signals. That's why access to secondary memory is much slower than access to main memory.

The **floppy disk** is a thin, round piece of plastic material, coated with a magnetic medium on which information is magnetically recorded, just as music is recorded on the surface of plastic cassette tapes. The flexible floppy disk is enclosed inside a sturdier, plastic jacket to protect it from damage. The disks used in personal computers are usually 3½ inches in diameter and can store 1.44 MB of data. Earlier PCs sometimes used 5¼ inch disks. The disks store information and can be used to exchange information between computers. The floppy disk drive stores data on and retrieves it from the magnetic material of the disk, which is in the form of a disk. It has two motors one that rotates the disk media and the other that moves two read-write heads, each on either surface of the disk, forward Floppy Disk Drive or backward.

A **hard disk** is a permanent memory device mounted inside the system unit. Physically, a hard disk consists of one or more metal (sometimes aluminum) platters, coated with a metal oxide that can be magnetized. The platters are all mounted on a spindle, which allows them to spin at a constant rate. Read/write heads are attached to metal arms and positioned over each of the platter surfaces. The arms can move the read/write heads radially inwards and outwards over the surfaces of the platters (see Fig. 1.5). Data and programs are stored on the hard disk by causing the write heads to make magnetic marks on the surfaces of the platters. Read heads retrieve the data by sensing the magnetic marks on the platters. The surface of each platter is divided into concentric rings called tracks. The tracks form concentric circles on the platter's surface. Each track is divided into a certain number of sectors. A sector is capable of generally 512 bytes or sometimes 1,024 bytes of data. The head is mounted on an arm, which moves or seeks from track to track. The vertical

group of tracks at the same position on each surface of each platter is called a cylinder. Cylinders are important, because all heads move at the same time. Once the heads arrive at a particular track position, all the sectors on the tracks that form a cylinder can be read without further arm motion. The storage capacity of a hard disk is very large and expressed in terms of gigabytes (GB). The data that is stored on the hard disk remains there until it is erased or deleted by the user.

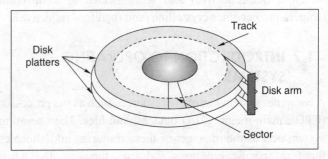

Fig. 1.5   Hard disk organization

The hard disk drive provides better performance and become mandatory for computer systems for the following reasons:

- Higher capacity of data storage
- Faster access time of data
- Higher data transfer rates
- Better reliability of operation
- Less data errors or data loss

A **CD** is a portable secondary storage medium. Various types of CDs are available: CD-R and CD-RW. CD-RW drives are used to create and read both CD-R and CD-RW discs. Once created (i.e. when it has been "burned"), data stored on CD-R (CD- Recordable) disc can't be changed. On the other hand, a CD-Rewritable (CD-RW) disc can be erased and reused. This disk is made of synthetic resin that is coated with a reflective material, usually aluminum. When information is written by a CD-writer drive, some microscopic pits are created on the surface of the CD. The information bit on a CD-ROM surface is coded in the form of ups and downs (known as pits and dumps), created by infrared heat. There is one laser diode on the reading head. The bits are read by shining a low - intensity laser beam onto the spinning disc. The laser beam reflects strongly from a smooth area on the disc but weakly from a pitted area. A sensor receiving the reflection determines whether each bit is a 1 or a 0 accordingly. CDs were initially a popular storage media for music; they were later used as general computer storage media. Most personal computers are equipped with a CD-Recordable (CD-R) drive. A CD-Rewritable (CD-RW) disc can be reused because the pits and flat surfaces of a normal CD are simulated on a CD-RW by coating the surface of the disc with a material that, when heated to one temperature becomes amorphous (and therefore non-reflective) and when heated to a different temperature becomes crystalline (and therefore reflective).

1.7 INTRODUCTION TO OPERATING SYSTEMS

A computer system has many resources such as the processor (CPU), main memory, I/O devices, and files. The operating system acts as the manager of these resources and allocates them to specific programs and uses them as and when necessary for the tasks.

An operating system may be defined as a system software which acts as an intermediary between the user and the hardware, an interface which isolates the user from the details of the hardware implementation. It consists of a set of specialized software modules that makes computing resources (hardware and software) available to users. Thus, the computer system is easier to use with the operating system in place than without it. Some of the operating systems used nowadays are Mac, MS Windows, Linux, Solaris, etc.

The common functions of an operating system includes –

Process(or) management   The process abstraction is a fundamental mechanism implemented by the operating system for management of the execution of programs. A process is basically a program in execution. The operating system decides which process gets to run, for how long and perhaps at what priority or level of importance.

Memory management   Operating system is responsible for keeping track of which parts of the memory are currently being used and by whom. It organizes and addresses memory; handle requests to allocate memory, frees up memory no longer being used, and rearranges memory to maximize the useful amount. Often several programs may be in memory at the same time. The operating system selects processes that are to be placed in memory, where they are to be placed, and how much memory is to be given to each.

Device management   The operating system allocates the various devices to the processes and initiates the I/O operation. It also controls and schedules accesses to the input/output devices among the processes.

File management   A file is just a sequence of bytes. Files are storage areas for programs, source codes, data, documents etc. The operating system keeps track of every file in the system, including data files, program files, compilers, and applications. The file system is an operating system module that allows users and programs to create, delete, modify, open, close, and apply other operations to various types of files. It also allows users to give names to files, to organize the files hierarchically into directories, to protect files, and to access those files using the various file operations.

Apart from these functions, an operating system must provide the facilities for controlling the access of programs, processes, memory segments, and other resources.

The *kernel* is that part of operating system that interacts with the hardware directly. The kernel represents only a small portion of the code of the entire OS but it is intensively used and so remains in primary storage while other portions may be transferred in and out of secondary storage as required. When a computer boots up, it goes through some initialization functions, such as checking the memory. It then loads the kernel and switches control to it. The kernel then starts up all the processes needed to communicate with the user and the rest of the environment.

The user interface is the portion of the operating system that users interact with directly. Operating systems such as MS-DOS and early versions of UNIX accepted only typed-in text commands. Now most operating systems provide users a graphical user interface for their interactions with the system. Operating systems such as Microsoft Windows, Solaris and Linux allow the user to interact with the operating system through icons, menus, keyboard and mouse movements. The user interface and way of interactions vary widely from one operating system to another.

1.7.1 Loading an Operating System

In some digital devices like controllers of small appliances, hand-held devices and videogame console, the operating system is relatively simple and small and is stored in ROM (Read-Only Memory). The operating system is also present in a ROM for systems such as industrial controllers and petrol-filling equipment. In such a system, it gains immediate control of the processor, the moment it is turned on.

In personal computer, the operating system is usually stored on hard disk. Because size of the operating system is large enough, it cannot be placed entirely in RAM. The kernel, the core part of the operating system, is loaded into RAM at start-up and is always present in memory. Other parts of the operating system are loaded into RAM as and when required. It is to be noted that there is no operating system resident in a new computer. The operating system is usually sold on a CD or DVD media and has to be permanently transferred from a CD or DVD media to the hard disk by expanding compressed files and initializing the whole system for use.

Booting is the general term for the process that a computer or other digital device follows from the instant it is turned on until the operating system is finally loaded and ready for use.

The Basic Input Output System (BIOS) is a small set of instructions stored on a PROM that is executed when the computer is turned on.

When the computer is switched on, the ROM circuitry receives power and begins the boot process. At first, an address is automatically loaded into the Program Counter (PC) register. This is done by hardware circuitry. The address given is the location of the first executable instruction of the BIOS. The code in the BIOS runs a series of tests called the POST (Power On Self Test) to make sure that system devices such as main memory, monitor, keyboard, the input/output devices are connected and functional. During POST, the BIOS compares the system configuration data obtained from POST with the system information stored on a Complementary Metal-Oxide Semiconductor (CMOS) memory chip located on the motherboard. The BIOS also sets various parameters such as the organization of the disk drive, using information stored in a CMOS chip. This CMOS chip gets updated whenever new system components are added and contains the latest information about system components.

The BIOS then loads only one block of data, called the *Master Boot Record*, from a specific and fixed place (the very first sector at cylinder 0, head 0, and sector 1) of the bootable device and is placed at a specific and fixed place of main memory. The master boot record is of 512 bytes in size and contains machine code instructions, called a *bootstrap loader*. Then the boot loader program starts the process of loading the OS and transfers control to the OS itself which completes the process.

The steps involved in the instruction cycle while executing a program are described below.

The Program Counter (PC) is the register that keeps track of what instruction has to be executed next. At the first step, the instruction is *fetched* from main memory and loaded into Instruction Register (IR), whose address is specified by PC register. Immediately the PC is incremented so that it points to the next instruction in the program. Once in IR, the instruction is *decoded* to determine the actions needed for its execution. The control unit then issues the sequence of control signals that enables *execution* of the instruction. Data needed to be processed by the instructions are either fetched from a register from RAM through an *address register*. The result of the instruction is *stored* (written) to either a register or a memory location. The next instruction of a program will follow the same steps. This will continue until there is no more instruction in the program or the computer is turned off, some sort of unrecoverable error occurs.

Fig. 1.6 A simplified view of an instruction cycle

Note

- *Cold boot* describes the process of starting the computer and loading its operating system by turning the power on. If the computer is running, one can carry out cold boot by first switching it off and then back on.
- *Warm boot* describes the process of restarting the computer and loading its operating system again without switching it off after it has already been running.

1.8 OPERATIONAL OVERVIEW OF A CPU

Any processing executed by central processing unit is directed by the instruction. The processing required for a single instruction is called an *instruction cycle*. The four steps which the CPU carries out for each machine language instruction are *fetch, decode, execute, and store* (Fig. 1.6).

Note

A register is a single, permanent storage location within the CPU used for a particular, defined purpose. CPU contains several important registers such as

- The *program counter(PC)* register holds the address of the current instruction being executed.
- The *instruction register (IR)* holds the actual instruction being executed currently by the computer.

To access data in memory, CPU makes use of two internal registers:

- The memory address register (MAR) holds the address of a memory location.
- The memory data register (MDR), sometimes known as the memory buffer register, will hold a data value that is being stored to or retrieved from the memory location currently addressed by the memory address register.

SUMMARY

A computer is defined as 'an automatic electronic apparatus for making calculations or controlling operations that are expressible in numerical or logical terms'.

Starting from the days of the abacus, the concept of developing a computing machine has led to the development of the modern electronic computing machine. There are five generations of computers. Today computers are available in various forms such as personal computers, laptop, palmtop, and mainframes. The electronic computer, of all sizes, perfected through years of development, has become a powerful machine capable of being employed in a variety of applications. A computer has a CPU, a fast-access primary memory (RAM), a non-volatile high storage capacity secondary memory (HDD), an easy-to-use keyboard, a video

color monitor console with a graphic pointer device such as mouse and a non-impact printer.

Thus, broadly, the basic computer system consists of a CPU, memory, and input and output devices. Memory can be classified into primary, secondary, and internal processor memory. Cache memory is a part of the primary memory and normally resides near the CPU. The rest of the primary memory consists of various types of ROMs and RAMs.

A PC consists of hardware and software. Software can be classified into system software and application software. The most important system software is the operating system that manages all resources of the computer system and acts as an interface between hardware and software. When the personal computer is switched on, a power on self test (POST) is executed and the operating system is loaded.

KEY TERMS

ALU The Arithmetic Logic Unit (ALU) performs arithmetic and logical operations on the data.

BIOS Basic Input-Output System (BIOS) is a small set of instructions stored in ROM which runs every time when the computer is switched on. BIOS is responsible for Power On Self Test to make sure every immediately required device is connected and functional and finally loading the core part of the operating system into RAM.

Cache memory It is a special high-speed memory that allows a microprocessor to access data more rapidly than from memory located elsewhere on the system board.

CMOS The Complementary Metal Oxide Semiconductor (CMOS) chip in the computer stores information about various attributes of the devices connected to the computer.

Control unit It interprets each instruction and determines the appropriate course of action.

Computer It is programmable device that can store, retrieve, and process data.

CPU It is an Integrated circuit chip which is the ultimate controller of the computer, as well as the place where all calculations are performed.

Hardware It refers to the physical components of a computer.

RAM Random Access Memory (RAM) is a volatile memory that is used to store data and instructions temporarily. It holds raw data waiting to be processed as well as the program instructions for processing that data. It also holds operating system instructions, which control the basic functions of a computer system.

ROM Read Only Memory (ROM) is permanent and nonvolatile memory. It is the place to store the "hard-wired" startup instructions of a computer. These instructions are a permanent part of the circuitry and remain in place even when the computer power is turned off.

Software It refers to the set of computer programs and to the data that the programs use.

FREQUENTLY ASKED QUESTIONS

1. What is a microprocessor?

A microprocessor is an integrated circuit chip that contains all of the essential components for the central processing unit (CPU) of a microcomputer system.

2. What is a chip?

A chip is a small, thin piece of silicon onto which the transistors making up the integrated circuits, e.g. microprocessors have been imprinted.

3. What is a chipset?

In personal computers a *chipset* is a group of integrated circuits that together perform a particular function.

4. What is booting?

The sequence of events that occurs between the time that a computer is

turned on and the time it is ready for use, is referred to as *booting*.

5. Where is the operating system stored?

In some digital devices— typically handhelds and videogame consoles— the entire operating system is small enough to be stored in ROM (read-only memory). For most other computers, the operating system program is quite large, so most of it is stored on a hard disk. During the boot process, the operating system kernel is loaded into RAM. The *kernel* provides essential operating system services. Other parts of the operating system are loaded into RAM as and when they are needed.

6. What is a plug-and-play device?

A device for which the installation process starts automatically by the operating system and which usually does not require any human intervention, is called a plug-and-play device.

7. If a computer contains RAM, why does it need ROM too?

Normally, the instructions and data are stored in a secondary storage devices permanently. In addition to data and program instructions currently being processed, RAM also holds operating system instructions that control the basic functions of a computer system. These instructions are loaded into RAM every time when the computer is booted, and they remain resident until the computer is turned off. But RAM is a volatile memory i.e. its content will be lost when the power is turned off. Now ROM plays the important role. ROM contains a small set of instructions called the BIOS (Basic Input Output System). These instructions access the hard disk, find the operating system, and load it into RAM. After the operating system is loaded, the system is ready to be used.

EXERCISES

1. Write full forms of the following:

   ENIAC, ALU, CU, RAM, ROM, EPROM, EEPROM, BIOS, POST, MIPS, CMOS

2. Briefly describe the functions of the different components of a conventional digital computer with the help of a suitable block diagram.

3. What is a CPU? What is its function? Mention its several components.

4. Explain the different memory units.

5. Discuss the memory hierarchy within a computer system.

6. What is cache memory? Why is it necessary?

7. Give three examples of system software.

8. Briefly state the role of the operating system in a computer system.

9. What is BIOS? Describe its functions.

10. What is meant by POST?

11. What is the boot sector?

12. Describe the bootstrap process.

13. Distinguish between the following:

    (a) Compiler and interpreter

    (b) System software and application software

    (c) RAM and ROM

    (d) Primary memory and secondary memory

    (e) Bit and byte

    (f) Hardware and software

Number Systems and Binary Arithmetic

After studying this chapter, the readers will be able to

- explain the number system used in computers
- learn about the digit symbols, base, and representation forms of various number systems developed and used
- explain the method of number system conversions
- add and subtract unsigned binary numbers
- differentiate signed magnitude, 1's complement, and 2's complement representation of binary numbers

- subtract signed numbers in 1's complement and 2's complement representation
- explain the technique of multiplication and division of binary numbers
- explain binary codes and their classification

2.1 INTRODUCTION TO NUMBER SYSTEMS

A number system defines a set of values used to represent quantity. For example, the number of mobile phones kept in a shop, the number of persons standing in a queue, and the number of students attending a class.

There are many ways to represent the same numeric value. Long ago, humans used sticks to count; they then learned how to draw pictures of sticks on the ground and eventually on paper. So, the number 5 was first represented as: ||||| (for five sticks).

Later on, the Romans began using different symbols for multiple numbers of sticks: ||| still meant three sticks, but a V meant five sticks, and a X was used to represent ten of them. Using sticks to count was a great idea at that time. And using symbols instead of real sticks was much better. One of the best ways to represent a number today is by using the modern decimal system. Why? Because it includes the major breakthrough of using a symbol to represent the idea of counting nothing. About 1500 years ago, in India, zero (0) was first used as a number. It was later used in the Middle East as the Arabic, *sifr*. It was finally introduced in the West as the Latin, *zephiro*. Soon it was seen how valuable the concept of zero was for all modern number systems.

2.2 BASE OF A NUMBER SYSTEM

The *base, or radix,* of any number system is determined by the number of digit symbols in the system. For example, binary is a base-2 number system since it uses two symbols and decimal is a base-10 system since it uses ten symbols.

In general, in any number system, a number N can be represented by any one of the following forms:

(a) Positional notation form:
$$N = d_{n-1}d_{n-2} \ldots d_1 d_0 \cdot d_{-1} d_{-2} \ldots d_{-m}$$

(b) Polynomial form:
$$N = d_{n-1} \times r^{n-1} + d_{n-2} \times r^{n-2} \ldots d_0 r^0$$
$$+ d_{-1} r^{-1} + d_{-2} r^{-2} \ldots d_{-m} r^{-m}$$

(c) Compact form:

$$N = \sum_{i=-m}^{n-1} d_i r^i$$

where
d = value of the digit symbol,
r = base or radix,
n = the number of integral digits to the left of the decimal point, and
m = the number of fractional digits or digits to the right of the decimal point.

2.3 WEIGHTING FACTOR

The numerical value of a number is the sum of the products obtained by multiplying each digit by the weight of its respective position. Decimal numbers are represented by arranging the symbols 0, 1, 2, 3, 4, 5, 6, 7, 8, and 9. These are known as decimal digits, in various sequences. The position of each digit in a sequence has a certain numerical weight, and each digit is a multiplier of the weight of its position. The decimal number system is hence an example of a weighted, positional number system. The weight of each position is a power of the base number 10.

Therefore, the weighting factor is the numerical value of the multiplier for each column (digit) position of the number. For instance, the decimal number system has a weighting factor of 10 raised to the power of value equal to the position of the digit symbol. For each column to the left, the value of the multiplier increases by 10 over the previous column on the right.

Let us consider the number 754 in the decimal number system.

$$7 \cdot \boxed{10}^2 + 5 \cdot 10^1 + 4 \cdot 10^{\boxed{0}} = 700 + 50 + 4 = 754$$

Base ⟶ Digit Position

Important note Any number raised to the power of zero is 1, even zero raised to the power of zero is 1, for example, $10^0 = 1, \quad 0^0 = 1, \quad x^0 = 1$

2.4 TYPES OF NUMBER SYSTEMS

There are several types number systems. Table 2.1 shows a list of number systems with their base and sets of valid digits.

2.4.1 Decimal Number System [Base-10]

Most people today use decimal representation to count. This number system uses TEN different symbols to represent values. In the decimal system there are 10 digit symbols 0, 1, 2, 3, 4, 5, 6, 7, 8, and 9 with 0 having the least value and 9 having the greatest value. For a number represented in decimal system, the digit on the extreme left has the greatest value, whereas the digit on the extreme right has the least value.

- Each position to the left increases by a weight of 10.

EXAMPLE

(i) 9 + 1 = 10 (nine plus one equals *zero, carry one* or 10)

(ii)

| 3 | 2 | 1 | 0 | ⟵ Digit position |
| 1 | 2 | 7 | 5 | ⟵ Decimal number |

$$5 \times 10^0 = 5$$
$$7 \times 10^1 = 70$$
$$2 \times 10^2 = 200$$
$$1 \times 10^3 = 1000$$
$$1275_{10}$$

Multiplier (in decimal)   Weight (in decimal)

Table 2.1 Number systems, bases, and symbols

Number system	Base	Digital symbols
Binary	2	0, 1
Ternary	3	0, 1, 2
Quaternary	4	0, 1, 2, 3
Quinary	5	0, 1, 2, 3, 4
Octal	8	0, 1, 2, 3, 4, 5, 6, 7
Decimal	10	0, 1, 2, 3, 4, 5, 6, 7, 8, 9
Duodecimal	12	0, 1, 2, 3, 4, 5, 6, 7, 8, 9, A, B
Hexadecimal	16	0, 1, 2, 3, 4, 5, 6, 7, 8, 9, A, B, C, D, E, F
Vigesimal	20	0, 1, 2, 3, 4, 5, 6, 7, 8, 9, A, B, C, D, E, F, G, H, I, J

2.4.2 Binary Number System [Base-2]

The binary number system uses TWO symbols to represent numerical values. These are 0 and 1 with 0 having the least value and 1 having the greatest value. Number representation in the binary system is similar to that in the decimal system, in which the digit on the extreme left represents the greatest value and is called the most significant digit (MSD), whereas the digit on the extreme right is known as the least significant digit (LSD).

- Each position to the left increases by a weight of 2.

EXAMPLE

(i) It should be noted that $1 + 1 = 10$ (one plus one equals *zero, carry one* or 10)

In a computer, a binary digit representing a binary value (0 or 1) is called a BIT. That is, each digit in a binary number is called a bit, 4 bits form a NIBBLE, 8 bits form a BYTE, two bytes form a WORD and two words form a DOUBLE WORD (rarely used).

An *n*-bit number can represent 2^n different number values, for example, for an 8-bit number, $2^8 = 256$ different values may be represented.

2.4.3 Octal Number System [Base-8]

The octal number system uses EIGHT digit symbols to represent numbers. The symbols are

0, 1, 2, 3, 4, 5, 6, and 7

with 0 having the least value and 7 having the greatest value. The number representation in the octal system is done in the same way as in the decimal system, in which the digit on the extreme left represents the most significant digit.

- Each position to the left increases by a weight of 8. Thus,
  (i) $7 + 1 = 10$ (seven plus one equals *zero, carry one* or 10)

2.4.4 Hexadecimal Number System [Base-16]

The hexadecimal number system uses SIXTEEN symbols to represent numbers. The symbols are

0, 1, 2, 3, 4, 5, 6, 7, 8, 9, A, B, C, D, E, and F

with 0 having the least value and F having the greatest value. Number representation in hexadecimal system is done in the same way as in the decimal system, in which the symbol on the extreme left represents the most significant digit.

- Each position to the left increases by a weight of 16. Thus,
  (i) $F + 1 = 10$ (F 'i.e. 15' plus one equals *zero, carry one* or 10)
(ii)

```
 2   1   0   ← Digit position (in decimal)
 2   A   6₁₆ ← Hexadecimal number
             ↘ 6 × 16⁰ =    6
               10 × 16¹ =  160
               2 × 16² =   512
                          ────
                          678₁₀
```

The hexadecimal system is often used to represent values (data and memory addresses) in computer systems. Table 2.2 shows the representation of decimal numbers ranging from 0 to 15 in binary, octal, and hexadecimal number systems.

Table 2.2 Number systems equivalency table

Decimal (Base-10)	Binary (Base-2)	Octal (Base-8)	Hexadecimal (Base-16)
0	0000	0	0
1	0001	1	1
2	0010	2	2
3	0011	3	3
4	0100	4	4
5	0101	5	5
6	0110	6	6
7	0111	7	7
8	1000	10	8
9	1001	11	9
10	1010	12	A
11	1011	13	B
12	1100	14	C
13	1101	15	D
14	1110	16	E
15	1111	17	F

2.4.5 Common Rules of Number Systems

All number systems follow the following set of rules:

Rule 1 The number of digit symbols available in a number system is equal to the base.

Examples:

For the decimal system having base 10, there are 10 digit symbols 0 through 9.

For the binary system having base 2, there are 2 digit symbols 0 and 1.

Rule 2 The value of the largest digit symbol is one less than the base.

Examples:

Decimal system—largest digit = $10 - 1 = 9$

Binary system—largest digit = $2 - 1 = 1$

Rule 3 Each position multiplies the value of the digit symbol by the base raised to the power of the value equal to the digit symbol position.

Examples:

Decimal system—consider the number

$125 = 1 \times 10^2 + 2 \times 10^1 + 5 \times 10^0$

Rule 4 A carry from one position to the next increases its weight base times.

Examples:

Decimal system—consider the number

$5 - 5 = 5 \times 10^0$ or 5 ones.

Moving the number, one place, to the left, it becomes—5×10^1 or 5 tens or 50.

Binary system—consider the number

$1 - 1 = 1 \times 2^0$ or 1 one.

Moving the number, one place, to the left, it becomes—1×2^1 or two 1's or 10

To avoid confusion, often a subscript is used with a number to indicate the number system base. For example,

162_h	'h' means hexadecimal
162_{16}	16 means base-16
162_d	'd' means decimal
162_{10}	10 means base-10
162_o	'o' means octal
162_8	8 means base-8
101_b	'b' means binary
101_2	2 means base-2

Note

- In all number system representations, the digit on the extreme left represents the greatest value and is called the most significant digit (MSD), whereas the digit on the extreme right is known as the least significant digit (LSD).
- The value of the largest digit symbol is one less than the base.
- A carry from one position to the next increases its weight base times.

2.5 NUMBER SYSTEM CONVERSIONS

Till now the different number systems have been discussed. But what happens when a number in one number system representation needs to be represented in another form? So it is necessary to understand how numbers from one form may be represented in other forms. The following sections discuss the way conversions from one number system to other number systems are carried out.

2.5.1 Working with Integer Numbers

Conversion of a decimal number to its binary equivalent

Method 1 Repeated-division-by-2 method

1. Divide the dividend, that is, the decimal number by two and obtain the quotient and remainder.
2. Divide the quotient by two and obtain the new quotient and remainder.
3. Repeat step 2 until the quotient is equal to zero (0).
4. The first remainder produced is the least significant bit (LSB) in the binary number and the last remainder is the most significant bit (MSB). Accordingly, the binary number is then written (from left to right) with the MSB occurring first (list the remainder values in reverse order). This is the binary equivalent.

EXAMPLE

Converting the decimal number 254 into its binary equivalent.

Thus, the binary equivalent is **11111110**.

Method 2 Power-of-2-subtraction method

1. Let D be the number that has to be converted from decimal to binary.
2. (a) Find the largest power of two that is less than or equal to D. Let this equal P.
   (b) If $|D| \geq P$, subtract P from D, obtain a result which is a decimal number. Put 1 in the digit position where the weighting factor is P.
   (c) Otherwise, if $|D| < |P|$, put 0 in the corresponding weighting factor column.
3. Repeat step 2 with D = remainder decimal number until $D = 0$, or $|D| < |P|$.

EXAMPLE

Converting the decimal number 247 into its binary equivalent.

The largest power of 2 that is less than 247 is $2^7 = 128$. Form the table with the weighting factor in the columns in the order shown, with 128 being the most significant weight. Put 1 in the digit position with weighting factor 128.

Weighting factor	128	64	32	16	8	4	2	1
Binary mumber	1							

This leaves a remainder $(247 - 128) = 119$. For 119, for which the highest power of 2 is 64, 1 is put in digit position with the weighting factor 64.

128	64	32	16	8	4	2	1
1	1						

This leaves a remainder $(119 - 64) = 55$. Weight 32 fits; therefore, 1 is put in the corresponding digit position as follows:

128	64	32	16	8	4	2	1
1	1	1					

This leaves a remainder $(55 - 32) = 23$. Weight 16 fits; thus 1 is put in the digit position with weight 16.

128	64	32	16	8	4	2	1
1	1	1	1				

This leaves $(23 - 16) = 7$ as remainder. This is smaller than the next digit position weight value 8. So 0 is put under 8. Next, find the weight that fits; thus, 1 is placed in the digit position with weight 4. Hence, $(7 - 4) = 3$ is left.

128	64	32	16	8	4	2	1
1	1	1	1	0	1		

Weight 2 fits; thus a 1 is put under the digit position with weight 2. Therefore, $(3 - 2) = 1$ is left, which is put in digit position with weight 1, that is, 2^0.

128	64	32	16	8	4	2	1
1	1	1	1				

Hence, 247 in base 10 is the same as 11110111 in base 2.

Conversion from binary to decimal

To express the value of a given binary number as its decimal equivalent, sum the binary digits after each digit has been multiplied by its associated weight.

EXAMPLE

Converting $(110101)_2$ to its decimal equivalent.

Conversion of a decimal number to its octal equivalent

To convert from decimal whole numbers to octal, the systematic approach called the **repeated-division-by-8 method** is used. This method is explained by the following example.

EXAMPLE

Converting $(359)_{10}$ to octal.

(a) Divide the decimal number by eight and obtain a quotient and a remainder.

(b) Divide the quotient by eight and obtain a new quotient and a remainder.

(c) Repeat step (b) until the quotient is equal to zero (0).

(d) The first remainder produced is the LSB in the octal number and the last remainder (R) is the MSB. Accordingly, the octal number is then written (from left to right) with the MSB occurring first.

Therefore, $(359)_{10} = (547)_8$

Conversion of an octal number to its decimal equivalent

To express the value of a given octal number as its decimal equivalent, add the octal digits after each digit has been multiplied by its associated weight.

EXAMPLE

Converting $(237)_8$ to decimal form.

Conversion of an octal number to its binary equivalent

Since each octal digit can be represented by a three-bit binary number (see Table 2.3), it is very easy to convert from octal to binary. Simply replace each octal digit with the appropriate three-bit binary number as indicated in the following example.

Table 2.3 Binary equivalents for octal digits

Octal digit	Equivalent binary number
0	000
1	001
2	010
3	011
4	100
5	101
6	110
7	111

EXAMPLE

Converting the octal number 236700321 to its equivalent binary number.

Octal number	Equivalent binary number
2	010
3	011
6	110
7	111
0	000
0	000
3	011
2	010
1	001

Conversion of a binary number to its equivalent octal number

Converting a binary number to an octal number is a simple process. Break the binary digits into groups of three starting from the binary point and convert each group into its appropriate octal digit. For whole numbers, it may be necessary to add zeros as the MSB, in order to complete a grouping of three bits. Note that this does not change the value of the binary number.

EXAMPLE

Converting $(010111)_2$ to its equivalent octal number.

Binary number	→	010	111
Equivalent octal number	→	2	7

Conversion of a decimal number to its hexadecimal equivalent

The decimal number to be converted is divided by 16 until the quotient is 0. The hexadecimal number is formed from the remainders.

Starting with the last remainder, convert the remainders into hexadecimal numbers:

1 5 11 14 10 = 15BEA = the hexadecimal number.

Conversion of a hexadecimal number to its decimal equivalent

To convert a hexadecimal to decimal, begin by multiplying each of the hexadecimal digits by their positional weight values as expressed in decimal. Then the resulting values are added to obtain the value of the decimal number.

EXAMPLE

Converting the hexadecimal number **A4D31** to its equivalent decimal number.

The decimal value of each digit in relation to its positional weight value is evaluated first:

Conversion of a hexadecimal number to its binary equivalent

As each hexadecimal digit can be represented by a four-bit binary number (see Table 2.4), it is very easy to convert from hexadecimal to binary. Simply replace each hexadecimal digit with the appropriate four-bit binary number as indicated in the following examples.

Table 2.4 Number systems equivalency

Decimal (Base-10)	Binary (Base-2)	Hexadecimal (Base-16)
0	0000	0
1	0001	1
2	0010	2
3	0011	3
4	0100	4
5	0101	5
6	0110	6
7	0111	7
8	1000	8
9	1001	9
10	1010	A
11	1011	B
12	1100	C
13	1101	D
14	1110	E
15	1111	F

--- EXAMPLE ---

Converting 1234_{16} to a binary number.

| Hexadecimal number | ⟶ | 1 | 2 | 3 | 4 |
| Equivalent binary number | ⟶ | 0001 | 0010 | 0011 | 0100 |

--- EXAMPLE ---

Converting $37B_{16}$ to a binary number.

| Hexadecimal number | ⟶ | 3 | 7 | B |
| Equivalent binary number | ⟶ | 0011 | 0111 | 1011 |

--- EXAMPLE ---

Converting the hexadecimal number AF376 to its equivalent binary number.

| Hexadecimal number | ⟶ | A | F | 3 | 7 | 6 |
| Equivalent binary number | ⟶ | 1010 | 1111 | 0011 | 0111 | 0110 |

Conversion of a binary number to its hexadecimal equivalent

Hexadecimal system works very much like the octal system, except that each digit needs exactly four bits to represent it. This means the binary number has to be divided into groups of four digits, again starting from the digit at the extreme right. The equivalent hexadecimals for each set of four digits are then written. For whole numbers, it may be necessary to add zeroes as the MSB in order to complete a grouping of four bits. Note that this addition does not change the value of the binary number.

--- EXAMPLE ---

Converting the binary number 1111011101101011011 to its equivalent hexadecimal number.

The conversion is done as follows:

A leading zero had to be added for the most significant group to have four bits.

| Binary Numbar | ⟶ | 0111 | 1011 | 1011 | 0101 | 1011 |
| Equivalent hexadecimal numbar | ⟶ | 7 | B | B | 5 | B |

Conversion from hexadecimal to octal, and octal to hexadecimal

To convert from hexadecimal to octal, each digit of the hexadecimal number is written as its equivalent four-bit binary number. The resulting binary number is divided into groups of three binary digits. Then corresponding octal numbers for each of these groups are written.

--- EXAMPLE ---

Converting the hexadecimal number AF35D02 to its equivalent octal number.

The given number is rewritten by replacing the hexadecimal digits by their equivalent four-bit binary numbers.

	In groups of three bits
A	1010
F	1111
3	0011
5	0101
d	1101
0	0000
2	0010

The binary number is regrouped as three-bit binary numbers that are replaced with octal symbols.

In groups of three bits	Octal number
001	1
010	2
111	7
100	4
110	6
101	5
110	6
100	4
000	0
010	2

Therefore, we see that $AF35D02_{16} = 1274656402_8$.

--- EXAMPLE ---

Converting the octal number 1273244 to its equivalent hexadecimal.

The given number is written by replacing the octal digits with equivalent three-bit binary numbers.

	In groups of 3 bits
1	001
2	010
4	111
7	111
3	011
2	010
4	100
4	100

The binary number is regrouped as four-bit binary numbers that are replaced with hexadecimal symbols.

In groups of 4 bits	Equivalent hexadecimal
0010	2
1011	B
1111	F
0110	6
1010	A
0100	4

Therefore, we see that $1273244_8 = 2BF6A4_{16}$.

However, there are easier conversion methods. Some ways to perform conversion between the bases are as follows.

Any base to decimal   Use expanded notation. Write down each digit as a product of a power of the base and add them all.

Decimal to any base   Use the division method. Divide the decimal number repeatedly with the base, writing down the remainder at each step. When the quotient becomes zero, the string of remainders is the number in the new base.

Octal to hexadecimal or vice versa   Use binary as an intermediate form.

2.5.2 Working with Fractional Numbers

One is familiar with the decimal (base-10) number system. Each digit within any given decimal number is associated with a weight. Furthermore, the value of that number is the sum of the digits after each has been multiplied by its weight. To illustrate, let us consider Table 2.5 and assume that the number 654.52, written as $(654.52)_{10}$ to specify base-10, is being represented. Note that the digits range from 0 to 9.

Table 2.5 Decimal number system

	Hundreds	Tens	Units	One-tenth	One-hundredth	
Weights	10^2	10^1	10^0	10^{-1}	10^{-2}	
Symbols	6	5	4	5	2	
Weighted value	600	50	4	0.5	0.02	Total 654.52

Just as the decimal system with its ten digits is a base-10 system, the binary number system with its two digits, 0 and 1, is a base-2 system. Table 2.6 shows the weighting for the binary number system up to two decimal places after and three places before the *binary point* (.) Note the similarity with the decimal system.

Table 2.6 Binary weights

Weights	2^2	2^1	2^0	2^{-1}	2^{-2}

The least significant bit (LSB) is the rightmost binary digit, which has the lowest binary weight of a given number. The most significant bit (MSB) is the leftmost binary digit, which has the highest binary weight of a given number.

Counting in binary is similar to the decimal number system. The LSB begins with zero (0) and is incremented until the maximum digit value is reached. The adjacent bit positions are then filled appropriately as the iterative counting process continues.

Note

- For conversion from any number base system to decimal use expanded notation.
- For conversion from decimal number system to any base use the division method.
- While converting octal number to hexadecimal number or vice versa use binary as an intermediate form.
- It is important to note that many decimal fractions do not have an exact representation in binary.

Conversion from decimal fractions to binary

When converting a fractional decimal value to binary, a slightly different approach is needed. Instead of dividing by 2, the decimal fraction is multiplied by 2. If the result is greater than or equal to 1, then 1 is to be put as the quotient. If the result is less than 1, then 0 is put as the quotient.

EXAMPLE

Converting $(0.375)_{10}$ to binary.

$0.375 \times 2 = 0.750$ 0
$0.750 \times 2 = 1.500$ 1
$0.500 \times 2 = 1.000$ 1
done.

Note that the last operation is complete when the fraction part equals zero. It is rarely possible to accurately represent a fractional value in binary. The answer to this problem is: .011

It is important to note that many decimal fractions do not have an exact representation in binary. This is illustrated in the following example.

EXAMPLE

Converting $(0.29)_{10}$ to binary.

$0.29 \times 2 = 0.58$	0
$0.58 \times 2 = 1.16$	1
$0.16 \times 2 = 0.32$	0
$0.32 \times 2 = 0.64$	0
$0.64 \times 2 = 1.28$	1
$0.28 \times 2 = 0.56$	0
$0.56 \times 2 = 1.12$	1
$0.12 \times 2 = 0.24$	0
$0.24 \times 2 = 0.48$	0
$0.48 \times 2 = 0.96$	0
$0.96 \times 2 = 1.92$	1
$0.92 \times 2 = 1.84$	1
$0.84 \times 2 = 1.68$	1
$0.68 \times 2 = 1.36$	1
$0.36 \times 2 = 0.72$	0
$0.72 \times 2 = 1.44$	1

The decimal point is at the top so the conversion of .29 to binary upto 16-bits of approximation is:

.0100101000111101

The whole number is ignored before multiplying again for the next digit. While using a calculator, just enter the decimal fraction value and multiply by 2. Writing a computer program to perform these operations is easy using this technique.

Conversion from binary fraction to decimal

To express the value of a given fractional binary number in equivalent decimal value, each bit is multiplied by its associated weight and the summation of these gives the desired decimal number.

EXAMPLE

Converting $(0.1011)_2$ to a decimal number.

$$1 \times 2^{-4} = 0.0625$$
$$1 \times 2^{-3} = 0.125$$
$$0 \times 2^{-2} = 0$$
$$1 \times 2^{-1} = 0.5$$
$$\overline{0.6875_{10}}$$

Multiplier Weight

Conversion from octal fraction to decimal

Just as the decimal system with its ten digit symbols is a number system with base 10, the octal number system with its 8 digit symbols, '0', '1', '2', '3', '4', '5', '6' and '7', has eight as its base. Table 2.7 shows the weights for an octal number that has three decimal places before and two digit places after the *octal point* (.).

Table 2.7 Octal weights

Weights	8^2	8^1	8^0	8^{-1}	8^{-2}

To express a given octal number as its decimal equivalent, each bit is multiplied by its associated weight and the summation of these gives the decimal number.

EXAMPLE

Converting $(237.04)_8$ to a decimal number.

$$4 \times 8^{-2} = 0.0625$$
$$0 \times 8^{-1} = 0$$
$$7 \times 8^0 = 7$$
$$3 \times 8^1 = 24$$
$$2 \times 8^2 = 128$$
$$\overline{159.0625_{10}}$$

Multiplier Weight

Conversion from decimal fractions to octal

The techniques used to convert decimal fractions to octal are similar to the methods demonstrated previously to convert decimal fractions to binary numbers. The **repeated-multiplication-by-8** method is used. In the multiplication-by-8 method, the fraction is repeatedly multiplied by eight, and the integer number is recorded until the fraction part is zero. The first integer produced is the MSD, while the last integer is the LSD. Remember that the octal point precedes the MSD. To illustrate, consider the following conversion.

EXAMPLE

Converting $(0.3125)_{10}$ to an octal number.

$0.3125 \times 8 = 2.5000$	2
$0.5 \times 8 = 4.0$	4

0.24_8

Thus, $(0.3125)_{10} = (0.24)_8$

Conversion from octal fraction to binary

The primary application of octal numbers is representing binary numbers, as it is easier to handle large numbers in octal form than in binary form. Because each octal digit can be represented by a three-bit binary number (see Table 2.8), it is very easy to convert from octal to binary. Simply replace each octal digit with the appropriate three-bit binary number as indicated in the following examples.

Table 2.8 Octal and binary numbers

Octal digit	Binary digit
0	000
1	001
2	010
3	011
4	100
5	101
6	110
7	111

--- EXAMPLE ---

(a) Converting 13_8 to equivalent binary number.

Octal number	1	3
Binary number	001	011

(b) Converting 37.12_8 to equivalent binary number.

Octal number	3	7	.	1	2
Binary number	011	111	.	001	010

Conversion from binary fraction to octal

Converting binary to octal is also a simple process. Arrange the binary number into groups of three bits starting from the binary point and convert each of these groups into its appropriate octal digit symbol. For whole numbers, it may be necessary to add a zero with the MSD in order to form a grouping of three bits. Note that this does not change the value of the binary number. Similarly, when representing fractions, it may be necessary to add a trailing zero in the LSD in order to form a complete grouping of three bits.

--- EXAMPLE ---

(a) Converting $(010.111)_2$ to octal

Thus, $(010.111)_2 = (2.7)_8$

(b) Converting $(0.110101)_2$ to octal

Thus, $(0.110101)_2 = (0.65)_8$

Hexadecimal number conversion

Just like the octal number system, the hexadecimal number system provides a convenient way to express binary numbers.

Table 2.9 shows the weight for the hexadecimal number system up to three digit places before and two places after the *hexadecimal point*. Based on the trend in previous number systems, the methods used to convert hexadecimal to decimal and vice versa should be similar.

Table 2.9 Hexadecimal weights

Weights	16^2	16^1	16^0	16^{-1}	16^{-2}

Table 2.10 lists the equivalent decimal, binary, and hexadecimal representations for the decimal numbers ranging from 0 to 15. Each hexadecimal number can be represented as a four-digit binary number.

Table 2.10 Number systems equivalency table

Decimal	Binary	Hexadecimal
0	0000	0
1	0001	1
2	0010	2
3	0011	3
4	0100	4
5	0101	5
6	0110	6
7	0111	7
8	1000	8
9	1001	9
10	1010	A
11	1011	B

Conversion from hexadecimal fraction to binary

Because each hexadecimal digit can be represented by a four-bit binary number, it is very easy to convert from hexadecimal to binary. Simply replace each hexadecimal digit with the appropriate four-bit binary number as indicated in the following example.

--- EXAMPLE ---

Converting $(37.12)_{16}$ to binary number.

Hexadecimal number	3	7	.	1	2
Binary number	0011	0111	.	0001	0010

Conversion from binary fraction to hexadecimal

Converting from binary to hexadecimal is also a simple process. Arrange the binary digits into groups of four starting from the binary point and convert each group into its appropriate hexadecimal digit symbol. For whole numbers, it may be necessary to add a zero with the MSD in order to form a grouping of four bits. Note that this addition does not change the value of the binary number. Similarly, while representing fractions, it may be necessary to add a trailing zero in the LSD in order to form a grouping of four bits.

EXAMPLE

Converting $(0.00111111)_2$ to hexadecimal

Binary number $\longrightarrow$	0 .	0011	1111
Hexadecimal number $\longrightarrow$	0 .	3	F

Thus, $(0.00111111)_2 = (0.3F)_{16}$

Check Your Progress

1. What is the binary equivalent of the decimal number 368
   - (a) 101110000
   - (c) 110110000
   - (c) 111010000
   - (d) 111100000

   Answer: (a)

2. The decimal equivalent of hex number 1A53 is
   - (a) 6793
   - (b) 6739
   - (c) 6973
   - (d) 6379

   Answer: (b)

3. $(734)_8 = (\ ?\ )_{16}$
   - (a) C 1 D
   - (b) D C 1
   - (c) 1 C D
   - (d) 1 D C

   Answer: (d)

4. The hexadecimal number for $(95.5)_{10}$ is
   - (a) $(5F.8)_{16}$
   - (b) $(9A.B)_{16}$
   - (c) $(2E.F)_{16}$
   - (d) $(5A.4)_{16}$

   Answer: (a)

5. Determine the binary number represented by 0.6875

   Answer: 0.1011_2

6. The octal equivalent of $(247)_{10}$ is
   - (a) $(252)_8$
   - (b) $(350)_8$
   - (c) $(367)_8$
   - (d) $(400)_8$

   Answer: (c)

2.6 BINARY ARITHMETIC

In computers, numbers are represented in binary form. The arithmetic operations performed by a computer therefore involves binary numbers. The next few sections describe how binary arithmetic operations like binary addition, subtraction, multiplication, and division are performed. In this context, it may be mentioned that such arithmetic operations are primarily performed by the ALU within the computer system.

2.6.1 Addition

Four basic rules are needed to perform binary addition. Table 2.11 lists these rules. The first three rules are quite simple and there is no difference between these binary rules and the corresponding decimal rules. The fourth rule, however, is different from the decimal rule. When two 1's are added together in binary, a carry gets generated which is placed in the next column. In the decimal system, because 10-digit symbols exist, a carry does not get generated until the sum of two digits is greater than or equal to 10 (e.g., $5 + 7 = 12$).

Table 2.11 Rules for binary addition

Rule 1	Rule 2	Rule 3	Rule 4
0	0	1	1
+ 0	+ 1	+ 0	+ 1
0	1	1	10

These rules can be used to derive another important rule for binary arithmetic. Consider what happens when three 1's are added together in binary. Let the problem be split into two addition problems; the answer is obtained by applying the rule for binary addition.

1. Apply Rule 4 to find the sum of the first two 1's.

$$\begin{array}{r} 1 \\ + 1 \\ \hline 10 \end{array}$$

2. Next, take the previous result of 10_2 and add the final 1 to it. Notice that Rule 2 ($0 + 1 = 1$) is used to find the answer to the first column, and Rule 3 ($1 + 0 = 1$) is used to find the answer to the second column.

$$\begin{array}{r} 10 \\ + 1 \\ \hline 11 \end{array}$$

3. Hence another rule has been derived for binary arithmetic. The sum of three 1's in binary is 11_2.

$$\begin{array}{r} 1 \\ + 1 \\ \hline 11 \end{array}$$

It is important to remember that in binary addition, two 1's always generate a carry to the next column. This happened in the preceding example. Adding the first two 1's gives a carry to the next column and the remaining 1 becomes the value for the current column.

EXAMPLE

Adding 1111_2 (15_{10}) and 0110_2 (6_{10}).

Solution: The binary numbers 1111_2 and 0110_2 can be added in the same way the decimal numbers 15_{10} and 6_{10} are added.

1. The numbers in the rightmost column are added. 1 plus 0 adds up to 1.

$$\begin{array}{r} 0 \quad \text{Carry} \\ 0\ 1\ 1\ 1\ 1 \\ +\ 0\ 0\ 1\ 1\ 0 \\ \hline 1 \quad \text{Result} \end{array}$$

2. The next column is added. 1 plus 1 equals 10_2, so a 1 is carried to the next column and the 0 is written under this column.

$$\begin{array}{r} 1\ 0 \quad \text{Carry} \\ 0\ 1\ 1\ 1\ 1 \\ +\ 0\ 0\ 1\ 1\ 0 \\ \hline 0\ 1 \quad \text{Result} \end{array}$$

3. Notice that the third column now contains three 1's. Adding the first two 1's gives 10_2. Adding this sum to the remaining 1 gives a total of 11_2, so a 1 is carried to the next column and a 1 is written under this column.

```
    1 1 0      Carry
  0 1 1 1 1
+ 0 0 1 1 0
      1 0 1   Result
```

4. The two ones in the fourth column total 10_2, so a 1 is carried to the final column, and a 0 is written below this column.

```
  1 1 1 0      Carry
  0 1 1 1 1
+ 0 0 1 1 0
    0 1 0 1   Result
```

5. Finally, the carry from the previous column plus the two 0's from this column add to 1.

```
  1 1 1 0      Carry
  0 1 1 1 1
+ 0 0 1 1 0
  1 0 1 0 1   Result
```

6. This gives a final answer of 10101_2.

```
  1 1 1 0      Carry
  0 1 1 1 1
+ 0 0 1 1 0
  1 0 1 0 1   Result
```

2.6.2 Subtraction

For subtraction in the decimal system, normally the borrow method is used. Consider the example on the right. Here a 10 is borrowed from the tens column in order to complete the subtraction in the ones column. Moving 10 to the ones column and subtracting 6 yields 4. The remaining 20 from the tens column is taken and 2 is written in the tens column to get the result of 24_{10}.

The borrow method can also be used to do binary subtraction. The basic rules for binary subtraction are listed in Table 3.2.

Table 2.12 Rules for binary subtraction

Rule 1	Rule 2	Rule 3	Rule 4
0	1	1	0
−0	−1	−0	−1
0	0	1	1

The first three rules are similar to the decimal system rules. The fourth rule, however, needs a little more explanation since it defines how borrowing is done from another column. Let us look at a simple example to see where this rule comes from. Consider the problem of subtracting 1_2 from 10_2.

1. To compute the first column, a 1 is borrowed from the next column. Recall that two 1's generate a carry in addition. If this process is reversed, a 1 can be borrowed from the second column and two 1's in the first column can be marked.

```
Second column ──┐ ┌── First column
             10 Minuend
            −1 Subtrahend
```

2. Following a borrow from the second column, the 1 is crossed out and a 0 is written above it to show that this column is now empty. The 1 from the second column is now represented by the two 1's in the first column.

```
   1 ⎫
 01 ⎬ Borrow
 10̶ Minuend
 −1 Subtrahend
```

3. Following a borrow from the second column, the 1 is crossed out and a 0 is written above it to show that this column is now empty. The 1 from the second column is now represented by the two 1's in the first column.

```
   1 ⎫
 01 ⎬ Borrow
 10̶ Minuend
 −1 Subtrahend
  1  Result
```

4. Note that the first column of the answer is identical to Rule 4. Since a 1 was borrowed from the next column, the second column becomes 0.

```
 10 Minuend
 −1 Subtrahend
  1  Result
```

The rules of subtraction can be applied to solve larger subtraction problems in binary arithmetic. The example below demonstrates how to subtract binary number 1110_2 from 10101_2.

EXAMPLE

Subtract 1110_2 from 10101_2.
Solution:

1. Consider subtraction of the extreme right column. 1 minus 0 equals 1.

```
  10101   Minuend
− 01110   Subtrahend
      1   Result
```

2. In order to subtract the second column, a 1 has to be borrowed. So, cross out the 1 in the third column, and represent it as two 1's in the second column.

```
     1 ⎫
    01 ⎬ Borrow
 10\01 Minuend
− 01110 Subtrahend
      1 Result
```

3. 1 can now be subtracted from the group of two borrowed 1's. This leaves a 1, so it is written below the second column.

```
     1 ⎫
    01 ⎬ Borrow
 10\01 Minuend
− 01110 Subtrahend
     11 Result
```

4. Now, subtraction of the next column is carried out. Since a 1 was borrowed from this column, the subtraction is 0 minus 1 and a borrow has to be made again. However, there is no borrow in the next column. So first, a borrow from the most significant column must be made.

```
  1 1 ⎫
      ⎬ Borrow
0101 ⎭
10101 Minuend
−01110 Subtrahend
   11 Result
```

5. Then borrow a 1 from the fourth column to the current column.

```
  1   ⎫
111   ⎬ Borrow
0101  ⎭
10101 Minuend
−01110 Subtrahend
   11 Result
```

6. Now the current column can be subtracted. A 1 is taken away from the group of two 1's. This leaves a single 1 which is written below the column.

```
  1   ⎫
111   ⎬ Borrow
0101  ⎭
10101 Minuend
−01110 Subtrahend
  111 Result
```

7. In the fourth column, a 1 is subtracted from a 1 for a result of 0.

```
  1   ⎫
111   ⎬ Borrow
0101  ⎭
10101 Minuend
−01110 Subtrahend
 0111 Result
```

8. The most significant column contains all zeros, so 0 is written below it. Hence, the result is 00111_2.

```
  1   ⎫
111   ⎬ Borrow
0101  ⎭
10101 Minuend
−01110 Subtrahend
00111 Result
```

2.6.3 Binary

So far in the study of binary arithmetic, only positive numbers have been considered. Now, a way is needed to represent numbers such as -32_{10}. When computations are done in decimal, a minus sign precedes a number to make it negative. Since computers can only work with 1's and 0's, it is necessary to modify this approach slightly.

One solution is to add an extra binary digit to the left of the binary number to indicate whether the number is positive or negative. In computer terminology, this digit is called a sign bit. Remember that a 'bit' is simply another name for a binary digit. When a number is positive, the sign bit is zero, and when the number is negative, the sign bit is one. This approach is called the **signed magnitude representation**. Note that this is very similar to adding a minus sign in decimal.

Still one small problem remains with the representation. It is necessary to specify how many bits are there in a number to know which bit is representing the sign. Let us convert the decimal numbers -5_{10} and -1_{10} to binary using signed magnitude representation. For these numbers, four bits will be enough to represent both.

1. 5 and 1 are converted to binary.   101 (5)
                                         1 (1)

2. Now a positive sign bit is added to each one. Notice that '1' is padded with zeros so that it has four bits.   0101 (5) 0001 (1)
   ↑
   sign bit
   ↓

3. To make the binary numbers negative, simply change the sign bit from 0 to 1.   1101 (−5) 1001 (−1)

One has to be sure not to mistake the number 1101_2 for 13_{10}. Since a four-bit signed magnitude representation is used, the first bit is the sign bit and the remaining three bits are for the magnitude (absolute value) of the number.

Therefore, the sign and magnitude of the integer are represented separately. A negative integer, for example, is represented by a 1 in the leftmost bit and the absolute value in the remaining bits. The range of integers that can be stored in signed magnitude is $-2^{n-1} + 1$ to $+2^{n-1} - 1$, where n is the number of bits in the signed magnitude number.

While representing negative numbers with signed magnitude is simple, performing arithmetic with signed magnitude is difficult. Consider the subtraction problem $30_{10} - 6_{10}$. This can be converted to an equivalent addition problem by changing 6_{10} to -6_{10}. Now, the problem may be restated as $30_{10} + (-6_{10}) = 24_{10}$. Something similar can be done in binary by representing negative numbers as complements. Two ways of representing signed numbers using complements will be discussed: 1's complement and 2's complement in the next section.

> **Note**
>
> - When a single bit number 1 is added with another single bit number 1 the sum bit is 0 and the carry bit is 1.
> - When a single bit number 1 is subtracted from a single bit number 0 the difference bit is 1 and the borrow bit is 1.
> - In the signed magnitude representation of binary numbers, the integer is represented by a sign bit in the most significant bit position followed by the binary representation of the magnitude. For a negative integer, the msb is 1 whereas for a positive integer the msb is 0.
> - Subtraction of integers in signed 2's complement representation produces results in true signed magnitude form.

1's Complement

A signed number with 1's complement is represented by changing all the bits that are 1 to 0 and all the bits that are 0 to 1. Reversing the digits in this way is also called complementing a number, as illustrated by the examples below.

EXAMPLE

Obtaining the 1's complement of (i) 10001 and (ii) 101001.
Solution:

Number	1's Complement
10001	01110
101001	010110

Note

- -0 and $+0$ are represented differently even though they are the same algebraically.
- This causes problems when carrying out tests on arithmetic results.
- Hence, 1's complement is an unpopular choice for integer representation.
- Most computers now use a variation of 1's complement (called 2's complement) that eliminates the problem.

2's Complement

The 2's complement of a binary number is obtained by adding 1 to the 1's complement representation as illustrated by the examples below.

EXAMPLE

Obtain 2's complement of (i) 10001 and (ii) 101001.
Solution:

Number	1's Complement	2's Complement
10001	01110	01111
101001	010110	010111

Subtraction using signed 1's complement representation

In this type of representation, subtraction is carried out by addition of 1's complement of the negative number. The sign bit is treated as a number bit in the subtraction method. For the sign bit being 0, i.e., positive, the magnitude part of the result is the true value. For the sign bit being 1, i.e., negative, the magnitude part of the result is in 1's complement form. For subtracting a smaller number from a larger number, the 1's complement method is implemented as follows.

1. Determine the 1's complement of the smaller number.
2. Add the 1's complement to the larger number.

3. Remove the final carry (overflow bit) and add it to the result, i.e., if the sum exceeds n bits, add the extra bit to the result. This bit is called the end-around carry.

EXAMPLE

Subtract 1_{10} from 7_{10} using 1's complement.
Solution:
Now, $1_{10} = 0001_2$ and $7_{10} = 0111_2$

1. The problem is stated with the numbers in binary.

2. Convert 0001_2 to its negative equivalent in 1's complement. To do this, change 1's complement all 1's to 0's and 0's to 1's in 0001_2 form. Notice that the most significant digit is now 1 since the number is negative.

3. Add the negative value 1110_2 to 0111_2. This gives the sum 10101_2.

4. Notice that the addition generated an overflow bit. Whenever an overflow bit occurs in such a method, add the bit to the sum to get the correct answer. If there is no overflow bit, leave the sum as it is.

5. This gives a final answer of 0110_2 (or 6_{10}).

EXAMPLE

Subtracting $1001_2 (9_{10})$ from $1101_2 (13_{10})$ using 1's complement.
Solution:
The subtraction between binary numbers $1101_2 (13_{10})$ and $1001_2 (9_{10})$ can be carried out by converting 1001_2 to its negative equivalent in 1's complement and adding this value to 1101_2.

1. The problem is stated in binary numbers.

2. Convert 01001_2 to its negative equivalent in 1's complement. To do this, change all the 1's to 0's and 0's to 1's. Notice that the most significant digit is now 1 since the number is negative.

$$01101 \longrightarrow 10110$$

3. Add the negative value 10110_2 to 01101_2. This gives the sum 1000011_2.

$$
\begin{array}{rr}
01101 & (13) \\
+\ 10110 & +\ (-1) \\
\hline
110001 & (?)
\end{array}
$$ True magnitude

4. Note that the addition caused an overflow bit. Whenever an overflow bit occurs in such a method, add this bit to the sum to get the correct answer. Hence, the result is 00100_2 (or 4_{10}).

$$
\begin{array}{r}
00011 \\
+\ 1 \\
\hline
00100
\end{array}
$$ (4) True magnitude

sign bit

For subtracting a larger number from a smaller number, the 1's complement method is as follows:

1. Determine the 1's complement of the larger number.
2. Add the 1's complement to the smaller number.
3. There is no carry (overflow). The result has the proper sign bit but the answer is in 1's complement of the true magnitude.
4. Take the 1's complement of the result to get the final result. The sign of the result is obtained from the sign bit of the result.

─────────────── **EXAMPLE** ───────────────

Subtracting 7_{10} from 1_{10} using 1's complement.
Solution:

1. State the problem with the numbers in binary.

$$
\begin{array}{rr}
0001 & (1) \\
-\ 0111 & -\ (7)
\end{array}
$$ Minuend / Subtrahend

2. Convert negative 0111_2 to 1's complement and add this to 0001_2.

sign bit

$$
\begin{array}{rr}
0001 & (1) \\
+\ 1000 & +\ (-7) \\
\hline
1001 & (?)
\end{array}
$$ Minuend / Subtrahend in 1's complement from

sign bit

3. The result does not cause an overflow, so the sum need not be adjusted. Note that the final result is a negative number since the sign bit is 1. Therefore, the result is in 1's complement notation; the correct decimal value for the result is -6_{10} and not 9_{10}. This is obtained by taking the 1's complement of the result.

sign bit

$$
\begin{array}{rr}
0001 & (1) \\
+\ 1000 & +\ (-7) \\
\hline
1001 & (-6)
\end{array}
$$ Result in signed 1's complement from / Magnitude in 1's

sign bit

─────────────── **EXAMPLE** ───────────────

Subtracting 1101_2 (13_{10}) from 1001_2 (9_{10}) using 1's complement.
Solution:

$$
\begin{aligned}
& 1001 - 1101 \\
& \text{Result from Step 1 } 0010 \\
& \text{Result from Step 2 } 1011 \\
& \text{Result from Step 3 } -0100 \\
& \text{To verify, note that } 9 - 13 = -4
\end{aligned}
$$

1. The problem is stated.

$$
\begin{array}{rr}
01001 & (9) \\
-\ 01101 & -\ (13)
\end{array}
$$

2. Convert 01101_2 to its negative equivalent in 1's complement and add to 01001_2.

$$
\begin{array}{rr}
01001 & (9) \\
+\ 10010 & (-13) \\
\hline
11011 &
\end{array}
$$ Magnitude in 1's complement

sign bit

3. The sign bit of the sum being 1, the resulting number is negative and the value is in 1's complement form.

sign bit

$$11011 \quad (-4)$$ Result in signed 1's complement

Subtraction using signed 2's complement representation

Subtraction for this representation is done by addition of the 2's complement of the negative number. The sign bit is treated as a number bit during subtraction. Thus, the result is obtained with the sign bit. When the sign bit is 0, i.e., positive, the magnitude part of the result is the true value. But when the sign bit is 1, i.e., negative, the magnitude part of the result is in 2's complement form. Therefore, the 2's complement of the magnitude part of the result gives the true value. The carry bit that evolves with the sum is ignored in the 2's complement method.

For subtracting a smaller number from a larger number, the 2's complement method is implemented as follows.

1. Determine the 2's complement of the smaller number.
2. Add the 2's complement to the larger number.
3. Discard the final carry (there is always one in this case).

─────────────── **EXAMPLE** ───────────────

Subtracting 1_{10} from 7_{10} using 2's complement.
Solution:

Now, $1_{10} = 0001_2$ and $7_{10} = 0111_2$.

sign bit

1. The problem is stated with numbers in binary.

$$
\begin{array}{rr}
0111 & (7) \\
+\ 0001 & +\ (-1)
\end{array}
$$

2. Convert 0001_2 to its negative equivalent in 2's complement. To do this change all the 1's to 0's and 0's to 1's and add one to the number. Notice that the most significant digit is now 1 since the number is negative.

$$0001 \rightarrow 1110$$
$$\underline{+\ 1}$$
2's complement $\rightarrow$ 1111
form

3. Add the negative value 1111_2 to 0111_2. This gives the sum 10110_2.

sign bit

$$
\begin{array}{ll}
\ \ 0111 & (7) \\
+ 1111 & + (-1) \\
\hline
10110 & (?)
\end{array}
$$
overflow bit

4. Notice that the addition caused an overflow bit. Whenever an overflow bit in 2's complement occurs, it is discarded. Hence, the final result is 0110_2 (or 6_{10}).

$$
\begin{array}{ll}
\ \ 0111 & (7) \\
- 1111 & - (1) \\
\hline
0110 & (6)
\end{array}
$$
sign bit — Result in true magnitude

--- EXAMPLE ---

Subtracting the binary number $1001_2 (9_{10})$ from $1101_2 (13_{10})$ by converting 1001_2 to its negative equivalent in 2's complement and adding this value to 1101_2.

Solution:

1. State the problem.

Magnitude part

$$
\begin{array}{ll}
\ \ 01101 & (13)\ \text{Minuend} \\
- 01001 & - (9)\ \text{Subtrahend}
\end{array}
$$

2. Convert 1001_2 to its negative equivalent in 2's complement. To do this, change all 1's to 0's and vice versa.

1's complement form

$$01001 \rightarrow 10110$$
sign bit

3. Add 1 to the number to obtain the negative equivalent. Notice that the most significant digit is now 1 since the number is negative.

$$
\begin{array}{l}
10110 \\
\underline{+\ \ \ 1} \quad (-9)\ \text{Subtrahend in} \\
10111 \qquad \text{2's complement}
\end{array}
$$

4. Add the negative value 10111_2 to 01101_2. This gives the sum 100100_2. However, the leftmost bit, which is the overflow bit, is discarded.

$$
\begin{array}{ll}
\ \ \ 01101 & (13) \\
- 10111 & + (-9) \\
\hline
1\ 00100 & (?)
\end{array}
$$
Overflow bit — sign bit

5. Hence, the final result is 00100_2 (or 4).

$$
\begin{array}{ll}
\ \ \ 01101 & (13) \\
+ 10111 & + (-9) \\
\hline
00100 & (4)
\end{array}
$$
sign bit — Ture magnitude

For subtracting a larger number from a smaller number, the 2's complement method is implemented as follows.

1. Determine the 2's complement of the larger number.

2. Add 2's complement to the smaller number.

3. There is no carry from the leftmost column. The result is in 2's complement form and is negative.

4. Take the 2's complement of the result to get the final answer.

--- EXAMPLE ---

Subtracting $1101_2 (13_{10})$ from $1001_2 (9_{10})$ using 2's complement.

Solution:

1. State the problem.

$$
\begin{array}{ll}
\ \ \ 01001 & (7) \\
- 01101 & - (13)
\end{array}
$$

2. Convert 1101_2 to its negative equivalent in 2's complement.

$$01101 \quad 10011$$
sign bit — 2's complement

3. Next, add 10011_2 to 01001_2. The sign bit being 1, the result is negative and the magnitude is in 2's complement.

$$
\begin{array}{l}
\ \ \ 01001 \\
+ 10011 \\
\hline
11100
\end{array}
$$
sign bit — 2's complement

4. Take the 2's complement of the sum to get $-0100_2 - 0100_2$, i.e., -4_{10}.

-0110_2

Points to remember: The steps for subtracting y from x, with an n-bit 1's complement representation are as follows.

1. Negate y using 1's complement, i.e., reverse all the bits in y to form $-y$.

2. Add $-y$, in 1's complement form, and x.

3. If the sum exceeds n bits, add the extra bit to the result.

4. If the sum does not exceed n bits, leave the result as it is.

The steps for subtracting y from x with an n-bit 2's complement representation are as follows.

1. Negate y using 2's complement, i.e., reverse all the bits in y and add 1 to form $-y$.

2. Add $-y$ in 2's complement form, and x.

3. If the sum exceeds n bits, discard the extra bit.

Notice that with 1's complement, it is necessary to check for an overflow bit each time subtraction is performed. If the result has an overflow bit, the extra bit is added to the result to obtain the correct result. However, with 2's complement, this extra bit is ignored. No other computations are required to find the correct result.

2.6.4 Multiplication

Binary multiplication uses the same techniques as decimal multiplication. In fact, binary multiplication is much easier because each multiplying digit is either zero or one. Consider the simple example of multiplying 110_2 by 10_2. This example is used to review some terminology and illustrate the rules for binary multiplication.

--- EXAMPLE ---

Multiplying 110_2 by 10_2.

Solution:

1. Note that 110_2 is the multiplicand and 10_2 is the multiplier.

   ```
    110    Multiplicand
   × 10    multiplier
   ```

2. Begin by multiplying 110_2 by the rightmost digit of the multiplier that is 0. Any number times zero is zero, so just zeroes are written below.

   ```
    110
   × 10
   ───
   000
   ```

3. Multiply the multiplicand by the next digit of the multiplier, which is 1. To perform this multiplication, just copy the multiplicand and shift it one column to the left as is done in decimal multiplication.

   ```
    110
   × 10
   ───
   000    Partial product
   110    Partial product
   ```

4. Add the partial products. Hence, the product of the multiplication is 1100_2.

   ```
    110
   × 10
   ────
   000
   110
   ────
   1100   Result
   ```

When performing binary multiplication, remember the following rules.

1. Copy the multiplicand when the multiplier digit is 1. Otherwise, write a row of zeros.

2. Shift the results one column to the left for a new multiplier digit.

3. Add the results using binary addition to find the product.

EXAMPLE

Multiplying 1111_2 by 1011_2.

Solution:

The binary numbers 1111_2 and 1011_2 can be multiplied using the same rules as decimal multiplication.

1. Multiply the multiplicand by the extreme right digit of the multiplier.

   ```
    1111   Multiplicand
   × 1011   multiplier
   ```

2. Since this number is 1 and any number multiplied by 1 equals itself, simply record the multiplicand below.

   ```
    1111
   × 1011
   ─────
   1111  ← First partial
          product
   ```

3. Now multiply the multiplicand by the next digit in the multiplier. Since this is the second multiplication, the second partial product obtained would be placed below the first and shifted one column to the left.

4. The second digit in the multiplier is 1 so the second partial product, which is same as the multiplicand, is placed as shown.

   ```
    1111
   × 1011
   ─────
   1111      Second partial
   1111   ←  product
   ```

5. Next, multiply by the third digit of the multiplier. Since this is the third multiplication, the third partial product is placed below the second partial product and shifted to the left by one column with respect to the latter.

   ```
    1111
   × 1011
   ─────
   1111
   1111
   ```

6. Notice that the third digit in the multiplier is 0. Since any number multiplied by zero is zero, place a row of zeroes as the third partial product as shown.

   ```
    1111
   × 1011
   ─────
   1111
   1111     Third partial
   0000  ←  product
   ```

7. Now, multiply with the most significant digit of the multiplier. Since this is the fourth multiplication, the fourth partial product is placed below the third partial product and shifted by one column to the left with respect to the latter.

   ```
    1111
   × 1011
   ─────
   1111
   1111
   0000
   ```

8. The most significant digit of the multiplier is 1, so the fourth partial product is the same as the multiplicand. This partial product is placed as shown.

   ```
    1111
   × 1011
   ─────
   1111
   1111
   0000      Fourth partial
   1111  ←   product
   ```

9. Now, all the partial products are added to get the final value of the multiplication product as 10100101_2.

   ```
    1111
   × 1011
   ─────
   1111
   1111
   0000
   1111
   ────────
   10100101
   ```

2.6.5 Division

Division of binary numbers uses the same technique as division in the decimal system. It will be helpful to review some of the basic terms of division. Consider the example given below.

EXAMPLE

Dividing 33_{10} by 6_{10}.

Solution:

1. In this problem, 6 is the divisor, 33 is the dividend, 5 is the quotient, and 3 is the remainder. The same terms describe binary division.

   ```
        5
   6 ⟌ 33
       30
       ──
        3
   ```

EXAMPLE

$11_2/10_2$ or $3_{10}/2_{10}$.

Solution:

Here, 10_2 is the divisor and 11_2 is the dividend. The steps that follow show how to find the quotient—1.1_2.

1. Find the smallest part of the dividend that is greater than or equal to the divisor. Since the divisor has two digits, start by checking the first two digits of the dividend.

   ```
   10 ⟌ 11
   ```

2. 11 is greater than 10. Thus a 1 is written as the quotient, the divisor is written below the dividend, and subtraction is carried out.

   ```
          1
   10 ⟌ 11
        10
        ──
         1
   ```

3. Since there are no more digits in the dividend, but there still is a remainder, therefore the answer must include a fraction. To complete the computation, it is necessary to mark the radix point and append a zero to the dividend.

$$\begin{array}{r} 1. \\ 10\,|\overline{11.0} \\ \underline{10} \\ 1 \end{array}$$

4. Bring down the extra zero and write it beside the remainder. Then check to see if this new number is greater than or equal to the divisor. Notice that the radix point is ignored in the comparison.

$$\begin{array}{r} 1. \\ 10\,|\overline{11.0} \\ \underline{10} \\ 10 \end{array}$$

5. 10 equals the divisor 10, so write a 1 in the quotient, copy the divisor below the dividend, and subtract. This completes the division because there are no more digits in the dividend and no remainder.

$$\begin{array}{r} 1. \\ 10\,|\overline{11.0} \\ \underline{10} \\ 10 \\ \underline{10} \\ 0 \end{array}$$

When doing binary division, some important rules need to be remembered.

(a) When the remainder is greater than or equal to the divisor, write a 1 in the quotient and subtract.

(b) When the remainder is less than the divisor, write a 0 in the quotient and add another digit from the dividend.

(c) If all the digits of the dividend have been considered and there is still a remainder, mark a radix point in the dividend and append a zero. Remember that some fractions do not have an exact representation in binary, so not all division problems will terminate.

EXAMPLE

Dividing 100001_2 by 110_2 using the same technique used in long division in the decimal system.

Solution:

1. Find the smallest part of the dividend that is greater than the divisor 110_2. Since the divisor has three digits, begin by examining the first three digits of the dividend. 100_2 is less than 110_2 so another digit from the dividend must be added.

$$110\,|\overline{100001}$$

2. Try the first four digits of the dividend. Since 1000_2 is greater than 110_2, the division is possible.

$$110\,|\overline{100001}$$

3. 110_2 divides 1000_2 once, so write 1 as the first digit of the quotient, copy the divisor below the dividend, and subtract using the borrow method.

$$\begin{array}{r} 1 \\ 110\,|\overline{100001} \\ \underline{110} \\ 10 \end{array}$$

4. Now bring down the next digit of the dividend and write it beside the remainder. Then check to see if this new number is greater than or equal to the divisor.

$$\begin{array}{r} 1 \\ 110\,|\overline{100001} \\ \underline{110} \\ 100 \end{array}$$

5. 100_2 is less than 110_2 so, write a 0 in the quotient and add another digit from the dividend to the reminder.

$$\begin{array}{r} 10 \\ 110\,|\overline{100001} \\ \underline{110} \\ 1001 \end{array}$$

6. 1001_2 is greater than 110_2, so write a 1 in the quotient and subtract 110_2 from 1001_2.

$$\begin{array}{r} 101 \\ 110\,|\overline{100001} \\ \underline{110} \\ 1001 \\ \underline{110} \\ 11 \end{array}$$

7. Note that after considering all the digits of the dividend a remainder still exists. This means that the result will include a fraction. To progress with the division, it is necessary to mark the radix point and append a zero to the dividend.

$$\begin{array}{r} 101. \\ 110\,|\overline{100001.0} \\ \underline{110} \\ 1001 \\ \underline{110} \\ 11 \end{array}$$

8. Now bring down the extra zero and compare the remainder with the divisor. Notice that the radix point is ignored in the comparison. 110_2 is equal to 110_2 so write another 1 in the quotient and subtract. This completes the division because no more digits exist in the dividend and there is no remainder.

$$\begin{array}{r} 101.1 \\ 110\,|\overline{100001.0} \\ \underline{110} \\ 1001 \\ \underline{110} \\ 110 \\ \underline{110} \\ 0 \end{array}$$

Note

- Multiplication and division of binary numbers uses the same rules as the decimal numbers.
- Some fractions do not have an exact representation in binary, so not all division computations will terminate.

Check Your Progress

1. The 2's complement of the number 1101101 is

   (a) 0101110   (b) 0111110

   (c) 0110010   (d) 0010011

Answer: (d)

2. −8 is equal to signed binary number

   (a) 10001000   (b) 00001000

   (c) 10000000   (d) 11000000

Answer: (a)

3. When signed numbers are used in binary arithmetic, then which one of the following notations would have unique representation for zero.

   (a) Sign-magnitude.   (b) 1's complement.

   (c) 2's complement.   (d) 9's complement

Answer: (a)

4. The result of adding hexadecimal number A6 to 3A is

   (a) DD   (b) E0

   (c) F0   (d) EF

Answer: (b)

5. Perform 2's complement subtraction of $(7)_{10} - (11)_{10}$

Answer: $(4)_{10}$ or (11111100) in signed 2's complement form.

6. Perform the following subtraction using 2's complement method: 0011.1001 − 0001.1110

Answer: 0001.1011   or   + 1.68625

7. Divide $(101110)_2$ by $(101)_2$

Answer: Quotient = $(1001)_2$ and   Remainder = 001_2

2.7 BINARY CODES

For practical reasons, it is very convenient to use the binary number system in digital systems or computers. Data is represented by symbols in the form of decimal numbers, alphabets, and special characters. To facilitate extensive communication between humans and digital machines, binary digits 1 and 0 are arranged according to certain defined rules and designated to represent symbols. The method of forming the binary representation is known as **encoding** and the complete group of binary representations corresponding to the symbols is known as **binary code**.

Binary codes may be broadly classified into four categories.

    (a) Numeric codes

    (b) Alphanumeric codes

    (c) Error-detecting codes

    (d) Error-correcting codes

Numeric codes are further classified as weighted, non-weighted, self-complementing, sequential, and cyclic codes as depicted in Fig. 2.1.

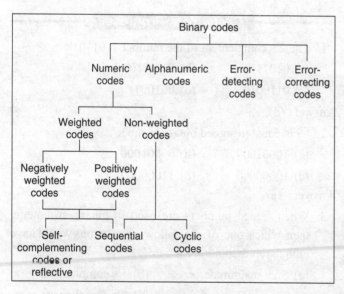

Fig. 2.1 Code classification

2.7.1 Numeric Codes

Numeric codes represent numeric data with a series of 0's and 1's. Decimal numbers 0 to 9 can be represented by four binary digits. Of the 16 possible combinations of the four binary digits, only 10 combinations are used to represent the decimal numbers 0 to 9. Each of these bit combinations that represent a specific decimal digit is called a **code word**.

The numeric codes devised to represent decimal digits are known as **binary coded decimal** (BCD) codes. There are several BCD codes. These are of two kinds: **weighted** and **non-weighted**.

Weighted codes

Weighted codes obey the position weighting principle, where each bit position is assigned a decimal weight. For such a code, the sum of the decimal weights of those bits whose value is '1' is equal to the decimal digit it represents. For example, in a four-bit weighted code, if w_1, w_2, w_3, and w_4 are the decimal weights of the binary digits and b_1, b_2, b_3, and b_4 are the corresponding bit values, then the decimal digit 'N' is given by

$$N = w_4.b_4 + w_3.b_3 + w_2.b_2 + w_1.b_1$$

whose BCD code representation is $b_4b_3b_2b_1$.

This binary sequence code is the code word for the decimal number N.

Weighted codes are of two types:

    (a) Positively weighted codes

    (b) Negatively weighted codes

Positively weighted codes are BCD codes in which all the weights assigned to the bits are positive. There are 17 positively weighted code in a four-bit BCD code. It should be noted that in every positively weighted code, the first weight should be 1, the second weight should either be 1 or 2, and the sum of all the weights should be greater than or equal to the decimal number 9.

Negatively weighted codes are BCD codes in which some of the weights assigned to the bits are negative. Table 2.13 depicts some of the weighted codes.

Table 2.13 Some weighted binary coded decimals

Decimal digits	Positive weights (w4, w3, w2, w1)				Negative weights (w3, w2, w1)	
	8421	5421	5211	2421	8 4 –2 –1	6 4 –2 –3
0	0000	0000	0000	0000	0000	0000
1	0001	0001	0001	0001	0111	0101
2	0010	0010	0011	0010	0110	0010
3	0011	0011	0101	0011	0101	1001
4	0100	0100	0111	0100	0100	0100
5	0101	1000	1000	1011	1011	1011
6	0110	1001	1001	1100	1010	0110
7	0111	1010	1011	1101	1001	1101
8	1000	1011	1101	1110	1000	1010
9	1001	1100	1111	1111	1111	1111

Self-complementing code A code is called self-complementing if the code word of the 9's complement of N, i.e. (9-N), can be obtained from the code word of N by interchanging all the 1's and 0's. The 9's complement of 1 is 8. In the (6, 4, 2, –3) code, decimal 1 is represented by 0101, while decimal 8 is represented by 1010, which is the 1's complement of 0101. The codes (2, 4, 2, 1), (5, 2, 1, 1), (4, 3, 1, 1), and (3, 3, 2, 1) are the four positively weighted self-complementing codes. There exist 13 negatively and positively weighted self-complementing codes like (8, 4, –2, –1) and (6, 4, 2, –3). The necessary condition for a weighted code to be self-complementing is that the sum of the weights should be equal to nine.

Table 2.14 Excess-3 code

Decimal number	8 4 2 1 code	Excess-3 code
0	0000	0011
1	0001	0100
2	0010	0101
3	0011	0110
4	0100	0111
5	0101	1000
6	0110	1001
7	0111	1010
8	1000	1011
9	1001	1100

Sequential code A sequential code is one in which each of its subsequent code words is one binary number greater than the preceding code word. The BCD code (8, 4, 2, 1) is a sequential code. In most cases BCD code means the (8, 4, 2, 1) code shown in Table 3.3.

Non-weighted codes

Codes that do not obey the position-weighting principle are called non-weighted codes. There are many non-weighted binary codes. Two of these are the Excess-3, or XS-3, and Gray Code. These are depicted in Tables 2.14 and 2.15.

Table 2.15 Gray code

Decimal number	Binary code b3, b2, b1, b0	Gray code g3, g2, g1, g0
0	0000	0000
1	0001	0001
2	0010	0011
3	0011	0010
4	0100	0110
5	0101	0111
6	0110	0101
7	0111	0100
8	1000	1100
9	1001	1101
10	1010	1111
11	1011	1110
12	1100	1010
13	1101	1011
14	1110	1001
15	1111	1000

The Excess-3 code is formed by adding 0011 to each code word of (8, 4, 2, 1) code or BCD. It is a self-complementing code.

The Gray code is a cyclic code. Cyclic code is one in which successive code words differ in only one digit. Such codes are also known as unit distance codes.

2.7.2 Alphanumeric Codes

Digital computers are capable of handling bits. Keyboards and printers, for example, are devices for transmitting and receiving data to and from computers, respectively. The user inputs data in the form of symbols representing alphabets, numbers, and special characters. These symbols must be represented by some code formed by a sequence of binary digits for the digital computer to process. Similarly, a bit code is sent by the computer to an output device, such as a printer, which must depict alphabetic, numeric, or special character information using the symbols.

There are several alphanumeric codes but two, ASCII and EBCDIC, are normally used. The ASCII code, known as the American Standard Code for Information Interchange, is used widely. This is a seven-bit code and hence it can form 2^7 (128) bit patterns thereby having an ability to encode 128 symbols. Table 2.16 shows the ASCII code representing capital letters/lowercase alphabets, decimal numbers, and special characters. Since the characters are assigned in ascending binary numbers, it is convenient for digital computers to convert from and to alphanumeric symbols.

The standard ASCII code defines 128 character codes (from 0 to 127), of which the first 32 are control codes (non-printable) and the other 96 are characters that can be represented. The above table is organized to easily read the ASCII code in hexadecimal form: row numbers represent the lower significant digit and the column numbers represent the most significant digit. For example, character **A** is located at row four column one. Thus the ASCII code for character **A** is represented in hexadecimal as 0x41, which in decimal is 65.

In addition to the 128 standard ASCII codes, there are other 128 that are known as extended ASCII, and these are platform-dependent. So, there is more than one extended ASCII character set.

The two most used extended ASCII character sets are OEM, which comes from the default character set incorporated in the IBM PC, and ANSI extend ASCII, which is used by the present operating systems.

Table 2.16 ASCII code

Hex LSD / MSD	0	1	2	3	4	5	6	7	8	9	A	B	C	D	E	F
0	NUL	SOH	STX	ETX	EOT	ENQ	ACK	BEL	BS	HT	LF	VT	FF	CR	SO	SI
1	DLE	DC1	DC2	DC3	DC4	NAK	SYN	ETB	CAN	EM	SUB	ESC	FS	GS	RS	US
2	SP	!	"	#	$	%	&	'	(	)	*	+	,	-	.	/
3	0	1	2	3	4	5	6	7	8	9	:	;	<	=	>	?
4	@	A	B	C	D	E	F	G	H	I	J	K	L	M	N	O
5	P	Q	R	S	T	U	V	W	X	Y	Z	[	\	]	^	_
6	`	a	b	c	d	e	f	g	h	i	j	k	l	m	n	o
7	p	q	r	s	t	u	v	w	x	y	z	{	|	}	~	DEL

The OEM character set is included in the majority of PC compatibles loaded with any operating system or MSDOS system. It includes diverse symbols, some marked characters and pieces to represent panels. However, it is usually redefined according to regional configurations to incorporate particular symbols in many countries.

OEM Extended ASCII

The ANSI character set is a standard that is incorporated in systems such as Windows, some UNIX platforms, and many applications. It includes many local symbols and marked letters so that it can be used without being redefined for other languages.

ANSI Extended ASCII (Windows)

Note

- Numeric codes represent numeric data with a series of 0's and 1's. Among the various available codes, the binary, hexadecimal and BCD codes are used mostly.
- Symbols representing capital letters/lowercase alphabets, decimal numbers, and special characters, which are termed as alphanumeric characters, are also represented by alphanumeric numeric codes formed with a combination of 1s and 0s. The ASCII code is the most widely used code used to represent alphanumeric symbols.

SUMMARY

A system in which quantities are represented by symbols bearing values is called a number system. The base of a number system has a value equal to the number of representation symbols the system has. A number in a number system, in general, can be represented by any one of the following forms: (a) positional notation form, (b) polynomial form, and (c) compact form. The number systems that are used in computers are binary, octal, and hexadecimal, whereas the decimal system is used by humans. Conversion of binary numbers to decimal numbers, and vice versa, uses the base of the binary number position of the digit. Conversion of binary to octal and vice versa, binary to hexadecimal and vice versa, and all other conversions between different number systems is possible.

Addition and subtraction of unsigned binary numbers are similar to the arithmetic rules followed for decimal numbers with the exception that the base here is 2. Signed magnitude representation of binary numbers consists of using a 0 for a positive number or a 1 for a negative number in the most significant digit position of the number. Using 1's and 2's complement representation, the signed binary number can be subtracted to obtain results correctly.

There are different classifications of binary codes used in computers. These are numeric codes, alphanumeric codes, error-detecting codes, and error-correcting codes.

KEY TERMS

Symbol It is any graphic character.

Number system It is a set of symbols that represents a set of quantitative values.

Base It represents the number of digit symbols in a number system.

Radix It represents the number of digit symbols in a number system.

Decimal number system It is a number system that has ten symbols 0,1,..........,9 which represents values.

Binary number system It is a number system that uses two symbols 0 and 1 to represent zero and one respectively.

Octal number system It is a number system that has eight symbols 0,1,..........,7 which represents values zero to seven respectively.

Hexadecimal number system a number system that has eight symbols 0,1,..........,F which represents values zero to sixteen respectively.

Bit It is a binary digit.

Carry In a number system, when the result of addition of two single digit numbers is greater than the largest representable number symbol, a carry is said to be generated. This carry is placed in the next left column.

Borrow In a number system, when a larger single digit number is subtracted from a smaller single digit, a borrow is generated.

Signed number A binary number in which the most significant bit represents the sign of the number and the rest the magnitude of the number.

1's complement A number system that was used in some computers to represent negative numbers. To form 1s complement of a number, each bit of the number is inverted which means zeros are replaced with ones and ones with zero.

2's complement A number formed by adding 1 to the 1's compliment of a number. The 2's complement representation has become the standard method of storing signed binary integers. It allows the representation of an n-bit number in the range $-2n$ to $2n-1$, and has the significant advantage of only having one encoding for 0.

BCD number Binary Coded Decimal (BCD) number is a number in which each of the digits of an unsigned decimal number is represented by the corresponding 4-bit binary equivalents.

ASCII code American Standard Code for Information Interchange is a 7-bit binary code formed to represent decimal numbers 0 to 9, alphabetic characters a to b(also A TO B), and special characters like ;, :, NUL, etc. for handling these characters in the digital computer and to also use this binary code for exchanging data between digital computers connected in a networked environment.

FREQUENTLY ASKED QUESTIONS

1. What is a binary number?

Answer:

A binary number is made of 0s and 1s. In the binary number system only two symbols, 0 and 1, are used to represent numeric values. The symbol "0" represents the value "zero" while the symbol "1" represents the value "one". Since there are only two symbols in the binary number system, the value "two" is represented by placing the symbol "1" on the left–hand side of the symbol "0" resulting in the binary equivalent "10". Next, the value "three" is represented by "11" in the binary number systemby replacing the " 0 " in "10" by the next higher value symbol "1". A sample table depicting the binary equivalent representation for different decimal numbers upto nine is shown below.

Decimal number (Number value)	Binary equivalent representation
0	0
1	1
2	10
3	11
4	100
5	101
6	110
7	111
8	1000
9	1001

Herein, it may be noted that as the number value increases the digit positions on the left-hand side of the binary equivalent number increases. Each increase of the digit position to the left signifies an increase by 2 in the value of the number represented in the binary number system. Since the number of symbols in the binary number system is two, the radix of this number system expressed in decimal is 2.

2. What is meant by 'bit'?

Answer:

The abbreviated form of " bi-nary dig-it " is known as bit. When a "bit" is mentioned, it means a single binary digit, which may either be a "0" or "1", is referred to.

3. Why do digital computers use binary numbers for their operations?

Answer:

A survey of the history of development of computers would reveal that the primary objective of computer designers as to construct a computer that would carry out all types of arithmetical calculations. This was achieved by initially employing mechanical devices and then improving it with the addition of electrical devices. But these computing machines were calculators with no programmable facilities. The need for programmability was also met using the mechanical and electrical devices. Meanwhile analog computers were in use for solving not only arithmetical problems but also mathematical problems which included integro-differential equations, etc. But with the availability of electronic devices and application of Boolean logic concepts digital computers were developed that execute jobs at much high speeds, consume less power, occupy much less space, weigh many times less, work reliably with very less maintenance effort and are easy to operate. As a consequence digital computers, that employed electronic devices and applied Boolean logic concepts, outperformed all earlier models of computers. And because the digital computers use Boolean logic concepts, binary numbers are obviously used in digital computers.

4. Where is the octal number representation used?

Answer:

The octal number representation is used to represent large binary numbers in a shorter form. This simplifies the manual handling of binary numbers while working with digital computers. For example, a binary number "1011001110010110" in octal number representation is "131626", which contains 6 digits instead of 16 in the binary form.

5. Where is the hexadecimal number representation used?

Answer:

The hexadecimal number representation, like the octal number representation, is a short-cut way to represent large binary numbers. Hence a binary number "1011001110010110" becomes B396 in hexadecimal number representation. From the (above example) it is evident that for the human computer user it is easier to handle the hexadecimal number than the big binary number shown.

6. How is the BCD representation useful?

Answer:

Human beings are accustomed to use the decimal number system. Hence an output from the computer or computer based system, in decimal number form is more acceptable than in binary or hexadecimal or octal number form. To achieve this, the Binary Coded Decimal number representation has been made.

7. Where is the Gray Code used?

Answer:

The gray code was primarily developed to prevent spurious output from electromechanical switches. It is widely used in digital communications to facilitate error correction. In position encoders, gray codes are used in preference to straightforward binary encoding.

8. How important is signed magnitude representation of binary numbers in digital computers?

Answer:

Normally, a " – " symbol is placed before a number to indicate the negative nature of the number. On the other hand, a positive number is indicated by putting " + " symbol or simply a blank before the number. But in a digital computer, these graphic symbols, " – " and " + ", cannot be used directly. All numbers and symbols are represented by a combination of " 0s " and " 1s ". Hence, the positive symbol, " + ", is represented by a " 0 " while the negative symbol, " – ", is represented by a " 1 ". The sign bit , a " 0 " or a " 1 ", occupies the most significant digit position of a number represented in binary. Therefore in an eight bit number, the most significant bit is a sign bit while the rest of the seven bits represent the magnitude or value. Such a representation is essential for the logic circuits, within the digital computer, to suitably carry out arithmetic operations.

9. Why is 2's complement representation preferred over 1's complement representation in binary arithmetic?

Answer:

In 1's complement representation, the carry, that occurs while adding the signed magnitude numbers, is added to the least significant bit of the result to obtain the proper result. This imposes an extra burden on the computer by way of providing additional logic circuitry to form the final result. In 2's compliment representation, the carry that occurs while adding the signed magnitude numbers, is discarded to obtain the result in true magnitude form. Therefore, the extra burden of adding the carry bit to obtain the final result is avoided in 2's complement representation. Hence, 2's complement representation is preferred.

EXERCISES

1. Convert the following.

   (i) $0110_2 =$ _____ $_{10}$

   (ii) $0110_2 =$ _____ $_8$

   (iii) $1101_2 =$ _____ $_{10}$

   (iv) $11_{10} =$ _____ $_2$

   (v) $11_{10} =$ _____ $_{16}$

   (vi) $20_{16} =$ _____ $_2$

   (vii) $20_{16} =$ _____ $_{10}$

   (viii) $259_{10} =$ _____ $_2$

   (ix) $259_{10} =$ _____ $_{16}$

   (x) $10000000_2 =$ _____ $_{10}$

   (xi) $10001010_2 =$ _____ $_{16}$

   (xii) $1024_{10} =$ _____ $_{16}$

2. Convert the following decimal numbers to equivalent binary numbers.

   (i) 702   (ii) 134

   (iii) 128   (iv) 1024

   (v) 563   (vi) 2047

   (vii) 17.75   (viii) 356.16

   (ix) 127.375   (x) 100.336

   (xi) 61.0625   (xii) 49.0125

   (xiii) 23.6125 (xiv) 36.625

   (xv) 0.0525

3. Convert the following binary numbers to equivalent decimal numbers.

   (i) 10110.101   (ii) 111001010.1011

   (iii) 110110.1101   (iv) 1011001.101

   (v) 110101.001   (vi) 0.011011

4. Determine the equivalent octal numbers for the following decimal numbers.

   (i) 4   (ii) 25
   (iii) 261   (iv) 73
   (v) 385   (vi) 621
   (vii) 10.25   (viii) 25.15
   (ix) 0.44   (x) 131.3
   (xi) 0.046   (xii) 0.5

5. Perform the following conversions from octal to decimal numbers.

   (i) 11   (ii) 42
   (iii) 507   (iv) 127
   (v) 100   (vi) 63.4
   (vii) 5.6   (viii) 0.1
   (ix) 13.5   (x) 36.05

6. Convert the following binary numbers to octal numbers.

   (i) 1101   (ii) 101101
   (iii) 1101111   (iv) 111111
   (v) 10100   (vi) 0.11
   (vii) 0.101   (viii) 1001.01101
   (ix) 11.110011   (x) 1100.1101

7. Find the equivalent binary numbers for the following octal numbers.

   (i) 36   (ii) 14
   (iii) 127   (iv) 251
   (v) 1723   (vi) 4.6
   (vii) 17.5   (viii) 64.05
   (ix) 231.44   (x) 1025.625

8. Convert the following decimal numbers to equivalent hexadecimal numbers.

   (i) 4181   (ii) 130
   (iii) 171   (iv) 4095
   (v) 30.10   (vi) 64.5
   (vii) 10.04   (viii) 15.64

9. Convert the following hexadecimal numbers to equivalent decimal numbers.

   (i) 4C   (ii) 512
   (iii) 100   (iv) BA2
   (v) B.2   (vi) 5.5
   (vii) 4A.25   (viii) F.2

10. Convert the following hexadecimal numbers to binary numbers.

    (i) A2;   (ii) B35;
    (iii) 54E;   (iv) DAE;
    (v) FE;   (vi) 4A.6;
    (vii) 74.5;   (viii) C7.9D;
    (ix) EF.2C;   (x) ABC.F

11. Convert the following binary numbers to hexadecimal numbers.

    (i) 101011
    (ii) 11001011
    (iii) 11110110101
    (iv) 10111111001010
    (v) 1101.01
    (vi) 1011110.1010
    (vii) 10110.0011
    (viii) 1001011.01101001

12. Perform the following conversions.

    (i) 567_{10} = _____ $_{16}$
                       = _____ $_8$
    (ii) $A6C2_{16}$ = _____ $_8$
                       = _____ $_2$
    (iii) $B.2C_{16}$ = _____ $_8$
                       = _____ $_{10}$
    (iv) 1011110011111.011_2
                       = _____ $_{16}$
                       = _____ $_8$
    (v) 101011000011_2
                       = _____ $_{16}$
                       = _____ $_8$

13. Give 1's complement representation of -7_{10}.

14. Give 2's complement representation of a number whose 1's complement representation is 10011_2. What is the number in binary representation?

15. Find the 1's complement of

    (i) 111001100_2 (ii) 11010111_2
    (iii) 10011111_2 (iv) 10000000_2
    (v) -1010_2 (vi) -1101_2

16. Find the 2's complement of

    (i) 10110_2 (ii) 1100111_2
    (iii) 01101_2 (iv) 01000_2
    (v) -1110_2 (vi) -1001_2

17. Add the following numbers

    (i) $1011_2 + 0101_2$
    (ii) $1111_2 + 0101_2$
    (iii) $11_2 + 111_2$
    (iv) $10011111_2 + 01101011_2$

18. Using 2's complement method, perform the following operations:

    (i) $31_{10} - 17_{10}$ (ii) $51_{10} - 27_{10}$
    (iii) $12_{10} - 19_{10}$ (iv) $25_{10} - 49_{10}$
    (v) $-19_{10} - 12_{10}$ (vi) $-10_{10} - 8_{10}$
    (vii) $-13_{10} + 10_{10}$ (viii) $-23_{10} + 45_{10}$
    (ix) $1001_2 + 0100_2$ (x) $1010_2 - 1101_2$

19. Perform the following operations. The most significant bit represents the sign bit and the negative numbers are in 2's complement form.
    (i) 00011011 + 00001101
    (ii) 00011111 − 11001111

20. If 2's complement of a number in four-bits is 1011_2, give its 2's complement representation in eight-bits.

21. Suppose a computer uses six-bits for base 2 unsigned integer and for 2's complement signed integers.
    (i) What range of values could be represented as an unsigned integer?
    (ii) What range of values could be represented as a signed integer?

22. Convert the following decimal numbers to BCD representation:
    (i) 8_{10}
    (ii) 26_{10}
    (iii) 37_{10}
    (iv) 145_{10}

23. What are the equivalent Excess-3 code representations for the following numbers in 8421 code:
    (i) 0011
    (ii) 0101
    (iii) 1001
    (iv) 1000

24. Find the decimal numbers represented by the given numbers in gray code:
    (i) 0011
    (ii) 1011
    (iii) 0111
    (iv) 1111

Boolean Algebra and Logic Gates

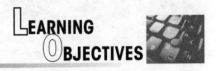

LEARNING
OBJECTIVES

After studying this chapter, the readers will be able to

- identify a binary logic variable
- explain the three basic operations of Boolean algebra
- explain some axioms and theorems of Boolean algebra
- analyse Boolean expressions and functions and their simplification methods
- explain the different forms of representing a Boolean function
- identify logic ` true' and `false' by high and low voltage levels

- explain the properties of the logic gates AND, OR, NOT, NAND, NOR, XOR, and XNOR
- explain the construction of logic gates using electronic devices such as diodes and transistors
- use Boolean algebra for describing the function of logic gates
- explain how complex logic circuits described by Boolean expressions are constructed using logic gates
- construct AND, OR, and NOT gates using NAND and NOR gates

3.1 INTRODUCTION TO BOOLEAN ALGEBRA

Boolean algebra deals with logic variables, which may either be 1, that is TRUE or 0, that is FALSE. It uses logic variables and logic operations to develop, manipulate, and simplify logic expressions, following set rules. Boolean algebra, introduced by George Boole in 1854, differs significantly from conventional algebra. The rules of Boolean algebra are simple and straightforward, and can be applied to any logical expression.

The rules of Boolean algebra that define three basic logic operations and some combinations of these, sometimes called axioms, are:

Boolean multiplication (·)

$0 \cdot 0 = 0$
$1 \cdot 0 = 0$
$0 \cdot 1 = 0$
$1 \cdot 1 = 1$

Boolean addition (+)

$0 + 0 = 0$
$1 + 0 = 1$
$0 + 1 = 1$
$1 + 1 = 1$

Boolean negation

$\overline{0} = 1$
$\overline{1} = 0$

Based on the axioms, the following laws have evolved:

AND law

$A \cdot 0 = 0$	(Null law)
$A \cdot 1 = A$	(Identity law)
$A \cdot A = A$	(Idempotence law)
$A \cdot \overline{A} = A$	(Complement law)

OR law

$A + 0 = A$	(Null law)
$A + 1 = 1$	(Identity law)
$A + A = A$	(Idempotence law)
$A + \overline{A} = 1$	(Complement law)

Complementation law

If A = 0 then $\overline{A} = 1$
If A = 1 then $\overline{A} = 0$
$\overline{\overline{A}} = A$ (Double negation law)

Associative law

$(A \cdot B) \cdot C = A \cdot (B \cdot C) = A \cdot B \cdot C$
$(A + B) + C = A + (B + C) = A + B + C$

Distributive law

$A \cdot (B + C) = (A \cdot B) + (A \cdot C)$
$A + (B \cdot C) = (A + B) \cdot (A + C)$

Commutative law

$A \cdot B = B \cdot A$
$A + B = B + A$

It should be evident from above that there are three basic logic operations in Boolean algebra, namely, AND, OR, and NOT. The common symbols used for each of these operations are given in Table 3.1.

Table 3.1 Boolean operations and their symbols

Operation	Symbol
AND	.
OR	+
NOT	⁻ or '

3.2 THEOREMS

From the axioms above, we can derive the following theorems.

Theorem 1: Idempotent	Proof
(a) $x + x = x$	(a) $x + x (x + x) \cdot 1$ (Identity) $(x + x) \cdot (x + \overline{x})$ (Complement) $x + x\overline{x}$ (Distributive) $x + 0$ (Complement) x (Null)
(b) $x \cdot x = x$ [Dual of (a)]	(b) It is not necessary to provide a separate proof for (b) which is the dual of (a) because of the principle of duality.

Duality

Any algebraic equality derived from the axioms of Boolean algebra remains true when the operators OR and AND are interchanged and the identity elements 0 and 1 are interchanged. This property is called duality. For example,

$x + 1 = 1$
$x \cdot 0 = 0$ (dual)

Because of the duality principle, for any given theorem its dual may be easily obtained.

Theorem 2: Operations with 0 and 1	Proof
(a) $x + 1 = 1$ (b) $x \cdot 0 = 0$ [Dual of (a)]	(a) $x + 1$ $x + x + \overline{x}$ (Complement) $x + \overline{x}$ (Idempotent theorem) 1 (Complement)

Theorem 3: Absorption	Proof
(a) $y \cdot x + x = 0$ (b) $(y + x) \cdot x = x$ [Dual of (a)]	(a) $y \cdot x + x$ $y \cdot x + x \cdot 1$ (Identity) $y \cdot x + 1 \cdot x$ (Commutative) $(y + 1) \cdot x$ (Distributive) $1 \cdot x$ (Operations with 0 and 1) x (identity)

Theorem 4: DeMorgan's Law	Proof
(a) $\overline{(x + y)} = \overline{x} \cdot \overline{y}$ (b) $\overline{(x \cdot y)} = \overline{x} + \overline{y}$ [Dual of (a)]	The proof for De Morgan's Law using the axioms of Boolean algebra is long. Another method (that also works for the other theorems just discussed) is to prove by the method of perfect induction, which uses the following truth tables:

x	y	$x + y$	$\overline{(x + y)}$	$\overline{x}$	$\overline{y}$	$\overline{x} \cdot \overline{y}$
0	0	0	1	1	1	1
0	1	1	0	1	0	0
1	0	1	0	0	1	0
1	1	1	0	0	0	0

3.2.1 Some Applications of Boolean Laws and Theorems

EXAMPLES

Proving the following:

1. $A + BC = (A + B)(A + C)$

Solution

R.H.S $= (A + B)(A + C)$
$= A \cdot A + A \cdot C + A \cdot B + B \cdot C$
$= A + AC + AB + BC$
$= A \cdot 1 + A \cdot C + AB + BC$
$= A(1 + C) + AB + BC$
$= A \cdot 1 + A \cdot B + BC$
$= A(1 + B) + BC$
$= A \cdot 1 + BC$
$= A + BC$

Or

L.H.S $= A + BC$
$= A \cdot (1 + B) + BC$
$= A \cdot 1 + AB + BC$
$= A(1 + C) + AB + BC$
$= A \cdot 1 + AC + AB + BC$
$= A + AC + AB + BC$
$= A \cdot A + AC + AB + BC$
$= A(A + C) + B(A + C)$
$= (A + B)(A + C)$

2. Prove $A + \overline{A}B = A$
   L.H.S. $= A \cdot 1 + A \cdot \overline{B} = A \cdot (1 + B) = A \cdot 1 = A$

3. Prove $A + \overline{A}B = 1$
   L.H.S. $= A + \overline{A} + \overline{B} = 1 + \overline{B} = 1$

4. Prove $A + AB = A$
   L.H.S. $= A \cdot 1 + A \cdot B = A \cdot (1 + B) = A$

5. Prove $A(\overline{A} + B) = AB$
   L.H.S. $= A \times \overline{A} + AB = 0 + AB = AB$

6. Prove $A(A + B) = A$
   L.H.S $= A \cdot A + A \cdot B = A + A \cdot B$
   $= A \cdot 1 + A \cdot B = A \cdot (1 + B)$
   $= A$

Note

- Boolean algebra deals with logic variables, which may either be 1 that is, TRUE or 0 that is, FALSE. It uses logic variables and logic operations to develop, manipulate, and simplify logic expressions, following set rules.
- The property of duality states that any algebraic equality derived from the axioms of Boolean algebra remains true when the operators OR and AND are interchanged and the identity elements binary values, 0 and 1, are interchanged.
- The two De Morgan's theorem are dual of each other.

3.3 BOOLEAN EXPRESSION

A Boolean or logic expression is a logic variable or a number of logic variables involved with one another through the logical '·' operations '.', '+', and '−'. For logic variables A and B, the following are some examples of Boolean expressions:

(a) A
(b) $\overline{A}$
(c) B
(d) $A \cdot B$
(e) $A + B$
(f) $A + \overline{AB}$

3.4 SIMPLIFICATION OF BOOLEAN EXPRESSIONS

The simplification of the following functions, using the theorems and axioms of Boolean algebra, is discussed here.

EXAMPLES

Simplifying the following Boolean expressions:

1. $XY + X\overline{Y}$

Solution:

It is easy to see the pattern in this example because of the similarity between the AND operator in Boolean algebra and the multiplication operator in regular algebra. Because they are both distributive, the pattern is easy to notice.

$XY + X\overline{Y}$
$= (Y + \overline{Y})X$ (Distributive)
$= (1)X$ (Complement)
$= X$ (Identity)

2. $(X + Y) \cdot (X + \overline{Y})$

Solution:

It is not so easy to spot the pattern in this example because one is not used to the symbol + being distributive. In Boolean algebra, the OR operator + is distriutive.

$(X + Y)(X + \overline{Y})$
$= X + (Y \cdot \overline{Y})$ (Distributive)
$= X + (0)$ (Complement)
$= X$ (Null)

3. $\overline{Y}Z + \overline{X}YZ + XYZ$

Solution:

$Y\overline{Z} + \overline{X}YZ + XYZ$
$= Y\overline{Z} + (\overline{X} + X)YZ$ (Distributive)
$= Y\overline{Z} + (1)YZ$ (Complement)
$= Y\overline{Z} + YZ$ (Identity)
$= Y(\overline{Z} + Z)$ (Distributive)
$= Y(1)$ (Complement)
(Identity)

4. $(X+Y)(\bar{X}+Y+Z)(\bar{X}+Y+\bar{Z})$

Solution:

$(X+Y)(\bar{X}+Y+Z)(\bar{X}+Y+\bar{Z})$

$=(X+Y)((\bar{X}+Y)+Z)((\bar{X}+Y)+\bar{Z})$ (Associative)

$=(X+Y)((\bar{X}+Y)+(Z\cdot\bar{Z}))$ (Distributive)

$=(X+Y)(\bar{X}+Y)+(0)$ (Complement)

$=(X+Y)(\bar{X}+Y)$ (Null)

$=(X\cdot\bar{X})+Y$ (Distributive)

$=(0)+Y$ (Complement)

$=Y$ (Null)

There are two instances in this problem that require the use of the distributive property of '+' to simplify the problem. Another way to solve this problem is to use the principle of duality:

$(X+Y)(\bar{X}+Y+Z)(\bar{X}+Y+\bar{Z})$

The dual of the expression above is:

$XY+\bar{X}YZ+\bar{X}Y\bar{Z}$

After simplifying this expression and obtaining an answer, the dual of the answer has to be taken so that the simplified form of the original expression is obained.

$XY+\bar{X}YZ+\bar{X}Y\bar{Z}$ simplifies to Y

So,

Dual $(X+Y)(\bar{X}+Y+Z)(\bar{X}+Y+\bar{Z})$ = Dual (Y)

The dual of Y is still Y, hence,

$(X+Y)(\bar{X}+Y+Z)(\bar{X}+Y+\bar{Z})=Y$

5. $X+XYZ+\bar{X}YZ+\bar{X}\cdot Y+W\cdot X+\bar{W}\cdot X$

Solution:

This example is long and uses many of the axioms and theorems discussed. A term has also been duplicated (see ine 9).

$X+XYZ+\bar{X}YZ+\bar{X}Y+WX+\bar{W}X$

$=X+(X+\bar{X})YZ+\bar{X}Y+(W+\bar{W})X$ (Distributive)

$=X+(1)YZ+\bar{X}Y+(1)X$ (Complement)

$=X+YZ+\bar{X}Y+X$ (Identity)

$=(X+X)+YZ+\bar{X}Y$ (Associative)

$=X+YZ+\bar{X}Y$ (Idempotent)

$=X(1)+YZ+\bar{X}Y$ (Identity)

$=X(Y+\bar{Y})+YZ+\bar{X}Y$ (Complement)

$=XY+X\bar{Y}+YZ+\bar{X}Y$ (Distributive)

$=XY+X\bar{Y}+X\bar{Y}+YZ+\bar{X}Y$ (Idempotent)

$=XY+X\bar{Y}+YZ+XY+\bar{X}Y$ (Associative)

$=X(Y+\bar{Y})+YZ+(X+\bar{X})Y$ (Distributive)

$=X(1)+YZ+(1)Y$ (Complement)

$=X+YZ+Y$ (Identity)

$=X+Y(Z+1)$ (Distributive)

$=X+Y(1)$ (Identity)

$=X+Y$ (Identity)

6. $(X\cdot(\overline{XY}))+(Y\cdot(\overline{XY}))$

Solution:

$(X\cdot(\overline{XY}))+(Y\cdot(\overline{XY}))$

$=(X\cdot(\bar{X}+\bar{Y}))+(Y\cdot(\bar{X}+\bar{Y}))$ (De Morgan's Law)

$=(X\bar{X}+X\bar{Y})+(Y\bar{X}+Y\bar{Y})$ (Distributive)

$=(0+X\bar{Y})+(Y\bar{X}+0)$ (Complement)

$=(X\bar{Y})+(Y\bar{X})$ (Null)

7. $XY+\bar{X}Z+YZ$

Solution:

Here, the expression needs to be expanded to obtain a simpler solution.

$XY+\bar{X}Z+YZ$

$=XY+\bar{X}Z+YZ\cdot1$ (Identity)

$=XY+\bar{X}Z+YZ\cdot(X+\bar{X})$ (Complement)

$=XY+\bar{X}Z+YZX+YZ\bar{X}$ (Distributive)

$=XY+YZX+\bar{X}Z+YZ\bar{X}$ (Commutative)

$=XY+XYZ+\bar{X}Z+\bar{X}ZY$ (Commutative)

$=XY(1+Z)+\bar{X}Z(1+Y)$ (Distributive)

$=XY(1)+\bar{X}Z(1)$ (Identity)

$=XY+\bar{X}Z$ (Identity)

8. $X\cdot X$

Solution:

This is the dual of the idempotent theorem that was proved; the equality is true because of the duality principle.

$X\cdot X$

$=X\cdot X+0$ (Null)

$=X\cdot X+(X\cdot\bar{X})$ (Complement)

$=X\cdot(X+\bar{X})$ (Distributive)

$=X\cdot(1)$ (Complement)

$=X$ (Identity)

Check Your Progress

1. The simplification of the Boolean expression $(\bar{A}\cdot B\cdot\bar{C})+(A\cdot\bar{B}\cdot C)$

(a) 0   (b) 1

(c) A (d) BC

Answer: (b)

2. The Boolean expression $\bar{A}\cdot B+A\cdot\bar{B}+A\cdot B$ is equivalent to

(a) $A+B$ (b) $\bar{A}\cdot B$

(c) $\overline{A+B}$ (d) $A\cdot B$

Answer: (a)

3. When simplified with Boolean Algebra, $(x+y)(x+z)$ simplifies to

(a) x (b) $x+x(y+z)$

(c) $x(1+yz)$ (d) $x+yz$

Answer: (d)

4. The simplification of $\overline{(\overline{AB}+\bar{A}+AB)}$ is

(a) 1   (b) 0

(c) A (d) AB

Answer: (b)

3.5 BOOLEAN FUNCTIONS AND TRUTH TABLES

A Boolean function of one or more logic variables, also known as Boolean variable, is a binary variable, the value of which depends on the values of these logic variables. For example, independent Boolean variables A and B may have arbitrarily chosen values while the Boolan function $f(A,B)$ has values that depend on the values of A and B, hence: $F_1 = AB\overline{C}$ means F_1 is 1 (TRUE) when $A = 1$ (TRUE), $B = 1$ (TRUE), and $C = 0$ (FALSE).

A table depicting the value of a given Boolean function, for all possible value combinations of its independent variables, is known as a truth table. Consider a Boolean function $f(A,B)$, of two logic variables A and B, which s given as:

$$f(A,B) = A \cdot B + \overline{A} \cdot \overline{B} \tag{3.1}$$

The truth table for this function is shown in the Table 3.2.

Table 3.2 For $f(A, B)$

A	B	f(A,B)
0	0	1
0	1	0
1	0	0
1	1	1

Four possible value combinations of A and B are depicted in the first two columns of the table. It may be verified whether the truth table truly represents the function expressed in Eqn (3.1). For row 1 of the truth table, $A = 0$, $B = 0$; therefore, putting these values in Eqn (3.1), $f(A,B) = 0 \cdot 0 + \overline{0} \cdot \overline{0} = 0 + 1 \cdot 1 = 0 + 1 = 1$. For row 2 of the truth table, $A = 0$, $B = 1$, hence $f(A,B) = 0 \cdot 1 + \overline{0} \cdot \overline{1} = 0 + 1 \cdot 0 = 0 + 0 = 0$. Also, for row 3 of the truth table, $A = 1$, $B = 0$, thus $f(A,B) = 1 \cdot 0 + \overline{1} \cdot \overline{0} = 0 + 0 \cdot 1 = 0 + 0 = 0$. Similarly, for row 4 of the truth table, $A = 1$, $B = 1$, $f(A,B) = 1 \cdot 1 + \overline{1} \cdot \overline{1} = 1 + 0 \cdot 0 = 1 + 0 = 1$.

All the computed values of $f(A, B)$ agree with the values shown in the corresponding rows of the truth table. Hence, the truth table of a given Boolean function truly represents the function.

3.6 CONSTRUCTING BOOLEAN FUNCTIONS FROM TRUTH TABLES

A Boolean function can be built from the value of a given truth table. Considering Table 3.2, the value of $f(A,B)$ is 1 when

$A = 0$ and $B = 0$
or $A = 1$ and $B = 1$
The above conditions may also be written as
$\overline{A} = 1$ and $\overline{B} = 1$
or $A = 1$ and $B = 1$

These conditions may further be rewritten as the following logical products:

$$\overline{A} \cdot \overline{B} = 1 \text{ or } A \cdot B = 1$$

It is, therefore, concluded that $f(A,B)$ is 1 when $\overline{A} \cdot \overline{B} = 1$ or $A \cdot B$ is 1, thus

$$f(A,B) = A \cdot B + \overline{A} \cdot \overline{B} \tag{3.2}$$

This function is the same as the function in Eqn (3.1). Hence, given a truth table, the corresponding Boolean function can be constructed.

The Boolean function in Eqn (3.2) was constructed from the truth table (Table 3.2) by considering a combination of values of variables A and B for which $f(A,B)$ is 1. Now from the same truth table, another Boolean function $f(A,B)$, for those combinations of values of A and B for which the function is 0, can also be built. From Table 3.2, the value of $f(A,B)$ is 0 when

$A = 0$ and $B = 1$
or $A = 1$ and $B = 0$
The above conditions may be written as
$A = 0$ and $\overline{B} = 0$
or $\overline{A} = 0$ and $B = 0$

The conditions can further be rewritten as the following logical smmations:

$$A + \overline{B} = 0 \text{ or } \overline{A} + B = 0$$

Hence, it is concluded that $f(A,B)$ is 0 for either of the two combinations being 0 Therefore,

$$f(A,B) = (A + \overline{B}) \cdot (\overline{A} + B) \tag{3.3}$$

Now,

$$\begin{aligned} f(A,B) &= (A + \overline{B}) \cdot (\overline{A} + B) \\ &= A \cdot \overline{A} + A \cdot B + \overline{B} \cdot \overline{A} + \overline{B} \cdot B \\ &= 0 + A \cdot B + \overline{A} \cdot \overline{B} + 0 \\ &= A \cdot B + \overline{A} \cdot \overline{B}, \end{aligned}$$

which is same as Eqn (3.2).

The function in Eqn (3.2) is a logical sum of logical products whereas the function in Eqn (3.3) is a logical product of logical sums. The functions are equal to one another but their forms are different. Hence, a truth table may be represented by at least two Boolean functions that are equal.

Terms A combination of logic variables forming a group in a Boolean function is called a term.

Literals Each complemented or uncomplemented variable in a term is called a literal.

3.7 CANONICAL AND STANDARD FORMS

In a Boolean function, if all terms are written as AND combinations of the Boolean variables, there are 2^n such AND 'terms' for n variables. These AND terms are called minterms. Minterms are designated as m_0, m_1, ... m_n, etc., where the subscripts represent the decimal values obtained from the equivalent binary value of the combined variables.

The minterms are also called standard products. Similarly, ORing the variables form maxterms. For three variables, the minterms and maxterms are determined as shown in Table 3.3.

Table 3.3 Summary of canonical and standard forms

Boolean variables			Minterm		Maxterm	
A	B	C	Term	Designation	Team	Designation
0	0	0	$\bar{A}\,\bar{B}\,\bar{C}$	m_0	$A+B+C$	M_0
0	0	1	$\bar{A}\,\bar{B}\,C$	m_1	$A+B+\bar{C}$	M_1
0	1	0	$\bar{A}\,B\,\bar{C}$	m_2	$A+\bar{B}+C$	M_2
0	1	1	$\bar{A}\,B\,C$	m_3	$A+\bar{B}+\bar{C}$	M_3
1	0	0	$A\,\bar{B}\,\bar{C}$	m_4	$\bar{A}+B+C$	M_4
1	0	1	$A\,\bar{B}\,C$	m_5	$\bar{A}+B+\bar{C}$	M_5
1	1	0	$A\,B\,\bar{C}$	m_6	$\bar{A}+\bar{B}+C$	M_6
1	1	1	$A\,B\,C$	m_7	$\bar{A}+\bar{B}+\bar{C}$	M_7

Since each minterm or the maxterm is formed by the combination of all the n complemented or uncomplemented variables, each of these is called a canonical term. Each minterm is obtained by ANDing the variables, with each variable having an overbar if its corresponding binary value is 0 and not having an overbar if its binary value is 1. Similarly, each maxterm is obtained by ORing the variables, with each variable having an overbar if its corresponding binary value is 1 and not having an overbar if it is 0. It may be noted that each maxterm is the complement of its corresponding minterm and vice versa.

Any Boolean function may be expressed as an OR combination of the minterms for which the function is 1. This form of the function is a 'sum' of minterms or standard 'products'. A Boolean function may also be expressed as an AND combination of maxterms for which the function is 0. The function, thus, is the 'product' of maxterms. A Boolean function written as a sum of minterms or product of maxterms is said to be in **canonical form**. De Morgan's theorem allows conversion between the two canonical forms. The two canonical forms of Boolean algebra are basic forms.

Another method of expressing a Boolean function is the *standard form*. There are two types of standard forms: *sum of products and product of sums*.

The sum of products is a Boolean expression containing AND terms, called product terms, formed with one or more logic variables. The sum denotes the ORing of these terms. Example: $f_1(A, B, C) = \bar{B} + AB + \overline{ABC}$

A product of sums is a Boolean expression containing OR terms called sum terms, comprising one or more logic variables. The product denotes the ANDing of these terms. Example: $f_2 = A \cdot (\bar{B} + C) \cdot (\bar{A} + B + \bar{C} + D)$

A Boolean function may be expressed in a non-standard form also. For example: $F_3 = (AB + CD)(\overline{AB} + \overline{CD})$ is neither in the sum of products nor in product of sums form. However, it can be transformed to a standard form using the distributive law, that is, $F_3 = \overline{AB}CD + AB\overline{CD}$.

3.8 NUMERICAL REPRESENTATION OF BOOLEAN FUNCTIONS IN CANONICAL FORM

A Boolean function, with the canonical sum of product terms, can be expressed in a compact form by listing the decimal value corresponding to the minterm for which the function value is 1.

As an example, the truth table of a three-variable function is shown below. Three variables, each of which can take the values 0 or 1, yield eight possible combinations of values for which the function may be true. These eight combinations are listed in ascending binary order and the equivalent decimal value is also shown in Table 3.4.

Table 3.4 Equivalent decimal value for Boolean terms

Decimal value	A	B	C	F
0	0	0	0	1
1	0	0	1	0
2	0	1	0	1
3	0	1	1	1
4	1	0	0	0
5	1	0	1	0
6	1	1	0	0
7	1	1	1	1

The function, has a value 1 for the variable combinations shown, therefore

$$f(A, B, C) = \overline{A} \cdot \overline{B} \cdot \overline{C} \cdot + \overline{A}B\overline{C} + \overline{A}BC + ABC \qquad (3.4)$$

This can also be written as

$$f(A, B, C) = (000) + (010) + (011) + (111)$$

The summation sign indicates that the terms are ORed together. The function can be expressed in the compact form as follows:

$$f(A, B, C) = \sum m(0, 2, 3, 7) = m_0 + m_2 + m_3 + m_7$$

Note (a) The position of the digits must not be changed.

(b) The expression must be in standard sum of products form.

Similarly, a Boolean function can be expressed in compact form by listing the decimal value corresponding to the maxterms for which the function value is 0.

From Table 3.4, consider the terms for which the function is 0, then

$$f(A, B, C) = (A + B + \overline{C}) \cdot (\overline{A} + B + C) \cdot (\overline{A} + B + \overline{C})$$
$$\cdot (\overline{A} + \overline{B} + C)$$

In compact form, this is expressed as

$$f(A, B, C) = \pi M(1, 4, 5, 6) = M_1 M_4 M_5 M_6$$

Note

- A Boolean or logic expression is a Boolean variable or a number of these variables involved with one another through the logic operators '·', '+', and '−'.
- A Boolean function of one or more logic variables, also known as Boolean variable, is a binary variable, the value of which depends on the values of these logic variables.
- A Boolean function may be represented by a truth table or as sum of product terms or by the product of sum terms.
- A Boolean function, with the canonical sum of product terms, can be expressed in a compact form by listing the decimal value corresponding to the minterm for which the function value is 1. Likewise, a Boolean function can also be expressed in compact form by listing the decimal value corresponding to the maxterms for which function value is 0.

3.9 LOGIC GATES

The boolean functions or expressions can be realized by using electronic gates. It must be understood that the logic '1' and logic '0', which are fed as input to the gates, are represented by two distinct voltage levels. Even the output, which is either logic '1' or '0', is represented by distinct voltage levels. There are three fundamental logical operations from which all other Boolean functions, no matter how much complex, can be derived. These operations are named *and, or,* and *not.* Each of these has a specific symbol and a clearly

defined behavior. These operations are implemented by three basic gates: AND, OR, and NOT. Four other gates NAND, NOR, XOR, and XNOR, which are derived gates, are also used to construct logic functions. NAND and NOR gates are known as universal gates.

3.9.1 AND Gate

The AND gate is an electronic circuit that has two or more inputs and only one output. It gives a HIGH output (1) only if all its inputs are HIGH. If A and B are logic inputs to a two input AND gate, then output Y is equal to $A \cdot B$. The dot (.) indicates an AND operation. This dot is usually omitted, as shown in the output in Fig. 3.1. The AND gate is also called an all or nothing gate. The truth table for the AND gate is given in Table 3.5.

Table 3.5 Truth table for a two-input AND gate

Inputs		Output
A	B	$Y = AB$
0	0	0
0	1	0
1	0	0
1	1	1

(a) AND Gate using electrical contacts

(b) AND gate using diodes

(c) Logic symbol for AND gate

Fig. 3.1 Two-input AND gate

In the AND gate formed by diodes in Fig. 3.1(b), when the voltage at A is $+V_{CC}$ volts and the voltage at B is $+V_{CC}$ volts, both diodes D_1 and D_2 do not conduct, which means the diodes are off. Therefore, no current flows through R. As a result no voltage is developed across R. This makes the voltage at Y almost equal to $+V_{CC}$ volt. But, if the voltage at A is zero volts or the voltage at B is zero volts or if both A and B be equal to zero volts, the respective diode D_1 or D_2 conducts or both the diodes conduct. This makes the voltage at $Y \approx 0.7V$, which is the drop across the diodes. In practice, this is considered to be zero volts. Thus, the output is $Y \approx 0$ V. The truth table for the gate circuit is given in Table 3.6.

Table 3.6 Truth table for a two-input AND gate (V_{CC} = +5 V)

Inputs		Output
A	B	Y
0 V	0 V	0 V
0 V	5 V	0 V
5 V	0 V	0 V
5 V	5 V	5 V

Figure 3.1(a) depicts two switches A and B connected in series. The output voltage is HIGH when A and B are on and the input is HIGH. But if either A or B is off or both are off, the output is LOW.

There is no functional limit to the number of inputs that may be applied to an AND function. However, for practical reasons, commercial AND gates are most commonly manufactured with two, three, or four inputs. A standard Integrated Circuit (IC) package contains 14 or 16 pins. A 14-pin IC package can contain four two-input gates, three three-input gates, or two four-input gates and still have room for two pins for power supply connections.

3.9.2 OR Gate

The OR gate is an electronic circuit that has two or more inputs and only one output. It gives a HIGH output if one or more of its inputs are HIGH. For a two-input OR gate, where A and B are the logic inputs, the output Y is equal to $A + B$. A plus (+) indicates an OR operation. The truth table for a two-input OR gate is given in Table 3.7.

Table 3.7 Truth table for a two-input OR gate

Inputs		Output
A	B	Y = A + B
0	0	0
0	1	1
1	0	1
1	1	1

In the OR gate in Fig. 3.2(b), when the voltage at A is zero volts and the voltage at B is zero volts, both diodes D1 and D2 do not conduct. Since, no current flows through R, no voltage exists across R. Thus, the voltage at Y is zero volts. But if either A or B or both are at voltage $+V_{CC}$, then the corresponding diode D1 or D2 or both conduct thereby making the voltage at $Y \approx +V_{CC}$. The truth table of this gate circuit is given in Table 3.8.

Fig. 3.2 Two-input OR gate

Figure 3.2(a) shows two switches A and B connected in parallel. The output voltage is HIGH, if any switch A or B or both are on, and the input is HIGH. When both switches are off, the output is LOW. As with the AND function, the OR function can have any number of inputs. However, practical, commercial OR gates are mostly limited to two, three, and four inputs, as with AND gates.

Table 3.8 Truth table (V_{CC} = +5V) for two-input OR gate

Inputs		Output
A	B	Y
0 V	0 V	0 V
0 V	5 V	5 V
5 V	0 V	5 V
5 V	5 V	5 V

3.9.3 NOT Gate or Inverter

The inverter is a little different from AND and OR gates as it has only one input and one output. Whatever logic state is applied to the input, the opposite state will appear at the output.

The NOT function is denoted by a horizontal bar over the value to be inverted, as shown in the Fig. 3.3. In some cases, a prime symbol (′) may also be used for this purpose: 0′ is 1 and 1′ is 0. For greater clarity in logical expressions, the overbar is used most of the time.

In the inverter symbol shown in Fig. 3.3, the triangle actually denotes only an amplifier, which does not change its logical sense. It is the circle at the output that denotes the logical inversion. The circle could have been placed at the input instead, and the logical meaning would still be the same. The truth table is given in Table 3.9.

Table 3.9 Truth table for NOT gate

Inputs	Output
A	$Y = \bar{A}$
0	1
1	0

The NOT gate in Fig. 3.3(b) uses a transistor. When the voltage applied to input A is zero volts, the transistor is reverse biased; so it is off. Hence the voltage at Y is $+V_{CC}$, i.e., HIGH. But when A is $+V_{CC}$, the transistor is forward biased thereby driving the transistor to an on state or saturation. The voltage at $Y \approx V_{CE}$ (sat), which is practically zero volts, i.e., Y is LOW. The truth table for this circuit is given in Table 3.10.

(a) Logic symbol for NOT gate

(b) NOT gate circuit using a transistor

Fig. 3.3 NOT gate

Table 3.10 Truth table for a NOT gate (V_{CC} = 5 V)

Inputs	Output
A	$Y = \bar{A}$
0 V	5 V
5 V	0 V

3.9.4 NAND Gate

The NAND gate implements the NAND function, which means NOT-AND. The inputs are ANDed and then NOTed to get a single output. The output of NAND gate is HIGH if any or all of the inputs are LOW. When all inputs are HIGH, the output is LOW. Table 3.11 depicts the truth table for a two-input NAND gate.

Table 3.11 Truth table for a two-input NAND gate

Inputs		Output
A	B	$Y = \overline{AB}$
0	0	1
0	1	1
1	0	1
1	1	0

In Fig. 3.4, the circle at the output of the NAND gate denotes the logical inversion, just as it did at the output of the inverter. Note that the output is the overbar of the ANDed input values. As shown in the figure, the NAND function can also be performed by a bubbled OR gate.

As with AND, there is no limit to the number of inputs that may be applied to a NAND function, so there is no functional limit to the number of inputs a NAND gate may have. However, for practical reasons, commercial NAND gates are most commonly manufactured with two, three, or four inputs to fit in a 14-pin or 16-pin IC package.

(a) AND gate followed by OR gate

(b) Two-input NAND gate logic symbol

(c) Bubbled OR gate as NAND gate

Fig. 3.4 Two-input NAND gate

3.9.5 NOR Gate

The NOR gate is an OR gate with inverted output. Whereas the OR gate allows the output to be HIGH (logic 1) if any one or more of its inputs are HIGH, the NOR gate inverts this and forces the output to logic 0 when any input is HIGH, i.e., the output of a NOR gate is LOW if any of the inputs are HIGH. The output is HIGH when all inputs are LOW. The truth table of a two-input NOR gate is given in Table 3.12.

The NOR function uses the plus sign (+) operator with the output represented by an expression with an overbar to indicate the OR inversion. In the logic diagram, shown in Fig. 3.5(b), the symbol designates the NOR gate. This is an OR gate with a circle to designate the inversion. The NOR function can also be performed by a bubbled AND gate, as depicted in Fig. 3.5(c).

The NOR function can have any number of inputs but only one output. As with other gates, practical commercial NOR gates are mostly limited to two, three, and four inputs to fit in standard IC packages.

(a) OR gate followed by NOT gate

(b) Two-input NOR gate logic symbol

(c) Bubbled AND gate as NOR gate

Fig. 3.5   Two-input NOR gate

Table 3.12   Truth table for a two-input NOR gate

Inputs		Output
A	B	$Y = \overline{A + B}$
0	0	1
0	1	0
1	0	0
1	1	0

3.9.6 Exclusive-OR or XOR Gate

The Exclusive-OR or XOR gate is a two-input circuit that will give a HIGH output if either, but not both, of the inputs are HIGH. The truth table of XOR gate is given in Table 3.13.

The XOR function is an interesting and useful variation of the basic OR function. Its function can be stated as 'Either A or B, but not both'. The XOR gate produces a logic 1 output only if the two inputs are different. If the inputs are the same, the output is a logic 0. XOR is also called an anti-coincidence gate or inequality detector.

The XOR symbol is a variation of the standard OR symbol, as can be seen in Fig. 3.6(a). An encircled plus $\oplus$ sign is used to show the XOR operation.

(a) Logic symbol for XOR gate

(b) XOR gate using AND, OR, and NOT gates

Fig. 3.6   XOR gate

There are a couple of interesting facts about Exclusive-OR. One is that if a bit is XORed with itself, the result is zero regardless of whether the original bit was zero or one. Unlike standard OR/NOR and AND/NAND functions, the XOR function always has exactly two inputs and commercially manufactured XOR gates are the same.

Generally, an XOR operation of an n-input variable would result in a logic 1 output if an odd number of the input variables are logic 1's. That is, the output of an XOR gate is HIGH when the number of one inputs is odd. This is useful in generating parity bits.

Table 3.13   Truth table for XOR gate

Inputs		Output
A	B	$Y = A \oplus B$
0	0	0
0	1	1
1	0	1
1	1	0

3.9.7 Exclusive-NOR or XNOR Gate

The Exclusive-NOR gate is a XOR gate followed by a NOT gate. XNOR gate is a two-input and one-output logic gate circuit. In the gate, the output is HIGH if both inputs are either LOW or HIGH. The logic symbol for a XNOR is shown in Fig. 3.7. Table 3.14 gives the truth table for the two-input XNOR gate.

Fig. 3.7   Logic symbol for a two-input XNOR gate

Table 3.14   Truth table for a two-input XNOR gate

Inputs		Output
A	B	$Y = A \odot B$
0	0	1
0	1	0
1	0	0
1	1	1

The output Y of the two-input XNOR, where A and B are the inputs, is given by

$$Y = \overline{A \oplus B} = \overline{\overline{A} \cdot B + A \cdot \overline{B}}$$
$$= \overline{\overline{AB}} \cdot \overline{\overline{A}\overline{B}} = (\overline{\overline{A}} + \overline{B}) \cdot (\overline{A} + \overline{\overline{B}}) \quad \text{De Morgan's Theorem}$$

$$= (A + \overline{B}) \cdot (\overline{A} + B)$$
$$= A \cdot \overline{A} + A \cdot B + \overline{A} \cdot \overline{B} + \overline{B} \cdot B = A \cdot B + \overline{A} \cdot \overline{B} = A \odot B$$

The XNOR gate output in Fig. 3.7 assumes a HIGH state whenever the inputs are similar, i.e., when both inputs are either 1 or 0; otherwise the output is LOW. It is, therefore, called a coincident gate. It can be used as a one-bit comparator or equality detector.

The symbol for the XNOR operation $\odot$, is shown in Fig. 3.7. The XNOR output is 1 if the number of 1's in its inputs is even, otherwise if the number is odd; the output is 0. This property of the XNOR gate is used to form an even-parity checker.

Note

- The three gates, AND, OR and NOT, can be used together to implement a Boolean function.
- If a bit is XOR-ed with itself, the result is zero regardless of whether the original bit was zero or one.
- An XOR operation of an n-input variable would result in a logic 1 output if an odd number of the input variables are logic 1's.
- In an XNOR operation, the output is 1 if the number of 1's in its inputs is even.

3.10 DESCRIBING LOGIC CIRCUITS ALGEBRAICALLY

Any logic circuit, no matter how complex, may be completely described using the Boolean operations because the OR, AND, and NOT gates are the basic building blocks of digital systems. The algebraic expression that relates the logic output of a logic circuit with the binary inputs of the logic circuit, is called a Boolean expression. Figure 3.8 shows a circuit diagram using Boolean expression.

Fig. 3.8 A circuit diagram using Boolean expression

If an expression contains both AND and OR operations, the AND operations are performed first. For example, in $Y = AB + C$, AB is performed first, unless there are parentheses in the expression, in which case the operation inside the parentheses is performed first. That is, in $Y = (A + B) + C$, $A + B$ is performed first.

Whenever an inverter is present in a logic-circuit diagram, its output expression is simply equal to the input expression

with an overbar ($^-$) over it. Figure 3.9 shows a circuit containing inverters.

Fig. 3.9 Circuit using inverters

3.11 REALIZATION OF LOGIC CIRCUITS FROM BOOLEAN EXPRESSIONS

If the operation of a circuit is defined by a Boolean expression, a logic-circuit diagram can be developed directly from the expression.

Suppose a circuit has to be constructed whose ouput is $Y = AC + B\overline{C} + \overline{A}BC$. This Boolean expression contains three terms ($AC, B\overline{C}, \overline{A}BC$), which are ORed together. This implies that a three-input OR gate is required with inputs that are equal to AC, $B\overline{C}$ and $\overline{A}BC$ respectively. Each OR gate input is an AND product term, which means that an AND gate with appropriate inputs can be used to generate each of these terms. Note that the use of inverters to produce the $\overline{A}$ and $\overline{B}$ terms is required in the expression. The logic circuit development is done in steps. These steps are shown in Figs 3.10 and 3.11 for the Boolean expression mentioned above.

Fig. 3.10 Step 1 of logic circuit developmnt for $Y = AC + B\overline{C} + \overline{A}BC$

Fig. 3.11 Step 2 of logic circuit development for $Y = AC + B\overline{C} + \overline{A}BC$

3.12 UNIVERSALITY OF NAND AND NOR GATES

NAND and NOR are called universal gates since the AND, OR, and NOT gates can be constructed with either of them.

It is possible to implement *any* logic expression using only NAND gates. This is because NAND gates, in the proper combination, can be used to perform each of the Boolean operations OR, AND, and NOT. Figure 3.12 shows how NAND gates are used to implement AND, OR, and NOT operations. Similarly, Fig. 3.13 depicts how NOR gates are used to implement AND, OR, and NOT operations.

Fig. 3.12 NAND gates performing OR, AND, and NOT operations

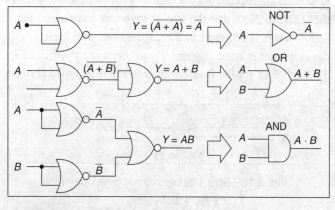

Fig. 3.13 NOR gates performing NOT, OR, and AND operations

Note

- The NAND and NOR gates can not only be used to implement the AND, OR and NOT gate functions but can also implement any complex Boolean function.

Check Your Progress

1. The NAND gate output will be low if the two inputs are

   (a) 00   (b) 01

   (c) 10   (d) 11

Answer: (d)

2. When an input signal $A = 11001$ is applied to a NOT gate serially, its output signal is

   (a) 00111   (b) 00110

   (c) 10101   (d) 11001

Answer: (b)

3. Write the expression for Boolean function:

   $F(A, B, C) = \sum m(1, 4, 5, 6, 7)$ in standard POS form.

Answer: $F = (A + B + C)(A + \bar{B} + C)(A + \bar{B} + \bar{C})$

4. A universal logic gate is one, which can be used to generate any logic function. Which of the following is a universal logic gate?

   (a) OR   (b) AND

   (c) XOR   (d) NAND

Answer: (d)

5. The "maxterm form" of a Boolean function is

   $F(A,B,C,D) = \sum_M(1, 2, 3, 4, 5, 6, 7, 8, 9, 10, 11, 12, 13, 14, 15)$. The equivalent "minterm form" of this function is

   (a) $\Sigma_m(0)$ (b) ABCD

   (c) ABC   (d) $\overline{ABCD}$

Answer: (a)

SUMMARY

A variable which can either be 'true' or 'false' is a logic variable. The basic operations of Boolean algebra are AND, OR, and NOT. The operations like AND, OR, Complementation, Associative, Distributive, and Commutative have evolved from these. The property of duality and De Morgan's theorems has also been derived from the basic boolean operations. Simplification of Boolean expressions can be performed with the help of the above laws and theorems. Boolean expressions or functions can be represented using truth tables, minterms, or maxterms.

The inputs and outputs of logic gates have two discrete voltage values. The AND gate is a circuit built with electronic devices which gives a 'true' output only if all inputs are 'true'. The OR gate, which is constructed with electronic devices, gives a 'true' output if any input is 'true'. In the NOT gate, whatever input is applied, the opposite logic state appears at the output, e.g., for a 'true' input, the output is 'false' and vice versa. The NAND gate is equivalent to NOT-AND and the NOR gate to NOT- OR. XOR gate is similar to OR gate with the exception that when both inputs are 1, the output is 0. The XNOR gate, also known as coincidence gate, gives 1 as output only if both inputs are 0 or if both inputs are 1. Any boolean expression can be implemented with logic gates as the building blocks. NAND and NOR are universal gates as these can be used to construct the basic logic gates.

KEY TERMS

TRUE   In Boolean algebra true means "1".

FALSE   In Boolean algebra false means "0".

Boolean algebra   Boolean algebra is the algebra of propositions. It deals with two values, 0 and 1 or true and false.

Boolean or logic variable   It is a variable that can be assigned any one of the two values, 0 or 1.

Axiom   It is an established statement or proposition.

AND   It is an operation in which the output is " true" only when all the inputs are true.

OR   It is an operation in which the output is true whenever at least one of the inputs is true.

NOT   It is an operation that produces an output which is the complement of the input.

NAND   It is an operation in which the output is formed by AND-ing all inputs and then complementing it.

NOR   It is an operation in which the output is formed by OR-ing all inputs and then complementing it.

Duality   It is the property in which any algebraic equality derived from the axioms of Boolean algebra remains true when the operators OR and AND are interchanged and the identity elements 0 and 1 are interchanged.

Literal   A literal is a variable or its complement. Example: $X, \bar{X}, Y, \bar{Y}$.

Boolean function   A Boolean function is a boolean variable that has a value, 0 or 1, which gets evaluated from logic computations involving boolean variables and logic operators like ' · ', ' + ', and ' — '.

Truth Table   It is a table that depicts the boolean value, 0 or 1, of the output boolean function for different sets of boolean values of the boolean inputs.

Term   A term is a collection of boolean variables formed by AND-ing or OR-ing , e.g. ABC or (a + c + d).

Product term   It is a term formed by AND-ing two or more boolean variables.

Sum term   It is a term formed by OR-ing two or more boolean variables.

Minterm   It is a special product of literals, in which each input variable appears exactly once. A function with n input variables has 2^n minterms , since each variable can appear complemented or un-complemented.

Maxterm   It is a sum of literals, in which each input variable appears exactly once. A function with n variables has 2^n maxterms, because each variable can appear complemented or un-complemented.

Sum of products   It is a function formed with the " sum " of product terms.

Product of sums   It is a function formed with the " product " of sum terms.

Canonical form   It is a function formed by minterms or maxterms.

FREQUENTLY ASKED QUESTIONS

1. What is a Boolean variable?

Answer:

A Boolean variable is a quantity which, at any point in time, can hold a value '1' or '0' in the Boolean algebraic system. The Boolean variable is denoted by an alphabetic symbol.

2. What is Boolean algebra?

Answer:

Boolean algebra is the algebra of propositions. It deals with three basic binary logic operators and Boolean variables that holds either a 0 or a 1. Based on this, this algebra has several laws and theorems. Any system where the output is " true" for different binary value combinations of a set of input variables, Boolean algebra helps in establishing a relationship between the output variable and input variables by means of a Boolean function.

3. What is a logic gate?

Answer:

It is a circuit that performs Boolean operations, like AND or OR or NOT, on one or more boolean variable inputs to produce a single Boolean output variable.

4. What is "inclusive-OR" gate?

Answer:

It is a gate in which the output is " true " even if one input, out of all the inputs, is "true" otherwise the output is "false".

5. What is "coincidence" gate?

Answer:

The XNOR gate is known as "coincidence" gate. Whenever the inputs to the gate are same, which means all inputs are either "1" or "0", the output is "1". This emphasizes the reason for the gate being called a "coincidence" gate.

6. How is a Boolean function constructed from a truth table?

Answer:

A truth table depicts the binary value of a function for all possible binary values of input variables. The Boolean expression for the function, in SOP form, can be developed by OR-ing the product terms, formed by the input variables, only for those values of the function where it is "1". An alternate method of building the Boolean expression for the function, in POS form, is to take the product of sum terms for those values of the function where it is "0". Whether the function is in SOP form or POS form, the expression developed, using either method, is equivalent. An example illustrating this is given below.

Example: A truth table, shown below, is given. Obtain the function in SOP and POS forms and show that both forms of expressing the Boolean function Y are equivalent.

Truth table

Input			Output
A	B	C	Y
0	0	0	0
0	0	1	1
0	1	0	0
0	1	1	1
1	0	0	1
1	0	1	0
1	1	0	1
1	1	1	0

The function Y in SOP form is given as follows:

$$Y = \bar{A}\bar{B}C + \bar{A}BC + A\bar{B}\bar{C} + AB\bar{C} = \bar{A}C + A\bar{C} \qquad \text{...(i)}$$

The function Y in POS form is given as follows:

$$\bar{Y} = \bar{A}\bar{B}\bar{C} + \bar{A}B\bar{C} + A\bar{B}C + ABC = \bar{A}\bar{C} + AC \cdot \qquad \text{...(ii)}$$

Complement of (ii) is given by

$$Y = (A + B + C) \cdot (A + \bar{B} + C) \cdot (\bar{A} + B + \bar{C}) \cdot (\bar{A} + \bar{B} + \bar{C})$$

⬇

$$Y = (A + C) \cdot (\bar{A} + \bar{C}) = \bar{A}C + A\bar{C}$$

The expression for Y is found to be the same in both SOP and POS forms.

7. How is a Boolean function realized using logic gates?

Answer:

A boolean function can be realized or implemented with the help of logic gates. This is best demonstrated by an example given below.

Consider the function $Y = A \cdot \bar{C} + \bar{A} \cdot C$. Here the first product term has to be implemented by NOT-ing C and then AND-ing this with A. The second term is implemented by NOT-ing A and then AND-ing this with C. These two terms are then OR-ed to yield the function Y. The circuit, using the gates AND, OR and NOT that realizes this function Y from the inputs A and C is shown below.

8. Why is it necessary to simplify a Boolean function?

Answer:

The expression representing a Boolean function has to be simplified or reduced for the simple reason of decreasing the number of terms in the expression. This in turn reduces the requirement of the number of logic gates for realizing the function. Hence the complexity, hardware and cost of the logic circuit for implementing a Boolean function can be reduced.

9. How is the compact form used to represent a Boolean function?

Answer:

A Boolean function, with the canonical sum of product terms, can be expressed in a compact form by listing the decimal value corresponding to the minterm for which the function value is 1. For example the following Boolean function expressed in SOP form can be expressed in compact form as shown below

$$Y = \bar{A} \cdot \bar{B} \cdot C + \bar{A} \cdot B \cdot C + A \cdot \bar{B} \cdot \bar{C} + A \cdot B \cdot \bar{C} + A \cdot B \cdot C$$

$$Y = \sum_m (1, 3, 4, 6, 7) = m_1 + m_3 + m_4 + m_6 + m_7$$

Similarly, a Boolean function can be expressed in compact form by listing the decimal value corresponding to the maxterms for which the function value is 0. Hence the following Boolean function represented in POS form can be expressed in compact form as shown below

$$Y = (A + B + C) \cdot (A + \bar{B} + C) \cdot (\bar{A} + B + \bar{C})$$

$$Y = \pi_M (0, 2, 5) = M_0 M_2 M_5$$

10. What is the difference in representing a Boolean function in SOP form and POS form ?

Answer:

The difference lies in the way the expression representing the Boolean function is formed. In the SOP form the expression is formed with OR-ing minterms, while in the POS form the expression is formed by AND-ing the maxterms. This is very well illustrated in the example given with the answer for the previous question.

EXERCISES

1. Solve the following.

   (i) $A + 1 = $ _____
   (ii) $A + 0 = $ _____
   (iii) $A \cdot 1 = $ _____
   (iv) $A + A = $ _____

   (v) $A + \bar{A} = $ _____
   (vi) $A \cdot 0 = $ _____
   (vii) $A \cdot A = $ _____
   (viii) $A \cdot \bar{A} = $ _____

2. State De Morgan's theorem.

3. Construct truth tables for the following Boolean functions.

- (i) $Q = A\bar{B} + \bar{A}B$
- (ii) $Q = A \cdot B$
- (iii) $Q = A + B$
- (iv) $Q = \bar{A}$
- (v) $Q = \overline{A + B}$
- (vi) $Q = \overline{A \cdot B}$
- (vii) $Q = A + B \cdot C$
- (viii) $Q = (A + B) \cdot C$
- (ix) $Q = A \cdot B + C \cdot D$
- (x) $Q = X(\bar{X} + Y) \cdot (\bar{X} + Z)$
- (xi) $f = \bar{A}BC + AB\bar{C} + ABC$
- (xii) $f = (\bar{A} + \bar{B} + \bar{C})(A + B + C) \cdot (A + \bar{B} + C)$

4. Simply the following Boolean expressions.

- (i) $AA + AB + AC + BC$
- (ii) $(A + B + C)\overline{(D + E)} + (A + B + C)(D + E)$
- (iii) $XZ + Z(\bar{X} + XY)$
- (iv) $\overline{(A + B)}(C + D + E) + \overline{(A + B)}$
- (v) $AB + ABC + ABCD + ABCDE + ABCDEF$
- (vi) $(A + B + C)\overline{(D + E)} + (\bar{A} + \bar{B} + \bar{C})(D + E)$
- (vii) $A \cdot (\bar{A} + C) + C$
- (viii) $(A + B) \cdot (B + \bar{A})$
- (ix) $\bar{a}bc + \bar{a}b\bar{c} + abc + ab\bar{c} + ab\bar{c}$
- (x) $(a + \bar{a}) \cdot (ab + ab\bar{c})$
- (xi) $\overline{(a + \bar{b})(\bar{c} + d)}$
- (xii) $\overline{ab + \overline{ac}(b + \bar{c})}$
- (xiii) $\overline{ab + a\bar{c} + b\bar{c}}$
- (xiv) $\overline{(a + b + \bar{c})(\bar{a} + b + \bar{c})}$

5. Find the dual of

- (i) $A + 1 = 1$
- (ii) $X + \bar{X}Y = X + Y$
- (iii) $A \cdot B = B \cdot A$
- (iv) $A(A + B) = A$
- (v) $A \cdot (B + C) = AB + AC$
- (vi) $\overline{(AB)} = \bar{A} + \bar{B}$
- (vii) $(A + C)(\bar{A} + B) = AB + \bar{A}C + BC$
- (viii) $A + B = AB + \bar{A}B + A\bar{B}$
- (ix) $A + B \cdot \overline{(C + DE)} = A + B\bar{C}DE$
- (x) $A + \bar{B}C(A + \bar{B}C) = A + \bar{B}C$

6. Prove the following.

- (i) $(X + Y) \cdot (\bar{X} + Z) = X \cdot Z + \bar{X} \cdot Y + YZ$
- (ii) $(A + D)(A + C)(B + C)(B + D) = AB + CD$
- (iii) $ABC(AB + \bar{C}(BC + AC)) = ABC$
- (iv) $\overline{AB}C + BC + AC = C$
- (v) $AB + A\bar{B}C + B\bar{C} = AC + B\bar{C}$
- (vi) $\overline{\overline{AB} + \bar{A} + AB} = 0$
- (vii) $(A + \bar{A})(AB + AB\bar{C}) = AB$

(viii) $\overline{ABC}\overline{(A + B + C)} = \overline{ABC}$

(ix) $\overline{(ABC + \overline{AB})} + BC = \overline{AB}$

(x) If $X\bar{Y} + \bar{X}Y = Z$ then $X\bar{Z} + \bar{X}Z = Y$

7. (i) Convert $Q = ABCD + \bar{A}BC$ into a sum of minterms by algebraic method.

(ii) Convert $Q = ABC + \bar{B}CD$ into a product of maxterms by algebraic method.

8. (i) To get into a physics program in University, Jagan needs to have Physics and either algebra or calculus. Assign Boolean variables to the conditions and write a Boolean expression for the program requirements.

(ii) Aman wants to go go-karting at Kart World. They have conditions on who can drive their go-karts. You must be either over sixteen or be over twelve years of age and have parental permission. Using Boolean variables create an expression for the karting requirements.

9. Find the output Y in each of the following when (a) $A = 1$ and (b) $A = 0$.

- (i)
- (ii)
- (iii)
- (iv)
- (v)
- (vi)
- (vii)
- (viii)

10. Construct the truth tables for each of the following. Find the Boolean expressions of output Y in each of the circuits. What conclusions can be drawn?

- (i)
- (ii)
- (iii)

(iv)

11. Construct the truth table for the given circuits and derive the output Boolean expressions for each.

(i)

(ii)

(iii)

(iv)

(v)

(vi)

(vii)

(viii)

(ix)

(x)

(xi)

(xii)

12. (a) Construct the circuits for the following Boolean expressions using AND, OR, and NOT gates without simplifying the expressions.

(i) $Q = A\bar{B} + \bar{A}B$

(ii) $Q = AA + AB + AC + BC$

(iii) $Q = AC + ABC$

(iv) $Q = (B + B)(B + \bar{A})$

(v) $Q = A(\bar{A} + C) + C$

(vi) $Q = (\bar{A} + \bar{B}) \cdot \overline{(C + D)}$

(vii) $Q = \overline{(A + B + C)}\overline{(\bar{A} + \bar{B} + \bar{C})} + \overline{A \cdot B \cdot C}$

(viii) $Q = \overline{A \cdot B \cdot C} \,(\bar{A} + \bar{B} + \bar{C})$

(b) For each of these, create a circuit using AND, OR, and NOT gates for the Boolean expression after simplification.

13. For each of the questions, 12a (i) to (viii), create a circuit using NAND or NOR gates for the Boolean expression after simplification.

14. With respect to questions 4 and 5, explain why simplifying Boolean expressions is useful when designing circuits.

Introduction to Software

LEARNING
OBJECTIVES

After studying this chapter, the readers will be able to

- identify system programs and application programs
- discuss basic concepts of high- and low-level languages

- briefly discuss compiler, interpreter, linker, and loader functions
- explain the software development steps

4.1 INTRODUCTION

The basic concepts of software have already been introduced in Chapter 1. As discussed earlier, there are different categories of software. Among them, *system software* controls the activities of computer resources (such as input/output devices, memory, processor), schedule the execution of multiple tasks, whereas *application software* is designed and developed for a specific or generic type of use which is sold in the market or for a user or an organization. The term 'application' refers to the specific usage such as creating documents, drawing images, playing video games, etc., which is accomplished by a computer system.

Nowadays, software is typically composed of several files among which at least one must be an *executable file* intended to be executed by users or automatically launched by the operating system. Apart from this main executable file, there are program files to be used in conjunction with the main executable file and additional data files and configuration files. Consequently, the installation of software is not just copying the files in the hard disk. It is typically dependent on the operating system on which it would execute and whether the software is a local, Web, or portable application. For *local application software*, its files are placed in the appropriate locations on the computer's hard disk and may require additional configurations with the underlying operating system so that it can be run as and when required. *Portable software* is basically designed to run from removable storage, such as a CD or USB flash drive without installing its program files or configuration data on the hard disk. Most interesting fact is that no trace is found when the removable storage media containing the portable software is removed from the computer. On the other hand, *web application software* is accessed through a Web browser and most of its program code runs on a remote computer connected to the Internet or other computer network.

4.2 PROGRAMMING LANGUAGES

A programming language can be defined formally as an artificial formalism in which algorithms can be expressed. It is composed of a set of instructions in a language understandable to the programmer and recognizable by a computer. Computer languages have been continuing to grow and evolve since the 1940's. Assembly language was the normal choice for writing system software like operating systems, etc. But, C has been used to develop system software since its emergence. The UNIX operating system and its descendants are mostly written in C. Application programs are designed for specific computer applications. Most programming languages are designed to be good for one category of applications but not necessarily for the other. For an instance, COBOL is more suitable for business applications whereas FORTRAN is more suitable for scientific applications.

The development of programming languages has been governed by a number of factors such as type and performance of available hardware, applications of computers in different fields, the development of new programming methodologies and its implementation etc.

4.2.1 Generation of Programming Languages

Just as hardware is classified into generations based on technology, computer languages also have a generation classification based on the level of interaction with the machine.

First generation language (1GL)—machine language

The instructions in machine language are written in the form of binary codes that can immediately be executed by the processor. A machine language instruction generally has three parts as shown in Fig. 4.1. The first part is the operation code that conveys to the computer what function has to be performed by the instruction. All computers have *operation codes* for functions such as adding, subtracting and moving. The second part "Mode" specifies the type of addressing used by the instruction to obtain the operand referred by the instruction. The third part of the instruction either specifies that the *operand* contains data on which the operation has to be performed or it specifies that the operand contains a location, the contents of which have to be subjected to the operation.

Fig. 4.1 General format of machine language instruction

Machine language is considered to be the first generation language (1GL). As it is the native language of the computer, CPU can directly start executing machine language instructions. But the limitations of using machine language in writing programs include the following.

Difficult to use and error prone It is difficult to understand and develop a program using machine language. Because it is hard to understand and remember the various combinations of 1's and 0's representing data and instructions. The programmer has to remember machine characteristics while preparing a program. Checking machine instructions to locate errors are about as tedious as writing the instructions. For anybody checking such a program, it would be difficult to forecast the output when it is executed. Nevertheless, computer hardware recognizes only this type of instruction code. Further, modifying such a program is highly problematic.

Machine independent As the internal design of the computer is different across types, which in turn is determined by the actual design or construction of the ALU, CU, and size of the word of the memory unit, the machine language also varies from one type of computer to another. Hence, it is important to note that after becoming proficient in the machine code of a particular computer, the programmer may be required to learn a new machine code and would have to write all the existing programs again in case the computer system is changed.

Second generation language (2GL)—assembly language

Assembly language is considered to be a second generation language (2GL). In this language, an instruction is expressed using mnemonic codes instead of binary codes. Normally an assembly language statement consists of a label, an operation code, and one or more operands. *Labels* are used to identify and reference instructions in the program. The *operation code* is a symbolic notation that specifies the particular operation to be performed, such as MOV, ADD, SUB, or CMP etc. The *operand* represents the register or the location in main memory where the data to be processed is located. For example, a typical statement in assembler to command the processor to move the hexadecimal number 0x80 into processor register R2 might be:

```
MOV R2, 080H
```

The following is an example of an assembly language program for adding two numbers A and B and storing the result in some memory location.

```
LDA, 2000h;   Load register A with content of
              memory address 2000h
MOV B, 10h;   Load register B with 10th.
ADD A, B      Add contents of A with contents of
              B and store result in register A
```

```
MOV (100), A    Save the result in the main memory
                location 100 from register A.
HALT            Halt process
```

An assembly language program cannot be executed by a machine directly as it is not in a binary machine language form. An *assembler* is a translator that produces machine language code from an assembly language code. It produces a single machine language instruction from a single assembly language statement. Therefore, the coding to solve a problem in assembly language has to be exercised at individual instruction level. That's why, along with machine language, assembly language is also referred to as a low level language.

Writing a program in assembly language is more convenient than writing in machine language. Instead of binary sequence, as in machine language, a program in assembly language is written in the form of symbolic instructions. This gives the assembly language program improved readability. It also offers several disadvantages.

- The most eminent disadvantage of assembly language is that it is *machine dependent*. Assembly language is specific to the internal architecture of a particular model of a processor and the programmer should know all about the internal architecture of the processor. A program written in assembly language for one processor will not work on a different processor if it is architecturally different.

- Though mnemonic codes are easier to be remembered than binary codes, programming with assembly language is still difficult and time-consuming.

Third generation language (3GL)—high-level language

High-level languages are called third generation languages (3GLs). High-level programming languages were developed to make programming easier and less error-prone. Languages like C, C++, COBOL, FORTRAN, BASIC, PASCAL etc., have instructions that are similar to English language that makes it easy for a programmer to write programs and identify and correct errors in them. The program shown below is written in BASIC to obtain the sum of two numbers.

```
10   LET X = 7
20   LET Y = 10
30   SUM = X + Y
40   PRINT SUM
50   END
```

Most third generation languages are procedural in nature. That is, the programmer must specify the sequential logically related steps to be followed by the computer in a program. As computer only understands machine language, a program written in a high level language must be translated into the basic machine language instruction set before it can be executed. This can be performed either by a *compiler*, or by *interpreter*. One statement in a high-level programming language will be translated into several machine language instructions.

Advantages of high-level programming languages are many fold which are as follows.

Readability Programs written in these languages are more readable than those written in assembly and machine languages.

Portability High-level programming languages can be run on different machines with little or no change. It is, therefore, possible to exchange software, leading to creation of program libraries.

Easy debugging Errors can be easily detected and removed.

Ease in the development of software Since the instructions or statements of these programming languages are closer to the English language, software can be developed with ease. The time and cost of creating machine and assembly language programs were quite high. This motivated the development of high-level languages.

Fourth generation languages (4GL)

The Fourth Generation Language (4GL) is a non-procedural language that allows the user to simply specify what is wanted without describing the steps that the computer has to follow to produce the result. This class of languages requires significantly fewer instructions to accomplish a particular task than does a third generation language. Thus, a programmer should be able to write a program faster in 4GL than in a third generation language.

The main areas and purviews of 4GLs are: database queries, report generators, data manipulation, analysis and reporting, screen painters, etc. An example of a 4GL is the query language that allows a user to request information from a database with precisely worded English-like sentences. A query language is used as a database user interface and hides the specific details of the database from the user. The following example shows a query in a common query language, SQL.

```
SELECT address FROM EMP WHERE empname = 'PRADIP DEY'
```

With a report generator, the programmer specifies the headings, detailed data, and other details to produce the required report using data from a file. 4GLs offer several advantages which include the following.

- Like third generation languages, fourth generation languages are mostly *machine independent*. They are primarily used mainly for developing business applications.

- Most of the fourth generation languages can be *easily learnt* and employed by end-users.

- All 4GLs are designed to reduce programming effort, the time it takes to develop software, and the cost of software development. *Programming productivity* is increased when 4GL is used in coding.

Fifth generation language (5GL)

Natural languages represent the next step in the development of programming languages belonging to Fifth Generation Language (5GL). Natural language is similar to query language, with one difference: it eliminates the need for the user or programmer to learn a specific vocabulary, grammar, or syntax.

Actually, 5GL is a programming language based around solving problems using constraints given to the program, rather than using an algorithm written by a programmer. Fifth generation languages are used mainly in artificial intelligence research. OPSS and Mercury are examples of fifth generation languages.

> **Note**
>
> - A low-level computer programming language is one that is closer to the native language of the computer. Machine and assembly languages are referred to as low-level languages since the coding for a problem is at the individual instruction level.
> - Program written in languages other than machine language is required to be translated into machine code.

4.2.2 Classification of Programming Languages

Programming languages can be classified in various ways. According to the extent of translation that is required to generate the machine instructions from a program, programming languages can be classified into *low-level* or *high-level lan-*

guages. Both assembly language and machine language are considered as *low-level languages*. Low-level languages are closer to the native language of the computer as program written in machine language does not require translation for a processor to execute them. Assembly language is also considered as a low-level language since each assembly language instruction accomplishes only a single operation and the coding for a problem is at the individual instruction level. On the other hand, high-level programming languages provide a high level of abstraction from the actual machine hardware.

High-level languages can further be characterized is by programming paradigm (Fig. 4.2). A programming paradigm refers to the way of problem solving that includes a set of methodologies, theories, practices and standards. The high-level programming languages may also be categorized into three groups—*procedural, non-procedural, and problem oriented.*

Procedural programming languages

In procedural programming, a program is conceived as a set of logically related instructions to be executed in order. In procedural programming, each program can be divided into small self-contained program segment, each of which performs a particular task and be re-used in the program as and when required without repeated explicit coding corresponding to the segment. These sections of code are known as procedures or subroutines or functions. It also makes it easier for programmers to understand and maintain program structure. There are mainly three classes of procedural programming languages.

Algorithmic Using this type of programming languages, the programmer must specify the steps the computer has to follow while executing a program. In these languages, a complex problem is solved using top-down approach

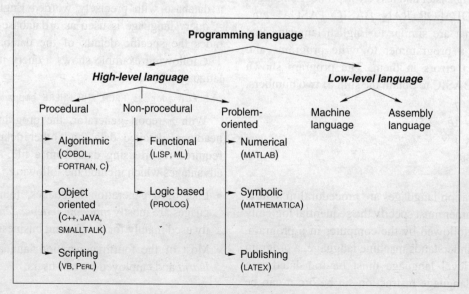

Fig. 4.2 Programming language classification

of problem solving in which the problem is divided into a collection of small problems and each small problem is realized in terms of subprogram. Each subprogram is implemented using procedure or function. Languages like C, COBOL, PASCAL and FORTRAN fall into this category.

Object-oriented language The basic philosophy of object-oriented programming is to deal with objects rather than functions or subroutines as in strictly algorithmic languages. Instead of procedures, object-oriented programming relies on software objects as the units of modularity. Data and associated operations are unified grouping objects with common properties, operations and semantics. The use of an object oriented programming language, advocates the reuse of not only code but also of entire design leading to creation of application framework. A program thus becomes a collection of cooperating objects, rather than a list of instructions. Objects are self-contained modules that contain data as well as the functions needed to manipulate the data within the same module. The most important object-oriented programming features are

Abstraction Abstraction is a technique of focussing on the essential and relevant details from a complex problem which are of interest to the application. It helps to simplify the understanding and using of any system. With data abstraction, data structures can be used without having to be concerned about the exact details of implementation. Object-oriented programming languages use classes and objects for representing abstractions. A class defines the specific structure of a given abstraction. It has a unique name that conveys the meaning of the abstraction. Class definition provides a software design which describes the general properties of something that the software is modeling. Object is an instance of class. An object's properties are exactly those described by its class.

Encapsulation and data hiding The process, or mechanism, by which the data and functions or methods for manipulating data into a single unit, is commonly referred to as encapsulation.

Inheritance Inheritance allows the extension and reuse of existing code, without having to repeat or rewrite the code from scratch. Inheritance involves the creation of new classes, also called *derived* classes, from existing classes (*base* classes). Object oriented languages are usually accompanied by a large and comprehensive library of classes. Members of these classes can either be used directly or reused by employing inheritance in designing new classes.

Polymorphism The purpose of polymorphism is to let one name be used to specify a general class of action. An operation may exhibit different behaviors in different instances.

The behaviour depends upon the types of data used in the operation. Polymorphism is a term that describes a situation where one name may refer to different methods. This means that a general kind of operations may be accessed in the same manner even though specific actions associated with each operation may differ.

Reusable code Object oriented programming languages enable programmer to make parts of program reusable and extensible by breaking down a program into reusable objects. These objects can then be grouped together in different ways to form new programs. By reusing code it is much easier to write new programs by assembling existing pieces.

Using the above features, object-oriented programming languages facilitate to produce reliable and reusable software in reduced cost and time. C++, JAVA, SMALLTALK, etc. are examples of object-oriented languages.

Scripting languages Few years back, the scripting languages were not considered as the languages, but rather thought of as auxiliary tool. A scripting language may be thought of as a glue language, which sticks a variety of components written in other languages together. These languages are usually interpreted. One of the earliest scripting languages is the UNIX shell. Now there are several scripting languages such as VBscript, Python, Tcl and Perl etc. Javascript language also belongs to this category and *defacto* standard for the implementation of client-side Web application.

Non-procedural languages

These *functional languages* solve a problem by applying a set of functions to the initial variables in specific ways to get the result. A program written in a functional language consists of a series of built-in function evaluation together with arguments to those functions. LISP, ML, Scheme, etc. are examples of functional languages.

Another non-procedural class of languages is called *rule based languages* or *logic programming languages*. A logic program is expressed as a set of atomic sentences, known as *facts*, and *horn clauses*, such as if-then rules. A query is then posed. Then the execution of the program begins and the system tries to find out if the answer to the query is true or false for the given facts and rules. Such languages include PROLOG.

Problem-oriented languages

These languages provide readymade procedures or functions which are pre-programmed. The user has to write the statements in terms of those pre-written functions. MATLAB is a very popular language among scientists and engineers to solve a wide class of problems in digital signal processing, control systems, modelling of systems described by differential equations, matrix computations, etc.

Another class of problem oriented languages is for *symbolic language* manipulation. For example, simplifying a complex algebraic expression or getting the indefinite integral of a complex expression. MATHEMATICA is a popular language of this type.

In the Internet era, a new category of languages has emerged, the *markup languages*. Mark-up languages are not programming languages. For instance, HTML, the most widely used mark-up language, is used to specify the layout of information in Web documents. However, some programming capability has crept into some extensions to HTML and XML. Among these are the Java Server Pages, Standard Tag Library (JSTL), and eXtensible Stylesheet Language Transformations (XSLT).

4.3 COMPILING, LINKING, AND LOADING A PROGRAM

A program, written in source language, is translated by the compiler to produce a program in a *target language*. The source language is usually a high-level language. The target language may or not necessarily be machine language. In most cases, the target language is assembly language, and in which case, the target program must be translated by an *assembler* into an object program. Then the object program is *linked* with other object programs to build an executable program, which is normally saved in a specified location of the secondary memory. When it is needed to be executed, the executable file is *loaded* into main memory before its execution. The whole process is managed, coordinated and controlled by the underlying operating system. Sometimes the target language may be a language other than machine or assembly language, in which case a translator for that language must be used to obtain an executable object program.

Conceptually, the compilation process can be divided into a number of phases, each of which is handled by different modules of a compiler, as shown in Fig. 4.3.

Lexical analysis In this phase, the source program is scanned for lexical units (known as *tokens*) namely, identifier, operator delimiter, etc. and classify them according to their types. A table, called *symbol table*, is constructed to record the type and attributes information of each user-defined name used in the program. This table is accessed in the other phases of compilation.

Syntax analysis In this phase, tokens are conflated into syntactic units such as expressions, statements, etc. that must conform to the syntax rules of the programming language.

This process is known as *parsing*. Syntax is similar to the grammar of a language. Syntax rules specify the way in which valid syntactic elements are combined to form the statements of the language. Syntax rules are often described using a notation known as BNF (*Backus Naur Form*) grammar.

Fig. 4.3 The process of compilation

As a result of parsing, a data structure, known as *parse tree*, is produced.

Semantic analysis The *semantics* of a statement in a programming language define what will happen when that statement is executed. Semantic rules assign meanings to valid statements of the language. In the semantic analysis phase, the parsed statements are analysed further to make sure that the operators and operands do not violate source language specification.

Intermediate code generation and optimization To make the target program a bit smaller or faster or both, many compilers produce an intermediate form of code for optimization. In most cases, the intermediate code is generated in assembly language or in a different language at a level between assembly language and machine language.

Code generation This is the final phase of a standard compilation which converts every statement of the optimized intermediate code into target code using predefined target language template. The target language template depends on the machine instructions of the processor, addressing modes and number of registers, etc.

If a system library containing pre-written subroutines or functions and/or separately compiled user-defined subroutines are used in a program a final linking and loading step is needed to produce the complete machine language program in an executable form.

Note
Conceptually, the compilation process can be divided into a number of phases

- In the first phase of compilation, termed as lexical analysis, each statement of a program is analyzed and broken into individual lexical units termed tokens and constructs a symbol table for each identifier.
- The second stage of translation is called syntax analysis; tokens are combined into syntactic units according to the syntax or grammar of the source language.
- In the third stage of compilation, the parsed statements are analysed further to make sure that the operators and operands do not violate source language specifications.
- Next, an intermediate representation of the final machine language code is produced. Optionally, the intermediate code is optimized to produce an optimized code.
- The last phase of translation is code generation whereby the optimized intermediate code is converted into target code.

4.4 TRANSLATOR, LOADER, AND LINKER REVISITED

4.4.1 Translators

There are three types of translators, namely *Assembler, Compiler* and *Interpreter*. Assembler converts one assembly language statement into a single machine language instruction. . Depending on its implementation, a high-level language employs a *compiler* or an *interpreter* or both for translation. One statement in a high-level programming language will be translated into several machine language instructions. Both compiler and interpreter translate a program written in high-level language into machine language but in different fashion. Compiler translates the entire source program into object program at once and then the object files are linked to produce a single executable file. Unlike compiler, an interpreter translates one line of source code at a time—then executes it—before translating the next one and it does this every time the program executes. BASIC is a language that is usually implemented with an interpreter. Translation using an interpreter is slower than that using a compiler. The interpreter translates each line of source code to machine code each time the program is executed. With respect to debugging, an interpreted language is better than the compiled language. In an interpreter, syntax error is brought to the attention of the programmer immediately so that the programmer can make necessary corrections during program development. The Java language uses both a compiler and an interpreter.

4.4.2 Linker

Most of the high-level languages provide libraries of subroutines or functions so that certain common operations may be reused by system-supplied routines without explicit coding. Hence, the machine language program produced by the translator must normally be combined with other machine language programs residing within the library to form a useful execution unit. This process of program combination is called linking and the software that performs this operation is variously known as a *linker*. The features of a programming language influence the linking requirements of a program. In languages like FORTRAN, COBOL, C, all program units are translated separately. Hence, all subprogram calls and common variable references require linking. Linking makes the addresses of programs known to each other so that transfer of control from one subprogram to another or a main program takes place during execution.

4.4.3 Loader

Loading is the process of bringing a program from secondary memory into main memory so it can run. The system software responsible for it is known as *loader*. The simplest type of loader is *absolute loader* which places the program into memory at the location prescribed by the assembler. *Bootstrap loader* is an absolute loader which is executed when computer is switched on or restarted to load the operating system.

In most of the cases, when a compiler translates a source code program into object code, it has no idea where the code will be placed in main memory at the time of its execution. In fact, each time it is executed, it would likely be assigned a different area of main memory depending on the availability of primary storage area at the time of loading. That is why, compilers create a special type of object code which can be loaded into any location of the main memory. When the program is loaded into memory to run, all the addresses and references are adjusted to reflect the actual location of the program in memory. This address adjustment is known as *relocation*. Relocation is performed before or during the loading of the program into main memory.

In modern languages, a prewritten subroutine is not loaded until it is called. All subroutines are kept on disk in a relocatable load format. The main program is loaded into memory and is executed. When a routine needs to call another routine, the calling routine first checks whether the other routine has been loaded. If not, the *linking loader* is called to load the desired routine into memory and to update the program's address tables to reflect this change. Then, control is passed to the newly loaded routine.

Note

- A high-level source program must be translated first into a form the machine can execute. This is done by the system software called the translator.
- The machine language program produced by the translator must normally be combined with other machine language programs residing within the library to form a useful execution unit. Linking resolves the symbolic references between object programs. It makes object programs known to each other. The system software responsible for this function is known as linker.
- Relocation is the process of assigning addresses to the various parts of the program, adjusting the code and data in the program to reflect the assigned addresses.
- A loader is a system software that places executable program's instructions and data from secondary memory into primary memory and prepares them for execution and initiates the execution

4.5 DEVELOPING A PROGRAM

We first discuss the step-by-step listing of the procedure involved in creating a computer program. Here we explain the seven important steps towards creating effective programs: definition, design, coding, testing, documentation, implementation, and maintenance.

1. The first step in developing a program is to **define the problem**. This definition must include the needed output, the available input, and a brief definition of how one can transform the available input into the needed output.

2. The second step is to **design the problem solution**. This detailed definition is an algorithm, a step-by-step procedure for solving a problem.

3. The third step in developing a program is to **code the program**; that is, state the program's steps in the language being used. The instructions must follow the language's syntax, or rules, just as good English must follow the rules of grammar in English.

4. The fourth step is to **test the program** to make sure that it will run correctly, no matter what happens. If the algorithm is wrong or the program does not match the algorithm, the errors are considered logic errors. Errors in a program are called bugs; the process of finding the bugs and correcting them is called debugging the program. To test or debug a program, one must create a sample-input data that represents every possible way to enter input.

5. The fifth step in developing a program is to complete the **documentation of the program**. Documentation should include: user instructions, an explanation of the logic of the program, and information about the input and output.

Documentation is developed throughout the program development process. Documentation is extremely important, yet it is the area in program development that is most often overlooked or downplayed.

6. The last step in developing a program is **implementation**. Once the program is complete, it needs to be installed on a computer and made to work properly. If the program is developed for a specific company, the programming team may be involved in implementation. If the program is designed to be sold commercially, the documentation will have to include directions for the user to install the program and begin working with it.

7. Even after completion, a program requires attention. It needs to be **maintained** and evaluated for possible changes.

4.6 SOFTWARE DEVELOPMENT

Programming is an individual's effort and requires no formal systematic approach. Software development is more than programming. A large number of people are involved in software development and it emphasizes on planned aspect of development process. Programming is one of the activities in software development. Other activities include requirement analysis, design, testing, deployment, maintenance etc. A software is built according to client's requirements. It is driven by cost, schedule and quality. That is, software should be developed at reasonable cost, handed over in reasonable time. Below the most basic steps in software development are explored.

4.6.1 Steps in Software development:

The entire process of software development and implementation involves a series of steps. Each successive step is dependent on the outcome of the previous step. Thus, team of software designers, developers and users are required to interact with each other at each stage of software development so as to ensure that the end product is as per the client's requirements.

Software development steps are described below.

Feasibility study

The feasibility of developing the software in terms of resources and cost is ascertained. In order to determine the feasibility of software developments, the existing system of the user is analysed properly. The analysis done in this step is documented in a standard document called feasibility report, which contains the observations and recommendations related to the task of software development. Activities involved in this step include the following.

Determining development alternatives This activity involves searching for the different alternatives that are available for the development of software.

Analysing economic feasibility This activity involves determining whether the development of new software will be financially beneficial or not. This type of feasibility analysis is performed to determine the overall profit that can be earned from the development and implementation of the software. This feasibility analysis activity involves evaluating all the alternatives available for development and selecting the one which is most economical.

Accessing technical feasibility It involves analysing various factors such as the performance of the technologies, ease of installation, ease of expansion or reduction in size, interoperability with other technologies, etc. The technical feasibility involves the study of the nature of technology as to how easily it can be learnt and the level of training required to understand the technology. This type of feasibility assessment greatly helps in selecting the appropriate technologies to be used for developing the software. The selection should be made after evaluating the requirement specification of the software.

Analysing operational feasibility It involves studying the software on operational and maintenance fronts. The operational feasibility of any software is done on the basis of several factors such as the following.

(a) Type of tools needed for operating the software
(b) Skill set required for operating the software
(c) Documentation and other support required for operating the software

Requirement analysis

In this step, the requirements related to the software, which is to be developed, are understood. Analysing the requirements analysis is an important step in the process of developing software. If the requirements of the user are not properly understood, then the software is bound to fall short of end user's expectations. Thus, requirements analysis is always the first step towards development of software.

The users may not be able to provide the complete set of requirements pertaining to the desired software during the requirement analysis stage. There should be continuous interaction between the software development team and the end users. The software development team also needs to take into account the fact that the requirement of the users may keep changing during the development process. Thus proper analysis of user requirements is quite essential for developing the software within a given time frame.

The customer requirements identified during the requirements gathering and analysis activity are organized into a System Requirements Specification Document. The important components of this document are functional requirements, the nonfunctional requirements, and the goals of implementation.

Design

After the feasibility analysis stage, the next step is creating the architecture and design of the new software. It involves developing a logical model or basic structure of the new software. Design of the software is divided into two stages – system design and detailed software design.

System design partitions the requirements to hardware or software systems. It establishes overall system architecture. The architecture of a software system refers to an abstract representation of that system. Architecture is concerned with making sure the software system meets the requirements of the product, as well as ensuring that future requirements can be addressed. The architecture step also addresses interfaces between the software system and other software products, as well as the underlying hardware or the host operating system. Detailed design represents the software system functions in a form that can be transformed into one or more executable programs. Specification is the task of precisely describing the software to be written, possibly in a rigorous way.

Implementation

In this step, the code for the different modules of the new software is developed. The code for the different modules is developed according to the design specifications of each module. The programmers in the software development team use development tools for this purpose. An important, and often overlooked, task is documenting the internal design of software for the purpose of future maintenance and enhancement.

Testing

It is basically performed to detect the prevalence of any errors in the new software and rectify those errors. One of the reasons for the occurrence of errors or defects in the new software is that the requirements of the client were not properly understood. Another reason for the occurrence of errors is the common mistakes committed by a programmer while developing the code. The two important activities that are performed during testing are verification and validation. Verification is the process of checking the software based on some predefined specifications, while validation involves testing the product to ascertain whether it meets the user requirements. During validation, the tester inputs different values to ascertain whether the software is generating the right output as per the original requirements.

Deployment

The newly developed and fully tested software is installed in its target environment. Software documentation is handed over to the users and some initial data are entered in the software to make it operational. The users are also given training on the software interface and its other functions.

Maintenance

In this phase, developed software is made operational. Users will have lots of questions and software problems which lead to the next phase of software development. Once the software has been deployed successfully, a continuous support is provided to it for ensuring its full time availability. The software may be required to be modified if the environment undergoes a change. Maintaining and enhancing software to cope with newly discovered problems or new requirements can take far more time than the initial development of the software.

SUMMARY

A programming language is an artificial formalism for expressing the instructions to be executed in a specified sequence. Programming languages can be classified into low-level and high level languages. Low-level programming languages include machine language and assembly language. In fact, assembly languages were so revolutionary that they became known as second-generation languages, the first generation being the machine languages themselves. Assembly languages are symbolic programming languages that use symbolic notation to represent machine-language instructions.

Most third generation languages are procedural languages. Compilers convert the program instructions from human understandable form to the machine understandable form. Interpreters also convert the source program to machine language instruction but execute each line as it is entered. The translation of the source program takes place for every run and is slower than the compiled code. The system software controls the activities of a computer, application programs, flow of data in and out of memory and disk storage. Compilation of a source code into target code follows successive stages. In lexical analysis phase, lexical units or tokens are produced from the statements. Also symbol table is constructed to record the type and attributes information of each user-defined name in the program. Next, syntax analysis takes place. In this phase, tokens are grouped into syntactic units such as expressions, and statements. that must conform to the grammatical rules of the source language to form a data structure called parse tree. In semantic analysis, the parse trees are analysed further to make sure that the operators and operands do not violate source language type specification. Then, to produce a more efficient target program, the intermediate code is generated which is then optimized. In the last phase, object code in target language is produced. Linking resolves symbolic references between object programs. A loader is a system program that accepts object programs and prepares them for execution and initiates the execution. Programming is an individual's effort and requires no formal systematic approach. Software development is more than programming. It involves a series of steps–feasibility study, requirement analysis, design, coding, testing, deployment and maintenance.

KEY TERMS

Loader It is a system program that accepts object programs and prepares these programs for execution by the computer and initialize the execution.

Linker It takes one or more object files or libraries as input and combines them to produce a single (usually executable) file.

Compiler It is a system software that translates the entire source program into machine language.

Interpreter An interpreter is a system software that translates the source program into machine language line by line.

Syntax It refers to the rules governing the computer operating system, the language, and the application.

Assembler It is a program that translates an assembly language program into machine code.

Bug It is a programming error.

Debugging It is the process of eliminating errors from a program.

Semantic It is the meaning of those expressions, statements, and program units.

FREQUENTLY ASKED QUESTIONS

1. Distinguish between 3GL and 4GL.

3GL	4GL
Meant for use by professional programmers.	May be used by non-professional programmers as well as by professional programmers.
Requires specifications of how to perform a task.	Requires specifications of what task to perform. System determines how to perform the task.
Requires large number of procedural instructions.	Requires fewer instructions.
Code may be difficult to read, understand, and maintain by the user.	Code is easy to understand and maintain.
Typically, file oriented.	Typically, database oriented.

2. What are the functions of a loader?

The functions of a loader are as follows:

- Assignment of load-time storage area to the program
- Loading of program into assigned area
- Relocation of program to execute properly from its load time storage area
- Linking of programs with one another

3. What is a debugger?

The debugger is a program that lets the programmer to trace the flow of execution or examine the value of variables at various execution points in the program. For example, GDB, the GNU debugger, is used with GNU

C Compiler. Debugger is always integrated in most of the Integrated Development Environment.

4. What does syntax and semantics of a programming language mean?

The **syntax** of a programming language is the form of its expressions, statements, and program units. Its **semantics** is the meaning of those expressions, statements, and program units.

5. What is a symbol table? What is its function?

The symbol table serves as a database for the compilation process. It records the type and attributes information of each user-defined name in the program. This table is used in sytax analysis, semantic analysis as well as in code generation phases of compilation.

6. Distinguish between a compiler and an interpreter.

Compiler	Interpreter
Scans the entire program before translating it into machine code.	Translates and executes the program line by line.
Converts the entire program to machine code and only when all the syntax errors are removed does execution take place.	Each time the program is executed, every line is checked for syntax error and then converted to the equivalent machine code.
Not much helpful in debugging.	Very helpful in debugging.
Compilation process is faster.	Interpretation process is slower.
Gives a list of all errors in the program.	Stops at the first error.

EXERCISES

1. What do you mean by a program?
2. Distinguish between system software and application software.
3. State the advantages and disadvantages of machine language and assembly language.
4. Compare and contrast assembly language and high-level language.
5. Differentiate between 3GL and 4GL.
6. What is a translator?
7. What are the differences between a compiler and an interpreter?
8. Briefly explain the compilation and execution of a program written in a high-level language.
9. Briefly explain linker and loader. Is there any difference between them?
10. Explain linking loader and linkage editor.
11. Classify the programming languages.
12. What is a functional language?
13. What is object-oriented language? Name five object-oriented programming languages.
14. What is the difference between linking loader and linkage editor?
15. What is relocation?

Basic Concepts of Operating Systems

After studying this chapter, the readers will be able to

- explain the basic role of an operating system in modern-day computers
- explain the general functions and components of an operating system
- discuss the interfacing between the operating system and application program or the user

- trace the history of the development of operating systems
- explain the different types of operating systems
- get an overview on some operating systems such as UNIX and MSDOS

5.1 INTRODUCTION

Without software, a computer is basically a useless equipment. With software, a computer can store, process, and retrieve information and engage in many other valuable activities. Computer software can be divided roughly into two parts: system programs, which manage the operation of the computer itself, and application programs, which perform the actual work the user wants. The most important system program is the operating system (OS) that controls all the computer resources and provides the base upon which the application program can be written.

A modern computer system consists of one or more processors, main memory, disk drives, printers, keyboard,

network interfaces, and other input/output devices. It is a complex system. Writing programs correctly is an extremely difficult job. If every programmer had to be concerned with how the disk drives work, and with all things that could go wrong when reading a disk, it is unlikely that many programs would be written at all.

Some way had to be found to shield programmers from the complexity of the hardware. The way that has evolved gradually is to put a layer of software on top of bare hardware to manage all the parts of the system. This layer of software is the operating system.

This is shown in Fig. 5.1. At the bottom lies the hardware. It is composed of two or more layers. The lowest layer contains physical devices consisting of integrated circuit chips, wires, power supplies, cathode ray tube (CRT) on LCD screen and similar physical devices.

Fig. 5.1   The software–hardware layers in a computer

Next comes primitive software that directly controls these devices. This software is called a micro-program and is usually located in a read only memory. The set of instructions that the micro-program interprets defines the machine language. In this layer, input/output devices are controlled by loading values into special device registers. The layer above is the operating system. One of the major functions of the operating system is to hide all this complexity and give the programmer a more convenient set of instructions to work with. Above the operating system is the rest of the system software consisting of command interpreter (shell), window system, compilers, editors, and similar application independent programs.

Finally, above the system programs come the application programs. These programs are purchased or written by users to solve their particular problems or for specific purposes, for example, word processing, spreadsheets, engineering calculations, games, etc.

5.2 INTRODUCTION TO OPERATING SYSTEM

An operating system is a collection of programs that acts as an interface between the user of a computer and the computer hardware. In fact, it provides an environment in which a user may execute programs.

An operating system is an important part of almost every computer system that comprises three main components:

- The hardware (memory, CPU, arithmetic-logic unit, various storage devices, I/O, peripheral devices, etc.)
- Systems programs (operating system, compilers, editors, loaders, utilities, etc.)
- Application programs (database systems, business programs, etc.)

The basic resources of a computer system are provided by its hardware, software, and data. The hardware provides the basic computing resources while the application programs define the way resources are used to solve the computing

problems with the data. The operating system controls and coordinates the use of all the hardware among the various system programs and application programs for the various users. It, thus, provides an environment within which other programs can do useful work.

An operating system can be viewed as a resource allocator. A computer system has many resources (hardware and software) that may be required to solve a problem: CPU time, memory space, files storage space, input/output devices, etc.

Viewing the operating system as a resource manager, each manager must do the following:

- Keep track of the resources
- Enforce policy that determines who gets what, when, and how much
- Allocate the resources
- Reclaim the resources

As the manager of these resources, the operating system allocates them to specific programs and users as necessary for their tasks. Since there may be many, possibly conflicting requests for resources, the operating system must decide which requests are allocated resources to operate the computer system fairly and efficiently.

An operating system is also a control program. It controls the execution of user programs to prevent errors and improper use of the computer. Therefore, it may be defined as follows: An operating system (OS) refers to the software on a computer that lets it run applications, control peripherals, and communicate with other computers.

> **Note**
>
> - Without software, a modern-day computer is unusable. Software comprising operating system, programming language compilers, etc. are essential to provide an 'user-friendly' interface to the user.
> - An operating system is a software that runs applications, manages all resources like memory and peripherals and communicates with other computers.

5.3 FUNCTIONS OF AN OPERATING SYSTEM

An operating system has the following functions.

Process management   The CPU executes a large number of programs. A process is a program in execution. In general, a process will need certain resources such as CPU time, memory, files, and I/O devices to accomplish its task. These resources are given to the process when it is created. It must be noted that a program by itself is not a process; a program is a passive entity, while a process is an active entity. Two processes may be associated with the same program; they are nevertheless considered two separate execution sequences.

Therefore, a process is the unit of work in a system. Such a system consists of a collection of processes, some of which are operating system processes that execute system code, with the rest being user processes that execute user code. All these processes can potentially execute concurrently.

The operating system is responsible for the following activities with respect to process management:

- The creation and deletion of user and system processes
- The suspension and resumption of processes
- Keep track of the resources (processors and the status of processes). Allocate the resources to a process by setting up the necessary hardware
- Reclaim the resources when the process relinquishes processor usage, terminates, or exceeds the allowed amount of usage
- The provision of mechanisms for process synchronization—decide which process gets the processor, when, and for how much time
- The provision of mechanisms for deadlock handling

Memory management

Primary memory management Memory is central to the operation of a modern computer system. Memory is a large array of words or bytes, each with its own address. Interaction is achieved through a sequence of reads or writes of specific memory address. The CPU fetches data from and stores it in memory.

In order that a program be executed, it must be loaded into memory. As the program executes, it accesses program instructions and data from memory by accessing memory locations.

In order to improve both the utilization of CPU and the speed of the computer's response to its users, several processes must be kept in the memory. There are many algorithms for allocation of memory space to different processes active concurrently and the choice of any particular algorithm depends on the particular situation. Selection of a memory management scheme for a specific system depends upon many factors, especially upon the hardware design of the system. Each algorithm requires its own hardware support.

The operating system is responsible for the following activities for fulfilling memory management functions.

- Keep track of the different parts of memory currently being used by various processes
- Decide which processes are to be loaded into memory when memory space becomes available
- Allocate and de-allocate memory space as needed

Secondary memory management The main purpose of a computer system is to execute programs. These programs, together with the data they access, must be in the main memory during execution. Since the main memory is too small to permanently accommodate all data and programs, the computer system must provide a secondary storage that is capable of providing large storage space to back up the main memory. Most modern computer systems use disks as the primary device for online storage of information, both programs and data. Most programs, such as compilers, assemblers, sort routines, and editors are stored on the disk and a copy of any of these is loaded into memory. The disk is thus used as both a source and destination while processing. Hence, the proper management of disk storage is of prime importance to a computer system.

There are few alternatives. Magnetic tape systems are generally too slow. In addition, they are limited to sequential access. Thus tapes are more suited for storing infrequently used files, where speed is not a primary concern.

The operating system is responsible for the following activities for accomplishing the disk management functions:

- Free space management
- Storage allocation
- Disk scheduling

Device (I/O) management

One of the purposes of an operating system is to hide the peculiarities of specific hardware devices from the user. For example, in UNIX, the peculiarities of I/O devices are hidden from the user by the I/O system. The I/O system consists of:

- a buffer memory system
- a general device driver program
- drivers for specific hardware devices

Only the device driver program can handle the peculiarities of a specific device.

File management

File management is one of the most visible services of an operating system. For convenient use of the computer system, the operating system provides a uniform logical view of information storage. The operating system extracts the physical properties of its storage devices to define a logical storage unit, the file. Files are mapped by the operating system onto physical devices.

A file is a collection of related information defined by its creator. Commonly, files contain programs (both source and object forms) and data. Data can be numeric, alphabetic, or alphanumeric. Files may be of free form, such as text files, or may be rigidly formatted. In general, a file is a sequence of bits, bytes, lines, or records whose meaning is defined by its creator and user.

The operating system implements the abstract concept of the file by managing mass storage device, such as tapes and disks. Also, files are normally organized into directories for easy use. Finally, when multiple users have access to files, it may be desirable to control the permission to users for accessing, creating, and amending the files.

The operating system is responsible for the following activities for accomplishing the file management functions:

- Creation and deletion of files
- Creation and deletion of directory
- Support of primitives for manipulating files and directories
- Mapping of files onto disk storage
- Backup of files on stable (non-volatile) storage

Protection

Protection refers to a mechanism for controlling the access of programs, processes, or users to the resources defined by a computer and the controls to be imposed, together with some means of enforcement. For example, the various processes in an operating system must be protected from each other's activities. The memory address management system ensures that a process can only execute within its own address space. The control mechanism ensures that no process can gain control of the CPU without the latter being relinquished by another process. Finally, no process is allowed to directly communicate with any I/O, to protect the integrity of the data from or to various peripheral devices.

Protection can improve reliability by detecting latent errors at the interfaces between component subsystems. Early detection of interface errors can often prevent contamination of a healthy subsystem by one that is malfunctioning. An unprotected resource cannot defend itself against use or misuse by an unauthorized or incompetent user.

5.4 COMPONENTS OF AN OPERATING SYSTEM

In general there are two main components of an operating system: command interpreter and kernel.

Command interpreter

Command interpreter is one of the most important components of an operating system. It is the primary interface between the user and the rest of the system.

Many commands are given to the operating system by control statements. A program that reads and interprets control statements is automatically executed. This program is variously called (a) the control card interpreter, (b) the command line interpreter, (c) the shell (in UNIX), and so on. Its function is quite simple: it gets the command statement and executes it.

The command statements deal with process management, I/O handling, secondary storage management, main memory management, file system access, protection, and networking.

Kernel

Kernel is a core part of the operating system and is loaded on the main memory when it starts up. It is the core library of functions; the operating system 'knows'. In the kernel, there are the functions and streams to communicate with the system's hardware resources.

The kernel provides the most basic interface between the machine and the rest of the operating system. The kernel is responsible for the management of the central processor. It includes the dispatcher that allocates the central processor to a process, determines the cause of an interrupt and initiates its processing, and makes some provision for communication among the various systems and user tasks currently active in the system.

The main functions of the kernel are as follows:

- To provide a mechanism for the creation and deletion of processes
- To provide CPU scheduling, memory management, and device management for these processes
- To provide synchronization tools so that the processes can synchronize their actions
- To provide communication tools so that processes can communicate with each other

Fig. 5.2 Operating system structure

The kernel-based design is often used for designing the operating system. The kernel, more appropriately called the nucleus, is a collection of primitive facilities over which the rest of the operating system is built and the latter uses the functions provided by the kernel (see Fig. 5.2). Thus, a kernel provides an environment to build an operating system in which the designer has considerable flexibility because policy and optimization decisions are not made at the kernel level. An operating system is an orderly growth of software over the kernel, where all decisions regarding process scheduling, resource allocation, execution environment, file system, resource protection, etc. are made.

Consequently, a kernel is a fundamental set of primitives that allows the dynamic creation and control of process as well as communication among them. Thus, the kernel only supports the notion of processes and does not include the concept of a resource. However, as operating systems have matured in functionality and complexity, more functionality has been related to the kernel. A kernel should contain a minimal set of functions that is adequate to build an operating system with a given set of objectives.

There are two different methodologies for designing a kernel: monolithic kernels and microkernels.

The monolithic kernel is the design that is used in operating systems such as Windows and Linux. In this case, the kernel is a set of tightly integrated packages that understand and handle the complete hardware of the machine.

An error in the monolithic kernel will bring the whole system crashing down. Since the integration level among the components of the kernel is very high, it is potentially difficult to distinguish and manage smaller parts separately.

A microkernel, on the other hand, takes a different approach. Microkernels usually provide only minimal services such as defining memory address spaces, interprocess communication methods and process, and thread management. All other features, such as hardware management or I/O locking and sharing, are implemented as processes running independently of the microkernel.

A microkernel does not suffer from the same ailments as monolithic kernels. If a certain subprocess of the kernel crashes, it is still possible to save the whole system from a crash by restarting the service which caused the error.

It was claimed that microkernels would revolutionize the way operating systems are designed. But no such thing has happened. Apparently, the improvements were not significant enough to force the majority of operating systems to use this approach. There are only a few operating systems today that use the microkernel approach, for instance, Mach microkernel (used in OS X), BeOS, and AIX.

5.5 INTERACTION WITH OPERATING SYSTEM

Broadly speaking, there are two ways to interact with an operating system:

- By means of operating *system calls* in a program
- Directly by means of *operating system commands*

System calls

System calls provide the interface between a running program and the operating system. These calls are generally available as assembly language instructions, and are usually listed in the manuals used by assembly language programmers. Some systems may allow system calls to be made directly from a high-level language program, in which case the calls normally resemble predefined function or subroutine calls. They may generate a call to a special run-time routine that makes

the system call, or the system call may be generated directly in-line. The C language allows system calls to be made directly. Some PASCAL systems also provide an ability to make system calls directly from a PASCAL program to the operating system. System calls can be roughly grouped into five major categories: *process control*, *file manipulation*, *device manipulation*, *information maintenance*, and *communications*.

A user program makes good use of the operating system. All interactions between the program and its environment must occur as the result of requests from the program to the operating system.

Operating system commands

Apart from system calls, users may interact with the operating system directly by means of commands. For example, if the user wants to list files or sub-directories in MSDOS, the DIR command is invoked. In either case, the operating system acts as an interface between users and the hardware of a computer system. The fundamental goal of a computer system is to solve user problems. The computer hardware is designed towards this goal. Since the bare hardware alone is not very easy to use, programs (software) are developed. These programs require certain common operations, such as controlling peripheral devices. The command function of controlling and allocating resources are then brought together into one piece of software, the operating system.

> **Note**
>
> - The operating system primarily manages processes, memory, input/output devices, and files and ensures proper control on all the resources to keep them from interfering with each other.
> - The *command interpreter* and the *kernel* are the two main components of the operating system.
> - The *system calls* and the *operating system commands* are the two ways of interacting with the operating system.

5.6 HISTORY OF OPERATING SYSTEMS

To understand what operating systems are and what they do, consider how they have developed over the last 30 years. By tracing that evolution, the common elements of operating systems can be identified as well as how and why they developed as they are now.

Operating systems and computer architecture have a great deal of influence on each other. Operating systems were developed to facilitate the use of the hardware. As operating systems were designed and used, it became obvious that changes in the design of the hardware could simplify it. This short historical review discusses how the introduction of new hardware features becomes the natural solution to many operating system problems.

As the history of computer operating systems run parallel to that of computer hardware, it can be generally divided into five distinct time periods, called generations, that are characterized by hardware component technology, software development, and mode of delivery of computer services.

The digital computer was designed by the English mathematician Charles Babbage (1792–1871). It was purely a mechanical design. After Babbage's efforts, little progress was made in constructing digital computers. First generation computers with vacuum tubes and plug boards evolved between 1945 and 1955. During this period, an individual group of people designed, built, programmed, operated, and maintained each machine. Programming was done in machine language.

5.6.1 First Generation (1945–55)

The first generation marked the beginning of commercial computing, including the introduction of Eckert's and Mauchly's Univac I in early 1951, and a little later, the IBM 701, also known as the Defense Calculator. The first generation computer was characterized by the vacuum tube as the active component technology.

The operation of computers continued without the benefit of an operating system for a certain period of time. This mode of computer operation was called 'closed shop' and was marked by the appearance of hired operators who would select the job to be run, then load the program in the system, run the program, select another job, and so on. Programs began to be written in high-level, procedure-oriented languages, and thus the operator's job expanded. The operator now selected a job, ran the translation program to assemble or compile the source program, combined the translated object program along with any existing library programs that the program might need for input to the linking program, and thereafter loaded and ran the composite linked program. The next job was handled in a similar fashion.

Application programs were run one at a time. The programs were translated with absolute computer addresses that bound them to be loaded and run from these pre-assigned main memory addresses set by the translator, obtaining their data from specific physical I/O devices. There was no provision for moving a program to different locations in main memory for any reason. Similarly, a program bound to specific devices could not be run at all, if any of these devices were busy or broken.

The inefficiencies inherent in the above methods of operation led to the development of the monoprogrammed operating system, which eliminated some of the human intervention in running a job and provided programmers with a number of desirable functions. The operating system consisted of a permanently resident kernel in main storage and a job scheduler as well as a number of utility programs kept in secondary storage. User application programs were preceded by control or specification cards (in those days, computer programs were submitted on punched cards), which informed the operating system about the system resources (software resources such as compilers and loaders; and hardware resources such as tape drives and printer) needed to run a particular application. The systems were designed for operation as a batch processing system.

These systems continued to operate under the control of a human operator who initiated operation by mounting a magnetic tape that contained the operating system's executable code onto a 'boot device', and then pushing the IPL (initial program load) or 'boot' button to initiate the bootstrap loading of the operating system. Once the system was loaded, the operator entered the date and time, and initiated the operation of the job scheduler program, which read and interpreted the control statements, secured the needed resources, executed the first user program, and recorded the timing and accounting information. The operator, thereafter, began processing another user program, and continued the process as long as there were programs waiting in the input queue to be executed.

The first generation saw the evolution from 'hands-on operation' to 'closed shop operation' to the development of monoprogrammed operating systems. At the same time, the development of programming languages was moving away from basic machine languages, first to assembly language, and later to procedure-oriented languages, the most significant being the development of FORTRAN by John W. Backus in 1956. However, several problems remained. The most obvious was the inefficient use of system resources. This was most evident when the CPU waited while the relatively slower mechanical I/O devices were reading or writing program data. In addition, system protection was a problem because the operating system kernel was not protected from being overwritten by an erroneous application program. Moreover, other user programs in the queue were not protected from destruction by executing programs.

5.6.2 Second Generation (1956–63)—Transistors and Batch System

Transistors replaced vacuum tubes as the hardware component technology in the second generation of computer hardware. In addition, some very important changes in hardware and software architectures occurred during this period. For the most part, computer systems remained card- and tape-oriented systems. Significant use of random access devices, that is, disks, did not appear until the end of the second generation. Program processing was, mostly, provided by large, centralized computers operated under monoprogrammed batch processing operating systems.

The most significant innovations addressed the problem of excessive central processor delay due to waiting for input/output operations. The programs were executed by processing the machine instructions in a strictly sequential order. As a result, the CPU, with its high-speed electronic components, was often forced to wait for completion of the I/O operations, which involved mechanical devices (card readers and tape drives) that were slower on an order of magnitude. This problem led to the introduction of the data channel, an integral and special-purpose computer with its own instruction set, registers, and control unit designed to process I/O operations separately and asynchronously from the operation of the computer's main CPU. This development took place near the end of the first generation, and was widely adopted in the second generation.

The data channel allowed some I/O to be buffered. That is, a program's input data could be read 'ahead' from data cards or tape into a special block of memory called a *buffer*. Then, when the user's program came to an input statement, the data could be transferred from the buffer locations at the faster main memory access speed rather than the slower I/O device speed. Similarly, a program's output could be written into another buffer and later moved from the buffer to the printer, tape, or card punch. What made this all work was the data channel's ability to work asynchronously and concurrently with the main processor. Thus, the slower mechanical I/O could be working concurrently with the main program processing. This process was called I/O overlap.

The data channel was controlled by a channel program set up by the operating system I/O control routines and initiated by a special instruction executed by the CPU. Then, the channel independently processed data to or from the buffer. This provided communication from the CPU to the data channel to initiate an I/O operation. It remained for the channel to communicate to the CPU such events as data errors and the completion of a transmission. At first, this communication was handled by polling; the CPU stopped its work periodically and polled the channel to determine if there was any message.

Polling was obviously inefficient (imagine stopping work periodically to go to the post office to see if an expected letter has arrived) and led to another significant innovation of the second generation—the interrupt. The data channel was now able to interrupt the CPU with a message, usually 'I/O complete'. In fact, the interrupt idea was later extended from I/O to allow signalling of a number of exceptional conditions such as arithmetic overflow, division by zero, and time-run-out. Of course, interval clocks were added in conjunction with the latter, and thus the operating system came to have a way of regaining control from an exceptionally long or indefinitely looping program.

These hardware developments led to enhancements of the operating system. I/O and data channel communication and control became functions of the operating system, both to relieve the application programmer from the difficult details of I/O programming and to protect the integrity of the system to provide improved service to users by segmenting jobs and running shorter jobs first (during 'prime time') and relegating longer jobs to lower priority or night time runs. System libraries became more widely accessible and more comprehensive as new utilities and application software components became available to programmers.

In order to further mitigate the I/O wait problem, systems were set up to spool the input batch from slower I/O devices such as the card reader to the much higher speed tape drive and, similarly, the output from the higher speed tape to the slower printer. Initially, this was accomplished by means of one or more physically separate small satellite computers. In this scenario, the user submitted a job at a window, a batch of jobs was accumulated and spooled from cards to tape, 'off line', the tape was moved to the main computer, the jobs were run, and their output collected on another tape that was later taken to a satellite computer for off line tape-to-printer output. Users then picked up their output at the submission windows.

Towards the end of this period, as random access devices became available, tape-oriented operating systems began to be replaced by disk-oriented systems. With more sophisticated disk hardware and the operating system supporting a greater portion of the programmer's work, the computer system that users saw was more and more removed from the actual hardware—users saw a virtual machine.

The second generation was a period of intense operating system development. It was also the period for sequential batch processing. But the sequential processing of one job at a time remained a significant limitation. Thus, there continued to be low CPU utilization for I/O-bound jobs and low I/O device utilization for CPU-bound jobs. This was a major concern, since computers were still very large (room-size) and expensive machines. Researchers began to experiment with multiprogramming and multiprocessing in their computing services called the time-sharing system. A noteworthy example is the Compatible Time Sharing System (CTSS) developed at MIT during the early 1960s.

5.6.3 Third Generation (1964–80)—Integrated Chips and Multiprogramming

The third generation officially began in April 1964 with IBM's announcement of its System/360 family of computers. Hardware technology began to use integrated circuits (ICs), which yielded significant advantages in both speed and economy.

Operating system development continued with the introduction and widespread adoption of multiprogramming. This was marked first by the appearance of more sophisticated I/O buffering in the form of spooling operating systems, such as the HASP (Houston Automatic Spooling) system that accompanied the IBM OS/360 system. These systems worked by introducing two new systems programs, a system reader to move input jobs from cards to disk and a system writer to move job output from disk to printer, tape, or cards. The operation of the spooling system was, as before, transparent to the computer user who perceived input as coming directly from the cards and output going directly to the printer.

The idea of taking fuller advantage of the computer's data channel I/O capabilities continued to develop. That is, designers recognized that I/O needed only to be initiated by CPU instructions—the actual I/O data transmission could take place under the control of separate and asynchronously operating channel programs. Thus, by switching control of the CPU between the currently executing user program, the system reader program, and the system writer program, it was possible to keep the slower mechanical I/O device running and minimize the amount of time the CPU spent waiting for I/O completion. The net result was an increase in system throughput and resource utilization, to the benefit of both users and providers of computer services.

This concurrent operation of three programs (more properly, apparent concurrent operation, since systems had only one CPU, and could, therefore execute just one instruction at a time) required that additional features and complexity be added to the operating system. First, the fact that the input queue was now on disk, a direct access device, freed the system scheduler from the first-come-first-served policy so that it could select the 'best' next job to enter the system (looking for either the shortest job or the highest-priority job in the queue). Second, since the CPU was to be shared by the user program, system reader, and system writer, some processor allocation rule or policy was needed. Since the goal of spooling was to increase resource utilization by enabling the slower I/O devices to run asynchronously with user program processing, and since I/O processing required the CPU only for short periods to initiate data channel instructions, the CPU was dispatched to the reader, writer, and program in that order. Moreover, if the writer or the user program was executing when something became available to read, the reader program would pre-empt the currently executing program to regain control of the CPU for its initiation instruction, and the writer program would pre-empt the user program for the same purpose. This rule, called the static priority rule with pre-emption, was implemented in the operating system as a system dispatcher program.

The spooling operating system in fact had multiprogramming, since more than one program was resident in the main storage at the same time. Later, this basic idea of multiprogramming was extended to include more than one active user program in memory at a time. To accommodate this extension, both the scheduler and the dispatcher were enhanced. The scheduler became able to manage the diverse resource needs of the several concurrently active user programs, and the dispatcher included policies for allocating processor resources among competing user programs. In addition, memory management became more sophisticated to ensure that the program code for each job or at least for the part of the code being executed, was resident in the main storage.

The advent of large-scale multiprogramming was made possible by several important hardware innovations. The first was the widespread availability of large-capacity, high-speed disk units to accommodate the spooled input streams and memory overflow, together with the maintenance of several concurrently active programs in execution. The second was relocation hardware, which facilitated the moving of blocks of code within memory without an undue overhead penalty. The third was the availability of storage protecting hardware to ensure that user jobs were protected from one another and that the operating system itself protected from user programs. Some of these hardware innovations involved extensions to the interrupt system in order to handle a variety of external conditions such as program malfunctions, storage protection violations, and machine checks in addition to I/O interrupts. In addition, the interrupt system became the technique for the user program to request services from the operating system kernel. Finally, the advent of privileged instructions allowed the operating system to maintain coordination and control over the multiple activities now going on within the system.

Successful implementation of multiprogramming opened the way for the development of a new method of delivering time shared computing services. In this environment, several terminals, sometimes up to 200 of them, were attached (hard wired or via telephone lines) to a central computer. Users at their terminals 'logged in' to the central system and worked interactively with the system. The system's apparent concurrency was enabled by the multiprogramming operating system. Users shared not only the system's hardware but also its software resources and file system disk space.

The third generation was an exciting period, indeed, for the development of both computer hardware and the accompanying operating system. During this period, the topic of operating systems became, in reality, a major element of the discipline of computing.

5.6.4 Fourth Generation (1980–present)— Personal Computers

With the development of LSI (Large Scale Integration) circuits, chips containing thousands of transistors in a square centimeter of silicon, the age of personal computers dawned. Personal computers are not that different from minicomputers. The most powerful personal computers used for business, universities, and government installations are usually called workstations (large personal computers). Usually they are connected together by hardware.

An interesting development that began during mid-1980s is the growth of hardware of personal computers, running operating system, and distributed operating system. In an operating system, the users are aware of the existence of multiple computers and can log in to remote machines and copy files from one machine to another.

5.7 TYPES OF OPERATING SYSTEMS

Modern computer operating systems may be classified into three groups according to the nature of interaction that takes place between the computer user and user's program during its processing. The three groups are called batch process, time-shared, and real-time operating systems.

5.7.1 Batch Process Operating System

In a batch process operating system, environment users submit jobs to a central place where these jobs are collected in batch, and subsequently placed in an input queue in the computer where they are run. In this case, the user has no interaction with the job during its processing, and the computer's response time is the turnaround time, that is, the time from submission of the job until execution is complete and the results are ready for return to the person who submitted the job.

A batch processing environment requires grouping of similar jobs that consist of programs, data, and system commands. When batch systems were first developed, they were defined by the 'batching' together of similar jobs. Card- and tape-based systems allowed only sequential access to programs and data, so only one application package (for instance, the FORTRAN compiler, linker, and loader, or the COBOL equivalents) could be used at a time. As online disk storage became feasible, it was possible to provide immediate access to all the application packages. Modern batch systems are no longer defined by the batching together similar jobs; other characteristics are used instead.

A batch operating system normally reads a stream of separate jobs (for example, from a card reader), each with its own control cards that predefine what the job does. When the job is complete, its output is usually printed (for example, on a line printer). The definitive feature of a batch system is the lack of interaction between the user and the job while the job is being executed. The job is prepared and submitted. The output appears later (perhaps after minutes, hours, or days). The delay between job submission and job completion, called the turnaround time, may result from the amount of computing needed or from delays before the operating system starts processing the job.

Process scheduling, i.e., allocation strategy for a process to a processor, memory management, file management, and I/O management in batch processing are quite simple. Jobs are typically processed in the order of submission, that is, on a first-come-first-serve basis.

A batch operating system generally manages the main memory by dividing it into two areas. One of them is permanently fixed for containing operating system routines and the other part contains only user programs to be executed; when one program is over, the next program is loaded into the same area. Since there is only one program in execution at a time, there is no competition for I/O devices. Therefore, allocation and de-allocation for I/O devices is very trivial. Access to files is also serial and there is hardly a need for protection and file access control mechanism.

This type of processing is suitable in programs with large computation time, with no need of user interaction or involvement. Some examples of such programs include payroll, forecasting, statistical analysis, and large, scientific, number-crunching programs. Users are not required to wait while the job is being processed. They can submit their programs to operators and return later to collect them.

A batch operating system has two major disadvantages and they are as follows.

Non-interactive environment There are some difficulties with a batch system from the point of view of a programmer or user. Batch operating systems allow little or no interaction between users and executing programs. The turnaround time is very high. Users have no control over the intermediate results of a program. This type of arrangement does not provide any flexibility in software development.

Offline debugging A programmer cannot correct bugs the moment they occur. Bugs are detected during program execution but are removed when not in execution.

5.7.2 Multiprogramming Operating System

A multiprogramming operating system allows more than one active user program (or part of user program) to be stored in the main memory simultaneously. Compared to batch operating systems, multiprogramming operating systems are fairly sophisticated. To have several jobs ready to run, the system must keep all of them in memory simultaneously. Having several programs in memory at the same time requires some form of memory management. In addition, if several jobs are ready to run at the same time, the system must choose the order in which each job has to be selected and executed one after the other. This decision is called CPU scheduling. Finally, multiple jobs running concurrently require that their ability to affect one another be limited in all phases of the operating system, including process scheduling, disk storage, and memory management.

Multiprogramming has significant potential for improving system throughput and resource utilization. Different forms of multiprogramming operating systems involve multitasking, multiprocessing, multi-user, or multi-access techniques. The main features and functions of such systems are discussed here briefly.

Multitasking operating systems

A program in execution is called a process or task. A multiprogramming operating system is one, which in addition to supporting multiple concurrent processes, several processes in execution states simultaneously, allows the instruction and data from two or more separate processes to reside in primary memory simultaneously. Note that multiprogramming implies multiprocessing or multitasking operation, but multiprocessing operation or multitasking does not imply multiprogramming. Therefore, multitasking operation is one of the mechanisms that the multiprogramming operating system employs in managing the totality of computer-related resources such as CPU, memory, and I/O devices.

The simplest form of multitasking is called serial multitasking or context switching. This is nothing more than stopping one process temporarily to work on another. If sidekick is used, then serial multitasking is used. While a program is running, the calculator, for instance, can be used by clicking it. When the work on the calculator is over, the program continues running. Some examples of multitasking operating systems are `UNIX, Windows 2000/XP`, etc.

Multi-user operating system

It allows simultaneous access to a computer system through one or more terminals. Although frequently associated with multiprogramming, a multi-user operating system does not imply multiprogramming or multitasking. A dedicated transaction processing system such as railway reservation system that has hundreds of terminals under the control of a single program is an example of a multi-user operating system. On the other hand, general-purpose time-sharing systems (discussed later in this section) incorporate the features of both multi-user and multiprogramming operating systems. Multiprocess operation without multi-user support can be found in the operating system of some advanced personal computers and in real systems (discussed later).

Some examples of multi-user operating systems include `Linux, UNIX,` and `Windows 2000/XP`.

Multiprocessing system

It is a computer hardware configuration that includes more than one independent processing unit. The term multiprocessing is generally used to refer to large computer hardware complexes found in major scientific or commercial applications. The words multiprogramming, multiprocessing, and multitasking are often confusing. There are, of course, some distinctions between these similar but different terms.

The term multiprogramming refers to the situation in which a single CPU divides its time between more than one job. Time sharing is a special case of multiprogramming, where a single CPU serves a number of users at interactive terminals. In multiprocessing, multiple CPUs perform more than one job at a time. Multiprogramming and multiprocessing are not mutually exclusive. Some mainframes and super minicomputers have multiple CPUs each of which can juggle several jobs.

The term multitasking is described as any system that runs or appears to run more than one application program at any given time. An effective multitasking environment must provide many services both to the user and to the application program it runs. The most important of these are resource management, which divides the computer's time, memory, and peripheral devices among competing tasks and interprocess communication, which helps to coordinate their activities by exchanging information. Some examples of multiprocessing operating systems are `Linux, UNIX,` and `Windows 2000/XP`.

Multiprocessing operating systems are multitasking systems by definition because they support simultaneous execution of multiple processes on different processors.

5.7.3 Time-sharing Operating Systems

Another mode for delivering computing services is provided by time-sharing operating systems. In this environment a computer provides computing services to several or many users concurrently online. Here, the various users share the central processor, memory, and other resources of the computer system in a manner facilitated, controlled, and monitored by the operating system. The user in this environment has nearly full interaction with the program during its execution, and the computer's response time may be expected to be no more than a few seconds.

A time-sharing operating system operates in an interactive mode with a quick response time. The user types a request to the computer through a keyboard. The computer processes it and a response, if any, is displayed on the user's terminal. A time-sharing system allows many users to simultaneously share the computer resources. Since each action or command in a time-shared system takes a very small fraction of time, only a little time of the CPU is needed for each user. As the CPU switches rapidly from one user to another, users have the impression that they have their own computer, while it is actually one computer that is being shared among many users.

Most time-sharing systems use time-slice (round robin) scheduling of CPU. In this approach, programs are executed with increasing priority in waiting state for an event and drops after the service is granted. In order to prevent a program from monopolizing the processor, a program executing longer than the system-defined time-slice is interrupted by the operating system and placed at the end of the queue of waiting programs.

Memory management in the time-sharing system provides for the protection and separation of user programs. The I/o management feature of a time-sharing system must be able to handle multiple users (terminals). However, the processing of terminal interrupts are not time critical due to the relatively slow speed of the terminals and users. As required by most multi-user environments, allocation and de-allocation of devices must be performed in a manner that preserves system integrity and provides for good performance.

Interactive processes are given a higher priority so that when I/O is requested (e.g., a key is pressed), the associated process is quickly given control of the CPU. This is usually done through the use of an interrupt that causes the computer to realize that an I/O event has occurred.

It should be mentioned that there are several different types of time-sharing systems. One type is represented by computers such as the vax/vms and UNIX workstations. In these computers, entire processes are in memory (albeit virtual memory) and the computer switches between executing codes in each. In other types of systems, such as airline reservation systems, a single application may actually do much of the time sharing between terminals. This way there is no need to have different running programs associated with each terminal.

It is evident that a time-sharing system is a multiprogramming system, but note that a multiprogramming system is not necessarily a time-sharing system. A batch or real-time operating system could, and indeed usually does, have more than one active user program simultaneously in main storage.

5.7.4 Real-time Operating Systems

The fourth class of operating systems, real-time operating systems, are designed to service those applications where response time is of essence in order to prevent error, misrepresentation, or even disaster. Examples of real-time operating systems are those that handle airlines reservations, machine tool control, and monitoring of a nuclear power station. In these cases, the systems are designed to be interrupted by external signals that require the immediate attention of the computer system.

It is another form of operating system that is used in environments where a large number of events, mostly external to computer systems, must be accepted and processed in a short time or within certain deadlines. Examples of such applications are flight control, real-time simulations, process control, etc. Real-time systems are also frequently used in military applications.

The primary objective of a real-time system is to provide quick response times. User convenience and resource utilization are of secondary concern here. In a real-time system, each process is assigned a certain level of priority according to the relative importance of the event it processes. The processor is normally allocated to the highest-priority process among those that are ready to execute. A higher-priority process usually pre-empts the execution of a lower-priority process. This form of scheduling, called priority-based pre-emptive scheduling, is used by the majority of real-time systems.

Memory management In real-time operating systems there is a swapping of programs between primary and secondary memory. Most of the time, processes remain in primary memory in order to provide quick response. Therefore, memory management in a real-time system is less demanding compared to other types of multiprogramming systems. On the other hand, processes in a real-time system tend to cooperate closely, thus providing for both protection and sharing of memory.

I/O management Time-critical device management is one of the main characteristics of a real-time system. It also provides a sophisticated form of interrupt management and I/O buffering.

File management The primary objective of file management in real-time systems is usually the speed of access rather than efficient utilization of secondary storage. In fact, some embedded real-time systems do not have secondary memory. However, where provided, file management of real-time systems must satisfy the same requirement as those found in time-sharing and other multiprogramming systems.

Some examples of real-time operating systems are CHIMERA, lynx, mtos, qnx, rtmx, and rtx.

5.7.5 Network Operating System

A networked computing system is a collection of physically interconnected computers. The operating system of each of the interconnected computers must contain, in addition to its own stand-alone functionality, provisions for handling communication and transfer of program and data among the other computers with which it is connected.

A network operating system is a collection of software and associated protocols that allow a set of autonomous computers interconnected by a computer network to be used together in a convenient and cost-effective manner. In a network operating system, the users are aware of the existence of multiple computers and can login to remote machines and copy files from one machine to another.

Some of the typical characteristics of network operating systems are the following.

- Each computer has its own private operating system instead of running as part of a global system-wide operating system.

- Users normally work on their systems; using a different system requires some kind of remote login instead of having the operating system dynamically allocate processes to CPUs.

- Users are typically aware of where each of their files are kept and must move a file from one system to another with explicit file transfer commands instead of having file placement managed by the operating system.

The network operating system offers many capabilities, including the following:

- Allowing users to access the various resources of the network hosts

- Controlling access so that only users with proper authorization are allowed to access particular resources
- Making use of remote resources, which appears to be identical to the use of local resources
- Providing up-to-the minute network documentation online

As was mentioned earlier, the key issue that distinguishes a network operating system from a distributed one is how aware the users are of the fact that multiple machines are being used. This visibility occurs in three primary areas: file system, protection, and program execution.

The important issue in file system is related to how a file is accessed on one system from another in a network. There are two important approaches to this problem.

Running a special file transfer program When connecting two or more systems together, the first issue that is faced is how to access the file system available on some other system. To deal with this issue, the user runs a special file transfer program that copies the needed remote file to the local machine, where it can then be accessed normally. Sometimes remote printing and mail is also handled this way.

Specifying a pathname The second approach in this direction is for programs on one machine to can open files on another machine by providing a pathname, thereby indicating where the file is located.

Some examples of the network operating systems are: Linux, Windows 2000 server/2003 server.

5.7.6 Distributed Operating System

A distributed computing system consists of a number of computers that are connected and managed so that they automatically share the job-processing load among the constituent computers, or separate the job load, as appropriate, to particularly configured processors. Such a system requires an operating system that in addition to the typical stand-alone functionality, provides coordination of the operations and information flow among the component computers.

The networked and distributed computing environments and their respective operating systems are designed with more complex functional capabilities. In a network operating system the users are aware of the existence of multiple computers, and can login to remote machines and copy files from one machine to another. Each machine runs its own local operating system and has its own user or users.

A distributed operating system, in contrast, is one that appears to its users as a traditional uniprocessor system, even though it is actually composed of multiple processors. In a true distributed system, users should not be aware of where their programs are being run or where their files are located; that should all be handled automatically and efficiently by the operating system.

Network operating systems are not fundamentally different from single processor operating systems. They obviously need a network interface controller and some low-level software to drive them, as well as programs to achieve remote login and remote file access, but these additions do not change the essential structure of the operating systems.

True distributed operating systems require more than just adding a little code to a uniprocessor operating system, because distributed and centralized systems differ in critical ways. Distributed systems, for example, often allow a program to run on several processors at the same time, thus requiring more complex processor scheduling algorithms in order to optimize the amount of parallelism achieved.

Advantages of distributed operating systems

Though the design and implementation is complex, there are certain advantages for which the distributed system is used. Some of these are given below.

Major breakthrough in microprocessor technology With microprocessors becoming very powerful and cheap compared to mainframes and minicomputers, it has become attractive to think about designing large systems consisting of small processors. These distributed systems clearly have a price/performance advantage over more traditional systems.

Incremental growth The second advantage is that if there is a need for 10 per cent more computing power, one should just add 10 per cent more processors. System architecture is crucial to the type of system growth. However, it is hard to increase computing power by 10 per cent for each user.

Reliability Reliability and availability can also be a big advantage. A few parts of the system can be down without disturbing people using the other parts. One of the disadvantages may be that unless one is very careful, it is easy for the communication protocol overhead to become a major source of inefficiency.

Now, let us discuss how the file system protection and program execution are supported in a distributed operating system.

File system

The distributed operating system supports a single global file system visible from all machines. When this method is used, there is one directory for executable programs (in UNIX, it is the bin directory), one password file, and so on.

The convenience of having a single global namespace is obvious. In addition, this approach means that the operating system is free to move files around machines to keep all the disks generally full and busy and that the system can maintain replicated copies of files if it chooses. The user of the program must specify the machine name as the system cannot decide on its own to move a file to a new machine. However, the user visible name, which is used to access the file, would change.

Thus in a network operating system, users must manually control file placement, whereas in a distributed operating system it can be done automatically by the system itself.

Protection

In a true distributed system, there is a unique UID for every user. That UID should be valid on all machines without any mapping. In this way no protection problems arise on remote access to files; a remote access can be treated like a local access with the same UID. There is a difference between network operating system and distributed operating system in implementing the protection issue. In a networking operating system, there are various machines, each with its own user to UID mapping while in a distributed operating system there is a single system-wide mapping that is valid everywhere.

Program execution

In the most distributed case, the system chooses a CPU by looking at the processing load of the machine, location of file to be used, etc. In the least distributed case, the system always run the process on one specific machine (usually the machine on which the user is logged in).

An important difference between network and distributed operating systems is in the way they are implemented. A common way to realize a networking operating system is to put a layer of software on top of the native operating system of the individual machines. For example, one could write a special library package that could intercept all the system calls and decide whether each one was local or remote. Most system calls can be handled this way without modifying the kernel, the part of operating system that manages all the resources of a computer. AMOEBA is an example of a distributed operating system.

> **Note**
> - Operating systems and computer architecture have a great deal of influence on each other.
> - From mono-program to multi-program handling, the operating system established itself as one of the most essential component of the modern day digital computer.
> - In general, the modern operating systems can be classified as batch processing, time-shared, or real-time operating systems.

5.8 AN OVERVIEW OF UNIX OPERATING SYSTEM

UNIX is an operating system. It was created in the late 1960s, in an effort to provide a multi-user, multitasking system for use by programmers. The philosophy behind the design of UNIX was to provide simple, yet powerful utilities that could be pieced together in a flexible manner to perform a wide variety of tasks.

5.8.1 Reasons for Success of UNIX

During the past 30 years, UNIX has evolved into a powerful, flexible, and versatile operating system. It is used on
(a) single user personal computers,
(b) engineering workstations, (c) multi-user microcomputers,
(d) minicomputers, (e) mainframes, and (f) supercomputers.

The reasons for this are the characteristics of UNIX, enumerated as follows:

Portability Because the UNIX operating system is written mostly in C, it is highly portable. It runs on a range of computers from microprocessors to the largest mainframe, provided the system has two components: a C compiler, and a modest amount of machine-dependent coding (machine-dependent I/O hardware service routines).

Open system It easily adapts to particular requirements. This openness has led to the introduction of a wide range of new features and versions customized to meet special needs. The code for UNIX is straightforward, modular, and compact. This has fostered the evolution of the UNIX system.

Rich and productive programming environment UNIX provides users with powerful tools and utilities. Some of these tools are simple commands that can be used to carry out specific tasks. Other tools and utilities are really small programmable languages that may be used to build scripts to solve problems. More importantly, the tools are intended to work together, like machine parts or building blocks.

Communication The UNIX system provides an excellent environment for networking. It offers programs and utilities that provide the services needed to build networked applications, the basis for distributed network computing.

Multi-user capability More than one user can access the same data at the same time. A computer system that can support multiple users is generally less expensive than the equivalent number of single-user machines.

Multitasking A given user can perform more than one task at the same time. One could update the client's database while printing the monthly sales report. The limit is about 20 simultaneous tasks per user and depending on the computer system, a system-wide limit of 50 or more tasks can be performed, which slows the response.

5.8.2 Components of UNIX

UNIX carries out various functions through three separate, but closely integrated parts: kernel, command interpreter, and file system.

Kernel

Known as the base operating system, kernel manages and allocates resources, interacts with I/O devices, and controls access to the processor. It controls the computer's resources.

When the user logs on, the kernel runs init and getty to check if the user is authorized and has the correct password. The kernel keeps track of all the programs being run, allots time to each running program, decides when one program stops and another program starts, assigns storage space for files, runs the shell program, and handles the transfer of information between the computer and the peripherals. In short, it provides the following functions:

- Process scheduling (process representation—structure, scheduling, and dispatching)
- Memory management
- Device management
- File management
- System call interface
- Process synchronization and inter-process communication
- Operator console interface

These functions are spread over a number of modules within the UNIX kernel. The utility programs and UNIX commands are not considered a part of the UNIX kernel, which consists of the layers closest to the hardware that are for the most part protected from the user. The kernel may be viewed with the help of a functional layer model (Fig. 5.3).

The kernel communicates directly with the hardware. When UNIX is adapted to a new machine, only the kernel has to be modified. The kernel does not deal directly with a user. It starts up a separate interactive program called a shell for each user, when the user logs on. The shell acts as an interface between the user and the system. The kernel serves as an interface between the shell, UNIX commands, and system hardware.

Everytime a process is loaded and started up, a chunk of main memory is allocated for program code and data. Additionally, main memory is required for buffers, system databases, and stack space. The device management routines in this layer start and stop devices, check and reset status, and read and write data from and to devices. Similarly, the disk management routines access the disk drive, and perform the basic block, read, and write functions.

The next layer consists of all kernel services. This layer provides the mapping between the user-level requests and device driver-level actions. The user system call is converted to calls to the kernel service routines that perform requested services. These services consist of process creation and termination, I/O services, receive data functions, and file access and terminal handling services.

The system call interface layer converts a process operating in the user mode to a protected kernel mode process so that the program code can invoke kernel routines to perform system functions.

The uppermost layer consists of user processes running shells, UNIX commands, utility programs, and user application programs. User programs are protected from inadvertent writes by other users. They have no direct access to the UNIX kernel routines and all access is channelled through the system call interface. Additionally, user programs cannot directly access memory used by the kernel routines.

Fig. 5.3 Functional layer model of the unix kernel

Command interpreter

This is a utility program and is called the *shell*. It interacts with the user and translates the user's request into actions on the part of the kernel and the other utility (Fig. 5.4). Each user opens one shell on logging on. Different types of shells are available such as Bourne shell, C shell, and Korn shell.

- protection of file data
- the treatment of peripheral devices as files

The shell translates typed commands into action; therefore, it is termed as a command interpreter. The shell has a few built-in commands, but the majority of the commands are separate programs stored elsewhere in the system. When a command is typed through the keyboard, it is collected and delivered to the kernel by the shell.

5.8.3 The UNIX File System

The file system is one of the major subsystems of the operating system. It is responsible for storing information on disk drives and retrieving and updating this information as directed by the user or by a program. The UNIX operating system regards practically every assemblage of information as a file. The formal definition of a file is a string of characters. Often, it is desirable to organize UNIX files as a set of lines. Every line is terminated by a new line character.

Fig. 5.4 The kernel–shell relationship

The files are identified by filenames that are kept in the file directory. Every user is allocated a personal file directory when the user's login name and password are authorized.

The file system is organized as a tree with a single root node called root (/). Every non-leaf node of the file system structure is a directory of files, and files at the leaf nodes of the tree are either directories, regular files, or special device files.

Filenames may contain up to 256 characters. The characters may include almost any printable character except a blank. The name of a file is given by a pathname that describes how to locate the file in the file system hierarchy. The file system hierarchy allows an entry only through the root.

The UNIX file system is characterized by the following:

- a hierarchical structure
- consistent treatment of file data
- the ability to create and delete files
- dynamic growth of files

The internal representation of a file is given by a unique *inode*. Inode stands for index node. Every file has one inode, but it may have several names, all of which map into the same inode. Each name is called a link. An inode contains a description of the disk layout of the file data and other information such as (a) file owner, (b) access permissions, (c) access times, (d) file size, and (e) location of file's data in the file system. The inode also contains (a) the time of the last modification of the file contents, (b) the time at which the file was last accessed, (c) the time at which the inode was changed (change permission), etc.

Processes access files by a well-defined set of system calls and specify a file by a character string that is a pathname. When a process refers to a file by name, the kernel parses the filename one component at a time and converts the filename to a file's inode. The kernel then checks that the process has permission to search the directories in the path and eventually retrieves the inode for the file. The system's internal name for the file is its i-number. When the following command is given:

    $ls   -i

(The output obtained shows the i-number and the filename.)

    i-nmbe filename
       ↓   ↓
    15768   junk
    15274   recipes
    15852   x

When a process creates a new file, the kernel assigns it an unused inode. Inodes are stored in the file system but the kernel reads them into an in-core inode table when manipulating the files. The kernel contains two other data structures: file table (global kernel structure) and user file descriptor table (per process).

Types of files

The UNIX system has the following types of files:

- Ordinary files
- Directory files
- Special files

Ordinary files   These are files that contain information entered by a user, an application program, or a system utility program. An ordinary file may contain text information (string of characters) and binary information (sequence of words). These files are also called byte streams.

An ordinary file is a string of bytes, stored on disk or on some other physical medium. There is no distinction between program files or data files. If all the bytes in the file represent printable characters, the file is termed a text file. It is often convenient to subdivide text files into lines, separated from each other with the new line character (ASCII 012 octal). The lines do not have fixed lengths.

Directory files   These are the files that manage the cataloging of the file system. A directory is a file that contains information about a group of files contained in the directory. A directory can contain sub-directories. Files can be accessed by selecting the corresponding directory or pathname.

The directory is defined as a file whose data is a sequence of entries, each consisting of an inode number and the name of a file, contained in the directory. A pathname is defined as a null terminated character string divided into separate components by the character slash, i.e., '/'. Every component in the pathname excepting the last one must be the name of a directory. The last component may be a directory or a non-directory file.

UNIX system restricts component names to a maximum of 256 characters, with a two-byte entry for the inode number. The size of a directory entry is 16 bytes. Every directory contains a '.' indicating the current directory and a '..' indicating the parent directory.

Empty directory entries are indicated by the inode number 0. Directories are created by the kernel. The 'read' permission allows a process to read the directory and the 'write' permission allows a process to create new directories.

The UNIX file directory structure is always in the form of a tree. Every directory is listed exactly in one predecessor directory, i.e., one directory can have only one predecessor directory. Normally, the predecessor directory is known as parent and the successor directories are known as children.

Special files   A special file represents a physical device such as a terminal, disk drive, magnetic tape drive, or communication link. Devices designated by special device files occupy node positions in the file system directory structure. The system reads from and writes to special files in the same way it does from and to an ordinary file. To the user, the UNIX system treats devices as if they were files. Programs access devices with the same syntax they use when accessing regular files; the semantics for the reading and writing devices are to a large degree the same as reading and writing regular files. Devices are protected in the same way as regular files.

Since device names look like the names of regular files and because the same operations work for devices and regular

files, most programs do not have to know internally the type of files they manipulate. However, the system's read/write requests do not activate the normal file access mechanism. Instead they activate the device handler associated with the file. For example, to print a file the system may be instructed to copy its content to another file called /dev/lp. This is a special file and the instruction

```
$cat newfile > /dev/lp
```

does not cause a file to be written on /dev/lp but causes the printer to be activated. The special file contains the rules according to which characters are treated by the peripheral device. Thus, there is no distinction between writing characters into a file, writing to the screen, or writing characters into a telephone coupler for transmission elsewhere.

Some commands related to file systems and privileged to be used by the system administrator are: mkfs makes a file system; fsck, fsdb repairs a file system; mknod builds a special file; clri removes a file forcefully; mount and umount mounts and unmounts a file system; and sync writes a disk block image from memory to disk.

File system structure

The file system in UNIX is organized in a hierarchical tree structure (Fig. 5.5). Each node of the tree consists of a directory file the branches of which contain other files.

Root directory   The directory at the root node is known as the root directory and is identified by '/'. The root directory acts as the first level of reference for any further reference to

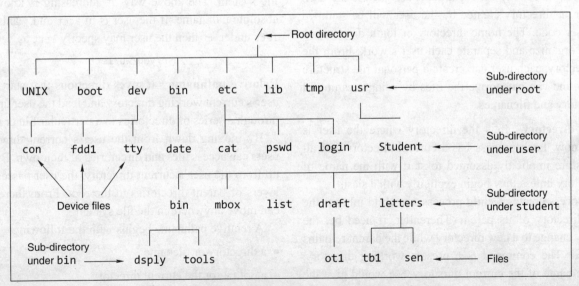

Fig. 5.5 The typical tree structure of the file system in UNIX

any particular file in the system. The other levels of reference are through the paths indicated by the branches and nodes connecting the file to the root node. Thus, /etc represents the directory etc which is a direct descendent of the root '/'.

The directory tree of a typical UNIX system contains a number of directories, each created by the system for specific

use and each housing files and directories containing logically related matter.

The root directory contains the files UNIX and boot and the directories /dev, /bin, /etc, /lib, /tmp, /usr, where each file and directory has a specific use.

'UNIX' contains the program for the UNIX kernel and boot contains the program for booting the system. When the system starts, boot is first read from the disk and stored in the main memory. Then, the program in boot reads UNIX. Each of these directories contain sub-directories and files.

/dev contains special files for physical devices such as the system console, terminals, disk drive, and line printers. /bin contains the basic programs such as who and ed. The user community is usually allowed the execute permission for files in /bin.

/lib contains libraries of system utilities and subroutines, C run-time support, system calls, I/O routines, etc. /etc contains restricted system data and special utility programs restricted to the system administrator, password file, login, etc. The general user does not have the execute permission for files in this directory.

/tmp stores temporary files. These files are created and used by the various system utilities such as editors and compilers. /usr stores the home directories of every authorized user. In addition, /usr houses directories, such as bin, tmp, and lib, which houses less-used system utilities of the types housed under the root directory.

Home directory Each user has a home directory allotted by the system administrator at the time of allocation of the user code. When the login procedure is successfully completed, the UNIX system places the user in a specific point in its file system structure, called the home directory. The name of this directory is usually the login name assigned to the user. Every file or directory created by the user will be stamped by his user code. The home directory or login directory is a way to organize and separate each user's work. From the login directory, each user can create a personal file structure hierarchy and can categorize the files by using meaningful sub-directory and filenames.

Current directory It is the directory where the user is working now. Each process has a current directory and all filenames are implicitly assumed to start with the name of this directory unless they begin explicitly with a slash.

If a process creates a child process, the child inherits the current directory of its parent. Thereafter, if need be, the child may change to a new directory while the parent remains unaffected. The command pwd, present working directory, prints the name of the current directory. pwd would give the user the directory where the user is residing at present.

Full pathname (absolute pathname) Every file and directory in the UNIX system is identified by a unique pathname. It is the full and proper name of the file. The pathname shows the location of the file and the directory in the structure of the file system. It is the list of directory tree nodes, which must be traversed to reach the desired file.

Every file is accessed by specifying the path to it through the directory tree. The successive node specifies the name of a directory and the pathname is created. To access any file the user has to use the pathname, giving the address of the file, depending upon its position within the file system structure, along with the filename. The absolute pathname gives directions from the root directory and leads the user down through a unique sequence of directories. For example, /usr/btech/letter/memo.

The following part of the file structure is examined. It concerns the user you whose home directory is you which is created directly under usr by the system administrator, when the user code is created.

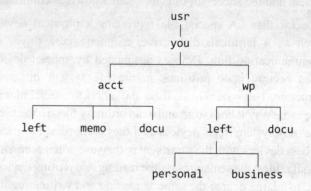

The pathname of you is /usr/you

The pathname of acct is /usr/you/acct

The pathname represents the position of the file within the file system. The above way of addressing is known as the absolute pathname. If the user is in acct and wants to reach lett under wp then the user may specify lett as

/usr/you/wp/left

Relative pathname It gives directions that start from the user's current working directory and lead the user up or down through a series of directories to a particular file or directory.

By moving down from the user's current directory, the users can access files and directories of their own. By moving up from the user's current directory, the user passes through layers of parent directories to the root. From there the user can move anywhere in the file system.

A relative pathname begins with the following:

- a directory or filename
- a dot (.) for the current directory
- a double dot (..) for the parent directory of the current directory

From acct
   .. is the pathname to you
   ../.. is the pathname to usr
   ../wp/docu is the pathname to docu

5.8.4 Account and Password

UNIX is security-conscious and can be used only by those persons who maintain an account with the computer system. A user cannot simply sit down at any terminal and start working as in DOS/Windows.

Users using UNIX workstations must set up their own user accounts. The system administrator will grant the user that authority. The user opens an account with a name, known as login name/user name, and enters a secret code called password when the system prompts for it.

5.8.5 Logging In

Logging in is a simple procedure that tells the UNIX system who the user is. The prompt appears as follows:

```
login:
```

The login prompt indicates that the terminal is available for login (i.e., connect). This message also indicates that the previous user has 'logged out' (disconnected). The procedure of login is: enter user name or login name and hit the <**Enter**> key after the string. The following happens:

```
$ login: manas
Password:
```

The system now requests the user to enter the secret code (password) given by the administrator. This code should be known only to the user. When the password is entered, the terminal does not display it. Then the <**Enter**> key is pressed.

--- EXAMPLE ---

```
$ login: Anand <Enter>
Password: *******<Enter>
```

The system crosschecks this password and if it is right, the system will allow the user to work.

5.8.6 UNIX Shell Commands

The basic form of a UNIX command is:

```
commandname [-options] [arguments]
```

The command name is the name of the program the user wants the shell to execute. The command options, usually indicated by a dash, allows the user to alter the behavior of the command. The arguments are the names of files, directories, or programs that the command needs to access.

The square brackets '[ ]' signify the optional parts of the command that may be omitted.

--- EXAMPLE ---

1. Type the command

```
ls -l /tmp
```

to get a long listing of the contents of the /tmp directory. In this example,

ls is the command name, -1 is an option that tells ls to create a long, detailed output, and /tmp is an argument naming the directory that ls is to list. The meaning of the other characters, and the ways to use them, will be introduced as the text progresses.

Aborting a shell command Most UNIX systems allow the user to abort the current command by typing **Control-C**. To issue a **Control-C** abort command, hold the control key down, and press the 'c' key.

Special characters in UNIX UNIX recognizes certain special characters as command directives. The special characters are: /, <, >, !, $, %, ^, &, *, |, {, }, ~, and ; . When creating files and directories on UNIX, it would be safe to use only the characters A-Z, a-z, 0-9, the period, dash, and underscore. The meaning of the other characters, and ways to use them, will be introduced later.

Printing current working directory The working directory of a user can be printed out by using the command pwd (present working directory).

When users log in to a UNIX system, they are located in their own directory space. Users are generally located off the /usr directory. The pwd command displays the pathname of the current directory the user is in. This is helpful when users want to know exactly where they are.

Creating a directory The UNIX command mkdir is used to create directories. The basic syntax is

```
mkdir directoryname
```

If the user does not specify the place where the directory should be created, by giving a path as part of the directory name, the shell assumes that the user wants the new directory placed within the current working directory.

--- EXAMPLE ---

2. Using a UNIX command, create a directory temp.
   Solution:

```
mkdir temp
```

This command creates a new directory named temp in the current directory. This example assumes that the user has the proper permission to create a new sub-directory in the current working directory.

--- EXAMPLE ---

3. Using UNIX commands, create three sub-directories.
   Solution:

```
mkdir memos letters email
```

This command creates three new sub-directories, memos, letters, and email, in the current directory.

--- EXAMPLE ---

4. Using a UNIX command, create a sub-directory within a directory.
   Solution:

```
mkdir /usr/it/tmp
```

This command creates a new directory named `tmp` under the directory `it`. `tmp` is now a sub-directory of `it`. This example assumes that the user has the proper permission to create a new directory in `/usr/it`.

Changing current directory `cd` stands for change directory. It is the primary command for moving around the file system.

EXAMPLE
---

5. Using a UNIX command, change directory.
   Solution:

   ```
   cd /usr/rcciit
   ```

   The command entry moves the choice to the `/usr/rcciit` directory.

EXAMPLE
---

6. Using a UNIX command, return to home directory.
   Solution:

   ```
   cd .
   ```

   Issuing the `cd` command without any arguments moves the choice to the home directory. This is very useful if the user is lost in the file system.

   The directories . and ..
   In UNIX, (.) means the current directory, so typing

   ```
   cd .
   ```

   means staying in the current directory. While (..) means the parent of the current directory, so typing

   ```
   cd ..
   ```

   will take the user one directory up the hierarchy, that is, back to the user's home directory. Note that there is a space between `cd` and the dot.

   Entering
   ```
   cd/
   ```
   moves the user to the root directory. / is the root directory.

EXAMPLE
---

7. Creating a directory called `bar`, within the directory called `rod`, which is within the home directory.
   Solution: Once the `rod` directory is created, the user could just type

   ```
   mkdir ~/rod/bar
   ```

   Alternately, the user could type

   ```
   cd ~/rod; mkdir bar
   ```

   In the second solution, two UNIX commands are given, separated by a semicolon. The first part of the command makes `rod` the current working directory. The second part of the command creates the `bar` directory in the current working directory.

Listing the contents of a directory The `ls` command allows the user to see the contents of a directory, and to view basic information such as size, ownership, and access permissions about files and directories. The `ls` command has numerous options.

The syntax for the `ls` command is:

```
ls [options] [directorynames]
```
The options are:

- `-a` Displays all files including the hidden files
- `-b` Displays non-printing characters in octal
- `-c` Displays files by file timestamp, i.e., by inode modification time
- `-C` Displays files in a columnar format (default)
- `-d` Displays only directories
- `-f` Interprets each name as a directory, not a file
- `-F` Flags filenames by appending / to directory, * to executable files, etc.
- `-g` Displays the long format listing, but excludes the owner name
- `-i` Displays the inode for each file
- `-l` Displays the long format listing
- `-L` Displays the file or directory referenced by a symbolic link
- `-m` Displays the names as a comma-separated list
- `-o` Displays the long format listing, but excludes group name
- `-p` Displays directories with /
- `-q` Displays all non-printing characters as ?
- `-r` Displays files in reverse order
- `-R` Displays sub-directories as well as current directory
- `-t` Displays newest files first
- `-u` Displays files by the file access time
- `-x` Displays files as rows across the screen
- `-1` Displays each entry on a line

EXAMPLE
---

8. Demonstrating the use of the `ls` command with different options.
   Solution:
   (i) `ls`

   This is the basic `ls` command, with no options. It provides a very basic listing of the files in the user's current working directory. Filenames beginning with a decimal are considered *hidden* files; they are not shown.

   (ii) `ls -a`

   The `-a` option tells the `ls` command to report information about all files, including hidden files.

   (iii) `ls -l`

   The `-l` option tells the `ls` command to provide a *long* listing of information about the files and directories it reports. The long listing will provide important information about file permissions, user and group ownership, file size, and creation date.

   (iv) `ls -la`

   This command provides a *long* listing of information about *all* files in the current directory. It combines the functionality of the `-a` and `-l` options. This is probably the most used version of the `ls` command. Remember that in `ls-1a` file listings, a directory is identified by a `d` in the front of the permissions (`drwxr-xr-x`).

(v) `ls -al /usr`

This command lists long information about all files in the `/usr` directory.

(vi) `ls -alR /usr | more`

This command lists long information about all files in the `/usr` directory, and all sub-directories of `/usr`. The `-R` option tells the `ls` command to provide a *recursive* listing of all files and sub-directories. `more` displays the list, one full screen at a time.

(vii) `ls -ld /usr`

Rather than list the files contained in the `/usr` directory, this command lists information about the `/usr` directory itself, without generating a listing of the contents of `/usr`. This is very useful when the user want to check the permissions of the directory, and not the files the directory contains.

(viii) Home directories can also be referred to by the tilde (~) character. It can be used to specify paths starting at the user's home directory. So typing

`ls ~/UNIXstuff`

will list the contents of the user's `UNIXstuff` directory, no matter where the user currently is in the file system.

5.8.7 Wildcards: The Characters * and?

The character * is called a wildcard and will match against one or more character(s) in a file (or directory) name. For example, in the user's UNIXstuff directory, type

`ls list*`

This will list all files in the current directory starting with `list`. Try typing

`% ls *list`

This will list all files in the current directory ending with `list`. The character ? will match exactly one character. So `ls ?ouse` will match files such as house and mouse, but not grouse, etc.

Creating a file

To create a file called `list1` containing a list of fruits, type

`cat > list1`

Then type in the names of some fruits. Press <**Return**> after each name.

        pear
        banana
        apple
        ^D (Control D to stop)

What happens is that the `cat` command reads the standard input (the keyboard) and the character '>' redirects the output, which normally goes to the screen, into a file called `list1`. Finally, press <**Ctrl-d**> to signify the end of input to the system.

Filename conventions

It should be noted that a directory is merely a special type of file. So the rules and conventions for naming files apply also to directories.

In naming files, characters with special meanings such as /, *, &, and % should be avoided. Also, avoid using spaces within names. The safest way to name a file is to use only alphanumeric characters, that is, letters and numbers, together with _ (underscore) and . (dot).

Filenames conventionally start with a lowercase letter and may end with a dot followed by a group of letters indicating the contents of the file. For example, all files consisting of C code may be named with the ending `.c`, for example, `prog1.c`. Then in order to list all files containing C code in the user's home directory, the user need only type `ls *.c` in that directory.

> **Note**
>
> - Some applications give the same name to all the output files they generate. For example, some compilers, unless given the appropriate option, produce compiled files named a.out. Should the user forget to use that option, the user is advised to rename the compiled file immediately, otherwise the next such file will overwrite it and it will be lost.

Viewing the contents of a file

Text files are intended for direct viewing and other files are intended for computer interpretation. The UNIX file command allows the user to determine whether an unknown file is in text format and suitable for direct viewing.

To see what kind of file the shell is, type the command

`file /bin/sh`

The shell is a shared executable code, indicating that the file contains binary instructions to be executed by the computer.

Viewing contents of files using cat command

The `cat` command reads one or more files and prints them on standard output. The operator '>' can be used to combine multiple files into one. The operator '>>' can be used to append to an existing file.

The syntax for the `cat` command is:

`cat [options] filename(s)`

or

`cat filename(s) [-n] [-b] [-u] [-s] [-v]`

where

filename The name of the file or files that the user wishes to look at or perform tasks on

-u The output is not buffered. The default is buffered output.

-s cat is silent about non-existent files.

-v Non-printing characters (with the exception of tabs, new lines and form-feeds) are printed. ASCII control characters (octal 000–037) are printed as ^n, where n is the corresponding ASCII character in the range octal 100–137 (@, A, B, C, . . ., X, Y, Z, [, \,], ^, and _); the DEL character (octal 0177) is printed ^?. Other non-printable characters are printed as M-x, where x is the ASCII character specified by the low order seven bits.

-e   A $ character will be printed at the end of each line (prior to the new line).

-t   Tabs will be printed as ^I's and form-feeds as ^L's.

Note that if -v is used, -e and -t will be ignored.

EXAMPLE

9. Write the command for displaying on screen the content of file abc. txt, whose absolute path is /usr/rcciit.
   Solution:

   ```
   cat /usr/rcciit/abc.txt
   ```

   This command displays the abc.txt file under /usr/rcciit on the screen.

EXAMPLE

10. Write a command that combines three files.
    Solution:

    ```
    cat file1 file2 file3
    ```

    This command combines the contents of the first three files one by one. The drawback of the cat command, when displaying file contents on the screen, is that the contents of the file may scroll off the screen. In cases where a file is too large to fit the screen, it is better to use the more command to display the file. In fact, it is probably easier to use the more command all the time, and just use the cat command to concatenate (merge) files.

more command   The more command displays a text file, one screen at a time. The user can scroll forward a line at a time by pressing the return key, or a screenful at a time by pressing the space bar. The user can quit at any time by pressing the q key.

EXAMPLE

11. Type

    ```
    more itfile
    ```

to the shell. Scroll down by pressing the spacebar. Stop the more command from displaying the rest of the file by typing q.

The user can also use one of the following commands.

    space bar: Display next screen of text

      <Return>: Display next line of text

      q: Exit from more. This can be done at any time

      d: Scroll forward about half a screen of text

      b: Skip backward one screen of text

      h: Display a list of commands (help)

The head and tail commands   The head command allows the user to see the top part of a file. The user may specify the number of lines required; by default it displays the first ten lines.

EXAMPLE

12. Type

    ```
    head -15 /etc/rc
    ```

to see the first 15 lines of the /etc/rc file. The tail command works like the head command, except that it shows the last ten lines of a file by default.

EXAMPLE

13. Type

    ```
    tail /etc/rc
    ```

to see the last ten lines of the file /etc/rc. Since the user did not specify the number of lines as an option, the tail command defaulted to ten lines.

less command   The command less writes the contents of a file onto the screen, a page at a time. Type

    ```
    less science.txt
    ```

the user must press the **<space bar>** to see another page and type q to quit reading. As can be seen, less is used in preference to cat for long files.

Clearing screen   The user may like to clear the terminal window of the previous commands so that the output of the following commands can be clearly understood.

At the prompt, type

    ```
    clear
    ```

This clears all text and leaves the command prompt at the top of the window.

wc (word count) command   A handy little utility is the wc command, short for word count. This utility displays a count of the number of characters, words, and lines in a file.

The syntax of the command is:

    ```
    wc [option] filename
    ```

There are several options for the wc command that simply print out the information requested. The options for this utility are:

      –l   print line count

      –c   print character count

      –w   print word count

To get a word count on science.txt, type

    ```
    wc -w science.txt
    ```

To find out how many lines the file has, type

    ```
    wc -l science.txt
    ```

Copying files and directories   The UNIX command to copy a file or directory is cp.

SYNTAX cp [options] sources target

where options are

-i Ask before updating a file or directory that exists in the destination with the same name.

-r Copy recursively each sub-directory of the directory given in the command.

To copy the profile file, one must have 'read permission' on the file. To create a new file one must have 'write permission' in the directory where the file will be created.

Make a copy in the current directory

    cp oldfilename newfilename

e.g.,

    cp file1.html file2.html

Make a copy in a sub-directory of the current directory

    cp filename dir-name

e.g.,

    cp file1.html public_html

This will make a copy of file1.html within the public_html directory (assuming the directory exists).

Copying (or moving) to the parent directory To move or copy a file to the parent directory, the following command has to be entered.

    cp filename ..

Copying from the parent directory into the current directory The following command is used to copy a file from the parent directory into the current directory:

    cp ../filename .

The dot at the end of this command stands for the current directory. Note that there is a space in front of this final dot.

EXAMPLE

14.

(i) cp .profile .profile.bak

This command copies the file .profile to a file named .profile.bak.

(ii) cp /usr/fred/Chapter1 .

This command copies the file named Chapter1 in the /usr/fred directory to the current directory. This example assumes that the user has write permission in the current directory.

(iii) cp /usr/fred/Chapter1 /usr/mary

This command copies the Chapter1 file in /usr/fred to the directory named/usr/mary. This example assumes that the user has write permission in the /usr/mary directory.

(iv) cp /vol/examples/tutorial/science.txt .

(**Note**: Do not forget the dot (.) at the end. Remember, in UNIX, the dot means the current directory).

The above command means copy the file science.txt to the current directory, without changing the name.

Moving and renaming file(s) The mv command allows the user to move and rename files.

SYNTAX mv [-f] [-i] oldname newname\directory

where

-f mv moves the file(s) without prompting, even if it is writing over an existing target. Note that this is the default if the standard input is not a terminal.

-i Prompts before overwriting another file

oldname The oldname of the file that is renamed

newname The newname of the file after renaming

filename The name of the file the user wants to move directory. The directory where you want the file to go

EXAMPLE

15.

(i) mv Chapter1 Chapter1.bad

This command renames the file Chapter1 as Chapter1.bad.

(ii) mv Chapter1 garbage

This command renames the file Chapter1 as garbage. Notice that if garbage is a directory, Chapter1 would be moved into that directory.

(iii) mv Chapter1 /tmp

This command moves the file Chapter1 into the directory named /tmp.

(iv) mv tmp tmp.old

Assuming in this case that tmp is a directory, this example renames the directory tmp as tmp.old.

(v) *Moving to the parent directory*

    mv filename ..

Note the space before the two dots. The two dots represent the parent directory.

(vi) *Moving from the parent directory into the current directory.* The user can use the following commands to move a file from the parent directory into the current directory

    mv ../filename .

The dot at the end of these commands stands for the current directory. Note that there is a space in front of this final dot.

Deleting file(s) This command deletes a file without confirmation (by default).

SYNTAX rm [-f] [-i] [-r] [filenames | directory]

where

-f Removes all files, whether write-protected or not, in a directory without prompting the user. In a write-protected directory, however, files are never removed, whatever their permissions are, but no messages are displayed. If the removal of a write-protected directory is attempted, this option will not suppress an error message.

-i Interactive. With this option, rm prompts for confirmation before removing any files. It over rides the -f option and remains in effect even if the standard input is not a terminal.

-r Recursively removes directories and sub-directories in the argument list. The directory will be emptied of files and removed. The user is normally prompted for removal of any write-protected files the directory contains. The write-protected files are removed without prompting, however, if the –f option is used, or if the standard input is not a terminal and the –i option is not used then the write-protected files are removed without prompting. Symbolic links that are encountered with this option will not be traversed. If the removal of a non-empty, write-protected directory is attempted, the utility will always fail (even if the –f option is used), resulting in an error message.

filenames A path of a filename that is to be removed.

EXAMPLE

16.

(i) `rm Chapter1.bad`

This command deletes the file named `Chapter1.bad`, assuming that the user has permission to delete this file.

(ii) `rm Chapter1 Chapter2 Chapter3`

This command deletes the files named `Chapter1`, `Chapter2`, and `Chapter3`.

(iii) `rm -i Chapter1 Chapter2 Chapter3`

This command prompts the user before deleting any of the three files specified. The –i option stands for *inquire*. The user must answer y (for yes) for each file the user wants deleted. This can be a safer way to delete files.

(iv) `rm *.html`

This command deletes all files in the current directory whose filenames end with `.html`.

(v) `rm index*`

This command deletes all files in the current directory whose filenames begin with `index`.

(vi) `rm -r newnovel`

This command deletes the directory named `newnovel`. This directory, and all its contents including any sub-directories and files, are erased from the disk.

(vii) Deleting several files using a wildcard

The following command uses the asterisk wildcard to stand for any characters (or no characters).

`rm file1.*`

This deletes the files called `file1.txt`, `file1.html`, `file1.html`, and so on. The user is asked to confirm deletion of each file in turn.

(viii) `rm public_html/*.html`

This deletes all the files with html after the dot, which is in the sub-directory called `public_html` under the current directory.

Removing a directory The UNIX `rmdir` command removes a directory from the file system tree. The `rmdir` command does not work unless the directory to be removed is completely empty.

SYNTAX `rmdir [-p] [-s] directory`

where

–p	Allows users to remove a directory and its parent directories that become empty. A message is printed for standard error if all or a part of the path could not be removed.
–s	Suppresses the message printed on the standard error when –p is in effect `directory`, the name of the directory that the user wishes to delete

---

EXAMPLE

17. Enter the command

`rmdir newfile`

It should be noted that `newfile` should be empty.

Online manuals There are online manuals that give information about most commands. The manual pages tell the user which options a particular command can take, and how each option modifies the behaviour of the command. Type man to read the manual page for a particular command.

For example, to find out more about the wc (word count) command, type

`man wc`

Redirection Most processes initiated by UNIX commands write onto the standard output (that is, they write onto the terminal screen) and many take their input from the standard input (that is, they read it from the keyboard). There is also the standard error, where processes write their error messages, by default, to the terminal screen.

It has been already seen that one use of the cat command is to write the contents of a file to the screen.

Now, type cat without specifying a file to read

`cat`

Then, type a few words on the keyboard and press the <**Return**> key. Finally, hold the <**Ctrl**> key down and press <**d**> (written as **^D** for short) to end the input.

What happens is that when the user runs the cat command without specifying a file to read, it reads the standard input (the keyboard), and on receiving the 'end of file' <**^D**>, copies it to the standard output (the screen). In UNIX, the user can redirect both the input and the output of commands.

Redirecting the output The > symbol is used to redirect the output of a command. For example, to create a file called `list1` containing a list of fruits, type

`cat > list1`

Then type in the names of some fruits. Press <**Return**> after each name.

`pear`

`banana`

`apple`

`^D` (Control D to stop)

What happens is that the cat command reads the standard input (the keyboard) and the > redirects the output, which normally goes to the screen, into a file called `list1`.

To read the contents of the file, type

```
cat list1
```
and type

```
cat > list2
```

Then type in the names of more fruits

```
peach
grape
orange
^D  (Control D to stop)
```
To read the contents of the file, type

```
cat list2
```

The user should now have two files. Both files contain names of three fruits. Now the cat command is used to join (concatenate) list1 and list2 into a new file called biglist. Type

```
cat list1 list2 > biglist
```

What this does is that it reads the contents of list1 and list2 in turn, then outputs the text to the file biglist.

To read the contents of the new file, type

```
cat biglist
```

Redirecting the input The < symbol is used to redirect the input of a command. The command sort alphabetically or numerically sorts a list. Type

```
sort
```

Then type in the names of some fruits. Press <**Return**> after each name.

```
apple
mango
banana
^D  (Control D to stop)
```

The output obtained would be

```
apple
banana
mango
```

With the help of < the user can redirect the input to come from a file rather than the keyboard. For example, to sort the list of fruits, type

```
sort < biglist
```
and the sorted list will be output to the screen. To output the sorted list to a file, type

```
sort < biglist > slist
```

Use cat to read the contents of the file slist.

Pipes As UNIX is a multi-user operating system, to see who all are using the system, a user may enter

```
who
```
One method to get a sorted list of user names is to type

```
who > names.txt
sort < names.txt
```

This is a bit slow and the user has to remember to remove the temporary file called names. What the user really wants to do is to connect the output of the who command directly to the input of the sort command. This is exactly what pipes do. The symbol for a pipe is the vertical bar | . For example, typing

```
who | sort
```
will give the same result as the earlier commands, and it will be faster and more effective.

To find out how many users are logged on, type

```
who | wc -l
```

Note

- The UNIX operating system can be used in various types of computers for its portability, openness, effective programming environment, networking capability, multi-programming and multi-tasking facilities.
- UNIX operating system carries out various functions through three separate, but closely integrated parts ---- kernel, command interpreter, and file system.

5.9 AN OVERVIEW OF MSDOS

5.9.1 A Brief History

The origin of MSDOS can be traced back to 1980 when Seattle Computer Producers developed a microcomputer operating system for in-house use. It was called QDOS. It was renamed 86-DOS in the late 1980 after modifications.

The rights on 86-DOS were bought by Microsoft, which had a contract with IBM to produce an operating system for the latter's new PC. The 86-DOS was modified and called PC-DOS 1.0. When PC compatible machines were produced, they used a similar version of pc-dos called MSDOS.

Version 1.0 of DOS was released in 1981, giving single-sided disk drive capability. Version 1.1 was released in 1982, giving double-sided disk drive capability and output to a serial printer. Version 2.0, released in 1983, gave hard disk support, sophisticated hierarchical file directory, installable device drivers, and file handles. Version 3.0, released in 1984, gave improved hard disk and network support. Version 3.3 released in 1987 continued this trend.

Version 4.0, released in 1988, provided the dosshell, expanded memory driver, and larger than 32MB hard disk partitions. Version 5.0, released in 1991, was designed as an upgrade. This version enabled device drivers to be placed in upper memory, leaving more conventional memory available to programs. MSDOS 6.22 was released in 1994.

The latest version of DOS is MSDOS 7, which is provided as a part of and inside the Windows system.

5.9.2 Role of Disk Drive for Loading DOS

A disk drive is a device that either stores data or reads data from the disk, which may be a floppy or a hard disk. A PC has floppy drives, hard disk drives, and CD-ROM drives. The first floppy drive is conventionally called drive A whereas the second floppy drive is designated as drive B and the first hard disk drive is designated as drive C.

Booting is synonymous with starting a computer. When the computer is switched on, the BIOS program, fused in the ROM, checks the memory and peripherals. Drive A of a microcomputer is the primary drive, which a computer first looks for when switched on. It reads the disk in drive A and checks for any boot record or system files. If drive A does not have these, it goes to drive C, skipping drive B. On finding drive C, the computer starts the process of loading the DOS into the RAM of the computer. Once the DOS is loaded, it is said that the DOS has booted the computer and is ready to accept the user's orders. The following prompt appears and awaits orders from the user:

```
A:>_  or  C:>_
```

The above prompt is displayed along with a flashing cursor, depending upon whether the system has been booted from drive A or C. When the booting is from drive A, there must be a DOS diskette in drive A. When the booting is from C drive, DOS must have been previously installed in the hard disk so that the system files are duly loaded into RAM.

5.9.3 Starting DOS

When the computer starts working, it does not have an ordinary program loaded into it. The computer does, however, have two special built-in programs it can rely on, and it does know how to do the following:

- How to do self-testing to see that things are in working order
- How to start up DOS

This start-up program is usually called a bootstrap loader, since it pulls DOS up by the bootstraps. This bootstrap operation works in two stages.

First, the tiny program built into the computer goes to work. It just knows how to read the beginning of a diskette or the hard disk, in case the diskette is not used, and runs whatever it finds there as any other operating system. However, this program in the computer does not actually know anything about DOS. The simple start-up program is located in the beginning of a diskette or hard disk. The start-up program, which is the DOS's own starting routine, knows how to set up DOS in the computer.

Second, the start-up program checks the memory. Then, it loads the DOS system files into the memory. There are three main system files in DOS. These are as follows:

```
IO.SYS
DOS.SYS
COMMAND.COM
```

First, the IO.SYS file is loaded into the memory and checks whether all the input and output devices are correctly connected to the computer. Then the program loads the DOS.SYS file, which starts the loading of COMMAND.COM into primary memory. COMMAND.COM is the command interpreter for DOS commands. It stays in the primary memory as long as the machine is on. The DOS.SYS also loads another system file known as HIMEM.SYS, which is a program that manages the memory. Then, it sets the configuration of the system by checking the file CONFIG.SYS. In the end, it checks for the existence of AUTOEXEC.BAT file. If it exists, then it executes the particular file. Eventually, the system prompt appears and the system is ready for use.

To run MSDOS, 640 KB of primary memory is required. This memory is called the conventional base memory. The primary memory of the personal computer is subdivided into three parts.

- Conventional memory
- Extended memory
- Expanded memory

Extended memory requires HIMEM.SYS to manage it.

5.9.4 The Command Prompt

When the personal computer is turned on, some cryptic information flashes by. MSDOS displays this information to let the user know how it is configuring the computer. This can be ignored now. When the display stops scrolling past the information, the following is seen on the screen:

```
C:\>
```

This is called the command prompt or DOS prompt. The flashing underscore next to the command prompt is called the cursor. The cursor shows the position where the command typed in would appear.

Any line in DOS that begins like this is a command prompt. The actual character that symbolizes the prompt is the 'greater than' symbol: '>'. This line prompt is a way of informing the users where they are in DOS. The characters that appear with '>' in the line prompt indicate the following:

- The C: means that the user is working within the file space (disk storage) on the hard drive, which is designated as C. C is usually reserved for the internal hard disk of a PC.
- The backslash (\) represents a level in the hierarchy of the file structure. There is always at least one, which represents the root directory. The root directory represents the very first level of the file structure on the hard disk.

Nowadays, while MSDOS is not commonly used, it can still be accessed from every version of Microsoft Windows by clicking Start/Run and typing command or by typing CMD in Windows NT, Windows 2000, or Windows XP.

If the command prompt does not look like that shown above, type the following at the command prompt, and then press <**Enter**>:

```
cd \
```

Note that the slash leans backwards, not forward. The cd command will be dealt with, in detail, later. If the command prompt still does not look like the above example, type the following at the command prompt and then press <**Enter**>:

```
prompt $p$g
```

The command prompt should now look like the example shown.

5.9.5 Communicating with DOS

MSDOS is a command-driven operating system. This means that there is a set of commands that the user gives to the operating system for the tasks the user wishes it to perform. These commands are entered following the command prompt (A, B, or C), at the place the user sees the blinking 'hyphen', which is the cursor. The user can type in commands from the keyboard. The system is not case-sensitive.

Typing a command

The user can type the command, in either capital letters or lowercase letters, after the command prompt. The user must press <**Enter**> after every command typed.

The user can correct any typographical mistakes that may have been made while entering the command before pressing <**Return**>. If the user makes a typing mistake, the <**Backspace**> or <**Del**> keys can be used to erase the mistake. The line at which the user enters the command is called the MSDOS command line. If the user makes a mistake while typing a DOS command, the following message appears:

```
Bad command or file name
```

Navigating disks A disk's storage comprises several parts of which two are covered here: directories and files. Directories are DOS' way of organizing the many files that can be placed on disk. Every disk has at least one directory. This is referred to as the 'root' directory. From the root directory of every disk the user is able to directly or indirectly access every file on the disk. The root directory can hold directories or files. Subsequent directories can also hold directories or files, and so on.

Naming a file While newer versions of DOS support longer filenames, the standard DOS filename format remains as follows: one to eight letters for a name, one dot for a period, and three letters for the extension. For example,

```
PROGRAM.EXE
DATA.DAT
LETTER.DOC
```

The extension to a file's name allows files of similar type to be grouped together. That is, all word processor files might have the extension .DOC, while all picture files might have the extension .PIC. Since the user can specify these extensions, many programs have used them to differentiate between formats. These extensions have gradually become standardized. For example, a .TXT file is expected to be a file containing unformatted text, whereas a .BMP file is considered to be a file in a bit mapped graphics file format.

To completely specify a file on a computer, the user must specify its drive, directory path, and filename. However, a file does not always have to be specified in this complete form. If it is in the current directory, then the user can just enter its filename.

Directories, sub-directories, and files

Every disk drive has a root directory that can have sub-directories, which are named in the same format as filenames though generally without any extension. The sub-directories can have sub-directories, and so on.

Directory structures comprise levels of directories with a parent/child relationship (Fig. 5.6). The root directory has no parent directory, only child directories.

Fig. 5.6   Directory structures in MSDOS

A directory pathname includes the disk drive and all sub-directories needed to specify a directory on a disk. The disk drive is specified by a single letter. The graphical representation of a file structure below shows how a file can be stored in different levels on a hard disk.

```
c:\
 ├── DEMO
 │     ├── DOS&WIN
 │     │      ├── SAMPLE
 │     │      └── SAMPLE
```

In DOS, the file, SAMPLE, is represented as follows:

```
C:\DEMO\DOS&WIN\SAMPLES\SAMPLE
```

So, what C:\DEMO\DOS&WIN\SAMPLES\SAMPLE means is that the file SAMPLE is on the internal hard disk, four levels deep, inside several nested directories. The list of directories, \DEMO\DOS&WIN\SAMPLES\, is referred to as a pathname and following the path of directories, it is possible to get to the file. The name of the file itself, SAMPLE, is referred to as the filename. '\' refers to the root directory. For reference to the parent directory of any given sub-directory, the following symbol is used: '..'.

A colon follows the drive letter, while directory pathnames are separated by backward slashes (\), not forward slashes like Internet addresses. For example, C:\PICTURES\HOLIDAY\FRANCE.

UNIX and DOS have an easy-to-use hierarchical file system. This means that files are organized in groups called directories. Windows users call them 'Folders'. Each directory may contain files as well as sub-directories. This provides a good way of organizing files on disk. This is one of the features that has made UNIX a popular server operating system. Any file on disk can also be accessed directly by specifying a full pathname. The pathname consists of all the names of the directories that have to be traversed to get to the file, starting at the top-level directory called the root directory. Each directory in the path is separated by a slash '/' and an additional slash separates the last directory name from the filename. Since, the Internet was made of mostly UNIX-based computers when it was born, the same slash character was used in Internet URLs (addresses).

Unlike mainframes, PCs did not have any type of fixed (versus removable) permanent storage when DOS was developed. Therefore, DOS had to be generic enough to run on a floppy disk-based system without much need for configuration data. It was decided that any disk devices were to be assigned generic letters: 'A' for the first disk drive and 'B' for a second disk drive. The drive letter was then used at the beginning of a pathname, followed by a colon and the rest of the pathname. For some odd reason, Microsoft decided to use a backslash ('\') for the directory separation character, rather than the regular forward slash.

Let us try to understand this with an example. Consider the following DOS pathname:

```
A:\WIN98\README.TXT
```

This means, on drive A (A:), start at the root directory (\), go to the WIN98 directory (WIN98\), then access README.TXT.

5.9.6 DOS Commands

There are two types of commands in DOS. These are classified as internal and external. Command programs that are in memory all the time once the DOS has been read off the disk and started up are called internal commands. Such commands can be easily accessible. Normally the internal commands are part of the file COMMAND.COM.

Commands that require separate executable programs, not available in COMMAND.COM, to perform the particular command are called external commands. These command programs are kept on the hard disk until they are needed. When the user calls for one of these commands, DOS loads the command program into the main memory.

Pressing <**Enter**> terminates all the commands. Some internal commands are given below.

CLS	Clears the screen.
VER	Finds out what version of DOS is in use.
Date	Shows the system date of that particular computer and prompts the user to enter a new date.
Time	Displays the system's time. It also prompts the user to enter the current time.

When the user types anything at the DOS prompt and presses <**Enter**>, it means the user is telling the DOS to run a program. It first checks if there is an internal command program with that name. If it does not find one, then it checks for a file on the disk with that name.

If it finds an external file with the extension .COM (command), or .EXE (executable) corresponding to the command, then the program is loaded and run. At this point, DOS loses control of the computer until the program has ended. However, parts of it are still used by the programs as they are running, e.g., to load and save files.

Viewing the contents of a directory

The DIR command is used to display a list of files and sub-directories in a directory. The syntax is

```
DIR [drive:]\[path]\[filename] [/P] [/W] [/A[[:]
    attributes]][/O[[:]sortorder]] [/S] [/B]
    [/L] [/V]
```

[drive:][path][filename]	Specifies drive, directory, and/or files to list
/P	Pauses after each screen of information
/W	Uses wide list format
/A	Includes only those files with specified attributes where attributes include
D =	Directories
R =	Read only files
H =	Hidden files
A =	Files ready for archiving
S =	System files
- Prefix meaning not	
/O	List by files in sorted order, where sort order is a letter indicating one of the following
N =	By name (alphabetic)
S =	By size (smallest first)
E =	By extension (alphabetic)
D =	By date and time (earliest first)
G =	Group directories first
- Prefix to reverse order	
/S	Displays files in specified directory and all sub-directories
/B	Uses bare format (no heading information or summary)

/L   Uses lowercase

`dir` Lists all files and directories in the current directory

`dir/ad` Lists only the directories in the current directory

`dir/s` Lists the files in the specified directory and all sub-directories within that directory. If the user is at the root directory, as seen from the prompt 'C:\>', and if the user types this command, then the command will list every file in the specified directory and all sub-directories that exist.

`dir/p` If the directory has a lot of files and the user cannot read all the files at once, this command will display all files one page at a time.

`dir/w` If the user does not need the date/time and other information on the files, the user can apply this command to list just the names of the files and directories by using the horizontal space, thereby taking as little vertical space as possible on the monitor screen.

`dir/s/w/p` This lists all the files and directories in the current directory and the sub- directories within it in a horizontal format one page at a time.

`dir/O:N/A:H` This displays only hidden files in alphabets call order.

Changing directories CD (Change Directory) is a command used to switch directories in MSDOS.

The syntax is

```
CHDIR [drive:]\[path]
CHDIR[..]
CD [drive:]\[path]
CD[..]
```

`cd\` Goes to the highest level directory, i.e., the root directory of the drive

`cd..` Goes back one directory, i.e., moves to the parent directory. For example, the prompt `C:\WINDOWS\COMMAND>` would change over to `C:\WINDOWS>`, if `CD..` is entered.

`cd windows` Takes the computer into the Windows directory. Windows can be substituted with any other name. It is to be noted that Windows is a sub-directory under current directory.

To go to a specific directory, use absolute or relative pathname. Suppose, the computer is at `c:\riit\btech` directory. To go to the `d:\mca\fyear` directory, the command will be `CD d:\mca\fyear`

Creating a directory The MD command allows the user to create directories in MSDOS. The syntax is

```
MKDIR [drive:]path
MD [drive:]path
```

`md test` creates a directory named `test` in the current directory

`md c:\riit\btech\test` creates a directory named `test` under `c:\riit\btech`

Creating a file The command to create a particular file within the current directory is

```
C:\> COPY CON <filename>
```

Here, `CON` is a special type of device file, which represents the console. To save the content of that particular file or to specify the end of the file mark, press **^Z**. Pressing the F6 key can also perform the same function.

Copying a file The COPY command copies one or more files to another location. The syntax is as follows:

```
COPY [/V] [/N] [/Y | /-Y] [/Z] [/A | /B ] source
   [/A | /B]
[+ source [/A | /B] [+ ...]] [destination [/A |
   /B]]
```

where

source	Specifies the file or files to be copied
/A	Indicates an ASCII text file
/B	Indicates a binary file
destination	Specifies the directory and/or filename for the new file(s)
/N	Uses short filename, if available, when copying a file with a non- 8 do t3 name
/V	Verifies that new files are written correctly
/Y	Suppresses prompting to confirm user's desire to overwrite an existing destination file
/-Y	Prompts to confirm user's desire to overwrite an existing destination file

The switch /Y may be preset in the COPYCMD environment variable. This may be over-ridden with /-Y on the command line. The default is to prompt on overwrites unless the COPY command is being executed from within a batch script.

To append files, specify a single file for destination, but multiple files for source (using wildcards or file1+file2+file3 format).

1. `copy c:\riit\test.txt.` This copies a text file named `test.txt` from `c:\riit` directory to current directory.

2. `copy c:\btech\*.dat *.bak /A/V` This copies all files with extension `.dat` with the same names and extension `.bak`. DOS honors end-of-file characters in all files, appends an end-of-file character on each new file it creates and verifies the copies that are made.

3. `copy a.txt + b.txt c.txt.` This combines `a.txt` and `b.txt` into one file `c.txt`.

Deleting file/files The command DEL is used to delete files from the computer. The syntax is

```
DEL [drive:][path]filename   [/P]
```

or

```
ERASE [drive:][path]filename [/P]
```

| [drive:][path]filename | Specifies the file(s) to be deleted. Specify multiple files by using wildcards. |
| /P | Prompts for confirmation before deleting each file |

EXAMPLE

1. `del test.tmp` Deletes the file `test.tmp` in the directory that the user currently is in, if the file exists.
2. `del c:\windows\test.tmp` Deletes the file `test.tmp` in the windows directory if it exists.
3. `del c:\windows\temp\?est.tmp` `?` is a single wild character for one letter. This command would delete any file ending with `est.tmp` such as `pest.tmp` or `zest.tmp` in the sub-directory 'temp'.

Removing directory The command RD removes empty directories in MSDOS. To delete directories with files or directories within them the user must use the deltree command or if the user is running Microsoft Windows 2000 or Windows XP, the /S option has to be used.

The syntax for this command is:

```
RMDIR [drive:]\path\directory name
RD [drive:]\path\directory name
```

Windows 2000 and Windows XP syntax for remove directory command:

```
RMDIR [/S] [/Q] [drive:]\path\directory name
RD [/S] [/Q] [drive:]\path\directory name
```

| /S | Removes all directories and files in the specified directory in addition to the directory itself. Used to remove a directory tree. |
| /Q | Quiet mode; do not ask if okay to remove a directory tree with /S. |

EXAMPLE

1. `rmdir c:\test` This removes the test directory, if empty. If the user desires to delete directories that are full, the deltree command must be used.
2. `rmdir c:\test /s` Windows 2000 and Windows XP users can use this option to permanently delete the test directory, all sub-directories and files with a prompt.

Renaming file/files The command REN is used to rename files and directories.

In earlier releases of MSDOS, instead of using `ren` or `rename`, the move command was used to rename the MSDOS directories or files. The syntax for renaming a file/directory or files/directories is

```
RENAME [drive:]\[path]\[directoryname1\
filename1] filename2
REN [drive:]\[path]\[directoryname1\ filename1]
filename2
```

Note that the user cannot specify a new drive or path for the destination.

EXAMPLE

To rename the directory `chope` to `hope`, the syntax is

```
rename c:\chope hope
```

Moving files This command allows the user to move files or directories from one folder to another or from one drive to another.

The syntax for the commands that move files and rename files and directories are

(a) To move one or more files:

```
MOVE [/Y | /-Y] [drive:]\[path]\filename1
destination
```

(b) To rename a directory:

```
MOVE [/Y | /-Y] [drive:]\[path]\dirname1
dirname2
```

`[drive:]\[path]\filename1`
Specifies the location and name of the file or files the user wants to move

`destination`
Specifies the new location of the file. Destination can consist of a drive letter and colon, a directory name, or a combination. If the user is moving only one file, and desires to rename the file when it is moved, then the user can also include a filename

`[drive:]\[path]\dirname1`
Specifies the directory the user wants to rename

`dirname2`
Specifies the new name of the directory

`/Y`
Suppresses the prompt to confirm that the user wants to overwrite an existing destination file

`/-Y`
Prompts to confirm the user's desire to overwrite an existing destination file

The switch /Y may be present in the COPYCMD environment variable. This may be over ridden with /-Y on the command line. The default is to prompt on overwrites unless the MOVE command is being executed from within a batch script.

EXAMPLE

`move c:\windows\temp\*.* c:\temp` This would move the files of `c:\windows\temp` to the temp directory in the root, assuming, of course, that the directory exists.

PROMPT command

This command is used to change the prompt of the computer.

```
C:\> PROMPT <new prompt>
```

There are several options to indicate a specified prompt.

$P Indicates the path

$G Indicates the greater than sign

5.9.7 Wildcards in DOS

There is a way to select more than one file at a time through a mechanism known as wildcards or global filename characters. Wildcards give the user a way to partly specify a filename so that several files may match the specification.

Either of the wildcard symbols can be in many ways used in file specification. When a question mark is used in a file specification, for example:

```
THISNAM?
```

then it will match with any letter in that particular position of the filename. So, THISNAM? would match with any of these filenames:

```
THISNAME
THISNAM1
THISNAM$
THISNAM
```

This works as long as all the characters, excepting that in the last position of the filename, match exactly. Wildcards can be used in both the filenames and the extension parts of the complete filename.

The asterisk (*) form of the wildcard is just shorthand for several question marks. A (?) is a wild card for the single character position that it occupies in a filename, or the end of the extension. An (*) acts as if there were as many (?) as there are position left in the filename or in the extension.

An (*) in the filename stops at the end of the filename, not at the end of the extension. If the question mark form is used then the user can be specific about the following positions in the name; but not with (*).

```
*.* is same as ????????.???
```

These wildcard specifications are mainly used with four commands, DIR, DEL/ERASE, REN, and COPY.

EXAMPLE

1. del c:\windows\temp*.* *.* indicates that the user would like to delete all files in the c:\windows\temp directory.
2. The command shown here renames all text files to files with .bak extension.

   ```
   rename *.txt *.bak
   ```
3. The following command renames all files to begin with A_. The asterisk (*) in this example is an example of a wild card character because nothing was placed before or after the first asterisk. This means all files that begin with A_ would be chosen for renaming. It will rename all files with same filenames and extenstion .bak.

```
ren A_*.* *.bak
```

5.9.8 Redirection

The DOS commands direct information to certain predictable places. For example, when the command DIR is used, the output is automatically directed to the screen.

In DOS terminology, the information moves from one of its standard input devices to one of its standard output devices. The user can break these default settings of DOS by using the redirection operator. There are two redirection operators:

> output symbol, i.e., send data from here to there

< input symbol, i.e., send data from there to here

EXAMPLE

1.

```
DIR > DIRLIST. TXT
```

This means the directory listing is now stored in the file DIRLIST.TXT instead of being displayed on the screen.

But the redirection operator works only for a limited variety of information. This means that the user can not redirect file data (that is not screen output). Likewise for input, the user can only redirect input that would be coming from the keyboard and is used by the program in a standard way.

EXAMPLE

2.

```
DIR >PRN
```

In the above command, directory listing is printed on the paper through a printer. Here PRN stands for printer, which is also a standard output device.

5.9.9 Pipelines

When the user needs the output of one DOS command as the input of another command, DOS provides a handy way to make this simple.

Suppose there are two commands, ONE and TWO. ONE creates data that is needed by the command TWO. The user can apply the redirection operator to do this.

```
ONE > WORK
TWO < WORK
```

The first command writes its data into the WORK file and the second program reads back from it. This is the basic function that DOS accomplishes with pipelines. A pipeline is just an automatic way of doing what the user did with WORK, ONE, and TWO.

To create a pipeline command, just write the program names on the same command line, separated by a vertical bar (|) that is the symbol for a pipeline.

```
ONE | TWO
```

A pipeline can have as many commands in it as the user wants to. For example, consider

```
ONE | TWO | THREE | FOUR | FIVE
```

There is an obvious difference between the commands at the beginning, middle, and end of the pipeline. Unless there is something unusual going on, the first command in a pipeline would be generating data. The ones in the middle would work with the data and pass it on. This kind of command is called a filter. The last command in a pipeline could be a consumer of data and a filter. If it is so, then it passes the finished result to DOS' standard device and the result appears on the screen.

EXAMPLE

```
TREE | MORE
DIR | SORT
TYPE A.TXT | SORT
```

ATTRIB command In a DOS file, there are normally two attributes to protect it from illegal users or commands. This command can control the files attribute settings for read only, archive, and hidden.

```
ATTRIB settings filename
```

The settings are either +H or –H, +A or –A, or +R or –R to set on or off the attributes of hidden, archive, and read only. Without any settings specified, this command will list the files and show how the attributes are currently set.

PATH command The term path is already known. It means the location of a particular file or directory. To search for a particular file, it is necessary to mention the exact path of the file. But in case of programs, path also describes a list of paths DOS should search for command program files.

Normally, the search always begins in the current directory. If the program file is not found there, it will display an error message. So path is a command that sets the extended program search paths. That is, if the program file is not found in the current directory, the search continues where the PATH command says it should. When the following command is typed in

```
C:\> PATH
```

the current path setting is displayed. The following command is given if the path settings are to be changed:

```
C:\> PATH = C:\; C:\DOS; C:\FPD26
```

That is, the command line gives all the directory names where the program or executable files are present. Every directory name is separated by a semicolon (;). The following command deactivates and discontinues the extended program search:

```
C:\> PATH;
```

TREE command A disk can have numerous sub-directories branching out from the root directory. The TREE command displays a list of all the branches of the directory tree for any disk, i.e., it shows the connection between all the branches of the tree. Such a command is written as follows:

```
C:\> TREE
```

SORT command This command is used to sort a particular file with respect to its column.

```
C:\> SORT <filename>
```

To sort the file in reverse order, use /R after the SORT command as follows:

```
C:\> SORT/R <filename>
```

FIND command FIND is a command that is used to search for a particular text from a file. This command is as follows:

```
C:\> FIND "string" <filename>/<option>
```

The above command displays all the lines that contain the word specified within the double quotation mark. Most commonly used options are /C and /I.

EXAMPLE
---

1. FIND "dos" sample.txt/c. This command reports the total number of lines in sample.txt that contains the string "dos".
2. FIND "rcciit" sample.dat/I. This command ignores lettercase when searching the string "rcciit" in the file sample.txt.

DISKCOPY command This command is used to read all the formatting and data from one diskette and copy it to another diskette, making literal duplicates of the original in the process.

```
C:\> DISKCOPY <source drive> <target drive>
```

The DISKCOPY command has some major disadvantages. It does not allow for bad areas on diskettes. If either of the diskettes has unusable bad areas, DISKCOPY will not work properly. On the other hand, the COPY command, the preferred way to copy data, works well in such situations. Copy can improve the use of space on a diskette, while DISKCOPY cannot. DISKCOPY will wipe out anything that is on the target diskette, while COPY will merge new files with old ones on a diskette.

DOSKEY command This command is used to create a buffer in the memory to store all the commands that have been given after that command. Such a command is written as follows:

```
C:\> DOSKEY
```

After the above command, if the following commands are given:

```
C:\> CD 1YEAR\XYZ
C:\> TYPE ABC.TXT
```

the computer stores all the commands in the buffer sequentially. To retrieve the commands that have been given before, just press the up arrow key continuously until the target is reached.

MORE command This command is an external command. It is used to show the information on the screen page-wise. That is, if the output of a command is too long with respect to the screen, the MORE command can break the output page-wise.

ssC:\> TREE | MORE

> **Note**
> - The MSDOS operating system has been primarily designed for Personal Computers.
> - MSDOS is portable and with the Window's user interface provides the user with an effective environment for handling the programming needs and the file system.

SUMMARY

The operating system is an important component of the modern computer. It is viewed as a manager that supervises, allocates, and reclaims resources according to certain predetermined policies. The two main components of an operating system are the command interpreter and the kernel. Programs can communicate with the operating system through system calls while the user can interact by means of commands directly.

The history of development of operating systems started with the need to effectively manage the various hardware and software resources in a computer with minimum user involvement. Modern computer operating systems may be classified into three groups: batch, time-shared, and real time. UNIX, MSDOS, and Windows are three very popular operating systems. UNIX and Windows are multi-user, multitasking operating systems. On the other hand, MSDOS is a single user operating system.

Command summary

	UNIX Command	DOS Command
Creating a directory	mkdir	md
Changing current directory	cd	cd
Removing a directory	rmdir	rd
Listing the contents of a directory	ls	dir
Creating a file (without using any editor)	cat > filename	copy filename con
Opening a file (using any editor)	vi filename	edit filename
Displaying the contents of a file	cat filename	type filename
Copying a file(s)	cp	copy
Deleting a file(s)	rm	del
Moving a file(s)	mv	move
Renaming a file(s)	mv	ren

KEY TERMS

Resource In the context of a computer system, it means memory or any input / output device.

Process It is a program in execution.

File It is a data storage unit that holds information.

System programs These could be operating system, compilers, editors, loaders, utilities, etc.

Application programs These are database systems, business programs, etc.

Process management These are jobs related to the unhindered execution of programs.

Memory management An activity or a set of activities associated with allocating and de-allocating memory space.

I/O device This refers to a proper activation and de-activation of input / output device management with appropriate hardware and software.

File management A set of jobs associated with creating, retrieving, deleting, amending data storage units on storage devices and keeping track of the same.

Protection It is the mechanism for controlling the access of programs, in Operating System processes, or users to the resources in the computer.

Command interpreter It a system program, which is an essential component of the operating system, that accepts, deciphers and executes the job related to the command statement.

Kernel It is the core library of functions that provides the most basic interface between the computer machine and the rest of the operating system.

System calls It provides the interface between a running program and the operating system.

Operating system commands These are commands through which the user interacts with the operating system directly.

Batch processing These are jobs that are executed with minimum user interaction and as and when the computer system is available following a schedule.

Multiprogramming Multiprogramming refers to the situation in which a single CPU divides its time between more than one job.

Multitasking Multitasking refers to execution of more than one application program at any given time.

Time-sharing In the context of a computer, time-sharing means sharing of the computer resources among many users by allocating them for a specified time.

Multiprocessing   Any simultaneous execution of multiple processes on different processors.

Real-time   In the context of an operating system, it is an operating system that provides quick and time critical response.

Networked computing   A collection of physically interconnected computers.

Distributed computing   This refers to processing of computing jobs by automatically sharing the job-processing load among the constituent computers connected to the same network.

FREQUENTLY ASKED QUESTIONS

1. What is a file?

A file is a collection of related information defined by its creator. In general, a file is a sequence of bits, bytes, lines, or records whose meaning is defined by its creator and user.

2. What is a directory?

Directories are treated as files which keep track of all other files. The directory contains information about the files such as location and owner of the file. The directory is itself a file, owned by the operating system and accessible by various file management routines.

3. What is a kernel?

Kernel refers to that part of the operating system that implements basic functionality and is always present in memory. This is the core part of the operating system and is loaded on the main memory when it starts up.

4. What is a microkernel?

A microkernel is a tiny operating system core that provides only minimal services such as defining memory address spaces, inter-process communication methods and process, and thread management. All other features, such as hardware management or I/O locking and sharing, are implemented as processes running independently of the microkernel.

5. What is a shell?

A shell is an interactive user interface to operating system services that allows the user to interact with the system by entering commands or through a graphical user interface. Different types of shells are available in UNIX such as Bourne shell, C shell, and Korn shell.

6. What are interrupts?

Interrupt is a mechanism to draw the system's attention to perform some specific task. They are asynchronous events that result in the interruption of execution of programs in order to handle the event. Program execution is resumed (in most cases) after completion of event handling. Interrupt

Service Routine is a program that is part of operating system and determines the nature of the interrupt and performs whatever actions are needed.

7. What is a process? How does it differ from a program?

Process is a program in execution. It is considered as a unit of execution for most operating systems. A process is an active entity as opposed to a program that is passive.

8. What is spooling?

Spool is an acronym for Simultaneous Peripheral Operation On-Line. It uses the disk as a large buffer for outputting data to line printers and other devices (like tape). It can be used for input, but is generally used for output. It also helps in reducing idle time and overlapped I/O and CPU. Spooling batch systems were the first and are the simplest of the multiprogramming systems.

9. What is the difference between spooling and buffering?

Buffering is a general idea which involves using an intermediate entity between two mismatched interacting components in order to reduce the effects of the mismatch. Thus, data buffering uses the storage between two components operating at different speeds to allow both of them to operate without waiting for each other up to an extent. Buffering is used to implement spooling.

10. What is multiprogramming?

Multiprogramming means that several (at least two) processes can be active within the system during any particular time interval.

11. What is multitasking?

Multitasking lets a single user have several programs in operation at the same time. Therefore, a multitasking operation is one of the mechanisms that the multiprogramming operating system employs in managing the totality of computer-related resources such as CPU, memory, and I/O devices.

EXERCISES

1. What is an operating system? What are the functions of an operating system?
2. What are system calls? Give an example of a system call.
3. What is a kernel? What is its function? What is a microkernel?
4. Define the essential differences between spooling and buffering.
5. Define the essential differences between the following types of operating systems:
   (a) Batch operating system
   (b) Time-sharing operating system
   (c) Real-time operating system
6. What are the disadvantages of a batch processing system?
7. Explain the terms: multiprogramming, multitasking, multi-user, and multiprocessing.
8. List the main differences between the network operating system and distributed operating system.
9. Outline the stages of evaluation of a modern operating system.
10. Define process. What is the difference between a process and a program?
11. Describe the components of the UNIX system.
12. Briefly explain the file system of UNIX.
13. What is inode in UNIX?
14. What is home directory in UNIX?
15. What are absolute path and relative path? Explain with an example.

16. Write DOS and UNIX commands for the following:

(a) Create the following tree structure under `root/home` directory.

(b) Create a `file result.txt` under cse sub-directory. The contents of the file may be anything that is typed in. Save it properly.

(c) Display the contents of the file `result.txt`.

(d) Make `mca` as the current directory.

(e) Copy the `result.txt` file from the `cse` sub-directory to the current directory. Confirm the copying.

(f) Without changing the current direc- tory, create a file `abc.txt` under it.

(g) Go to the root directory.

(h) Change the current directory to home directory (for UNIX only).

(i) List the contents of the root directory. Use several options with the command and observe the output carefully.

(j) List the files with `.txt` extension under the root directory.

(k) List the files under the root directory that begin with '`r`'.

(l) Rename the file `result.txt` as `exam.dat` under mca sub-directory without changing the current directory.

(m) Change the current directory to cse.

(n) Go to the parent directory using relative path specification.

(o) Move the file `result.txt` from cse sub-directory to its sub-directory.

The Internet

After studying this chapter, the readers will be able to

- define a computer network and the Internet
- trace the evolution of the Internet
- explain the various uses and applications of the Internet

- explain the World Wide Web
- define basic Internet terminology
- differentiate the types of Internet connections
- analyse the possible threats posed by the Internet

6.1 INTRODUCTION

The Internet is best defined as 'the biggest network of computer networks on earth'. A computer network is a data communications system. It comprises hardware and software for transmitting data between computers. The hardware part of a computer network includes physical infrastructure such as wires, cables, fibre optic lines, undersea cables, and satellites. Software refers to the programs used to operate a computer network. Computer networks can be connected to other computer networks. The Internet is one such network of computer networks. It can be defined as a global network connecting millions of computers. The Internet makes it possible for any computer connected to it to send and receive data from any other computer connected to it. A hypothetical diagram of the Internet is depicted in the Fig. 6.1. The Internet

can also be referred to as a 'meta network', that is, a network of networks that spans the entire world. It is impossible to give an exact count of the number of networks or users that comprise the Internet. Computers on the Internet use the client–server architecture. The Internet employs a set of standardized protocols, which allow for the sharing of resources among different kinds of computers that communicate with each other on the network. These standards, sometimes referred to as the Internet Protocol Suite, are the rules that govern the exchange of data and communication functions for the Internet. All computers on the Internet communicate with one another using the Transmission Control Protocol/Internet Protocol suite, abbreviated as TCP/IP. These protocols are used to manage communication between computers using any type of operating system.

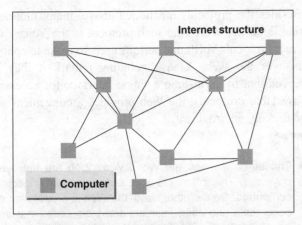

Internet structure

Computer

Fig. 6.1 Hypothetical diagram of the Internet

6.2 EVOLUTION OF INTERNET

It was way back in 1957, when the erstwhile Soviet Union, now known as the Commonwealth of Independent States (CIS), launched the first man-made satellite, named Sputnik, in space. This brought immediate concern to USA's defence and scientific establishments with visions of Soviet Union weapons placed in space capable of striking USA. Hence, USA adopted a strategy of setting up their defence establishments at different locations. Therefore, the need for establishing communication links between computers at different locations arose during that period. In 1959, the US administration formed the Advanced Research Projects Agency (ARPA) within the Pentagon to establish an American lead in military science and technology.

By the early 1960s the first theories of computer networking were shaped and in 1965, ARPA sponsored a study on 'co-operative network of time-sharing computers'. Lawrence G. Roberts, of the Massachusetts Institute of Technology (MIT), formed the first such plan in early 1967. Designs for such a network were put forward the following year and in 1968, the Pentagon sent out requests for proposals for ARPANET—a computer network to unite USA's military and scientific establishments.

Meanwhile, J.C.R. Licklider of MIT had proposed a global network of interconnected computer networks in 1962. In 1969, the ARPANET connected four universities—University of California, Los Angeles (UCLA); Stanford Research Institute; University of California, Santa Barbara (UCSB); and the University of Utah. They exchanged the first information over the new computer network. However, the system crashed several times.

In 1974, Vint Cerf joined Bob Kahn to present their 'Protocol for Packet Network Interconnection' specifying the detailed design of the Transmission Control Program (TCP)—the basis of the modern Internet. In 1975, the ARPANET was handed over to Defense Communication Agency (now

known as The Defense Information Systems Agency), and subsequently, the US military part of the ARPANET was hived off into a separate network. Another branch of the US government, the National Science Foundation (NSF), became heavily involved in Internet research and started to work on a successor to the ARPANET. The research resulted in the development of the Computer Science Network (CSNET) in 1984—the first wide area network specifically designed to use the TCP/IP to connect to ARPANET. TCP/IP, in simpler words, is a 'common universal' protocol through which the computers in a network can communicate with each other. Around this time, the term Internet was coined and adopted with a general definition as any network that adopts the TCP/IP technologies.

By the end of the 1980s, the website of CERN, the European particle research laboratory in Geneva, was one of the premier Internet sites in Europe. At that time, CERN was desperately looking for an optimum method of locating its files, documents, and other resources.

Tim Berners-Lee, a young British scientist, working as a consultant for CERN, had the answer. His 'world wide web' system assigned a common system of written addresses and hypertext links to all information. Hypertext is the organization of information units into connections that a user can make; the association is referred to as a link. In October 1990, Berners-Lee started working on a hypertext graphical user interface (GUI) browser and editor. In 1991, the first www files were made available on the Internet for download using File Transfer Protocol (FTP).

By 1993, the world was starting to wake up to the World Wide Web. In October that year, there were around 200 known HTTP servers. By 1996, the load on the first Web server at CERN was 1,000 times more than what it had been three years earlier.

Internet technology is a primitive precursor of the information superhighway, a theoretical goal of computer communications to provide schools, libraries, businesses, and homes universal access to quality information that will educate, inform, and entertain. In early 1996, the Internet interconnected more than 25 million computers in over 180 countries and continues to grow at a dramatic rate. Today, the number of Internet users is nearing the billion mark and is destined to grow further in the coming years.

6.3 WORLD WIDE WEB

The World Wide Web consists of several servers connected together to form a unified network which supports hypertext to access various Internet protocols on a single interface. It is popularly known as the Web or www. The Web operation utilizes hypertext as a primary means of accessing information. Hypertext is a document that holds information which is utilized to link the user to other documents. Such information are selected by the user and these are known as *links*. Any single hypertext document is capable of containing links to several documents. An application software, termed the Web browser, residing on computers are responsible to interpret and display text, graphics, etc. present in the Web document. A software, known as *Web server*, installed at the remote computer receives the requests for Web documents and responds by sending them over the Internet to the Web browser resident on the user's computer from where the request was sent by clicking hyperlinks or specifying addresses.

The World Wide Web was developed by Tim Berners-Lee of CERN in 1989. Initially, the purpose of World Wide Web was to provide suitable communication between its members, spread over various countries, by using networked hypertext. The following facilities are supported by www:

Multimedia information Includes textual document, pictures, movies, sound, programs, etc.

Hypertext information Refers to information that links to other information resources.

Graphic user interface Enables users to point and click for requested information instead of typing in text commands.

The Hypertext Markup Language (HTML) is used to develop documents for the Web.

Using HTML, tags are put within the text to accomplish document formatting, visual features like font size, bold or italics, and develop the hypertext links. Graphics may also be created in an HTML document. Led by web founder Tim Berners-Lee, the World Wide Web Consortium (W3C) assists the efforts for standardizing HTML.

Nearly all protocol type obtainable on the Internet may be accessible on the Web. Each Internet protocol is a set of rules that is followed for establishing communication between machines connected to the Internet. Some of the frequently used protocols that are available on the web are:

Simple mail transport protocol or SMTP Popularly known as e-mail, this protocol manages the delivery and receipt of electronic messages and files between one or more electronic mail-boxes.

Telnet protocol Known as just "Telnet", it allows the user to login to a host computer to execute requested commands.

File transfer protocol Generally termed "FTP", this protocol manages the transfer of text or binary files between an FTP server and client.

Network news transfer protocol or NNTP Also called "Usenet", this protocol manages the distribution of news articles prepared from topical discussions on newsgroups.

Hypertext transfer protocol Better known as "HTTP", it is a protocol that is responsible for transmitting hypertext through the networks and also handle the details needed to retrieve documents.

Besides the protocols mentioned above, many more are available on the Web. One such protocol is the Voice over Internet Protocol (VoIP) that permits users to make telephone calls over the Web. As a concluding remark it may be observed that by furnishing a single interface for accessing all available protocols, the Web provides a convenient and user-friendly environment.

Note

- The terms Internet and World Wide Web are not synonymous. The Internet is a collection of interconnected computers. On the other hand, the Web is a collection of documents and other interconnected resources that are accessible by means of hyperlink and addresses.

6.4 BASIC INTERNET TERMINOLOGY

6.4.1 Web Page

Web page is the basic unit of information available on the Web. The World Wide Web consists of files, known as pages or web pages, containing information and links to resources throughout the Internet. A website is a set of intimately connected web pages which are inter-linked by logical pointers called *hyperlinks*. Generally, a single page is designed as the website's home page. This home page is the entry point comprising of a content list or index for people to view the request information on this website and may also provide leads to other websites containing again a set of web pages that holds the desired subject matter.

6.4.2 Web Browser

A Web browser or, in short, a browser is an application program that makes the content on the Internet viewable. It interprets the HTML code embedded within the Web page and converts the data of the Internet in the graphical interface that one sees on a website and displays and plays all elements such as images, sounds, motion, and other features of a website at their designated positions. Web browsers provide the way to send request for a web page by specifying its internet address that is processed by the corresponding web server. The Web server residing at remote computer sends the desired web page to the browser. There are two types of browsers—graphical and text.

Graphical browser Text, images, audio, and video are retrievable through a graphical software program such as Internet Explorer, Firefox, Netscape, Mozilla, and Opera. These browsers are available for Windows, Apple, Linux, and other operating systems. Pointing and clicking with a mouse on highlighted words and graphics accomplish navigation.

Text browser It is a browser that provides access to the web only in the text mode. Navigation is accomplished by highlighting emphasized words in the screen with the arrow up and down keys, and then pressing the forward arrow (or Enter) key to follow the link. One example of such a browser is the Lynx text mode browser. In this era of graphical browsers, it may be hard to believe that Lynx was once very popular.

6.4.3 Web Server

A Web server is an application program that runs on the host computer and manages the web pages stored on the website's repository. Its purpose is to provide the information and services to the Web users. Typically, users can request an initial web page, known as home page, from the Web server through the browser that displays the page. Once the home page is displayed, the user can begin *surfing* the Web. The process of looking at different things on the Internet is known as *surfing*. Whenever the mouse pointer is clicked on a hyperlink, a page request is sent by it through the browser, at the client end, to the Web server of the desired page. In return, the Web server sends a copy of the requested page to the client's browser. The browser, at the client end, receives the page and then displays it.

6.4.4 Internet Service Provider

An *Internet Service Provider* (ISP) is an establishment that offers Internet access against monthly or annual subscription to its customers who might be an individual, organizations, or smaller ISPs. Some of the major ISPs in India are NICNet, VSNL, Satyam, and so on.

6.4.5 Gateway

A network node that works as an entrance to some other network is called a gateway. A node or a stopping junction, in the Internet jargon, may be a host node or a gateway node. The host node is an end point node. The computers that serve the pages on the Internet on request and the Internet users computers are termed as host nodes. On the other hand, the gateway nodes are computers that regulate the information traffic within an organization's network or an Internet Service Provider's (ISP) network. Generally, *Transmission Control Protocol*/Internet Protocol (TCP/IP) is used by the Internet to transfer information. To identify individual nodes on the Internet and also on LANs, a low-level protocol, called IP, is used. At a given time, each node on the Internet is assigned a number which is called the IP address. Since it is difficult for the user to remember an IP address, each node is allotted a *domain name* using which a corresponding IP address can be obtained. In the current scenario, instead of assigning permanent IP address to a user, the moment the user's computer gets connected to the Internet, the computer at the user's ISP allocates a temporary IP address from a range of addresses assigned to that ISP. These are known as dynamic IPs. On the other-hand, TCP works at a different level over the IP and provides features like message tracking, error checking, and retransmitting. Since IP does not have any error checking feature, TCP is used alongside IP to provide reliable transmission from sender to receiver.

> **Note**
>
> - HTTP is the basic communication protocol for providing Web services. It ensures that all parts of the web page are delivered. Web servers and Web browsers communicate via HTTP. Web users request services through Web browser. Web servers deliver the information and services that are requested by Web users. Web browser decides how these items are displayed. Web document files are made available on the Internet for download using File Transfer Protocol (FTP).

6.4.6 URL

URL is the abbreviation of *Uniform Resource Locator*. It provides a uniform way of identifying resources that are available at host computer (The computer on which a website is physically located). It specifies the Internet address of a file stored on the host computer connected to the Internet. Web browsers use the URL to retrieve a file from host computer. The simplest format for a URL is as follows.

$$protocol://host/path/filename$$

where

Protocol

Protocol is a mutually agreed set of rules or methods for transmitting data between two devices. Here the term 'protocol' means the HTTP, which designates the Web's standard communications protocol through which a client establishes a TCP connection to the host server for the resource to be accessed. The double slash (//) indicates that the protocol uses the format defined by the Common Internet Scheme Syntax (CISS). Apart from http, other protocols available include ftp, gopher, and mailto.

Host

It specifies a particular host on the Internet by a unique numeric identifier, known as an IP address or by a unique name that can be resolved into the IP address. The *domain* is a set of nodes that are administered as a unit. The *domain name* is the hierarchical name assigned to a host address using the Domain Name System (DNS). A domain name consists of two to four words separated by dots. Starting from the right is a *top-level domain name*, such as com for commercial. The top-level domain names are assigned by the Internet Corporation for Assigned Names and Numbers (ICANN). An organization's domain name is assigned to a host computer that is linked to the Internet. Every domain name has a suffix that indicates the purpose for which it is used. The most widespread domain suffix is '.com' and even though it stands for commercial, it is used by many non-commercial websites as well. Also, every country has a specific suffix. A few examples are as follows

.com—this identifies a business enterprise (commercial)

.us—this is intended for use by US websites

.de—this is intended for use by German websites

.org—this identifies an organization

.edu—this identifies an educational organization

.gov—this identifies a government agency

Path

This is the location of a file or a program (JSP, PHP, Perl, CGI, etc.) on the server relative to a document root specified by the Web server. The document root is a directory where resources are stored.

Figure 6.2 provides a suitable explanation for the URL.

Fig. 6.2 Description of URL

For physical transmission of a message to the destination node, its physical Media Access Control (MAC) address is required. MAC address is a unique built-in number that permanently identifies a network adapter of a computer. The Address Resolution Protocol (ARP) translates the IP address to a MAC address. The message is then routed to the destination computer. Internet address translation is depicted in Fig. 6.3.

Fig. 6.3 Internet address translation

6.4.7 Search Engines

Search engines are application programs that allow searching the Web by typing in a topic of interest. Examples of search engines used are—Google, HotBot, Altavista, etc. These search engines find exact matches from what has been typed in the search screen to either documents (files) or subjects of files on the www. Different search engines have different ways of categorizing and indexing information. Typing in the URL of that engine or using a browser's compilation of search engines in its Internet search function accesses search engines.

> **Note**
>
> - The *webpage* is a basic unit of information available on the web. A website is a set of web pages inter-connected by hyperlink and URL. A web browser or, in short, a browser is an application program that makes the content of a web page viewable. HTTP is the basic communication protocol through which a browser establishes a TCP connection to the host server for the resource to be accessed. Web users request services through web browser. Web document files can be downloaded using File Transfer Protocol (FTP).
> - An *Internet Service Provider* (ISP) is a company that offers Internet access to its customers. Each time the computer is connected to the Internet, the ISP provides a temporary IP to the computer. IP is a low-level protocol that is used to identify each internet node. Internet typically uses TCP/IP alongside IP to provide reliable transmission on the internet. Web browsers use the URL to retrieve the resources from host computer.

6.5 TYPES OF INTERNET CONNECTIONS

6.5.1 Dial-up Connection

The most general type of Internet connections, available from ISPs, are the dial-up connections that use a telephone line to transmit and receive data. It blocks the telephone line and is the slowest and the most inexpensive among the different types of available Internet connections. This type of connection permits the user to connect to the Internet through a local server using an analog modem and the Public Switched Telephone Network. To get connected to the Internet, the PC literally dials a phone number, provided by the ISP and connects to the local server. The maximum data rate with dial-up access is 56 Kbps (56,000 bits per second), but technologies such as Integrated Services Digital Network (ISDN), which uses the Public Switched Telephone Network, provide faster data rates of 128 Kbps.

Phone line

Computer

The Internet

Internet service

Internet Service Provider (ISP)

Modem

Fig. 6.4 Dial-up connection

6.5.2 Leased Lines

An alternative way to connect computers to the Internet is through a leased line, which is a dedicated wire or an optical fibre cable or a wireless channel that directly connects them to the Internet using Public Switched Telephone Network. Leased lines provide faster throughput and better quality connections, but they are more expensive. These are mostly used by large business houses and big establishments.

Another old technology, known as the T-carrier lines, is also available as leased lines. Under this category the fractional T1/T3 lines provide data rates between 56 and 1,500 kbit/s. Some types of special termination equipment are necessary for such lines. These are installed in some multi-resident dwellings, fractional. T1/T3 lines are typically underground fibre or copper cables that connect directly to the service provider, with individual home connections switched over Ethernet cables.

6.5.3 Digital Subscriber Line (DSL)

This is a connection using a phone line and a special modem. The modem does not interfere with the normal telephone operation. Most connections average about 400–650K per second in download (some are faster), while some average about 128–256K per second upload speed as well.

6.5.4 Satellite Internet

A satellite Internet connection is a system in which a computer receives(downloads) and sends(uploads) data streams through a satellite. In such a connection, every user computer is provided with a transmitter-receiver unit and a satellite dish antenna. The upstream data transfer rate is much less than the down-stream rate in these systems.

In areas where DSL or any other type of wire internet connections are difficult to reach, the satellite internet connection is the only option for accessing the Internet. For people in the rural areas and those living on hilly areas or in

places where the basic utilities are lacking satellite Internet connection is an effective means of availing the Internet. However such systems are expensive and are slower than the land-based systems.

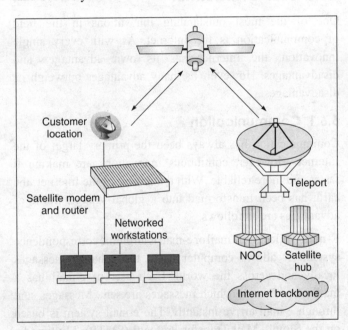

Customer location

Satellite modem and router

Networked workstations

Teleport

NOC

Satellite hub

Internet backbone

Fig. 6.5 Internet via satellite

6.5.5 Broadband Versus Power Line

Broadband over Power Line (BPL) supports Internet connections over residential power lines. The technology behind power line BPL works analogous to phone line DSL, using unused signalling space on the wire to transmit the Internet traffic. BPL requires specialized (but not expensive) equipment to connect to a home network.

6.5.6 Cable Modem Broadband

Cable modem broadband is a connection through an ordinary coax cable through the user's digital cable provider and is the easiest and most common way to connect to the Internet at high speeds. Most connections average about 400K/second download and 128K upload. A cable's biggest advantage is its availability and ability to produce multiple upstream (when sending). Cable connections are always on; eliminating long waits to make a connection. Cable connections are not available in every area; the users will need to contact a cable company of their choice to ensure that they have coverage.

6.5.7 Other forms of Internet Connectivity

Cellular Internet Mobile Internet connections can be made over digital cell phones. Due to high costs, cellular Internet is usually used in homes only during emergencies.

Wireless Broadband Internet WiMax technology supports high-speed wireless Internet via base stations such as cellular networks. The WiFi community or 'mesh' networks serve a similar function using different technologies.

6.6 USES OF INTERNET

One of the most outstanding innovations in the field of communication is the Internet. As with every single innovation, the Internet has its own advantages and disadvantages. However, its many advantages outweigh its disadvantages.

6.6.1 Communication

Communication has always been the primary target of the Internet. However, continuous innovations are making it faster and more reliable. With the advent of the Internet, the earth has been transformed into a global village. Some of advantages are as follows.

E-mail Electronic mail or e-mail is an online correspondence system. It allows computer users to exchange messages locally and across the world. Each user of e-mail has a mailbox address to which messages are sent. Messages sent through e-mail arrive instantly. The e-mail system is based on the Simple Mail Transfer Protocol (SMTP). Multimedia Internet Mail Extension (MIME) was originally developed to help e-mail software handle a variety of binary (non-ASCII) file attachments. The use of MIME has expanded to the Web.

Chat and Instant messaging Chat programs allow users to communicate with each other through the Internet by typing in real time. Sometimes, they are included as a feature of a website, where users can log into chat rooms to exchange remarks and information about the topics addressed on the site. Chat may take many other wide-ranging forms. For example, America Online is well-known for sponsoring a number of topical chat rooms. Internet Relay Chat (IRC) is a service through which participants can communicate with

each other on hundreds of channels. The discussions on these channels are generally based on specific topics. To access IRC, a user must use an IRC software program. A variation of chat is the phenomenon of instant messaging. With instant messaging, a user on the Web can contact another logged-in user and start a conversation. One of the most popular Internet relay chat sites is America Online's (AOL) instant messenger. ICQ, MSN, and Yahoo also offer chat programs.

Telnet It is a program which assists the user to get connected with computers on the Internet and access chat services, library catalogues, online databases, etc. However, Telnet sessions use graphics and not text. To get connected on to a computer using Telnet, the user must know its address. This can consist of words (judde.ac.in) or numbers (.140.147.254.3). Some services require the specification of a specific port on the remote computer. In such a case, the user has to type the port number after the Internet address. A link to a Telnet resource may appear like any other link, but it will launch a Telnet session to provide the connection. In order to work, a Telnet program must be installed on the user's local computer and configured to his or her Web browser. With the popularity of the Web, Telnet is less frequently used as a means of access to information on the Internet.

6.6.2 Information

The biggest advantage the Internet offers is probably information. It is a virtual treasure trove of information. Any kind of information on any topic is available on the Internet.

Search engines such as Google, Yahoo!, and others help in retrieving information from the Internet. People can get almost any type of data on almost any kind of subject that they are looking for. There is a massive amount of information available on the Internet on just about every subject known to man—ranging from government law and services, market information, technical support, new ideas, trade fairs and conferences, etc.

Usenet news is a collection of news groups that have nothing to do with news. Usenets are ongoing discussion groups on the Internet, among people who share mutual interest. Usenet News is a global electronic bulletin board system in which millions of computer users exchange information on a vast range of topics. The major difference between Usenet News and e-mail discussion groups is the fact that Usenet messages are stored on central computers, and users must connect with these computers to read or download the messages posted to these groups. This is distinct from email distribution, in which messages arrive in the electronic mailboxes of each listed member. Usenet itself is a set of machines that exchange messages or articles from Usenet discussion forums, known as newsgroups. Usenet administrators control their own sites, and decide which (if any) newsgroups to sponsor and which remote newsgroups to allow into the system.

Web blog or simply blog is a new form of online update-able diary that can be created with the help of the Internet. Many people, groups of people, and organizations post their information or knowledge or their views, etc. to share. It has organizational and personal roles. Blogger provides one of the most popular and oldest web blog services which have been owned by google since 2003.

Students and children are among the major users who surf the Internet for research purposes. Today, it is essential for students to access the Internet for research and for gathering resources. Teachers give assignments that require research on the Internet. Due to the Internet, it has now become possible to locate information on ever-changing fields such as medical research. Numerous websites available on the Internet offer loads of information for people to research about diseases and discuss health issues with online doctors. During 1998, over 20 million people were reported to have used online resources to retrieve information about health issues.

6.6.3 Entertainment

Many people prefer to surf the Internet in search of entertainment. In fact, the Internet has become quite successful in providing multifaceted entertainment options. Some of the uses people have discovered are—downloading games, visiting chat rooms, or just surfing the Web. There are lots of games that may be downloaded from the Internet for free. The online gaming industry has tasted dramatic success due to the phenomenal interest shown by game lovers. Chat rooms are popular because users can meet new and interesting people. News, music, hobbies, and many more areas of interest can be found and shared on the Internet. Apart from these, there are plenty of messenger services to facilitate this. With the help of such services, it has become very easy to establish global friendship where people can share their thoughts. Social networking websites such as Facebook, and MySpace extend the new form of interactions that outspreads socialization.

6.6.4 Services

Many services are now provided on the Internet such as job seeking, guidance services on a variety of topics, online banking, online share trading, purchasing tickets for movies, and hotel reservations. Some of these services may not be available off-line and can cost less if purchased online.

6.6.5 E-commerce

The concept of any type of commercial activity or business deal that involves the transfer of information across the globe through the Internet is known as e-commerce. It has become a phenomenon that is associated with any type of online business transaction. E-commerce, with its giant tentacles engulfing every single product and service, will make almost all services and products available at one's doorstep. It covers an amazing and wide range of products from household needs to technology and entertainment.

> **Note**
> - A computer can be connected to the Internet through modem or another communication channel (DSL or ISDN or broadband etc.). The Internet Service Provider (ISP) provides the infrastructure and communication software for Internet access.
> - Services available on the Internet include instant access to online information, e-mail and chat, remote access to the computer for file sharing and collaborative work, leisure activities, online services and voice telephony, and many more.

6.7 HAZARDS OF INTERNET

Despite the numerous advantages of the Internet, it also endures the security and protection hazards, some of which are discussed as follows:

- *Virus* is a piece of code which on execution disrupts the normal functioning of computer systems. Computers attached to the Internet are more susceptible to virus attacks which can end up with mischievous behaviour or crashing the system.
- Hackers utilize one type of virus called *Trojans* to gain access to the computer to intercept personal or secret information (such as password, credit card number) there by invading users' privacy, or use the intended victim's computer for their purposes.
- *Spamming* refers to sending unsolicited bulk e-mails, which provide no purpose and needlessly obstruct the entire system.

Such illegal activities can be very frustrating for the users, and so instead of just ignoring them, they should make an effort to try and stop these activities so that using the Internet can become much safer.

Internet addiction is another important menace to the society. the Internet has established its potential for encompassing new forms of social interactions and leisure activities. Websites like Facebook, Orkut, and Myspace have shaped socialization in such a dimension that people especially students get addicted to surfing the Internet.

Pornography There are thousands of pornographic sites on the Internet that can be easily accessed; hence, children should use the Internet with parental supervision.

SUMMARY

Computer network is a data communications system made up of hardware and software that transmits data from one computer to another. Computer networks can connect to other computer networks to get an even bigger computer network. The Internet can be defined as a worldwide network connecting millions of computers. It employs a set of standardized protocols, which allow for the sharing of resources among different kinds of computers that communicate with each other on the network. In 1969, the ARPANET connected four universities (UCLA, Stanford Research Institute, UCSB, and the University of Utah) and exchanged the first information over the new computer network. In 1974, Vint Cerf joined Bob Kahn to present 'Protocol for Packet Network Interconnection' specifying the detailed design of the 'Transmission Control Program' (TCP)—the basis of the modern Internet. All computers on the Internet communicate with one another using the Transmission Control Protocol/Internet Protocol suite (TCP/IP). Tim Berners-Lee, a young British scientist at CERN, devised a better way of locating all the files, documents, and other resources. His World Wide Web system assigned a common system of written addresses and hypertext links to all information. In 1991 the first www files were made available on the Internet for download using File Transfer Protocol (FTP). The Internet is one of the most outstanding innovations in the field of communication. It provides a means to communicate between people located at various places. The biggest advantage the Internet offers is information. Any kind of information on any topic is available on the Internet. Many people prefer to surf the Internet in search of entertainment. The Internet also covers an amazing and wide range of services catering to household needs, technology, and entertainment. The world wide web (www) is a system of Internet servers that supports hypertext to access several Internet protocols on a single interface. The operation of the Web relies primarily on hypertext as its means of information retrieval. Hypertext is a document containing words that connect to other documents. Almost every protocol type available on the Internet is accessible on the Web. Internet protocols are sets of rules that allow for inter-machine communication on the Internet. Some of these major protocols accessible on the Web are SMTP, Telnet, FTP, Usenet, and HTTP. The different types of Internet connections are Digital Subscriber Link (DSL), Dial-up, Satellite Internet, Broadband over Power Line (BPL), Cable Modem Broadband, and other forms of Internet connectivity. There are some drawbacks of the Internet. It is prone to the spreading of unwanted messages and damaging programs. The unwanted messages are known as spam, while the damaging programs are known as viruses. The Internet also contains information unsuitable for children. However, the Internet is a wonderful and powerful tool for people, who want to use it for communication and exchange of information.

KEY TERMS

Browser   It is a program for accessing the Internet.

Domain   It is a set of nodes that are administered as a unit.

Download   It means transferring of file from the Internet to the local computer.

Host   The computer on which a website is physically located is referred to as a host.

http   Hypertext Transfer Protocol (HTTP) is the protocol of the Web to handle the details needed to retrieve documents.

hypertext   It is the organization of information units into connected associations that a user can choose to make.

Internet Protocol   It is a set of rules that govern the exchange of data and communication functions for the Internet.

ISP   An *Internet Service Provider* (ISP) is an organization which offers Internet access against monthly or annual subscription to its customers.

TCP/IP   Transmission Control Protocol/Internet Protocol is used to manage communication between computers using any type of operating system.

Upload   It means transferring files from a local computer to another remote computer through the Internet.

URL   It provides a uniform way of identifying the Internet address of a resource stored on a host computer connected to the Internet.

VoIP   Voice over Internet Protocol (VoIP) allows users to place a telephone call over the Web.

website   It is a collection of viewable 'www files' stored on one or more computers connected to the Internet.

www   World Wide Web (www) is a system that assigns a common system of written addresses and hypertext links to all information.

FREQUENTLY ASKED QUESTIONS

1. What is browsing?

Viewing information and documents in the Internet is known as browsing.

2. Explain hyperlink, hypertext, and hypermedia.

A website is a set of closely related web pages that are interconnected by logical pointers known as *hyperlink*. On clicking a hyperlink (usually underlined), the linked document can be accessed or displayed on the browser. It is used as a cross-referencing to other documents on the Web. This creates a non-linear form of text, known as *hypertext*. Web pages can also contain hyperlinked multimedia content that are named as *hypermedia*.

3. What is a Web server?

A Web server is a computer in which a software program is running to provide Web services. The software manages the HTTP whereabouts and makes the information stored on the Web server accessible through the Web.

4. What is a web page?

Web page is a digital document file, created and designed using Hyper Text Markup Language (HTML) that can be accessed using Web browser. HTML is the standard language to design a web page. It defines the way information, pictures, and other elements of the web page would be displayed regardless of the browser used or the type of computer.

5. What is meant by home page of a website?

A website is composed of several web pages. The first or opening page of a website is known as the home page. It is similar to the table of contents in a book.

6. What is an ISP?

ISP stands for Internet Service Provider. ISP is a company that delivers a point of access to the Internet against monthly or annual subscription to an individual, organization, and smaller ISPs.

Each ISP maintains a network of routers and communication links for providing access to the Internet.

7. What is a search engine?

Search engine is a Web server that collects data from other Web servers into a database. The database is used to provide links to the web pages containing the information that the user is looking for.

EXERCISES

1. What is the Internet?
2. What functions does an Internet Service Provider (ISP) perform?
3. How is a workstation on a local network linked to the Internet?
4. What is a domain?
5. What is domain name system (DNS)?
6. What is an IP address? Explain the significance of each of the numbers in an IP address.
7. Explain how the DNS maps a domain name to an IP address.
8. What is a protocol?
9. What is Transmission Control Protocol/Internet Protocol (TCP/IP)?
10. What is a browser? How does a browser work?
11. What is a Uniform Resource Locator (URL)?
12. What is a search engine?

Introduction to Algorithms and Programming Concepts

LEARNING OBJECTIVES

After studying this chapter, the readers will be able to

- explain algorithms and the key features of an algorithm—sequence, decision, and repetition
- learn the different ways of stating algorithms—step-form, flowchart, etc.
- define variables, types of variables, and naming conventions for variables
- decide a strategy for designing algorithms

- explain the concept of tracing the correctness of an algorithm
- discuss the method of implementing an algorithm in a program
- explain structural programming and the process of programming

7.1 ALGORITHMS

To solve any problem a plan is needed. This plan is a procedure to solve the problem in question. The procedure has to be based on definite reasoning and logic to obtain a result. How can such plans be formed? The following sections discuss the various ways a procedure-wise plan can be made to solve any problem.

7.1.1 What is an Algorithm?

Computer scientist Niklaus Wirth stated that

Program = Algorithms + Data

An algorithm is a part of the plan for the computer program. In fact, an algorithm is 'an effective procedure for solving a problem in a finite number of steps'.

It is effective, which means that an answer is found and it has a finite number of steps. A well-designed algorithm will always provide an answer; it may not be the desired answer but there will be an answer. It may be that the answer is that there is no answer. A well-designed algorithm is also guaranteed to terminate.

7.1.2 Different Ways of Stating Algorithms

Algorithms may be represented in various ways. There are four ways of stating algorithms.
These are as follows:

- Step-form
- Pseudo-code
- Flowchart

• Nassi-Schneiderman

In the step-form representation, the procedure of solving a problem is stated with written statements. Each statement solves a part of the problem and these together complete the solution. The step-form uses just normal language to define each procedure. Every statement, that defines an action, is logically related to the preceding statement. This algorithm has been discussed in the following section with the help of an example.

The pseudo-code is a written form representation of the algorithm. However, it differs from the step form as it uses a restricted vocabulary to define its action of solving the problem. One problem with human language is that it can seem to be imprecise. But the pseudo-code, which is in human language, tends toward more precision by using a limited vocabulary.

Flowchart and Nassi-Schneiderman are graphically oriented representation forms. They use symbols and language to represent sequence, decision, and repetition actions. Only the flowchart method of representing the problem solution has been explained with several examples. The Nassi-Schneiderman technique is beyond the scope of this book.

> **Note**
>
> • An algorithm is an effective procedure for solving a problem in a finite number of steps.
> • A program is composed of algorithm and data.
> • The four common ways of representing an algorithm are the step-form, pseudo-code, flowchart, and Nassi-Schneiderman.

7.1.3 Key Features of an Algorithm and the Step-form

Here is an example of an algorithm, for making a pot of tea.

1. If the kettle does not contain water, then fill the kettle.
2. Plug the kettle into the power point and switch it on.
3. If the teapot is not empty, then empty the teapot.
4. Place tea leaves in the teapot.
5. If the water in the kettle is not boiling, then go to step 5.
6. Switch off the kettle.
7. Pour water from the kettle into the teapot.

It can be seen that the algorithm has a number of steps and that some steps (steps 1, 3, and 5) involve decision-making and one step (step 5 in this case) involves repetition, in this case the process of waiting for the kettle to boil.

From this example, it is evident that algorithms show these three features:

• Sequence (also known as process)
• Decision (also known as selection)

• Repetition (also known as iteration or looping)

Therefore, an algorithm can be stated using three basic constructs: sequence, decision, and repetition.

Sequence

Sequence means that each step or process in the algorithm is executed in the specified order. In the above example, each process must be in the proper place otherwise the algorithm will fail.

The decision constructs—if ... then, if ... then ... else...

In algorithms the outcome of a decision is either true or false; there is no state in between. The outcome of the decision is based on some condition that can only result in a true or false value. For example,

if today is Friday then collect pay

is a decision and the decision takes the general form:

if proposition then process

A proposition, in this sense, is a statement, which can only be true or false. It is either true that 'today is Friday' or it is false that 'today is not Friday'. It can not be both true and false. If the proposition is true, then the process or procedure that follows the then is executed. The decision can also be stated as:

if proposition

  then process1

else process2

This is the if ... then ... else ... form of the decision. This means that if the proposition is true then execute process1, else, or otherwise, execute process2.

The first form of the decision if proposition then process has a null else, that is, there is no else.

The repetition constructs—repeat and while

Repetition can be implemented using constructs like the repeat loop, while loop, and if.. then .. goto .. loop.

The Repeat loop is used to iterate or repeat a process or sequence of processes until some condition becomes true. It has the general form:

Repeat

  Process1

  Process2

  ....

  ....

  ProcessN

Until proposition

Here is an example.

Repeat

  Fill water in kettle

Until kettle is full

The process is 'Fill water in kettle,' the proposition is 'kettle is full'.

The Repeat loop does some processing before testing the state of the proposition.

What would happen if in the above example the kettle is already full? If the kettle is already full at the start of the Repeat loop, then filling more water will lead to an overflow.

This is a drawback of the Repeat construct.

In such a case the `while` loop is more appropriate. The above example with the `while` loop is shown as follows:

```
while kettle is not full
        fill water in kettle
```

Since the decision about the kettle being full or not is made before filling water, the possibility of an overflow is eliminated. The while loop finds out whether some condition is true before repeating a process or a sequence of processes.

If the condition is false, the process or the sequence of processes is not executed. The general form of `while` loop is:

```
while proposition
begin
Process 1
Process 2
...........
...........
Process N
end
```

The `if .. then goto ..` is also used to repeat a process or a sequence of processes until the given proposition is false. In the kettle example, this construct would be implemented as follows:

1. Fill some water in kettle
2. `if` kettle not full `then goto` 1

So long as the proposition 'kettle not full' is true the process, 'fill some water in kettle' is repeated. The general form of `if .. then goto ..` is:

```
Process1
Process2
..........
..........
ProcessN
if proposition then goto Process1
```

Termination

The definition of algorithm cannot be restricted to procedures that eventually finish. Algorithms might also include procedures that could run forever without stopping. Such a procedure has been called a computational method by Knuth or calculation procedure or algorithm by Kleene. However, Kleene notes that such a method must eventually exhibit 'some object.' Minsky (1967) makes the observation that, if an algorithm has not terminated, then how can the following question be answered: "Will it terminate with the correct answer?" Thus the answer is: undecidable. It can never be

known, nor can the designer do an analysis beforehand to find it out. The analysis of algorithms for their likelihood of termination is called termination analysis.

Correctness

The prepared algorithm needs to be verified for its correctness. Correctness means how easily its logic can be argued to satisfy the algorithm's primary goal. This requires the algorithm to be made in such a way that all the elements in it are traceable to the requirements.

Correctness requires that all the components like the data structures, modules, external interfaces, and module interconnections are completely specified.

In other words, correctness is the degree to which an algorithm performs its specified function. The most common measure of correctness is defects per Kilo Lines of Code (KLOC) that implements the algorithm, where defect is defined as the verified lack of conformance to requirements.

> **Note**
> - The key features of an algorithm are sequence, selection, and repetition.
> - The stepwise form has sequence, selection, and repetition constructs.
> - Termination means the action of closing. A well-designed algorithm has a termination.
> - Correctness of algorithm means how easily its logic can be argued to meet the algorithm's primary goal.

7.1.4 What are Variables?

So long, the elements of algorithm have been discussed. But a program comprises of algorithm and data. Therefore, it is now necessary to understand the concept of data. It is known that data is a symbolic representation of value and that programs set the context that gives data a proper meaning. In programs, data is transformed into information. The question is, how is data represented in programs?

Almost every algorithm contains data and usually the data is 'contained' in what is called a variable. The variable is a container for a value that may vary during the execution of the program. For example, in the tea-making algorithm, the level of water in the kettle is a variable, the temperature of the water is a variable, and the quantity of tea leaves is also a variable.

Each variable in a program is given a name, for example,

- Water_Level
- Water_Temperature
- Tea_Leaves_Quantity

and at any given time the value, which is represented by Water_Level, for instance, may be different to its value at some other time. The statement if the kettle does not contain water then fill the kettle could also be written as

if Water_Level is 0 then fill the kettle

or

if Water_Level = 0 then fill the kettle

At some point Water_Level will be the maximum value, whatever that is, and the kettle will be full.

Variables and data types

The data used in algorithms can be of different types. The simplest types of data that an algorithm might use are

- numeric data, e.g., 12, 11.45, 901, etc.
- alphabetic or character data such as 'A', 'Z', or 'This is alphabetic'
- logical data, that is, propositions with true/false values

Naming of variables

One should always try to choose meaningful names for variables in algorithms to improve the readability of the algorithm or program. This is particularly important in large and complex programs.

In the tea-making algorithm, plain English was used. It has been shown how variable names may be used for some of the algorithm variables. In Table 7.1, the right-hand column contains variable names which are shorter than the original and do not hide the meaning of the original phrase. Underscores have been given to indicate that the words belong together and represent a variable.

Table 7.1 Algorithm using variable names

Algorithm in plain English	Algorithm using variable names
1. If the kettle does not contain water, then fill the kettle.	1. If kettle_empty then fill the kettle.
2. Plug the kettle into the power point and switch it on.	2. Plug the kettle into the power point and switch it on.
3. If the teapot is not empty, then empty the teapot.	3. If teapot_not_empty then empty the teapot.
4. Place tea leaves in the teapot.	4. Place tea leaves in the teapot.
5. If the water in the kettle is not boiling then go to step 5.	5. If water_not_boiling then go to step 5.
6. Switch off the kettle.	6. Switch off the kettle.
7. Pour water from the kettle into the teapot.	7. Pour water from the kettle into the teapot.

There are no hard and fast rules about how variables should be named but there are many conventions. It is a good idea to adopt a conventional way of naming variables.

The algorithms and programs can benefit from using naming conventions for processes too.

> **Note**
> - Data is a symbolic representation of value.
> - A variable, which has a name, is a container for a value that may vary during the execution of the program.

7.1.5 Subroutines

A simple program is a combination of statements that are implemented in a sequential order. A statement block is a group of statements. Such a program is shown in Fig. 7.1(a). There might be a specific block of statement, which is also known as a procedure, that is run several times at different points in the implementation sequence of the larger program. This is shown in Fig.7.1(b). Here, this specific block of statement is named 'procedure X'. In this example program, the 'procedure X' is written twice in this example. This enhances the size of the program. Since this particular procedure is required to be run at two specific points in the implementation sequence of the larger program, it may be treated as a separate entity and not included in the main program. In fact, this procedure may be called whenever required as shown in Fig.7.1(c). Such a procedure is known as a subroutine.

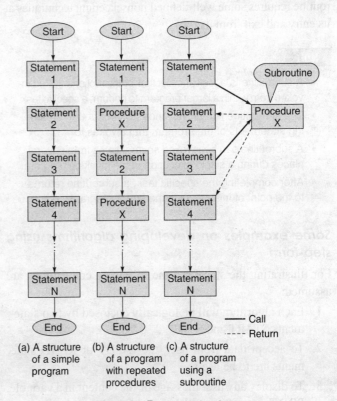

Fig. 7.1 Program structures

Therefore, a subroutine, also known as procedure, method or function, is a portion of instruction that is invoked from within a larger program to perform a specific task. At the same time the subroutine is relatively independent of the remaining statements of the larger program. The subroutine behaves in much the same way as a program that is used as one step in a larger program. A subroutine is often written so that it can be started ("called") several times and/or from several places during a single execution of the program, including from other subroutines, and then branch back (*return*) to the next instruction after the "call", once the subroutine's task is done. Thus, such subroutines are invoked with a CALL statement with or without passing of parameters from the calling program. The subroutine works on the parameters if given to it, otherwise it works out the results and gives out the result by itself and returns to the calling program or pass the results to the calling program before returning to it.

The technique of writing subroutine has some distinct advantages. The subroutine reduces duplication of block of statements within a program, enables reuse of the block of statements that forms the subroutine across multiple programs, decomposes a complex task into simpler steps, divides a large programming task among various programmers or various stages of a project and hides implementation details from users.

However, there are some disadvantages in using subroutines. The starting or invocation of a subroutine requires some computational overhead in the call mechanism itself. The subroutine requires some well-defined housekeeping techniques at its entry and exit from it.

Note

- A subroutine is a logical collection of instructions that is invoked from within a larger program to perform a specific task.
- The subroutine is relatively independent of the remaining statements of the program that invokes it.
- A subroutine can be invoked several times from several places during a single execution of the invoking program.
- After completing the specific task, a subroutine returns to the point of invocation in the larger program.

Some examples on developing algorithms using step-form

For illustrating the step-form the following conventions are assumed:

1. Each algorithm will be logically enclosed by two statements START and STOP.
2. To accept data from user, the INPUT or READ statements are to be used.
3. To display any user message or the content in a variable, PRINT statement will be used. Note that the message will be enclosed within quotes.
4. There are several steps in an algorithm. Each step results in an action. The steps are to be acted upon sequentially in the order they are arranged or directed.

4. The arithmetic operators that will be used in the expressions are
   (i) '←' ….Assignment (the left-hand side of '←' should always be a single variable)
   Example: The expression $x \leftarrow 6$ means that a value 6 is assigned to the variable x. In terms of memory storage, it means a value of 6 is stored at a location in memory which is allocated to the variable x.
   (ii) '+' ….. Addition
   Example: The expression $z \leftarrow x + y$ means the value contained in variable x and the value contained in variable y is added and the resulting value obtained is assigned to the variable z.
   (iii) '−' ….. Subtraction
   Example: The expression $z \leftarrow x - y$ means the value contained in variable y is subtracted from the value contained in variable x and the resulting value obtained is assigned to the variable z
   (iv) '*' ….. Multiplication
   Example: Consider the following expressions written in sequence:
   $$x \leftarrow 5$$
   $$y \leftarrow 6$$
   $$z \leftarrow x * y$$
   The result of the multiplication between x and y is 30. This value is therefore assigned to z.
   (v) '/' ….. Division
   Example: The following expressions written in sequence illustrates the meaning of the division operator :
   $$x \leftarrow 10$$
   $$y \leftarrow 6$$
   $$z \leftarrow x/y$$
   The quotient of the division between x and y is 1 and the remainder is 4. When such an operator is used the quotient is taken as the result whereas the remainder is rejected. So here the result obtained from the expression x/y is 1 and this is assigned to z.

5. In propositions, the commonly used relational operators will include
   (i) '>' ….. Greater than
   Example: The expression $x > y$ means if the value contained in x is larger than that in y then the outcome of the expression is true, which will be taken as 1. Otherwise, if the outcome is false then it would be taken as 0.
   (ii) '<=' …..Less than or equal to
   Example: The expression $x <= y$ implies that if the value held in x is either less than or equal to the

value held in y then the outcome of the expression is true and so it will be taken as 1.

But if the outcome of the relational expression is false then it is taken as 0.

(iii) '<' ...... Less than

Example: Here the expression x < y implies that if the value held in x is less than that held in y then the relational expression is true, which is taken as 1, otherwise the expression is false and hence will be taken as 0.

(iv) '=' ...... Equality

Example: The expression x = y means that if the value in x and that in y are same then this relational expression is true and hence the outcome is 1 otherwise the outcome is false or 0.

(v) '>=' ...... Greater than or equal to

Example: The expression x >= y implies that if the value in x is larger or equal to that in y then the outcome of the expression is true or 1, otherwise it is false or 0.

(vi) '!=' ...... Non- equality

Example: The expression x != y means that if the value contained in x is not equal to the value contained in y then the outcome of the expression is true or 1, otherwise it is false or 0.

Note: The 'equal to (=)' operator is used both for assignment as well as equality specification. When used in proposition, it specifies equality otherwise assignment. To differentiate 'assignment' from 'equality' left arrow (←) may be used. For example, a ←b is an assignment but a = b is a proposition for checking the equality.

6. The most commonly used logical operators will be AND, OR and NOT. These operators are used to specify multiple test conditions forming composite proposition. These are

(i) 'AND' ...... Conjunction

The outcome of an expression is true or 1 when both the propositions AND-ed are true otherwise it is false or 0.

Example: Consider the expressions

$$x \leftarrow 2$$
$$y \leftarrow 1$$
$$x = 2 \text{ AND } y = 0$$

In the above expression the proposition 'x = 2' is true because the value in x is 2. Similarly, the proposition 'y = 0' is untrue as y holds 1 and therefore this proposition is false or 0. Thus, the above expression may be represented as 'true' AND 'false' the outcome for which is false or 0.

(ii) 'OR' ...... Disjunction

The outcome of an expression is true or 1 when any-one of the propositions OR-ed is true otherwise it is false or 0.

Example: Consider the expressions

$$x \leftarrow 2$$
$$y \leftarrow 1$$
$$x = 2 \text{ OR } y = 0$$

Here, the proposition 'x = 2' is true since x holds 2 while the proposition 'y = 0' is untrue or false. Hence the third expression may be represented as 'true' OR 'false' the outcome for which is true or 1.

(iii) 'NOT' ...... Negation

If outcome of a proposition is 'true', it becomes 'false' when negated or NOT-ed.

Example: Consider the expression

$$x \leftarrow 2$$
$$\text{NOT } x = 2$$

The proposition 'x = 2' is 'true' as x contains the value 2. But the second expression negates this by the logical operator NOT which gives an outcome 'false'.

EXAMPLES

1. Write the algorithm for finding the sum of any two numbers.

Solution Let the two numbers be *A* and *B* and let their sum be equal to *C*. Then, the desired algorithm is given as follows:

1. START
2. PRINT "ENTER TWO NUMBERS"
3. INPUT A, B
4. C ← A + B   — Add values assigned to A and B and assign this value to C
5. PRINT C
6. STOP

Explanation The first step is the starting point of the algorithm. The next step requests the programmer to enter the two numbers that have to be added. Step 3 takes in the two numbers given by the programmer and keeps them in variables A and B. The fourth step adds the two numbers and assigns the resulting value to the variable C. The fifth step prints the result stored in C on the output device. The sixth step terminates the procedure.

2. Write the algorithm for determining the remainder of a division operation where the dividend and divisor are both integers.

Solution Let *N* and *D* be the dividend and divisor, respectively. Assume *Q* to be the quotient, which is an integer, and *R* to be the remainder. The algorithm for the given problem is as follows.

1. START
2. PRINT "ENTER DIVIDEND"
3. INPUT N
4. PRINT "ENTER DIVISOR"

```
5. INPUT D
6. Q ← N/D (Integer division)
7. R ← N - Q * D
8. PRINT R
9. STOP
```

> Only integer value is obtained and remainder ignored

Explanation The first step indicates the starting point of the algorithm. The next step asks the programmer to enter the dividend value. The third step keeps the dividend value in the variable N. Step 4 asks for the divisor value to be entered. This is kept in the variable D. In step 6, the value in N is divided by that in D. Since both the numbers are integers, the result is an integer. This value is assigned to Q. Any remainder in this step is ignored. In step 7, the remainder is computed by subtracting the product of the integer quotient and the integer divisor from integer dividend N. The computed value of the remainder is an integer here and obviously less than the divisor. The remainder value is assigned to the variable R. This value is printed on an output device in step 8. Step 9 terminates the algorithm.

3. Construct the algorithm for interchanging the numeric values of two variables.

   Solution Let the two variables be *A* and *B*. Consider *C* to be a third variable that is used to store the value of one of the variables during the process of interchanging the values.

   The algorithm for the given problem is as follows.
```
1. START
2. PRINT "ENTER THE VALUE OF A & B"
3. INPUT A, B
4. C ← A
5. A ← B
6. B ← C
7. PRINT A, B
8. END
```

Explanation Like the previous examples, the first step indicates the starting point of the algorithm. The second step is an output message asking for the two values to be entered. Step 3 puts these values into the variables A and B. Now, the value in variable A is copied to variable C in step 4. In fact the value in A is saved in C. In step 5 the value in variable B is assigned to variable A. This means a copy of the value in B is put in A. Next, in step 6 the value in C, saved in it in the earlier step 4 is copied into B. In step 7 the values in A and B are printed on an output device. Step 8 terminates the procedure.

4. Write an algorithm that compares two numbers and prints either the message identifying the greater number or the message stating that both numbers are equal.

   Solution This example demonstrates how the process of selection or decision making is implemented in an algorithm using the step-form. Here, two variables, A and B, are assumed to represent the two numbers that are being compared. The algorithm for this problem is given as follows.
```
1. START
2. PRINT "ENTER TWO NUMBERS"
3. INPUT A, B
4. IF A > B THEN
          PRINT "A IS GREATER THAN B"
```

```
5. IF B > A THEN
          PRINT "B IS GREATER THAN A"
6. IF A = B THEN
          PRINT "BOTH ARE EQUAL"
7. STOP
```

Explanation The first step indicates the starting point of the algorithm. The next step prints a message asking for the entry of the two numbers. In step 3 the numbers entered are kept in the variables A and B. In steps 4, 5 and 6, the values in A, B and C are compared with the IF ...THEN construct. The relevant message is printed whenever the proposition between IF and THEN is found to agree otherwise the next step is acted upon. But in any case one of the message would be printed because at least one of the propositions would be true. Step 7 terminates the procedure.

5. Write an algorithm to check whether a number given by the user is odd or even.

   Solution Let the number to be checked be represented by *N*. The number *N* is divided by 2 to give an integer quotient, denoted by *Q*. If the remainder, designated as *R*, is zero, *N* is even; otherwise *N* is odd. This logic has been applied in the following algorithm.
```
1. START
2. PRINT "ENTER THE NUMBER"
3. INPUT N
4. Q ← N/2 (Integer division)
5. R ← N — Q * 2
6. IF R = 0 THEN
          PRINT "N IS EVEN"
7. IF R != 0 THEN
          PRINT "N IS ODD"
8. STOP
```

Explanation The primary aim here is to find out whether the remainder after the division of the number with 2 is zero or not. If the number is even the remainder after the division will be zero. If it is odd, the remainder after the division will not be zero. So by testing the remainder it is possible to determine whether the number is even or odd.

The first step indicates the starting point of the algorithm while the next prints a message asking for the entry of the number. In step 3, the number is kept in the variable N. N is divided by 2 in step 4. This operation being an integer division, the result is an integer. This result is assigned to Q. Any remainder that occurs is ignored. Now in step 5, the result Q is multiplied by 2 which obviously produces an integer that is either less than the value in N or equal to it. Hence in step 5 the difference between N and Q * 2 gives the remainder. This remainder value is then checked in step 6 and step 7 to print out that it is either even or odd respectively. Step 8 just terminates the procedure.

6. Print the largest number among three numbers.

   Solution Let the three numbers be represented by *A*, *B*, and *C*. There can be three ways of solving the problem. The three algorithms, with some differences, are given below.
```
1. START
2. PRINT "ENTER THREE NUMBERS"
3. INPUT A, B, C
4. IF A >= B AND B >= C
          THEN PRINT A
```

```
5. IF B >= C AND C >= A
          THEN PRINT B
          ELSE
                PRINT C
6. STOP
```

Explanation To find the largest among the three numbers A, B and C, A is compared with B to determine whether A is larger than or equal to B. At the same time it is also determined whether B is larger than or equal to C. If both these propositions are true then the number A is the largest otherwise A is not the largest. Step 4 applies this logic and prints A.

If A is not the largest number as found by the logic in step 4, then the logic stated in step 5 is applied. Here again, two propositions are compared. In one, B is compared with C and in the other C is compared with A. If both these propositions are true then B is printed as the largest otherwise C is printed as the largest.

Steps 1, 2, 3 and 6 needs no mention as it has been used in earlier examples.

Or

This algorithm uses a variable *MAX* to store the largest number.

```
1. START
2. PRINT "ENTER THREE NUMBERS"
3. INPUT A, B, C
4. MAX ← A
5. IF B > MAX THEN MAX ← B
6. IF C > MAX THEN MAX ← C
7. PRINT MAX
8. STOP
```

Explanation This algorithm differs from the previous one. After the numbers are stored in the variables A, B and C, the value of any one of these is assigned to a variable MAX. This is done in step 4. In step 5, the value assigned to MAX is compared with that assigned to B and if the value in B is larger only then it's value is assigned to MAX otherwise it remains unchanged. In step 6, the proposition " IF C > MAX " is true then the value in C is assigned to MAX. On the other hand, if the proposition is false then the value in MAX remains unchanged. So at the end of step 6, the value in MAX is the largest among the three numbers. Step 1 is the beginning step while step 8 is the terminating one for this algorithm.

Or

Here, the algorithm uses a **nested if** construct.

```
1. START
2. PRINT "ENTER THREE NUMBERS"
3. INPUT A, B, C
4. IF A > B THEN
     IF A > C THEN
     PRINT A
     ELSE
     PRINT C
     ELSE IF B > C THEN
     PRINT B
     ELSE
     PRINT C
5. STOP
```

Explanation Here, the nested if construct is used. The construct "IF p1 THEN action1 ELSE action2" decides if the proposition " p1" is true then action1 is implemented otherwise if it is false action2 is implemented. Now, action1 and action2 may be either plain statements like PRINT X or INPUT X or another "IF p2 THEN action3 ELSE action4" construct, were p2 is a proposition. This means that a second "IF p1 THEN action1 ELSE action2" construct can be interposed within the first "IF p1 THEN action1 ELSE action2" construct. Such an implementation is known as "nested" if construct.

Step 4 implements the nested if construct. First the proposition "A > B "is checked to find whether it is true or false. If true, the proposition "A > C " is verified and if this is found to be true, the value in A is printed otherwise C is printed. But if the first proposition "A > B" is found to be false then the next proposition that is checked is "B > C". At this point if this proposition is true then the value in B is printed whereas if it is false C is printed.

7. Take three sides of a triangle as input and check whether the triangle can be drawn or not. If possible, classify the triangle as equilateral, isosceles, or scalene.

Solution Let the length of three sides of the triangle be represented by *A*, *B*, and *C*. Two alternative algorithms for solving the problem are given, with explanations after each step, as follows:

```
1. START
```
   Step 1 starts the procedure.
```
2. PRINT "ENTER LENGTH OF THREE SIDES OF A
   TRIANGLE"
```
   Step 2 outputs a message asking for the entry of the lengths for each side of the triangle.
```
3. INPUT A, B, C
```
   Step 3 reads the values for the lengths that has been entered and assigns them to A, B and C.
```
4. IF A + B > C AND B + C > A AND A + C > B THEN
   PRINT "TRIANGLE CAN BE DRAWN"
   ELSE
       PRINT "TRIANGLE CANNOT BE DRAWN": GOTO 6
```

It is well known that in a triangle, the summation of lengths of any two sides is always greater than the length of the third side. This is checked in step 4. So for a triangle all the propositions "A + B > C", "B + C > A" and "A + C > B" must be true. In such a case, with the lengths of the three sides, that has been entered, a triangle can be formed. Thus, the message "TRIANGLE CAN BE DRAWN" is printed and the next step 5 is executed. But if any one of the above three propositions is not true then the message "TRIANGLE CANNOT BE DRAWN" is printed and so no classification is required. Thus in such a case the algorithm is terminated in step 6.

```
5. IF A = B AND B = C THEN
            PRINT "EQUILATERAL"
      ELSE
            IF A != B AND B != C AND C !=A THEN
            PRINT "SCALENE"
      ELSE
            PRINT "ISOSCELES"
```

After it has been found in step 4 that a triangle can be drawn, this step is executed. To find whether the triangle is an "EQUILATERAL" triangle the propositions "A = B" and "B = C" are checked.

If both of these are true, then the message "EQUILATERAL" is printed which means that the triangle is an equilateral triangle. On the other hand if any or both the propositions "A = B" and "B = C" are found to be untrue then the propositions "A != B" and "B != C" and "C !=A" are checked. If none of the sides are equal to each other then all these propositions are found to be true and so the message "SCALENE" will be printed. But if these propositions "A != B" and "B != C" and "C !=A" are false then the triangle is obviously an isosceles triangle and hence the message "ISOSCELES" is printed.

6. STOP

The procedure terminates here.

Or

This algorithm differs from the previous one and applies an alternate way to test whether a triangle can be drawn with the given sides and also identify its type.

```
1. START
2. PRINT "ENTER THE LENGTH OF 3 SIDES OF A TRIANGLE"
3. INPUT A, B, C
4. IF A + B > C AND B + C > A AND C + A > B
   THEN
            PRINT "TRIANGLE CAN BE DRAWN"
   ELSE
            PRINT "TRIANGLE CANNOT BE DRAWN"
                 : GO TO 8
5. IF A = B AND B = C THEN
            PRINT "EQUILATERAL TRIANGLE"
                 : GO TO 8
6. IF A = B OR B = C OR C = A THEN
            PRINT "ISOSCELES TRIANGLE"
                 : GO TO 8
7. PRINT "SCALENE TRIANGLE"
8. STOP
```

Having followed the explanations given with each of the earlier examples, the reader has already understood how the stepwise method represents the algorithm with suitable statements.

In a similar way the following example exhibits the stepwise representation of algorithms for various problems using the stepwise method.

8. In an academic institution, grades have to be printed for students who appeared in the final exam. The criteria for allocating the grades against the percentage of total marks obtained are as follows.

Marks	Grade	Marks	Grade
91–100	O	61–70	B
81–90	E	51–60	C
71–80	A	<= 50	F

The percentage of total marks obtained by each student in the final exam is to be given as input to get a printout of the grade the student is awarded.

Solution The percentage of marks obtained by a student is represented by N. The algorithm for the given problem is as follows.

```
1. START
2. PRINT
    "ENTER THE OBTAINED PERCENTAGE MARKS"
```

```
3. INPUT N
4. IF N > 0 AND N <= 50 THEN
       PRINT "F"
5. IF N > 50 AND N <= 60 THEN
       PRINT "C"
6. IF N > 60 AND N <= 70 THEN
       PRINT "B"
7. IF N > 70 AND N <= 80 THEN
       PRINT "A"
8. IF N > 80 AND N <= 90 THEN
       PRINT "E"
9. IF N > 90 AND N <= 100 THEN
       PRINT "O"
10. STOP
```

9. Construct an algorithm for incrementing the value of a variable that starts with an initial value of 1 and stops when the value becomes 5.

Solution This problem illustrates the use of iteration or loop construct. Let the variable be represented by C. The algorithm for the said problem is given as follows.

```
1. START
2. C ← 1
3. WHILE C <= 5
4. BEGIN
5. PRINT C
6. C ← C + 1
7. END
8. STOP
```

While loop construct for looping till C is greater than 5

10. Write an algorithm for the addition of N given numbers.

Solution Let the sum of N given numbers be represented by S. Each time a number is given as input, let it is assigned to the variable A. The algorithm using the loop construct 'if ... then goto ...' is used as follows:

```
1. START
2. PRINT "HOW MANY NUMBERS?"
3. INPUT N
4. S ← 0
5. C ← 1
6. PRINT "ENTER NUMBER"
7. INPUT A
8. S ← S + A
9. C ← C + 1
10. IF C <= N THEN GOTO 6
11. PRINT S
12. STOP
```

11. Develop the algorithm for finding the sum of the series $1 + 2 + 3 + 4 + \ldots$ up to N terms.

Solution Let the sum of the series be represented by S and the number of terms by N. The algorithm for computing the sum is given as follows.

```
1. START
2. PRINT "HOW MANY TERMS?"
3. INPUT N
4. S ← 0
5. C ← 1
6. S ← S + C
7. C ← C + 1
8. IF C <= N THEN GOTO 6
```

```
 9. PRINT S
10. STOP
```

12. Write an algorithm for determining the sum of the series 2 + 4 + 8 + ... up to *N*.

    Solution Let the sum of the series be represented by *S* and the number of terms in the series by *N*. The algorithm for this problem is given as follows.

    ```
     1. START
     2. PRINT "ENTER THE VALUE OF N"
     3. INPUT N
     4. S ← 0
     5. C ← 2
     6. S ← S + C
     7. C ← C * 2
     8. IF C <= N THEN GOTO STEP 6
     9. PRINT S
    10. STOP
    ```

13. Write an algorithm to find out whether a given number is a prime number or not.

    Solution The algorithm for checking whether a given number is a prime number or not is as follows.

    ```
     1. START
     2. PRINT "ENTER THE NUMBER"
     3. INPUT N
     4. IF N = 2 THEN
            PRINT "CO-PRIME" GOTO STEP 12
     5. D ← 2
     6. Q ← N/D (Integer division)
     7. R ← N - Q*D
     8. IF R = 0 THEN GOTO STEP 11
     9. D ← D + 1
    10. IF D <= N/2 THEN GOTO STEP 6
    11. IF R = 0 THEN
            PRINT "NOT PRIME"
        ELSE
            PRINT "PRIME"
    12. STOP
    ```

14. Write an algorithm for calculating the factorial of a given number *N*.

    Solution The algorithm for finding the factorial of number *N* is as follows.

    ```
     1. START
     2. PRINT "ENTER THE NUMBER"
     3. INPUT N
     4. F ← 1
     5. C ← 1
     6. WHILE C <= N
     7. BEGIN
     8. F ← F * C
     9. C ← C + 1
    10. END
    11. PRINT F
    12. STOP
    ```

    While loop construct for looping till C is greater than *N*

15. Write an algorithm to print the Fibonacci series up to *N* terms.

    Solution The Fibonacci series consisting of the following terms 1, 1, 2, 3, 5, 8, 13, ... is generated using the following algorithm.

    ```
     1. START
     2. PRINT "ENTER THE NUMBER OF TERMS"
     3. INPUT N
     4. C ← 1
     5. T ← 1
     6. T1 ← 0
     7. T2 ← 1
     8. PRINT T
     9. T ← T1 + T2
    10. C ← C + 1
    11. T1 ← T2
    12. T2 ← T
    13. IF C <= N THEN GOTO 8
    14. STOP
    ```

16. Write an algorithm to find the sum of the series $1 + x + x^2 + x^3 + x^4 + \ldots$ up to *N* terms.

    Solution

    ```
     1. START
     2. PRINT "HOW MANY TERMS"
     3. INPUT N
     4. PRINT "ENTER VALUE OF X"
     5. INPUT X
     6. T ← 1
     7. C ← 1
     8. S ← 0
     9. S ← S + T
    10. C ← C + 1
    11. T ← T * X
    12. IF C <= N THEN GOTO 9
    13. PRINT S
    14. STOP
    ```

17. Write the algorithm for computing the sum of digits in a number.

    Solution

    ```
     1. START
     2. PRINT "ENTER THE NUMBER"
     3. INPUT N
     4. S ← 0
     5. Q ← N/10 (Integer division)
     6. R ← N - Q * 10
     7. S ← S + R
     8. N ← Q
     9. IF N > 0 THEN GOTO 5
    10. PRINT S
    11. STOP
    ```

18. Write an algorithm to find the largest number among a list of numbers.

    Solution The largest number can be found using the following algorithm.

    ```
     1. START
     2. PRINT "ENTER,
            TOTAL COUNT OF NUMBERS IN LIST"
     3. INPUT N
     4. C ← 0
     5. PRINT "ENTER FIRST NUMBER"
     6. INPUT A
     7. C ← C + 1
    ```

```
  8.  MAX ← A
  9.  PRINT "ENTER NEXT NUMBER"
 10.  INPUT B
 11.  C ← C + 1
 12.  IF B > MAX THEN
          MAX ← B
 13.  IF C <= N THEN GOTO STEP 9
 14.  PRINT MAX
 15.  STOP
```

19. Write an algorithm to check whether a given number is an Armstrong number or not. An Armstrong number is one in which the sum of the cube of each of the digits equals that number.

Solution If a number 153 is considered, the required sum is $(1^3 + 5^3 + 3^3)$, i.e., 153. This shows that the number is an Armstrong number. The algorithm to check whether 153 is an Armstrong number or not, is given as follows.

```
  1.  START
  2.  PRINT "ENTER THE NUMBER"
  3.  INPUT N
  4.  M ← N
  5.  S ← 0
  6.  Q ← N/10 (Integer division)
  7.  R ← N – Q * 10
  8.  S ← S + R * R * R
  9.  N ← Q
 10.  IF N > 0 THEN GOTO STEP 6
 11.  IF S = M THEN
          PRINT "THE NUMBER IS ARMSTRONG"
          ELSE PRINT "THE NUMBER IS NOT ARMSTRONG"
 12.  STOP
```

20. Write an algorithm for computing the sum of the series $1 + x + x^2/2! + x^3/3! + x^4/4! + \ldots$ up to N terms.

Solution

```
  1.  START
  2.  PRINT "ENTER NUMBER OF TERMS"
  3.  INPUT N
  4.  PRINT "ENTER A NUMBER"
  5.  INPUT X
  6.  T ← 1
  7.  S ← 0
  8.  C ← 1
  9.  S ← S + T
 10.  T ← T * X/C
 11.  C ← C + 1
 12.  IF C <= N THEN GO TO STEP 9
 13.  PRINT S
 14.  STOP
```

Pseudo-code

Like step-form, Pseudo-code is a written statement of an algorithm using a restricted and well-defined vocabulary. It is similar to a 3GL, and for many programmers and program designers it is the preferred way to state algorithms and program specifications.

Although there is no standard for pseudo-code, it is generally quite easy to read and use. For instance, a sample pseudo-code is written as follows:

```
dowhile kettle_empty
    Add_Water_To_Kettle
end dowhile
```

As can be seen, it is a precise statement of a while loop.

Flowcharts

A flowchart depicts appropriate steps to be followed in order to arrive at the solution to a problem. It is a program design tool which is used before writing the actual program. Flowcharts are generally developed in the early stages of formulating solutions to problems.

A flowchart comprises a set of standard shaped boxes that are interconnected by flow lines. Flow lines have arrows to indicate the direction of the flow of control between the boxes. The activity to be performed is written within the boxes in English. In addition, there are connector symbols that are used to indicate that the flow of control continues elsewhere, for example, the next page.

Flowcharts facilitate communication between programmers users and business persons. These flowcharts play a vital role in the programming of a problem and are quite helpful in understanding the logic of complicated and lengthy problems. Once the flowchart is drawn, it becomes easy to write the program in any high-level language. Often flowcharts are helpful in explaining the program to others. Hence, a flowchart is a must for better documentation of a complex program.

Standards for flowcharts The following standards should be adhered to while drawing flow charts.

- Flowcharts must be drawn on white, unlined 8½″ × 11″ paper, on one side only.
- Flowcharts start on the top of the page and flow down and to the right.
- Only standard flowcharting symbols should be used.
- A template to draw the final version of flowchart should be used.
- The contents of each symbol should be printed legibly.
- English should be used in flowcharts, not programming language.
- The flowchart for each subroutine, if any, must appear on a separate page. Each subroutine begins with a terminal symbol with the subroutine name and a terminal symbol labeled return at the end.
- Draw arrows between symbols with a straight edge and use arrowheads to indicate the direction of the logic flow.

Guidelines for drawing a flowchart Flowcharts are usually drawn using standard symbols; however, some special symbols can also be developed when required. Some standard symbols frequently required for flowcharting many computer programs are shown in Fig.7.2.

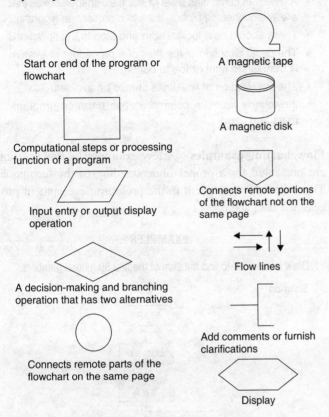

Start or end of the program or flowchart

A magnetic tape

Computational steps or processing function of a program

A magnetic disk

Input entry or output display operation

Connects remote portions of the flowchart not on the same page

Flow lines

A decision-making and branching operation that has two alternatives

Connects remote parts of the flowchart on the same page

Add comments or furnish clarifications

Display

Fig. 7.2 Flowchart symbols

The following are some guidelines in flowcharting.

- In drawing a proper flowchart, all necessary requirements should be listed out in a logical order.
- There should be a logical **start** and **stop** to the flowchart.
- The flowchart should be clear, neat, and easy to follow. There should be no ambiguity in understanding the flowchart.
- The usual direction of the flow of a procedure or system is from left to right or top to bottom.
- Only one flow line should emerge from a process symbol.

- Only one flow line should enter a decision symbol, but two or three flow lines, one for each possible answer, can leave the decision symbol.

- Only one flow line is used in conjunction with a terminal symbol.

- The writing within standard symbols should be brief. If necessary, the annotation symbol can be used to describe data or computational steps more clearly.

This is a top secret data

- If the flowchart becomes complex, connector symbols should be used to reduce the number of flow lines. The intersection of flow lines should be avoided to make the flowchart a more effective and better way of communication.
- The validity of the flowchart should be tested by passing simple test data through it.
- A *sequence* of steps or processes that are executed in a particular order is shown using process symbols connected with flow lines. One flow line enters the first process while one flow line emerges from the last process in the sequence.

First process in sequence

Last process in sequence

- *Selection* of a process or step is depicted by the decision making and process symbols. Only one input indicated by one incoming flow line and one or more output flowing out of this structure exists. The decision symbol and the process symbols are connected by flow lines.

- *Iteration* or *looping* is depicted by a combination of process and decision symbols placed in proper order. Here flow lines are used to connect the symbols and depict input and output to this structure.

Advantages of using flowcharts

Communication Flowcharts are a better way of communicating the logic of a system to all concerned.

Effective analysis With the help of flowcharts, problems can be analysed more effectively.

Proper documentation Program flowcharts serve as a good program documentation needed for various purposes.

Efficient coding Flowcharts act as a guide or blueprint during the systems analysis and program development phase.

Proper debugging Flowcharts help in the debugging process.

Efficient program maintenance The maintenance of an operating program becomes easy with the help of a flowchart.

Limitations of using flowcharts

Complex logic Sometimes, the program logic is quite complicated. In such a case, a flowchart becomes complex and clumsy.

Alterations and modifications If alterations are required, the flowchart may need to be redrawn completely.

Reproduction Since the flowchart symbols cannot be typed in, the reproduction of a flowchart becomes a problem.

Loss of objective The essentials of what has to be done can easily be lost in the technical details of how it is to be done.

Note

- A flowchart comprises a set of standard shaped boxes that are interconnected by flow lines to represent an algorithm.
- There should be a logical start and stop to the flowchart.
- The usual direction of the flow of a procedure or system is from left to right or top to bottom.
- The intersection of flow lines should be avoided.
- Flowcharts facilitate communication between programmers and users.

Flowcharting examples A few examples on flowcharting are presented for a proper understanding of the technique. This will help the student in the program development process at a later stage.

EXAMPLES

21. Draw a flowchart to find the sum of the first 50 natural numbers.

Solution

22. Draw a flowchart to find the largest of three numbers *A*, *B*, and *C*.

Solution

23. Draw a flowchart for computing factorial N ($N!$) where $N! = 1 \times 2 \times 3 \times \ldots \times N$.

Solution

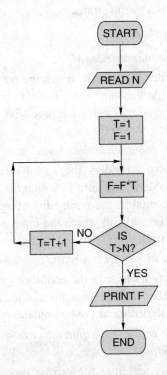

24. Draw a flowchart for calculating the simple interest using the formula $SI = (P * T * R)/100$, where P denotes the principal amount, T time, and R rate of interest. Also, show the algorithm in step-form.

Solution

Step 1: START

Step 2: Read P, T, R

Step 3: Calculate I=P*R*T/100

Step 4: PRINT I

Step 5: STOP

25. The XYZ Construction Company plans to give a 5% year-end bonus to each of its employees earning Rs 5,000 or more per year, and a fixed bonus of Rs 250 to all other employees. Draw a flowchart and write the step-form algorithm for printing the bonus of any employee.

Solution

Step 1: START

Step 2: Read salary of an employee

Step 3: IF salary is greater than or equal to 5,000 THEN Step 4 ELSE Step 5

Step 4: Calculate Bonus = 0.05 * Salary Go to Step 6

Step 5: Calculate Bonus = 250

Step 6: Print Bonus

Step 7: STOP

26. Prepare a flowchart to read the marks of a student and classify them into different grades. If the marks secured are greater than or equal to 90, the student is awarded Grade A; if they are greater than or equal to 80 but less than 90, Grade B is awarded; if they are greater than or equal to 65 but less than 80, Grade C is awarded; otherwise Grade D is awarded.

Solution

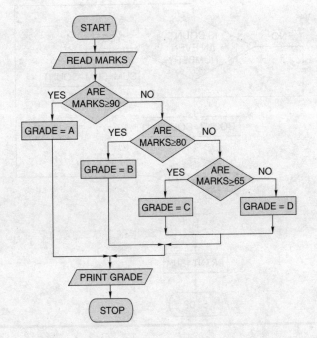

27. Draw a flowchart to find the roots of a quadratic equation.

Solution

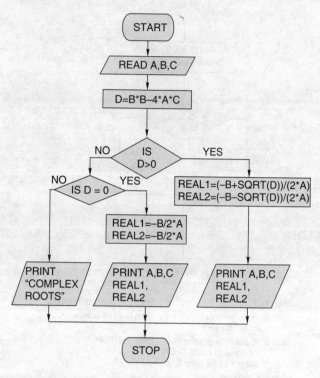

28. Draw a flowchart for printing the sum of even terms contained within the numbers 0 to 20.

Solution

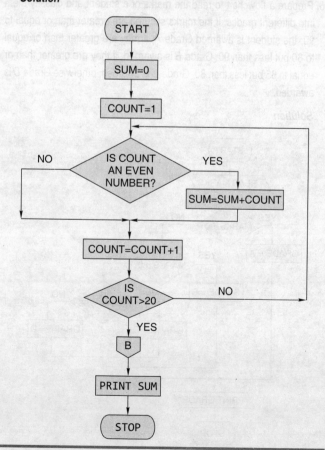

7.1.6 Strategy for Designing Algorithms

Now that the meaning of algorithm and data has been understood, strategies can be devised for designing algorithms. The following is a useful strategy.

Investigation step

1. *Identify the outputs needed.*

   This includes the form in which the outputs have to be presented. At the same time, it has to be determined at what intervals and with what precision the output data needs to be given to the user.

2. *Identify the input variables available.*

   This activity considers the specific inputs available for this problem, the form in which the input variables would be available, the availability of inputs at different intervals, the ways in which the input would be fed to the transforming process.

3. *Identify the major decisions and conditions.*

   This activity looks into the conditions imposed by the need identified and the limitations of the environment in which the algorithm has to be implemented.

4. *Identify the processes required to transform inputs into required outputs.*

   This activity identifies the various types of procedures needed to manipulate the inputs, within the bounding conditions and the limitations mentioned in step 3, to produce the needed outputs.

5. *Identify the environment available.*

   This activity determines the kind of users and the type of computing machines and software available for implementing the solution through the processes considered in steps.

Top–down development step

1. *Devise the overall problem solution by identifying the major components of the system.*

   The goal is to divide the problem solution into manageable small pieces that can be solved separately.

2. *Verify the feasibility of breaking up the overall problem solution.*

   The basic idea here is to check that though each small piece of solution procedure are independent, they are not entirely independent of each other, as they together form the whole solution to the problem. In fact, the different pieces of solution procedures have to cooperate and communicate in order to solve the larger problem.

Stepwise refinement

1. *Work out each and every detail for each small piece of manageable solution procedure.*

Every input and output dealt with and the transformation algorithms implemented in each small piece of solution procedure, which is also known as process, is detailed. Even the interfacing details between each small procedure are worked out.

2. *Decompose any solution procedure into further smaller pieces and iterate until the desired level of detail is achieved.*

   Every small piece of solution procedure detailed in step 1 is checked once again. If necessary any of these may be further broken up into still smaller pieces of solution procedure till it can no more be divided into meaningful procedure.

3. *Group processes together which have some commonality.*

   Some small processes may have to interface with a common upper level process. Such processes may be grouped together if required.

4. *Group variables together which have some appropriate commonality.*

   Certain variables of same type may be dealt as elements of a group.

5. *Test each small procedure for its detail and correctness and its interfacing with the other small procedures.*

   Walk through each of the small procedures to determine whether it satisfies the primary requirements and would deliver the appropriate outputs. Also, suitable tests have to be carried out to verify the interfacing between various procedures. Hence, the top-down approach starts with a big and hazy goal. It breaks the big goal into smaller components. These components are themselves broken down into smaller parts. This strategy continues until the designer reaches the stage where he or she has concrete steps that can actually be carried out.

   It has to be noted that the top-down approach does not actually take into account any existing equipment, people, or processes. It begins with a "clean slate" and obtains the optimal solution. The top-down approach is most appropriate for large and complex projects where there is no existing equipment to worry about. However, it may be costly because, sometimes, the existing equipments may not fit into the new plan and it has to be replaced. However, if the existing equipments can be made to fit into the new plan with very less effort, it would be beneficial to use it and save cost.

> **Note**
> - Investigation phase determines the requirements for the problem solution.
> - The top-down development phase plans out the way the solution has to be done by breaking it into smaller modules and establishing a logical connection among them.
> - The step-wise refinement further decomposes the modules, defines the procedure in it and verifies the correctness of it.

7.1.7 Tracing an Algorithm to Depict Logic

An algorithm is a collection of some procedural steps that have some precedence relation between them. Certain procedures may have to be performed before some others are performed. Decision procedures may also be involved to choose whether some procedures arranged one after other are to be executed in the given order or skipped or implemented repetitively on fulfillment of conditions arising out of some preceding manipulations. Hence, an algorithm is a collection of procedures that results in providing a solution to a problem. *Tracing* an algorithm primarily involves tracking the outcome of every procedure in the order they are placed. *Tracking* in turn means verifying every procedure one by one to determine and confirm the corresponding result that is to be obtained. This in turn can be traced to offer an overall output from the implementation of the algorithm as a whole. Consider Example 26 given in this chapter for the purpose of tracing the algorithm to correctly depict the logic of the solution. Here at the start, the "mark obtained by a student in a subject" is accepted as input to the algorithm. This procedure is determined to be essential and alright. In the next step, the marks entered is compared with 90. As given, if the mark is greater than 90, then the mark obtained is categorized as Grade A and printed, otherwise it is be further compared. Well, this part of the algorithm matches with the requirement and therefore this part of the logic is correct.

For the case of further comparison, the mark is again compared with 80 and if it is greater, then Grade B is printed. Otherwise, if the mark is less than 80, then further comparison is carried out. This part of the logic satisfies the requirement of the problem. In the next step of comparison, the mark is compared with 65. If the mark is lesser than 65, Grade C is printed, otherwise Grade D is printed. Here also, the flowchart depicts that the correct logic has been implemented.

The above method shows how the logic of an algorithm, planned and represented by a tool like the flowchart, can be verified for its correctness. This technique, also referred to as *deskcheck* or *dry run*, can also be used for algorithms represented by tools other than the flowchart.

7.1.8 Specification for Converting Algorithms into Programs

By now, the method of formulating an algorithm has been understood. Once the algorithm, for solution of a problem, is formed and represented using any of the tools like step-form or flowchart or pseudo code, etc., it has to be transformed into some programming language code. This means that a program, in a programming language, has to be written to represent the algorithm that provides a solution to a problem.

Hence, the general procedure to convert an algorithm into a program is given as follows:

Code the algorithm into a program—Understand the syntax and control structures used in the language that has been selected and write the equivalent program instructions based upon the algorithm that was created. Each statement in an algorithm may require one or more lines of programming code.

Desk-check the program—Check the program code by employing the desk-check method and make sure that the sample data selected produces the expected output.

Evaluate and modify, if necessary, the program—Based on the outcome of desk-checking the program, make program code changes, if necessary, or make changes to the original algorithm, if need be.

Do not reinvent the wheel—If the design code already exists, modify it, do not remake it.

Note

- An algorithm can be traced by verifying every procedure one by one to determine and confirm the corresponding result that is to be obtained.
- The general procedure to convert an algorithm into a program is to code the algorithm using a suitable programming language, check the program code by employing the desk-check method and finally evaluate and modify the program, if needed.

Because the reader has not yet been introduced to the basics of the C language, the reader has to accept the use of certain instructions like `#include <stdio.h>`, `int main()`, `printf()`, `scanf()`, and `return` without much explanation at this stage in the example program being demonstrated below.

However, on a very preliminary level, the general form of a C program and the use of some of the necessary C language instructions are explained briefly as follows:

1. All C programs start with:
```
#include <stdio.h>
    int main ()
    {
```

2. In C, all variables must be declared before using them. So the line next to the two instruction lines and {, given in step 1 above should be any variable declarations that is needed.

For example, if a variable called "a" is supposed to store an integer, then it is declared as follows:
```
    int a;
```

3. Here, `scanf()` is used for inputting data to the C program and `printf()` is used to output data on the monitor screen.
4. The C program has to be terminated with a statement given below:
```
    return 0;
    }
```
Here is an example showing how to convert some pseudocode statements into C language statements:

Pseudocode	C language code
LOOP {	while(1) {
EXIT LOOP	break;
IF (conditions) {	if (conditions) {
ELSE IF (conditions) {	else if (conditions) {
ELSE {	else
INPUT a	scanf("%d",&a);
OUTPUT "Value of a:" a	printf("Value of a: %d",a);
+ - * / %	+ - * / %
=	==
<–	=
!=	!=
AND	&&
OR	||
NOT	!

To demonstrate the procedure of conversion from an algorithm to a program in C, an example is given below.

Problem statement: Write the algorithm and the corresponding program in C for adding two integer numbers and printing the result.

Solution

Algorithm

1. START
2. PRINT "ENTER TWO NUMBERS"
3. INPUT A, B
4. R = A + B
5. PRINT "RESULT ="
6. PRINT R
7. STOP.

Program in C

```
int main( )
{
    int A, B;
    printf("\n ENTER TWO NUMBERS:");
    scanf("%d%d",&A,&B);
    R = A + B;
    printf("\n RESULT = ");
    printf("%d",R);
    return 0;
}
```

7.2 STRUCTURED PROGRAMMING CONCEPT

In 1968, computer scientist Edsger Dijkstra of Netherlands published a letter to the editor in the journal of the Association of Computing Machinery with the title 'GoTo statement considered harmful'. goto is a command available in most programming languages to transfer a control to a particular statement. For three decades, Dijkstra had been crusading for a better way of programming—a systematic way to organize programs—called structured programming.

Structured programming has been called a revolution in programming and is considered as one of the most important advancements in software in the past two decades. Both academic and industrial professionals are inclined towards the philosophy and techniques of structured programming. Today, it can be safely said that virtually all software developers acknowledge the merits of the structured programming approach and use it in software development.

There is no standard definition of structured programs available but it is often thought to be programming without the use of a goto statement. Indeed, structured programming does discourage the frequent use of goto but there is more to it than that.

Structured programming is:

- concerned with improving the programming process through better organization of programs and better programming notation to facilitate correct and clear description of data and control structure.
- concerned with improved programming languages and organized programming techniques which should be understandable and therefore, more easily modifiable and suitable for documentation.
- more economical to run because good organization and notation make it easier for an optimizing compiler to understand the program logic.
- more correct and therefore more easily debugged, because general correctness theorems dealing with structures can be applied to prove the correctness of programs.

Structured programming can be defined as a

- top–down analysis for program solving
- modularization for program structure and organization
- structured code for individual modules

7.2.1 Top–Down Analysis

A program is a collection of instructions in a particular language that is prepared to solve a specific problem. For larger programs, developing a solution can be very complicated. From where should it start? Where should it terminate? Top-down analysis is a method of problem solving and problem analysis. The essential idea is to subdivide a large problem into several smaller tasks or parts for ease of analysis.

Top-down analysis, therefore, simplifies or reduces the complexity of the process of problem solving. It is not limited by the type of program. Top-down analysis is a general method for attending to any problem. It provides a strategy that has to be followed for solving all problems.

There are two essential ideas in top-down analysis:

- subdivision of a problem
- hierarchy of tasks

Subdivision of a problem means breaking a big problem into two or more smaller problems. Therefore, to solve the big problem, first these smaller problems have to be solved.

Top-down analysis does not simply divide a problem into two or more smaller problems. It goes further than that. Each of these smaller problems is further subdivided. This process continues downwards, creating a hierarchy of tasks, from one level to the next, until no further break up is possible.

The four basic steps to top-down analysis are as follows:

Step 1: Define the complete scope of the problem to determine the basic requirement for its solution. Three factors must be considered in the definition of a programming problem.

Input What data is required to be processed by the program?

Process What must be done with the input data? What type of processing is required?

Output What information should the program produce? In what form should it be presented?

Step 2: Based on the definition of the problem, divide the problem into two or more separate parts.

Step 3: Carefully define the scope of each of these separate tasks and subdivide them further, if necessary, into two or more smaller tasks.

Step 4: Repeat step 3. Every step at the lowest level describes a simple task, which cannot be broken further.

7.2.2 Modular Programming

Modular programming is a program that is divided into logically independent smaller sections, which can be written separately. These sections, being separate and independent units, are called modules.

- A module consists of a series of program instructions or statements in some programming language.
- A module is clearly terminated by some special markers required by the syntax of the language. For example, a BASIC language subroutine is terminated by the return statement.
- A module as a whole has a unique name.
- A module has only one entry point to which control is transferred from the outside and only one exit point from which control is returned to the calling module.

The following are some of the advantages of modular programming.

- Complex programs may be divided into simpler and more manageable elements.

- Simultaneous coding of different modules by several programmers is possible.
- A library of modules may be created, and these modules may be used in other programs as and when needed.
- The location of program errors may be traced to a particular module; thus, debugging and maintenance may be simplified.

7.2.3 Structured Code

After the top-down analysis and design of the modular structure, the third and final phase of structured programming involves the use of structured code. Structured programming is a method of coding, i.e., writing a program that produces a well-organized module.

A high-level language supports several control statements, also called structured control statements or structured code, to produce a well-organized structured module. These control statements represent conditional and repetitive type of executions. Each programming language has different syntax for these statements.

In C, the if and case statements are examples of conditional execution whereas for, while, and do...while statements represent repetitive execution. In BASIC, for-next and while-wend are examples of repetitive execution. Let us consider the goto statement of BASIC, which is a simple but not a structured control statement. The goto statement can break the normal flow of the program and transfer control to any arbitrary point in a program. A module that does not have a normal flow control is unorganized and unreadable.

The following example is a demonstration of a program using several goto statements. Note that at line numbers 20, 60, and 80, the normal flow control is broken. For example, from line number 60, control goes back to line 40 instead of line 70 in case value of $(R - G)$ is less than 0.001.

```
10      INPUT X
20      IF X < 0 THEN GOTO 90
30      G = X/2
40      R = X/G
50      G = (R + G)/2
60      IF ABS(R - G) < 0.001 THEN GOTO 40
70      PRINT G
80      GOTO 100
90      PRINT "INVALID INPUT"
100     END
```

The structured version of this program using while-wend statement is given below.

```
INPUT X
IF X > 0
        THEN
G = X/2
R = X/G
        WHILE ABS (R - G) < 0.001
                R = X/G
                G = (R + G)/2
```

```
        WEND
        PRINT G
ELSE
        PRINT "INVALID INPUT"
END
```

Now if there is no normal break of control flow, gotos are inevitable in unstructured languages but they can be and should be always avoided while using structured programs except in unavoidable situations.

7.2.4 The Process of Programming

The job of a programmer is not just writing program instructions. The programmer does several other additional jobs to create a working program. There are some logical and sequential job steps which the programmer has to follow to make the program operational.
These are as follows:

1. Understand the problem to be solved
2. Think and design the solution logic
3. Write the program in the chosen programming language
4. Translate the program to machine code
5. Test the program with sample data
6. Put the program into operation

The first job of the programmer is to understand the problem. To do that the requirements of the problem should be clearly defined. And for this, the programmer may have to interact with the user to know the needs of the user. Thus this phase of the job determines the 'what to' of the task.

The next job is to develop the logic of solving the problem. Different solution logics are designed and the order in which these are to be used in the program are defined. Hence, this phase of the job specifies the 'how to' of the task.

Once the logics are developed, the third phase of the job is to write the program using a chosen programming language. The rules of the programming language have to be observed while writing the program instructions.

The computer recognizes and works with 1's and 0's. Hence program instructions have to be converted to 1's and 0's for the computer to execute it. Thus, after the program is written, it is translated to the machine code, which is in 1's and 0's with the help of a translating program.

Now, the program is tested with dummy data. Errors in the programming logic are detected during this phase and are removed by making necessary changes in either the logic or the program instructions.

The last phase is to make the program operational. This means, the program is put to actual use. Errors occurring in this phase are rectified to finally make the program work to the user's satisfaction.

Note

- Structured programming involves top–down analysis for program solving, modularization of program structure and organizing structured code for individual module.
- Top-down analysis breaks the whole problem into smaller logical tasks and defines the hierarchical link between the tasks.
- Modularization of program structure means making the small logical tasks into independent program modules that carries out the desired tasks.
- Structured coding is structured programming which consists of writing a program that produces a well-organized module.

SUMMARY

An algorithm is a statement about how a problem will be solved and almost every algorithm exhibits the same features. There are many ways of stating algorithms; three of them have been mentioned here. These are step-form, pseudo code, and flowchart method. Of these flowchart is a pictorial way of representing the algorithm. Here, the START and STOP are represented by an ellipse-like figure, ⬭, decision construct by the rhombus-like figure, ⬦, the processes by rectangles, ▭ and input/output by parallelograms, ▱. Lines and arrows connect these blocks. Every useful algorithm uses data, which might vary during the course of the algorithm. To design algorithms, it is a good idea to develop and use a design strategy.

Generally the design strategy consists of three stages. The first stage is investigation activity followed by the top-down development approach stage and eventually a stepwise refinement process. Once the design strategy is decided the algorithm designed is traced to determine whether it represents the logic. Eventually, the designed and checked, algorithm is transformed into a program.

A program is a sequence of instructions and the process of writing a program is called programming. Nowadays, structured programming technique is used to develop a program in a high-level programming language.

KEY TERMS

Algorithm   An algorithm specifies a procedure for solving a problem in a finite number of steps.

Correctness   Correctness means how easily its logic can be argued to meet the algorithm's primary goal.

Data   It is a symbolic representation of value.

Debug   It means to search and remove errors in a program.

High-level programming language   A language similar to human languages that makes it easy for a programmer to write programs and identify and correct errors in them.

Investigation step   It is a step to determine the input, output and processing requirements of a problem.

Low-level programming language   Closer to the native language of the computer, which is 1's and 0's.

Machine language   Machine language is a language that provides instructions in the form of binary numbers consisting of 1's and 0's to which

the computer responds directly

Portability of language   A programming language that is not machine dependent and can be used in any computer.

Program   A set of logically related instructions arranged in a sequence that directs the computer in solving a problem.

Programming language   A language composed of a set of instructions understandable by the programmer.

Programming   It is a process of writing a program.

Termination   It denotes closure of a procedure.

Top-down analysis   It means breaking up a problem solution into smaller modules and defininig their interconnections to provide the total solution to a problem.

Variable   It is a container or storage location for storing a value that may or may not vary during the execution of the program.

FREQUENTLY ASKED QUESTIONS

1. What is a programming language?

A programming language is an artificial formalism in which algorithms can be expressed. More formally, a *computer program* is a sequence of instructions that is used to operate a computer to produce a specific result.

A programming language is the communication bridge between a programmer and computer. A programming language allows a programmer to create sets of executable instructions called programs that the computer can understand. This communication bridge is needed because computers

understand only machine language, which is a low-level language in which data is represented by binary digits.

2. What is a token?

A token is any word or symbol that has meaning in the language, such as a keyword (reserved word) such as if or while. The tokens are *parsed* or grouped according to the rules of the language.

3. What is a variable?

A variable is a name given to the location of computer memory that holds the relevant data. Each variable has a data type, which might be number, character, string, a collection of data elements (such as an array), a data record, or some special type defined by the programmer.

4. What is Spaghetti code?

Non-modular code is normally referred to as spaghetti code. It is named so because it produces a disorganized computer program using many GOTO statements.

5. What is structured programming?

Structured programming is a style of programming designed to make programs more comprehensible and programming errors less frequent. This technique of programming enforces a logical structure on the program being written to make it more efficient and easier to understand and modify. It usually includes the following characteristics:

Block structure The statements in the program must be organized into functional groups. It emphasizes clear logic.

Avoidance of jumps A lot of GOTO statements makes the programs more error-prone. Structured programming uses less of these statements. Therefore it is also known as 'GOTO less programming'.

Modularity It is a common idea that structuring the program makes it easier for us to understand and therefore easier for teams of developers to work simultaneously on the same program.

6. What are the advantages and disadvantages of structured programming?

Structured programming provides options to develop well-organized codes which can be easily modified and documented.

Modularity is closely associated with structured programming. The main idea is to structure the program into functional groups. As a result, it becomes easier for us to understand and therefore easier for teams of developers to work simultaneously on the same program.

Another advantage of structured programming is that it *reduces complexity*. Modularity allows the programmer to tackle problems in a logical fashion. This improves the programming process through better organization of programs and better programming notations to facilitate correct and clear description of data and control structure.

Structured programming also *saves time* as without modularity, the code that is used multiple times needs to be written every time it is used. On the other hand, modular programs need one to call a subroutine (or function) with that code to get the same result in a structured program.

Structured programming *encourages stepwise refinement*, a program design process described by Niklaus Wirth. This is a top-down approach in which the stages of processing are first described in high-level terms, and then gradually worked out in their details, much like the writing of an outline for a book.

The disadvantages of structured programming include the following:

Firstly, error control may be harder to manage. Managing modifications may also be difficult.

Secondly, debugging efforts can be hindered because the problem code will look right and even perform correctly in one part of the program but not in another.

7. What is a pseudocode?

Pseudocode is an informal description of a sequence of steps for solving a problem. It is an outline of a computer program, written in a mixture of a programming language and English. Writing pseudocodes is one of the best ways to plan a computer program.

The advantage of having pseudocodes is that it allows the programmer to concentrate on how the program works while ignoring the details of the language. By reducing the number of things the programmer must think about at once, this technique effectively amplifies the programmer's intelligence.

8. What is top-down programming?

Top-down programming is a technique of programming that first defines the overall outlines of the program and then fills in the details.

This approach is usually the best way to write complicated programs. Detailed decisions are postponed until the requirements of the large program are known; this is better than making the detailed decisions early and then forcing the major program strategy to conform to them. Each part of the program (called a *module*) can be written and tested independently.

EXERCISES

1. What do you mean by structured programming? State the properties of structured programming.
2. What is top-down analysis? Describe the steps involved in top-down analysis.
3. What is a structured code?
4. What is an algorithm?
5. Write down an algorithm that describes making a telephone call. Can it be done without using control statements?
6. Write algorithms to do the following:
   (a) Check whether a year given by the user is a leap year or not.
   (b) Given an integer number in seconds as input, print the equivalent time in hours, minutes, and seconds as output. The recommended output format is something like:
   7,322 seconds is equivalent to 2 hours 2 minutes 2 seconds.
   (c) Print the numbers that do not appear in the Fibonacci series.

The number of terms to be printed should be given by the user.
   (d) Convert an integer number in decimal to its binary equivalent.
   (e) Find the prime factors of a number given by the user.
   (f) Check whether a number given by the user is a Krishnamurty number or not. A Krishnamurty number is one for which the sum of the factorials of its digits equals the number. For example, 145 is a Krishnamurty number.
   (g) Print the second largest number of a list of numbers given by the user.
   (h) Print the sum of the following series:
   (i) $1 - \frac{x^2}{2!} + \frac{x^4}{4!} +$ up to n terms where n is given by the user
   (ii) $1 - \frac{1}{2} + \frac{1}{3} - \cdots$ up to n terms where n is given by the user

(iii) $1 + \frac{1}{2!} + \frac{1}{3!} + \cdots$ up to n terms where n is given by the user

7. By considering the algorithmic language that has been taught, answer the following:

   (a) Show clearly the steps of evaluating the following expressions:

   (i) $x - y + 12 * \frac{3}{6} + k \wedge x$ where $x = 2$, $y = 6$, $k = 5$

   (ii) a AND b OR (m < n) where a = true, b = false, m = 7, n = 9

   (b) State whether each of the following is correct or wrong. Correct the error(s) where applicable.

   (i) The expression ('35' = '035') is true.

   (ii) x_1 x_2 * 4 value

   (iii) INPUT K, Y – Z

8. Write an algorithm as well as draw a flowchart for the following:

   Input

   - the item ID number
   - the Number On Hand
   - the Price per item
   - the Weight per item in kg
   - the Number Ordered
   - the Shipping Zone (1 letter, indicating the distance to the purchaser)

   Processing

   The program will read each line from the user and calculate the following:

   Total Weight = Weight Per Item * Number Ordered

   Weight Cost = 3.40 + Total Weight / 5.0

   Shipping cost is calculated as follows:

   ```
   If Shipping Zone is 'A'
       Then Shipping Cost is 3.00
   If Shipping Zone is 'B'
       Then Shipping Cost = 5.50
   If Shipping Zone is 'C'
       Then Shipping Cost = 8.75
       Otherwise Shipping Cost is 12.60
   ```

   Handling Charges = 4.00, a constant

   New Number On Hand = Number On Hand Number Ordered

   Discount is calculated as follows:

   ```
   If New Number On Hand < 0
       Then Discount = 5.00
       Else Discount = 0
   ```

   Here the purchaser is being given a discount if the item has to be repeat ordered. Total cost is calculated as follows:

   Total Cost

   ```
           = Price of Each * Number Ordered +
             Handling Charge + Weight Cost +
             Shipping Cost – Discount
   ```

   For each purchase, print out the information about the purchase in a format approximately like this:

   ```
   Item Number:     345612
   Number Ordered: 1
   Number On Hand: 31
   Price of Each:  19.95
   Weight of Each: 3
   Shipping Zone:  A
   Total Cost:     30.95
   ```

   After all the purchases are finished, print two lines stating the total number of purchases and the total cost of all purchases.

9. Fill in the blanks.

   (i) A program flowchart indicates the _____ to be performed and the _____ in which they occur.

   (ii) A program flowchart is generally read from _____ to _____.

   (iii) Flowcharting symbols are connected together by means of _____.

   (iv) A decision symbol may be used in determining the _____ or _____ of two data items.

   (v) _____ are used to join remote portions of a flowchart.

   (vi) _____ connectors are used when a flowchart ends on one page and begins again on another page.

   (vii) A _____ symbol is used at the beginning and end of a flowchart.

   (viii) The flowchart is one of the best ways of _____ a program.

   (ix) To construct a flowchart, one must adhere to prescribed symbols provided by the _____.

   (x) The programmer uses a _____ to aid him in drawing flowchart symbols.

10. Define a flowchart. What is its use?

11. Are there any limitations of a flowchart?

12. Draw a flowchart to read a number given in units of length and print out the area of a circle of that radius. Assume that the value of pi is 3.14159. The output should take the form: The area of a circle of radius _____ units is _____ units.

13. Draw a flowchart to read a number N and print all its divisors.

14. Draw a flowchart for computing the sum of the digits of any given number.

15. Draw a flowchart to find the sum of N odd numbers.

16. Draw a flowchart to compute the sum of squares of integers from 1 to 50.

17. Write a program to read two integers with the following significance.

   The first integer value represents a time of day on a 24-hour clock, so that 1245 represents quarter to one mid-day.

   The second integer represents a time duration in a similar way, so that 345 represents three hours and 45 minutes.

   This duration is to be added to the first time and the result printed out in the same notation, in this case 1630 which is the time 3 hours and 45 minutes after 1245.

   Typical output might be: start time is 1415. Duration is 50. End time is 1505.

Basics of C

LEARNING OBJECTIVES

After studying this chapter, the readers will be able to

- analyse the basic structure of a C program
- discuss the commands used in UNIX/Linux and MS-DOS for compiling and running a program in C
- enumerate the various keywords in C
- list the data types, variables, constants, operators, and

expressions in C
- discuss the precedence and associativity rules of operators in C
- explain the rules of type conversions in C

8.1 INTRODUCTION

The story started with the Common Programming Language (CPL), which Martin Richards at the University of Cambridge turned into Basic Combined Programming Language (BCPL). This was essentially a type-less language, which allowed the user direct access to the computer memory. This made it useful to system programmers.

Ken Thompson at Bell Labs, USA, wrote his own variant of this and called it B. In due course, the designers of UNIX modified it to produce a programming language called C. Dennis Ritchie, also at Bell Labs, is credited for designing C in the early 1970s. Subsequently, UNIX was rewritten entirely in C. In 1983, an ANSI standard for C emerged, consolidating its international acceptance.

In UNIX operating system and its descendants, 90 per cent of the code is written in C. The name C is doubly appropriate being the successor of B and BCPL. It has often been said, and with some justification, that C is the FORTRAN of systems software. Just as FORTRAN compilers liberated programmers from creating programs for specific machines, the development of C has freed them to write systems software without having to worry about the architecture of the target machine. Where architecture-dependent code, i.e., assembly code, is necessary, it can usually be invoked from within the C environment.Today, it is the chosen language for systems programming for the development of 4GL packages such as dbase, and also for the creation of user-friendly interfaces for special applications. But application programmers admire C for its elegance, brevity, and the versatility of its operators and control structures. C may be termed as a mid-level language, not as low-level as assembly and not as high-level as BASIC.

C is a high-level language which also provides the capabilities that enable the programmers to 'get close' with the hardware and allows them to interact with the computer on a much lower level.

8.1.1 Why Learn C?

There are a large number of programming languages in the world today—C++, Java, Ada, BASIC, COBOL, Perl, Pascal, Smalltalk, FORTRAN, etc. Even so, there are several reasons to learn C, some of which are stated as follows.

C is a core language   In computing, C is a general-purpose, cross-platform, block structured, procedural, imperative computer programming language. A number of common and popular computer languages are based on C. Having learnt C, it will be much easier to learn languages that are largely or in part based upon C. Such languages include *C++, Java,* and *Perl*.

C is a small language   C has only thirty-two keywords and only about twenty of them are in common use. This makes it relatively easy to learn compared to bulkier languages.

C is quick   We can write codes which run quickly, and the program can be very 'close to the hardware'. This implies that you can access low-level facilities in your computer quite easily, without the compiler or run-time system stopping you from doing something potentially dangerous.

C is portable   C programs written on one system can be run with little or no modification on other systems. If modifications are necessary, they can often be made by simply changing a few entries in a header file accompanying the main program. The use of compiler directives to the preprocessor makes it possible to produce a single version of a program which can be compiled on several different types of computer. In this sense, C is said to be very portable. The function libraries are standard for all versions of C so they can be used on all systems.

8.1.2 The Future of C

The story about C is not yet over. During the time when the X3J11 committee moved steadily towards producing the ANSI C standard, another researcher, Bjarne Stroustrup of Bell Laboratories began experimenting with an object-oriented flavour of C that he called C++ (pronounced C *plus plus*). C++ extended C, and according to Stroustrup, refined the language, making C++, in his words, 'a better C'.

Apparently, the X3J11 committee agreed, if not completely, and they adopted some of Stroustrup's proposals into the ANSI C standard. Subsequently, a new committee was formed to investigate a standard for ANSI C++ that is now ready. Does this new standard mean that ANSI C is destined to join its ancestors BCPL, B, and K&R C on the heap of discarded programming languages?

The answer is a solid no. Frankly, C++ is not for everyone. When learning C, it is best to stick to the basics, and readers would be well advised to ignore some of the more advanced elements found in C++. For example, C++ provides classes for *object-oriented programming*, or OOP as it is known. Until one knows C, one is not ready for OOP.

On the other hand, because C++ is based on ANSI C, one may as well use modern next-generation C++ compilers to write C programs. That way, one can take advantage of both worlds. After learning C, one is ready to tackle OOP and other advanced C++ subjects.

8.2 STANDARDIZATIONS OF C LANGUAGE

Both UNIX and C were created at AT&T's Bell Laboratories in the late 1960s and early 1970s. During the 1970s the C programming language became increasingly popular. Many universities and organizations began creating their own variations of the language for their own projects.

During the late 1970s and 1980s, various versions of C were implemented for a wide variety of mainframe computers, minicomputers, and microcomputers, including the IBM PC. In the early 1980s, a need was realized to standardize the definition of the C language which in turn would help C become more widespread in commercial programming.

In 1983, the American National Standards Institute (ANSI) formed a committee to establish a standard specification of C known as 'ANSI C'. This work ended in the creation of the so-called C89 standard in 1989. Part of the resulting standard was a set of software libraries called the ANSI C standard library. This version of the language is often referred to as ANSI C, Standard C, or sometimes C89. ISO/IEC standard was thereafter adopted by ANSI and people referred to this common standard as simply 'standard' or simply 'C89'.

In 1990, the ANSI C standard (with a few minor modifications) was made by the International Organization for Standardization (ISO) as ISO/IEC 9899:1990. This version is sometimes called C90. Therefore, the terms 'C89' and 'C90' refer to essentially the same language.

Changes included in C89 are as follows:

- The addition of truly standard library
- New preprocessor commands and features
- Function prototypes which specify the argument types in a function declaration
- Some new keywords *const, volatile,* and *signed*
- Wide characters, wide strings, and multi-byte characters
- Many smaller changes and clarification to conversion rules, declarations, and type checking

C89 is supported by current C compilers, and most C code being written nowadays is based on it. In 1995, amendments to C89 include

- Three new library headers: `iso646.h`, `wctype.h`, and `wchar.h`
- Some new formatting codes for the `printf` and `scanf` family of functions
- A large number of functions plus some types and constants for multi-byte and wide characters

With the evolution of C++, the standardization of C language began to be revised again. Some amendments and corrections to C89 standard were made and a new standard for the C language was created in 1995. In 1999, a more extensive revision to the C standard began. It was completed and approved in 1999. This new version is known as 'ISO/IEC 9899:1999' or simply 'C99' and has now become the official standard C. The following features were included:

- Support for complex arithmetic
- inline functions
- several new data types, including `long long int`, optional extended integer types, an explicit `boolean` data type, and a `complex` type to represent complex numbers
- Variable length arrays
- Better support for non-English characters sets
- Better support for floating-point types including math functions for all types
- C++ style comments (`//`)
- New header files, such as `stdbool.h` and `inttypes.h`
- Type-generic math functions (`tgmath.h`)
- Improved support for IEEE floating point
- Variable declaration no longer restricted to file scope or the start of a compound statement

GCC and other C compilers now support many of the new features of C99. However, there has been less support from vendors such as Microsoft and Borland that have mainly focused on C++, since C++ provides similar functionality improvement. According to Sun Microsystems, Sun Studio (which is freely downloadable) now supports the full C99 standard.

A new standard C 11 has been proposed at the end of 2012 by the C standards committee. The C standards committee has adopted guidelines that should limit the adoption of new features that have not been tested by existing implementations.

Most C implementations are actually C/C++ implementations giving programmers a choice of which language to use. It is possible to write C code in the common subset of the standard C/C++ language compilers so that code can be compiled either as a C program or a C++ program.

8.3 DEVELOPING PROGRAMS IN C

There are mainly three steps in developing a program in C:

1. Writing the C program
2. Compiling the program
3. Executing the program

For these steps, some software components are required, namely an operating system, a text editor, the C compiler, assembler, and linker. The editor is used to create and modify the program code while the compiler transforms the source program to object code. Operating system is responsible for the execution of the program. There are several editors which provide a complete environment for writing, managing, developing, and testing the C programs. This is sometimes called an integrated development environment, or IDE.

The stages of C program development that are followed, regardless of the operating system or compiler used, are illustrated in Fig. 8.2. A brief explanation of each of the processes involved in the compilation model are given in the following sections.

8.3.1 Writing or Editing

This involves writing a new program code or editing an existing source program using a text editor or an IDE and saving it with `.c` extension.

Programming environment

Most programming language compilers come with a specific editor that can provide facilities for managing the programs. Such an editor offers a complete environment for writing, developing, modifying, deploying, testing, and debugging the programs. Such software is referred to as an **integrated development environment** or **IDE**. An IDE is typically dedicated to a specific programming language. It thus incorporates features compatible with the particular programming paradigm.

Many IDEs have a Build option, which compiles and links a program in one step. This option will usually be found within an IDE in the Compile menu; alternatively, it may have a menu of its own. In most IDEs, an appropriate menu command allows one to run or execute or debug the compiled program. In Windows, one can run the `.exe` file for the corresponding source program like any other executable program. The processes of editing, compiling, linking, and executing are essentially the same for developing programs in any environment and with any compiled language.

A simple programming environment specially designed for C and C++ programming on Windows is the Quincy IDE. Figure 8.1(a) shows a screenshot of the Quincy environment. Quincy can be freely downloaded from `http://www.codecutter.com`.

There are many other IDEs available. DevC++ is one of the most popular C++ IDEs amongst the student community. DevC++ is a free IDE distributed under the GNU General Public License for programming in C/C++. It is bundled with MinGW, a free compiler. It can be downloaded from the URL `http://www.bloodshed.net`.

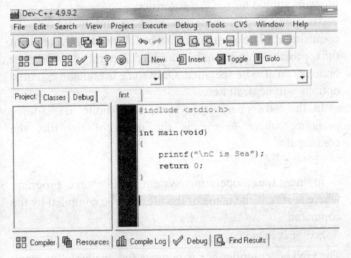

Fig. 8.1(a)   The screenshot of quincy

Fig. 8.1(b)   The screenshot of Dev C++

In UNIX or Linux, the most common text editor is the vi editor. Alternatively, one might prefer to use the emacs editor. The vi editor is simpler, smaller, and faster, and has limited customization capabilities, whereas emacs has a larger set of commands and is extensible and customizable. On a PC, a user can use one of the many freeware and shareware programming editors available. These will often help in ensuring the code to be correct with syntax highlighting and auto-indenting of the code.

8.3.2 Compiling the Program

Compiling involves preprocessing, compilation, assembly, and linking.

Preprocessing   It is the first phase of C compilation. It processes include-files, conditional compilation instructions, and macros. The C preprocessor is used to modify the program according to the preprocessor directives in the source code. A preprocessor directive is a statement (such as #define) that gives the preprocessor specific instructions on how to modify the source code. The preprocessor is invoked as the first part of the compiler program's compilation step. It is usually hidden from the programmer because it is run automatically by the compiler.

Compilation   It is the second step of the compiling process. It takes the output of the preprocessor and the source code, and generates assembler source code. The compiler examines

each program statement contained in the source program and checks it to ensure that it conforms to the syntax and semantics of the language. If mistakes are discovered by the compiler during this phase, they are reported to the user. The errors then have to be corrected in the source program (with the use of an editor), and the program has to be recompiled.

Assembly   It is the third stage of compilation. It takes the assembly source code and produces an assembly listing with offsets. The assembler output is stored in an object file. After the program has been translated into an equivalent assembly language program, the next step in the compilation process is to translate the assembly language statements into actual machine instructions. On most systems, the assembler is executed automatically as part of the compilation process. The assembler takes each assembly language statement and converts it into a binary format known as *object code*, which is then written into another file on the system. This file typically has the same name as the source file under UNIX, with the last letter an 'o' (for *object*) instead of a 'c'. Under Windows, the suffix letters "obj" typically replace the "c" in the filename.

Linking   It is the final stage of compilation. After the program has been translated into object code, it is ready to be linked. The purpose of the linking phase is to get the program into a final form for execution on the computer. The functions are the part of the standard C library, provided by every C compiler. The program may use other source programs that were previously processed by the compiler. These functions are stored as separate object files which must be linked to the object file. Linker handles this linking.

The process of compiling and linking a program is often called *building*. The final linked file, which is in an *executable object* code format, is stored in another file on the system ready to be run or *executed*. Under UNIX, this file is called a.out by default. Under Windows, the executable file usually has the same name as the source file, with the .c extension replaced by an exe extension.

8.3.3 Executing the Program

When the program is executed, each of the statements of the program is sequentially executed. If the program requests any data from the user, known as *input*, the program temporarily suspends its execution so that the input can be entered. Or, the program might simply wait for an *event*, such as a mouse being clicked, to occur. Results that are displayed by the program, known as *output*, appear in a window, sometimes called the *console*. Or, the output might be directly written to a file on the system.

Errors

If all goes well, the program performs its intended task. If the program does not produce the desired results, it is necessary to go back and reanalyse the program. Three types of errors may occur:

Compile errors   These are given by the compiler and prevent the program from running.

Linking errors   These are given by the linker or at run time and ends the program. The linker can also detect and report errors, for example, if part of the program is missing or a non-existent library component is referenced.

Run-time errors   These are given by the operating system.

Debugging

Removing errors from a program is called *debugging*. Any type of error in a program is known as a *bug*. During *debugging,* an attempt is made to remove all the known problems or *bugs* from the program. By tracing the program step-by-step, keeping track of each variable, the programmer monitors the program state. The *program state* is simply the set of values of all the variables at a given point in program execution. It is a snapshot of the current state of computation.

A *debugger* is a program that enables the programmer to run another program step-by-step and examine the value of that program's variables. Debuggers come in various levels of ease of use and sophistication. The more advanced debuggers show which line of source code is being executed.

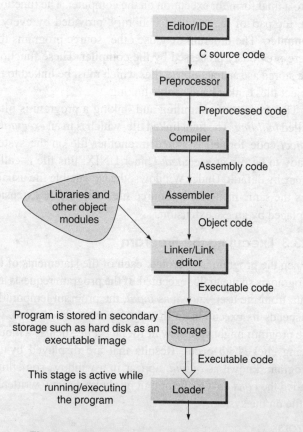

Fig. 8.2   Typical steps for entering, compiling, and executing C programs

In the UNIX/Linux operating system environment, the program is stored in a file, the name of which ends in '.c'. This means that the extension of the file will be '.c'. This identifies it as a C program. The easiest way to enter text is by using a text editor such as vi, emacs, or xedit. The editor is also used to make subsequent changes to the program. To create or edit a file called 'first.c' using vi editor, the user has to enter vi first.c.

Most of the Windows-based C compilers have an inbuilt context-sensitive editor to write C programs. The program filename should have a '.c' extension.

To compile a C program in UNIX simply invoke the command cc. The command must be followed by the name of the C program that has to be compiled. A number of compiler options can also be specified. Only some useful and essential options will be dealt here.

In the UNIX operating system, to compile a C source program, where first.c is the name of the file, the command is

```
cc first.c
```

In the Linux operating system, a C source program, where first.c is the name of the file, may be compiled by the command

```
gcc first.c
```

The GNU C compiler gcc is popular and available for many platforms. If there are syntax errors in the program due to wrong typing, misspelling one of the keywords, or omitting a semicolon, the compiler detects and reports them. There may, of course, still be logical errors that the compiler cannot detect. The program code may be directing the computer to do the wrong operations.

When the compiler has successfully translated the program, the compiled version or the executable program code is stored in a file called a.out or if the compiler option -o is used, the executable program code is put in the file listed after the -o option specified in the compilation command.

It is more convenient to use -o and file name in the compilation as shown.

```
cc -o program first.c
```

This puts the compiled program into the file program or any filename following the -o argument, instead of putting it in the file a.out.

PC users may also be familiar with the Borland C compiler. Borland International has introduced many C compilers such as Turbo C, Turbo C++, and Borland C++. It should be noted here that C++ is the superset of C and has the same syntax. A C program can be compiled by a C++ compiler. In all these cases, the actual computer program development environment comes in two forms.

To run the executable file, the command for both UNIX and Linux operating systems is

```
./a.out
```

To run an executable program in UNIX, simply type the name of the file that contains it; in this case first instead of—a.out. This executes the program, displaying the results on the screen. At this stage there may be run-time errors, such as division by zero, or it may become evident that the program has produced incorrect output. If so, the programmer must return to edit the source program, recompile it, and run it again.

For compiling a C program in the Borland C compiler, the steps are as follows.

1. Open MS-DOS prompt.
2. At the prompt

   ```
   c:\windows>
   ```
   give the following command:
   ```
   c:\windows>cd c:\borland\bcc55\bin
   ```
   Press **<Enter>**
   This changes the directory to c:\borland\bcc55\bin and the following prompt appears:
   ```
   c:\borland\bcc55\bin>
   ```
   Now, enter
   ```
   bcc32 -If:\borland\bcc55\include
         -Lf:\borland\bcc55\Lib c:\cprg\first.c
   ```
3. Press **<Enter>**

To run a C program in the Borland environment, the steps are as follows:

1. If the MSDOS prompt obtained while compiling has not been closed, the following prompt would be visible on the screen:
   ```
   c:\borland\bcc55\bin>
   ```
2. Enter
   ```
   c:\borland\bcc55\bin> cd c:\cprg
   ```
3. Press **<Enter>**. This changes the directory to one where the following MSDOS prompt would be seen:
   ```
   c:\cprg>
   ```
4. Enter first.exe or simply first, and the screen will display
   ```
   c:\cprg>first.exe or c:\cprg>first
   ```
5. Press **<Enter>** to run the program and its output will be available.

8.4 A SIMPLE C PROGRAM

The best way to learn C or any programming language is to begin writing programs in it.

Let us write the first program named first.c as follows:

```
/* A Simple C Program */
#include <stdio.h>
int main(void)
{
    printf("C is Sea\n");
    return 0;
}
```

There are a few important points to note about this program. These are common to all C programs.
```
/* A Simple C Program */
```
This is a comment line.

In C, the comments can be included in the program. The comment lines start with /* and terminate with */. These statements can be put anywhere in the program. The compiler considers these as non-executable statements.

The comment lines are included in a program to describe the variables used and the job performed by a set of program instructions or an instruction. Comment lines may also be written to record any other information that may be necessary for the programmer and relevant to the program.

According to C99, a comment also begins with // and extends up to the next line break. So the above comment line can be written as follows:
```
// A Simple C Program
```
// comments were added for C99 due to their utility and widespread existing practice, especially in dual C and C++ translators.
```
#include <stdio.h>
```
In C, all lines that begin with # are directives for the preprocessor, which means that all these directives will be processed before the program is actually compiled. The #include directive includes the contents of a file during compilation. In this case, the file stdio.h is added in the source program before the actual compilation begins. stdio.h is a header file that comes with the C compiler and contains information about input and output functions, e.g., printf().

For now it may be noted that there are two ways in which the preprocessor directives differ from program statements: (a) they must begin in the first column and no spaces are allowed between # and include and (b) they are not terminated by a semicolon.
```
int main(void)
```
Every C program contains a function called main. This is the starting point of the program. A C program may contain one or more functions one of which must be main(). Functions are the building blocks of a C program. For now, the functions may be recognized by the presence of parentheses after their names. When a C program is executed, main() is where the action starts. Then, other functions maybe 'invoked' or called.

A function is a sub-program that contains instructions or statements to perform a specific computation or processing. When its instructions have been executed, the function returns control to the calling point, to which it may optionally return the results of its computations. Since main() is also a function from which control returns to the operating system at program termination, in ANSI C it is customary, although not required, to include a statement in main() which explicitly returns control to the operating environment.

For the Watcom C/C++, IBM VisualAge C/C++, and Microsoft Visual C/C++ compilers, the function `main` can also be declared to return `void`. The compilers MetaWare High C/C++ and EMX C/C++ do not allow `main` to have a return type `void`. For these compilers, the return type of `main` has to be declared as `int`. Borland C/C++, Comeau C/C++, and Digital Mars C/C++ compilers do not explicitly list `void main()` as a legal definition of `main`, but somewhat ironically there are example codes using this non-conforming definition on `main`.

```
{}
```

This is a *brace*. As the name implies, braces come in packs of two, i.e., for every open brace there must be a matching close. Braces allow to lump pieces of program together. Such a lump of program is often called a *block*. A block can contain the declaration of variable used within it, followed by a sequence of program statements which are executed in order. In this case, the braces enclose the working parts of the function `main`. When the compiler sees the matching close brace at the end, it knows that it has reached the end of the function and can look for another (if any).

By enclosing the program instructions, `printf()` and `return 0` within the opening brace '{' and the closing brace '}', a block of program instruction is formed. Such a block of program instructions, within these braces, form the body of the function `main()`.

```
printf("C is Sea\n");
```

`printf()` is a 'library function'.

The `\n` (pronounced backslash n) in the string argument of the function `printf()`

```
"C is Sea\n"
```

is an example of an escape sequence. It is used to print the new line character. If the program is executed, the `\n` does not appear in the output. Each `\n` in the string argument of a `printf()` causes the cursor to be placed at the beginning of the next line of output. Think of an escape sequence as a 'substitute character' for outputting special characters or some positional action on the printing point, known as cursor, when the output device is a visual diaplay unit.

All escape sequences available in C are given in Table 8.1. Placing any of these within a string causes either the indicated action or the related character to be output.

```
return 0;
```

This statement indicates that the value returned by the function `main()`, after the program instructions in its body are executed, to the operating system is 0. Though the value, recognized by the OS as *status*, is returned using the `return 0` statement, the OS may not always use it.

The return statement is not mandatory; if it is missing, the program will still terminate. In C89, the value returned to the operating system is undefined. In C99, if `main()` is declared to return an `int`, the program returns 0 (zero) to the operating

system or operating environment; otherwise the program returns an unspecified value.

Throughout this book, at the end of every function definition for `main()`, the `return 0` instruction must be written. Function definition means the sequence of instructions that form the body of the function which performs the desired task. Similarly, `main()` should always be written as `int main(void)` in every program given in this book.

The above discussion is summarized in Fig. 8.3.

Table 8.1 Backslash codes

Code	Meaning
\a	Ring terminal bell (a is for alert) [ANSI extension]
\?	Question mark [ANSI extension]
\b	Backspace
\r	Carriage return
\f	Form feed
\t	Horizontal tab
\v	Vertical tab
\0	ASCII null character
\\	Backslash
\"	Double quote
\'	Single quote
\n	New line
\o	Octal constant
\x	Hexadecimal constant

Note

- C uses a semicolon as a statement terminator; the semicolon is required as a signal to the compiler to indicate that a statement is complete.
- All program instructions, which are also called statements, have to be written in lower-case characters.

8.5 PARTS OF C PROGRAM REVISITED

Header files

A header file is a file containing C declarations and macro definitions to be shared among the source files, compiler, preprocessor, C library, and other header files.

In C, the usual convention is to give header files names that end with .h. Functions in the ANSI C library are declared in a set of standard headers. This set is self-consistent and is free of name space pollution, when compiling in the pure ANSI mode. The ISO C standard library consists of 24 header files which can be included into a programmer's project with a single directive. Each header file contains one or more function declarations, data type definitions, and macros. Later revisions of the C standard have added several new required header files to the library:

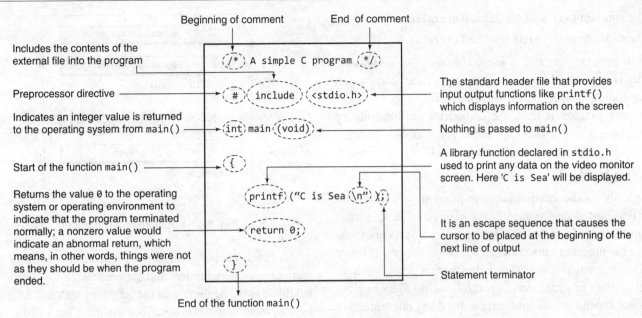

Includes the contents of the external file into the program

Beginning of comment End of comment

Preprocessor directive

Indicates an integer value is returned to the operating system from main()

Start of the function main()

Returns the value 0 to the operating system or operating environment to indicate that the program terminated normally; a nonzero value would indicate an abnormal return, which means, in other words, things were not as they should be when the program ended.

The standard header file that provides input output functions like printf() which displays information on the screen

Nothing is passed to main()

A library function declared in stdio.h used to print any data on the video monitor screen. Here 'C is Sea' will be displayed.

It is an escape sequence that causes the cursor to be placed at the beginning of the next line of output

Statement terminator

End of the function main()

Fig. 8.3 An Illustrated version of first.c

- The headers `<iso646.h>`, `<wchar.h>`, and `<wctype.h>` were added with Normative Addendum 1 (hereafter abbreviated as NA1), an addition to the C Standard ratified in 1995.
- The headers `<complex.h>`, `<fenv.h>`, `<inttypes.h>`, `<stdbool.h>`, `<stdint.h>`, and `<tgmath.h>` were added with C99, a revision to the C Standard published in 1999.

The following list contains the set of standard headers:

assert.h	inttypes.h	signal.h	stdlib.h
complex.h	iso646.h	stdarg.h	string.h
ctype.h	limits.h	stdbool.h	tgmath.h
errno.h	locale.h	stddef.h	time.h
fenv.h	math.h	stdint.h	wchar.h
float.h	setjmp.h	stdio.h	wctype.h

There are two ways of including files in C program. The first way is to surround the file you want to include with the angled brackets < and > that is like #include <filename>. This method of inclusion tells the preprocessor to look for the file in the predefined default location. This predefined default location is often an INCLUDE environment variable that denotes the path to the include files. On UNIX systems, standard include files reside under /usr/include.

The second way to include files is to surround the file that is required to be included with double quotation marks like #include "filename". This method of inclusion tells the preprocessor to look for the file in the current directory first, then look for it in the predefined locations the programmer set up. The #include <filename> method of file inclusion is often used to include standard headers such as stdio.h or stdlib.h. This is because these headers are rarely (if ever) modified, and they should always be read from the compiler's standard include file directory.

The #include "file" method of file inclusion is often used to include nonstandard header files that the programmer creats

for use in the program. This is because these headers are often modified in the current directory, and the programmer will want the preprocessor to use the newly modified version of the header rather than the older, unmodified version.

Philosophy of *main()*

main() is a user-defined function. main() is the first function in the program which gets called when the program executes. The startup code calls main() function. The programmer cannot change the name of the main() function.

According to ANSI/ISO/IEC 9899:1990 International Standard for C, the function called at program startup is named main. The implementation declares no prototype for this function. It can be defined with no parameters:

```
int main(void) { /* ... */ }
```
or with two parameters (referred to here as argc and argv, though any names may be used, as they are local to the function in which they are declared):

```
int main(int argc, char *argv[ ]) { /* ... */ }
```

On many operating systems, the value returned by main() is used to return an exit status to the environment. On UNIX, MS-DOS, and Windows systems, the low eight bits of the value returned by main( ) are passed to the command shell or calling program. It is extremely common for a program to return a result indication to the operating system. Some operating systems require a result code. And the return value from main(), or the equivalent value passed in a call to the exit() function, is translated by the compiler into an appropriate code.

There are only three completely standard and portable values to return from main() or to pass to exit():

- The plain old ordinary integer value 0

- The constant EXIT_SUCCESS defined in stdlib.h
- The constant EXIT_FAILURE defined in stdlib.h

If 0 or EXIT_SUCCESS is used, the compiler's run-time library is guaranteed to translate this into a result code which the operating system considers as successful.

If EXIT_FAILURE is used, the compiler's run-time library is guaranteed to translate this into a result code which the operating system considers as unsuccessful.

main() is Must

It depends on the environment the program is written for. If it is a hosted environment, then main function is a must for any standard C program. Hosted environments are those where the program runs under an operating system. If it is a freestanding environment, then main function is not required. Freestanding environments are those where the program does not depend on any host and can have any other function designated as startup function. Freestanding implementation need not support all the standard libraries; usually only a limited number of I/O libraries will be supported and no memory management functions will be supported. Examples of freestanding implementations are embedded systems and the operating system kernel.

The following will give a linker error in all compilers:

```
MAIN()
{
    printf("hello, world\n");
}
```

Along with the user-supplied main() function, all C programs include something often called the run-time support package which is actually the code that the operating system executes when starting up your program. In case, the user has supplied MAIN() rather than main(), then "MAIN" is a perfectly valid C function name but it is not "main". If there is no user-supplied main(), then the linker cannot finish the installation of the run-time package.

8.6 STRUCTURE OF A C PROGRAM

The general structure of a C program is depicted in Fig. 8.4.

Declaration is the program statement that serves to communicate to the language translator information about the name and type of the data objects needed during program execution. As discussed before, *preprocessor directives* tell the preprocessor to look for special code libraries, make substitutions in the code, and in other ways prepare the code for translation into machine language.

The basic idea behind the *global declaration* is that it is visible to all parts of the program. A more detailed discussion on global declarations has been included in Chapter 12.

Fig. 8.4   Structure of a C program

All functions including main() can be divided into two sections—local definition and statements. *Local definitions* would be at the beginning of the functions which is followed by statement section. It describes the data that will be used in the function. Data objects in local definitions as opposed to global declarations are visible only to the function that contains them. *Statement section* consists of the instructions that cause the computer to do something.

The difference between a declaration and a definition is important. A *declaration* announces the properties of a data object or a function. The main reason for declaring data objects and functions is type checking. If a variable or function is declared and later reference is made to it with data objects that do not match the types in the declaration, the compiler will complain. The purpose of the complaint is to catch type errors at compile time rather than waiting until the program is run, when the results can be more fatal.

A *definition*, on the other hand, actually sets aside storage space (in the case of a data object) or indicates the sequence of statements to be carried out (in the case of a function).

Note

- Declaration means describing the type of a data object to the compiler but not allocating any space for it.
- Definition means declaration of a data object and also allocating space to hold the data object.

8.7 CONCEPT OF A VARIABLE

Programs operate on data. The instructions that make up the program and the data that it acts upon have to be stored somewhere while the computer is executing that program. A programming language must provide a way of storing the data that is to be processed, otherwise it becomes useless. In this context, it may be mentioned that a computer provides a random access memory (RAM) for storing the executable program code and the data the program manipulates.

A computer memory is made up of registers and cells which are capable of holding information in the form of binary digits 0 and 1 (bits). It accesses data as a collection of bits, typically 8 bits, 16 bits, 32 bits or, 64 bits. Data is stored in the memory at physical memory locations. These locations are known as the memory address. Therefore, each byte can be uniquely identified by its address (see Fig. 8.5).

Fig. 8.5   Bits and bytes in memory

The amount of bits on which it can operate simultaneously is known as the *word length* of the computer. A *word* is the natural unit of memory for a given computer design. For 8-bit microcomputers, such as the original Apple computers, a word is just 1 byte. IBM compatibles using the 80286 processor are 16-bit machines. This means that they have a word size of 16 bits, which is 2 bytes. Machines like the Pentium-based PCs and the Macintosh PowerPCs have 32-bit words. More powerful computers can have 64-bit words or even larger. When we say that Pentium 4 is a 32-bit machine, it means that it simultaneously operates on 32 bits of data.

A variable is an identifier for a memory location in which data can be stored and subsequently recalled. Variables are used for holding data values so that they can be utilized in various computations in a program.

Variables are a way of reserving memory to hold some data and assign names to them so that we do not have to remember numbers like 46735; instead we can use the memory location by simply referring to the variable. Every variable is mapped to a unique memory address. Variables are used for holding data values so that they can be utilized in various computations in a program.

The C compiler generates an executable code which maps data entities to memory locations. For example, the variable definition

```
int salary = 65000;
```

causes the compiler to allocate a few bytes to represent salary. The exact number of bytes allocated and the method used for the binary representation of the integer depends on the specific C implementation, but let it be said that two bytes contain the encoded data as a binary number 1111110111101000. The compiler uses the *address* of the first byte at which salary

is allocated to refer to it. The above assignment causes the value 65000 to be stored as a binary number in the two bytes allocated (see Fig. 8.6).

(A 2-byte Integer whose address is 1214)

Fig. 8.6   Representation of an integer in memory

While the exact binary representation of a data item is rarely of interest to a programmer, the general organization of memory and use of addresses for referring to data items is very important.

All variables have three important attributes.

- A *data type* that is established when the variable is defined, e.g., integer, real, character. Once defined, the type of a C variable cannot be changed.
- The *name* of the variable.
- A *value* that can be changed by assigning a new value to the variable. The kind of values a variable can assume depends on its type. For example, an integer variable can only take integer values, e.g., 2, 100, –12.

The number of characters that you can have in a variable name will depend upon your compiler. A minimum of 31 characters must be supported by a compiler that conforms to the C language standard, so you can always use names up to this length without any problem. It can be suggested not to make the variable names longer than this anyway, as they become cumbersome and make the code harder to follow. Some compilers will truncate names that are too long.

Variable names are case sensitive, which means that the names NUM and num are distinct.

In C, a variable must be declared before it can be used. Variables can be declared at the start of any block of code, but these are mostly found at the start of each function. This serves two purposes. First, it gives the compiler precise information about the amount of memory that will be given over to a variable when a program is finally run and what sort of arithmetic will be used on it (e.g., only integer or floating point or none). Second, it provides the compiler with a list of the variables in a convenient place so that it can cross-check names and types for any errors.

8.8 DATA TYPES IN C

The type or data type of a variable determines the set of values that a variable might take and the set of operations that can be applied to those values. Data types can be broadly classified as shown in Fig. 8.7.

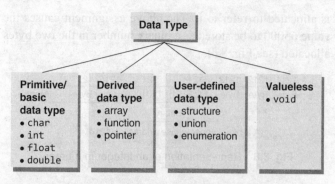

Fig. 8.7 Classification of data types

C provides a standard, minimal set of basic data types. Sometimes these are called 'primitive' types. More complex data types can be built up from these basic types. C has five basic data types (Refer Fig. 8.8) and they are as follows:

- character—Keyword used is char
- integer—Keyword used is int
- floating-point—Keyword used is float
- double precision floating point—Keyword used is double
- valueless—Keyword used is void

Fig. 8.8 Basic data types

Table 8.2(a) lists the sizes and ranges of basic data types in C for a 16-bit computer and Table 8.2(b) lists the sizes and ranges of basic data types in C for a 32-bit computer.

Table 8.2(a) Sizes and ranges of basic data types in C for a 16-bit computer

Data type	Size (in bits)	Range
char	8	–128 to 127
int	16	–32768 to 32767
float	32	1.17549×10^{-38} to 3.40282×10^{38}
double	64	2.22507×10^{-308} to 1.79769×10^{308}
void	8	valueless

Table 8.2(b) Sizes and ranges of basic data types in C for a 32-bit computer

Data type	Size (in bits)	Range
char	8	–128 to 127
int	32	–2147483648 to 2147483647
float	32	1.17549×10^{-38} to 3.40282×10^{38}
double	64	2.22507×10^{-308} to 1.79769×10^{308}
void	8	valueless

The C standard does not state how much precision the float and double types provide, since different computers may store floating point numbers in different ways. According to IEEE, the precisions for *float* and *double* are 6 and 15, respectively.

The void type has no values and only one operation, assignment. The void type specifies an empty set of values. It is used as the type returned by functions that generate no value. The void type never refers to an object and therefore, is not included in any reference to object types. According to ISO/IEC draft, 'The void type comprises an empty set of values; it is an incomplete type that cannot be completed.'

In addition, C has four type specifiers or modifiers and three type qualifiers.

The following points should be noted:

(a) Each of these type of modifiers can be applied to the base type int.

(b) The modifiers signed and unsigned can also be applied to the base type char.

(c) In addition, long can be applied to double.

(d) When the base type is omitted from a declaration, int is assumed.

(e) The type void does not have these modifiers.

The specifiers and qualifiers for the data types can be broadly classified into three types:

- *Size specifiers*—short and long
- *Sign specifiers*—signed and unsigned
- *Type qualifiers*—const, volatile, and restrict

The *size qualifiers* alter the size of the basic data types. There are two such qualifiers that can be used with the data type int; these are short and long.

The specifier short, when placed in front of the int declaration, tells the C compiler that the particular variable being declared is used to store fairly small integer values. The motivation for using short variables is primarily of conserving memory space, which can be an issue in situations in which the program needs a lot of memory and the amount of available memory is limited.

In any ANSI C compiler, the sizes of short int, int, and long int are restricted by the following rules:

- The minimum size of a short int is two bytes.
- The size of an int must be greater than or equal to that of a short int.
- The size of a long int must be greater than or equal to that of an int.
- The minimum size of a long int is four bytes.

In most of the DOS based compilers that work on 16-bit computers, the size of a short int and an int is the same, which is two bytes. In such compilers, a long int occupies four bytes. On the other hand, in the 32-bit machine compilers such as GNU C(gcc), `int` and `long int` take four bytes while a `short int` occupies two bytes. For UNIX based compilers, a `short int` takes two bytes, while a `long int` takes four bytes.

The `long` qualifier is also used with the basic data type `double`. In older compilers, this qualifier was used with `float`, but it is not allowed in the popular compilers of today. As mentioned earlier, it may be noted here that the sign qualifiers can be used only with the basic data types `int` and `char`.

Table 8.3 lists the sizes of the `short int`, `int` and `long int` data types in different machines.

Table 8.3 Sizes in number of bytes of the `short int`, `int` and `long int` data types in different machines.

	16-bit machine	32-bit machine	64-bit machine
short int	2	2	2
int	2	4	4
long int	4	4	8

C99 provides two additional integer types: `long long int` and `unsigned long long int`. For `long long`, the C99 standard specified at least 64 bits to support. Table 8.4 summarizes the size and range of different variations of `long long` type.

Table 8.4 Size and range of `long long` type

	Size (in bytes)	Range
long long int	8	− 9223372036854775808 to + 9223372036854775807
unsigned long int or unsigned long	4	0 to 4294967295
unsigned long long int or unsigned long long	8	0 to + 18446744073709551615

The C89 Committee added to C two *type qualifiers*, `const` and `volatile`; and C99 adds a third, `restrict`. Type qualifiers control the way variables may be accessed or modified. They specify the variables that will never (`const`) change and those variables that can change unexpectedly (`volatile`).

Both keywords require that an associated data type be declared for the identifier, for example,

```
const float pi = 3.14156;
```

specifies that the variable `pi` can never be changed by the program. Any attempt by code within the program to alter the value of `pi` will result in a compile time error. The value of a `const` variable must be set at the time the variable is declared. Specifying a variable as `const` allows the compiler to perform better optimization on the program because of the data type being known. Consider the following program:

```
#include <stdio.h>
int main(void)
{
const int value = 42;
/* constant, initialized integer variable */
value = 100;
/* wrong! – will cause compiler error */
return 0;
}
```

Note

- `const` does not turn a variable into a constant. A variable with `const` qualifier merely means the variable cannot be used for assignment. This makes the value read only through that variable; it does not prevent the value from being modified in some other ways, e.g., through pointer.

The `volatile` keyword indicates that a variable can unexpectedly change because of events outside the control of the program. This is usually used when some variable within the program is linked directly with some hardware component of the system. The hardware could then directly modify the value of the variable without the knowledge of the program. For example, an I/O device might need to write directly into a program or data space. Meanwhile, the program itself may never directly access the memory area in question. In such a case, we would not want the compiler to optimize-out this data area that never seems to be used by the program, yet must exist for the program to function correctly in a larger context. It tells the compiler that the object is subject to sudden change for reasons which cannot be predicted from a study of the program itself, and forces every reference to such an object to be a genuine reference.

The `restrict` type qualifier allows programs to be written so that translators can produce significantly faster executables. Anyone for whom this is not a concern can safely ignore this feature of the language.

Size and range of different combinations of basic data types and modifiers are listed in Table 8.5.

Several new types that were added in C89 are listed below:

- void
- void*
- signed char
- unsigned char
- unsigned short
- unsigned long
- long double

Moreover, new designations for existing types were added in C89:

- signed short for short
- signed int for int
- signed long for long

Table 8.5 Allowed combinations of basic data types and modifiers in C for a 16-bit computer

Data type	Size (bits)	Range	Default type
char	8	−128 to 127	signed char
unsigned char	8	0 to 255	None
signed char	8	−128 to 127	char
int	16	−32768 to 32767	signed int
unsigned int	16	0 to 65535	unsigned
signed int	16	−32768 to 32767	int
short int	16	−32768 to 32767	short, signed short, signed short int
unsigned short int	16	0 to 65535	unsigned short
signed short int	16	−32768 to 32767	short, signed short, short int
long int	32	−2147483648 to 2147483647	long, signed long, signed long int
unsigned long int	32	0 to 4294967295	unsigned long
signed long int	32	−2147483648 to 2147483647	long int, signed long, long
float	32	3.4E−38 to 3.4E+38	None
double	64	1.7E−308 to 1.7E+308	None
long double	80	3.4E−4932 to 1.1E+4932	None

C99 also adds new types:

- _Bool
- long long
- unsigned long long
- float _Imaginary
- float _Complex
- double _Imaginary
- double _Complex
- long double _Imaginary
- long double _Complex

C99 also allows extended integer types <inttypes.h>, and <stdint.h>) and a boolean type <stdbool.h>).

char A character variable occupies a single byte that contains the *code* for the character. This code is a numeric value and depends on the *character coding system* being used, i.e., it is machine-dependent. The most common coding system is ASCII (American Standard Code for Information Interchange). For example, the character 'A' has the ASCII character code 65, and the character 'a' has the ASCII code 97.

Since character variables are accommodated in a byte, C regards char as being a sub-range of int (the sub-range that fits inside a byte), and each ASCII character is for all purposes equivalent to the decimal integer value of the bit picture that defines it. Thus 'A', of which the ASCII representation is 01000001, has the arithmetical decimal value of 65. This is the decimal value of the sequence of bits 01000001, which may be easily verified. In other words, the memory representation of the char constant 'A' is indistinguishable from that of the int constant, decimal 65.

It may be observed that small int values may be stored in char variables and char values may be stored in int variables. Character variables are therefore signed quantities restricted to the value range [−128 to 127]. However, it is a requirement of the language that the decimal equivalent of each of the printing characters be non-negative.

It may thus be concluded that in any C implementation in which a char is stored in an 8-bit byte, the corresponding int value will always be a non-negative quantity whatever the value of the leftmost (sign) bit. Now, identical bit patterns within a byte may be treated as a negative quantity by one machine and as a positive quantity by another. For ensuring the portability of programs that store non-character data in char variables, the unsigned char declaration is useful: it changes the range of chars to [0 to 255].

The signedness of characters is an important issue because the standard I/O library routines which may normally return characters from files, return a negative value when end-of-file is reached.

Let us now discuss these data types in detail.

Signed integer types

There are four standard integer types — short, int, long, long long.

The precise range of values representable by a signed integer type depends not only on the number of bits used in the representation, but also on the encoding techniques.

The most common binary encoding technique for integers is called *2's complement notation* in which a signed integer represented with *n* bits will have a range from (-2^{n-1}) through $(2^{n-1} - 1)$ encoded in the following fashion:

1. The highest order(left-most) bit (of the word) is the sign bit. If the sign bit is 1, the number is negative; otherwise the number is positive.

2. To negate an integer, complement all bits in the word and then add 1 to the result; thus to form the integer −1, start with 1 $(00....001_2)$, complement the bits 11 ..... 110_2, and add 1 giving $11....111_2 = -1$.

3. The maximum negative value, $10\ldots0000_2$ or -2^{n-1}, has no positive equivalent; negating this value produces the same value.

Other binary integer encoding techniques are 1's complement notation, in which negation simply complements all bits of the word, and sign magnitude notation, in which negation involves simply complementing the sign bit. These alternatives have a range from (-2^{n-1}) through $(2^{n-1}-1)$; they have one less value and two representations for zero (positive and negative). All three notations represent positive integers identically. All are acceptable in standard C.

In C89, information about the representation of integer types is provided in the header file limits.h. In C99, the files stdint.h and inttypes.h contain additional information.

The system file limits.h available in ANSI C-compliant compilers contains the upper and lower limits of integer types. The user may #include it before main() precisely like #include <stdio.h>, as shown

    #include <limits.h>

and thereby give the program access to the constants defined in it.

The permitted minimum and maximum values are shown in Table 8.6.

Unsigned integer types

For each signed integer types, there is a corresponding unsigned type that occupies the same amount of storage but has a different integer encoding.

All unsigned types use straight binary notation regardless of whether the signed types use 2's complement, 1's complement, or sign magnitude notation, the sign bit treated as an ordinary data bit. Therefore, an n-bit word can represent the integers 0 through $2^n - 1$. Most computers are easily able to interpret the value in a word using either signed or unsigned notation. For example, when the 2's complement notation is used, the bit pattern $11\ldots1111_2$ (n bits long) can represent either -1 (using the signed notation) or $2^n - 1$ (using the unsigned notation). The integers from 0 through $2^{n-1} - 1$ are represented identically in both signed and unsigned notations. The particular ranges of the unsigned types in a standard C implementation are documented in the header file limits.h.

unsigned The declaration of unsigned int variable 'liberates' the sign bit and makes the entire word (including the freed sign bit) available for the storage of non-negative integers. It should be noted that the sign bit is the leftmost bit of a memory word. It determines the sign of the contents of the word: when it is set to 1, the value stored in the remaining bits is negative. Most computers use 2's complement arithmetic in which the sign bit is 'weighted', i.e., it has an associated place value, which is negative. Thus on a 16-bit machine, its value is -2^{15} or $-32,768$. So a 16-bit signed number such as 10000000 00111111 would have the value $2^0 + 2^1 + 2^2 + 2^3 + 2^4 + 2^5 - 2^{15} = -32,705$. As an unsigned integer, this string of bits would have the value $2^{15} + 2^5 + 2^4 + 2^3 + 2^2 + 2^1 + 2^0 = 32831$. On PCs, the unsigned declaration allows for the int variables a range 0 to 65535 and is useful when one deals with quantities which are known beforehand to be both large and non-negative, e.g., memory addresses, a stadium's seating capacity, etc.

short The short int declaration may be useful in instances where an integer variable is known beforehand to be small. The declaration above ensures that the range of short int will not exceed that of ints, but on some computers the range may be shorter (e.g., -128 through 127); short int may be accommodated in a byte, thus saving memory. In the early days of computing when main memory was an expensive resource, programmers tried to optimize core memory usage to

Table 8.6 Constants in limit.h

Name	Meaning	Values
CHAR_BIT	Bits in a char	8
CHAR_MAX	Maximum value of char	UCHAR-MAX or SCHAR_ MAX
CHAR_MIN	Minimum value of char	0 or SCHAR _ MIN
INT_MAX	Maximum value of int	32767
INT_MIN	Minimum value of int	-32767
LONG_MAX	Maximum value of long	2147483647
LONG_MIN	Minimum value of long	-2147483647
SCHAR_MAX	Maximum value of signed char	127
SCHAR_MIN	Minimum value of signed char	-127
SHRT_MAX	Maximum value of short	32767
SHRT_MIN	Minimum value of short	-32767
UCHAR_MAX	Maximum value of unsigned char	255
UINT_MAX	Maximum value of unsigned int	65535
ULONG_MAX	Maximum value of unsigned long	4294967295
USHRT_MAX	Maximum value of unsigned short	65535

the extent possible using such declarations and other methods. The VAX computer uses two bytes to store short ints, which is half the amount it uses for ints; but for present-day PCs, with cheap and plentiful memory, most compiler writers make no distinction between int and short int.

unsigned short For the unsigned short int variable, the range of values does not exceed that of the unsigned int; it may be shorter.

unsigned long The unsigned long variable declaration transforms the range of long int to the set of 4-byte non-negative integers with values ranging from 0 to 4294967295.

long On most computers, long int variables are 4-byte integers with values ranging over the interval [–2147483648 to 2147483647].

float Integer and character data types are incapable of storing numbers with fractional parts. Depending on the precision required, C provides two variable types for computation with floating-point numbers, i.e., numbers with a decimal (internally a binary) point. floats are stored in four bytes and are accurate to about seven significant digits.

Note

- It must be remembered that the floating point numbers held in a computer's memory are at best approximations to real numbers. The finite extent of the word size of any computer forces a truncation or round-off of the value to be stored; whether a storage location is two bytes wide, or four, or even eight, the value stored therein can be precise only to so many binary digits. In any computation with floating point numbers, errors of round-off or truncation are necessarily introduced. Therefore, any number with a long string of digits after the decimal point, given by a computer as the result of a computation, may not be quite as accurate as it seems.

double Because the words of memory can store values that are precise only to a fixed number of figures, any calculation involving floating-point numbers almost invariably introduces round-off errors. At the same time, scientific computations often demand a far greater accuracy than that provided by single precision arithmetic, i.e., arithmetic with the four-byte float variables. Thus, where large-scale scientific or engineering computations are involved, the double declaration becomes the natural choice for program variables. The double specification allows the storage of double precision floating-point numbers (in eight consecutive bytes) that are held correct to 15 digits and have a much greater range of definition than floats.

Boolean data type _Bool A _Bool variable is defined in the language to be large enough to store just the values 0 and 1. The precise amount of memory that is used is unspecified. _Bool variables are used in programs that need to indicate a Boolean condition. For example, a variable of this type might be used to indicate whether all data has been read from a file.

By convention, 0 is used to indicate a false value and 1 indicates a true value. When assigning a value to a _Bool variable, a value of 0 is stored as 0 inside the variable, whereas any nonzero value is stored as 1.

To make it easier to work with _Bool variables in a program, the standard header file stdbool.h defines the values for bool, as true, and false.

8.9 PROGRAM STATEMENT

A statement is a syntactic construction that performs an action when a program is executed. All C program statements are terminated with a semicolon (;). A program statement in C can be classified as shown in Fig. 8.9.

Declaration is a program statement that serves to communicate to the language translator information about the name and type of the data objects needed during program execution.

Fig. 8.9 Different types of program statements available in C

Expression statement is the simplest kind of statement which is no more than an expression followed by a semicolon. An *expression* is a sequence of operators and operands that specifies computation of a value.

```
x = 4
```

is just an expression (which could be part of a larger expression), but

```
x = 4;
```

is a statement.

Compound statement is a sequence of statements that may be treated as a single statement in the construction of larger statements.

Labeled statements can be used to mark any statement so that control may be transferred to the statement by switch statement.

Control statement is a statement whose execution results in a choice being made as to which of two or more paths should be followed. In other words, the control statements determine the 'flow of execution' in a program.

The types of control flow statements supported by different languages vary, but can be categorized by their effect:

- Continuation of program execution from a different statement
- Executing a set of statements only if some condition is met
- Executing a set of statements zero or more times, until some condition is met
- Executing a set of distant statements, after which the flow of control usually returns
- Stopping the program, preventing any further execution (unconditional halt)

Selection statements   allow a program to select a particular execution path from a set of one or more alternatives. Various forms of the `if..else` statement belong to this category.

Iteration statements   are used to execute a group of one or more statements repeatedly. `while`, `for`, and `do..while` statements falls under this group.

Jump statements   cause an unconditional jump to some other place in the program. `goto` statement falls in this group.

The first four types of program statements shown in the figure are defined and explained in the next few sections of this chapter. The program statement control, which is of three types, is dealt with in Chapter 9.

8.10 DECLARATION

Declaration introduces one or more variables within a program. Definition, on the other hand, directs the compiler to actually allocate memory for the variable. A declaration statement begins with the type, followed by the name of one or more variables. The general form is

```
data_type  variable_name_1,  variable_name_2,  ...,
variable_name_n;
```

Declaration of multiple variables of the same data types can be done in one statement. For example,

```
int a;
int b;
int c;
```

can be rewritten as

```
int a, b, c;
```

Variables are declared at three basic places. First, when these are declared inside a function, they are called local variables. Second, when the variables are declared in the definition of function parameters, these variables are called formal parameters. Third, when the variables are declared outside all functions, they are called global variables. Variables used in expressions are also referred to as operands.

8.11 HOW DOES THE COMPUTER STORE DATA IN MEMORY?

It is necessary to understand the *word size* of your computer. The word size is the computer's preferred size for moving units of information around; technically it is the width of the processor's *registers*, which are the data holding areas the processor uses to do arithmetic and logical calculations. This is what they mean when people refer to computers as 32-bit or 64-bit computers.

Most computers now have a word size of 64 bits. In the recent past (early 2000s), many PCs had 32-bit words. The old 286 machines back, in the 1980s, had a word size of 16 bits. Old-style mainframes often had 36-bit words.

The computer views the memory as a sequence of words numbered from zero up to some large value dependent on the memory size.

8.11.1 How are Integers Stored?

Storing *unsigned integers* is a straightforward process. The number is changed to the corresponding binary form and the binary representation is stored.

Fig. 8.10(a)   Range of an unsigned integer stored in a 16-bit word

An unsigned integer can be represented with a circle as shown in Fig. 8.10(b).

0 is placed at the top of the circle and values are placed around the circle clockwise until the maximum value adjacent to the value 0. In other words, storing numbers is a modulo process. The number to be stored is represented as modulus, the maximum value that can be stored plus one; in this case it is 65535.

$$65535 + 1 = 65536 \% 65536 = 0.$$

Fig. 8.10(b)   Cyclic view of the range of an unsigned integer stored in a 16-bit word

For *signed integer* types, the bits of the object representation shall be divided into three groups: *value bits*, *padding bits*, and the *sign bit*. There need not be any padding bits; there shall be exactly one sign bit. Each bit that is a value bit shall have the same value as the same bit in the object representation of the corresponding unsigned type (if there are M value bits in the signed type and N in the unsigned type, then $M \leq N$). If the sign bit is zero, it shall not affect the resulting value. If the sign bit is one, the value shall be modified in one of the following ways:

- The corresponding value with sign bit 0 is negated (*sign and magnitude*).
- The sign bit has the value (2^N) (2's complement).
- The sign bit has the value $(2^N - 1)$ (1's complement).

Which of these applies is implementation-defined, as is whether the value with sign bit 1 and all bits in magnitude are zero (for the first two), or with sign bit and all bits in magnitude are 1 (for ones' complement), is a representation of a normal value. In the case of sign and magnitude and ones' complement, if this representation is a normal value it is called a *negative zero*.

Sign and magnitude

In this method, one bit (the left-most) represents sign bit; 0 for positive and 1 for negative. The leftover bits of the word represent the absolute value of the number. Therefore, the maximum positive value is one half of the unsigned value. There are two zero values, a plus zero and a minus zero. This method is not used to store values in today's computers.

Fig. 8.11   Range of a signed integer stored in a 16-bit word in sign and magnitude form

One's complement

In this method, negative numbers are stored in their complemented format. Like sign and magnitude form, the one's complement has two zero values (plus zero and minus zero). Figure 8.12 shows the format of one's complement values.

Fig. 8.12   Range of a signed integer stored in 16-bit word in one's complement form

Like sign and magnitude method, this method is not used in general purpose computers.

Two's complement form

All bits change when the sign of the number changes. So the whole number, not just the most significant bit, takes part in the negation processes. However, we have only one 0.

With a little thought, you should recognize that 0 and –1 are complement of each other. Likewise +32767 and – 32768 are the complement of each other. The range of integers in 2's complement format is shown Fig. 8.14.

Fig. 8.13   Range of a signed integer stored in 16-bit word in two's complement form

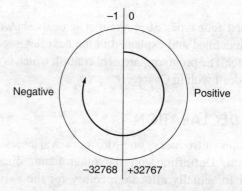

Fig. 8.14   Cyclic view of the range of a signed integer stored in a 16-bit word in two's complement form

32767 is at the bottom of the circle. When we add 10, we move clockwise 10 positions which puts us in the negative portion of the number range. The value at that position is –32759. Thus, the geometric depiction of 2's complement numbers may help to understand how overflow conditions can be determined using this representation for negative numbers. Starting at any point on the circle, you can add positive k (or subtract negative k) to that number (the starting point number) by moving k positions clockwise. Similarly, you can subtract positive k (or add negative k) from that number by moving k positions counter-clockwise. If an arithmetic operation results in traversal of the point where the endpoints are joined, an incorrect answer will result.

8.11.2 How are Floats and Doubles Stored?

Floats and doubles are stored in *mantissa* and *exponent* forms except that instead of the exponent representing the power of 10, it represents the power of 2, since base 2 is the computer's natural format. The number of bytes used to represent a floating-point number depends on the precision of the variable. float is used to declare *single-precision* variables, whereas the type double denotes *double-precision* values. The representation of the mantissa and exponent in these variables is in accordance with the IEEE floating-point standards. This representation is followed by most of the C compilers. The IEEE format expresses a floating-point number in a binary form known as a *normalized* form. Normalization involves adjusting the exponent so that the *binary point* (the binary analog of the decimal point) in the mantissa always lies to the right of the most significant non-zero digit. In binary representation, this means that the most significant digit of the mantissa is always 1. This property of the normalized representation is exploited by the IEEE format when storing the mantissa. Consider an example of generating the normalized form of a floating-point number. For instance, the binary equivalent to represent the decimal number 5.375 can be obtained as shown in the following example.

EXAMPLE

Integer part conversion to binary

2	5	
2	2	1
2	1	0
	0	1

Quotient Remainder

Writing the remainders in reverse order, the integer part in binary is 101

Fraction part conversion to binary

0.375 × 2 = 0.750 0
0.750 × 2 = 1.500 1
0.500 × 2 = 1.000 1

← Whole numbers

Writing the whole numbers part in the same order in which they are obtained, the fraction part in binary is 011

Thus, the binary equivalent of 5.375 would be 101.011. The normalized form of this binary number is obtained by adjusting the exponent until the decimal point is to the right of the most significant 1. In this case, the result is 1.01011×2^2. The IEEE format for floating-point storage uses a sign bit, a mantissa, and an exponent for representing the power of 2. The sign bit denotes the sign of the number: 0 represents a positive value and 1 denotes a negative value. The mantissa is represented in binary. Converting the floating point number to its normalized form results in a mantissa whose most significant digit is always 1. The IEEE format takes advantage of this by not storing this bit at all. The exponent is an integer stored in unsigned binary format after adding a positive integer bias. This ensures that the stored exponent is always positive. The value of the bias is 127 for floats and 1023 for doubles. Thus, 1.01011×2^2 is represented as follows:

Consider another example. Suppose the number –0.25 has to be represented in IEEE format. On conversion to binary, this number would become –0.01 and in its normalized form it would be -1.0×2^{-2}. This normalized form when represented in IEEE format would look like

Now it is known that converting the floating point number to its normalized form results in a mantissa whose most significant digit is always 1. The IEEE format takes advantage of this by not storing this bit at all. The exponent is an integer stored in an unsigned binary format after adding a positive integer bias. This ensures that the stored exponent is always positive. The value of the bias is 127 for floats and 1023 for doubles. Figure 8.15 shows how any float and double are generally represented in the IEEE format.

Fig. 8.15 IEEE format for representing float and double

According to most C literature, the valid range for floats is 10^{-38} to 10^{38}. But, how is such an odd range used? Well, the answer lies in the IEEE representation. Since the exponent of a float in IEEE format is stored with a positive bias of 127, the smallest positive value that can be stored in a float variable is 2^{-127}, which is approximately 1.175×10^{-38}. The largest positive value is 2^{128}, which is about 3.4×10^{38}. Similarly for a double variable, the smallest possible value is 2^{-1023}, which is approximately 2.23×10^{-308}. The largest positive value that can be held in a double variable is 2^{1024}, which is approximately 1.8×10^{308}.

There is one more quirk. After obtaining the IEEE format for a float, when the time comes to actually store it in memory, it is stored in the reverse order. That is, if the user calls the four-byte IEEE form as ABCD, then while storing in memory, it is stored in the form DCBA. This can be understood with an example. Suppose the floating-point number in question is 5.375. Its IEEE representation is 01000000101011000000000000000000 0000. Expressed in Hex, this is 40 AC 00 00. While storing this in memory, it is stored as 00 00 AC 40.

The representation of a `long double` (10-byte entity) is also similar. The only difference is that unlike `float` and `double`, the most significant bit of the normalized form is specifically stored. In a `long double`, 1 bit is occupied by the sign, 15 bits by the biased exponent (bias value 16383), and 64 bits by the mantissa.

8.12 TOKEN

Tokens are the basic lexical building blocks of source code. In other words, tokens are one or more symbols understood by the compiler that help it interpret the program code. Characters are combined into tokens according to the rules of the programming language. The compiler checks the tokens so that they can be formed into legal strings according to the syntax of the language. There are five classes of tokens: *identifiers*, *reserved words*, *operators*, *separators*, and *constants*.

Identifier   It is a sequence of characters invented by the programmer to identify or name a specific object, and the name is formed by a sequence of letters, digits, and underscores.

Keywords   These are explicitly reserved words that have a strict meaning as individual tokens to the compiler. They cannot be redefined or used in other contexts. Use of variable names with the same name as any of the keywords will cause a compiler error.

Operators   These are tokens used to indicate an action to be taken (usually arithmetic operations, logical operations, bit operations, and assignment operations). Operators can be simple operators (a single character token) or compound operators (two or more character tokens).

Separators   These are tokens used to separate other tokens. Two common kinds of separators are indicators of an end of an instruction and separators used for grouping.

Constant   It is an entity that does not change.

Consider the following piece of code

```
if(x<5)
    x = x + 2;
else
    x = x + 10;
```

Here, the tokens that will be generated are

```
Keywords   : if , else
Identifier : x
Constants  : 2, 10,5
```

```
Operators  : +,=
Separator  : ;
```

8.12.1 Identifier

Identifier or name is a sequence of characters created by the programmer to identify or name a specific object. In C, variables, arrays, functions, and labels are named. Describing them may help to learn something about the character of the language since they are elements that C permits the programmer to define and manipulate. Some rules must be kept in mind when naming identifiers. These are stated as follows:

1. The first character must be an alphabetic character (lower-case or capital letters) or an underscore '_'.
2. All characters must be alphabetic characters, digits, or underscores.
3. The first 31 characters of the identifier are significant. Identifiers that share the same first 31 characters may be indistinguishable from each other.
4. A keyword cannot be duplicated by an identifier. A keyword is word which has special meaning in C.

Some examples of proper identifiers are `employee_number`, `box_4_weight`, `monthly_pay`, `interest_per_annum`, `job_number`, and `tool_4`.

Some examples of incorrect identifiers are `230_item`, `#pulse_rate`, `total~amount`, `/profit margin`, and `~cost_per_item`.

8.12.2 Keywords

Keywords are the vocabulary of C. Because they are special to C, one cannot use them for variable names.

There are 32 words defined as keywords in C. These have predefined uses and cannot be used for any other purpose in a C program. They are used by the compiler to compile the program. They are always written in lower-case letters. A complete list of these keywords is given in Table 8.7.

Table 8.7 Keywords in C

auto	double	int	struct
break	else	long	switch
case	enum	register	typedef
char	extern	return	union
const	float	short	unsigned
continue	for	signed	void
default	goto	sizeof	volatile
do	if	static	while

Several keywords were added in C89: const, enum, signed, void, and volatile. The new keywords in C99 are inline, restrict, _Bool, _Complex, and _Imaginary.

Table 8.8 Full set of keywords upto C99

auto	enum	restrict	unsigned
break	extern	return	void
case	float	short	volatile
char	for	signed	while
const	goto	sizeof	_Bool
continue	if	static	_Complex
default	inline	struct	_Imaginary
do	int	switch	
double	long	typedef	
else	register	union	

Note that compiler vendors (like Microsoft and Borland) provide their own keywords apart from the ones mentioned above. These include extended keywords such as near, far, and asm. Though it has been suggested by the ANSI committee that every such compiler-specific keyword should be preceded by two underscores (as in __asm), not every vendor follows this rule.

8.12.3 Constant

A constant is an explicit data value written by the programmer. Thus, it is a value known to the compiler at compiling time. The compiler may deal with this value in any of several ways, depending on the type of constant and its context. For example, the binary equivalent of the constant may be inserted directly into the output code stream. The value of the constant may be stored in a special data area in memory. The compiler may decide to use the constant's value for its own immediate purpose, e.g., to determine how much storage it should allocate to a data array.

C permits integer constants, floating-point constants, character constants, and string constants. Table 8.9 depicts the types of constants that C allows. An integer constant consists of a sequence of digits. It is normally interpreted as a decimal value. Thus, 1, 25, and 23456 are all decimal integer constants.

A literal integer (e.g., 1984) is always assumed to be of type int, unless it has an 'L' or 'l' suffix, in which case it is treated as a long. Also, a literal integer can be specified to be unsigned using the suffix U or u. For example,

```
1984L  1984l  1984U  1984u  1984LU  1984ul
```

Literal integers can be expressed in decimal, octal, and hexadecimal notations. The decimal notation is the one that has been used so far. An integer is taken to be octal if it is preceded by a zero (0), and hexadecimal if it is preceded by a 0x or 0X. For example,

```
92    /* decimal          */
0134  /* equivalent octal    */
0x5C  /* equivalent hexadecimal */
```

Note

- In ANSI C, a decimal integer constant is treated as an unsigned long if its magnitude exceeds that of the signed long. An octal or hexadecimal integer that exceeds the limit of int is taken to be unsigned; if it exceeds this limit, it is taken to be long; and if it exceeds this limit, it is treated as an unsigned long. An integer constant is regarded as unsigned if its value is followed by the letter 'u' or 'U', e.g., 0x9999u; it is regarded as unsigned long if its value is followed by 'u' or 'U' and 'l' or 'L', e.g., 0xFFFFFFFFul.

A floating-point constant consists of an integer part, a decimal point, a fractional part, and an exponent field containing an e or E followed by an integer. Both integer and fractional parts are digit sequences. Certain portions of this format may be missing as long as the resulting number is distinguishable from a simple integer. For example, either the decimal point or the fractional part, but not both, may be absent. A literal real (e.g., 0.06) is always assumed to be of type double, unless it has an 'F' or 'f' suffix, in which case it is treated as a float, or an 'L' or 'l' suffix, in which case it is treated as a long double. The latter uses more bytes than a double for better accuracy (e.g., 10 bytes on the programmer's PC), for example,

```
0.06F   0.06f   3.141592654L   3.1415926541
```

In addition to the decimal notation used so far, literal reals may also be expressed in *scientific* notation. For example, 0.002164 may be written in scientific notation as

```
2.164E-3   or   2.164e-3
```

The letter E (or e) stands for *exponent*. The scientific notation is interpreted as follows:

$$2.164E-3 = 2.164 \times 10^{-3}$$

The following are examples of long long:

```
12345LL
12345ll
```

The following are examples of unsigned long long:

```
123456ULL
123456ull
```

A character constant normally consists of a single character enclosed in single quotes. Thus, for example, 'b' and '$' are both character constants. Each takes on the numeric value of its character in the machine's character set. Unless stated otherwise, it will henceforth be assumed that the ASCII code is used. This table is provided in Appendix B. Thus, for example, writing down the character constant 'A' is equivalent to writing down the hex value 41 or the octal value 101. The 'A' form is preferable, of course, first, because its meaning is unmistakable, and second, because it is independent of the actual character set of the machine.

In C, certain special characters, in particular, non-printing control characters are represented by special, so-called escape character sequences, each of which begins with the special backslash (\) escape character. Most of these escape codes are designed to make visible, on paper, any of those characters whose receipt by a printer or terminal causes a special, non-printing control action.

Character constants can also be defined via their octal ASCII codes. The octal value of the character, which may be found from the table in Appendix B, is preceded by a backslash and enclosed in single quotes.

```
char terminal_bell = '\07';
                /* 7 = octal ASCII code for beep */

char backspace = '\010';
                /* 10 = octal code for backspace */
```

For ANSI C compilers, character constants may be defined by hex digits instead of octals. Hex digits are preceded by x, unlike 0 in the case of octals. Thus, in ANSI C,

```
char backspace = '\xA';
```
is an acceptable alternative declaration to
```
char backspace = '\010';
```

Any number of digits may be written, but the value stored is undefined if the resulting character value exceeds the limit of char.

On an ASCII machine, both '\b' and '\010' are equivalent representations. Each will print the backspace character. But the latter form, the ASCII octal equivalent of '\b', will not work on an EBCDIC machine, typically an IBM mainframe, where the collating sequence of the characters (i.e., their gradation or numerical ordering) is different. In the interests of portability, it is therefore preferable to write '\b' for the backspace character rather than its octal code. Then the program will work as faultlessly on an EBCDIC machine as it will on an ASCII.

Note that the character constant 'a' is not the same as the string "a". A string is really an array of characters that is a bunch of characters stored in consecutive memory locations, the last location containing the null character; so the string "a" really contains two chars, an 'a' immediately followed by '\0'. It is important to realize that the null character is not the same as the decimal digit 0, the ASCII value of which is 00110000.

A string constant is a sequence of characters enclosed in double quotes. Whenever the C compiler encounters a string constant, it stores the character sequence in an available data area in memory. It also records the address of the first character and appends to the stored sequence an additional character, the null character '\0', to mark the end of the string.

The length of a character string is the number of characters in it (again, excluding the surrounding double quotes). Thus, the string "messagen" has a length of eight. The actual number of stored characters is one more as a null character is added.

The characters of a string may be specified using any of the notations for specifying literal characters. For example,
```
"Name\tAddress\tTelephone" /* tab-separated words */
"ASCII character 65: \101"/* 'A' specified as '101' */
```

A long string may extend beyond a single line, in which case each of the preceding lines should be terminated by a backslash. For example,
```
"Example to show \
the use of backslash for \
writing a long string"
```

The backslash in this context means that the rest of the string is continued on the next line. The preceding string is equivalent to the single-line string.
```
"Example to show the use of backslash for writing a
long string"
```

Note

- A common programming error results from confusing a single-character string (e.g., "A") with a single character (e.g., 'A'). These two are *not* equivalent. The former consists of two bytes (the character 'A' followed by the character '\0'), whereas the latter consists of a single byte.

The shortest possible string is the null string (" "). It simply consists of the null character. Table 8.9 summarizes the different constants.

Table 8.9 Specifications of different constants

Type	Specification	Example
Decimal	nil	50
Hexadecimal	Preceded by 0x or 0X	0x10
Octal	Begins with 0	010
Floating constant	Ends with f/F	123.0f
Character	Enclosed within single quotes	'A' 'o'
String	Enclosed within double quotes	"welcome"
Unsigned integer	Ends with U/u	37 u
Long	Ends with L/l	37 L
Unsigned long	Ends with UL/w	37 UL

C89 added the suffixes U and u to specify unsigned numbers. C99 adds LL to specify long long.

More than one \n can be used within a string enabling multi-line output to be produced with a single use of the printf() function. Here's an example.
```
int main()
{
    printf("This sentence will \n be printed\nin\
    multi-line \n");
    return 0;
}
```

When the program was compiled and run, it produced the following output:

```
This sentence will
be printed
in multi-line
```

However if the string is too long to fit on a single line, then it is possible to spread a string over several lines by escaping the actual new-line character at the end of a line by preceding it with a backslash. The string may then be continued on the next line as shown in the following program:

```
int main()
{
  printf("hello,\
    world\n");
  return 0;
}
```

The output is

```
hello, world
```

The indenting spaces at the start of the string continuation have been taken as part of the string. A better approach is to use *string concatenation* which means that two strings which are only separated by *whitespaces* are regarded by the compiler as a single string. Space, newline, tab character, and comment are collectively known as *whitespace*. The use of string concatenation is shown by the following example:

```
int main()
{
  printf("hello," "world\n");
  return 0;
}
```

8.12.4 Assignment

The assignment operator is the single equal to sign (=). The general form of the assignment statement is

```
variable_name = expression;
```

Some examples are given below.

```
i = 6;
i = i + 1;
```

The assignment operator replaces the content of the location 'i' with the evaluated value of the expression on its right-hand side. The assignment also acts as an expression that returns the newly assigned value. Some programmers use the feature to write statements like the following:

```
y = (x = 2 * x);
```

This statement puts x's new value in y. The operand to the left of the assignment operator must be a variable name. C does not allow any expression, constant, or function to be placed to the left of the assignment operator. Thus, its left operand should be a variable and its right operand may be an arbitrary expression. The latter is evaluated and the outcome is stored in the location denoted by the variable name. For example, the mathematical expression x + 2 = 0 does not become an assignment expression in C by typing x + 2 = 0. It is wrong in C, as the left-hand side of the 'equal to' operator (assignment operator) must not have an expression, value, or constant.

The operand to the left of the assignment operator is an lvalue that denotes left value. An lvalue is anything that denotes a memory location in which a value may be stored. The only kind of lvalue identified so far in this book is a variable. It will be discussed in detail later in this chapter. Other types of lvalues, based on pointers and references, will be described later in the book.

8.12.5 Initialization

When a variable is declared, the C compiler does not assign any value to the variable, unless it is instructed to do so. Such declaration is called a *tentative declaration*. For example,

```
int i; /* This declaration is tentative */
int x;
x = i + 5;
/* variable i is not assigned any known value, and
therefore the value of x is undefined. This is a bug
*/
```

To prevent such pitfalls, always assign a value to the variable during the declaration of variables. This is known as initialization. The value of initialization is called the initializer. The general form of the initialization statement is

```
data type variable_name=constant;
```

For example,

```
int i = 100; /* 100 is an initializer */
int x;
x = i + 5;
/* since i has been given a value during its declaration,
x is evaluated to hold a value 105 */
```

Check Your Progress

1. What will be the output of the following program?
   (a)
   ```
   #include <stdio.h>
   int main()
   {
     int a=010;
     printf("\n a=%d",a);
     return 0;
   }
   ```
   Output a = 8

   (b)
   ```
   #include <stdio.h>
   int main()
   {
     int a=010;
   ```

```
printf("\n a=%o",a);
return 0;
}
```
Output a = 10

Explanation: In (a), the integer constant 010 is taken to be octal as it is preceded by a zero (0). Here the variable 'a' is printed with %d specifier. The decimal equivalent of the octal value 10, which is 8, will be printed. Whereas in (b) the same variable is printed with %o format specifier, so 10 is printed on the screen.

(c)
```
#include <stdio.h>
int main()
{
    int a=010;
    printf("\n a=%x",a);
    return 0;
}
```
Output a = 8

Explanation: In (c), the octal value 10 is printed with %x format specifier, i.e., hexadecimal equivalent of 10, which is 8, will be printed.

(d)
```
#include <stdio.h>
int main()
{
    int a=53;
    printf("\n a=%o",a);
    return 0;
}
```
> Decimal value "53" is stored in "a".

Output a = 65

Explanation: In (d), an integer constant 53 is stored in the variable 'a' but is printed with %o. The octal equivalent of 53, which is 65, will be printed.

(e)
```
#include <stdio.h>
int main()
{
    int a=53;
    printf("\n a=%X",a);
    return 0;
}
```
Output a = 35

Explanation: In (e), an integer constant 53 is stored in the variable 'a' but is printed with %X. The hexadecimal equivalent of 53, which is 35, will be printed.

8.13 OPERATORS AND EXPRESSIONS

An operator is a symbol that specifies the mathematical, logical, or relational operation to be performed. This section introduces the built-in C operators for composing expressions

with variables. An expression is any computation that yields a value. Figure 8.16 gives the classification of operators in C language. Table 8.10 gives the different types of operators.

Table 8.10 Types of operators

Type of operator	Operator symbols with meanings		
Arithmetical	Unary		
	+	(Unary)	
	−	(Unary)	
	++	Increment	
	−−	Decrement	
	Binary		
	+	Addition	
	−	Subtraction	
	*	Multiplication	
	/	Division	
	%	Modulo	
	Ternary		
	?:	Discussed later	
Assignment	Simple Assignment		
	=		
	Compound Assignment		
	+=, −=, *=, /=, %=, &=, ^=, |=		
	Expression Assignment		
	A= 5+(b=8 + (c=2)) -4		
Relational	>, <, >=, <=		
Equality	==	(Equal to)	
	!=	(Not equal to)	
Logical	&&	(Logical AND)	
	||	(Logical OR)	
	!	(Logical NOT)	
Bitwise	&	(Bitwise AND)	
	|	(Bitwise OR)	
	~	(Complement)	
	^	(Exclusive OR)	
	>>	(Right Shift)	
	<<	(Left Shift)	
Others	,	(Comma)	
	*	(indirection),	
	.	(membership operator)	
	->	(membership operator)	

When discussing expressions, the term evaluation is often used. For example, it is said that an expression evaluates to a certain value. Usually the final value is the only reason for evaluating the expression. However, in some cases, the expression may also produce side effects. These are permanent changes in the program state. In this sense, C expressions are different from mathematical expressions.

C provides operators for composing arithmetic, relational, logical, bitwise, and conditional expressions. It also provides operators that produce useful side effects, such as assignment, increment, and decrement. Each category of operators will be discussed in turn. The precedence rules that govern the order of operator evaluation in a multi-operator expression will also be discussed.

Fig. 8.16   Classification of operators in C language

8.13.1 Arithmetic Operators in C

There are three types of arithmetic operators in C: binary, unary, and ternary.

Binary operators

C provides five basic arithmetic binary operators. These are summarized in Table 8.11.

Table 8.11   Arithmetic binary operators

Operator	Name	Example
+	Addition	12 + 4.9 /* gives 16.9*/
-	Subtraction	3.98 - 4 /* gives -0.02*/
*	Multiplication	2 * 3.4 /* gives 6.8 */
/	Division	9 / 2.0 /* gives 4.5 */
%	Remainder	13 % 3 /* gives 1 */

Except for remainder (%), all other arithmetic operators can accept a mix of integer and real operands. Generally, if both operands are integers, the result will be an integer. However, if one or both of the operands are reals, the result will be a real (or double to be exact).

When both operands of the division operator (/) are integers, the division is performed as an integer division and not the normal division. Integer division always results in an integer outcome, i.e., the result is always rounded off by ignoring the remainder. For example,

```
9/2   /* gives 4, not 4.5 */

-9/2  /* gives -4, not 4 */
```

Unintended integer divisions are a common source of programming errors. To obtain a real division when both operands are integers, cast one of the operands to be real, which means forcing the data type of the variable to real. Typecasting will be explained in detail later in this chapter. The following example demonstrates the case of real division.

```
int    cost = 100;

int    volume = 80;

double unitPrice;

unitPrice = cost/(double) volume; /* gives 1.25 */
```

The remainder operator (%) always expects integers for both of its operands. It returns the integer part of the remainder obtained after dividing the operands. For example, 13%3 is calculated by integer division of 13 by 3 to give a remainder of 1; the result is therefore 1.

It is possible for the outcome of an arithmetic operation to be too large for storing in a designated variable. This situation is called an overflow. The outcome of an overflow is machine-dependent and therefore undefined. For example,

```
unsigned char k = 10 * 92;  /* overflow: 920 > 255  */
```

It is not possible to divide a number by zero. This operation is illegal and results in a run-time *division-by-zero* exception that typically causes the program to terminate.

The effects of attempting to divide by zero are officially undefined. The ANSI standard does not require compiler writers to do anything special, so anything might happen. Of course we tried this by changing the value of a variable to zero in a program. Turbo C spotted what was going on and displayed the message

```
Divide error
```

The UNIX systems were slightly less informative producing the following messages:

```
Arithmetic exception (core dumped)
```
```
Breakpoint - core dumped
```

A few examples on the use of various arithmetic operators are given below.

EXAMPLES

```
1.  #include <stdio.h>

    int main( )

    {

        int a = 100;

        int b = 2;

        int c = 25;

        int d = 4;

        int result;

        result = a-b;              /*subtraction */

        printf("a - b = %d \n", result);
```

```
    result = b * c;          /* multiplication */
    printf("b * c = %d \n", result);
    result = a / c;                /* division */
    printf("a / c = %d \n", result);
    result = a + b * c;
    printf("a + b * c = %d \n", result);
    printf("a * b + c * d = %d\n", a* b+c*d);
    return 0;
}
```

Output

```
a - b = 98
b * c = 50
a / c = 4
a + b * c = 150
a * b + c * d = 300
```

```
2.  #include <stdio.h>
    int main()
    {
      int a = 25;
      int b = 2;
      int result;
      float c = 25.0;
      float d = 2.0;
      printf("6 + a / 5 * b = %d \n", 6 + a / 5 * b);
      printf("a / b * b = %d\n", a / b * b);
      printf("c / d * d = %f\n", c / d * d);
      printf("-a = %d\n",-a);
      return 0;
    }
```

Output

```
6 + a / 5 * b = 16
a / b * b = 24
c / d * d = 25.000000
-a = -25
```

Note the difference between this and the previous program. When we evaluate 6 + a / 5 * b, we have not stored its value in any variable, but it is evaluated in the printf statement itself and printed straight away.

Note

```
op1/op2
op1%op2
```

For / and %, op2 must be non-zero; op2 = 0 results in an error (We cannot divide by zero.). When op1 and op2 are integers and the quotient is not an integer, then the following points have to be noted:

- If op1 and op2 have the same sign, op1/op2 is the largest integer less than the true quotient, then op1%op2 has the sign of op1.
- If op1 and op2 have opposite signs, op1/op2 is the smallest integer greater than the true quotient, then op1%op2 has the sign of op1.

It is to be noted that rounding off is always towards zero.

- % operator returns the remainder of an integer division. i.e., x%y = x − (x/y)*y, where x and y both are of integer types. This operator can be applied only to integer operands and cannot be applied to operands of type float or double. The following example shows the occurrence of compiler error when the % operator is applied on a floating-point number:

```
#include <stdio.h>
  int main()
  {
    float c= 3.14;
    printf("%f", c%2);
    return 0;
  }
```

Check Your Progress

1. What will be the output of the following programs?
   (a)
```
#include <stdio.h>
    int main()
    {
      int x = 5, y = 7, z;
      z = x + y;
      printf("The value of x is: %d\n", x);
      printf("The value of y is: %d\n", y);
      printf("Their sum, z, is: %d\n", z);
      return 0;
    }
```

   Output
```
The value of x is: 5
The value of y is: 7
Their sum, z, is: 12
```

   (b)
```
#include <stdio.h>
    int main()
    {
      int a, b, c; /* a, b and c are undefined. */
      c= a + b ;
      printf("The value of a is: %d\n", a);
      printf("The value of b is: %d\n", b);
      printf("Their sum, c, is: %d\n", c);
      return 0;
    }
```

   Output
```
The value of a is: 2146744409
The value of b is: 2146744417
Their sum, c, is: -1478470
```

Now, look at the output of this program. Could it be possible to predict the values a, b, and c? Never assume a variable to have a meaningful value, unless a value is assigned to it.

Unary operators

The unary '–' operator negates the value of its operand (clearly, a signed number). A numeric constant is assumed positive unless it is preceded by the negative operator. That is, there is no unary '+'. It is implicit. Remember that -x does not change the value of x at the location where it permanently resides in memory.

Apart from this, there is another group of unary operators available in C that are described next.

Unary increment and decrement operators The unary '++' and '--' operators, respectively, increment or decrement the value of a variable by 1. There are 'pre' and 'post' variants for both operators that do slightly different things as explained below.

var++ increment 'post' variant var-- decrement 'post' variant

++var increment 'pre' variant --var decrement 'pre' variant

The following examples illustrate the use of increment and decrement operators on a variable not placed in an expression.

EXAMPLE

```
3. int i = 42;
   i++; /* increment contents of i, same as i = i + 1; */
                                    /* i is now 43 */
   i—; /* decrement contents of i, same as i = i - 1; */
                                    /* i is now 42 */
   ++i; /* increment contents of i, same as i = i + 1; */
                                    /* i is now 43 */
   --i; /* decrement contents of i, same as i = i - 1; */
                                    /* i is now 42 */
```

Basic rules for using ++ and -- operators

- The operand must be a variable but not a constant or an expression.
- The operator ++ and -- may precede or succeed the operand.

EXAMPLES

```
4. #include <stdio.h>
   int main()
   {
      int a=5, b=3;
      printf("\n %d", ++(a*b+2));
      return 0;
   }
```

Output

```
Compiler error - Lvalue required
```

```
5. #include <stdio.h>
   int main()
   {
      printf("\n %d", ++2));
      return 0;
   }
```

Output

```
Compiler error - Lvalue required
```

It is to be noted that i++ executes faster than i = i + 1 because the expression i++ requires a single machine instruction such as INR to carry out the increment operation whereas i = i + 1 requires more instructions to carry out this operation.

Pre- and post-variations of ++ and -- operators The pre- and post- (++ and --) operators differ in the value used for the operand n when it is embedded inside expressions.

If it is a 'pre' operator, the value of the operand is incremented (or decremented) before it is fetched for computation. The altered value is used for computation of the expression in which it occurs.

A few examples are shown here to demonstrate the use of the increment and decrement operators for postfix and prefix operations in expressions.

EXAMPLES

6. **Postfix operation**

(a) x = a++;

First action: store value of a in memory location for variable x.

Second action: increment value of a by 1 and store result in memory location for variable a.

(b) y = b--;

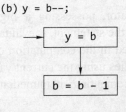

First action: put value of b in memory location for variable y.

Second action: decrement value of b by 1 and put result in memory location for variable b.

7. **Prefix operation**

(a) x = ++a;

First action: increment value of a by 1 and store result in memory location for variable a.

Second action: store value of a in memory location for variable x.

(b) `y = --b;`

First action: decrement value of b by 1 and put result in memory location for variable b.

Second action: put value of b in memory location for variable y.

To clarify, suppose that an `int` variable `a` has the value 5. Consider the assignment

`b = ++a;`

Pre-incrementation implies

Step 1: increment a; /* a becomes 6 */

Step 2: assign this value to b; /* b becomes 6 */

Result: a is 6, b is 6

If it is a 'post' operator, the value of the operand is altered after it is fetched for computation. The unaltered value is used in the computation of the expression in which it occurs.

Suppose again that `a` has the value 5 and consider the assignment

`b = a++;`

Post-incrementation implies

Step 1: assign the unincremented a to b;

/* b becomes 5 */

Step 2: increment a; /* a becomes 6 */

Result: a is 6, b is 5

The placement of the operator before or after the operand directly affects the value of the operand that is used in the computation. When the operator is positioned before the operand, the value of the operand is altered before it is used. When the operator is placed after the operand, the value of the operand is changed after it is used. Note in the examples above that the variable a has been incremented in each case.

Suppose that the `int` variable `n` has the value 5. Now consider a statement such as

`x = n++ / 2;`

The post-incrementation operator, possessing a higher priority than all other operators in the statement, is evaluated first. But the value of n that is used in the computation of x is still 5. Post-incrementation implies using the current value of n in the computation and incrementing; it immediately afterwards.

So x gets the value 5/2 = 2, even though n becomes 6. The rule is repeated; in an expression in which a post-incremented or post-decremented operand occurs, the current (unaltered) value of the operand is used; only then, is it changed. Accordingly, in the present instance, 5 is the value of n that is used in the computation. n itself becomes 6.

Now, consider the following statement.

`x = ++n / 2;`

where n is initially 5.

Pre-incrementation or pre-decrementation first alters the operand n; it is this new value that is used in the evaluation of x. In the example, n becomes 6, as before; but this new value is the value used in the computation, not 5. So x gets the value 6/2 = 3.

Now, consider the following program:

```
int main()
{
    int x=5;
    printf("Values are %d and %d\n",x++,++x);
    return 0;
}
```

Before revealing the results, let us see if we can work out what the output of the program will be. Here, it is needed to consider the values passed to the printf() function. The first part of the expression is "x++". This is a post-increment(use-and-increment) expression, so the value of the expression is 5 and as a side effect of evaluating the expression the value of x is increased to 6. Next, the value of the expression "++x" is calculated. This is the pre-increment (increment-and-use) expression, so the value of the expression is clearly 7. Thus the expected output is

`Values are 5 and 7`

Some compilers give this expected output but trying the same program using the Turbo C as well as GCC based compiler for example in Quincy 2005 resulted in the output

`Values are 6 and 7`

This is rather surprising but it can easily be explained. The C programming language standard rules quite specifically allow the parameters to be passed to a function to be evaluated in any convenient order. Some compilers worked left to right, which seems more natural, whereas others worked right to left which may be more efficient in some circumstances.

This must be remembered when writing programs that are to be compiled on many different machines. A similar difficulty arises when considering the output of a program such as

```
int main()
{
    int x = 4;
    printf("Result = %d\n",x++ + x);
    return 0;
}
```

Since the standard allows expressions involving commutative associative operators such as "+" to be evaluated in any order, a moment's thought shows that the value printed out would be 8 for right-to-left evaluation and 9 for left-to-right evaluation. On the Quincy 2005, the output was

```
Result = 8
```
whereas the Turbo C compiler gave the result
```
Result = 9
```
Strictly the behaviour of the program is undefined, which means the C standard fails to define what the result should be.

The following statements are undefined
```
i = ++i + 1;
a[i++] = i;
```
while allowing the following statements
```
i = i + 1;
a[i] = i;

#include <stdio.h>
int main(void)
{
  int number = 5;
  printf("the number is: %d\n", number);
  return 0;
}
```
When compiled and executed, this program should display the following on the screen:
```
the number is: 5
```
If the %d specifier is omitted, the value 5 vanishes from the output.

The values of several variables of different types are shown in a single statement in the following example:
```
#include <stdio.h>
int main(void)
{
  int i = 5;
  char ch= 'A';
  float f=12.345;
  printf("\n i = %d ch = %c f = %f", i, ch, f);
  return 0;
}
```

Output
```
i = 5 ch = A f = 12.345000
```

The conversion specifiers are replaced in order by the values of the variables that appear as the second and subsequent arguments to the printf() function, so the value of i corresponds to the first specifier %d, and the value of ch corresponds to the second one, i.e. %c, and so on.

One important point to note is that when a variable is not initialized with some values, then what is printed on the screen if the following program is compiled and run:
```
#include <stdio.h>
int main(void)
{
  int number;
  printf("the number is: %d\n", number);
  return 0;
}
```

The output will be anything, which means that the values are indeterminate; this means that one cannot make any assumptions about what values are initially in a location. On many systems we will find that the initial value is zero but you must not rely on this.

Abbreviated (compound) assignment expressions It is frequently necessary in computer programs to make assignments such as
```
n = n + 5;
```
C allows a shorter form for such statements, as shown.
```
n += 5;
```
Assignment expressions for other arithmetic operations may be similarly abbreviated as shown.
```
n -= 5; /* is equivalent to n = n - 5; */
n *=5;  /* is equivalent to n = n * 5; */
n /= 5; /* is equivalent to n = n / 5; */
n %= 5; /* is equivalent to n = n % 5; */
```
The priority and direction of association of each of the operators +=, -=, *=, /=, and %= is the same as that of the assignment operator.

8.13.2 Relational Operators in C

C provides six relational operators for comparing numeric quantities. These are summarized in Table 8.12. Relational operators evaluate to 1, representing the *true* outcome, or 0, representing the *false* outcome.

Note that the <= and >= operators are only supported in the form shown. In particular, =< and => are both invalid and do not mean anything.

The operands of a relational operator must evaluate to a number. Characters are valid operands since they are represented by numeric values. For example (assuming ASCII coding),
```
'A' < 'F' /* gives 1 (is like 65 < 70) */
```

Table 8.12 Relational operators

Operator	Action	Example
==	Equal	5 == 5 /* gives 1 */
!=	Not equal	5 != 5 /* gives 0 */
<	Less than	5 < 5.5 /* gives 1 */
<=	Less than or equal	5 <= 5 /* gives 1 */
>	Greater than	5 > 5.5 /* gives 0 */
>=	Greater than or equal	6.3 >= 5 /* gives 1 */

The relational operators should not be used for comparing strings because this will result in string *addresses* being compared, not string contents. For example, the expression

Computer Fundamentals and Programming in C

164

"HELLO" < "BYE"

causes the address of "HELLO" to be compared to the address of "BYE". As these addresses are determined by the compiler (in a machine-dependent manner), the outcome may be 0 or may be 1, and is therefore undefined.

C provides library functions (e.g., strcmp) for the lexicographic comparison of strings. These will be described later in the book.

8.13.3 Logical Operators in C

C provides three logical operators for forming logical expressions. These are summarized in Table 8.13. Like the relational operators, logical operators evaluate to 1 or 0.

Logical *negation* is a unary operator that negates the logical value of its single operand. If its operand is non-zero, it produces 0, and if it is 0, it produces 1. Logical AND produces 0 if one or both its operands evaluate to 0. Otherwise, it produces 1. Logical OR produces 0 if both its operands evaluate to 0. Otherwise, it produces 1.

Table 8.13 Logical operators

Operator	Action	Example	Result
!	Logical Negation	!(5 == 5)	0
&&	Logical AND	5 < 6 && 6 < 6	0
||	Logical OR	5 < 6 || 6 < 5	1

Note that here, zero and non-zero operands are mentioned, not zero and 1. In general, any non-zero value can be used to represent the logical *true*, whereas only zero represents the logical *false*. The following are, therefore, all valid logical expressions.

```
!20        gives 0
10 && 5    gives 1
10 || 5.5  gives 1
10 && 0    gives 0
```

C does not have a built-in Boolean type. It is customary to use the type int for this purpose instead. For example,

```
int   sorted = 0;    /* false */
int   balanced = 1;  /* true */
```

Exceptions in the evaluation of logical expressions containing && and || If the left operand yields a false value, the right operand is not evaluated by a compiler in a logical expression using &&. If the left operand evaluates true value, the right operand is not evaluated by the compiler in a logical expression with the || operator. The operators && and || have left to right associativity. Hence the left operand is evaluated first and, depending on the output, the right operand may or may not be evaluated.

EXAMPLE

```
8. #include <stdio.h>
   int main()
   {
       int i=0, j=1;
       printf("\n %d", i++ && ++j);
       printf("\n %d %d", i,j);
       return 0;
   }
```

Output

```
0
1 1
```

8.13.4 Bitwise Operators in C

C provides six bitwise operators for manipulating the individual bits in an integer quantity. These are summarized in Table 8.14.

Table 8.14 Bitwise operators

Operator	Action	Example
~	Bitwise Negation	~'\011' /* gives '\066' */
&	Bitwise AND	'\011' & '\027' /* gives '\001' */
|	Bitwise OR	'\011' | '\027' /* gives '\037' */
^	Bitwise Exclusive OR	'\011' ^ '\027' /* gives '\036' */
<<	Bitwise Left Shift	'\011' << 2 /* gives '\044' */
>>	Bitwise Right Shift	'\011' >> 2 /* gives '\002' */

Bitwise operators expect their operands to be integer quantities and treat them as bit sequences. Bitwise *negation* is a unary operator that complements the bits in its operands. Bitwise AND compares the corresponding bits of its operands and produces a 1 when both bits are 1, and 0 otherwise. Bitwise OR compares the corresponding bits of its operands and produces a 0 when both bits are 0, and 1 otherwise. Bitwise *exclusive OR* compares the corresponding bits of its operands and produces a 0 when both bits are 1 or both bits are 0, and 1 otherwise.

Bitwise *left shift* operator and bitwise *right shift* operator both take a bit sequence as their left operand and a positive integer quantity *n* as their right operand. The former produces a bit sequence equal to the left operand but which has been shifted *n* bit positions to the left. The latter produces a bit sequence equal to the left operand but which has been shifted *n* bit positions to the right. Vacated bits at either end are set to 0. The general form of the right shift statement is variable_name >> number of bit positions;

and that of the left shift statement is

variable_name << number of bit positions;

Table 8.15 illustrates bit sequences for the sample operands. To avoid worrying about the sign bit (which is machine dependent), it is common to declare a bit sequence as an unsigned quantity.

```
unsigned char x = '\011';
unsigned char y = '\027';
```

Table 8.15 Effect of bit-wise operator implementation

Example	Octal value	Bit sequence							
x	011	0	0	0	0	1	0	0	1
y	027	0	0	0	1	0	1	1	1
~x	366	1	1	1	1	0	1	1	0
x & y	001	0	0	0	0	0	0	0	1
x | y	037	0	0	0	1	1	1	1	1
x ^ y	036	0	0	0	1	1	1	1	0
x << 2	044	0	0	1	0	0	1	0	0
x >> 2	002	0	0	0	0	0	0	1	0

8.13.5 Conditional Operator in C

The conditional operator has three expressions. It has the general form

expression1 ? expression2 : expression3

First, *expression1* is evaluated; it is treated as a logical condition. If the result is non-zero, then *expression2* is evaluated and its value is the final result. Otherwise, *expression3* is evaluated and its value is the final result. For example,

```
int m = 1, n = 2, min;
min = (m < n ? m : n); /* min is assigned a value 1 */
```

In the above example, because m is less than n, m<n expression evaluates to be true, therefore, min is assigned the value m, i.e., 1.

The same code can also be written using the if-else construct, described in Chapter 10.

```
int m=1, n=2, min;
if(m<n)
  min=m;
else min=n;
```

Note that out of the second and the third expressions of the conditional operator, only one is evaluated. This may be significant when one or both contain side effects, that is, their evaluation causes a change to the value of a variable. For example, in

```
min = (m < n ? m++ : n++);
```

m is incremented because m++ is evaluated but n is not incremented because n++ is not evaluated.

8.13.6 Comma Operator

The comma operator allows the evaluation of multiple expressions, separated by the *comma*, from left to right in order and the evaluated value of the rightmost expression is accepted as the final result. The general form of an expression using a *comma* operator is

```
expressionM = (expression1, expression2, …,
              expressionN);
```

where the expressions are evaluated strictly from left to right and their values discarded, except for the last one, whose type and value determine the result of the overall expression. Here, it may be stated that in the preceding general form, the left hand side expression, expiressonM, may be omitted. In such a case, the right hand side expressions exist and the comma operator evaluates these from left to right. Finally, the value of the last expression is returned as the outcome. The application of the comma operator is best explained by the following examples.

EXAMPLES

9.
```
int i = 0;
int j;
j = (i += 1, i += 2, i + 3);
```
In this example, the *comma* operator is used with three expressions on the right hand side of the assignment operator. Hence, the comma operator takes these three expressions and evaluates them from left to right and returns the value of the rightmost expression. Thus, in this example, the operator first evaluates "i += 1" which increments the value of i. Then the next expression "i += 2" is evaluated which adds 2 to i, leading to a value of 3. The third expression is evaluated and its value is returned as the operator's result. Thus, j is assigned a value of 6.

10.
```
int m = 1;
int n;
n = (m = m+3, m%3);
```
Here, the comma operator takes two expressions. The operator first evaluates "m = m+3" which assigns a value 4 to m. Then the expression m%3 is evaluated to 1. Thus n is assigned a value of 1.

11.
```
int m, n, min;
int mCount = 0, nCount = 0;
.
.
.
min = (m < n ? mCount++, nCount++, n);
```
Here, when m is less than n, mCount++ is evaluated and the value of m is stored in min. Otherwise, nCount++ is evaluated and the value of n is stored in min.

12. Swapping of two integer variables using the comma operator:
```
#include <stdio.h>
int main()
{
```

```
int a=2,b=3,c;
c=a,a=b,b=c;  /* comma operator is used */
printf("\n a=%d b=%d",a,b);
return 0;
}
```
Output a=3 b=2

From these examples, it may be concluded that the comma operator is used to ensure that parts of an expression are performed in a left to right sequence. The comma allows for the use of multiple expressions where normally only one would be allowed. It is used most often in the for loop statement where one statement is called for, but several actually need to be coded.

The comma operator forces all operations that appear to the left to be fully completed before proceeding to the right of the comma. This helps eliminate any inaccuracy in the evaluation of the expression. For example,

```
num1 = num2 + 1, num2 = 2;
```

The comma operator ensures that num2 will not be changed to a 2 before num2 has been added to 1 and the result placed in num1. The other similar operators that are also considered to be sequence points like the comma operator are as follows:

```
&&
||
?:
```

When any of these operators are encountered all activity associated with any operator to the left is completed before the new operator begins executing. Both the semicolon and the comma also perform this service, ensuring that there is a way to control the order of executions in a program. The commas that separate the actual arguments in a function call are punctuation symbols, not sequence points. A punctuation symbol, in a function, does not guarantee that the arguments are either evaluated or passed to the function in any particular order.

8.13.7 sizeof Operator

C provides a useful operator, sizeof, for calculating the size of any data item or type. It takes a single operand that may be a type name (e.g., int) or an expression (e.g., 100) and returns the size of the specified entity in bytes. The outcome is totally machine-dependent. The following program illustrates the use of sizeof on the built-in types we have encountered so far.

```
#include <stdio.h>
int main()
{
    printf("char size = %d bytes\n", sizeof(char));
    printf("short size = %d bytes\n", sizeof(short));
    printf("int size = %d bytes\n", sizeof(int));
```

```
    printf("long size = %d bytes\n", sizeof(long));
    printf("float size = %d bytes\n", sizeof(float));
    printf("double size = %d bytes\n", sizeof(double));
    printf("1.55 size = %d bytes\n", sizeof(1.55));
    printf("1.55L size = %d bytes\n", sizeof(1.55L));
    printf("HELLO size = %d bytes\n", sizeof("HELLO"));
    return 0;
}
```

When run, the program will produce the following output (on the programmer's PC):

```
char size = 1 bytes
short size = 2 bytes
int size = 2 bytes
long size = 4 bytes
float size = 4 bytes
double size = 8 bytes
1.55 size = 8 bytes
1.55L size = 10 bytes
HELLO size = 6 bytes
```

8.13.8 Expression Evaluation—Precedence and Associativity

Evaluation of an expression in C is very important to understand. Unfortunately there is no 'BODMAS' rule in C language as found in algebra. Operators have rules of precedence and associativity that are used to determine how expressions are evaluated.

When there is more than one operator in an expression, it is the relative priorities of the operators with respect to each other that will determine the order in which the expression will be evaluated. This priority is known as precedence. The precedence of operators determines the order in which different operators are evaluated when they occur in the same expression. Operators of higher precedence are applied before operators of lower precedence.

Consider the following expression:

```
4 + 3 * 2
```

the operator '*' has higher precedence than '+', causing the multiplication to be executed first, then the addition. Hence, the value of the expression is 10. An equivalent expression is

```
4 + (3 * 2)
```

But what happens when an expression consists of operators with same precedence. For example

```
4 / 2 *3
```

The associativity of operators determines the order in which operators of equal precedence are evaluated when they occur in the same expression. The associativity defines the direction, left-to-right or right-to-left, in which the operator acts upon its operands.

Both * and / have the same precedence. Here, division operation will be executed first followed by multiplication. The value of the expression is 6.

Table 8.16 lists the operators in order of decreasing operator priority and states their direction of grouping.

Let's illustrate a statement as written below. Assume that *n* is a variable of type int:

```
n = 5 - 2 * 7 - 9;
```

The '*' has a higher precedence than '−' so it is evaluated first, and the statement is equivalent to:

```
n = 5 - 14 - 9;
```

The minus has left-to-right associativity, so the statement is equivalent to:

```
n = -18;
```

Also, the '=' has lower precedence than either '−' or '*' or any other arithmetic, logical, or relational operator, and this is how C enforces the rule that the expression to the right of the '=' gets evaluated first and then the resulting value gets assigned to the variable to the left of the '='. Here is another valid statement in C language:

```
x = x + 1;
```

The expression to the right of the equal sign is evaluated first, and its value is then assigned to the variable to the left. So let's assume the value stored in x is equal to 5. When this statement is executed, the expression to the right of '=' evaluates to 6, and the value of 6 is assigned back to x.

It makes sense for the priority of the assignment operator to be lower than the priorities of all the arithmetic operators, and for it to group from right to left. Naturally it is very important for programmers to become familiar with the precedence and grouping properties of all C operators. But if programmers are not sure of the order in which operators will be evaluated in a computation, they may use the parentheses operator, (), to override default priorities. Yes, even the parenthesis is an operator in C. The parenthesis operator has a priority higher than any binary operator, such as that for multiplication; it groups from left to right. Thus, in the statement

```
w = x * (y * z);
```

the product y * z will be computed first; the value obtained will then be multiplied by x; lastly, the assignment of the result will be made to w. Had the parentheses been absent, the order of the computation would first be, the multiplication of x by y, with the result stored as an intermediate quantity; second, the multiplication of this quantity by z; and third, the assignment of the result to w.

The parentheses are an example of a primary operator. C has in addition three other primary operators: array [ ], the dot (.), and arrow (→), which will be encountered in later chapters. All these operators have the same priority, higher than that of any other operator. They all group from left to right.

Aside from the primary operators, C operators are arranged in priority categories depending on the number of their operands. Thus, a unary operator has a single operand and a higher priority than any binary operator, which has two operands. Binary operators have a higher priority than the ternary operator, which has three operands. The comma operator may have any number of operands, and has the lowest priority of all C operators. Table 8.16 illustrates this rule.

One readily available example of a unary operator is the operator for negation, the (-). It changes the sign of the quantity stated on it. Since the unary operators have higher priority than the assignment operator, in the statement

```
x = -3;
```

the 3 is first negated, and only then is this value assigned to x. The negation operator has a priority just below that of the parentheses operator; it groups from right to left. Right to left association is a property the operator for negation shares in common with all unary operators. In the following statement

```
x = -(3 * 4);
```

the presence of the parentheses ensures that the expression 3 * 4 is evaluated first. It is then negated. Finally, x is assigned the value -12.

A question that might be asked is: Does C have a unary plus operator, +? In other words, can an assignment of the form a = + 5 be made? Not in compilers conforming to the K&R standard, though ANSI C does provide a unary plus operator. See Table 8.16.

Table 8.16 Precedence and associativity of operators

Operators	Associativity
( ) [ ] . ++ (postfix) -- (postfix)	L to R
++ (prefix) -- (prefix) !~ sizeof(type) + (unary) - (unary) & (address) * (indirection)	R to L
* / %	L to R
+ -	L to R
<< >>	L to R
< <= > >=	L to R
== !=	L to R
&	L to R
^	L to R
|	L to R
&&	L to R
||	L to R
?:	R to L
= += -= *= /= %= >>= <<= &= ^= |=	R to L
, (comma operator)	L to R

Note

- In the division of one integer by another, the remainder is discarded. Thus, 7/3 is 2, and 9/11 is 0. The % operator can only be used with the integer variables. It cannot be used with the variables of float or double.

- The multiplication, division, and residue-modulo operators have the same priority. The addition and subtraction operators also have equal priority, but this is lower than that of the former three operators, *, /, and %. All these operators group from left to right. In a C program, is the value of 3/5 + 2/5 the same as (3 + 2)/5? Is 3 * (7/5) the same as 3 * 7/5? The answer to both questions is 'No'.

EXAMPLES

In the examples below, let x be an integer variable.

13. `x = 2 * 3 + 4 * 5;`

    The products 2 * 3 and 4 * 5 are evaluated first; the sum 6 + 20 is computed next; finally the assignment of 26 is made to x.

14. `x = 2 * (3 + 4) * 5;`

    The parentheses guarantee that 3 + 4 be evaluated first. Since multiplication groups from left to right, the intermediate result 7 will be multiplied by 2 and then by 5, and the assignment of 70 will finally be made to x.

15. `x = 7*6 % 15/9;`

    Each of the operators above has equal priority; each groups from left to right. Therefore, the multiplication 7 * 6 (= 42) is done first, then the residue-modulo with respect to 15 (42 % 15 = 12), and finally the division (of 12) by 9. Since the division of one integer by another yields the integer part of the quotient and truncates the remainder, 12/9 gives the value 1. x is therefore assigned the value 1.

16. `x = 7 * (6 % 15)/9;`

    The parentheses ensure that 6 % 15 is evaluated first. The remainder, when 6 is divided by 15, is 6. In the second step, this result is multiplied by 7, yielding 42. Integer division of 42 by 9 gives 4 as the quotient, which is the value assigned to x.

17. `x = 7*6 % (15/9);`

    Here, 15/9 is performed first and yields 1. The next computation in order is 7 * 6 % 1, i.e., the remainder, on division of 42 by 1, is 0. x gets the value 0.

18. `x = 7 * ((6 % 15)/9);`

    The innermost parentheses are evaluated first: 6 % 15 is 6. The outer parentheses are evaluated next—6/9 is 0. x gets the value 7 * 0 = 0.

19. An example of the use of precedence of operators

```c
#include <stdio.h>
int main()
  {
    int a;
    int b = 4;
```

```c
    int c = 8;
    int d = 2;
    int e = 4;
    int f = 2;
    a = b + c / d + e * f;
                /* result without parentheses */
    printf("The value of a is = %d \n", a);
    a = (b + c) / d + e * f;
                /* result with parentheses */
    printf("The value of a is = %d \n", a);
    a = b + c / ((d + e) * f);
                /* another result with parentheses */
    printf("The value of a is = %d \n", a);
    return 0;
}
```

Output

```
The value of a is = 16
The value of a is = 14
The value of a is = 4
```

8.14 EXPRESSIONS REVISITED

An expression in C consists of a syntactically valid combination of operators and operands that computes to a value. An expression by itself is not a statement. Remember, a statement is terminated by a semicolon; an expression is not. Expressions may be thought of as the constituent elements of a statement, the 'building blocks' from which statements may be constructed. The important thing to note is that every C expression has a value. The number 7 as we said a while ago, or any other number by itself, is also an expression, the value of the number being the value of the expression. For example,

    3 * 4 % 5

is an expression with value 2.

    x = 3 * 4

is an example of an assignment expression. Note the absence of the semicolon in the assignment above. The terminating semicolon would have converted the expression into a statement. Like any other C expression, an assignment expression also has a value. Its value is the value of the quantity on the right-hand side of the assignment operator. Consequently, in the present instance, the value of the expression (x = 3 * 4) is 12. Consider a C statement such as

    z = (x = 3 * 4) / 5;

Here, the parentheses ensure that x is assigned the value 12 first. It is also the value of the parenthetical expression (x = 3 * 4), from the property that every expression has a value. Thus, the entire expression reduces to

    z = 12/5

Next, in order of evaluation, the integer division of 12 by 5 yields 2. The leftmost assignment operator finally gives the value 2 to z. x continues to have the value 12. Consider the expression

```
x = y = z = 3
```

The assignment operator groups from right to left. Therefore, the rightmost assignment

```
z = 3
```

is made first. z gets the value 3; this is also the value of the rightmost assignment expression, z = 3. In the next assignment towards the left the expression is

```
y = z = 3
```

Since the sub-expression z = 3 has the value 3, so

```
y = (z = 3)
```

i.e., y = 3

The assignment to y is again of the value 3. Equally then the entire expression

```
y = z = 3
```

gets the value 3. In the final assignment towards the left, x gets the value of this latter expression

```
x = (y = (z = 3))
```

Each parenthetical expression is 3. Thus x is 3. One statement that often confuses novice programmers is

```
x = x * x;
```

For those who have studied algebra, the immediate reaction may well be, 'This cannot be right, unless x is 0 or x is 1; and x is neither 0 nor 1 in the program.' However, the statement

```
x = x * x;
```

is not an algebraic equation. It is an instruction to the computer, which in English translates to the following:

Replace x by x times x.

Or, more colloquially, after its execution

(new value of x) is (old value of x) * (old value of x)

8.15 LVALUES AND RVALUES

An lvalue is an expression to which a value can be assigned. An rvalue can be defined as an expression that can be assigned to an lvalue. The lvalue expression is located on the *left side* of an assignment operator, whereas an rvalue is located on the *right side* of an assignment operator.

The address associated with a program variable in C is called its lvalue; the contents of that location are its rvalue, the quantity that is supposed to be the value of the variable. The rvalue of a variable may change as program execution proceeds; but never its lvalue. The distinction between lvalues and rvalues becomes sharper if one considers the assignment operation with variables a and b.

```
a = b;
```

b, on the right-hand side of the assignment operator, is the quantity to be found at the address associated with b, i.e.,

an rvalue. a is assigned the value stored in the address associated with b. a, on the left-hand side, is the address at which the contents are altered as a result of the assignment. a is an lvalue. The assignment operation deposits b's rvalue at a's lvalue.

An lvalue cannot be a constant. For example, consider the following statements:

```
1 = x;
x + y = a + b;
x + b = 5;
```

In each of the above cases, the left side of the statement evaluates to a constant value that cannot be changed because constants do not represent storable locations in memory. Therefore, these two assignment statements *do not* contain lvalue and will generate compiler errors.

Unlike an lvalue, an rvalue can be a constant or an expression, as shown here:

```
int x, y;
x = 5; /* 5 is an rvalue; x is an lvalue */
y = (x + 1); /* (x + 1) is an rvalue; y is an lvalue */
```

The difference between lvalue and rvalue is shown in Table 8.17.

Table 8.17 Lvalue versus rvalue

Lvalue	Rvalue
Consider the following assignment statement: a = b;	
Refers to the address that 'a' represents.	Means the content of the address that b represents.
is known at compile time.	is not known until run time.
Says where to store the value.	Tells what is to be stored.
Cannot be an expression or a constant.	Can be an expression or a constant.

8.16 TYPE CONVERSION IN C

Though the C compiler performs *automatic type conversions*, the programmer should be aware of what is going on so as to understand how C evaluates expressions.

8.16.1 Type Conversion in Expressions

When a C expression is evaluated, the resulting value has a particular data type. If all the variables in the expression are of the same type, the resulting type is of the same type as well. For example, if x and y are both of int type, the expression x + y is of int type as well.

What if the variables of an expression are of different types? In that case, the expression has the same data type as that of the variable with the largest size data type present in it. The smallest to the largest data types with respect to size are given as follows:

```
char
int
long
float
double
```

Thus, an expression containing an int and a char evaluates to type int, an expression containing a long and a float evaluates to type float, and so on. Within expressions, individual operands are promoted as necessary to match the associated operands in the expression. Operands are promoted in pairs for each binary operator in the expression. If both operands are of the same type, promotion is not needed. If they are not, promotion follows these rules:

- float operands are converted to double.
- char or short (signed or unsigned) are converted to int (signed or unsigned).
- If any one operand is double, the other operand is also converted to double, and that is the type of the result; or if any one operand is long, the other operand is treated as long, and that is the type of the result.
- If any one operand is of type unsigned, the other operand is converted to unsigned, and that is the type of the result; or the only remaining possibility is that both operands must be int, and that is also the type of the result.

Figure 8.16 illustrates the rule for data type promotion in an expression.

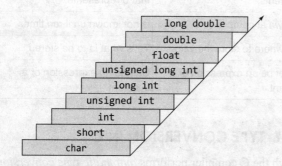

Fig. 8.16 Rule for data type promotion in an expression

For example, if x is an int and y is a float, evaluating the expression x/y causes x to be promoted to float type before the expression is evaluated. This does not mean that the type of variable x is changed. It means that a float type copy of x is created and used in the evaluation of the expression. The value of the expression is the float type. Likewise, if x is a double type and y is a float type, y will be promoted to double.

Figure 8.17 shows how the rule of type promotion is followed in a typical expression containing variables of mixed types. The data type of r evaluates to double.

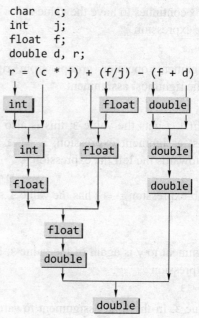

Fig. 8.17 Conversion of types in a mixed expression

8.16.2 Conversion by Assignment

Promotions also occur with the assignment operator. The expression on the right side of an assignment statement is always promoted to the type of the data object on the left side of the assignment operator. Note that this might cause a 'demotion' rather than a promotion. If f is a float type and i is an int type, i is promoted to float type in this assignment statement:

```
f = i;
```

In contrast, the assignment statement

```
i = f;
```

causes f to be demoted to type int. Its fractional part is lost on assignment to i. Remember that f itself is not changed at all; promotion affects only a copy of the value. Thus, after the following statements are executed

```
float f = 1.23;
int i;
i = f;
```

the variable i has the value 1, and f still has the value 1.23. As this example illustrates, the fractional part is lost when a floating point number is converted to an integer type.

The programmer should be aware that when an integer type is converted to a floating point type, the resulting floating point value might not exactly match the integer value. This is because the floating point format used internally by the computer cannot accurately represent every possible integer number.

In most cases, any loss of accuracy caused by this would be insignificant. To be sure, however, keep integer values in int type or long type variables.

Conversions of characters and integers

There are six basic methods of converting values from one type to another. The methods are:

Sign extension   This technique is adopted when converting a signed object to a wider signed object, e.g. converting a short int to a long int. It preserves the numerical value by filling the extra leading space with 1's or 0's.

Zero extension   This is used when converting an unsigned object to a wider unsigned object. It works by simply prefixing the value with the relevant number of zeroes.

Preserve low order data-truncate   This is used when converting an object to a narrower form. Significant information may be lost.

Preserve bit pattern   This is used when converting between signed and unsigned objects of the same width.

Internal conversion   This uses special hardware to convert between floating point types and from integral to floating point types.

Truncate at decimal point   This is used to convert from floating point types to integral types, and may involve loss of significant information.

The basic conversions listed above are those that take place on assignment.

Conversion of a shorter integer to a longer integer preserves the sign. Traditional C uses 'unsigned preserving integer promotion' (unsigned short to unsigned int), while ANSI C uses 'value preserving integer promotion' (unsigned short to int).

A longer integer is truncated on the left when converted to a shorter integer or to a char. Excess bits are discarded.

When an unsigned integer is converted to a longer unsigned or signed integer, the value of the result is preserved. Thus, the conversion amounts to padding with zeroes on the left.

When an unsigned integer is converted to a shorter signed or unsigned integer, the value is truncated on the left. If the result is signed, this truncation may produce a negative value.

Consider the following program which illustrates the above facts:

```c
#include <stdio.h>
int main()
{
    short    int    si;
    long     int    li;
    unsigned        short   int     usi;
    unsigned        long    int     uli;
    si = -10;
    li = si; /* sign extension - li should be -10 */
```

```c
    printf("si = %8hd li = %8ld\n",si,li);
    usi = 40000U;    /* unsigned decimal constant */
    uli = usi;
            /* zero extension - uli should be 40000 */
    printf("usi = %8hu uli = %8lu\n",usi,uli);
    uli = 0xabcdef12;          /* sets most bits ! */
    usi = uli;
                    /* will truncate - discard more
                                    sigficant bits */
    printf("usi = %8hx uli = %8lx\n",usi,uli);
    si = usi;              /* preserves bit pattern */
    printf("si = %8hd usi = %8hu\n",si,usi);
    si = -10;
    usi = si;              /* preserves bit pattern */
    printf("si = %8hd usi = %8hu\n",si,usi);
    return 0;
}
```

Output

```
si = -10      li = -10
usi = 40000 uli = 40000
usi = ef12   uli = abcdef12
si = -4334   usi = 61202
si = -10     usi = 65526
```

It may be interesting to note that the difference between the pairs of values on the last two lines is 65536. Conversions between signed long and unsigned short are typically undefined. The next program shows conversions to and from floating point types.

There is an extra complication concerning variables of type char. The conversion rules to be applied depend on whether the compiler regards char values as signed or unsigned. Basically the ANSI C standard says that variables of type char are promoted to type unsigned int or type signed int depending on whether the type char is signed or unsigned. An unsigned int may then be further converted to a signed int by bit pattern preservation. This is implementation dependent. The following program shows what might happen.

```c
#include <stdio.h>
int main()
{
    int si;
    unsigned int usi;
    char ch = 'a';
                // Most significant bit will be zero
    si = ch;    // will give small +ve integer
    usi = ch;
    printf("c = %c\n  si = %d\n usi = %u\n", ch,\
            si,usi);
    ch = '\377';             /* set all bits to 1 */
    si = ch;    /* sign extension makes negative */
    usi = ch;
```

```
    printf("si = %d\n usi = %u\n",si,usi);
    return 0;
}
```

Output

```
    c = a
    si = 97
    usi = 97
    si = -1
    usi = 4294967295
```

The Turbo C compiler regarded *char* as a signed data type applying sign extension when assigning the *signed char* c to the *signed int* si . The conversion from *signed char* c to *unsigned int* usi is more interesting. This took place in two stages—the first being sign extension and the second being bit pattern preservation. On the IBM 6150, *char* is treated as an unsigned data type, both assignments using bit pattern preservation.

The conversion of the unsigned char to either the signed int si or the unsigned int usi is by bit pattern preservation.

Conversions of float and double

ANSI C considers all floating point constants to be implicitly double precision, and operations involving such constants therefore take place in double precision. To force single precision arithmetic in ANSI C, use the f or F suffix on floating point constants. To force long double precision on constants, use the l or L suffix. For example, 3.14l is long double precision, 3.14 is double precision, and 3.14f is single precision in ANSI C.

What happens if you try to make a float variable exceed its limits? For example, suppose you multiply 1.0e38f by 1000.0f (overflow) or divide 1.0e-37f by 1.0e8f (underflow)? The result depends on the system. Either could cause the program to abort and to print a run-time error message. Or overflows may be replaced by a special value, such as the largest possible float value; underflows might be replaced by 0. Other systems may not issue warnings or may offer you a choice of responses. If this matter concerns you, check the rules for your system. If you cannot find the information, do not be afraid of a little trial and error.

Conversion of floating and integral types

When a floating value is converted to an integral value, the rounded value is preserved as long as it does not overflow. When an integral value is converted to a floating value, the value is preserved unless a value of more than six significant digits is being converted to single precision, or fifteen significant digits is being converted to double precision.

Whenever a floating-point value is assigned to an integer variable in C, the decimal portion of the number gets truncated. Assigning an integer variable to a floating variable does not cause any change in the value of the number; the value is simply converted by the system and stored in the

floating variable. The following program shows conversions to and from floating point types.

```
#include <stdio.h>
int main()
{
    double  x;
    int     i;
    i = 1400;
    x = i;  /* conversion from int to double */
    printf("x = %10.6le i = %d\n",x,i);
    x = 14.999;
    i = x;  /* conversion from double to int */
    printf("x = %10.6le i = %d\n",x,i);
    x = 1.0e+60;     /* a LARGE number */
    i = x;  /* won't fit - what happens ?? */
    printf("x = %10.6le i = %d\n",x,i);
    return 0;
}
```

Producing the output

```
    x = 1.445000e+03 i = 1445
    x = 1.499700e+01 i = 14
    x = 1.000000e+60 i = 2147483647
```

The loss of significant data, a polite way of saying the answer is wrong, in the final conversion should be noted.

8.16.3 Casting Arithmetic Expressions

Casting an arithmetic expression tells the compiler to represent the value of the expression in a certain way. In effect, a cast is similar to a promotion, which was discussed earlier. However, a cast is under the programmer's control, not the compiler's. For example, if i is a type int, the expression

```
    (float)i
```

casts i to float type. In other words, the program makes an internal copy of the value of i in floating point format.

When is a typecast used with an arithmetic expression? The most common use is to avoid losing the fractional part of the answer in an integer division. Consider the following example.

EXAMPLE
---

20. When one integer is divided by another, any fractional part of the answer is lost.

```
    #include <stdio.h>
    int main()
    {
        int a = 100,b = 40;
        float c;
        …
        …
```

```
    c = a/b;
    return 0;
}
```

If the value of c is printed, the output will be 2.000000. The answer displayed by the program is 2.000000, but 100/40 evaluates to 2.5. What happened? The expression a/b contains two int type variables. Following the rules explained earlier in this chapter, the value of the expression is int type itself. As such, it can represent only whole numbers, so the fractional part of the answer is lost.

It may be assumed that assigning the result of a/b to a float type variable promotes it to float type. This is correct, but it is too late; the fractional part of the answer is already gone.

To avoid this sort of inaccuracy, one of the int type variables must be cast to float type. If one of the variables is cast to type float, the previous rules say that the other variable is promoted automatically to float type, and the value of the expression is also float type. The fractional part of the answer is thus preserved. To demonstrate this, change the statement

```
    c= a/b;
```

in the source code so that the assignment statement reads as follows:

```
    c = (float)a/b;
```

The program will then display the correct answer.

Rounding a floating point value to a whole number

A floating point value can be rounded to an integer simply by adding 0.5 before storing it in an integer storage location. Normally, when a floating point value is assigned to an integer storage location, all fractional values (digits to the right of the decimal point) are 'truncated' (chopped-off). If we declare an integer variable named *N* with the statement

```
    int N;
```

and then attempt to assign a floating point value into it with the statement

```
    N = 2.8;
```

the variable *N* would receive the whole value 2, not the value 2.8 or the rounded value 3. Therefore, to assign the rounded result of 2.8 into variable *N*, we would use the simple expression

```
    N = 2.8 + 0.5;
```

which would increase the value to 3.3 and then truncate the .3 portion, resulting in the rounded value 3.

If you had a floating point value stored in a variable named *A* and you wanted to round it to a whole number and store that in an integer variable named *B*, the statement would be

```
    B = A + 0.5;
```

If you had a complex formula such as

```
    (X + 8.5) / (Y - 4.2)
```

that would result in a floating point value and if you want to round off the result to a whole number and store that in an integer variable named *C*, the statement would be

```
    C = (X + 8.5) / (Y - 4.2) + 0.5;
```

Rounding a floating point value to a specific decimal precision

A floating point value can be rounded to a specific decimal precision by following the four major steps described above, but with special care given to production of the appropriate data type during each part of the process. Using casting, we can force a value into an integer data type during calculation. This would be done just before the step in which we truncate unwanted digits to the right of the offset decimal point. Normally, when a floating point value is converted into an integer, all fractional values (digits to the right of the decimal point) are 'truncated' (chopped-off).

Consider the following example in which a stored floating point value is rounded to 2 decimal places, as are the results of most monetary calculations.

Given the following floating point variables

```
    float F;  /* A floating point value that needs to
                 be rounded */

    float R;  /* A floating point value that has been
                 rounded */
```

If we assign a floating point value into F with the statement

```
    F = 2.468;
```

the variable F would receive the value 2.468, not the rounded value of 2.47 which would be appropriate for most monetary uses. To assign the rounded result of 2.47 into variable R, we would use the expression

```
    R = (int) (F*100+0.5) / 100.0;
```

which would offset the decimal point two places by multiplying F by 100 (resulting in 246.8), then sum the value to 247.3, and then truncate the .3 portion by casting the value into integer form, and finally reposition the decimal point by dividing the result by 100.0. It is essential to write the value 100 in floating point notation (with the .0 attached) to prevent C from performing integer division which would corrupt the results.

When rounding the results of a floating point calculation, simply substitute that expression in place of F in the expression above. But pay careful attention to data types and the order of precedence of operators in the larger expression. For example, if the expression was

```
    X+Y;
```

where X and Y were double precision floating point values (long floats), then the larger expression made by inserting X+Y in place of F in the rounding formula above would be

```
    R = (long int) ((X+Y)*100+0.5) / 100.0;
```

Notice the enclosure of the X+Y inside of parentheses to force the weak addition operator to be performed before the stronger multiplication by 100. Notice also the use of the long int data type in the casting to allow for the high precision floating point result required by double precision floating point values.

If our intention was to round the floating point value F to three decimal places, then we would use a factor of 1000 (10 raised to the 3rd power) in steps 1 and 4, as in

```
R = (int) (F*1000+0.5) / 1000.0;
```

All the programs will have #include <stdio.h> preceding the main().

1. Which of the following is an incorrect assignment statement?
   (a) n = m = 0
   (b) value += 10
   (c) mySize = x < y ? 9 : 11
   (d) testVal = (x > 5 || x < 0)
   (e) none of the above
   Answer: (e)

2. What will be the output?
   (a) int main()
   ```
   {
       float c= 3.14;
       printf("%f", c%2);
       return 0;
   }
   ```
   Output Compiler error

Explanation: In example (a), % operator is applied on a variable of type float. The operands of the % opearator cannot be of float or double. This is why it causes a compiler error.

   (b) int main()
   ```
   {
       printf("%d", 'A');
       return 0;
   }
   ```
   Output 65

Explanation: In example (2), 'A' is a character constant and it is printed with format specifier %d. The ASCII equivalent of the character A is 65. So 65 will be printed.

   (c) int main()
   ```
   {
       double d= 1/2.0 - 1/2;
       printf("d=%.2lf", d);
       return 0;
   }
   ```
   Output d=0.50

Explanation: The value of 1 / 2.0 is evaluated as 0.50, as one of this expression is of type double and the result would be in double. Whereas in case of 1 / 2, both operands are of type int. The result of this expression is 0 as an integer division of 1 / 2 gives 0. So the value of d is equal to 0.50 – 0, i.e. 0.50. Now, the value of d is printed with %g format specifier; so, 0.50 will be printed instead of 0.500000.

   (d) int main()
   ```
   {
       unsigned int c= -2;
       printf("c=%u", c);
       return 0;
   }
   ```
   Output c=65534

   (Considering Turbo C compiler)

Explanation: An overflow occurs during an operation on unsigned integers, though the result is defined. A signed integer constant −2 is assigned to an unsigned integer variable. Such an operation on numbers is a modulo process. The number to be stored is represented as the maximum value that can be stored plus one; in this case, it is 65535 + 1, i.e. 65536, minus the signed value, here is −2. (65535 + 1) − 2 = 65534. Hence the output.

   (e) int main()
   ```
   {
       char c = 'A';
       printf("%c", c + 10);
       return 0;
   }
   ```
   Output K

Explanation: The chatracter constant 'A' is stored in the variable c. When 10 is added with c, then 10 is added to the ASCII value of 'A' (i.e. 65), the result is 75. As the result is printed with %c, the character equivalent of 75, which is 'K', is printed on the screen.

   (f) int main()
   ```
   {
       int a=5;
       a=printf("Good")+ printf("Boy");
       printf("%d",a);
       return 0;
   }
   ```
   Output GoodBoy7

Explanation: printf() function returns the number of characters printed on the screen. 'Good' and 'Boy' will be printed consecutively. The first printf () returns 4 and the second one returns 3. So 4 + 3 = 7 is stored in a. When it is printed, 7 would be printed at the end of 'GoodBoy'.

```
(g) void int main()
    {
        printf("Work" "Hard");
        return 0;
    }
```
Output WorkHard

Explanation: In example (g), adjacent string literals will automatically be joined together as one at compile time. So "WorkHard" will be printed on the screen.

```
(h) int main()
    {
        int c= - -2;
        printf("c=%d", c);
        return 0;
    }
```
Output c = 2;

Explanation: In example (h) unary minus (or negation) operator is used twice. Here, math-rule 'minus * minus = plus' is to be applied. However, one cannot give --2 instead of - -2 because the -- operator can only be applied to variables as a decrement operator (eg., i--). 2 is a constant and not a variable.

```
(i) int main()
    {
        int a=5;
        i=!a >10;
        printf("i=%d",i);
        return 0;
    }
```
Output i = 0

Explanation: In the expression !a>10, the NOT (!) operator has more precedence than the '>' symbol. ! is a unary logical operator. !a (!5) is 0 (NOT of true is false). 0>10 is false (zero).

```
(j) int main()
    {
        printf("\nab");
        printf("\bsi");
        printf("\rha");
        return 0;
    }
```
Remember that   \n - newline
                \b - backspace
                \r - linefeed

Output hai

Explanation: The escape sequences \n, \b and \r stand for newline, backspace, and line feed respectively. At first, 'ab' is printed on console. The \b deletes the character 'b' of 'ab' and appends 'si'. Therefore, 'asi' is printed. Then, \r causes to position the cursor at 'a' of

'asi' and replace 'as' with 'ha'. As a result, finally 'hai' is printed on the screen.

```
(k) int main()
    {
        int i=5;
        printf("%d%d%d",i++, i, ++i);
        return 0;
    }
```
Output 666

Explanation: The arguments in a function call are pushed into the stack from left to right. The evaluation is by popping out from the stack and the evaluation is from right to left, hence the result.

```
(l) int main()
    {
        int i;
        printf("%d",scanf("%d",&i));
                /* value 10 is given as input here */
        return 0;
    }
```
Output 1

Explanation: scanf returns the number of items successfully read. Here, 10 is given as input that should have been scanned successfully. So the number of items read is 1.

```
(m) int main()
     {
         char n;
         n=!2;
         printf("%d",n);
         return 0;
     }
```
Output 0

Explanation: ! is a logical operator. In C, the value 0 is considered to be FALSE, and any non-zero value including negative value, is considered to be the Boolean value TRUE. Here, 2 is a non-zero value, so TRUE. !TRUE is FALSE (0), so it prints 0.

```
(n) int main()
    {
        int i=-2;
        printf("-i = %d \n",-i,);
        return 0;
    }
```
Output -i = 2

Explanation: –i is executed and this execution does not affect the value of i. In printf first just print the value of i. After that the value of the expression -i = -(-2) is printed.

```
(o) int main()
```

```
{
    int x=10,y=15,a,b;
    a=x++;
    b=++y;
    printf("%d%d\n",a,b);
    return 0;
}
```
Output 1016

Explanation: a = x++ is evaluated as a =x then x = x + 1. So the value of a is 10 and the value of x is 11. The statement b= ++y, ++y is incremented before it is assigned to b. Then b = ++y is evaluated as y = y+1 followed by b = y. So the value of b is 16; hence the output.

(p) int main()
```
{
    int x=10,y=15;
    x=x++;
    y=++y;
    printf("%d%d\n",x,y);
    return 0;
}
```
Output 1116

Explanation: In this example, x = x++ is evaluated as x = x followed by x = x + 1. That is, value of x will be 11. Similarly, y is also evaluated.

(q) int main()
```
{
    int x=1,y=5;
    printf("%d ",++(x+y));
    return 0;
}
```
Output Compiler error - Lvalue required

Explanation: The increment operator (++) cannot be used with expressions. The expression ++(x+y) stands for (x+y) = (x+y) +1. We cannot write expression in the left-hand side of the assignment operator (=).

(r) int main()
```
{
    int x=1,y=5;
    printf("%d ",++x+y);
    return 0;
}
```
Output 7

Explanation: In the expression ++x + y, before addition ++x is evaluated first. The ++x yields 2 and the value of y is 5. The result of x + y is 7; hence the output.

3. How do we round off numbers?

   Answer: The simplest and most straightforward way is with a code like (int)(x + 0.5) This technique will not work properly for negative numbers, though.

4. Use the following values for the next four questions.
```
int a = 8, b = 3, x1, x2, x3, x4
x1 = a * b          x2 = a / b
x3 = a % b          x4 = a && b
```
   (a) The value of x1 is
   - (i) 0
   - (ii) 1
   - (iii) 2
   - (iv) 3
   - (v) none of these
   Output (v)

   (b) The value of x2 is
   - (i) 0
   - (ii) 1
   - (iii) 2
   - (iv) 3
   - (v) none of these
   Output (iii)

   (c) The value of x3 is
   - (i) 0
   - (ii) 1
   - (iii) 2
   - (iv) 3
   - (v) none of these
   Output (iii)

   (d) The value of x4 is
   - (i) 0
   - (ii) 1
   - (iii) 2
   - (iv) 3
   - (v) none of these
   Output (ii)

5. Find the output:
   (a) int main()
```
{
    int a = 7, b = 2;
    float c;
    c = a/b;
    printf("\n%f",c);
    return 0;
}
```
   Output 3.000000

(b)
```
int main()
{
    int c = 1;
    c=c+2*c++;
    printf("\n%f",c);
    return 0;
}
```
Output 4.000000

(c) Is `i % 2 == 0`
equivalent to `(i % 2) == 0`?
Output Yes,
`==` has lower precedence than `%`

(d)
```
int main()
{
    int a=2,b=3, c=3;
    a=b==c;
    printf("a=%d", a);
    return 0;
}
```
Output a=1

8.17 WORKING WITH COMPLEX NUMBERS

A *complex number* is a number with a real part and an imaginary part. It is of the form a + bi, where i is the square root of minus one, and a and b are real numbers. Here a is the real part, and bi is the imaginary part of the complex number. A complex number can also be regarded as an ordered pair of real numbers (a, b).

According to C99, three complex types are supported:

```
float complex
double complex
long double complex
```

C99 implementations support three imaginary types also:

```
float imaginary
double imaginary
long double imaginary
```

To use the complex types, the complex.h header file must be included. The complex.h header file defines some macros and several functions that accept complex numbers and return complex numbers. In particular, the macro I represents the square root of −1. It enables to do the following:

```
double complex c1 = 3.2 + 2.0 * I;
float imaginary c2= -5.0 * I;
```

The following program illustrates the use of complex and imaginary types:

```
#include <stdio.h>
#include <limits.h>
#include <complex.h>
#include <stdio.h>
int main(void)
{
    double complex cx = 3.2 + 3.0*I;
    double complex cy = 5.0 - 4.0*I;
    printf("Working with complex numbers:");
    printf("\nStarting values: cx = %g  + %gi cy = %g +\
     %gi",creal(cx), cimag(cx), creal(cy), cimag(cy));\
    double complex sum = cx+cy;
    printf("\n\nThe sum cx + cy = %g + %gi",
    creal(sum),cimag(sum));
    return 0;
}
```

Output
```
Working with complex numbers:
Starting values: cx = 3.2  + 3i cy = 5  + -4i
The sum cx + cy = 8.2 + -1i
```

The creal() function returns the real part of a value of type that is passed as the argument, and cimag() returns the imaginary part. For details of the functions that can be applied on these types, the header file complex.h, which is supplied with the compiler, may be explored.

SUMMARY

C is a programming language that can be used to solve problems. Each of the 32 keywords of C has a fixed meaning and forms the building block for program statements. Variables are given names.

Variables holds data at memory locations allocated to them. There are five basic data types in C, namely, char, int, float, double, and void. Except type void, the basic data types can have various modifiers such as signed, unsigned, long, and short that precedes them. The computer and the data type determine the memory space allocated to a variable. Constants in C have fixed values. There are several operators

in C that can be classified as arithmetic, relational, logical, assignment, increment and decrement, conditional, bit-wise, and special. Expressions are formed with variables and operators. Operators in C have certain precedence and associativity rules that are followed while evaluating expressions. Automatic type conversion takes place according to set rules in expressions with mixed types. Forced type conversion is also possible in C.

For handling complex numbers the complex, h header file should be included while writing the program.

KEY TERMS

ASCII It is a standard code for representing characters as numbers and is used on most microcomputers, computer terminals, and printers. In addition to printable characters, the ASCII code includes control characters to indicate carriage return, backspace, etc.

Assembler It creates the object code.

Associativity The *associativity* of operators determines the order in which operators of equal precedence are evaluated when they occur in the same expression. Most operators have a left-to-right associativity, but some have right-to-left associativity.

Compiler It is a system software that translates the source code to assembly code.

Constant It is an entity that does not change.

Data type The type or *data type* of a variable determines a set of values that the variable might take and a set of operations that can be applied to those values.

Debugger It is a program that enables you to run another program step-by-step and examine the value of that program's variables.

IDE An Integrated Development Environment or *IDE* is an editor which offers a complete environment for writing, developing, modifying, deploying, testing, and debugging the programs.

Identifier It is a symbolic name used in a program and defined by the programmer.

Identifier An *identifier* or name is a sequence of characters invented by the programmer to identify or name a specific object.

Keywords These are explicitly reserved words that have a strict meaning as individual tokens to the compiler. They cannot be redefined or used in other contexts.

Linker If a source file references library functions or functions defined in other source files, the *linker* combines these functions to create an executable file.

Lvalue It is an expression to which a value can be assigned.

Precedence The *precedence* of operators determines the order in which different operators are evaluated when they occur in the same expression. Operators of higher precedence are applied before operators of lower precedence.

Preprocessor The C preprocessor is used to modify the source program before compilation according to the preprocessor directives specified.

Rvalue It can be defined as an expression that can be assigned to an lvalue.

Token It is one or more symbols understood by the compiler that help it interpret the code.

Variable It is a named memory location. Every variable has a type, which defines the possible values that the variable can take, and an identifier, which is the name by which the variable is referred.

Whitespace Space, newline, tab character and comment are collectively known as *whitespace*.

Word The natural unit of memory for a given computer design. The word size is the computer's preferred size for moving units of information around; technically it is the width of the processor's *registers*.

FREQUENTLY ASKED QUESTIONS

1. What is the difference between compiling and linking?

Compiler converts each source file into an object file. Linker takes all generated object files, as well as the system libraries that are relevant, and builds an executable file that is stored on disk.

2. What is a bug?

Any type of error in a program is known as *bug*. There are three types of errors that may occur:

Compile errors These are given by the compiler and prevent the program from running.

Linking errors These are given by the linker or at run time and ends the program. The linker can also detect and report errors, for example, if part of the program is missing or a non-existent library component is referenced.

Run time errors These are given by the operating system.

3. Why do we need header files?

The header files primarily contain declarations relating to standard library functions and macros that are available with C. During compilation, the compilers perform type checking to ensure that the calls to the library and other user-defined functions are correct. This form of checking helps to ensure the semantic correctness of the program. The header files, which usually incorporate data types, function declarations and macros, resolves this issue. The file with .h extension is called header file, because it is usually included at the head of a program. Every C compiler that conforms to the international standard (ISO/IEC 9899) for the language will have a set of standard header files supplied with it.

4. What is a library?

A library is a collection of functions. A library file stores each function individually. When the program uses a function contained in a library, the linker looks for the function and adds its code to the program. Note the contents of the entire library are added to the executable file.

5. What is the difference between declaring a variable and defining a variable?

Declaring a variable means informing the compiler about its type without allocating any space for it. To put it simply, a declaration says to the compiler, 'Somewhere in the program there will be a variable with this name, and this is the kind of data type it is.' Defining a variable means declaring it as well as allocating space to hold the variable. Here is a declaration of a variable and a variable definition:

```
extern int x; /* this is a declaration */
int y; /* this is a definition */
```

The following is a definition of a variable with initialization.

```
int y=10;
```

It is to be noted that a variable can be declared many times, but it must be defined exactly once. For this reason, definitions do not belong in header files, function definitions are placed in library files.

6. Why is data type specified for a variable declaration?

The type or data type of a variable determines a set of values that the variable might take and a set of operations that can be applied to those values.

7. What are the uses of `void` in C?

`Void` has three uses. When it specifies the return type of a function, it means the function returns no value to the calling function. It is also used to declare that a function has no parameters. Moreover, it can create a generic pointer.

8. Which one is correct: `main()` or `void main()` or `int main()`?

Under C89, `main()` is acceptable, although it is advisable to use the C99 standard, under which only `int main(void)` is acceptable. There are some compilers where `void main()` is allowed, but these are on specialized systems only. If the programmer is not sure of whether he/she is using one of these specialized systems, then the programmer should simply avoid using `void main()`.

9. Is `main()` must?

It depends on the environment your program is written for. If it is a hosted environment, then main function is a must for any standard C program. Hosted environments are those where the program runs under an operating system. If it is a freestanding environment, then main function is not required. Freestanding environments are those where the program does not depend on any host and can have any other function designated as start-up function. Freestanding implementation need not support complete support of the standard libraries; usually only a limited number of I/O libraries will be supported and no memory management functions will be supported. Examples of freestanding implementations are embedded systems and the operating system kernel.

10. Can the prototype for `main()` be included?

Absolutely; it is legal in C though it is not required.

11. Should `main()` always return a value?

Yes, unless it encounters a call for `exit()`. When a program runs, it usually terminates with some indication of success or some error code. The return statement is not mandatory; if it is missing, the program will still terminate. In C89, the value returned to the operating system is undefined. In C99, if `main()` is declared to return an `int`, the program returns 0 (zero) to the operating system or operating environment; otherwise the program returns an unspecified value.

12. How can you check what value is returned from `main()`? Is the executed program terminated normally or not?

A "batch file" or "shell script" can be used for this purpose.

In UNIX, each shell has its own method for testing the status code. In the Bourne shell, after executing the C program, the variable $? contains the status of the last program executed. The C shell has similar variable, but its name is $status.

13. What is the need of `unsigned char`?

The signedness of characters is an important issue because the standard I/O library functions which normally read characters from files and return a negative value (-1 or its symbolic constant EOF) when the end of file is reached.

14. In some compilers like Turbo C the size occupied by an integer variable is 2 bytes; again in most of the compilers an integer variable takes 4 bytes of memory. What is the size of an integer variable?

The size of an `int` is usually the same as the word length of the execution environment of the program.

15. Both `%d` and `%i` can be used to read and print integers. What is the difference between `%d` and `%i`?

If `%d` is used in `scanf()`, it can only match an integer in decimal form. On the other hand if `%i` is used with `scanf()`, it can match an integer expressed in octal, decimal or hexadecimal form. If the input number is prefixed with a 0, `%i` treats it as an octal number; if it is prefixed with 0x or 0X, it will be treated as a hexadecimal number.

With `printf()`, there is no such difference between these two format specifiers. The aforesaid facts are evident from the following program:

```c
#include <stdio.h>
int main(void)
{
        int n;
        printf("\n Enter an integer: ");
        scanf("%d",&n);
        printf("\n n = %d", n);
        printf("\n Enter the same integer again: ");
        scanf("%i",&n);
        printf("\n n = %i", n);
        return 0;
}
```

Sample run:
```
Enter an integer: 023
n = 23
Enter the same integer again: 023
n = 19
```

16. What is the difference between %f, %g, and %e format specifiers when used to display a real value?

The `%f` characters are used to display values in a standard manner. Unless size and width are specified, `printf()` always displays a float or double value rounded up to six decimal places.

The `%e` characters are used to display the value of a float or double variable in scientific notation.

With the `%g` characters, `printf()` automatically removes from displaying any trailing zeroes. If no digits follow the decimal point, it does not display that either. For illustration consider the following program:

```c
#include <stdio.h>
int main()
{
    float x=12.34;
    printf("\n %f", x);
    printf("\n %g", x);
    printf("\n %e", x);
    return 0;
}
```

Output
```
12.340000
12.34
1.234000+e001
```

17. What is lvalue and rvalue?

An `lvalue` is an expression to which a value can be assigned. An `rvalue` can be defined as an expression that can be assigned to an `lvalue`. The `lvalue` expression is located on the *left side* of an assignment statement, whereas an `rvalue` is located on the *right side* of an assignment statement.

The address associated with a program variable in C is called its `lvalue`; the contents of that location are its `rvalue`, the quantity that is supposed to be the value of the variable. The `rvalue` of a variable may change as program execution proceeds; but never its `lvalue`. The distinction between `lvalues` and `rvalues` becomes sharper if one considers the assignment operation with variables a and b.

a = b;

b, on the right-hand side of the assignment operator, is the quantity to be found at the address associated with b, i.e., an `rvalue`. a is assigned the value stored in the address associated with b. a, on the left-hand side, is the address at which the contents are altered as a result of the assignment. a is an `lvalue`. The assignment operation stores b's `rvalue` at a's `lvalue`.

18. What are the differences between l-value and r-value?

l-value	r-value
The l-value expression is located on the *left side* of an assignment statement.	An r-value is located on the *right side* of an assignment statement.
An l-value means the address that it represents.	An r-value means the contents of the address that it represents which is a value.
An l-value says where to store the result.	An r-value says what is to be stored.
An l-value is known at compile time.	An r-value is not known until run time.

19. Why is the statement a + b = c + d not valid in C?

The given statement is not valid in C because the left side of the statement evaluates to a constant value that cannot be changed and do not represent storable locations in memory. Therefore, this assignment statement do not contain an lvalue and will generate compiler errors.

20. Why should we use i++ instead of i = i + 1?

Most C compilers produce very fast and efficient object code for increment and decrement operations. For these reasons, we should use the increment and decrement operators when we can.

21. Can we apply ++ and -- operators on floating point numbers?

++ and -- operators can be applied to floating point numbers as well as integers.

22. What is the difference between the prefix and postfix forms of the ++ operator?

The prefix form increments first, and the incremented value goes on to participate in the surrounding expression (if any). The postfix form increments later; the previous value goes on to participate in the surrounding expression.

23. The % operator fails to work on float numbers. Can we get the remainder of a floating point division?

The % operator cannot be used with floating point values. But if it is required to get the remainder of floating point division, one may use the function `fmod()`. The `fmod()` function returns the remainder as a floating-point division. Following program illustrates the use of `fmod()` function.

```
#include <math.h>
int main( )
{
    printf ("%f", fmod (7.25, 3.0));
    return 0;
}
```

The above code snippet would give the output as 1.250000.

24. What is precedence of operators?

Operator precedence determines the sequence in which operators in an expression are evaluated. In fact, each operator in C has a precedence associated with it. The operator with the higher precedence is evaluated first. In the expression

a + b * c

the operations of multiplication and division are given precedence over the operations of addition and subtraction. Therefore, the expression

a + b * c

is evaluated as

(a + (b * c))

by the C system.

25. What is associativity?

The sequence of execution for operators of equal precedence is determined by their associativity, which determines whether they are selected from left to right or from right to left.

In the expression

a * b / c

the operations of multiplication and division are of same precedence. Here associativity breaks the tie. Therefore, the expression

a * b / c

is evaluated as

((a * b) / c)

by the C system.

26. What is short-circuiting in C expressions?

Short-circuiting in an expression means that the right hand side of the expression is not evaluated if the left hand side determines the outcome. This means that if the left hand side is true for || or false for &&, the right hand side will not be evaluated.

27. What does the term cast refer to? Why is it used?

Casting is a mechanism built into C language that allows the programmer to force the conversion of data types. This may be needed because most

Basics of C **181**

C functions are very particular about the data types they process. A programmer may wish to override the default way the C compiler promotes data types. An example of a type cast which ensures that an expression evaluates to type float is as follows:

x = (float) x / 2;

28. When should a type cast be used?

There are two situations in which the type casting may be used.

- To change the type of an operand to an arithmetic operation so that the operation will be performed properly.
- To cast pointer types to and from void * in order to port with functions that return void pointers, e.g. malloc() has to be casted to the return

type of the pointer to which returned address to be stored.

29. When should a type cast not be used?

There are two cases where type casting should not be used.

- To override a const or volatile declaration, overriding these type modifiers can cause the program to fail to run correctly.
- To turn a pointer to one type of structure into another.

30. Why is the output of sizeof('a') 2 and not 1?

Character constants in C are of type int, hence sizeof ('a') is equivalent to sizeof(int), i.e. 2. Hence the output comes out to be 2 bytes.

EXERCISES

1. What is the purpose of a header file? Is the use of a header file absolutely necessary?
2. What is the return type of a program's main() function?
3. What is meant by a variable? What is meant by the value of a variable?
4. Name and describe the basic data types in C.
5. What is ASCII? How common is its use?
6. How can values be assigned to variables?
7. How can the % symbol be printed using a printf() statement?
8. What is an escape sequence? What is its purpose?
9. Describe the different types of operators that are included in C.
10. What are unary operators? State the purpose of each.
11. Describe two different ways of using the increment and decrement operators.
12. What is meant by precedence? Explain with an example.
13. What is meant by associativity? Explain with an example. What is the associativity of arithmetic operators?
14. What is the order of precedence and associativity of arithmetic operators?
15. What are bit-wise operators? Explain.
16. What is the difference between prefix and postfix of -- and ++ operators?
17. Describe the use of the conditional operator to form a conditional expression.
18. Which of the algebraic expressions matches the C expression given below?

sqrt(x*x + y*y)/sqrt(x*x - 1)

(a) $\sqrt{\dfrac{x^2+y^2}{x^2+1}}$ (b) $\sqrt{\dfrac{x^2+y^2}{x^2-1}}$

(c) $\sqrt{\dfrac{x^2+y^2}{x^2-1}}$ (d) $\sqrt{\dfrac{x^2+y^2}{x^2-y^2}}$

(e) none of the above

19. Find the value that is assigned to the variables x, y, and z when the following program is executed.

```
int main()
 {
 int x, y, z;
```

```
x = 2 + 3 - 4 + 5 - (6 - 7);
y = 2 * 33 + 4 * (5 - 6);
z = 2 * 3 * 4 / 15 % 13;
x = 2 * 3 * 4 / (15 % 13);
y = 2 * 3 * (4 / 15 % 13);
z = 2 + 33 % 5 / 4;
x = 2 + 33 % - 5 /4;
y = 2 - 33 % - 5 /- 4;
z =-2*-3/-4%-5;
x =50 % (5 * (16 % 12 * (17/3)));
Y=-2*-3%-4 /-5-6+-7;
z = 8 /4 / 2*2*4*8 %13 % 7 % 3;
return 0;
}
```

By inserting appropriate calls to printf(), verify the answers obtained.

20. Give the output of the following program:

```
#include <stdio.h>
int main( )
 {
 int x = 3,y = 5,z = 7,w;
 w = x % y + y % x - z % x - x % z;
 printf("%d \n", w);
 w = x / z + y / z + (x + y) / z;
 printf("%d\n", w);
 w = x / z * y / z + x * y / z;
 printf("%d\n", w);
 w = x % y % z + z % y % (y % x);
 printf("%d\n", w);
 w = z / y / y / x + z / y / (y / x);
 printf("%d\n", w);
 return 0;
 }
```

21. What does the following program print?

```
#include <stdio.h>
int main()
 {
 printf("%d\n", - 1 + 2 - 12 * -13 / -4);
 printf("%d\n", - 1 % - 2 + 12 % -13 % - 4);
 printf("%d \n",-4/2 - 12/4 - 13 % -4);
 printf("%d\n", (- 1 + 2 - 12) * (- 13 / - 4));
```

```
printf("%d\n", (- 1 % - 2 + 12) %(- 13 % - 4));
printf("%d\n", (- 4 /2 - 12) / (4 - 13 % - 4));
return 0;
}
```

22. Find the outputs of the following programs:

(a)
```
#include <stdio.h>
int main()
{
int x = 3, y = 5, z = 7, w =9;
w += x;
printf("w = %d\n", w);
w -= y;
printf("w = %d\n", w);
x *= z;
printf("x = %d\n", x);
w += x + y - (z -= w);
printf("w = %d, z=%d\n",w,z);
w += x -= y %= z;
printf("w = %d, x = %d, y = %d\n", w, x, y);
w *= x / (y += (z += y));
printf("w = %d, y = %d, z = %d\n", w, y, z);
w /= 2 + (w %= (x += y - (z -= -w)));
printf("w = %d, x = %d, z = %d\n", w, x, z);
return 0;
}
```

(b)
```
#include <stdio.h>
int main()
{
int x = 7, y = -7, z = 11,
    w =- 11, S = 9, t = 10;
x += (y -= (z *= (w /= (s %= t))));
printf("x = %d, y = %d, z = %d, w = %d,\
        s = %d, t = %d\n", x, y, z, w, s, t);
t += s -= w *= z *= y %= x;
printf("x = %d, y %d, z = %d, w = %d,\
        s = %d, t = %d\n", x, y, z, w, s, t);
return 0;
}
```

(c)
```
#include <stdio.h>
int main()
{
int amount = 7;
printf("If I give you");
printf("Rs.%05d\n", amount);
printf("You will owe me");
printf("Rs.%-05d\ n", amount);
return 0;
}
```

23. Given that x, y, z, and w are integers with the respective values 100, 20, 300, and 40, find the outputs from the following printf() statements.

```
printf("%d\n%d\n%d\n%d", x,*y, z, w);
printf("\t%d\n\t%d\n\t%d\n\t%d", x, y, z, w);
printf("%d %d %d %d %d %d %d %d", x, y,\
```

```
w, z, y, w, z, x);
printf("%d %d", x + z - y * y,\
        (y - z % w) * x);
```

24. Execute the following program to verify the rules stated above for the output of floating point variables.

```
#include <stdio.h>
int main()
{
double pi = 3.14159265;
printf("%15f\n", pi);
printf("%15.12f\n", pi);
printf("%-15.12f\n", pi);
printf("%15.4f\n", pi);
printf("%15.0f\n", pi);
printf("%15.3g\n", pi);
printf("%15g\n", pi);
printf("%15.4e\n", pi);
printf("%15e\n", pi);
return 0;
}
```

25. What does the following program print?

```
#include <stdio.h>
int main()
{
printf("%-40.24s", "Left\
        justified printing.\n");
printf("%-40.20s", "Left\
        justified printing.\n");
printf("%-40.16s", "Left\
        justified printing.\n");
printf("%-40.12s", "Left\
        justified printing.\n");
printf("%-40. 8s", "Left\
        justified printing.\n");
printf("%-40.4s", "Left\
        justified printing.\n");
printf("%-40.0s", "Left\
        justified printing.\n");
printf("%40.25s", "Right\
        justified printing.\n");
printf("%40.20s", "Right\
        justified printing.\n");
printf("%40.15s", "Right\
        justified printing.\n");
printf("%40.10s", "Right\
        justified printing.\n");
printf("%40.5s", "Right\
        justified printing.\n");
printf("%40.0s", "Right\
        justified printing.\n");
printf("%40.0s", "Right\
        justified printing.\n");
return 0;
}
```

Input and Output

After studying this chapter, the readers will be able to

- discuss what C considers as standard input and output devices
- list the input and output streams that exist in C to carry out the input and output tasks
- understand that C provides a set of input and output functions

- analyse the use of single character unformatted input and output functions getchar() and putchar()
- use the formatted input and output functions scanf() and printf() for handling multiple inputs and output

9.1 INTRODUCTION

For carrying out an arithmetic calculation using C, there is no way other than writing a program, which is equivalent to using a pocket calculator. Different outcomes are obtained when different values are assigned to variables involved in the arithmetic calculation.

Hence, there is a need to read values into variables as the program runs. Notice the words here: 'as the program runs'. Values can be stored in variables using the assignment operator. For example, a=100; stores 100 in the variable a each time the program is run, no matter what the program does. Without some sort of input command, every program would produce exactly the same result every time it is run. This would certainly make debugging easy. But in practice, of course, the user may need programs to do different jobs

that give different outcomes each time they are run. For this purpose, C has been provided with some input instructions that are in fact a set of functions. For the present, it may be said that a function is a code segment that is complete in itself and does some particular task as and when it is called. Functions will be dealt in greater detail in Chapter 12.

When a program is in execution, each of its statements are executed one after the other or in a particular order. When this process of execution reaches an input instruction, also referred to as an input statement, the most common being the scanf() function, the program execution pauses to give the user time to enter something on the keyboard. The execution of the program continues only after the user enters some data (or nothing) and presses <**Enter**> or <**Return**> to signal that the procedure of entering input data has been completed. The program execution then continues with the inputted value stored in the memory location reserved for the variable. In this way, each time the program is run, users get a chance to type in different values for the variable and the program also gets a chance to produce different results.

The final missing piece in the jigsaw is using an output command or statement, the commonly used one being the printf() function, the one that has already been used in some example programs in the previous chapter, to print the value currently stored in a variable.

In the context of the above example, it should be understood that the input function, scanf(), is used to read the data entered through the keyboard. On the other hand, the printf() function is used to display the data on the screen.

The original C specification did not include commands for input and output. Instead, the compiler writers were supposed to implement library functions to suit their machines. In practice, all chose to implement printf() and scanf() and, after a while, C programmers started to think of these functions as I/O keywords. It sometimes helps to remember that they are functions like any other function.

To make C a more uniform language, it has been provided with standard libraries of functions that perform common tasks. Though these libraries are termed standard but until the ANSI committee actually produced a standard, there was, and still is, some variation in what the standard libraries contained and exactly how the functions worked. However, in practice, the situation is not that bad; most of the functions that are used frequently are standard on all implementations. In particular the input and output functions vary very little.

This chapter will, therefore, primarily consider input functions that read data from the keyboard and output functions that display data on the screen.

Note

- The scanf() function does not prompt for an input. It is a good programming practice to always use a printf() function before a scanf() function for users of the program to know what they should enter through the keyboard.

9.2 BASIC SCREEN AND KEYBOARD I/O IN C

C provides several functions that give different levels of input and output capability. These functions are, in most cases, implemented as routines that call lower-level input/output functions.

The input and output functions in C are built around the concept of a set of standard data streams being connected from each executing program to the basic input/output devices. These standard data streams or files are opened by the operating system and are available to every C and assembler program for use without having to open or close the files. These standard files or streams are called

- stdin : connected to the keyboard
- stdout : connected to the screen
- stderr : connected to the screen

The following two data streams are also available on MS-DOS-based computers, but not on UNIX or other multi-user-based operating systems.

- stdaux: connected to the first serial communications port
- stdprn: connected to the first parallel printer port

A number of functions and macros exist to provide support for streams of various kinds. The <stdio.h> header file contains the various declarations necessary for the functions, together with the macros and type declarations needed for the input and output functions. The input/output functions fall into two categories: non-formatted read (input) and display (output) functions and formatted read (input) and display (output) functions.

Note

- The input and output functions in C are implemented through a set of standard data streams which connect each executing program to the basic input/output devices.
- The input/output functions are of two kinds: non-formatted and formatted functions.

9.3 NON-FORMATTED INPUT AND OUTPUT

Non-formatted input and output can be carried out by standard input–output library functions in C. These can handle one character at a time. For the input functions, it does not require <Enter> to be pressed after the entry of the character. For output functions, it prints a single character on the console.

9.3.1 Single Character Input and Output

A number of functions provide for character-oriented input and output. The declaration formats of two of these are given as follows:

```
int getchar(void);
//function for character input

int putchar(int c);
//function of character output
```

getchar() is an input function that reads a single character from the standard input device, normally a keyboard. putchar() is an output function that writes a single character on the standard output device, the display screen.

There are two other functions, gets() and puts(), that are used to read and write strings from and to the keyboard and the display screen, respectively. A string may be defined as an arranged collection of characters. These two functions will be dealt with in greater detail in the chapter on arrays and strings.

9.3.2 Single Character Input

The getchar() input function reads an unsigned char from the input stream stdin. The character obtained from the input stream is treated as an unsigned char and is converted to an int, which is the return value. On end of file, the constant EOF is returned and the end-of-file indicator is set for the associated stream. On error, the error indicator is set for the stream. Successive calls will obtain characters sequentially.

To read a single character from the keyboard, the general form of the statement used to call the getchar() function is given as follows:

```
char_variable = getchar();
```

where char_variable is the name of a variable of type char. The getchar() input function receives the character data entered through the keyboard and places it in the memory location allotted to the variable char_variable. The code

```
int ch;
ch = getchar();
```

places the character read from the keyboard in the lower byte of the variable named ch.

Two bytes are allotted in memory to the integer variable 'ch'; but the typed in character 'x' is stored in the lower order byte while the content of the higher-order byte has no relevance when a character is typed in.

It has to be noted here that getchar() reads a single character from the input data stream, but does not return the character to the program until the '\n' (<**Return**> or <**Enter**>) key is pressed.

There is an important observation that has to be made about the ch = getchar(); function. Though the data entered through the keyboard is perceived to be of character type, the data is actually stored as an integer. Here, this integer is the variable ch. This is because everytime ch = getchar(); reads a data from the keyboard, it checks whether it is a character data or an EOF. The problem is distinguishing the end of input from valid data. The solution is that getchar() returns a distinctive value when there is no more input, a value that cannot be confused with any real character. This value is called EOF, i.e., end of file. So ch must be declared to be of a type big enough to hold any value that getchar() returns. Therefore, char cannot be used since ch must be big enough to hold EOF in addition to any possible char. Therefore, int is used.

9.3.3 Single Character Output

The putchar() function is identical in description to the getchar() function except the following difference. putchar()

writes a character to the stdout data stream. On success, putchar() returns the character. On error, putchar() returns EOF. There is no equivalent to end of file for an output file. To write a single character on the screen, the general form of the statement used to call the putchar() function is given as follows:

```
putchar(char_variable);
```

where char_variable is the name of a variable that is of type char. The character data stored in the memory location allotted to the variable char_variable is displayed on the display screen.

The following program code displays the character entered through getchar() on the screen.

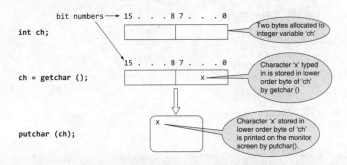

It has to be noted that the character 'x' remains stored in the lower order byte of ch even after putchar(ch) copies it and displays it on the monitor screen.

9.3.4 Additional Single Character Input and Output Functions

Other than getchar() and putchar(), there are some more single character input and output functions that are available in Turbo C only. These are as follows:

getch() This input function reads, without echoing on the screen, a single character from the keyboard and immediately returns that character to the program. General statement form:

```
ch = getch(); /* 'ch' is a character variable */
```

getche() This input function reads, with echo on the screen, a single character from the keyboard and immediately returns that character to the program. General statement form:

```
ch = getche(); /* 'ch' is a character variable */
```

putch() This output function writes the character directly to the screen. On success, the function putch() returns the character printed. On error, it returns EOF. General statement form:

```
putch(ch); /* 'ch' is a character variable */
```

When used in programs, the above functions require the header file conio.h to be included. It should be noted here that the data held by the variable in all the input and output functions are in ASCII value.

Note

- getchar(), the single character input function, reads a one byte character input from the keyboard and stores it in the lower order byte of an integer variable.
- putchar(), the single character output function, displays a one-byte character on the monitor screen.

EXAMPLES

1. Display a given character.

Solution

```
#include<stdio.h>
int main(void)
{
  int ch;
  ch='A';
  putchar(ch);
  return 0;
}
```

Output A

Explanation: In this example, the variable ch is declared as an integer. In the next statement, the character A is assigned to this variable, which results in the ASCII equivalent of the character A being stored in the lower order byte of the integer variable ch as shown below:

Next, when the output statement putchar( ), actually an output function, is executed, the ASCII equivalent of A is taken from the lower order byte of the integer variable ch and displayed on the monitor screen.

2. Display a keyed-in character.

Solution

```
#include<stdio.h>
int main(void)
{
  int ch;
  ch=getchar();
  putchar(ch);
  return 0;
}
```

Input A
Output A

Explanation: Here, the typed-in character is read and stored in the lower order byte allocated to the integer ch by the input function getchar(). This character is then copied on to the monitor screen by the output function putchar(ch).

3. Accept a given character and display the next character from the ASCII table.

Solution

```
#include<stdio.h>
int main(void)
{
  int ch;
  ch='A';
  ch=ch + 1;
  putchar(ch);
  return 0;
}
```

Output B

Explanation: Here, the character A is assigned to the integer variable ch. This results in the ASCII equivalent, 41h, of the character A being stored in the lower order byte of the integer variable ch. As 1 is added to the contents of ch, it becomes 42h, which is the ASCII representation for the character B. So when putchar(ch) is executed, the character displayed on the screen is B. The figure below illustrates the contents of the variable ch as it changes from A to B.

4. Display the keyed-in character and the next character from the ASCII table.

Solution

```
#include<stdio.h>
int main(void)
{
  int ch;
  ch=getchar();
  ch=ch++;
  putchar(ch);
  return 0;
}
```

Input a
Output b

Explanation: This example is similar to the previous one except that the integer variable ch is assigned a character read in by getchar() from the keyboard. Hence, the output obtained after executing this program is similar to the previous example.

5. Double the output of next two characters from the ASCII table.

Solution
```
#include<stdio.h>
int main(void)
{
  int ch;
  ch=getchar();
  putchar(++ch); /* first putchar() */
  putchar(ch++); /* second putchar()*/
  putchar(ch);   /* third putchar() */
  putchar(ch--); /* fourth putchar()*/
  putchar(ch);   /* fifth putchar() */
  return 0;
}
```
(i) **Input** a

   Output bbccb

(ii) **Input** h

   Output iijji

Explanation: Here when the program is executed, getchar() obtains the typed-in character and places its ASCII equivalent in the integer variable ch. As shown, the typed-in character is chosen to be a. Next, in the first putchar(), at the beginning, the content of ch is incremented by 1 to represent b, then this is displayed on the monitor screen. In the second putchar(), the content of ch, which is b, is displayed on the monitor screen and then its content is incremented by 1 to represent c in ASCII. In the third putchar(), the content of ch, which is c, is displayed on the monitor screen and the content in ch does not get altered. During the fourth putchar(), the content in ch, which is c, is first displayed on the monitor screen and then the content in ch is decremented to represent b in ASCII. Therefore, during the fifth putchar(), the content of ch is displayed as b on the monitor screen.

Similar result is obtained when the program is run for the second time with h as the input data.

6. Print a keyed-in character.

Solution
```
#include<stdio.h>
int main(void)
{
    int ch;
    putchar(ch=getchar());
    return 0;
}
```
Input x

Output x

Explanation: The program in this example is similar to Example 2 except that the statement ch=getchar() is placed as a parameter of the output function putchar(). So when putchar() is executed, getchar()gets invoked and it obtains the character

data from the keyboard which is passed to putchar(). Then putchar() displays the data entered through the keyboard.

7. Print a keyed-in character.

Solution
```
#include<stdio.h>
int main(void)
{
    putchar(getchar());
    return 0;
}
```
Input y

Output y

Explanation: This example is almost similar to Example 6. The only difference is that the integer variable ch has been omitted. But otherwise this program executes similarly as that in Example 6.

8. Obtain an ASCII number that is ahead by two positions from the keyed-in number.

Solution
```
#include<stdio.h>
int main(void)
{
    int ch;
    putchar(ch=(getchar())+2);
    return 0
}
```
Reads a typed in character in ASCII representation.

Content of 'ch' is {ASCII equivalent of character typed in} + 2

Input a

Output c

Explanation: Here, the ASCII equivalent of the typed-in character a, read in by getchar(), is 61h. To this, 2 is added to make it 63h. The alphabetic character represented by 63h is c. Therefore, putchar() displays this character on the monitor screen.

9. Compare two numbers.

Solution
```
#include<stdio.h>
#include<conio.h>
int main(void)
{
  int a=2,b=5;
  int t,f,x;
  t=getchar();
  fflush(stdin);  /* the fflush() function clears */
                  /* the input stream stdin      */
```

```
f=getchar();
x=((a>b)?t:f);
putchar(x);
putch(x);
return 0;
}
```

Input 1
      0

Output 00

Explanation: In this example, the character entered in variable t is 1 while that for f is 0. During evaluation of the expression x=((a>b)?t:f), the relation a > b is found to be false, so f is assigned to x. Since f contains 0, thus x is assigned this character 0. Therefore, putchar(x) displays a 0 on the monitor screen. Since there is no new-line command following the display of 0, the cursor positions itself next to this character. Now, when putch(x) is executed, it displays the value in x at the cursor positioned next to the earlier display. So the output finally appears as 00.

10. Convert alphabets from lower-case letters to capital letters.

Solution
```
#include<stdio.h>
int main(void)
{
  int ch,n;
  ch=getchar();
  n=(ch>='a')&&(ch<='z')?
                  putchar(ch+'A'-'a'): putchar(ch);
  putchar(n);
  return 0;
}
```

  (i) **Input** m
      Output MM
  (ii) **Input** b
      Output BB
  (iii) **Input** $
      Output $$

Explanation: In this example program, once the typed-in character is read in by getchar(), its ASCII equivalent is stored in the integer variable ch. Next, the expression (ch>='a')&&(ch<='z') is evaluated. The ASCII equivalent value in ch is compared with the ASCII equivalent value of the beginning (means a) and ending (means z) characters of the alphabet. In short, this expression checks to see whether the character entered is among the characters a to z of the alphabet. If this is true, then the function putchar(ch+'A'-'a') is executed and its return value is assigned to n; otherwise the function putchar(ch)is executed. Here, it may be noted that on evaluating the expression (ch +'A'-'a'), an ASCII value representing the upper-case alphabet corresponding to the lower-case value is obtained. So putchar(ch+'A'-'a') displays the upper-case alphabet and assigns this character to n. On the other hand, if the typed-in character is none

among the alphabets a to z, then the typed-in character is displayed. In any case, the output function putchar(n) displays the character once again.

The following two programs depict what happens when getch() and getche() are used.

11. Write a program to show the usefulness of getch().

Solution
```
#include <stdio.h>
int main()
{
  int ch;
  printf("\nContinue(Y/N)?");
  ch = getch();
  putch(ch);
  return 0;
}
```
> This typed-in character is read in by getch() and kept in variable 'ch'. putch(ch) just displays ch content.

Output Continue(Y/N)? Y

Explanation: Upon pressing the Y or N key, the character is stored in ch, but the character pressed is not automatically shown on the screen.

The functions getch() and putch(ch) are available only with Turbo C compilers.

12. Write a program to show the usefulness of getche().

Solution
```
#include <stdio.h>
int main()
{
  int ch;
  printf("\nContinue(Y/N)?");
  ch = getche();
  return 0;
}
```
> This typed-in character is read in by getche() which keeps it in variable ch and displays it.

Output Continue(Y/N)?N

Explanation: Upon pressing the Y or N key, the character is stored in ch and is also displayed on the screen without using any output function like putch(ch). Such input and output functions are available only with Turbo C compilers.

9.4 FORMATTED INPUT AND OUTPUT FUNCTIONS

When input and output is required in a specified format, the standard library functions scanf() and printf() are used. The scanf() function allows the user to input data in a specified format. It can accept data of different data types. The printf() function allows the user to output data of different data types on the console in a specified format.

9.4.1 Output Function print f ( )

The printf() [and scanf()] functions differ from the kind of functions that are created by the programmer as they can take a variable number of parameters. In the case of printf(), the first parameter is always a *control string*, for example, 'Hello World', but after that the programmer can include any number of parameters of any type. The general form of a call to the printf() function is

```
printf("control_string",variable1,variable2,
    variable3,...);
```

where '...' means a list of variables that can be written separated by commas and this list may be as long as is desired. The control string is all-important because it specifies the type of each variable in the list and how the user wants it printed. The control string is also called the *format string*.

The *control string*, which is written within "and", contains *data type* with *format specifiers* indicated by the characters that follow the % symbol. These are arranged in order so that they correspond to the respective variables. In between the % symbol with the specifiers, character strings may be inserted. When the printf() function executes, it scans the control string from left to right and prints out the character string as it is while printing the values of the listed variables according to the information specified with the respective format specifiers. For example,

```
printf("Hello World");
```

has a control string only and has no % characters. The above statement displays Hello World only. The format specifier %d means convert the next value to a signed decimal integer, and hence

```
printf("Total = %d",total);
```

will print Total = and then the value passed by the variable named total as a decimal integer.

The C view of output is at a lower level than one might expect. The %d is known as a format specifier, while it also acts as a *conversion code*. It indicates the data type of the variable to be printed and how that data type should be converted to the characters that appear on the screen. Thus %d says that the next value to be printed is a signed integer value, i.e., a value that would be stored in a standard int variable, which should be converted into a sequence of characters, where digits represent the value in decimal. If by some accident the variable that is to be displayed happens to be a float or a double, then the user will still see a value displayed but it will not correspond to the actual value of the float or double. The reason for this is twofold.

- An int uses two bytes (considering 16-bit machine) to store its value, while a float uses four and a double uses eight. If an effort is made to display a float or a double using %d, then only the first two bytes of the value are actually used.

- Even if there was no size difference, int, float, and double use a different binary representation and %d expects the bit pattern to be a simple signed binary integer.

This is all a bit technical, but that is in the nature of C. These details can be ignored as long as two important facts are remembered.

- The conversion code following % indicates the type of variable to be displayed as well as the format in which that value should be displayed.

- If the programmer uses a conversion code with the wrong type of variable, then some strange things will be seen on the screen and the error often propagates to other items in the printf() list.

Though this appears a bit complicated, it should also be pointed out that the benefit lies in being able to treat what is stored in a variable in a more flexible way than other languages allow. In fact, the programmer need not know that the numeric number stored in a variable is in binary form. But while printing this number using the printf() function, it would appear to be a decimal number. Of course, whether this is viewed as an advantage depends on what the programmer is trying to do. It certainly brings the user closer to the way the machine works.

The *format string* in printf(), enclosed in quotation marks, has three types of objects:

Ordinary characters These are copied to output.

Conversion specifier field It is denoted by % containing the codes listed in Table 9.1 and by optional modifiers such as *width*, *precision*, *flag*, and *size*.

Control code It includes optional control characters such as \n, \b, and \t.

Table 9.1 Format specifiers for printf()

Conversion code	Usual variable type	Display
%c	char	single character
%d (%i)	int	signed integer
%e (%E)	float or double	exponential format
%f	float or double	signed decimal
%g (%G)	float or double	use %f or %e, whichever is shorter
%o	int	unsigned octal value
%p	pointer	address stored in pointer
%s	array of char	sequence of characters (string)
%u	int	unsigned decimal integer
%x (%X)	int	unsigned hex value
%%	none	no corresponding argument is converted, prints only a %.
%n	pointer to int	the corresponding argument is a pointer to an integer into which the number of characters displayed is placed.

% format specifiers in printf ( )

The % format specifiers, also termed here as the conversion code, that can be used in ANSI C are given in Table 9.1.

Formatting the output in printf ()

The type conversion code only does what is asked of it. This means that it converts a given bit pattern into a sequence of characters that a human can read. If the programmer wants to format the characters, then more needs to be known about the `printf()` function's *control string* or *format string*.

The *format string* in `printf()` has the following general form:

> "<control code><character string><%conversion specifier field> <control code>"

The programmer has the option of changing the order of the objects, such as `character string`, the `% conversion specifier field`, and the `control code` within the *format string*. Except for the `% conversion specifier field`, the other two objects, that is, the `character string` and the `control code`, are optional when the list of variables is present in `printf()`. Figure 9.1 shows the parts of a `conversion specifier` field for `printf()`.

Fig. 9.1 Parts of conversion specifier field for `printf()`

The character string is a sequence of ordinary characters that is to be printed without any alteration. The `control code` and `conversion specifier` may be embedded within the `character string`. Each conversion specifier field is coded as follows:

> %<flag(s)><width><precision><size><conversion code>

The `%` and `conversion code` are required but the other modifiers such as `width` and `precision` are optional. The `width` modifier specifies the total number of characters used to display the value and `precision` indicates the number of characters used after the decimal point. The `precision` option is only used with `floats` or `strings`. Its use with `strings` will be discussed in a later chapter; for now, its use with `floats` will be considered.

When used to modify a `float`, precision indicates how many digits should be printed after the decimal point. If the `precision` option is used, the number of digits must be preceded by a period. Extra digits will be omitted, and zero digits will be added to the right if necessary. If `precision` is not specified, the default value of 6 is assumed.

So, the `width` option is used to specify the minimum number of positions that the output will take. If the output would normally take less than the specified number, the output is padded, usually with empty spaces to the left of the value. If the output requires more space than the specified number, it is given the space that it needs. For example, `%10.3f` will display the `float` using ten characters with three digits after

the decimal point. Notice that the ten characters include the decimal point and a '–' sign if there is one.

Here are some examples.

```
printf("number=%3d\n", 10);
printf("number=%2d\n", 10);
printf("number=%1d\n", 10);
printf("number=%7.2f\n", 5.4321);
printf("number=%.2f\n", 5.4391);
printf("number=%.9f\n", 5.4321);
printf("number=%f\n", 5.4321);
```

The outputs of these five statements in order are as follows:

Output screen

The first example prints one space to the left of 10 since a width of 3 was specified. The second case adds no spaces, since 10 takes up the entire width of 2. In the third case, the specified width is just 1, but the value of 10 requires two spaces so it is given.

In the fourth case, a precision of 2 is specified for a `float`, so only two digits are printed after the decimal place, and a width of 7. So the value, which would normally contain four characters including the decimal point has three additional spaces. In the fifth case, no width is specified, so the value of width is taken to be exactly what it needs, and a precision of 2 is specified; but this time, the hundredth digit is rounded up.

In the sixth case, a precision of 9 is specified, so five zeroes are added to the end of the value, and in the final case, a default precision of 6 is used, so two zeroes are added to the end of the value.

The `flag` option allows one or more print modifications to be specified. The flag can be any one of the characters shown in Table 9.2.

The specifier `%-10d` will display an `int` left justified in a ten-character space. The specifier `%+5d` will display an `int` using the next five character locations and will add a '+' or '–' sign to the value.

Table 9.2 Flag characters used in `printf()`

Flag	Meaning
–	Left justify the display
+	Display positive or negative sign of value
space	Display space if there is no sign
0	Pad with leading zeroes
#	Use alternate form of specifier

Here are a couple of examples using the `flag` options.

```
printf("number=%06.1f\n", 5.5);

printf("%-+6.1f=number\n", 5.5);
```

The output of these two statements in order is as follows:

```
number = | 0 | 0 | 0 | 5 | . | 5 |
```

```
| + | 5 | . | 5 |   |   | = number
```

In the first statement, a `float` is printed with a precision of 1 and width of 6. Because the 0 `flag` is used, the three extra positions that need to be filled are occupied by zeroes instead of spaces. In the second statement, the minus sign causes the value to be left justified, spaces are added to the right instead of the left, and the positive sign causes the sign of the number to be printed with the number.

Similarly, for

```
printf("%-6.3f\n",17.23478);
```

the output on the screen will show

```
| 1 | 7 | . | 2 | 3 | 5 |
```

which is left justified and the total width being 6, only three digits after the decimal point are printed. Also, for

```
printf("VAT=17.5%%\n");
```

the output on the screen will be

```
| V | A | T | = | 1 | 7 | . | 5 | % |
```

Strings will be discussed later but for now it is enough to remember that if a string is printed using the `%s` specifier, then all of the characters stored in the array up to the first null will be printed. If a width specifier is used, the string will be right justified within the space. If a precision specifier is included, only that number of characters will be printed. For example, consider the program given as follows:

```
#include <stdio.h>
int main()
{
  printf("%s","hello");        /* first printf()  */
  printf("\n%3s","hello");     /* second printf()*/
```

```
  printf("\n%10s","hello");   /* third printf() */
  printf("\n%-10s","hello");  /*fourth printf()*/
  printf("\n%10.3s","hello"); /* fifth printf() */
  return 0;
}
```

The output for the respective `printf()` functions would be as follows:

The third `printf()` prints 10 characters with `hello` right justified, while the fourth `printf()` prints 10 characters with `hello` left justified. The fifth `printf()` prints only the first three characters considered from the left of `hello` because the precision specifier has been given as 3. Also notice that it is normal to pass a constant value to `printf()` as in `printf("%s", "hello")`.

Output screen

```
Quincy 2005                                    _ □ ×
hello
hello
        hello
hello
      hel
```

Among the flags, the only complexity is in the use of the # modifier. What this modifier does depends on the type of format specifier, that is, the conversion code it is used with.

Table 9.3 depicts the actions that take place when this flag is used with the different allowed format specifiers.

Table 9.3 Uses of # flag with format specifier

flag with format specifier	Action
%#0	Adds a leading 0 to the octal number printed
%#x or X	Adds a leading 0x or 0X to the hex number printed
%#f or e	Ensures that the decimal point is printed
%#g or G	Displays trailing zeroes in g or G type conversion and ensures decimal point is printed in floating-point number, even though it is a whole number

The effects of the size modifiers that transform the conversion code are shown in Table 9.4.

Table 9.4 Size modifiers used in `printf()`

Size modifier	Conversion code	Converts to
l	d i o u x	long int
h	d i o u x	short int
l	e f	double
L	e f	long double

Examples of the use of size modifiers are as follows:

```
%hd /* short integer */
%ld /* long integer  */
%Lf /* long double    */
```

Adding a 1 in front of a conversion code will mean a long form of the variable type and a h will indicate a short form. For example, %ld means a long integer variable, usually four bytes, and %hd means a short int. Notice that there is no distinction between a four-byte float and an eight-byte double. The reason is that a float is automatically converted to a double precision value when passed to printf. Therefore, the two can be treated in the same way. In pre-ANSI, all floats were converted to double when passed to a function but this is no longer true.

Finally there are the *control codes* also known as escape sequences that have already been described and listed in Chapter 8. Some of the commonly used control codes are listed in Table 9.5.

Table 9.5 List of commonly used control codes

Control code	Action
\b	Backspace
\f	Form feed
\n	New line
\r	Carriage return
\t	Horizontal tab
\'	Single quote
\0	Null

If any of these are included in the format string, the corresponding ASCII control code is sent to the screen, or output device, which should produce the effect listed. In most cases, the programmer only needs to remember \n for new line.

The conversion specifier field is used to format printed values, often to arrange things nicely in columns. Here are some illustrations of the use of printf() with brief explanations.

EXAMPLES

13. `printf( "Hello there" );`

Puts Hello there on the screen. The cursor remains at the end of the text, which is where the next printf() statement will place its text.

14. `printf("Goodbye.\n");`

This prints Goodbye. on the screen. The \n does not show on the screen; it means 'new line'; it moves the cursor to the next line downwards and to the left.

15. `int int_var;`

`int_var = 10;`

`printf("Integer is: %d", int_var);`

Integer variable int_var contains a value of 10. This prints Integer is: 10 on the screen, as the %d is replaced by the contents of the int_var variable.

16. `int i1, i2; i1 = 2; i2 = 3;`

`printf( "Sum is: %d", i1 + i2);`

Integer variable i1 contains 2 and i2 contains 3. This prints Sum is: 5 on the screen.

The result of i1+i2 is calculated (2+3=5) and this replaces the %d in the string.

17. `printf( "%3d\n%3d\n%3d\n", 5, 25, 125 );`

This displays three values on the screen, each followed by a new line. The %3d means 'replace this with an integer, but ensure it takes up at least three spaces on the screen'. This is good for lining up columns of data. There are three of these, so we need three extra parameters to fill them in (5, 25, and 125). So the output is

```
  5
 25
125
```

18. `float pi;`

`pi = 3.1415926535;`

`printf( "Pi is %4.2f to 2dp\n", pi);`

This example sets a floating-point variable pi to be 3.1415926535. The %4.2f is replaced by this value, but the 4.2 part indicates that the number can be maximum four characters wide (including the decimal point), and has two decimal places (i.e., digits after the decimal point). This means that only 3.14 will show. Note that if pi had been 3.146, then 3.15 would have been shown due to rounding off. In this case, what shows is pi, which is 3.14, followed by a new line.

19. `char color[11] = "red";`

`printf( "Color is: %s\n", color );`

The %s is replaced by a character array (or string). In this case, Color is: red is displayed, followed by a new line.

Note: After the printf() function is executed, the output is printed out on the standard device, which is normally the Video Display Unit (VDU); it returns a number that is equal to the number of characters printed.

To illustrate that the printf() function returns a number that is equal to the number of characters printed, the following program is used:

```
#include<stdio.h>
#include<stdlib.h>
```

```
#define length 40
int  main( )
{
    int n;
    printf("Oxford University%n Press", &n);
    printf("\n n = %d",n);
    return 0;
}
```

> There are 17 characters, including one space in this string of characters that precedes %n.

> Address of the variable n, where the character count 17 is stored.

Output

```
Oxford University
n = 17
```

Run-time adjustment and precision in printf()

The correct way to adjust field *width* and *precision* at run time is to replace the *width* and/or *precision* with a star (*) and include appropriate integer variables in the parameter list. The values of these integer variables representing width and precision will be used before the actual variable to be converted is taken from the parameter list. Here is a program showing the described feature in use.

```
#include <stdio.h>
int main()
{
    double x=1234.567890;
    int i=8,j=2;
    while(i<12)
    {
        j=2;
        while(j<5)
        {
            printf("width = %2d precision = %d display \
            >>%*.*lf<<\n",i,j,i,j,x);
        }
        j++;
    }
    return 0;
}
```

> Total number of digit positions provided for output

> Total number of digit positions provided for decimal part in the output

> *.* takes the values assigned to i and j as width and precision for outputting the value in x.

The program displays the effects of various widths and precisions for output of a double variable. The following is the output.

```
width =  8 precision = 2 display >> 1234.57<<
width =  8 precision = 3 display >>1234.568<<
width =  8 precision = 4 display >>1234.5679<<
width =  9 precision = 2 display >>  1234.57<<
width =  9 precision = 3 display >> 1234.568<<
width =  9 precision = 4 display >>1234.5679<<
width = 10 precision = 2 display >>   1234.57<<
width = 10 precision = 3 display >>  1234.568<<
width = 10 precision = 4 display >> 1234.5679<<
```

```
width = 11 precision = 2 display >>    1234.57<<
width = 11 precision = 3 display >>   1234.568<<
width = 11 precision = 4 display >>  1234.5679<<
```

The >> and << symbols are used to indicate the limits of the output field. Note that the variables i and j appear twice in the parameter list, the first time to give the values in the annotation and the second time to actually control the output.

Note

- A control string, also termed as format string, and variable names are specified for the `printf()` output function to display the values in the variables in the desired form on the monitor screen.
- The format string in `printf()`, enclosed in quotation marks, has three types of objects: (i) Character string (ii) Conversion specifier (iii) Control code, with the programmer's option of changing the order of these three objects within the format string.
- Except for the % conversion specifier field, the other two objects, that is, the character string and the control code, are optional when the list of variables is present in `printf()`.
- The control code and conversion specifier may be embedded within the character string.

9.4.2 Input Function scanf ( )

The `scanf()` function works in much the same way as the `printf()`. It has the general form

```
scanf("control_string",variable1_address, variable2_
address,...);
```

where the *control string*, also known as the *format string* is a list of *format specifiers* indicating the format and type of data to be read from the standard input device, which is the keyboard, and stored in the corresponding address of variables. There must be the same number of format specifiers and addresses as there are input fields.

`scanf()` returns the number of input fields successfully scanned, converted, and stored. The return value does not include scanned fields that were not stored. If `scanf()` attempts to read end-of-file, the return value is EOF. If no fields were stored, the return value is 0. However, there are a number of important differences as well as a number of similarities between `scanf()` and `printf()`.

The most obvious is that `scanf()` has to change the values stored in parts of the computer's memory associated with variables. Until functions are covered in more detail, understanding this fully has to wait. But, just for now, understand that to store values in memory locations associated with variables, the `scanf()` function should have the addresses of the variables rather than just their values. This means that simple variables have to be passed with a preceding &.

There is no need to use & for strings stored in arrays because the array name is already a pointer. This issue will be dealt with in the chapter on arrays and strings. Moreover, the format string has some extra attributes to cope with the problems of reading and data writing, which are described below. However, almost all of the conversion specifiers, or format specifiers, listed in connection with `printf()` can be used with `scanf()` also.

As with `printf()`, the format string in `scanf()` is enclosed in a set of quotation marks and it may contain the following:

White space This causes the input stream to be read up to the next non-white-space character.

Ordinary character string Anything except white space or % characters. The next character in the input stream must match this character.

Conversion specifier field This is a % character, followed by an optional * character, which suppresses the conversion, followed by an optional non-zero decimal integer specifying the maximum field width, an optional h, 1, or L to control the length of the conversion, and finally a non-optional conversion specifier. Note that the use of h, 1, or L will affect the type of pointer that must be used.

Format specifiers in scanf ( )

The format string in `scanf()` has the following general form:

```
"< character string >< % conversion specifier field >"
```

Here, character string is optional and has to be used with care. Each *conversion specifier* field is coded as follows:

```
%[*]<width><size><conversion-code>
```

Each *conversion* (or *format*) *specifier* begins with the per cent character, %, after which come the following, in the given order.

1. An optional assignment-suppression character, *, which states that the value being read will not be assigned to an argument, but will be dropped.

2. An optional *width specifier*, <width>, which designates the maximum number of characters to be read that compose the value for the associated argument.

    Encountering white space, before the entire width is scanned, terminates the input of this value and moves to the next.

3. An optional conversion-code modifier, <size>, which modifies the conversion code to accept format for a type of

    h = short int,

    1 = long int, if the format specifiers provide for an integer conversion,

    1 = double, if the format specifiers provide for a floating-point conversion, and

    L = long double, which is valid only with floating-point conversions.

The format specifiers in `scanf()` are shown in Fig. 9.2.

Fig. 9.2 Parts of conversion specifier field for `scanf()`

The format specifiers, or the conversion code, that apply to `scanf()` are given in Table 9.6.

Table 9.6 Format specifiers for `scanf()`

Conversion code	Usual variable type	Action
%c	char	Reads a single character.
%d(%i)	int	Reads a signed decimal integer.
%e(%E)	float or double	Reads signed decimal.
%f	float or double	Reads signed decimal.
%g(%G)	float or double	Reads signed decimal.
%o	int	Reads octal value.
%p	pointer	Reads in hex address stored in pointer.
%s	array of char	Reads sequence of characters (string).
%u	int	Reads unsigned decimal integer.
%x(%X)	int	Reads unsigned hex value.
%%	none	A single % character in the input stream is expected. There is no corresponding argument.
%n	pointer to int	No characters in the input stream are matched. The corresponding argument is a pointer to an integer into which the number of characters read is placed.
[...]	array of char	Reads a string of matching characters.

Formatted input in scanf ()

Typically, the format string for a `scanf()` will not contain constant text. If it does, that means the input must contain the same text in the same position. For example, consider the following simple program.

─────────── **EXAMPLE** ───────────

20.
```c
#include <stdio.h>
int main(void)
{
    int x;
    scanf("Number=%d", &x);
    printf("The value of x is %d.\n", x);
    return 0;
}
```

If the user wants the value of x to be 25, the user would have to type `Number=25` exactly, or the behaviour of this little program is unpredictable. To avoid this type of problem, it is usually a good idea not to include constant text in format strings when using `scanf()`.

When reading in integers or floats, the `scanf()` function skips leading white space. This means that all spaces, tabs, and new line characters will be ignored, and `scanf()` will keep reading input until it reaches a number. When reading in a character, `scanf()` will read exactly one character, which can be any valid ASCII character or other valid character for the system. If the user wants to skip a space before a character, the space has to be explicitly included in the character string. For example, consider the following code, assuming that a, b, and c are integers and x is a character.

```
scanf("%d%d%d%c", &a, &b, &c, &x);
```

Assume that the user wants a, b, c, and x to be 1, 2, 3, and z. The user would have to type

```
1 2 3Z
```

If, instead, the user types

```
1 2 3 Z
```

then the value of x will be a space because z has been typed with a space preceding it.

If the user wants to be able to enter the line this way, the `scanf()` needs to be coded as follows:

```
scanf("%d%d%d %c", &a, &b, &c, &x);
```

Using spaces between integer field specifications is optional. For example, while reading integers x, y, and z

```
scanf("%d%d%d", &x, &y, &z);
```

is equivalent to

```
scanf("%d %d %d", &x, &y, &z);
```

Normally, when reading a numeric value, `scanf()` reads until it sees trailing white space. The rule is that `scanf()` processes the format string from left to right and each time it reaches a specifier it tries to interpret what has been typed as a value. If multiple values are input, these are assumed to be separated by white space, i.e., spaces, new line, or tabs. This means, the user can type

```
3 4 5
```

or

```
3
4
5
```

and it does not matter how many spaces are included between items. For example,

```
scanf("%d %d",&i,&j);
```

will read in two integer values into i and j. The integer values can be typed on the same line or on different lines as long as there is at least one white space character between them. The only exception to this rule is the `%c` specifier that always reads in the next character typed no matter what it is.

If a width modifier is used, it specifies the maximum number of characters to be read.

Then `scanf()` will read either as many characters as specified by the width modifier or until it sees white space, whichever happens first. In this case, its effect is to limit the number of characters accepted to the width. For example,

```
scanf("%10d",&i);
```

would use at most the first ten digits typed as the new value for i. There are two other reasons that can cause `scanf()` to stop. One is if an end-of-file character is encountered. When reading from an actual disk file, there is automatically an end-of-file character at the end of the file. When reading from a keyboard, the user can simulate one by pressing a specific character sequence. On UNIX machines, the user can enter an end-of-file character by pressing <**Ctrl-d**>.

The other reason that may cause `scanf()` to stop is when it encounters an invalid input. For instance, if `scanf()` is expecting to read a numeric value and it comes across a non-numeric character, this is an error.

The following are the reasons because of which `scanf()` will stop reading a value for a variable.

- A white space character is found after a digit in a numeric sequence.
- The maximum number of characters has been processed.
- An end-of-file character is reached.
- An error is detected.

The `scanf()` function returns the number of variables successfully read in. For example, consider the following program.

EXAMPLE

```
21. #include <stdio.h>
    int main(void)
    {
      int a, b, c;
      int num;
      num = scanf("%d %d %d", &a, &b, &c);
      printf("I have read %d values.\n", num);
      return 0;
    }
```

When run, the user must type `10 20 30` for the program to output

```
I have read 3 values.
```

If the user types `10 20 hello`, the program will output

```
I have read 2 values.
```

If the user types `hello 10 20 30`, the program will output

```
I have read 0 values.
```

When reading standard input from the keyboard, the input is buffered. In other words, the program does not see the text directly as it is typed in; the characters are being temporarily stored in a buffer somewhere. When the user hits <**Enter**>, the buffer is sent to the program. Until then, the user can edit the buffer by adding (typing) new characters, or by hitting the backspace or delete key to remove the last character from the buffer. The program will never see these deleted characters. Consider the following simple program.

EXAMPLE

22.
```c
#include <stdio.h>
int main(void)
{
    int x;
    scanf("%d", &x);
    printf("You typed %d.\n", x);
    return 0;
}
```

If an input 45 is given to this program, the printed output will be

You typed 45.

Another thing to note about `scanf()` is that the format string should *never* end with a new line character. This will always lead to some form of error. For example,

```c
scanf("%d\n", &x);
```

This code will not work correctly because of the `\n` at the end of the `scanf()` format string. The last thing to remember about `scanf()` is that each variable must be preceded by the & symbol. This symbol is the address operator. It takes the address in memory of the variable following the symbol. If the values of the variables are passed to `scanf()`, it would be unable to change the values of the variables. By passing the memory address where these values are stored, the function is able to write new values into memory.

At this point it must be clear that both the functions `scanf()` and `printf()` use the `stdin` and `stdout` streams, respectively, and require the header file `stdio.h` to be included in the program when they are used.

Note

- In `scanf()`, the control string or format string that consists of a list of format specifiers indicates the format and type of data to be read in from the standard input device, which is the keyboard, for storing in the corresponding address of variables specified.
- There must be the same number of format specifiers and addresses as there are input variables.
- The format string in `scanf()` is enclosed in a set of quotation marks and it may contain the following:
  (a) White space
  (b) Ordinary character string
  (c) Conversion specifier field

EXAMPLES
---

23. Add two integer numbers and print the input numbers and result.
    Solution
    ```c
    #include <stdio.h>
    int main()
    {
        int a,b,c;
        printf("\nThe first number is ");
        scanf("%d",&a);
        printf("\nThe second number is ");
        scanf("%d",&b);
        c=a+b;
        printf("The answer is %d \n",c);
        return 0;
    }
    ```
    Output
    ```
    The first number is 5
    The second number is 9
    The answer is 14
    ```

24. Print formatted numbers.
    Solution
    ```c
    #include <stdio.h>
    int main()
    {
        printf("/%d/\n",336);
        printf("/%2d/\n",336);
        printf("/%10d/\n",336);
        printf("/%-10d/\n",336);
        return 0;
    }
    ```
    Output
    ```
    /336/
    /336/
    /       336/
    /336       /
    ```

25. Print formatted floating-point number.
    Solution
    ```c
    #include <stdio.h>
    int main()
    {
        printf("/%f/\n",1234.56);
        printf("/%e/\n",1234.56);
        printf("/%4.f/\n",1234.56);
        printf("/%3.1f/\n",1234.56);
        printf("/%-10.3f/\n",1234.56);
        printf("/%10.3f/\n",1234.56);
        printf("/%10.3e/\n",1234.56);
        return 0;
    }
    ```
    Output
    ```
    /1234.560000/
    /1.234560e+03/
    /1235/
    /1234.6/
    ```

```
    /1234.560   /
    /   1234.560/
    / 1.235e+03/
```

26. Print character strings.

    Solution

    ```c
    #include <stdio.h>
    #define BLURB "Outstanding Program!"
    int main()
    {
      printf("/%2s/\n",BLURB);
      printf("/%22s/\n",BLURB);
      printf("/%22.5s/\n",BLURB);
      printf("/%-22.5s/\n",BLURB);
      return 0;
    }
    ```

    Output

    ```
    /Outstanding Program!/
    /   Outstanding Program!/
    /                 Outst/
    /Outst                 /
    ```

27. Write a program that prints the next character for the corresponding three characters given to the program.

    Solution

    ```c
    #include <stdio.h>
    int main()
    {
      char a,b,c;
      scanf("%c%c%c",&a,&b,&c);
      a++;
      b++;
      c++;
      printf("a=%c b=%c c=%c",a,b,c);
      return 0;
    }
    ```

    Input PQR
    Output a=Q b=R c=S

28. Determine how much money is in a piggy bank that contains several 50, 25, 20, 10 , and 5 paise coins. Use the following values to test the program: five 50 paise coins, three 25 paise coins, two 20 paise coins, one 10 paise coin, and fifteen 5 paise coins.

    Solution

    ```c
    /* To determine how much money there is in a piggy
            bank */
    #include <stdio.h>
    #include <string.h>
    int main(void)
    {
      float coin1=0.50,coin2=0.25,coin3=0.20,
            coin4=0.10, coin5=0.05,total=0.0;
      int ncoins;
      printf("How many 50 paise coins : ");
      scanf("%d",&ncoins);
      total += (ncoins * coin1);
      printf("** %.2f **",total);

      printf("\nHow many 25 paise coins : ");
      scanf("%d",&ncoins);
      total += (ncoins * coin2);
      printf("** %.2f **",total);

      printf("\nHow many 20 paise coins : ");
      scanf("%d",&ncoins);
      total += (ncoins * coin3);
      printf("** %.2f **",total);

      printf("\nHow many 10 paise coins : ");
      scanf("%d",&ncoins);
      total += (ncoins * coin4);
      printf("** %.2f **",total);

      printf("\nHow many 5 paise coins : ");
      scanf("%d",&ncoins);
      total += (ncoins * coin5);
      printf("\n\nThe total amount is
            Rs.%.2f",total);
      return 0;
    }
    ```

    Output

    ```
    How many 50 paise coins : 5
    ** 2.50 **
    How many 25 paise coins : 3
    ** 3.25 **
    How many 20 paise coins : 2
    ** 3.65 **
    How many 10 paise coins : 1
    ** 3.75 **
    How many 5 paise coins : 15
    The total amount is Rs 4.50
    ```

29. Modify the program given in Example 28 to accept the total amount (in rupees) and convert them into paise (vice-versa of Example 28).

    Solution

    ```c
    #include <stdio.h>
    #include <string.h>
    int main(void)
    {
      int nc1,nc2,nc3,nc4,nc5,temp;
      float total;
      printf("Enter the amount : ");
      scanf("%f",&total);
      temp = total * 100;
      nc1 = temp / 50;
      temp = temp % 50;

      nc2 = temp / 25;
      temp = temp % 25;

      nc3 = temp / 20;
      temp = temp % 20;
    ```

```
nc4 = temp / 10;
temp = temp % 10;

nc5=temp;

printf("\n\nNo. of 50 paise coins = %d",nc1);
printf("\nNo. of 25 paise coins = %d",nc2);
printf("\nNo. of 20 paise coins = %d",nc3);
printf("\nNo. of 10 paise coins = %d",nc4);
printf("\nNo. of 5 paise coins = %d",nc5);
return 0;
}
```

Output

```
Enter the amount: 7.65
No. of 50 paise coins = 15
No. of 25 paise coins = 0
No. of 20 paise coins = 0
No. of 10 paise coins = 1
```

30. Write a program for computing product cost. The program should output the computed cost and the delivery date of the product.

   Solution

```
#include <stdio.h>

int main()
{
  int quantity, day, month, year;
  float cost, total;
  int prod_code;

  printf("Enter quantity: ");
  scanf("%d", &quantity);

  printf("Enter cost: ");
  scanf("%f", &cost);
  total = cost * quantity;
```

```
printf("Enter product code: ");
scanf("%d", &prod_code);

printf("Enter date in format dd/mm/yyyy: ");
scanf("%d/%d/%d", &day, &month, &year);

month+=1;
if( month > 12 )
{
    month = 1; year++;
}

printf("Order for %d should be with you by\
    %d/%d/%d at a total cost of %6.2f\n",prod_\
    code, day, month, year, total);
return 0;
}
```

Result:

```
                                                       Inputs
Enter quantity: 3         ◄─────────────────────
Enter cost: 1.25          ◄─────────────────────
Enter product code: 1 2   ◄─────────────────────
Enter date in format dd/mm/yy: 17/12/2003 ◄──────
```

Output

```
Order for 1 should be with you by 17/1/2004 at a total
cost of 3.75
```

> **Note**
> - The scanf() function returns the number of variables successfully read in.
> - The printf() function returns a number that is equal to the number of characters printed.

SUMMARY

Generally, input and output in C, from and to standard devices, are managed through standard streams. The standard input and output devices are the keyboard and the screen. To carry out the input and output, a number of standard functions such as getchar(), putchar(), scanf(), and printf() are in-built in C.

getchar() and putchar() functions are single-character input and output functions, respectively.

So, these do not need any formatted inputs or outputs. The functions scanf() and printf() handle multiple variables of all the allowed data types in C. These, therefore, require formatted inputs and outputs.

KEY TERMS

Character string It is a chain of characters, placed one after another, that is dealt as one unit.

Control codes There are special characters that specify some positional action on the printing point, also known as cursor.

Conversion specifier It is same as format specifier.

Flag modifier It is a character that specifies one or more of the following:

- Displays space if no sign symbol precedes the output

- Inclusion of + or – sign symbol preceding the output
- Padding the output with leading 0s
- The positioning of the output to be displayed
- Use of alternate form of specifier

Format specifier It is identifies the data type, along with width, precision, size, and flag, for the respective variables to be outputted to or read in from a standard device.

Format string   It is a group of characters that contain ordinary character string, conversion code, or control characters arranged in order so that they correspond to the respective control string variables placed next to it in `printf( )` function.

Precision modifier   It indicates the number of characters used after the decimal point in the output displayed. The precision option is used only with floats or strings.

Size modifier   It precedes the conversion code and specifies the kind of data type thereby indicating the number of bytes required for the corresponding variable.

White space   It is the blank space that causes the input stream to be read up to the next non-white-space character.

Width modifier   When used in context with the format string, with modifier specifies the total number of characters used to display the output or to be read in.

FREQUENTLY ASKED QUESTIONS

1. How can you print % character using `printf()`?

Conversion specifiers always start with a % character so that the `printf()` function can recognize them. Because a % in a control string always indicates the start of a conversion specifier, if one wants to output a % character you must use the sequence %%.

2. What is the return type of `printf()` ?

The return value for `printf()` is incidental to its main purpose of printing output, and it usually isn't used. The return type of `printf()` function is `int`. Under ANSI C, `printf()` function returns the number of characters it printed. If there is an output error, `printf()` returns a negative value. The following program illustrates the fact:

```
#include <stdio.h>
int main(void)
{
    int c;
    c=printf("One");
    printf("\nc = %d",c);
    return 0;
}
```
Output
```
One
c = 3
```

3. What is the return type of `scanf()`?

The `scanf()` function returns the number of variables that it successfully reads. If it reads no variables, which happens if you type a non-numeric string when it expects a number, `scanf()` returns the value 0. It returns EOF if it detects end of file. This condition can occur if we press **CTRL-z** in Windows or **CTRL-d** in UNIX/Linux.

```
#include <stdio.h>
int main(void)
{
    int a,b,c;
    c=scanf("%d %d",&a,&b);
    printf("\nc = %d",c);
    return 0;
}
```

Output

Sample run 1:
```
2 3
c = 2
```

Sample run 2:
```
 2 a
 c = 2
```

Sample run 3:
```
 a b
 c = 0
```

Sample run 4:
```
 ^z
 c = -1
```

4. How do I write `printf()` so that the width of a field can be specified at run-time?

This is shown in the following program:

```
int main( )
{
    int w, no;
    printf ("Enter number and the width for the\
            number field:");
    scanf ("%d%d", &no, &w);
    printf ("%*d", w, no);
    return 0;
}
```

Here, * in the format specifier in `printf()` indicates that an `int` value from the argument list should be used for the field width.

5. What is EOF?

EOF is a special character called the end-of-file character. In fact, the symbol EOF is defined in `<stdio.h>` and is usually equivalent to the value −1. However, this is not necessarily always the case, so one should use EOF in the programs rather than as an explicit value. EOF generally indicates that no more data is available from a stream. Incidentally EOF can be entered manually from the keyboard by pressing **CTRL + D** on a UNIX/Linux type machine or by pressing **CTRL + Z** on a Windows type machine.

EXERCISES

1. What will be the value of each variable after the following input command?

   data input: Tom 34678.2 AA4231

   ```
   scanf("%s %3d %f %c %*c %1d",
         name,&m,&x,&ch,&i,&j);
   ```

   (a) name: _____

(b) m: _____

(c) x: _____

(d) ch: _____

(e) i: _____

(f) j: _____

2. What output does each of the following produce?

   (a) putchar('a'); _____

   (b) putchar('\007'); _____

   (c) putchar('\n'); _____

   (d) putchar('\t'); _____

   (e) n = 32; putchar(n); _____

   (f) putchar('\"'); _____

3. For the different values of n, what is the output?

   printf("%x %c %o %d",n,n,n,n);

   (a) n = 67 _____

   (b) n = 20 _____

   (c) n = 128 _____

   (d) n = 255 _____

   (e) n = 100 _____

4. What is wrong with each of the following?

   (a) scanf("%d",i); _____

   (b) #include stdio.h _____

   (c) putchar('/n'); _____

   (d) printf("\nPhone Number:(%s) %S", phone);

   _____

   (e) getch(ch); _____

   (f) putch() = ch; _____

   (g) printf("\nEnter your name:", name);

   _____

5. Which numbering system is not handled directly by the printf() conversion specifiers?

   (a) decimal

   (b) binary

   (c) octal

   (d) hexadecimal

6. What are formatted input and output statements in C? Give suitable examples.

7. What do the getchar() and putchar() functions do?

8. How can a % character be printed with printf()?

9. How can printf() use %f for type double if scanf() requires %lf?

10. How can a variable field width be implemented with printf()?

11. How can numbers be printed with commas separating the thousands?

12. Will the call scanf("%d", i) work? Give reasons for your answer.

13. Explain why the following code is not going to work.

    double d;

    scanf("%f",&d);

14. How can a variable width be specified in a scanf() format string?

15. When numbers are read from the keyboard with scanf "%d\n", they seem to hang until one extra line of input is typed. Explain.

16. Why does everyone advise against using scanf()? What should be used instead?

17. On the screen how do you write the following words?

    she sells seashells by the seashore

    (a) all in one line

    (b) in three lines

18. Write a program that asks interactively the user's name and age and responds with

    Hello name, next year you will be next_age.

    where next_age is age + 1.

19. Write programs to read the values of the variables and print the results of the computed expressions given below:

    (a) a = (b+c)*(b−c)

    (b) $y = ax^2 + bx + c$

    (c) I = (P*R*T)/100

    (d) C = (F−32)/100

    (e) A = −(R1/R2+R3)

    (f) a = 0.5*float1 + 0.25*integer1 + integer2/0.4 + integer3

20. What will be printed by the code given below?

    int value = 5;

    printf("%s", !(value % 2) ? "yes": "no");

21. What will be the output of the following program?

    int main()

    {

    char a,b,c;

    scanf("%c %c %c",&a,&b,&c);

    printf("a=%c b=%c c=%c",a,b,c);

    return 0;

    }

    [Note: The user input is:ABC DEF GHI]

    (a) a=ABC b=DEF c=GHI

    (b) a=A b=B c=C

    (c) a=A b=D c=G

    (d) None of these

22. What will be the output of the following program?

    int main()

    {

    int a,b,c;

    scanf("%1d %2d %3d",&a,&b,&c);

    printf("Sum=%d",a+b+c);

    return 0;

    }

    [Note: The user input is: 123456 44 544]

(a) Sum=480

(b) Sum=594

(c) Sum=589

(d) None of these

23. What will be the output of the following program?

```
int main()
{
    int x=20,y=35;
    x = y++ + x++;
    y = ++y + ++x;
    printf("x=%d,y= %d\n",x,y);
    return 0;
}
```

24. What will be the output of the following program?

```
int main()
{
    int x=5;
    printf("%d %d %d\n",x,x<<2,x>>2);
    return 0;
}
```

25. What will be the output of the following program?

```
int main()
{
    int a=2, b=3;
    printf(" %d ", a+++b);
    printf("a=%d,b=%d",a,b);
    return 0;
}
```

26. What will be the output of the following program?

```
int main()
{
    int a,b;
    printf("\n enter integer values");
    printf("for a and b within 0");
    printf("to 100\n");
    scanf("%d%d",&a,&b);
    b=b^a;
    a=b^a;
    b=b^a;
    printf("a=%d, b=%d\n",a,b);
    return 0;
}
```

[Note: The user input is 23 67]

27. What will be the output of the following program?

```
int main(void)
{
    int var1,var2,var3,minmax;
    var1=5;
    var2=5;
    var3=6;
    minmax=(var1>var2)?(var1>var3)?
            var1:var3:(var2>var3)? var2:var3;
    printf("%d\n",minmax);
    return 0;
}
```

28. What will be the output of the following program?

```
int main(void)
{
    int a=19,b=4;
    float c,d;
    c=a/b;
    d=a%b;
    printf("/c=%12f/\nd=%);
    printf("-12.4f/",c,d);
    return 0;
}
```

29. Pick the correct output of the given program.

```
int main(void)
{
    int i=5;
    printf("%d %d %d %d %d",i, i++, i++, i++, ++i);
    return 0;
}
```

(a) Compile-Time Error

(b) 10 9 8 7 6

(c) 9 8 7 6 6

(d) 10 8 7 6 6

Answers to objective type questions and problems

20. no,   21. (b),   22. (a),   23. x=57, y=94,

24. 5 201,   25. 5 a=3, b=3 *Explanation*: Here

it evaluates as a+++b,   26. a=67, b=23,   27. 6,

28. /c=4.000000/

    /d=4.0000 /

29. (d)

Control Statements

After studying this chapter, the readers will be able to

- discuss the meaning of a statement and a statement block
- explain decision type control constructs in C and the way these are used
- explain looping type control constructs in C and the

technique of putting them to use
- discuss the use of special control constructs such as goto, break, continue, and return
- describe nested loops and their utility

10.1 INTRODUCTION

So far, every program in this book has executed sequentially in the order in which they appear, i.e., statements in a program are normally executed one after another until the last statement completes. A C application begins executing with the first line of the main() function and proceeds statement by statement until it reaches to the end of the main() function.

In C, any sequence of statements can be grouped together to function as a syntactically equivalent single statement by enclosing the sequence in braces. This grouping is known as *statement block* or *compound statement*. Compound statements were originally designed to make control structures simpler.

In C89, one must declare all local variables at the start of the block prior to any executable statements. However in

C99, local variables can be declared at any point within the block prior to their first use.

Consider the following program that illustrates variable declaration at the beginning of a statement block.

```c
#include <stdio.h>
int main(void)
{
  int a=5;
  printf("\n a = %d", a);
  /* A statement block follows */

  {
    int b=10;
    printf("\n a = %d", a);
    printf("\n b = %d", b);
  }
}
```

'b' is visible only within this block.

```
  printf("\n a = %d", a);
  return 0;
}
```
Output
```
a = 5
a = 5
b = 10
a = 5
```

In C99 compliant compiler, the above program can be written as follows giving the same output:

```
#include <stdio.h>
int main(void)
{
  int a=5;
  printf("\n a = %d", a);
  /* A statement block follows */
  {
    printf("\n a = %d", a);
    int b=10;
    printf("\n b = %d", b);
  }
  printf("\n a = %d", a);
  return 0;
}
```

Take a note of the highlighted line. The visibility or accessibility of the variable 'b' is limited to the block in which it was declared. Consider the modified version of the above program. Here an attempt is made to access the variable out of the block. We should definitely get a compilation error.

```
#include <stdio.h>
int main(void)
{
  int a=5;
  printf("\n a = %d", a);
  {
    int b=10;
    printf("\n b = %d", b);
  }
  printf("\n b = %d", b);
  return 0;
}
```

Every function has a function body consisting of a set of one or more statements, i.e., a statement block. For that reason, every function body including main() is confined within a set of curly braces and may optionally include variable declarations after the open curly brace. Inside a function, execution proceeds from one statement to the next, top to bottom. However, depending on the requirements of a problem, it might be required to alter the normal sequence of execution in a program. The order in which statements are executed in a running program is called the *flow of control*. Controlling the flow of a program is a very important aspect of programming. Control flow relates to the order in which the operations of a program are executed.

Control statements embody the decision logic that tells the executing program what action to carry out next depending on the values of certain variables or expression statements. The control statements include *selection*, *iteration*, and *jump statements* that work together to direct program flow.

A *selection statement* is a control statement that allows choosing between two or more execution paths in a program. The selection statements in C are the *if* statement, the *if-else* statement, and the *switch* statement. These statements allow us to decide which statement to execute next. Each decision is based on a *Boolean expression* (also called a *condition* or *test expression*), which is an expression that evaluates to either true or false. The result of the expression determines which statement is executed next.

The programming mechanism that executes a series of statements repeatedly a given number of times, or until a particular condition is fulfilled, is called a *loop*. The construct used for loop is known as *iteration statement*. C language offers three language elements to formulate iteration statements: *while, do-while,* and *for*.

Jump statements transfer the control to another point of the program. Jump statements include *goto, break, continue,* and *return*.

After a very brief introduction to the different types of control structures, it is explained how each type can be used. The subsequent sections will discuss the use of control statements in C. It is also explained how these statements can be used to write efficient programs by using the following:

- Selection or branching statements
- Iteration or loop statements
- Jump statements

The various types of program control statements are shown in Fig. 10.1.

10.2 SPECIFYING TEST CONDITION FOR SELECTION AND ITERATION

A test condition used for selection and iteration is expressed as a test expression. If an expression evaluates to true, it is given the value of 1. If a test expression evaluates to false, it is given the value of 0. Similarly, if a numeric expression is used to form a test expression, any non-zero value (including negative) will be considered as true, while a zero value will be considered as false.

Test expression is a Boolean expression that is either true or false. It is formed in terms of relational expression or logical expression or both. The expressions used to compare the operands are called *boolean expressions* in terms of relational operators. In addition to using simple relational expressions as conditions, compound conditions can be formed using the logical operators.

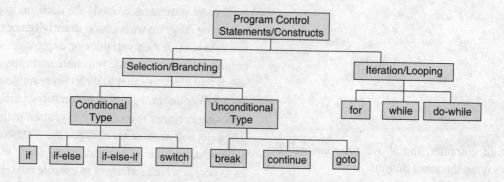

Fig. 10.1   Program control statements/constructs in C

Several relational and logical operators are available to specify the test condition used in the control constructs of C. Relational operators are used to specify individual test expression. More than one test expression can be connected through the logical operator. Tables 10.1 and 10.2 list the several relational, equality, and logical operators used in C.

When the AND operator, &&, is used between two relational expressions, the result is true only if each of both the expressions are true by themselves. When using the OR operator, ||, the condition is true if either one or both of the two individual expressions is true.

The NOT operator, !, is used to change any expression to its opposite state. That is, if the expression has any nonzero value (true), !expression produces a zero value (false). If an expression is false to begin with (has a zero value), !expression is true and evaluates to 1.

Table 10 .1   Relational operators

To specify	Symbol used
less than	<
greater than	>
less than or equal to	<=
greater than or equal to	>=

Among the relational, equality, and logical operators only the '!' operator is unary; the rest are binary operators.

Table 10.2   Equality and logical operators

To specify	Symbol used
Equal to	==
Not equal to	!=
Logical AND	&&
Logical OR	||
Negation	!

10.3 WRITING TEST EXPRESSION

Relational expression can be formed using relational operators. A relational operator takes two operands and compares them to each other, resulting in a value of true (1) or false (0). The syntax for relational expression is as follows:

```
⎧ Variable  ⎫              ⎧ Variable  ⎫
⎪ OR        ⎪              ⎪ OR        ⎪
⎨ Expression⎬ Relational_Operator ⎨ Expression⎬
⎪ OR        ⎪              ⎪ OR        ⎪
⎩ Constant  ⎭              ⎩ Constant  ⎭
```

The relational operators may be used with integer, float, double, or character operands.

EXAMPLES

1. Some examples of expressions are given below.

   - a>2
   - a < b + c
   - a == 3
   - a! = 0
   - a <= b
   - a >= 2

   A test expression involving relational and/or equality and/or logical operators, yields either integer 1 or 0 after evaluation. Consider the following example programs.

2. (a)
```c
#include <stdio.h>
int main()
{
    int a=3;
    printf("\n%d",a>3);
    return 0;
}
```
Output 0

(b)
```c
#include <stdio.h>
int main()
{
    int a=3;
    printf("\n%d",a>2);
    return 0;
}
```
Output 1

The reason for the above output is that in C, false is represented by the value 0 and true is represented by the value 1 as it is a relational expression. In C, if such a value is zero, it is interpreted as a logical value false. If such a value is not zero, it is interpreted as the logical value true. The value for false may be any zero value, e.g., 0, 0.0, '\0' (null character) or the NULL pointer value, discussed later.

3. The following declarations and initializations are given.

```
int x=1, y=2, z=3;
```

Then,

- The expression `x>=y` evaluates to `0` (false).
- The expression `x+y` evaluates to 3 (true).

  The expression `x+y` is basically a concise syntax for the full relational expression (`x+y != 0`), written for coding convenience, as it is only a relational expression which can be used for testing. When `x+y` evaluates to 3, (`x+y !=0`) evaluates to true, as it should be.

- The expression `x=y` evaluates to 2 (true).

  The expression `x=y` would again be translated by the compiler to a relational expression (`(x=y)!=0`). When `x=y` evaluates to 2, (`(x=y)!= 0`) evaluates to true.

- The expression `x==y` evaluates to `0` (false).
- The expression `z%2==0` evaluates to `0` (false).
- The expression `x<=y` evaluates to non-zero (true), i.e., 1.

10.3.1 Understanding How True and False is Represented in C

C does not have predefined true and false values. The value zero (0) is considered to be *false* by C. Any positive or negative value is considered to be *true*. Conventionally, it is assumed that only positive one is *true* but C evaluates any non-zero value to be *true*.

- The following expressions have the resulting value of *true*, assuming that the integer variables `a`, `b`, and `c` have the values a = 1, b = 2, and c = 3.

  - `(a < 2)`   `(a + 1 == b)`   `1==a`
  - `a + b >=c`   `c <= (a + b)`   `(a > 0)`
  - `(a)`   `(-a)`   `(a = 3)`

Note that in the expression (`a = 3`) where the assignment operator is sometimes accidentally used instead of the relational operator '`==`', C evaluates the expression as true even if the variable '`a`' is previously assigned some value other than zero (`0`).

It is better to develop the habit of writing the literal first, e.g., (`3==i`). Then, if an equal sign is accidently left out, the compiler will complain about the assignment, as lvalue can never be constant.

The expression (`a`) where the variable '`a`' was previously assigned the value 1 is true since C considers any expression that evaluates a non-zero value to be true. Even if the value –3 was assigned to the variable '`a`' the expression (`a`) would evaluate to true.

- The following expressions evaluate to *true* where a = 1, b = 2, and c = 3.

  - `(b)`   `(c+a)`   `(2*b)`
  - `(c-2*-30)`   `(0+b)`   `(c-a+b)`

- The following expressions evaluate to *false* where a = 1, b = 2, and c = 3.

  - `(a - 1)`   `(!(a))`   `(0 * c)`
  - `(c - a - b)`

Note that the ' `!` ' symbol, the logical NOT operator, changes a true to a false.

- The following expressions have the resulting value of *false* assuming that the integer variables `a`, `b`, and `c` have the values a = 1, b = 2, and c = 3.

  - `(a > 1)`
  - `(b == 1)`
  - `(a/b + a/b)= = 1`
  - `(c % 3)`
  - `(a > 0 + 4)`

Care should be taken when one compares two values for equality. Due to truncation, or rounding up, some relational expressions, which are algebraically true, may return `0` instead of `1`.

For example, look at the relational expression: `(a/b + a/b)==1` which is `1/2 + 1/2==1`.

This is algebraically true and is supposed to return `1` . The expression, however, returns `0`, which means that the equal-to relationship does not hold. This is because the truncation of the integer division `1/2` produces `0`, not `0.5`. The following program proves this.

```
#include <stdio.h>
int main()
{
    int a=1,b=2;
    printf("\n (a/b + a/b) == 1 evaluates %d",
        (a/b + a/b) == 1);
    return 0;
}
```

Output

```
(a/b+a/b) == 1 evaluates to 0
```

Another example is `1.0/3.0`, which produces `0.33333....`. This is a number with an infinite number of decimal places. But the computer can only hold a limited number of decimal places. Therefore, the expression `1.0/3.0 + 1.0/3.0 + 1.0/3.0 == 1.0` might not return `1` on some computers, although the expression is theoretically true.

- Consider a relational expression such as `a < b`. If '`a`' is less than '`b`', then the expression has the integer value 1, which is true. If '`a`' is not less than '`b`', then the expression has the integer value `0`, which is false. Mathematically, the value of `a < b` is the same as the value of `a - b < 0`. Because the precedence of the relational operators is less than that of the arithmetic operators, the expression `a - b < 0` is equivalent to `(a - b) < 0`.

On many machines, an expression such as a < b is implemented as a - b < 0. The usual arithmetic conversions occur in relational expressions.

Let a and b be the arbitrary arithmetic expressions. Table 10.3 shows how the value of a - b determines the values of relational expressions.

Table 10.3 Values of relational expressions

a - b	a < b	a > b	a <= b	a >= b
Positive	0	1	0	1
Zero	0	0	1	1
Negative	1	0	1	0

An equality expression like a == b evaluates to either true or false. An equivalent expression is a - b == 0. If a equals b, then a - b evaluates to 0 and 0 == 0 is true. In this case a == b results in the integer value 1 which is true in C. If a is not equal to b, then the expression yields 0, which might be thought of as false.

> **Note**
>
> - If an expression, involving the relational operator, is true, it is given a value of 1. If an expression is false, it is given a value of 0. Similarly, if a numeric expression is used as a test expression, any non-zero value (including negative) will be considered as true, while a zero value will be considered as false.
> - Space can be given between operand and operator (relational or logical) but space is not allowed between any compound operator like <=, >=, ==, !=. If the operators are reversed, a compiler error would result.
> - a == b and a = b are not similar, as == is a test for equality, a = b is an assignment operator. Therefore, the equality operator has to be used carefully.
> - The relational operators have lower precedence than all arithmetic operators.

C has three logical operators for combining logical values, which are listed in Table 10.2. && and || are used to connect two or more expressions to form a test condition. && means a conjunction, i.e., all the expressions connected by it must be true to satisfy the test condition. || means a disjunction, i.e., either of the expressions connected by it must be true to satisfy the test condition.

Like arithmetical operators, the relational, equality, and logical operators have rules of precedence and associativity for evaluating expressions involving these operators. Logical operators may be mixed within relational expressions but one must abide by their *precedence rule which is as follows* (see Table 10.4 for complete list).

NOT operator (!), AND operator (&&), OR operator (||) →

One must remember that the && operation is always performed before the || operation because && is similar to multiplication in normal arithmetic while || is similar to addition.

The == (equal to) and != (not equal to) operators are analogous to the relational operators except for their lower precedence.

Table 10.4 Precedence and associativity of operators

Operators	Associativity
( ) ++ (postfix) – (postfix)	left to right
+ (unary) – (unary)	right to left
++ (prefix) – (prefix) * / %	left to right
+ -	left to right
< <= > >=	left to right
== !=	left to right
&&	left to right
||	left to right
?:	right to left
= += –= *= /=	right to left
, (comma operator)	left to right

Given the following declarations and initializations:

```
int a=3, b=-5, c=0;
```

consider Table 10.5 which illustrates the use of the logical operators.

Table 10.5 Illustration of the use of logical operators

Expression	Result
a>0 && c>0	0(false)
a>=0 && c>=0	1(true)
a && c	0(false)
a && b	1(true)
a || c	1(true)
!a && c	0(false)
5 && !c	1(true)

In addition to numerical operands, character data can also be compared using relational operators.

```
'a' < 'e'    returns 1(true)
'9' > '1'    returns 1(true)
'A' > 'a'    returns 0 (false)
```

as ASCII value of 'A' is 65 and that of 'a' is 97. Consider the following declaration:

```
Char ch = 'A';
```

To check whether ch contains upper-case letter the conditional expression can be written as follows:

```
ch>='A' && ch<='Z'
```

It is also possible to use the ASCII value corresponding to a character in relational expression. The above expression can also be written as

```
ch >= 65 && ch <= 90
```

- Although C does not have an exclusive OR (XOR) logical operator, outcome of XOR is true if and only if one operand is true but not both. It can be implemented by the following expression:

```
(a || b) && !(a && b)
```

Short-circuiting evaluation in C

It is to be noted that in case of && when the first operand is false, it is evident that the result must be false. So, the other operand of the expression will not be evaluated. Likewise, in case of ||, when the first operand is true, there is no need to evaluate the other operand of the expression, so the resulting value is set to true immediately. C uses this short-circuit method which is summarized as follows:

Sometimes, it can cause problems when the second operand contains side effects. For instance, consider the following example:

```
r= a && b++;
```

When the first operand is non-zero, that is, if a=2, b=3 then the expression evaluates to give r=1, a=2, and b=4. But if the first variable is zero, then the second variable will never be evaluated. That is, if a=0, b=3; then r=0, a=0, and b=3. Same thing would happen in case of

```
r = a || b++;
```

If the first operand is non-zero, then the second operand would never be incremented. It is important to understand the complement of relational and equality operators. Table 10.6 illustrates the complements.

Table 10.6 Relational operator complement

Operator	Complement
>	< =
<	>=
==	! =

For example, !(a<b) is equivalent to a>=b, !(a>=b) is equivalent to a<b.

- An expression such as a < b < c is syntactically correct but often confusing. This is illustrated with an example. In mathematics,

```
3 < j < 5
```

indicates that the variable j has the property of being greater than 3 and less than 5. It can also be considered as a mathematical statement that, depending on the value of j, may or may not be true. For example, if $j = 4$, then the mathematical statement is true. But if $j = 7$, then the mathematical statement is false. Now consider the C code

```
j =7;
printf("%d\n", 3 < j < 5);
                /* 1 gets printed, not 0 */
```

By analogy with mathematics, it might be expected that the expression is false and that 0 is printed. However, that is not the case because relational operators associate from left to right.

```
3 < j < 5 is equivalent to  (3 < j) < 5
```

Because the expression 3 < j is true, it has value 1. Thus,

```
(3 < j) < 5 is equivalent to 1 < 5
```

which has value 1. In C, the correct way to write an expression for testing both 3 < j and j < 5 is

```
3 < j && j < 5
```

Because relational operators have higher precedence than binary logical operators, this is equivalent to

```
(3 < j) && (j < 5)
```

and, as will be seen later, this expression is true if and only if both operands of the && expression are true.

- Like arithmetic operators, the relational and logical operators have rules of precedence and associativity for evaluating expressions involving these operators (shown in Table 10.4).

The precedence of the relational operators is less than that of the arithmetic operators, including + and –, and greater than that of assignment operators. This means, a > b + 5 means the same as a > (b + 5). The expression a = b > 5 means a = (b > 5). That is, a is assigned 1 if b is greater than 5 and 0; otherwise a is not assigned the value of b.

The relational operators are themselves organized into two different priorities:

Higher-priority group: <<= >>=
Lower-priority group: !=

Like most other operators, the relational operators associate from left to right. Therefore,

```
expr1 != expr2 == expr3
```

is the same as

```
(expr1 != expr2) == expr3
```

First, C checks to see if expr1 and expr2 are unequal. Then the resulting value of 1 or 0 (true or false) is compared to the value of expr3. It is not recommended to write a relational expression like this but this has been pointed out for a clearer understanding of the precedence and associativity of the relational operator.

Initially, C language did not provide any Boolean data type. In C99, a new data type _Bool has been provided which remedied the lack of Boolean type in C language. In this version of C, a Boolean variable can be declared as follows:

```
_Bool isPrime;
```

_Bool is actually an integer type (More precisely an unsigned integer type). Unlike an ordinary integer variable, _Bool variable can only be assigned 0 or 1. When converting any scalar values to type _Bool, all non-zero values are converted to 1 while zero values are converted to 0. Consider the following program:

```
#include <stdio.h>
int main(void)
{
  _Bool isPrime =5;
  printf("\n isPrime = %d", isPrime);
  return 0;
}
```

Output isPrime = 1

Because a relational operator produces a Boolean result, it is possible to store the result in a variable of type _Bool. For example

```
_Bool result = 5 < 4; /* result will be false */
```

In addition to _Bool type, C99 also provides a new header file stdbool.h for working with Boolean values. This header file provides a macro bool which is synonymous with _Bool and defines false and true to be 0 and 1 respectively.

If stdbool.h is included then the following declaration can be written:

```
bool flag;
```

This header file also provides macros like true, false which stands for 1 and 0, respectively making it possible to write the following statement:

```
flag=true;
```

10.4 SELECTION

Selection and iteration statements are the basic tools of thought when designing a logical process. The ability to control the order in which the statements are executed adds enormous value to the programming.

Selection is used to take a decision between one or two or more alternatives. Decision in a program is concerned with choosing to execute one set of statement over the others. Selection is also known as *branching*. There are different types of selection that can be employed in a program as shown in Fig. 10.2.

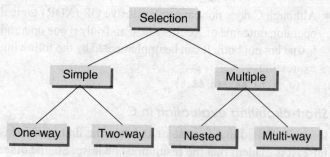

Fig. 10.2 Types of selection constructs

For one-way selection. if..... without else part is used. The if...else... construct is used to implement two-way selection. Nested-if and if...elseif... ladder is used to implement nested selection construct. For implementing multi-way selection switch case is used.

10.4.1 Selection Statements

When dealing with selection statements, there are generally three versions: *one-way*, *two-way*, and *multi-way*. One-way decision statements do a particular thing or they do not. Two-way decision statements do one thing or do another. Multi-way decision statements can do one of many different things depending on the value of an expression.

One-way decisions using if statement

One-way decisions are handled with an if statement that either do some particular thing or do nothing at all. The decision is based on a 'test expression' that evaluates to either true or false. If the test expression evaluates to true, the corresponding statement is executed; if the test expression evaluates to false, control goes to the next executable statement. Figure 10.3 demonstrates this. The form of this one-way decision statement is as follows:

```
if(TestExpr)
  stmtT;
```

TestExpr is the test expression. stmtT can be a simple statement or a block of statements enclosed by curly braces {}.

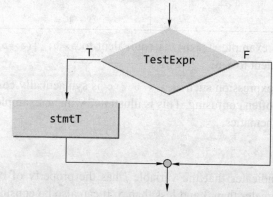

Fig. 10.3 Flowchart for if construct

The if construct can be illustrated with the help of the following example.

---

4. Write a program that prints the largest among three numbers.

Algorithm	C Program
1. START	`#include <stdio.h>`
2. PRINT "ENTER THREE NUMBERS"	`int main()`
	`{`
3. INPUT A, B, C	`int a, b, c, max;`
4. MAX←A	`printf("\nEnter 3 numbers");`
	`scanf("%d %d %d", &a, &b, &c);`
	`max=a;`
5. IF B>MAX THEN MAX←B	`if(b>max)`
	`    max=b;`
6. IF C>MAX THEN MAX←C	`if(c>max)`
7. PRINT "LARGEST NUMBER IS", MAX	`    max=c;`
	`printf("Largest No is %d", max);`
8. STOP	`return 0;`
	`}`

if and the comma operator

Normally, the comma operator is used to combine statements. For example, the statements:

```
x = 1;
y = 2;
```

are treated as a single statement when written as:

```
x = 1, y = 1;
```

With simple statements, the comma operator is not very useful. However it can be used in conjunction with if statement to provide the programmer with a unique shorthand.

```
if (flag)
    x =1, y = 1;
```

This example is syntactically equivalent to:

```
if (flag)
{
    x = 1;
    y = 1;
}
```

The problem with the comma operator is that when you use it, you break the rule of one statement per line, which obscures the structure of the program. Therefore, do not use the comma operator when you can use braces instead.

Two-way decisions using if-else statement

Two-way decisions are handled with if-else statements that either do one particular thing or do another. Similar to one-way decisions, the decision here is based on a test expression. The form of a two-way decision is as follows:

```
if(TestExpr)
    stmtT;
else
    stmtF;
```

If the test expression TestExpr is true, stmtT will be executed; if the expression is false, stmtF will be executed. stmtT and stmtF can be single or a block of statements. Remember that a block of statements is always enclosed within curly braces {}. Figure 10.4 depicts the flowchart of the if-else construct.

Fig. 10.4 Flowchart of if-else construct

The if-else construct is illustrated with the help of an example.

5. Write a C program to check whether a number given by the user is odd or even.

Algorithm	C Program
1. START	`#include <stdio.h>`
2. PRINT "ENTER THE NUMBER"	`int main()`
3. INPUT N	`{`
4. Q←N/2 (Integer Division)	`int n,r;`
5. R←N−Q*2	`printf("\nEnter the number");`
6. IF R=0 THEN PRINT "EVEN" ELSE PRINT "ODD"	`scanf("%d", &n);`
	`r=n%2;`
7. STOP	`if(r==0)`
	`    printf("EVEN");`
	`else`
	`    printf("ODD");`
	`return 0;`
	`}`

An absolutely classic pitfall is to use assignment (=) instead of comparison (==). This is probably the single most common error made by beginners in C programming. The problem is that in such a case the compiler is of no help—it is unable to distinguish this non-syntax error. Consider the following example program.

EXAMPLE

---

6. Check whether the two given numbers are equal.

(a)
```c
#include <stdio.h>
int main()
{
  int a=2, b=3;
  if(a == b)
  printf("EQUAL");
  else
  printf("UNEQUAL");
  return 0;
}
```
Output UNEQUAL

(b)
```c
#include <stdio.h>
int main()
{
  int a=2, b=3;
  if(a = b)
  printf("EQUAL");
  else
  printf("UNEQUAL");
  return 0;
}
```
Output EQUAL

The explanation for the above outputs is that when a condition is specified with = instead of ==, the C compiler checks the value of the test expression. If it is non-zero including negative, it evaluates the test condition as true; otherwise it evaluates the test condition as false. Example 6(a) simply checks the equality and gives the result as expected. But in Example 6(b), the value of b is assigned to a first. Since the value assigned to a is 3, which is non-zero, the condition will be true and the program outputs EQUAL. If the value of b was assigned as zero, then following the above explanation, the second program would print UNEQUAL as now a would be zero.

So the test expression using the equality operator must be specified carefully. If the value of a variable is assigned a constant value, the same thing may not occur. The example statement,

```c
if(x = 3) stmT;
```

does not test whether x is 3. This sets x to the value 3, and then returns x to the if construct for testing. Now, 3 is not 0, so it is deduced as true. The actual test expression should

be x==3. Such a problem can be overcome by writing the expression as 3==x. It is safe to write. If the expression is written 3=x by mistake, then the compiler will complain because 3 cannot be a lvalue.

In case it is desired to test whether variable x has a non-zero value, one could write

```c
if(x)
```

rather than

```c
if(x != 0)
```

However, this can sometimes be confusing. In general, it is better to write whatever is meant rather than writing something that has the same effect.

The following three if() statements are functionally equivalent.

```c
if(x)
  printf("true\n");
if(x!=0)
  printf("true\n");
if(!(x==0))
  printf("true\n");
```

The *unsigned preserving* approach (K&R C) says that when an unsigned type mixes with an int or smaller signed type, the result is an unsigned type. This is the simple rule independent of hardware but as in the following example, it does something to force a negative result to lose its sign. The value preserving approach (ANSI C) says that when an integral operand type is mixed like this, the result type is signed or unsigned depending on the relative sizes of the operand type. Consider the following example.

```c
#include <stdio.h>
int main()
{
  int i=-1;
  unsigned int u=1;
  if(i<u)
    printf("\n i is less than u");
  else
    printf("\n i is not less than u");
  return 0;
}
```

Output i is not less than u (in GCC compiler)

Depending on whether this program is compiled and executed under K&R or ANSI C, the expression i<u will be evaluated differently. The same bit patterns are compared but interpreted as either a negative number or as an unsigned (hence positive number).

If either operand is unsigned, the result is unsigned, and is defined to be modulo 2^n, where n is the word size. If both operands are signed, the result is *undefined*.

Suppose, for example, a and b are two integer variables known to be non-negative, and you want to test whether a+b might overflow. One obvious way to do it looks something like this:

```
if (a + b < 0)
    printf("\OVERFLOW");
```

In general, this does not work. The point is that once a + b has overflowed, all bits in the register holding the result will be zero. If the operation overflowed, the register would be in overflow state, and the test would fail. One correct way of doing this particular test relies on the fact that unsigned arithmetic is well defined for all values, as are the conversions between signed and unsigned values:

```
if ((int) ((unsigned) a + (unsigned) b) < 0)
printf("\OVERFLOW");
```

EXAMPLES

7. Suppose a C code has to be written that will calculate the earnings by workers who are paid an hourly wage, with weekly hours greater than 40 being paid 'time and a half'. Suppose weekly hours and hourly rate are known in the program. Two options of the code to handle this situation are as follows.

Option 1 Using simple statements:

```
if(weeklyHours <= 40)
    earnings = hourlyRate * weeklyHours;
else
    earnings = 40 * hourlyRate + (weeklyHours -
        40) *hourlyRate* 1.5;
```

Option 2 Using a simple and compound statement:

```
if(weeklyHours <= 40)
    earnings = hourlyRate * weeklyHours;
else
    {
      offHours = weeklyHours - 40;
      regpay = 40 * hourlyRate;
      earnings = regpay + offHours * hourlyRate *
          1.5;
    }
```

A complete program in C is illustrated as follows.

8. Write a program that determines if a year is a leap year.

```
#include<stdio.h>
int main()
{
    int year, rem_4,rem_100,rem_400;
    printf("Enter the year to be tested:");
    scanf("%d", &year);
    rem_4 = year % 4;
    rem_100 = year % 100;
    rem_400 = year % 400;
    if( (rem_4 == 0 && rem_100 != 0) || rem_400 = = 0)
        printf("It is a leap year.\n");
```

```
    else
        printf("It is not a leap year.\n");
    return 0;
}
```

Given below are the outputs obtained for different inputs from the above program executed in a computer.

Test run no. 1

```
Enter the year to be tested: 1955
It is not a leap year.
```

Test run no. 2

```
Enter the year to be tested: 2000
It is a leap year.
```

Test run no. 3

```
Enter the year to be tested: 1800
It is not a leap year.
```

Multi-way decisions

Multi-way decision statements use if-else-if nested if or switch statements. They are used to evaluate a test expression that could have several possible values. if-else-if statements are often used to choose between ranges of values. Switch statements are discussed in the next section.

- if-else-if ladder

  The form of a multi-way decision construct using if-else if statements is as follows:

```
if(TestExpr1)
    stmtT1;
else if(TestExpr2)
    stmtT2;
else if(TestExpr3)
    stmtT3;
        .
        .
        .
    else if(TestExprN)
        stmtTN;
    else
        stmtF;
```

If the first test expression TestExpr1 is evaluated to true, then stmtT1 is executed. If the second test expression TestExpr2 is true, then stmtT2 is executed, and so on. If none of the test expressions are true, then the statement stmtF is executed. The flowchart of the above construct is shown in Fig. 10.5.

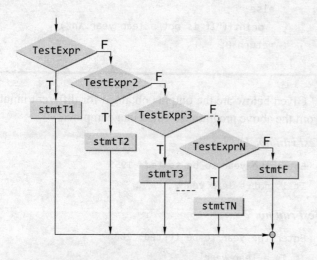

Fig. 10.5 Flowchart of an `if-else-if` construct

EXAMPLES

9. The following program checks whether a number given by the user is zero, positive, or negative.

```c
#include <stdio.h>
int main()
{
int x;
printf("\n ENTER THE NUMBER:");
scanf("%d", &x);
if(x > 0)
  printf("x is positive \n");
else if(x == 0)
    printf("x is zero \n");
  else
    printf("x is negative \n");
return 0;
}
```

10. This program prints the grade according to the score secured by a student.

```c
#include <stdio.h>
int main()
{
int score;
char grade;
printf("\n ENTER SCORE : ");
scanf("%d", &score);
if(score >= 90)
  grade = 'A';
```

```c
else if(score >= 80)
  grade = 'B';
else if(score >= 70)
  grade = 'C';
else if(score >= 60)
  grade = 'D';
else
  grade = 'F';
printf("GRADE IS:%c", grade);
return 0;
}
```

Nested `if`

When any `if` statement is written under another `if` statement, this cluster is called a nested `if`. A simple illustration of a nested `if` is given below.

The `if` statement that tests for divisibility by 5 is located inside of the `if` statement that tests for divisibility by 3; therefore, it is considered to be a nested `if` statement.

```c
if (number % 3 == 0)
{
  printf("number  is divisible by 3. \n");
  if (number % 5 == 0)
  {
    printf("number  is divisible by 3 and 5. \n");
  }
}
```

Another example is given below.

```c
if(a > b)
  if(a > c)
  printf("%d", a);
```

Here, a will be printed in case both `if` conditions are true. The indentation makes the logic of the statements explicitly clear. Next, the nested loop is further explained with the example given below.

```c
if(a > b)
  if(a > c)
    printf("%d",  a);
  else
    printf("%d",  c);
```

An important fact to be noted here is that an `else` always associates itself with the closest (innermost) `if`. In the above example, the `else` part corresponds to the inner `if`, that is, if(a > c). If another `else` is added, the last `else` corresponds to if(a > b). The syntax for the nested `if` is as follows.

Construct 1	Construct 2
`if(TestExprA)`	`if(TestExprA)`
`    if(TestExprB)`	`    if(TestExprB)`
`        stmtBT;`	`        stmtBT;`
`    else`	`    else`
`        stmtBF;`	`        stmtBF;`
`else`	`else`
`    stmtAF;`	`    if(TestExprC)`
	`        stmtCT;`
	`    else`
	`        stmtCF;`

`stmtBT`, `stmtBF`, `stmtCT`, and `stmtCF` can be a simple statement or a block of statements. It is to be remembered that a block of statements is always enclosed within curly braces {}.

In construct 1, `stmtBT` will be executed if both `TestExprA` and `TestExprB` evaluate to true. `stmtBF` will be executed if `TestExprA` evaluates to true and `TestExprB` evaluates to false. `stmtAF` will be executed if `TestExprA` is false and does not check for `TestExprB`.

In construct 2, `stmtBT` will be executed if both `TestExprA` and `TestExprB` evaluate to true. `stmtBF` will be executed if `TestExprA` evaluates to true and `TestExprB` evaluates to false. If `TestExprA` is false, then the test expression `TestExprC` will be checked. If it is true, then `stmtCT` will be executed, otherwise `stmtCF` will be executed.

Finally, a program to find the largest among three numbers using the nested loop follows. The required flowchart is shown in Fig. 10.6. The C code is given as follows:

```c
#include <stdio.h>
int main()
{
  int a, b, c;
  printf("\nEnter the three numbers");
  scanf("%d %d %d", &a, &b, &c);
  if(a > b)
   if(a > c)
     printf("%d", a);
   else
     printf("%d", c);
  else
   if(b > c)
     printf("%d", b);
   else
     printf("%d", c);
  return 0;
}
```

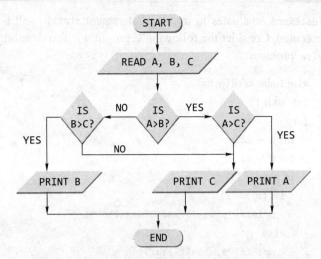

Fig. 10.6 Flowchart for finding the largest of three numbers

Dangling *else* Problem

This classic problem occurs when there is no matching `else` for each `if`. To avoid this problem, the simple C rule is that always pair an `else` to the most recent unpaired `if` in the current block. Consider the following illustration.

```c
if(TestExprA)
    if(TestExprB)
        stmtBT;
    else
        stmtAF;
```

If `TestExprA` is evaluated to true, then the execution moves to the nested `if` and evaluates `TestExprB`. If `TestExprB` is evaluated to true, then `stmtBT` will be executed. If `TestExprA` is evaluated to false, then `stmtAF` is executed. But in the code above, the `else` is automatically paired with the closest `if`. But, it is needed to associate an `else` with the outer `if` also. The solution is either of the following:

- Use of a null `else`
- Use of braces to enclose the true action of the second `if`

Each of these has the following form:

With null else	With braces
`if(TestExprA)`	`if(TestExprA)`
`    if(TestExprB)`	`{`
`        stmtBT;`	`    if(TestExprB)`
`    else`	`        stmtBT;`
`        ;`	`}`
`else`	`else`
`    stmtAF;`	`    stmtAF;Z`

Now, in both the solutions, if the expression `TestExprA` evaluates to false then the statement `stmtAF` will be executed. If it evaluates to true, then it checks for `TestExprB`. If

TestExprB evaluates to true then statement stmtBT will be executed. Consider the following C program with a dangling else problem.

```c
#include <stdio.h>
int main()
{
  int a = 2;
  int b = 2;
  if (a == 1)
    if (b == 2)
      printf("a was 1 and b was 2\n");
    else
      printf("a wasn't 1\n");
  return 0;
}
```

When compiled and run, this program did not produce any output. With the program in its original form it is quite likely that the programmer thought the else statement

```c
else
  printf("a wasn't 1\n");
```

would be associated with the first if but it was not. An else always associates with the immediately preceding if as is clear by the alternative version of the program. The reason for the complete absence of output is that there is no else statement associated with the first if.

In order to achieve the effect that the programmer probably originally intended, it is necessary to re-arrange the program in the following form.

```c
int main()
{
  int a = 2;
  int b = 2;
  if (a == 1)
  {
    if (b == 2) printf("a was 1 and b was 2\n");
  }
  else printf("a wasn't 1\n");
  return 0;
}
```

Note

- Multi-way decision statements are used to evaluate a test expression that could have several possible values.
- An else is always associated with the closest unmatched if.

Check Your Progress

1. What will be the output of the following programs?

```c
(a)  int main()
     {
       printf("Hi!");
       if(-1)
```

```c
         printf("Bye");
       return 0;
     }
```
Output Hi!Bye

```c
(b)  int main()
     {
       printf("Hi!");
       if(!1)
         printf("Bye");
       return 0;
     }
```
Output Hi!

```c
(c)  float x = 199.9;
     if( x < 100)
       printf("one ");
     if(x < 200)
       printf("two ");
     if(x < 300)
       printf("three ");
```
Output two three

```c
(d)  int main()
     {
       int i= -1;
       unsigned int j =1;
       if(i<j)
         printf("Less");
       else
         printf("Greater");
       return 0;
     }
```
Output Greater

10.4.2 The Conditional Operator

Consider the situation in which there are two or more alternatives for an expression. Such a situation arises frequently in programming. For example, depending on existing conditions, there may be two or more alternative values evaluated from the expression. There may be two or more alternative expressions, based on existing conditions, for the value to be returned by a specific function. There may be two or more alternative expressions, again based on existing conditions, for the value of a specific argument in a function call. The conditional operator of C is specifically tailored for such situations. It has the following simple format:

```c
expr1 ? expr2  :  expr3
```

It executes by first evaluating expr1, which is normally a relational expression, and then evaluates either expr2, if the first result was true, or expr3, if the first result was false.

For instance, if the larger of two integer numbers has to be printed, the program using conditional operator will be

```c
#include <stdio.h>
int main()
{
  int a,b,c;
  printf("\n ENTER THE TWO NUMBERS: ");
  scanf("%d %d", &a, &b);
  c=a>b?a:b;
  printf("\n LARGER NUMBER IS %d",c);
  return 0;
}
```

The following is a more refined version of the program. Here, the conditional operator has to be nested.

```c
#include <stdio.h>
int main()
{
  int a,b,c;
  printf("\n ENTER THE TWO NUMBERS: ");
  scanf("%d %d", &a, &b);
  c=a>b? a : b>a ? b :-1;
  if(c==-1)
    printf("\n BOTH NUMBERS ARE EQUAL");
  else
    printf("\n LARGER NUMBER IS %d",c);
  return 0;
}
```

For illustration, let us consider the program that will print the largest among three integer numbers. If the program is written using the nested if construct, it will be as follows:

```c
#include <stdio.h>
int main()
{
  int a,b,c;
  printf("\n ENTER THE THREE NUMBERS: ");
  scanf("%d %d %d", &a, &b, &c);
  if(a>b)
   if(a>c)
     printf("\n LARGEST NUMBER IS: %d", a);
   else
     printf("\n LARGEST NUMBER IS: %d", c);
  else
   if(b>c)
     printf("\n LARGEST NUMBER IS: %d", b);
   else
```

```c
     printf("\n LARGEST NUMBER IS: %d", c);
  return 0;
}
```

Now, the above program is converted into one that uses the nested conditional operator.

```c
#include <stdio.h>
int main()
{
  int a,b,c, max;
  printf("\n ENTER THE THREE NUMBERS: ");
  scanf("%d %d %d", &a, &b, &c);
  max=a>b ? a>c ? a : c: b>c? b : c;
  /* This statement is equivalent to
    max= a>b? (a>c? a: c):(b>c? b: c)*/
  printf("\n LARGEST NUMBER IS: %d", max);
  return 0;
}
```

Similarly, the following program finds the largest number among four integer numbers.

```c
#include <stdio.h>
int main()
{
  int a, b, c, d, e;
  printf("\n Enter the four numbers one by one \n");
  scanf("%d %d %d %d", &a, &b, &c, &d);
  e=a>b?(a>c?(a>d?a:d):(c>d?c:d)):(b>c?(b>d?b:d):(c
      >d?c:d));
  printf("\nLargest number is %d\n", e);
  return 0;
}
```

The use of the conditional expression frequently shortens the amount of source code that must be written. For example, a lengthy function call which has several argument expressions, one of which is conditional, needs to be written only once.

The conditional expression is not only a shorthand; it may also result in less object code than would be generated by other alternative means, e.g., by the use of one or more if statements.

Observe that parentheses are normally not needed around the expressions that are separated by the characters '?' and because, as the operator precedence table shows, the '?:' operator has a very low precedence, i.e., it is usually applied last.

10.4.3 The switch Statement

When there are a number of else alternatives as above, another way of representing this multi-way selection is by the switch statement (shown in Fig. 10.6). The general format of a switch statement is

```
switch(expr)
{
  case constant1: stmtList1;
                  break;
  case constant2: stmtList2;
                  break;
  case constant3: stmtList3;
                  break;

  ...............
  ...............
  default: stmtListn;
}
```

When there is a switch statement, it evaluates the expression expr and then looks for a matching case label. If none is found, the default label is used. If no default is found, the statement does nothing.

The expanded flowchart of the switch statement is shown in Fig. 10.7.

Fig. 10.7 The C switch construct

This construct evaluates the expression expr and matches its evaluated value with the case constants and then the statements in the corresponding statement list are executed. Otherwise, if there is a default (which is optional), then the program branches to its statement list when none of the case constants match with the evaluated value of expr. The case constants must be integer or character constants. The expression must evaluate to an integral type. Single quotes must be used around char constants specified with each case.

Once again, it is emphasized that the default case, if present, will be selected if none of the prior cases are chosen. A default case is not required but it is good programming practice to include one.

Perhaps the biggest defect in the switch statement is that cases do not break automatically after the execution of the corresponding statement list for the case label. Once the statement list under a case is executed, the flow of control continues down, executing all the following cases until a break statement is reached.

The break statement must be used within each case if one does not want the following cases to execute after one case is selected. When the break statement is executed within a switch, C executes the next statement outside the switch construct. However, sometimes it may be desirable not to use the break statement in a particular case.

EXAMPLES

The following is an example where the control expression is a char variable ch. Notice the use of single quotes around the character variable in each case.

11. ```
switch(ch)
    {
      case 'A':
        printf("You entered an A");
        break;
      case 'B':
        printf("You entered a B");
        break;
      default:
        printf("Illegal entry");
        break;
    }
```

Another example is depicted where the variable Choice is an int variable. Note that single quotes are not used around the integer values in each of the case statements.

12. ```
switch(Choice)
    {
      case 1:
        printf("You entered menu choice #1");
        break;
      case 2:
        printf("You entered menu choice #2");
        break;
      case 3:
        printf("You entered menu choice #3");
        break;
      default:
        printf("You failed to enter a valid menu choice");
      break;
    }
```

13. ```
switch(donationLevel)
    {
      case 1:
        printf("You donated over Rs 1,000.");
```
```

```
case 2:
  printf("You donated over Rs 500.");

case 3:
  printf("You donated over Rs 250.");

case 4:
  printf("You donated over Rs 100.");

  break;

default:
  printf("Please be a little more generous.");

  break;
}
```

The break statement causes flow of control to exit from the entire switch block and resume at the next statement outside the switch. Technically, the break statement is optional, although most applications of the switch will use it. If a break statement is omitted in any case of a switch statement, the compiler will not issue an error message. The flow of control continues to the next case label.

The redundancy in the code can be minimized by placing the cases next to each other, as in the following example. That is, several case values can be associated with one group of statements.

14.
```
switch(number)
{
  case 1:
  case 3:
  case 5:
  case 7:
  case 9:
    printf(" %d is an odd number.", number);

    break;

  case 2:
  case 4:
  case 6:
  case 8:
    printf(" %d is an even number\n", number);

    break;

  default:
    printf(" %d is a value not between or including
         1 and 9.", number);

    break;
}
```

Note

- The switch statement enables you to choose one course of action from a set of possible actions, based on the result of an integer expression.
- The case labels can be in any order and must be constants.
- No two case labels can have the same value.
- The default is optional and can be put anywhere in the switch construct.
- The case constants must be integer or character constants. The expression must evaluate to an integral type.
- The break statement is optional. If a break statement is omitted in any case of a switch statement, the program flow is followed through the next case label.
- C89 specifies that a switch can have at least 257 case statements. C99 requires that at least 1023 case statements be supported. The case cannot exist by itself, outside of a switch.

Switch vs nested *if*

The switch differs from the else-if in that switch can test only for equality, whereas the if conditional expression can be a test of an expression involving any type of relational operators and/or logical operators. A switch statement is usually more efficient than nested ifs.

The switch statement can always be replaced with a series of else-if statements. One may only use switch and case statements if an expression is required to check against a finite amount of constant, integral, or character values. If there are too many values and if any of the values depends on variables, or if the values are not integers or characters, one must use a series of else-if statements. Even when one can use switch efficiently, it is just a matter of personal preference whether one decides to use a switch statement or else-if statements.

--- **EXAMPLES** ---

15. Write a program using a switch statement to check whether a number given by the user is odd or even.

Solution:
```
#include <stdio.h>
int main()
{
  int n;
  printf("\n Enter the number:");
  scanf("%d", &n);
  switch(n%2)
  {
    case 0: printf("\n EVEN");
```

```
        break;
    case 1: printf("\n ODD");
        break;
    }
    return 0;
}
```

16. Write a program to carry out the arithmetic operations addition, subtraction, multiplication, and division between two variables.

Solution:

Use the switch construct to choose the operations.

```
#include<stdio.h>
int main()
{
    int value1, value2;
    char operator;
    printf("Type in your expression. \n");
    scanf("%d %c %d ",&value1,&operator,&value2);
    switch(operator)

    case '+':
        printf("%d \n", value1 + value2);
        break;
    case '-':
        printf("%d \n", value1 - value2);
        break;
    case '*':
        printf("%d \n", value1 * value2);
        break;
    case '/':
        if(value2 == 0)
        printf("division by zero. \n");
        else
        printf("%d \n", value1 / value2);
        break;
    default:
        printf("Unknown Operator \n");
        break;
    }
    return 0;
}
```

17. Write a program that checks whether a character entered by the user is a vowel or not.

Solution:

```
#include <stdio.h>
int main(void)
{
    char c;
    printf("Enter a character: ");
    scanf("%c", &c);
    switch(c)
    {
        case 'a': case 'A':
        case 'e': case 'E':
        case 'i': case 'I':
        case 'o': case 'O':
        case 'u': case 'U':
        printf("%c is always a vowel!\n", c);
        break;
        case 'y': case 'Y':
        printf("%c is sometimes a vowel!\n", c);
        break;
        default:
        printf("%c is not a vowel!\n", c);
        break;
    }
    return 0;
}
```

Check Your Progress

1. What will be printed by the code below?
```
float x =  123.4;
if( x < 100)
    printf("one ");
if(x < 200)
    printf("two ");
if(x < 300)
    printf("three ");
```
Output two three

2. What will the following switch statement print?
```
char c = 'Y'; switch(c)
{
    case 'Y': printf("Yes/No");
    case 'N': printf("No/Yes"); break;
    default: printf("Other");
}
```
Output Yes/NoNo/Yes

3. What will the following `switch` statement print?

(a)
```
char c = 'y';
switch(c)
{
    case 'Y': printf("Yes/No");
    break;
    case 'N': printf("No/Yes");
    break;
    default: printf("Other");
}
```
Output Other

(b)
```
int main()
{
    int choice=3;
    switch(choice)
    {
        default:
            printf("Default");
        case 1:  printf("Choice1");
        break;
        case 2: printf("Choice2");
        break;
    }
    return 0;
}
```
Output DefaultChoice1

10.5 ITERATION

A loop allows one to execute a statement or block of statements repeatedly. There are mainly two types of iterations or loops – *unbounded iteration* or *unbounded loop* and *bounded iteration* or *bounded loop*. In bounded iteration, repetition is implemented by constructs that allow a determinate number of iterations. That is, bounded loops should be used when we know, ahead of time, how many times we need to loop. C provides `for` construct as bounded loop.

There are also many occasions when one does not know, ahead of time, how many iterations may be required. Such occasions require *unbounded loops*. C provides two types of unbounded loops: `while` loop and `do...while` loop. These types of loops are also known as *indeterminate* or *indefinite* loops.

A loop can either be a *pre-test loop* or a *post-test loop*. In a *pre-test loop*, the condition is checked before the beginning

of each iteration. If the test expression evaluates to true, the statements associated with the pre-test loop construct are executed and the process is repeated till the test expression becomes false. On the other hand, if the test expression evaluates to false, the statements associated with the construct are skipped and the statement next to the loop is executed. So for such a construct, the statements associated with the construct may not be executed even once.

In the *post-test loop*, the code is always executed once. At the completion of the loop code, the test expression is tested. If the test expression evaluates to true, the loop repeats; if the expression is false the loop terminates. The flowcharts in Fig. 10.8 illustrate these loops.

C has three loop constructs: `while`, `for`, and `do-while`. The first two are pre-test loops and `do-while` is a post-test loop.

Fig. 10.8 Loop variations: pre-test and post-test loops

In addition to the test expression, two other processes are associated with almost all loops. These are initialization and updating. The test expression always involves a variable, which is known as a *loop control variable*. *Initialization* is the statement that assigns the initial value to the loop control variable. Now how can the test expression, which controls the loop, be true for a while and then change to false? The answer is that something must happen inside the loop so that the test expression becomes false. The action that changes the test expression from true to false, so that the loop is terminated, is the updating statement. This involves updating the value of the control variable. *Updating* is done in each iteration. Comparison between a pre-test and post-test loop is given in Table 10.7.

A loop can be characterized as either event controlled or counter controlled. In an event-controlled loop, an event changes the test expression of the loop from true to false. When the number of repetitions is known, then a counter-controlled loop is used. Here, it is needed to initialize the counter, test it, and update it. All the loops used in C are either event controlled or counter controlled.

Table 10.7 Comparison between a pre-test and post-test loop

	Pre-test loop	Post-test loop
Initialization	once	once
Number of tests	n+1	n
Actions executed	n	n
Updating executed	n	n
Minimum iteration	not even once	at least once

10.5.1 While Construct

while statement is a pre-test loop. It uses a test expression to control the loop. Since it is a pre-test loop, it evaluates the test expression before every iteration of the loop. The basic syntax of the while statement is shown in Fig. 10.9.

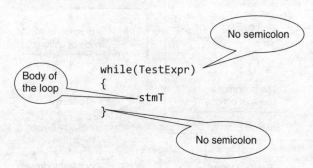

Fig. 10.9 While construct

stmT will be executed repeatedly till the value of TestExpr becomes 0. stmT may be a single statement or multiple statements terminated by a semicolon.

To use the while statement, the test expression should contain a loop control variable. The initialization of the loop control variable has to be done before the loop starts and updating must be included in the body of the loop. The expanded form of the while statement is given in Fig. 10.10.

Fig. 10.10 Expanded syntax of while and its flowchart representation

18.
```c
#include <stdio.h>
int main()
{
  int c;
  c=5;            // Initialization
  while(c>0)
  {               // Test Expression
  printf(" \n %d",c);
  c=c-1;          // Updating
  }
  return 0;
}
```

This loop contains all the parts of a while loop. When executed in a program, this loop will output

5
4
3
2
1

The operation of the looping construct in the above example is traced step by step as follows. First, the loop initialization, with 'c' being assigned the value of 5, is carried out. Then, the instructions within the while construct are executed repetitively so long as the test expression, c > 0, is true. The moment the test expression in the while construct evaluates as false, the program is terminated.

Now, when the while statement is encountered, the test expression, similar to an if-test expression, is evaluated. In this case, since c is 5 and c > 0, the test expression evaluates to true. Hence the statement body of the loop is executed sequentially. A printf statement writes the current value of c on the screen. After this, c is updated by subtracting 1. Thus, c now has the value of 4. On reaching the end of the loop, the loop condition is checked again. If it is true, which it is because 4 > 0, the loop is executed once again. In a similar way, the loop is executed five times.

At the end of the fifth iteration, c has the value of 0 for which the condition will fail since 0 is not greater than 0. Thus the term loop being applied to this repeating control structure can be understood since all statements inside the while loop construct will be executed several times until the condition has failed.

19. Program to print a horizontal row of 50 asterisks

The program is written using while loop. Here are three versions of same program. They differ only in the use of test expression and the initialization of the control variable.

Version 1

```c
#include <stdio.h>
int main()
{
  int times = 0;
  while (times < 50)
  {
    printf( "*");
    times++;
  }
  return 0;
}
```

Version 2

```c
#include <stdio.h>
int main()
{
  int times = 1;
  while (times <= 50)
  {
    printf( "*");
    times++;
  }
  return 0;
}
```

Version 3

```c
#include <stdio.h>
int main()
{
  int times = 50;
  while (times > 0)
  {
    printf("*");
    times--;
  }
  return 0;
}
```

Notice the various ways of accomplishing the same task. Run the above three versions and see the output. If a loop is to be executed for a specified number of times and the counter variable is used within the loop, the loop may be written as given in version 3 using countdown instead of count up. This is called *loop inversion*.

The following program takes age as input from user and quits when a –1 is entered:

```c
int main()
{
  int count = 0;
  int age;
  printf("\n Please enter an age(enter -1 to quit)");
  scanf("%d",&age);
  while(age != -1)
  {
    count++;
```

```c
    printf("\n Age # %d is %d",count, age);
    printf("\n Enter an age(enter -1 to quit)");
    scanf("%d",&age);
  }
  return 0;
}
```

20. Consider a general while loop that accepts input from the keyboard and counts the positive integers until a negative number is entered.

```c
#include <stdio.h>
int main( )
{
  int x = 1;
  int count = 0;
  printf("\n Enter the Number:");
  while(x >= 0)
  {
    scanf("%d",&x);
    count += 1;
  }
  return 0;
}
```

The following are some observations on the above while loop.

- Variables have been declared and initialized at the same time.
- The loop condition logically says, 'While x is a positive number, repeat.'
- The count variable keeps track of how many numbers are entered by the user.
- This can be a useful loop when accepting input from the keyboard for a certain number of times.

21. Consider a more extensive example of a program that asks the user to enter some numbers and then find their average.

The program that would be written would either ask the user in advance how many numbers will be supplied or ask the user to enter a special value after the last number is entered, e.g., negative for test scores. This special value is known as *sentinel* value.

The algorithm of the C program using the first approach is given as follows:

Algorithm

```
1. START
2. PRINT  "HOW MANY NUMBERS:"
3. INPUT N
4. S = 0
5. C=1
```

```
    6.  PRINT  "ENTER THE NUMBER"
    7.  INPUT A
    8.  S←S+A
    9.  C←C+1
   10.  IF C<=N THEN GOTO STEP 6
```
```
   11.  AVG←S/N
   12.  PRINT  "AVERAGE IS"   AVG
   13.  STOP
```

C Program

```c
#include <stdio.h>

int main()

{

  int n, a, c=1,s=0;

  float avg;

  printf("\n HOW MANY NUMBERS?");

  scanf("%d",  &n);

  while(c<=n)
  {

    printf("\n Enter the number:   ");

    scanf("%d",  &a);

    s+=a;

    c++;

  }

  avg=(float)s/n;

  printf(" \n AVERAGE IS %f  ", avg);

  return 0;

}
```

In this example, typecasting is needed as both s and n are integers and avg is a float. Otherwise the program evaluates avg as an integer.

A better way to implement the program in Example 21 is given as follows.

22. *Algorithm*

```
    1.  START
    2.  S←0
    3.  N←0
    4.  ANS←'Y'
```
```
    5.  PRINT "ENTER THE NUMBER"
    6.  INPUT A
    7.  S←S+A
    8.  N←N+1
    9.  PRINT "WILL U ADD MORE (Y/N)?"
   10.  INPUT ANS
```
```
   11.  IF ANS='Y' THEN GOTO STEP 5
```

```
   12.  AVG←S/N
   13.  PRINT "AVERAGE IS", AVG
   14.  STOP
```

C Program

```c
#include <stdio.h>

int main()

{

  int n=0, a, s=0;

  float avg;

  char ans='y';

  while(ans == 'y' || ans == 'Y')
  {

    printf("\n Enter the number: ");

    scanf("%d", &a);

    s+=a;

    n++;

    printf("\n will U add more(y/ n)?");

    scanf("%c",&ans);

  }

  avg=(float)s/n;

  printf(" \n AVERAGE IS %f", avg);

  return 0;

}
```

23. Consider the two versions of the same program that prints the sum of digits of a number.

Version 1

```c
#include <stdio.h>
int main()
{
  int n, s=0, r;
  printf("Enter the Number");
  scanf("%d", &n);
  while(n>0)
  {
    r=n%10;
    s=s+r;
    n=n/10;
  }
  printf("\nSum of digits %d", s);
  return 0;
}
```

Version 2

```c
#include <stdio.h>
int main()
{
  int n, s=0, r;
```

```
  printf("Enter the Number");
  scanf("%d", &n);
  while(n)
  {
    r=n%10;
    s=s+r;
    n=n/10;
  }
  printf("\nSum of digits %d", s);
  return 0;
}
```

Notice the conditions specified in the two versions—in version 1 `while(n>0)`, in version 2 `while(n)`. When an expression or variable is used instead of a relational expression, if the result of the expression or the value of the variable is non-zero (including negative), the statements within the `while` loop will be executed. Both versions will run fine.

Care must be taken in using expressions in a `while` loop. It should be noted that that there is no semicolon after the right parenthesis ending the expression that 'while' is checking. If there were, it would mean that the program would repeat the null statement until the condition becomes false.

Consider the use of the `scanf()` function in a loop. Suppose one needs to read and process a list of numbers from the keyboard. The loop ends when EOF is reached (when **<Ctrl+d>** in UNIX or **<Ctrl+z>** in DOS is pressed). The loop logic is shown in the following example:

```
r=scanf("%d",&a);
while(r!=EOF)
{
  _____-
  _____-
  r=scanf("%d",&a);
}
or
while((r=scanf("%d",&a))!=EOF)
{
  _____-
  _____-
}
```

Developing infinite loop using while construct   Consider the following programs:

```
#include <stdio.h>
int main()
{
  int c=5;
  while(c)
  {
    printf("\t %d",c);
    c--;
```

```
}
  return 0;
}
```

Here, the output will be

```
54321
```

Now, the above program is rewritten to print the odd numbers between 5 and 0.

```
#include <stdio.h>
int main()
{
  int c=5;
  while(c)
  {
    printf("\t %d",c);
    c=c-2;
  }
  return 0;
}
```

It will print

```
5      3      1      -1      -3      -5    ...
```

That is, it leads to an infinite loop. This is so because after printing 1, the value of 'c' will be -1 and `while(c)` evaluates true as the value of ' c' is non-zero. As a result, the program will print -1, -3, -5, and so on.

An infinite loop can also be built using the following construct:

```
while(1)
{
  ...
  ...
}
```

The `while(1)` loop will iterate forever because the while will exit only when the expression 1 is 0. The only way to exit this loop is through a break statement.

It should be noted that any non-zero value including a negative value may be used instead of 1 in the condition expression of the `while` construct.

Some do's and don'ts for testing floating point 'equality'

Representation error   Consider the following program fragment that uses C's floating-point arithmetic.

```
double hundred = 100.0;
double number = 95.0;
if(number == number / hundred * hundred)
  printf("Equal\n");
else
  printf("Not equal\n");
```

On some machines, the above fragment prints 'Not equal', because 95.0/100.0 cannot be accurately represented in binary. It might be 0.94999999999, 0.9500000001, or some other value, and when multiplied by 100 it does not exactly equal 95.0.

Compiler optimizations In the case of Borland compilers used on PCs, the following program fragment, identical to the above except that the variables have been replaced with their constant values, prints 'Equal'.

```
if(95.0 == 95.0 / 100.0 * 100.0)
  printf("Equal\n");
else
  printf("Not equal\n");
```

The best guess is that the compiler 'optimizes' the constant division and multiplication, causing the statement to appear as "95.0 == 95.0', which is trivially true.

Testing for floating-point 'equality' As the preceding examples show, floating-point numbers cannot be compared for exact equality. Here is a second example. Using a floating-point number as an 'exact' terminating condition in a loop is not a good idea. Since floating-point numbers are approximations, a test for exact equality will often be wrong. An example of a program code is given as follows:

```
float x;
x = 0.0;
while(x != 1.1)
{
  x = x + 0.1;
  printf("1.1 minus %f equals %.20g\n", x, 1.1 - x);
}
```

The above loop never terminates on many computers, because 0.1 cannot be accurately represented using binary numbers. At each iteration, the error increases and the sum of eleven 'tenth' never becomes 1.1. Do not test floating-point numbers for exact equality, especially in loops. Since floating-point numbers are approximations, the correct way to make the test is to see if the two numbers are 'approximately equal'.

The usual way to test for approximate equality is to subtract the two floating-point numbers and compare the absolute value of the difference against a very small number, *epsilon*. Such an approach is shown in the following program code.

```
#define EPSILON 1.0e-5   /* a very small value */
double hundred=100.0;
double number=95.0;
```

```
double n1, n2;
n1 = 95.0;
n2 = number / hundred * hundred;
if(fabs(n1-n2) < EPSILON)
  printf("Equal\n");
else
  printf("Not equal\n");
```

`fabs()` is the C library function that returns the floating-point absolute value of its argument.

Epsilon is chosen by the programmer to be small enough so that the two numbers can be considered 'equal'. The larger the numbers being compared, the larger will be the value of epsilon. For example, if the floating-point numbers are in the range 1.0e100, epsilon will probably be closer to 1.0e95, which is still a very big number but small compared to 1.0e100. (1.0e95 is ten-thousandth of 1.0e100.) If two numbers of magnitudes 1.0e100 and 1.0e95 differ by only 0.0e05, they may be close enough to be considered equal.

Note that just as adding a very small floating-point value to a very large floating-point value may not change the latter, subtracting floating-point numbers of widely differing magnitudes may have no effect. If the two numbers differ in magnitude by more than the *precision* of the data type used, the addition or the subtraction will not affect the larger number. For the float data type on most microcomputers, the precision is about six to seven decimal digits. An example of a program code follows:

```
float big, small, sum;
big = 1.0e20;
small = 1.0;
sum = big - small;
if(sum == big)
  printf("Equal\n");   /* this prints */
else
  printf("Not Equal\n");
```

On executing the program code, the computer would print 'Equal', as observed earlier.

10.5.2 for Construct

A loop formed by using the for statement is generally called a determinate or definite loop because the programmer knows exactly how many times it will repeat. The number of repetitions can be determined mathematically by manually checking the logic of the loop. The general form of the for statement is as follows:

```
for(initialization; TestExpr; updating)
  stmT;
```

Initialization This part of the loop is the first to be executed. The statement(s) of this part are executed only once. This statement involves a loop control variable.

`TestExpr` `TestExpr` represents a test expression that must be true for the loop to continue execution.

`stmT` `stmT` is a single or block of statements.

Updating The statements contained here are executed every time through the loop before the loop condition is tested. This statement also involves a loop control variable.

C allows the updating of a loop control variable to be written inside the body of the loop. An example of a `for` loop is shown as follows:

```c
int main(void)
{
  int i;
  for(i = 0; i < 10; i++)
    printf("%d",i);
  return 0'
}
```

The above `for` loop operates as follows:

1. Set i equal to 0.
2. If i is less than 10, execute the body of the loop, that is, 'printf' and go to step 3; otherwise, go to the next instruction after the `for` loop and continue.
3. Increment i.
4. Go to step 2.

The following figure explains the three expressions in the `for` loop used in the above program that are separated by semicolons and that control the operation of the loop.

This loop would produce the following output:

```
0123456789
```

Note that 'running the loop' from 0 to 9 executes the body of the loop 10 times. The flowchart of the `for` construct is given in Fig. 10.11.

Fig. 10.11 `for` construct flowchart

It is to be noted that all four parts of the previous loops are present in the `for` loop, although they are compressed into one line. In general, a `for` loop can be written as an equivalent `while` loop and vice versa.

The equivalence of bounded and unbounded loops

We should now be able to understand that the `for` and `while` control flow statements are both closely related. To fully understand this, however, one needs to interpret that the three 'pieces' of the `for` construct, are not always *initialization*, *condition*, and *modification*.

In general, a `for` loop can be written as an equivalent `while` loop and vice versa. The `for` loop

```c
for(initialization; TestExpr; updating)
{
    stmT;
}
```

is equivalent to the following `while` construct:

```c
initialization;
while (TestExpr)
{
    stmT;
    updating;
}
```

The following example illustrates a `for` loop that prints 1, 2, 3, 4, 5.

In both cases, `TestExpr` is expected to produce a Boolean value, either true or false, as the truth value is needed to determine whether the loop should keep going on.

Let us illustrate the similarities between 'while' and 'for' loop constructs using an example which prints 1, 2, 3, 4, and

5. The algorithm for the above problem is given below:

1. START
2. C ← 1
3. PRINT C
4. C ← C+1
5. IF C<=5 THEN GO TO STEP 3
6. STOP

The C program corresponding to the problem can use either while or for construct. The two versions, one using for construct and another using while construct, and their equivalence are shown below:

To test the understanding of the while and for loops, conversion of one to the other would be implemented. Suppose, a while loop, given in the following illustration, has to be converted to a well-constructed for loop.

```
float C = 2.0;
char chr = 'F';
while(C > 0.01) {
  printf("%f \n",C);
  C /= 10;
}
```

To make this an easy conversion, note the four parts of a loop.

```
float C = 2.0;        /* initialization */
char chr = 'F';
while(C > 0.01){      /* test expression */
printf("%f \n",C);    /* body of the loop */
  C /= 10;            /* updating */
}
```

Given such information, the transition to the for loop is made. The for loop is

```
float C;
char chr = 'F';
```

```
for(C = 2.0; C > 0.01; C /= 10)
{
  printf("%f \n",C);
}
```

There was a small trick in this case. Even though two variables were declared and initialized, only one was used in the while loop. Therefore, only that specific variable, C, is initialized in the for loop.

Now, consider the conversion of the following for loop to its respective while loop.

```
int index;
int Total;
for(Total = 0, index = 0; index < 10; index += 1)
{
  if(index > 5)
      Total += index;
  else if(index < 5)
      Total -= index;
}
```

Again, noting the four parts of the loop, the conversion is given as follows:

```
int index = 0;
int Total = 0;
while(index < 10)
{
  if(index > 5) Total += index;
    else if(index < 5)
      Total -= index;
  index += 1;
}
```

It must be emphasized that in a for construct, the condition is tested before the statements contained in body and updating are executed; it is possible that the body of the loop is never executed or tested.

The sequence of events that generate the iteration using the for loop are as follows.

1. Evaluate the *initialization* expression.
2. If the value of the *test expression* is false, terminate the loop, which means go to step 6; otherwise go to step 3.
3. Execute the statement or blocks of statements.
4. Evaluate the *update* expression.
5. Go to step 2.
6. Execute the next statement.

An execution cycle for a for construct is drawn to help understand the concept.

```
for(initialization; TestExpr; updating)
    stmT;
```

Here is a program that adds a sequence of integers. Assume that the first integer read with scanf() specifies the number of input values to be summed. The program should read only one value each time scanf() is executed. A typical input sequence might be

5 102 125 352 54 9

where 5 indicates that the subsequent five values are to be summed.

Next Instruction

F = false
T = true

```c
#include <stdio.h>
int main()
{
    int sum = 0, number, value, i;
    printf("Enter no. of values to be processed: \n");
    scanf("%d", &number);
    for(i = 1; i <= number; i++)
    {
        printf("Enter a value: \n");
        scanf("%d", &value);
        sum += value;
    }
    printf("Sum of %d values is: %d\n", number, sum);
    return 0;
}
```

In general, how many times does the body of a for() loop execute?

(a) The following loop is executed (n-m)+1 times.
```c
for(i=m;  i<=n;  i++)
...
```

(b) The following loop is executed (n-m) times.
```c
for(i=m;  i<n;  i++)
...
```

(c) The following loop is executed (n-m)/x times.
```c
for(i=m;  i<n;  i+=x)
...
```

Considering the above, the previous program may be rewritten as follows:

```c
#include <stdio.h>
int main()
{
```

```c
    int sum = 0, number, value, i;
    printf("Enter no. of values to be processed: \n");
    scanf("%d", &number);
    for(i = 0; i < number; i++)
    {
        printf("Enter a value: \n");
        scanf("%d", &value);
        sum += value;
    }
    printf("Sum of %d values is: %d\n", number, sum);
    return 0;
}
```

Now, let us calculate the factorial of a number given by the user. The factorial of a positive integer n, written as n!, is equal to the product of the positive integers from 1 to n. The following is an example program that calculates the factorial of a number.

```c
int main()
{
    int n, c;
    long int f=1;
    printf("\n Enter the number: ");
    scanf("%d",&n);
    for(c=1;c<=n;++c)
     f*=c;
    printf("\n Factorial  is %ld",f);
    return 0;
}
```

It can be implemented in another way too. Here, the variable 'c' is not required. The alternate program is shown as follows:

```c
int main()
{
    int n;
    long int f=1;
    printf("\n Enter the number: ");
    scanf("%d",&n);
    for(;n>0;n--)
     f*=n;
    printf("\n Factorial  is %ld",f);
    return 0;
}
```

The following program inputs a series of ten integer numbers and determines and prints the largest of them.

```c
#include <stdio.h>
```

```
int main()
{
  int counter = 2, number, max;
  printf("Enter an integer number\n");
  scanf("%d", &max);
  while(counter <= 10)
  {
    printf("Enter an integer number\n");
    scanf("%d", &number);
    if(number > max)
    max = number;
    counter++;
  }
  printf("The maximum number is %d\n", max);
  return 0;
}
```

There must be no semicolon after a for statement or it will lead to a different output. Consider the following program.

```
#include <stdio.h>
int main()
{
  int c;
  for(c=1; c<=5; c++);
    printf("%d", c);
    return 0;
}
```

A semicolon before the printf statement implies that the loop only increments the value of c. No executable statement is included in this for loop, i.e., there is no statement in the statement block. The output will be 6, as the loop continues up to c=5. When the value of c is 6, the loop terminates as the test expression evaluates false.

Some variations of for loop

From a syntactic standpoint, all the three expressions initialization, test expression, and updating need not be present in a for statement, though semicolon must be present. However, the criteria and consequences of an omission should be clearly understood.

Any initialization statement can be used in the first part of the for loop. Multiple initializations should be separated with a comma operator.

EXAMPLE
---

24. Print the sum of the series 1+2+3+4+... up to n terms.
   Program 1
```
#include <stdio.h>
int main()
```

```
{
  int c, s=0, n;
  printf("\n Enter the No. of terms");
  scanf("%d", &n);
  for(c=1; c<=n; c++)
    s+=c;
    printf("\n Sum is %d", s);
    return 0;
}
```
Program 2 Equivalent to Program 1
```
#include <stdio.h>
int main()
{
  int c=1, s, n;
  printf("\n Enter the No. of terms");
  scanf("%d", &n);
  for(s=0; c<=n; c++)
    s+=c;
    printf("\n Sum is %d", s);
    return 0;
}
```
Program 3
```
#include <stdio.h>
int main()
{
  int c, s, n;
  printf("\n Enter the No. of terms");
  scanf("%d", &n);
  for(c=1, s=0; c<=n; c++)
    s+=c;
    printf("\n Sum is %d", s);
    return 0;
}
```

- If initialization is not required or is done before the for loop, the initialization statement can be skipped by giving only a semicolon. This is illustrated using the previous program.

```
#include <stdio.h>
int main()
{
  int c=1, s=0, n;
  printf("\n Enter the No. of terms");
  scanf("%d", &n);
  for(; c<=n; c++)
    s+=c;
    printf("\n Sum is %d", s);
    return 0;
}
```

- Multiple conditions in the test expression must be connected using the logical operator && or ||.

- In the third expression of the for statement, the increment or decrement statement may contain any expression which involves unary and/or assignment operator. It is not true that increment or decrement statements must be used with ++ or − − only. This is illustrated in the following example where the sum of digits of a given number has to be found.

EXAMPLE

25.
```c
#include <stdio.h>
int main()
{
  int n, s=0, r;
  printf("\n Enter the Number");
  scanf("%d", &n);
  for(;n>0;n/=10)
  {
    r=n%10;
    s=s+r;
  }
  Printf("\n Sum of digits %d", s);
  return 0;
}
```

- If the increment or decrement is done within the statement block, then the third part can be skipped. The following is the equivalent variation of the program in Example 25 (sum of digits of a number).

```c
#include <stdio.h>
int main()
{
  int n, s=0, r;
  printf("\n Enter the Number");
  scanf("%d", &n);
  for(;n>0;)
  {
    r=n%10;
    s=s+r;
    n=n/10;
  }
  printf("Sum of digits %d", s);
  return 0;
}
```

- Multiple statements can be written in the third part of the for statement with the help of the comma operator. The preceding program can be rewritten as follows:

```c
#include <stdio.h>
int main()
{
  int n, s=0, r;
  printf("\n Enter the Number");
  scanf("%d", &n);
  for(;n>0;s+=r, n=n/10)
    r=n%10;
    printf("\n Sum of digits %d", s);
    return 0;
}
```

It is to be noted that comma operator associates from the left to right. The code

```c
for(s=0,i=1;i<=n;++i)
  s+=i;
```

can be written as

```c
for(s=0,i=1;i<=n; s+=i, ++i);
```

but not as

```c
for(s=0,i=1;i<=n; ++i, s+=i);
```

Because, in the comma expression ++i, s+=i, the expression ++i is evaluated first and this will cause s to have a different value.

- If ++ or − − operators are used in the increment or decrement part of the for loop, pre-increment or post-increment and post-decrement or pre-decrement has the same effect. So, both the following codes yield the same output 1, 2, 3, 4, 5.

Version 1
```c
#include <stdio.h>
int main()
{
  int c;
  for(c=1; c<=5; c++)
    printf("%d", c);
    return 0;
}
```

Version 2
```c
#include <stdio.h>
int main()
{
  int c;
  for(c=1; c<=5; ++c)
    printf("%d", c);
    return 0;
}
```

But the post- and pre-operations play a different role when they are specified in the test_expression.

```c
#include <stdio.h>
int main()
{
  int c;
  for(c=0; c++; c++)
    printf("%d", c);
    return 0;
}
```

Output Prints nothing as c has been initialized as zero and the post-increment of c makes a difference. The condition is evaluated first, followed by increment. The condition is evaluated false as c contains zero at that moment. The printf() statement will not be executed as the condition becomes false.

```c
#include <stdio.h>
int main()
{
  int c;
  for(c=0;++c; ++c)
    printf("%d", c);
return 0;
}
```

Output This is an infinite loop. As the first pre-increment takes place, it results in c=1. Then the test expression evaluates to 1 as c contains a non-zero value. Thus the loop continues.

- It is possible to have a variable increase by a value other than one. For example, the following loop would iterate four times with the variable num taking on the values 1, 4, 7, and 10. The step expression adds 3 to the value of num on each iteration.
  ```c
  for(num = 1; num <= 10; num = num + 3)
  ```

  It is a common error for students to use the following for statement, which causes a compilation error:
  ```c
  for(num = 1; num <= 9 ; num + 3)
  ```

  Consider the following program where the increment operator is used at a place other than the third part of the for statement.

  ```c
  #include <stdio.h>
  int main()
  {
    int c;
    for(c=1; c<=5; )
    printf("%d", c++);
  ```

```c
  return 0;
}
```
Output 12345

```c
#include <stdio.h>
int main()
{
  int c;
  for(c=1; c<=5;)
  printf("%d", ++c);
  return 0;
}
```

Output 23456

- Any or all of the three expressions in a for loop can be omitted, but the two semicolons must remain. When all three expressions in a for loop are omitted, it acts as a infinite loop. For example,

  ```c
  for(;;)
  {
    printf("hello\n");
  }
  ```

This loop will run forever. Although there are some programming tasks, such as operating system command processors, which require an infinite loop, most 'infinite loops' are really just loops with special termination requirements.

- Often, the variable that controls a for loop is needed only for the purposes of the loop and is not used elsewhere. When this is the case, it is possible to declare the variable inside the initialization portion of the for loop in modern compiler. Some compilers, however, do not. You will need to check this feature in the environment you are using. Consider the following program which prints the sum of the following series

```c
#include <stdio.h>
int main()
{
  int s=0, n;
  printf("\n Enter the No. of terms");
  scanf("%d", &n);
  for(int c=1; c<=n; c++)
  s+=c;
  printf("\n Sum is %d", s);
  return 0;
}
```

Here, c is declared inside the for loop.

The variable c is only known throughout the execution of the for loop (it's called a local variable) and cannot be accessed outside the loop. The ANSI/ISO Standard restricts the variable to the scope of the for loop.

Note

- If the test expression is omitted, however, it will be assumed to have a permanent value of true; thus the loop will continue indefinitely unless it is terminated by some other means, such as a break or a return statement (see Section 10.8).
- Multiple initializations should be separated with a comma operator.
- Multiple relational expressions in the test expression must be connected using logical operators && or ||.
- A floating-point variable should not be used as the control variable because floating-point values are sometimes approximated and may result in imprecise counter values and inaccurate test for termination.

Check Your Progress

1. Is there any difference between the following for statements? Explain.

    (a) `for(x = 1; x < 100; x++)`

    (b) `for(x = 1; x < 100; ++x)`

    (c) `for(x = 1; x < 100; x = x + 1)`

    (d) `for(x = 1; x < 100; x += 1)`

    Output There is no difference between these for statements. This is because x is incremented in the same manner at the end of the for structure. One may, equivalently, use the while structure to represent these for statements.

    ```
    x = 1;
    while(x < 100)
    {
        ...
        ++x; /* This can be replaced with x++ or x += 1 or*/
            /* x = x + 1 */
    }
    ```

2. What would be the output from the given program?

    ```
    int main()
    {
      int i=9;
      for(i--; i--; i--)
        printf("%d", i);
        return 0;
    }
    ```

    Output 7 5 3 1

3. What would be the output from the given program?

    ```
    int main()
    {
        int i;
        for(i=5; ++i; i-=3)
          printf("%d", i);
          return 0;
    }
    ```

    Output 6 4 2

4. What would be the output from the given program?

    ```
    int main()
    {
      for(;printf("C"););
      return 0;
    }
    ```

    Output This is an infinite loop and it will repeatedly print 'c'.

5. Examine the given program and predict the output.

    ```
    int main()
    {
        int i;
        for(i=5; --i;)
          printf("%d",i);
          return 0;
    }
    ```

    Output 4321

6. What output is obtained from the given program?

    ```
    int main()
    {
        int i=3;
        for(i--; i<7; i=7)
          printf("%d",i++);
          return 0;
    }
    ```

    Output 2

7. Read the program code and guess the output.

    ```
    int main()
    {
        int i;
        for(i=-10; !i; i++);
          printf("%d",-i);
          return 0;
    }
    ```

    Output No output

10.5.3 do-while Construct

do while construct is another construct that is very closely related to the while construct.

The do keyword is placed on a line of code at the top of the loop. A block of statements follows it with a test expression after the keyword while, at the bottom of the loop. Figure 10.12 illustrates this. The form of this loop construct is as follows:

```
do
{
    stmT;  /* body of statements would be placed here*/
}while(TestExpr);
```

The test expression TestExpr must evaluate to 'true' for the do-while loop to iterate after the first time. StmT may be a single statement or a block of statements. The main difference between the while and do-while loop is the placement of the test expression. Since the do-while has the test expression at the end of the loop, it is guaranteed that the body of the loop will execute at least once.

In the while loop, it is possible to come upon a condition that is not satisfied and hence does not enter the loop. What are the reasons of placing the condition at the end of the loop in terms of coding? They are few but important. The order of the statements may have to change to reflect the effect of the condition being at the end.

Consider the simple while loop illustrated in Example 20. It can be rewritten as a do-while loop as follows:

```
#include <stdio.h>
int main()
{
    int x = 1;
    int count = 0;
    do {
        scanf("%d", &x);
        if(x >= 0)
            count += 1;
    } while(x >= 0);
    return 0;
}
```

Notice that an extra if statement was added to the loop.

Fig. 10.12 The C do-while loop

Explanation: Consider the case when the first number entered is a negative number. Without the if statement, the count would be 1. Beware of the ramifications of allowing at least one execution of the loop when using the do-while loop. The following examples will help understand this loop.

```
#include <stdio.h>
int main()
{
    int c=5;
    while(c<5)
    {
        printf(" Hello");
        c++;
    }
    return 0;
}
```

Output The program will print nothing. As the condition c<5 fails, neither the printf() statement nor c++ will be executed.

```
#include <stdio.h>
int main()
{
    int c=5;
    do
    {
        printf("Hello");
        c++;
    } while(c<5);
    return 0;
}
```

Output Hello

Here, the statements within the loop are executed at least once.

Suppose, one wants to write a code that reads in a positive integer only. The following code will serve the purpose.

```
do
{
    printf("\n INPUT A POSITIVE INTEGER:   ");
    scanf("%d",&n);
    if(error=(n<=0))
        printf("\n ERROR Do it again\n");
}while(error);
```

while and do-while loops

Like a while loop, a do-while loop is considered to be an indeterminate or unbound loop. The important difference between the while and do-while loops lies with the question

'When is the loop controlling `test expression` checked?'. A `do-while` loop is considered to be a *post-test loop*, since the `test expression` is located after the body of the loop and after the `while` keyword. A `do-while` loop is guaranteed to execute at least once even if the test expression evaluates to false.

With a `while` statement, the Boolean expression is checked *before* the loop body is executed. If the `test expression` evaluates to false, the body is not executed at all.

Note

- With a `do-while` statement, the body of the loop is executed first and the `test expression` is checked after the loop body is executed. Thus, the `do-while` statement always executes the loop body at least once.

EXAMPLE
---

26. Euler's number *e* is used as the base of natural logarithms. It may be approximated using the following formula:

$$e = \frac{1}{0!} + \frac{1}{1!} + \frac{1}{2!} + \frac{1}{3!} + \ldots + \frac{1}{(n-1)!} + \frac{1}{n!}$$

where *n* is sufficiently large. Write a program that approximates *e* using a loop that terminates when the difference between the two successive values of *e* is less than 0.0000001.

```
#include <stdio.h>
int main()
{
  double term = 1.0;
  double sum = 1.0;
  int n = 0;
  while (term >= 0.0000001)
    {
      n++;
      term = term/n;
      sum = sum + term;
    }
  printf("\n Approximate value of e is: %lf ",sum);
  return 0;
}
```

Check Your Progress
---

1. How many times will the following `while` loop repeat, i.e., how many x's are printed?

   ```
   int i = 5; while(i-- > 0) printf("x");
   ```

   Output 5

2. How many x's are printed by the following code?

   ```
   int i = 5;
   ```

```
while(i-- > 0)
  printf("x");
  printf("x");
```
Output 6

3. What does the following `do-while` loop print?

   ```
   int i = 0; char c = '0';
   do {
     putchar(c + i);
     ++i;
   } while(i < 5);
   ```
   Output 01234

4. ```
   int main()
   {
     float s=1.0;
       int a=4;
         while(a<=10)
           {
             s = a*1.2;
             printf("%f",s);
           }
     return 0;
   }
   ```
   Output It never ends because 'a' is always 4, an infinite loop!

5. What will be the output of the following program?

   ```
   # define infiniteloop while(1)
   int main()
   {
     infiniteloop;
     printf("DONE");
     return 0;
   }
   ```
   Output No output

   Explanation: The `infiniteloop` in `main` ends with ';'. So the loop will not reach an end; and the 'no output' too will not print.

10.6 WHICH LOOP SHOULD BE USED?

A question that must be asked is why are there `while`, `do-while`, and `for` loops? Is it a matter of style?

The `while` and `for` constructs are pre-test loops and the `do-while` construct is post-test loop. The `while` and `do-while` loops are event-controlled whereas the `for` loop is counter-controlled. The `for` loop is appropriate when one knows in advance how many times the loop will be executed. The `while` and `do-while` loops are used when it is not known in advance when the loop should terminate; the `while` loop is used when one may not want to execute the loop body even once, and the `do-while` loop when one wants to execute the loop body
   ```

at least once. These criteria are somewhat arbitrary and there is no hard-and-fast rule regarding which type of loop should be used.

Note

When using loops, always ask the following:
- Under what condition(s) will the loop body be executed?
- Under what condition(s) will the loop terminate?
- What is the value of the loop control variable(s) when the loop halts?

Some methods of controlling repetition in a program will be discussed in the following subsections. There are three ways of doing this: sentinel values, prime reads, and counters.

10.6.1 Using Sentinel Values

A sentinel value is not a legitimate data value for a particular problem, but is of a proper type, that is used to check for a 'stopping' value. It is like a flag or an indicator. There may be times when users of the program must be allowed to enter as much information as they want to about something. When the user has finished entering all the information, the user can enter a sentinel value that would let the program know that the user has finished with inputting information.

EXAMPLES
---

27. [-1] may be used as a sentinel value.
```c
int main()
{
  int age;
  printf("\n Enter an age(-1 to stop ):");
  scanf("%d",&age);
  while(age != -1)
  {
    .
    printf("\n Enter an age(-1 to stop ):");
    scanf("%d",&age);
  }
  return 0;
}
```

28. [-99] may also be used as a sentinel value. Read a list of text scores and calculate their average. An input of -99 for a score denotes end-of-data for the user.
```c
#include <stdio.h>
int main()
{
  int n, sum, score;
  float average;
  sum = 0;
```

```c
  n = 0;
  printf("\n Enter a test score(-99 to quit):");
  scanf("%d", &score);
  while(score != -99)
  {
    sum += score;
    n++;
    printf("\n Enter a test score(-99 to quit):");
    scanf("%d",&score);
  }
  average = (float)sum/ n;
  printf("\n The average is %f", average);
  return 0;
}
```

10.6.2 Using Prime Read

Another method of controlling repetition is to use a prime read. A prime read and sentinel value often go hand in hand. A prime read is a data input before the loop statement that allows the first actual data value to be entered so that it can be checked in the loop statement. The variable that is inputted by the user and being tested by the expression in the loop is the prime read; the value of the prime read is what one calls a sentinel value [see Section 10.6.1].

EXAMPLES
---

29. [age] is used as a prime read.
```c
#include <stdio.h>
int main()
{
  int age;
  printf("\n Enter an age(-1 to stop):");
  scanf("%d",&age);
  while(age != -1)
  {
    .
    .
    .
    printf("\n Enter an age(-1 to stop):");
    scanf("%d",&age);
  }
  .
  .
  .
  return 0;
}
```

30. `[score]` is used as a prime read. Read a list of text scores and calculate their average. An input of `-99` for a score denotes end-of-data for the user.

```c
#include <stdio.h>

int main()
{
  int n, sum, score;
  float average;
  sum = 0;
  n = 0;
  printf("\n Enter a test score(-99 to quit):");
  scanf("%d", &score);
  while(score != -99)
  {
    sum += score;
    n++;
    printf("\n Enter a test score(-99 to quit):");
    scanf("%d", &score);
  }
  average = (float)sum / n;
  printf("\n The average is %f", average);
  return 0;
}
```

EOF can also be used in prime read. Consider the following program.

```c
#include <stdio.h>
#include <stdlib.h>

int main()
{
  int n, sum, score;
  float average;
  sum = 0;
  n = 0;
  printf("\n Enter test scores one by one(EOF to
          quit): ");
  while(scanf("%d", &score) != EOF)
  {
    sum += score;
    n++;
  }
  average = (float)sum / n;
  printf("\n The average is %f", average);
  return 0;
}
```

10.6.3 Using Counter

Yet another method for controlling repetition during the execution of a program is by using a counter. Using a counter requires knowledge of the exact number of times something needs to be repeated. For example, if a user of the program had to be instructed to input ten numbers, a counter variable could be set to 0, and then a loop set up to continue cycles while the value of the counter is less than ten (this loop would equal ten cycles: 0, 1, 2, ..., 9).

EXAMPLES

31. Write a section of code that would output the numbers from 1 to 10.

```c
#include <stdio.h>
int main()
{
  int count;
  count = 0;
  int numTimesNeeded = 10;
  while(count < numTimesNeeded)
  {
    printf("\n%d", (count + 1)) ;
    count++;
  }
  return 0;
}
```

32. Write a section of code that will allow the user to input ten test scores in order to find the average of the scores.

```c
#include <stdio.h>
int main()
{
  int count, score;
  float average;
  count = 0;
  int numTimesNeeded = 10;
  int total = 0;
  while(count < numTimesNeeded)
  {
    printf("\n Enter a test score");
    scanf("%d", &score);
    total += score;
    count++;
  }
  average = (float)total/ numTimesNeeded;
  printf("\n The average is %f" , average);
  return 0;
}
```

10.7 GOTO STATEMENT

The goto statement is another type of control statement supported by C. The control is unconditionally transferred to the statement associated with the label specified in the goto statement. The form of a goto statement is

```
goto label_name;
```

Because the goto statement can interfere with the normal sequence of processing, it makes a program more difficult to read and maintain. Often, a break statement, a continue statement, or a function call can eliminate the need for a goto statement.

A *statement label* is defined in exactly the same way as a variable name, which is a sequence of letters and digits, the first of which must be a letter. The statement label must be followed by a colon (:) just like a CASE label in a SWITCH. Like other statements, the goto statement ends with a semicolon. Some examples of goto statements are in order

EXAMPLE

33. The following program is used to find the factorial of a number.

```c
#include <stdio.h>
int main()
{
  int n, c;
  long int f=1;
  printf("\n Enter the number:");
  scanf("%d",&n);
  if(n<0)
    goto end;
  for(c=1; c<=n; c++)
    f*=c;
  printf("\n FACTORIAL IS %ld", f);
  end:
  return 0;
}
```

The goto statement can be used for looping as follows. Here, the goto statement is used in conjunction with an if statement.

```c
#include <stdio.h>
int main()
{
  int n, c;
  long int f=1;
  printf("\n Enter the number:");
  scanf("%d",&n);
  if(n<0)
    goto end;
  c=1;
  loop:
  f=f*c;
```

```c
  c++;
  if(c<=n)
    goto loop;
  printf("\n FACTORIAL IS %ld", f);
  end:
  return 0;
}
```

In theory it is always possible to avoid using the goto statement, but there are one or two instances in which it is a useful option. But the goto statement is not considered a good programming statement when overused. Because the goto statement can interfere with the normal sequence of processing, it makes a program more difficult to read and maintain. When too many goto statements are used in a program then the program branches all over the place, it becomes very difficult to follow. Some authors call programs with many goto statements '*spaghetti code*'. So, it is best to avoid the goto statement as far as possible. Often, a break statement, a continue statement, or a function call can eliminate the need for a goto statement.

10.8 SPECIAL CONTROL STATEMENTS

There are certain control statements which terminate either a loop or a function. There are three such statements, namely: return, break, and continue.

return statement The return type is used in the definition of a function to set its returned value and the return statement is used to terminate execution of the function. The return statement has two forms. Functions with return type void use the following form:

```
return;
```

Functions with non-void return type use the following form:

```
return expression;
```

Here, expression yields the desired return value. This value must be convertible to the return type declared for the function. This will be explained in more detail in the chapter on functions.

break statement The break statement is used in loop constructs such as for, while, and do-while, and switch statement to terminate execution of the loop or switch statement. The form of a break statement is

```
break;
```

After a break statement is executed within a loop or a case in a switch construct, execution proceeds to the statement that follows the loop construct or switch statement. The following is an example of the use of a break statement.

```c
#include <stdio.h>
int main( )
{
  int c=1;
  while(c<=5)
  {
    if(c==3)
      break;
    printf("\t %d", c);
    c++;
  }
  return 0;
}
```

Or

```c
#include <stdio.h>
int main( )
{
  int c=1;
  for(;c<=5;c++)
  {
    if(c==3)
      break;
    printf("\t %d", c);
  }
  return 0;
}
```

The program will print 1 2 instead of 1 2 3 4 5.

The statement while(1) leads to an infinite loop but by using the break statement it can be made a finite loop. This is illustrated in the following example.

— **EXAMPLE** —

34. **Program 1**

```c
#include <stdio.h>
int main( )
{
  int c=1;
  while(1)
  {
    printf("\t %d", c);
    c++;
  }
  return 0;
}
```

It is an infinite loop. It will print
1   2   3   4...

Program 2

```c
#include <stdio.h>
```

```c
int main( )
{
  int c=1;
  while(1)          <-- Note this
  {
    if(c==5)
      break;
    printf("\t %d", c);
    c++;
  }
  return 0;
}
```

Or

```c
#include <stdio.h>
int main( )
{
  int c;
  for(;;)          <-- Note this
  {
    if(c==5)
      break;
    printf(" \t %d", c);
    c++;
  }
  return 0;
}
```

It is a finite loop. It will print
1   2   3   4

A break statement may be used to check whether a number is a prime number or not. The following program illustrates this.

```c
#include <stdio.h>
int main( )
{
  int n, r, d=2;
  printf( "\n Enter the number :");
  scanf("%d", &n);
  r = n%d;
  while(d <=n/2)
  {
    r = 1;
    if(r ==0)
      break;
    d++;
  }
  if(r==0)
    printf("\n IT IS NOT A PRIME NUMBER");
```

```
else
  printf("\n IT IS A PRIME NUMBER");
return 0;
}
```

continue statement The `continue` statement does not terminate the loop but goes to the test expression in the `while` and `do-while` statements and then goes to the updating expression in a `for` statement. The form of a `continue` statement is

```
continue;
```

The jumps by `continue` in different pre-test and post-test loops are shown here.

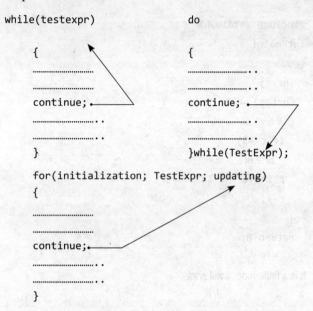

```
while(testexpr)              do

    {                            {
    ...................          ...................  ..
    ...................          ...................  ..
    continue; .                  continue; .
    ...................  ..      ...................  ..
    ...................  ..      ...................  ..
    }                            }while(TestExpr);

for(initialization; TestExpr; updating)
    {
    ...................
    ...................
    continue;.
    ...................  ..
    ...................  ..
    }
```

The difference between `break` and `continue` statements is summarized in Table 10.8.

Table 10.8 `Break` and `continue` statements

Break	Continue
It helps to make an early exit from the block where it appears.	It helps in avoiding the remaining statements in a current iteration of the loop and continues with the next iteration.
It can be used in all control statements including switch construct.	It can be used only in loop constructs.

This can be illustrated by the following programs.

Program code with break

```
#include <stdio.h>
int main( )
{
  int c=1;
```

```
  while(c<=5)
  {
    if(c==3)
      break;
    printf("\t %d", c);
    c++;
  }
  return 0;
}
```

Output 1 2

Program code with continue

```
#include <stdio.h>
int main()
{
  int c = 0;
  while(c<=5)
  {
    c++;
    if(c==3)
      continue;
    printf("\t %d", c);
  }
  return 0;
}
```

Output 1 2   4 5 6

10.9 NESTED LOOPS

A nested loop refers to a loop that is contained within another loop. If the program has to repeat a loop more than once, it is a good candidate for a nested loop. In nested loops, the inside loop (or loops) executes completely before the outside loop's next iteration. It must be remembered that each inner loop should be enclosed completely in the outer loop; overlapping loops are not allowed. Thus, the following is not allowed.

```
for(count = 1; count < 100; count++)
{
  do
  {
    /* the do...while loop */
  } /* end of for loop */
}while(x != 0);
```

If the `do-while` loop is placed entirely in the `for` loop, there is no problem. For example,

```
for(count = 1; count < 100; count++)
{
  do
  {
    /* the do...while loop */
  }while(x != 0);
} /* end of for loop */
```

An example of the nested loop is to print the following:

```
*
* *
* * *
* * * *
```

In each row, there are several ' *' to be printed. In row one, one star has to be printed; in row two, two stars have to be printed; in row three, three stars have to be printed, and so on. So an outer loop is required to keep track of the number of rows to be printed and in each iteration of the outer loop, an inner loop is required to keep track of the printing of stars that corresponds to the row. The program will then read as follows:

```
#include <stdio.h>
int main()
{
  int row,col;
  for(row=1;row<=4;++row)
  {
    for(col=1;col<=row;++col)
      printf("* \t");
    printf("\n");
  }
  return 0;
}
```

If the following output has to be obtained on the screen

```
1
2 2
3 3 3
4 4 4 4
```

then the corresponding program will be

```
#include <stdio.h>
int main()
{
  int row,col;
  for(row=1;row<=4;++row)
```

```
  {
    for(col=1;col<=row;++col)
      printf("%d \t", row);
    printf("\n");
  }
  return 0;
}
```

The variant of the preceding program is

```
#include <stdio.h>
int main()
{
  int row,col, k=1;
  for(row=1;row<=4;++row)
  {
    for(col=1;col<=row;++col)
      printf("%d \t", k++);
    printf("\n");
  }
  return 0;
}
```

It will print the following on the screen.

```
1
2 3
4 5 6
7 8 9 10
```

When nested loops are used, remember that changes made in the inner loop might affect the outer loop as well. Note, however, that the inner loop might be independent of any variables in the outer loop; in the above examples, they are not.

Good indenting style makes a code with nested loops easier to read. Each level of loop should be indented one step further than the last level. This clearly identifies the code associated with each loop.

Let us take a look at a trace of two nested loops. In order to keep the trace manageable, the number of iterations has been shortened.

```
for(num2 = 0; num2 <= 3;  num2++)
{
  for(num1 = 0; num1 <= 2; num1++)
  {
    printf("\n %d  %d",num2,num1);
  }
}
```

Memory		Screen
num 2	*num 1*	
0	0	0 0
	1	0 1
	2	0 2
	3 (end)	
1	0	1 0
	1	1 1
	2	1 2
	3 (end)	
2	0	2 0
	1	2 1
	2	2 2
	3 (end)	
3	0	3 0
	1	3 1
	2	3 2
	3 (end)	
4 (end)		

Remember that, in the memory, for loops will register a value one beyond (or the step beyond) the requested ending value in order to disengage the loop.

Here is an example of nested loops which prints out a multiplication table.

EXAMPLE

35.
```c
#include <stdio.h>
int main ()
{
int i,j;
for (i = 1; i <= 10; i++)
 {
 for (j = 1; j <= 10; j++)
  {
     printf ("%5d",i * j);
  }
 printf ("\n");
 }
 return 0;
}
```

Output

```
1    2    3    4    5    6    7    8    9   10
2    4    6    8   10   12   14   16   18   20
3    6    9   12   15   18   21   24   27   30
4    8   12   16   20   24   28   32   36   40
5   10   15   20   25   30   35   40   45   50
6   12   18   24   30   36   42   48   54   60
7   14   21   28   35   42   49   56   63   70
8   16   24   32   40   48   56   64   72   80
9   18   27   36   45   54   63   72   81   90
10   20   30   40   50   60   70   80   90  100
```

Note that after the inner for loop (at the end of each iteration of the outer for loop), a '\n' is used which causes the next line of the output to be printed in a fresh line.

If a break statement is encountered in a nested loop, the control of the program jumps to the first statement after the innermost loop. For instance, to print the diagonal lower half of the multiplication table (below the diagonal line from the top left to the bottom right), for each row(denoted by i here), once the column (denoted by j) equals the row, the rest of the inner for loop has to be skipped and the line that prints the newline character should be executed. Similarly, the next row has to be printed. The output would be as follows.

```
1
2    4
3    6    9
4    8   12   16
5   10   15   20   25
6   12   18   24   30   36
7   14   21   28   35   42   49
8   16   24   32   40   48   56   64
9   18   27   36   45   54   63   72   81
10   20   30   40   50   60   70   80   90  100
```

The C program to achieve the preceding output is as follows.

```c
#include <stdio.h>
int main()
{
  int i,j;
  for (i = 1; i <= 10; i++)
  {
    for (j = 1; j <= 10; j++)
    {
      printf ("%5d",i * j);
      if(i==j)
      break;
    }
    printf ("\n");
  }
  return 0;
}
```

To put everything together as well as demonstrate the use of the break statement, here is a program for printing prime numbers between 1 and 100.

```
#include <stdio.h>
#include <math.h>
int main()
{
int i, j;
printf("%d\n", 2);
for(i = 3; i <= 100; ++i)
  {
  for(j = 2; j < i; ++j)
    {
    if(i % j == 0)
      break;
    if(j > sqrt(i))
      {
      printf("%d\n", i);
      break;
      }
    }
  }
  return 0;
}
```

The outer loop steps the variable 'i' through the numbers from 3 to 100; the code tests to see if each number has any divisors other than 1 and itself. The trial divisor 'j' increments from 2 to 'i'. 'j' is a divisor of 'i' if the remainder of 'i' divided by 'j' is 0, so the code uses C's 'remainder' or 'modulus' operator % to make this test. Remember that i % j gives the remainder when 'i' is divided by 'j'.

If the program finds a divisor, it uses break to come out of the inner loop, without printing anything. But if it evaluates that 'j' has risen higher than the square root of 'i', without its having found any divisors, then 'i' must not have any divisors. Therefore, 'i' is prime, and its value is printed. Once it has been determined that 'i' is prime by noticing that j > sqrt(i), there is no need to try the other trial divisors. Therefore, a second break statement can be used to break out of the loop in that case, too. The following program is a simplified form of the previous program.

```
#include <stdio.h>
#include <math.h>
main()
{
  int i, j,r;
  for(i = 2; i <= 100; ++i)
  {
    r=1;
    for(j = 2; j <= sqrt(i); ++j)
    {
      r=i%j;
```

```
      if(r == 0)
        break;
    }
    if(r!=0)
    printf("%d\n", i);
  }
}
```

Nested loops and the goto *statement*

Occasionally, it is needed to come out of all the nested loops from the innermost loop and then continue with the statement following the outermost loop. A break statement in the innermost loop will only break out of that loop, and execution will continue with the loop which is the immediate outer loop. To escape the nested loops completely using break statements therefore requires quite complicated logic to break out of each level until you escape the outermost loop. This is one situation in which the goto can be very useful (as shown below) because it provides a way to avoid all the complicated logic.

Consider the following code segment:

```
for (i = 0; i < n; ++i)
  for (j = 0; j < m; ++j)
    for (k = 0; k < s; ++k)
    {
      scanf("%d", &n);
      if (n == 0)
        goto GoOut;
      x= n*(i+j+k)
      ……………………….
      ……………………….
    }
GoOut:
```

A naive attempt is as follows:

```
for (done = 0, i = 0; !done && i < n; ++i)
  for (j = 0; !done && j < m; ++j)
    for (k = 0; !done && k < s; ++k)
    {
      scanf("%d", &n);
      if (n == 0)
        done = 1;
      x= n*(i+j+k)
      ……………………….
      ……………………….
    }
```

C89 specifies that at least 15 levels of nesting must be supported by the compiler. C99 raises this limit to 127. In practice, most compilers allow substantially more levels. However, nesting beyond a few levels is seldom necessary, and excessive nesting can quickly confuse the meaning of an algorithm.

Common programming errors

Writing expressions like `a<b<c` or `a==b==c`, etc. These expressions are legal in C but do not have meaning that might be expected. For example, in `a<b<c`, the operator < is left associative, this expression is equivalent to `(a<b) < c`.

Using = instead of == `a == b` and `a = b` are not similar as `==` is a test for equality `a = b` is an assignment operator. Be careful when writing the equality operator.

Forgetting to use braces for compound statement If the number of statements to be executed is more than one, i.e. compound statements and those statements are to be executed if the test expression is true for once (`if` used with `if...else`) or repeatedly (if used with `while` or `for` or `do-while`), then the compound statement must be enclosed within braces.

Dangling else An `else` is always associated with the closest unmatched `if`. If this is not the required branching, impose the proper association between `if` and `else` by means of braces. One should be careful when framing `if-else-if` ladder.

Use of semicolon in loop Also, remember not to put a semicolon after the close parenthesis at the end of the `for` loop (this immediately ends the loop). As an illustration, the following code, segment will print 12345.

```
for (int c = 1; c <= 5; ++c)
    printf("%d",c);
```

But the following code would print 6.

```
for (int c = 1; c <= 5; ++c);
    printf("%d",c);
```

Similar problems can arise with a *while* loop. Be careful not to place a semicolon after the closing parenthesis that encloses the test expression at the start of a *while* loop. A do-while loop has just the opposite problem. You must remember always to end a do-while loop with a semicolon.

Floating point equality Do not use the equality operator with floating point numbers. When equality of floating point values is desired, it is better to require that the absolute value of the difference between operands be less than some extremely small value. To test for equality of floating point operands such as `a == b`, use

```
if(fabs(a-b) < 0.000001)
```

where the value 0.000001 can be altered to any other acceptably small value. Thus, if the difference between the two operands is less than 0.000001 (or any other user selected value), the two operands are considered essentially equal.

SUMMARY

A statement is a syntactic construction that performs an action when a program is executed. It can alter the value of variables, generate output, or process input. In C, any sequence of statements can be grouped together to function as a syntactically equivalent single statement by enclosing the sequence in braces. These groupings are called *statement blocks,* which means a final semicolon after the right brace is not needed.

The program statements in C fall into three general types: assignment, input/output, and control. C has two types of control structures: *selection (decision)* and *repetition (loops).* The decision control constructs are of two types: conditional and unconditional. The conditional control constructs are `if`, `if-else`, `if-else-if`, and `switch`. The unconditional control constructs are `break`, `continue`, and `goto`. The loop control constructs are `for`, `while`, and `do-while`. Relational and logical operators are used to specify test conditions used in the control constructs of C. The test conditions give shape to test expressions, which are evaluated to give a value of zero or non-zero, irrespective of its sign. In C, the zero value is taken as *false* and any non-zero value, either positive or negative, is taken as *true*.

One-way decisions are handled with an `if` statement that either does some particular thing or does nothing at all. The decision is based on a test expression that either evaluates to true or false. Two-way decisions are handled with `if-else` statements that either do one particular thing or

do another. Similar to one-way decisions, the decision is based on a test expression. Multi-way decision statements use `if-else-if`, `nested if`, or `switch` statements. They are all used to evaluate a test expression that can have several possible values selecting different actions.

The `while` statement is a pre-test loop declaration construct. This is a top-driven loop. The *condition* is tested *before* the execution of the code in the body of the loop. It is tested before the body is executed the very first time and if it is false, the body of the loop will not be executed at all. So the loop may execute zero times. A `while` loop is considered to be an *indeterminate* or *indefinite loop* because it is usually only at run time that it can be determined how many times it will iterate.

A loop formed by using the `for` statement is generally called a *determinate* or *definite* loop because the programmer knows exactly how many times it will repeat. The number of repetitions can be determined mathematically by manually checking the logic of the loop.

A `do-while` loop is considered to be a bottom-checking loop since the control expression is located after the body of the loop and after the `while` keyword. A `do-while` loop is guaranteed to execute at least once even if the control expression evaluates to false.

A `goto` statement causes control to be transferred unconditionally to the statement associated with the label specified in the statement. There are some special statements such as `break`, `return`, and `continue` that are used with the control constructs. The break statement is used in loop constructs, such as for, while, and do-while, and switch statement to terminate execution of the loop or switch statement.

The return statement has two forms. In one instance, it is used in the definition of a function to set its returned value and in the other instance it is used to terminate the execution of the function. The continue statement is used in while, for, or do-while loops to terminate an iteration of the loop.

A *nested loop* refers to a loop that is contained within another loop. It must be remembered that each inner loop should be enclosed completely in the outer loop; overlapping loops are not allowed.

KEY TERMS

Block Any sequence of statements can be grouped together to function as a syntactically equivalent single statement by enclosing the sequence in braces.

Boolean expression It is an expression that evaluates to either true or false.

Loop It is a programming construct in which a set of statements in a computer program can be executed repeatedly.

Sentinel It is a value that is not a legitimate data value for a particular problem, but is of a proper type, that is used to check for a 'stopping' value.

Spaghetti code It comprises programs with many goto statements.

FREQUENTLY ASKED QUESTIONS

1. Is the relational expression a < b < c legal in C?

Yes, it is legal but does not have the meaning that might be expected. Since the operator < is left associative, this expression is equivalent to (a < b) < c. The result from the evaluation of this expression would either be 0 or 1 depending on the values of a, b, and c.

2. There is no logical exclusive OR operator in C; can it be simulated anyway?

The result of the logical exclusive OR operation on two integers is true if and only if one operand (but not both) is true. It can be simulated by the following expression.

```
(a||b) && !(a && b)
```
where a and b are both of type int.

3. The floating point numbers are seldom equal to required value or variable; then how can two floating point values or variables be tested for equality?

The following code segment may be used.

```
float a, b;
if(fabs(a-b) < 0.000001)
        printf("equal");
else
        printf("\n not equal ");
```

4. What is a null statement?

A null statement is an expression statement consisting solely of the terminating semicolon. A null statement can appear on its own, or (most frequently) as the statement body of an iteration statement. "0;"or "1;"
can also be used as null statements. Note that {}(which contains nothing within braces, i.e., it is empty) is not a null statement. {} is a compound statement. An empty block (called a null block) is not the same as a null statement.

5. Which form of loop should you use- while or for or do-while?

The decision of selecting while or do-while depends on the situation. It is to be decided whether one needs a pre-test loop or a post-test loop. In such a situation where either while or do-while can be used, the computer scientists usually consider a pre-test loop superior. A program is easier to read if the test for iteration (i.e., loop) is found at the beginning of the loop. In many uses, it is important that the loop be skipped entirely if the test is not initially met.

The choice between a for or a while is partly a matter of taste.

6. What is the difference between a break and continue statement?

Sometimes when executing a loop, it becomes desirable to leave the loop as soon as a certain condition occurs. The break statement can be used for this purpose. Execution of the break statement causes the program to immediately exit from the loop it is executing, whether it is a for, while, or do-while loop. Subsequent statements in the loop are skipped, and execution of the loop is terminated.

The continue statement causes the next iteration of the enclosing for, while, or do-while to begin. In the while and do-while, this means that the test part is executed immediately; in the for, control passes to the increment step. The continue statement applies only to loops, not to switch. A continue inside a switch causes the next loop iteration if it is placed within a loop.

EXERCISES

1. What do you mean by control statements in C?
2. What is the purpose of the if-else statement?
3. Compare the use of the if-else statement with the use of the '?:' operator. In particular, in what way can the '?:' operator be used in place of an if-else statement?
4. What is the purpose of the switch statement? What are labels, i.e., case prefixes? What type of expression must be used to represent a case label?

5. What is the purpose of the comma operator? Within which control statement does the comma operator usually appear?

6. Why is the use of the `goto` statement generally discouraged? Under what conditions might the `goto` statement be helpful? What types of usage should be avoided and why?

7. Differentiate between a `for` loop and a `while` loop. Discuss the usage of each.

8. Distinguish between the following:
   (a) `do-while` and `while` loop
   (b) `break` and `continue`

9. Write a program using conditional operators to determine whether a year entered through the keyboard is a leap year or not.

10. The factorial of an integer n is the product of consecutive integers from 1 to n. That is, factorial n = n! = n x (n - 1) x (n - 2) x (n - 3) x ... x 3 x 2 x 1. Write a C program to find the factorial value of n.

11. Write a C program to print the quotient of an integer number without using '/'.

12. Write a program to print all the even and odd numbers of a certain range as indicated by the user.

13. Write a C program to convert the binary equivalent of an integer number without using an array.

14. Write a C program to find the prime factors of a number given by the user.

15. Write a C program to check whether a number is a power of 2 or not.

16. Write a program to find the GCD of two numbers.

17. Write a program to find the sum of digits of a number given by the user.

18. Write a C program to calculate the sum of prime numbers in a range.

19. Write a C program to print the sum of the following series up to n terms where n is given by the user.

   $1 + x + x^2/2! + x^3/3! + ...$ (The value of x is also given by the user.)

20. Write a C program to print the sum of the following series up to n terms where n is given by the user.

   $x - x^3/3! + x^5/5! - ...$ (The value of x is given by the user.)

21. Write a C program to print the following series: 0 1 1 2 3 5 8 13 .... The number of terms to be printed should be given by the user.

22. Write a C program to print the numbers that do not appear in the Fibonacci series. The number of such terms to be printed should be given by the user.

23. Write a program to convert a decimal number into any base.

24. Write a program to check whether a number is a Krishnamurty number or not. A Krishnamurty number is one whose sum of factorial of digits equals the number.

25. Write a program to print the second largest number among a list of numbers without using array.

26. Write programs to print the sum of the following series (with and without `pow()` library function).

   (a) $S = 1 + x + x^2 + x^3 + x^4 + ...$ n terms
   (b) $S = -x + x^2 + x^3 + ...$ n terms
   (c) $S = 1 + x + x^2/2! + x^3/3! + ...$ n terms
   (d) $S = 1 + (1+2) + (1+2+3) + ...$ n terms
   (e) $S = 1 - x + x^2/2! - x^3/3! + ...$ n terms
   (f) $S = x - x^3/3! + x^5/5! + ...$ n terms
   (g) $S = 2 + 22 + 222 + 2222 + ...$ n terms
   (h) $S = 1 + x/4 + x2/8 + ...$ n terms
   (i) $S = x - x^2/2! + x^3/3! - x^4/4! ...$ n terms

27. Write a program to print the prime numbers in a range.

28. Given a number, write a program using `while` loop to reverse the digits of the number. For example, the number 12345 should be written as 54321.

29. Write a program to print the following triangle.

   (a) *

       * *   * * *

       * * * *   ... up to nth line
   (b) *

       * *

       * * *

       * * * * *   ... up to nth line
   (c) 1

       1 2

       1 2 3

       1 2 3 4   ... up to nth line
   (d) 1

       2 1 2

       3 2 1 2 3   ... up to nth line
   (e) 1

       2 2

       3 3 3

       4 4 4 4

       5 5 5 5 5   ... up to nth line

30. Write a program to check whether a number is a prime number or not.

31. Write a program to print all the prime numbers of a certain range given by the user.

32. Write a program to print the Floyd's triangle.

33. Write a program to add the prime numbers of a certain range given by the user.

PROJECT QUESTIONS

1. Write a C program that prompts the user to enter the date as three integer values for the month, the day in the month, and the year. The program should then output the date in the form 31st December 2003 when the user enters, say 12 31 2010. The program has to work out when superscripts "th", "nd", "st", and "rd" need to be appended to the day value. The programmer should not forget 1st, 2nd, 3rd, 4th; and then 11th, 12th, 13th, 14th; and 21st, 22nd, 23rd, and 24th.

2. This is a well-known game with a number of variants. The following variant has an interesting winning strategy. Two players alternately take marbles from a pile. In each move, a player chooses how many marbles to take. The player must take at least one but at most half of the marbles. Then the other player takes a turn. The player who takes the last marble loses. Write a C program in which the computer plays against a human opponent. Generate a random integer between 10 and 100 to denote the initial size of the pile. Generate a random integer between 0 and 1 to decide whether the computer or the human takes the first turn. Generate a random integer between 0 and 1 to decide whether the computer plays *smart* or *stupid*. In stupid mode the computer simply takes a random legal value (between 1 and n/2, where n is the total number of marbles) from the pile whenever it has a turn. In smart mode the computer takes off enough marbles to make the size of the pile a power of two minus 1—that is, 3, 7, 15, 31, or 63. That is always a legal move, except when the size of the pile is currently one less than a power of two. In that case, the computer makes a random legal move. It should be noted that the computer cannot be beaten in smart mode when it has the first move, unless the pile size happens to be 15, 31, or 63. Of course a human player who has the first turn and knows the winning strategy can win against the computer.

Arrays and Strings

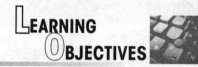

LEARNING **O**BJECTIVES

After studying this chapter, the readers will be able to

- define an array
- explain one-dimensional arrays, their declaration, initialization, ways to access individual array elements, representation of array elements in memory, and other possible operations
- discuss one-dimensional strings and the way they are declared, initialized, manipulated, inputted, and displayed

- explain two-dimensional arrays, initialization of sized and unsized two-dimensional arrays, accessing elements in such arrays, and their uses
- explain array of strings, their declaration, initialization, other operations, manipulations, and uses
- get a brief idea of three-dimensional arrays or even larger ones

11.1 INTRODUCTION

The variables used so far have all had a common characteristic: each variable can only be used to store a single value at a time. For example, each of the variables ch, n, and price declared in the statements

```
char ch;
int n;
float price;
```

are of different data types and each variable can only store one value of the declared data type. These types of variables are called *scalar variables*. A scalar variable is a single variable whose stored value is an atomic type. This means that the value cannot be further subdivided or separated into a legitimate data type.

In contrast to atomic types, such as integer, floating point, and double precision data, there are aggregate types. An aggregate type, which is referred to as both a *structured type* and a *data structure*, is any type whose values can be decomposed and are related by some defined structure. Additionally, operations must be available for retrieving and updating individual values in the data structure. Such a *derived data type* is an array.

Why array?

Consider a brand-new problem: a program that can print its input in reverse order. If there are two values, this is easy and the program is

```
#include <stdio.h>
int main()
{
  int v1, v2;
  printf("Enter two values:");
  scanf("%i %i", &v1, &v2);
  printf("%i\n%i\n", v2, v1);
  return 0;
}
```

If there are three values, this is still relatively easy and the program is

```
#include <stdio.h>
int main()
{
  int v1, v2, v3;
  printf("Enter three values: ");
  scanf("%d %d %d", &v1, &v2, &v3);
  printf("%d\n %d\n %d \n", v3, v2, v1);
  return 0;
}
```

But what if there are ten or twenty or one hundred values? Then it is not so easy.

Besides that, the solutions work only if the number of inputs exactly matches with those expected by the user.

Consider another problem: the average of *n* integer numbers given by the user can easily be computed as follows.

```
#include <stdio.h>
int main()
{
  int count,s=0, n, num;
  float avg;
    printf("\n How many numbers?");
    scanf("%d", &n);
  for(count=1;count<=n;++count)
  {
    printf("\n Enter the Number:");
    scanf("%d", &num);
    s+=num;
  }
  avg=(float)s/n;
  printf("Average is %f", avg);
  return 0;
}
```

Now if the problem is given as 'Print the numbers that are greater than the average', then one solution is to read the numbers twice, that is,

- read in all the numbers and calculate the average.

- read in all the numbers again, this time checking each as it is read against a previously calculated average.

If input is from the keyboard, then the user has to enter each number twice and accurately, with no mistakes. This is not a viable solution. Because, for 25 numbers entered, the user has to remember all the numbers. But what if there are 50 or 100 numbers? Then, it is not so easy. To solve this problem, an array is required. It is a collection of numbered elements.

An array is a fundamental data structure that enables the storing and manipulation of potentially huge quantities of data. An array stores an *ordered* sequence of *homogeneous* values. Homogeneous means that all the values are of the same data type. The order of the values are also preserved, i.e., the integer array {1, 2, 3, 4} is different from {1, 4, 3, 2}.

An array can be defined as a data structure consisting of an ordered set of data values of the homogeneous (same) type. An array is a collection of individual data elements that are

- Ordered—one can count off the elements 0, 1, 2, 3, ...
- Fixed in size
- Homogeneous—all elements have to be of the same type, e.g., int, float, char, etc.

In C, each array has two fundamental properties: the data type and the size. Individual array elements are identified by an integer index. In C, the index begins at zero and is always written inside square brackets.

> **Note**
>
> - A scalar variable is a single variable whose stored value is an atomic data type.
> - An array is a collection of individual data elements that are ordered, fixed in size, and homogeneous.
> - An array is considered to be a derived data type.
> - Array enables the storing and manipulation of potentially huge quantities of data.

11.2 ONE-DIMENSIONAL ARRAY

There are several forms of an array used in C: one-dimensional or single-dimensional and multidimensional array. In this section, one-dimensional arrays will be discussed.

Since the array is one dimensional, there will be a single subscript or index whose value refers to the individual array element which ranges from 0 to (*n*–1), where *n* is the total number of elements in the array.

11.2.1 Declaration of a One-dimensional Array

To use an array variable in a program, it must be declared. When defining an array in a program, three things need to be specified.

- The type of data it can hold, i.e., int, char, double, float, etc.

- The number of values it can hold, i.e., the maximum number of elements it can hold

- A name

A one-dimensional array declaration is a data type followed by an identifier with a bracketed constant integral expression. The value of the expression, which must be positive, is the *size* of the array. It specifies the number of elements in the array. The array subscripts can range from 0 to (size –1). The lower bound of the array subscripts is 0 and the upper bound is (size –1). Thus, the following relationships hold.

```
int a[size]; /* memory space for a[0],a[1],…, a[size -1]
                 allocated */

lower bound = 0
upper bound = size -1
size = upper bound + 1
```

The syntax for declaration of a one-dimensional array is

```
data_type  array_name [SIZE];
```

- All the array elements hold values of type <data type>.

- The size of the array is indicated by <SIZE>, the number of elements in the array. <SIZE> must be an int constant or a constant expression.

For example, to declare an array that can hold up to 10 integers, the following statement has to be written.

```
int ar[10];
```

This reserves *space* for 10 integers. Similarly,

```
int a[100]; /* an array with 100 int elements */
```

declares an array 'a' that can hold 100 integers. Once declared, an array element can be referenced as

```
<array name>[<index>]
```

where <index> is an integer constant or variable ranging from 0 to <SIZE> - 1.

In the above example, the array index starts at 0, so for this array there are elements named a[0], a[1], ..., a[99]. The idea is that if there is an array variable named a, its elements can be accessed with a[0], a[1], ..., a[99]. This means that a particular element of the array can be accessed by its 'index', a number that specifies which element is needed.

In a single-dimensional array of integers, the array is composed of individual integer values where integers are referred to by their position in the list. Indexed variables provide the means of accessing and modifying the specific values in the array. For instance, in an array named 'number'

number[0] refers to the first number stored in the 'number' array

number[1] refers to the second number stored in the 'number' array

number[2] refers to the third number stored in the 'number' array

number[3] refers to the fourth number stored in the 'number' array

number[4] refers to the fifth number stored in the 'number' array

Figure 11.1 illustrates the array named 'number' in memory with the correct designation for each array element.

Each individual array element is called an *indexed variable* or a *subscripted variable*, since both a variable name and an index or a subscript value must be used to reference the element. Remember that the index or subscript value gives the position of the element in the array. Internally, unseen by the programmer, the computer uses the index as an offset from the array's starting position.

Fig. 11.1 Identifying individual array elements

As illustrated in Fig. 11.2, the index indicates how many elements to skip over, starting from the beginning of the array, to get the desired element. At the time of declaration, the size of the array must be given; it is mandatory. Otherwise the compiler generates an error.

Fig. 11.2 Accessing element 3

The following declaration is invalid.

```
#include <stdio.h>
int main()
{
    double x[], y[];
    ...
    return 0;
}
```
(No size is specified.)

C does not allow declaring an array whose number of elements is unknown at compile time. So the above declaration statement is not valid. Now, consider the following code:

```
#include <stdio.h>
int main()
{
    int N;
    double x[N], y[N];
    ...
    scanf("%d",&N);
    return 0;
}
```
(An integer variable is used as size of the array. It must be an integer constant or constant integer variable.)

Here, the variable size array declaration, e.g.,

```
double x[N], y[N];
```

is used where `N` is an integer variable. This kind of declaration is illegal in C and results in a compile-time error.

It is sometimes convenient to define an array size in terms of a symbolic constant, rather than a fixed integer quantity. This makes it easier to modify a program that utilizes an array, since all references to the maximum array size can be altered by simply changing the value of the symbolic constant. This approach is used in many of the sample programs given in this book. Consider the following sample program, which uses this approach.

```
/* Define a symbolic constant for the size of
the array */
#include <stdio.h>        The symbolic
                          constant N is
#define N 100             assigned the
                          value 100.
int main()
{
   double x[N], y[N];
   ...
   return 0;              N is replaced with the
}                         assigned value 100.
```

It is a good programming practice to define the size of an array as a symbolic constant.

Hence, it may be observed that a literal number or a previously declared #defined symbolic constant must be used in an array declaration for the size of the array. No variables are allowed for the size of the array.

Since the number of array elements can also be given by an expression, the declarations depicted below can be used.

```
int x[N+1];
double y[M+5*N];
```

However, the C compiler must be able to evaluate the expression, which implies that all components of the expression must be available for evaluation of the expression when the program is compiled—there must be no unknowns. This means that the expression must be composed of constants. In the preceding examples, identifiers consisting of capital letters have been used, which is the convention for symbols defined with #define directives.

Thus the following expressions accessing elements of array arr are valid.

```
/* Give N a value so that the examples are concrete! */
#define N 20
int i = 1, j = 3, k = 2;
float arr[N];

arr[0]          The evaluated value
arr[3]          of this expression is
arr[9]          the index of arr here.
arr[i*j+k]  /* given values of i,j,k evaluates i*j+k to 5 */
```

```
arr[N-10]
arr[N-1]
```

The following array references are not valid.

```
arr[-1]
arr[N-21]
arr[N+20]
arr[N]
```

In the previous example, `arr[N-1]` is the cause of many problems for new C programmers. It must be remembered that C array indices start at 0. Thus for an array with `N` elements, the index of the last element is `N-1`. It may be of help to think of the array index as an offset from the beginning of the array, so that the first element, at offset 0 from the beginning, is `arr[0]` and the last, at offset N-1, must be `arr[N-1]`.

Thus, expressions such as `arr[N]` are happily accepted by the compiler. (C compilers usually make the assumption that programmers know what they are doing.) The results of running such programs are entirely unpredictable, since the space at the end of the array may have arbitrary data in it. The results from a program may even vary from one run to another, as the memory space in which the compiler assumes the (N+1)th object to be stored may well have been allocated to some other object.

Note

- In C, arrays are of two types: one-dimensional and multidimensional.
- An array must be declared with three attributes: *type of data* it can hold, the number of data it can hold(size), and an identifier(name) before it is used.
- The array *size* must be a positive integer number or an expression that evaluates to a positive integer number that must be specified at the time of declaration with the exception that it may be unspecified while initializing the array.
- In C, the array index starts at 0 and ends at (size–1) and provides the means of accessing and modifying the specific values in the array.
- C never checks whether the array index is valid—either at compile time or when the program is running.

11.2.2 Initializing Integer Arrays

Variables can be assigned values during declaration like the following example.

```
int x = 7;
```

Arrays can be initialized in the same manner. However, since an array has multiple elements, braces are used to denote the entire array of values and commas are used to separate the individual values assigned to the elements in the array initialization statements as shown.

```
(a) int A[10] = {9, 8, 7, 6, 5, 4, 3, 2, 1, 0};
```

```
9 8 7 6 5 4 3 2 1 0  ← values stored in array elements

0 1 2 3 4 5 6 7 8 9  ← index values of array elements
```

(b) double a[5] = {3.67, 1.21, 5.87, 7.45, 9.12}

Automatic sizing While initializing, the size of a one-dimensional array can be omitted as shown.

```
int arr[] = {3,1,5,7,9};
```

Here, the C compiler will deduce the size of the array from the initialization statement.

From the above initialization statement, the size of the array is deduced to be 5.

11.2.3 Accessing Array Elements

Single operations, which involve entire arrays, are not permitted in C. Thus, if x and y are similar arrays (i.e., of the same data type, dimensionality, and size), then assignment operations, comparison operations, etc., involving these two arrays must be carried out on an element-by-element basis. This is usually accomplished within a loop, or within nested loops for multidimensional arrays.

For initializing an individual array element, a particular array index has to be used. For example, in an array A, for initializing elements 0 and 3, the following statements are used,

```
A[0] = 3;
A[3] = 7;
```

Subscripted variables can be used at any place where scalar variables are valid. Examples using the elements of an array named 'numbers' are shown here:

```
numbers [0] = 98;
numbers [1] = numbers [0] – 11
numbers [2] = 2 * (numbers [0] – 6);
numbers [3] = 79;
numbers [4] = (numbers [2] + numbers [3] – 3)/2;
total = numbers[0] + numbers[1] + numbers[2] +
        numbers[3] + numbers[4];
```

One extremely important advantage of using integer expressions as subscripts is that it allows sequencing through an array using a for loop. This makes statements such as

```
total = numbers[0] + numbers[1] + numbers[2] +
        numbers[3] + numbers [4];
```

unnecessary. The subscript value in each of the subscripted variables in this statement can be replaced by the counter in a for loop to access each element in the array sequentially. For example, the C statements,

```
total = 0;              /*initialize total to zero */
for(i = 0; i <5; ++i)
total = total + numbers[i]; /* add in a number */
```

sequentially retrieve each array element and adds the element to the total. Here the variable 'i' is used both as the counter in the for loop and as a subscript. As 'i' increases by one each time through the for loop, the next element in the array is referenced. The procedure for adding the array elements within the for loop is the same as that used before.

The following code

```
/* Initialization of all of the elements of the sample
array to 0 */

for(i = 0; i < 5; i++)
{
  a[i] = 0;
}
```

would cause all the elements of the array to be set to 0. Consider the following program that would use the above code segment.

```
#include <stdio.h>
#define ARRAY_SIZE 10
int main()
{
  int index, a[ARRAY_SIZE];
  for(index = 0; index < ARRAY_SIZE; index++)
  {
    a[index] = 0;
    printf("a[%d] = %d\n", index, a[index]);
  }
  printf("\n");
  return 0;
}
```

The output from the above example is as follows:

```
a[0] = 0
a[1] = 0
a[2] = 0
a[3] = 0
a[4] = 0
a[5] = 0
a[6] = 0
a[7] = 0
a[8] = 0
a[9] = 0
```

Arrays are a real convenience for many problems, but there is not a lot that C can do with them automatically. In particular, neither can all elements of an array be set at once nor can one array be assigned to another. Both assignments

```
a = 0;    /* WRONG */
```

and

```
int b[10];
b = a;    /* WRONG */
```

are illegal, where a is an array.

So, for example, to assign values to (i.e., store values into) an array, ar[10], the following program statements may be used.

```
ar[0] = 1;
ar[1] = 3;
ar[2] = 5;
```

```
...
ar[9] = 19;
```

Or

```
for(i = 0; i < 10; i++)
    ar[i] = (i*2) + 1;
```

Notice how the variable i, used as a subscript, increments from 0 to 'less than' 10, i.e., from 0 to 9. To access values in an array, the same subscripted notation has to be utilized as shown.

```
printf("%d", ar[2]);
thirdOdd = ar[2];
nthOddSquared = ar[n-1] * ar[n-1];
```

11.2.4 Other Allowed Operations

These operations include the following, for an array named 'ar'.

(a) To increment the ith element, the given statements can be used.
```
ar[i]++;
ar[i] += 1;
ar[i] = ar[i] + 1;
```

(b) To add n to the ith element, the following statements may be used,
```
ar[i] += n;
ar[i] = ar[i] + n;
```

(c) To copy the contents of the ith element to the kth element, the following statement may be written.
```
ar[k] = ar[i];
```

(d) To copy the contents of one array 'ar' to another array 'br', it must again be done one by one.
```
int ar[10],br[10];
for(i = 0; i < 10; i = i + 1)
br[i] = ar[i];
```

(e) To exchange the values in ar[i] and ar[k], a 'temporary' variable must be declared to hold one value, and it should be the same data type as the array elements being swapped. To perform this task, the following C statements are written
```
int temp;
temp = ar[i]; /* save a copy of value in ar[i] */
ar[i] = ar[j]; /* copy value from ar[j] to ar[i]  */
ar[j] = temp; /* copy saved value of ar[i] to ar[j]  */
```

Storing values given by the user in an array   Reading the input into an array is done as shown.

```
int a[10]; /* an array with 10 "int" elements */
int i;
```

```
for(i=0 ; i< 10; i++)
    scanf("%d", &a[i]);
```

The idea is that first a value must be read and copied into a[0], then another value read and copied into a[1], and so on, until all the input values have been read.

Printing an array   The following code segment prints the elements of an array, a[10].

```
for(i=0 ; i< 10; i++)
    printf("%d", a[i]);
```

Now the problem posed earlier can be solved. For printing of numbers entered by the user in the reverse order, the program will be as follows:

```
#include <stdio.h>
#include <stdlib.h>
int main()
{
    int a[30],n,i;
    /* n = number of array elements and i=index */
    printf("\n Enter the number n");
    scanf("%d",&n);
    if(n>30)
    {
      printf("\n Too many Numbers");
      exit(0);
    }
    for(i=0 ; i< n; i++)
        scanf("%d", &a[i]);
    printf("\n Numbers entered in reverse order \n");
    for(i=n-1 ; i>=0; i--)
        printf("%d", a[i]);
    return 0;
}
```

A program for printing numbers that are greater than the average is as follows:

```
#include <stdio.h>
#include <stdlib.h>
int main()
{
    int a[30],n,i,s=0;
    float avg;
    printf("\n Enter the number of entries");
    scanf("%d",&n);
    if(n>30)
    {
      printf("\n Too many Numbers");
      exit(0);
    }
    for(i=0 ; i< n; i++)
    {
```

```
    scanf("%d", &a[i]);
    s+=a[i];
}
avg=(float)s/n;
printf("\n Numbers greater than the average: \n");
for(i=0 ; i< n; i++)
if(a[i]>avg)
printf("%d",a[i]);
return 0;
}
```

11.2.5 Internal Representation of Arrays in C

Understanding how arrays work in C requires some understanding of how they are represented in the computer's memory. In C, an array is implemented as a single block of memory, with element 0 occupying the first 'slot' in that block, that is, arrays are allocated contiguous space in memory. As a result, C subscripts are closely related to actual memory addresses and to the notion of 'pointer' that will be discussed in Chapter 13.

The possible consequences of the misuse of arrays should motivate one to pay close attention to the array indices.

For a simple variable (e.g., int, double, etc.) of data type X, the compiler allocates sizeof(X) bytes to hold it. For an array of length L and data type X, the compiler allocates L* sizeof (X) bytes.

Given an array like int scores[100], the compiler allocates 200 bytes starting at some location, say 64789. Given an expression like scores[5], the compiler accesses the value stored at the memory location 64789+(5*2). In general, a[i] is located at byte: base address of a + i * sizeof (type of array).

References to elements outside of the array bounds It is important to realize that there is no array bound checking in C. If an array x is declared to have 100 elements, the compiler will reserve 100 contiguous, appropriately sized slots in computer memory on its behalf. The contents of these slots can be accessed via expressions of the form x[i], where the integer i should lie in the range 0 to 99. As seen, the compiler interprets x[i] as the contents of the memory slot which is i slots away from the beginning of the array. Obviously, accessing elements of an array that do not exist will produce some sort of error. Exactly what sort of error is very difficult to say—the program may crash, it may produce an absurdly incorrect output, it may produce plausible but incorrect output, it may even produce correct output—it all depends on exactly what information is being stored in the memory locations surrounding the block of memory reserved for x. This type of error can be extremely difficult to debug, since it may not be immediately apparent that something has gone wrong when

the program is executed. It is, therefore, the programmer's responsibility to ensure that all references to array elements lie within the declared bounds of the associated arrays.

A bit of memory allocation It has been seen how arrays can be defined and manipulated. It is important to learn how to do this because in more advanced C programs it is necessary to deal with something known as dynamic memory management. This is where the memory management of the programs is taken over by the programmer so that they can do more advanced things. To understand this, it is important to have a rough idea of what is going on inside the computer's memory when the program runs. Basically, it is given a small area of the computer's memory to use. This memory, which is known as the *stack*, is used by variables in the program

```
int a = 10;
float values[100];
```

The advantage of this is that the memory allocation is very simple. When a variable or an array is required, the user can define it. When the variable or array goes out of scope, it is destroyed and the memory is freed up again. A variable goes out of scope when the program control (the place of the program in the code) reaches the next closing curly bracket. This is normally at the end of a function or even at the end of an if-else/for/while structure.

This is why it is necessary to be careful when getting functions to fill in arrays. If the function declares the array and then returns it, what actually happens is that only the pointer is kept safe (copied back to the calling function); all the memory allocated for the array is de-allocated. This is a disadvantage.

Another disadvantage is that the size of memory allocated from the stack must be fixed at compile time. For example, it is impossible to declare an array using a variable for the size because at compile time the compiler does not know how big the array will be. For this reason, the following code will not work.

```
int size;
printf("How big do you want the array?\n");
scanf("%d", &size);
int array[size];
```

Therefore, doing things dynamically is a real problem. Perhaps the biggest problem with using memory from the stack is that the stack is not very big. It is typically 64k in size, even on a machine with tens of megabytes of memory. The rest of this memory is left alone by the compiler but the user can access it explicitly; it is called the *heap*.

11.2.6 Variable Length Arrays and the C99 changes

With the earlier version of C(C89) compilers, the size of an array must be a *constant integral expression* so that it can be calculated at compile time. This has already been mentioned in earlier sections. But in the C99 compilers, an array size can be an *integral expression* and not necessarily a constant. This allows the programmer to declare a *variable-length array* or an array whose size is determined at run time. However, such arrays can exist within a block or a function thereby signifying its scope to be limited within a set of instructions contained within a pair of left ({) and right (}) braces. This means that storage allocation to such an array is made at run time and during its existence within the scope of a block or a function and relinquishes this storage the moment it exits its scope.

The following program illustrates the concept:

```
#include <stdio.h>
int main(void)
{
  int n,i;
  printf("\n enter the value of n: ");
  scanf("%d", &n);
  int a[n];
  printf("\n enter the values one by one\n");
  for(i=0;i<n; ++i)
    scanf("%d", &a[i]);
  printf("\n entered numbers are.....\n");
  for(i=0;i<n;++i)
    printf("\n %d",a[i]);
  return 0;
}
```

Some changes in initializing an array have been made in C99. Here, the element number of an array can be specified explicitly by using a format called a *specification initializer*. When an array is initialized in C89, each element needs to be initialized in order from the beginning. In C99, initial values can be set only for certain elements, with uninitialized elements being initialized as 0. This is useful when the elements requiring initialization are limited, or when arrays have large element counts.

──── EXAMPLE ────

1. `int arr[6] = { [2] =3, [5] = 7 };`

   Here, array elements `arr[2]` and `arr[5]` are assigned the value 3 and 7 respectively, while all other elements in arr are assigned the value 0.

11.2.7 Working with One-dimensional Array

Printing binary equivalent of a decimal number using array

Here, the remainders of the integer division of a decimal number by 2 are stored as consecutive array elements.

The division procedure is repeated until the number becomes 0.

```
#include <stdio.h>
int main()
{
  int a[20],i,m,n,r;
  printf("\n Enter the decimal Integer");
  scanf("%d",&n);
  m=n;
  for(i=0;n>0;i++)
  {
    r=n%2;
    a[i]=r;
    n=n/2;
  }
  printf("\n Binary equivalent of %d is \t",m);
  for(i--;i>=0;i--)
  printf("%d",a[i]);
  return 0;
}
```

Fibonacci series using an array This example will introduce another application of the array. The program prints out an array of Fibonacci numbers. These are defined by a series in which any element is the sum of the previous two elements. This program stores the series in an array, and after calculating the terms, prints the numbers out as a table.

```
#include <stdio.h>
int main()
{
  int fib[15];
  int i;
  fib[0] = 0;
  fib[1] = 1;
  for(i = 2; i < 15; i++)
  fib[i] = fib[i-1] + fib[i-2];
  for(i = 0; i < 15; i++)
        printf("%d\n", fib[i]);
  return 0;
}
```

Output:
```
0
1
1
2
3
5
8
```

```
13
21
34
55
89
144
233
377
```

Searching an element within an array

Consider an array of *n* elements, where each element is a key (e.g., a number). The task is to find a particular key in the array. The simplest method is a sequential search or linear search. The idea is to simply search the array, element by element, from the beginning until the key is found or the end of the list is reached. If found, the corresponding position in the array is printed; otherwise, a message will have to be displayed that the key is not found. Now, the implementation of the program will be

```c
#include <stdio.h>
#include <stdlib.h>
int main()
{
  int a[30],n,i,key, FOUND=0;
  printf("\n How many numbers");
  scanf("%d",&n);
  if(n>30)
  {
    printf("\n Too many Numbers");
    exit(0);
  }
  printf("\n Enter the array elements \n");
  for(i=0 ; i<n; i++)
  scanf("%d", &a[i]);
  printf("\n Enter the key to be searched \n");
  scanf("%d",&key);
  for(i=0 ; i<n; i++)
  if(a[i] == key)
  {
    printf("\n Found at %d",i);
    FOUND=1;
  }
  if(FOUND = = 0)
  printf("\n NOT FOUND...");
  return 0;
}
```

Sorting an array

Bubble sort A bubble sort compares adjacent array elements and exchanges their values if they are out of order. In this way, the smaller values 'bubble' to the top of the array (towards element 0), while the larger values sink to the bottom of the array. This sort continues until no exchanges

are performed in a pass. If no exchanges are made, then all pairs must be in order. For this reason, a flag named 'sorted' is used.

The way bubble sort works is that it iterates through the data set comparing two neighbouring items at a time and swapping them if the first item is larger than the second item.

The following example depicts the different stages of bubble sort.

	Pass 1	Pass 2	Pass 3	Pass 4	Pass 5
42	42	26	26	26	26
60	26	42	34	28	28
26	55	34	28	34	34
55	34	28	42	42	42
34	28	55	55	55	55
28	60	60	60	60	60

Now the implementation of the above algorithm will be as follows:

```c
#include <stdio.h>
#include <stdlib.h>
int main()
{
  int a[30],n,i,j,temp, sorted=0;
  printf("\n How many numbers");
  scanf("%d",&n);
  if(n>30)
  {
    printf("\n Too many Numbers");
    exit(0);
  }
  printf("\n Enter the array elements \n");
  for(i=0 ; i< n; i++)
    scanf("%d", &a[i]);
  for(i = 0; i < n-1 && sorted==0; i++)
  {
    sorted=1;
    for(j = 0; j < (n - i) -1; j++)
      if(a[j] > a[j+1])
      {
        temp = a[j];
        a[j] = a[j+1];
        a[j+1] = temp;
        sorted=0;
      }
  }
  printf("\n The numbers in sorted order \n");
  for(i=0 ; i<n; ++i)
    printf("\n %d", a[i]);
  return 0;
}
```

Output

```
How many numbers 6
Enter the array elements
42
```

```
60
26
55
34
28
The numbers in sorted order
26
28
34
42
55
60
```

Binary searching

The drawbacks of sequential search can be eliminated if it becomes possible to eliminate large portions of the list from consideration in subsequent iterations. The binary search method does just that; it halves the size of the list to search in each iteration.

Binary search can be explained simply by the analogy of searching for a page in a book. Suppose a reader is searching for page 90 in a book of 150 pages. The reader would first open the book at random towards the latter half of the book. If the page number is less than 90, the reader would open at a page to the right; if it is greater than 90, the reader would open at a page to the left, repeating the process till page 90 was found. As can be seen, by the first instinctive search, the reader dramatically reduced the number of pages to be searched.

Binary search requires sorted data to operate on, since the data may not be contiguous like the pages of a book. It is not possible to guess in which quarter of the data set the required item may be. So, the array is divided in the centre each time.

Binary search will first be illustrated with an example before going on to formulate the algorithm and analysing it.

In binary search, implement the following procedure.

- Look at the middle element of the list.
- If it is the value being searched, then the job is done.
- If the value that is being searched is smaller than the middle element, then continue with the bottom half of the list.
- If the value that is being searched is larger than the middle element, then continue with the top half of the list.

In effect, binary search splits the array in half and then repeats the algorithm on the half that must contain the value that it is searching for, if it is there at all.

EXAMPLE

2. Consider the array

```
1 2 3 4 5 6 7 8 9
```

Construct the binary search algorithm for finding the Key = 7.

1st iteration
```
HIGH = 8, LOW = 0; because the array index begins with
'0' and ends with '8'
MID = 4, Array[4] = 5, 5<7 : TRUE
LOW = 5
New List = 6 7 8 9
```

2nd iteration
```
HIGH = 8, LOW = 5
MID = 6, Array[6] = 7, 7<7 : FALSE
HIGH = 6
New List = 6 7
```

3rd iteration
```
HIGH = 6, LOW = 5
MID = 5, Array[5] = 6, 6<7 : TRUE
LOW = 6
New List = 7
```

4th iteration
```
HIGH = 6, LOW = 6
MID = 6, Array [MID] = Array [6] = 7 == Key
then Found = TRUE
```

Tabular illustration Table 11.1 shows an example of the operation of the binary search algorithm. The rows of the table, starting from the top, are the array indices, the data stored at the indexed location, and the index values used for high (H), low (L), and middle (M) at each iteration of the algorithm. If the target value is 52, its location is found in the thirrd iteration.

Implementation of binary search algorithm This represents the binary search method to find a required item in a list sorted in increasing order.

Table 11.1 Depiction of binary search algorithm

Index	0	1	2	3	4	5	6	7	8	9	10	11	12	13	14	15
Data	23	27	29	32	34	41	46	47	49	52	55	68	71	74	77	78
1st iteration	L						M									H
2nd iteration								L				M				H
3rd iteration								L	M	H						

EXAMPLE
---

3. Sort an array `LIST` of size `N` and find the position of the target value `T`.

   Algorithm: The algorithm determines the position of `T` in the `LIST`.

   1. START
   2. PRINT "ENTER THE NO. OF ELEMENTS IN THE ARRAY"
   3. INPUT N
   4. I=0
   5. PRINT "ENTER ARRAY ELEMENT IN ASCENDING ORDER"
   6. INPUT LIST(I)
   7. I=I+1
   8. IF I<N THEN GOTO STEP 5
   9. PRINT "ENTER THE ELEMENT TO SEARCH"
   10. INPUT T
   11. HIGH = N - 1
   12. LOW = 0
   13. FOUND = 0
   14. MID = (HIGH + LOW)/ 2
   15. IF T = LIST [MID]
             FOUND = 1
       ELSE IF T < LIST[MID]
             HIGH = MID-1
       ELSE
             LOW = MID+1
   16. IF (FOUND =0) and (HIGH > = LOW) THEN GOTO STEP 14
   17. IF FOUND =0 THEN PRINT "NOT FOUND"
   18. ELSE PRINT "FOUND AT", MID.
   19. STOP

The C program for this algorithm is as follows:

```c
#include <stdio.h>
#include <stdlib.h>
int main()
{
    int a[30],n,i,t,low,mid,high,found=0;
    printf("\n Enter the NO. of elements in the array:");
    scanf("%d",&n);
    if(n>30)
    {
      printf("\n Too many Numbers");
      exit(0);
    }
    printf("\n Enter the elements of the array:");
    for(i=0 ; i< n; i++)
        scanf("%d", &a[i]);
    printf("\n Enter the element to search :");
    scanf("%d",&t);
    low = 0;
    high = n - 1;
    while(high >= low)
    {
      mid = (low + high) / 2;
      if(a[mid] == t)
      {
```

```c
        found = 1;
        break;
      }
      else if (t < a[mid])
              high = mid - 1;
          else
              low = mid + 1;
    }
    if(found==0)
    printf("\n NOT FOUND");
    else
    printf("\n FOUND AT %d",mid);
    return 0;
}
```

Output

```
Enter the number of elements in the array: 9
Enter the elements of the array:
1
2
3
4
5
6
7
8
9
Enter the element to search: 7
FOUND AT 6
Enter the number of elements in the array 9
Enter the elements of the array:
1
2
3
4
5
6
7
8
9
Enter the element to search: 11
NOT FOUND
```

Here is a slightly bigger example on the use of arrays. Suppose one wants to investigate the behaviour of rolling a pair of dice. The total roll value can range from 2 to 12, and how often each roll comes up is to be counted. An array is to be used to keep track of the counts: `a[2]` will count how many times 2 have been rolled, etc.

The simulation of the roll of a dice is done by calling C's random number generation function, `rand()`. Each time `rand()` is called, it returns a different, pseudo-random integer. The values that `rand()` returns typically span a large range, so C's *modulus* (or remainder) operator `%` will be used to produce random numbers in the required range. The expression `rand() % 6` produces random numbers in the range 0 to 5, and `rand() % 6 + 1` produces random numbers in the range 1 to 6.

Here is the program.

```c
#include <stdio.h>
#include <stdlib.h>
int main()
{
  int i;
  int d1, d2;
  int a[13]; /* uses [2..12] */
  for(i = 2; i <= 12; i = i + 1)
    a[i] = 0;
  for(i = 0; i < 100; i = i + 1)
  {
    d1 = rand() % 6 + 1;
    d2 = rand() % 6 + 1;
    a[d1 + d2] = a[d1 + d2] + 1;
  }
  for(i = 2; i <= 12; i = i + 1)
  printf("%d: %d\n", i, a[i]);
  return 0;
}
```

The header `<stdlib.h>` has to be included because it contains the necessary declarations for the `rand()` function. The array of size 13 has to be declared so that its highest element will be `a[12]`. Space for `a[0]` and `a[1]` will be wasted; this is no great loss. The variables `d1` and `d2` contain the roll values of the two individual dice; they are added together to decide which cell of the array to increment in the line

```c
a[d1 + d2] = a[d1 + d2] + 1;
```

After 100 rolls, the array is printed out. Typically, mostly 7's are seen as output, and relatively few 2's and 12's. However, using the `%` operator to reduce the range of the `rand()` function is not always a good idea.

Check Your Progress

1. Given the array declaration

```c
int myArray[] = {0, 2, 4, 6, 8, 10};
```

   What is the value of `myArray[myArray[2]];`?

   Output 8

2.
```c
#include <stdio.h>
main()
{
  float a[10];
  printf("%d", sizeof(a));
}
```
   What is the output of this program?

   Output 40

3.
```c
#include <stdio.h>
main()
{
```

```c
  int a[5],i;
  for(i=0;i<5;++i)
  printf("%d",a[i]);
}
```
   What is the output of this program?

   Output Garbage

4. An array has been declared as `int a[] = {1, 2, 3, 4, 5, ...};` How can you find the number of elements (i.e., size) of the array without manually counting them?

   Output `printf("%d",sizeof(a)/sizeof(a[0]));`

> **Note**
> - Single operations, which involve entire arrays, are not permitted in C.
> - Neither can all elements of an array be set at once nor can one array be assigned to another.
> - For an array of length L and data type X, the compiler allocates L* sizeof (X) bytes of contiguous space in memory.
> - It is not possible to declare an array using a variable for the *size*.

11.3 STRINGS: ONE-DIMENSIONAL CHARACTER ARRAYS

Strings in C are represented by arrays of characters. The end of the string is marked with a special character, the *null character*, which is a character whose bits are all zero, i.e., a NUL (not a NULL). (The null character has no relation except in name to the *null pointer*. In the ASCII character set, the null character is named NUL.) The null or string-terminating character is represented by another character escape sequence, `\0`.

Although C does not have a string data type, it allows string constants. For example, "hello students" is a string constant.

11.3.1 Declaration of a String

Strings can be declared like one-dimensional arrays. For example,

```c
char str[30];
char text[80];
```
illustrates this feature.

11.3.2 String Initialization

Character arrays or strings allow a shorthand initialization, for example,

```c
char str[9] = "I like C";
```
which is the same as

```c
char str[9] = {'I',' ','l','i','k','e',' ','C','\0'};
```

Whenever a string, enclosed in double quotes, is written, C automatically creates an array of characters containing that string, terminated by the \0 character. C language allows the alternative notation

```
char msg[] = "Hello";
```

that is always used in practice. The rules for writing string constants are exactly the same as those that were discussed earlier in this book when the use of `printf()` was introduced. It should be noted that the size of the aggregate 'msg' is six bytes, five for the letters and one for the terminating NUL.

There is one special case where the null character is not automatically appended to the array. This is when the array size is explicitly specified and the number of initializers completely fills the array size. For example,

```
char c[4] = "abcd";
```

Here, the array c holds only the four specified characters, a, b, c, and d. No null character terminates the array.

> **Note**
>
> - An array formed by characters is a string in C.
> - The end of the string is marked with a null character.
> - When the character array size is explicitly specified and the number of initializers completely fills the array size, the null character is not automatically appended to the array.

11.3.3 Printing Strings

The conversion type 's' may be used for output of strings using `printf()`. Width and precision specifications may be used with the `%s` conversion specifier. The width specifies the minimum output field width; if the string is shorter, then space padding is generated. The precision specifies the maximum number of characters to display. If the string is too long, it is truncated. A negative width implies left justification of short strings rather than the default right justification. For example,

```
printf("%7.3s",name)
```

This specifies that only the first three characters have to be printed in a total field width of seven characters and right justified in the allocated width by default. We can include a minus sign to make it left justified (%-7.3). The following points should be noted.

- When the field width is less than the length of the string, the entire string is printed.

- The integer value on the right side of the decimal point specifies the number of characters to be printed.

- When the number of characters to be printed is specified as zero, nothing is printed.

- The minus sign in the specification causes the string to be printed as left justified.

The following program illustrates the use of the `%s` conversion specifier.

```
#include <stdio.h>
int main()
{
  char s[]="Hello, World";
  printf(">>%s<<\n",s);
  printf(">>%20s<<\n",s);
  printf(">>%-20s<<\n",s);
  printf(">>%.4s<<\n",s);
  printf(">>%-20.4s<<\n",s);
  printf(">>%20.4s<<\n",s);
  return 0;
}
```

This program produces the output

```
>>Hello, World<<
>>        Hello, World<<
>>Hello, World        <<
>>Hell<<
>>Hell                <<
>>                Hell<<
```

The `>>` and `<<` symbols are included in this program so that the limits of the output fields are clearly visible in the output.

There is another way to print a string. The library function `puts()` writes a line of output to the standard output. It terminates the line with a new line, '\n'. It returns an EOF if an error occurs. It will return a positive number upon success. The use of `puts()` is given as follows:

```
#include <stdio.h>
int main()
{
  char s[]="Hello, World";
  puts(s);
  return 0;
}
```

The library function `sprintf()` is similar to `printf()`. The only difference is that the formatted output is written to a memory area rather than directly to a standard output. It is particularly useful when it is necessary to construct formatted strings in memory for subsequent transmission over a communications channel or to a special device. Its relationship with `printf()` is similar to the relationship between `sscanf()` and `scanf()`. The library function `puts()` may be used to copy a string to the standard output, its single parameter is the start address of the string. `puts()` writes a new-line character to standard output after it has written the string.

The following is a simple example of the use of `sprintf()` and `puts()`.

```
#include <stdio.h>
int main()
{
    char buf[128];
    double x = 1.23456;
    int i = 0;
    sprintf(buf,"x = %7.5lf",x);
    while(i<10)
    puts(buf+i++);
    return 0;
}
```

The output produced is as follows:

```
x = 1.23456
= 1.23456
= 1.23456
1.23456
1.23456
.23456
23456
3456
456
56
```

If '\n' had been incorporated in the format string of the `sprintf()`, the output would have been double-spaced because the function would have put a new-line character in the generated string and `puts()` would then generate a further new line.

11.3.4 String Input

The following sections will describe the methods of taking input from the user.

Using %s control string with scanf()

Strings may be read by using the `%s` conversion with the function `scanf()` but there are some restrictions. The first is that `scanf()` only recognizes a sequence of characters delimited by white space characters as an external string. The second is that it is the programmer's responsibility to ensure that there is enough space to receive and store the incoming string along with the terminating null which is automatically generated and stored by `scanf()` as part of the `%s` conversion. The associated parameter in the value list must be the address of the first location in an area of memory set aside to store the incoming string.

Of course, a field width may be specified and this is the maximum number of characters that are read in, but remember that any extra characters are left unconsumed in the input buffer. A simple use of `scanf()` with `%s` conversions is illustrated in the following program.

```
int main()
{
    char str[50];
    printf("Enter a string");
```

```
    scanf("%s",str);
    printf("The string was :%s\n",str);
    return 0;
}
```

Output of sample runs:

```
(a) Enter a string    manas
    The string was :manas
(b) Enter a string    manas ghosh
    The string was :manas
(c) Enter a string    "manas and ghosh"
    The string was : "manas"
```

Dissimilar to the integer, float, and characters, the `%s` format does not require the ampersand before the variable `str`.

It will also be observed that attempts to quote a string with internal spaces or to escape the internal spaces (both of which normally work in the UNIX command environment) did not work. C supports variable field width or precision, e.g.,

```
printf("%*.*s",w,d,str);
```

prints the first `d` characters of the string in the field width of `w`. For example,

```
int main()
{
    char str[50];
    printf("\n Enter a string:");
    scanf("%s",str);
    printf("\n %*.*s\n",2,3,str);
    return 0;
}
```

Specifies that the first three characters of the string will be printed.

Sample run:

```
Enter a string:Manas
Man
```

First three characters of entered string "Manas" is displayed on the screen.

As an illustration, the following program converts a decimal number into its hexadecimal equivalent.

```
#include <stdio.h>
int main(void)
{
    int n, r, i, a[50];
    char hexdigit[]="0123456789ABCDEF";
    printf("\n Enter the decimal number: ....\t");
    scanf("%d", &n);
    i=0;
    while(n>0)
    {
        r=n%16;
        a[i]=r;
        i++;
        n=n/16;
    }
    printf("\n Hexadecimal equivalent is...: \t");
    for(--i;i>=0;--i)
```

```
    printf("%c", hexdigit[a[i]]);
    return 0;
}
```

Here, at each iteration, remainder of the integer division of n by 16 is stored as an element of the array variable 'a'. It continues until the number 'n' becomes 0. After storing the remainders as elements of the array 'a', it is needed to print the elements in reverse order. When the control comes out of the while loop the value of 'i' would be incremented.

So it is needed to decrement i by 1 and it has been performed at the initialization part of the for loop. The expression hexdigit[a[i]] would print the corresponding hexadecimal digit at each iteration. If the value stored in a[i] is 5 then printf("%c", hexdigit[5]) would print 5. If the value stored in a[i] is 13 then printf("%c", hexdigit[13]) would print D. The trace of the above program is given below.

```
n= 28
n=28  i=0  r=12  a[0]=12
n=1   i=1  r=1   a[1]=1
n=0   i=2
```

The value of i is 2 when the control is outside the while loop. 'i' becomes 1 at the initialization step. In the first iteration, hexdigit[1] that is '1' will be printed because the value stored in a[1] is 1. In the second iteration, hexdigit[0] that is 'C' will be printed because the value stored in a[0] is 12.

The above program can be rewritten where the remainders are stored in the string hexdigit.

```c
#include <stdio.h>
#include <string.h>
int main(void)
{
  int n, r, i;
  char hexdigit[50];
  printf("\n Enter the decimal number: ....\t");
  scanf("%d", &n);
  i=0;
  while(n>0)
  {
   r=n%16;
   if(r<10)
     hexdigit[i]=r+48;
   else
     hexdigit[i]=r%10+65;
   i++;
   n=n/16;
  }
  hexdigit[i]='\0';
  printf("\n Hexadecimal equivalent is...: \t");
  for(i=strlen(hexdigit)-1;i>=0;--i)
        printf("%c", hexdigit[i]);
  return 0;
}
```

Using scanset

The scanset conversion facility provided by scanf() is a useful string input method. This conversion facility allows the programmer to specify the set of characters that are (or are not) acceptable as part of the string. A scanset conversion consists of a list of acceptable characters enclosed within square brackets. A range of characters may be specified using notations such as 'a-z', meaning all characters within this range. The actual interpretation of a range in this context is implementation-specific, i.e., it depends on the particular character set being used on the host computer. If an actual '-' is required in the scanset, it must be the first or last character in the set. If the first character after the '[' is a '^' character, then the rest of the scanset specifies unacceptable characters rather than acceptable characters.

The following program shows the use of scansets.

```c
int main()
{
    char str[50];
    printf("Enter a string in lower case:");
    scanf("%[a-z]",str);
    printf("The string was : %s\n",str);
    return 0;
}
```

Three sample runs are given below.

(a) Enter a string in lower case: hello world
    The string was: hello world

(b) Enter a string in lower case: hello, world
    The string was: hello

(c) Enter a string in lower case: abcd1234
    The string was : abcd

In the second case, the character, ',' (comma) is not in the specified range. Note that in all cases, conversion is terminated by the input of something other than a space or lower-case letter.

Single-line input using scanset with ^

The circumflex (^) plays an important role while taking input. For a single-line text input, the user presses the <**Return**> or <**Enter**> key to terminate the string. The maximum number of characters typed by the user might be 80 because the screen can print a maximum of 80 characters in a line. All characters are allowed to be typed as input except '\n'. In the example that follows, the computer takes this (\n) as a clue indicating that the string has ended.

```c
#include <stdio.h>
int main()
{
    char str[80];
    printf("Enter a string in lower case");
    scanf("%[^\n]",str);
    printf("The string was : %s\n", str);
    return 0;
}
```

Multiline input using scanset

One can use a bracketed string read, %[..] where the square brackets [] are used to enclose all characters which are permissible in the input. If any character other than those listed within the brackets occurs in the input string, further reading is terminated. Reciprocally, those characters may be specified with the brackets which, if found in the input, will cause further reading of the string to be terminated. Such input terminators must be preceded by the caret (^). For example, if the tilde (~) is used to end a string, the following scanf() shows how it is coded.

```
char string [200];

scanf("%[^~]", string);
```

Then, if the input for string consists of embedded spaces, no matter what, they will all be accepted by scanf(); and reading will stop when a tilde (~) is entered. This is illustrated in the following program and its output.

```
#include <stdio.h>

int main( )
{
  char string [80];
  printf("Enter a string, terminate with a tilde\
     (~)...");
  scanf("%[^~]", string);
  printf("%s", string);
  return 0;
}
```

Output

```
Enter a string, terminate with a tilde (~) ... I am
a string. ~
I am a string.
```

Though the terminating tilde is not itself included as an element of the string read, it stays in the 'read buffer'—the area of memory designated to store the input—and will be picked up by the next call to scanf(), even though it is not required. This is illustrated by the following program and its output. Here, when the second call to scanf() is executed automatically, the tilde (~) character is assigned to the character variables x. The call to putchar() prints the value of x.

```
#include <stdio.h>
int main( )
{
  char string [80];
  char x;
  printf("Enter a string, terminate with a tilde\
     (~)...");
  scanf("%[^~]", string);
```

```
  scanf("%c", &x); /* The leftover from the last
       scanf is read here. This scanf() does not
       wait for the user to enter another char.*/
  printf("%s", string);
  putchar(x);
  return 0;
}
```

Output

```
Enter a string, terminate with a tilde (~) ... I am a
string. ~
I am a string. ~
```

Compile and execute the program. It will be found that the machine executes the second scanf() without much fuss. Such dangling characters must be 'absorbed away' by a subsequent call to scanf() with %c, or to getchar() or they may interfere in unexpected ways with subsequent calls to scanf() or getchar().

String input using scanf() with conversion specifier %c

An alternative method for the input of strings is to use scanf() with the %c conversion which may have a count associated with it. This conversion does not recognize the new-line character as special. The count specifies the number of characters to be read in. Unlike the %s and %[] (scanset) conversions, the %c conversion does not automatically generate the string terminating NUL and strange effects will be noted if the wrong number of characters is supplied. The following program demonstrates its use.

```
int main()
{
  char str[10];
  int i;
  while(1)
  {
    printf("Enter a string of 9 characters:");
    scanf("%10c",str);
    str[9]='\0';             /* Make it a string */
    printf("String was :%s\n",str);
    if(str[0] == 'Z')
    break;
  }
  return 0;
}
```

The output of the sample runs is given below.
```
(a) Enter a string of 9 characters: 123456789
    String was : 123456789
(b) Enter a string of 9 characters: abcdefghi
    String was : abcdefghi
(c) Enter a string of 9 characters: abcdefghijklmnopqr
    String was :abcdefghi
(d) Enter a string of 9 characters: 123456789
    String was :klmnopqr
(e) Enter a string of 9 characters: ttttttttt
    String was :23456789
```

Some other points need to be noted here. The first is that, contrary to the prompt, 10 characters are being converted. This is done so that the new-line character at the end of the input line is also read in; otherwise it would be left in the input buffer to be read as one of the input characters the next time round. The effect of providing too many input characters is that 'unconsumed' input characters (including new-line characters) are left in the input buffer. These will be 'consumed' by the next call to scanf(). If too few input characters are provided, scanf() hangs (or blocks) until it gets enough input characters. Both types of behaviour can be seen in the above example.

The complexities in using the scanf() function suggest that it is not really suitable for a reliable, general-purpose string input.

Using gets()

The best approach to string input is to use a library function called gets(). This takes the start address of an area of memory suitable to hold the input as a single parameter. The complete input line is read in and stored in the memory area as a null-terminated string. Its use is shown in the program below.

```
int main()
{
    char str[150];
    printf("Enter a string");
    gets(str);
    printf("The string was :%s\n",str);
    return 0;
}
```

Sample run:

```
(a) Enter a string    manas
    The string was :manas
(b) Enter a string    manas ghosh
    The string was :manas ghosh
```

gets() can be implemented using getchar() or scanf() with %c conversion specifier as follows:

```
#include <stdio.h>
int main()
{
    char s[80], ch;
    int i;
    printf("\n Enter the text:");
    for(i=0; i<80 ;i++)
    {
        ch=getchar();
        if(ch=='\n')
        break;
        s[i]=ch;
    }
    s[i]='\0';
    printf("\n Entered text is:");
```

```
    puts(s);
    return 0;
}
```

Be careful not to input more characters than can be stored in the string variable used because C does not check array bounds. gets() and puts() functions can be nested. The following statements can be written in C.

```
printf("%s", gets(s));
puts(gets(s));
```

sscanf()

There are a variety of library functions for handling input data. The most useful include sscanf() and the function atoi(). The function sscanf() applies scanf() type conversions to data held in a program buffer as a single string but not to read data from standard input. The atoi() function converts a character string from external decimal form to internal binary form.

The use of sscanf() in conjunction with gets() is illustrated by the following program. The purpose of the program is to read an integer. Unlike simple uses of scanf(), input errors are detected and the prompt repeated until a valid integer is entered.

```
#include <stdio.h>
int main()
{
    int error;
    char inbuf[256];
    int i;
    char c;
    while(1)
    {
        error = i = 0;
        printf("Enter an integer");
        gets(inbuf);        /* get complete input line */
        while(inbuf[i] == ' ')
        i++;                            /* skip spaces */
        if(inbuf[i] == '-' || inbuf[i] == '+')
        i++;
        while((c = inbuf[i++])!='\0')
                        /* while string end with NUL */
        {
            if(c>'9' || c<'0')          /* non-digit ? */
            {
                printf("Non-Numeric Character %c\n",c);
                error = 1;
                break;
            }
        }
        if(!error)          /* was everything OK ? */
        {
```

```
    int num;                /* local variable */
    sscanf(inbuf,"%d",&num);    /* conversion */
    printf("Number was %d\n",num);
    break;
  }
 }
 return 0;
}
```

Sample outputs are shown below:

```
(a) Enter an integer a123
    Non-Numeric Character a
(b) Enter an integer 123a
    Non-Numeric Character a
(c) Enter an integer 1234.56
     Non-Numeric Character .
(d) Enter an integer    1234
    Number was 1234
(e) Enter an integer    +43
    Number was 43
```

There are some interesting points about this program. The main processing loop first skips any leading spaces pointing to the first non-blank character in the input text. An initial sign is also skipped. After the optional initial sign, all input characters must be digits until the input string terminating NUL is encountered. If anything other than a digit, including trailing blanks, is encountered, the loop is broken and an error indicator is set. The condition

```
c = inbuf[i++]
```

associated with the loop that checks for digits is a typical piece of C code that does several things in one go. The value of the expression `inbuf[i++]` is the next character from the input buffer `inbuf`. In the course of shifting of the character, the variable `i` is incremented as a side effect. The character value is assigned to the variable `c` to be used in the test for being a digit on the following line, the value of the assignment expression being, of course, the value assigned. The value of this expression becomes zero and terminates the loop when the character in question is the string terminating NUL that is represented with '\0'.

In practice the code of this program would be incorporated into a user-defined function that might return the value of the entered integer.

The function `sscanf()` is similar to `scanf()` except that it has an extra parameter, which is the address of the start of the memory area that holds the character string to be processed. The library function `atoi()` could have been used instead of `sscanf()` in this example by changing the appropriate line to read.

```
num = atoi(inbuf);
```

The function `atoi()` takes the address of an area of memory as parameter and converts the string stored at that location to an integer using the external decimal to internal binary conversion rules. This may be preferable to `sscanf()` since `atoi()` is a much smaller, simpler, and faster function. `sscanf()` can do all possible conversions whereas `atoi()` can only do single decimal integer conversions. This type of function will be discussed in later sections.

String input and output using fscanf() and fprintf()

`stdin`, `stdout`, and `stderr`: Each C program has three I/O streams.

The input stream is called standard-input (`stdin`); the usual output stream is called standard-output (`stdout`); and the side stream of output characters for errors is called standard error (`stderr`). Internally they occupy file descriptors 0, 1, and 2 respectively.

Now, one might think that calls to `fprinf()` and `fscanf()` differ significantly from calls to `printf()` and `scanf()`. `fprintf()` sends formatted output to a stream and `fscanf()` scans and formats input from a stream. See the following example.

```
#include <stdio.h>
int main()
{
    int first, second;
    fprintf(stdout,"Enter two ints in this line:  ");
    fscanf(stdin,"%d %d", &first, &second);
    fprintf(stdout,"Their sum is: %d.\n", first + second);
    return 0;
}
```

There is a third defined stream named `stderr`. This is associated with the standard error file. In some systems such as MSDOS and UNIX, one can redirect the output of the programs to files by using the redirection operator. In DOS, for example, if fl.exe is an executable file that writes to the monitor, then it can be redirected to output to a disk file. Output that would normally appear on the monitor can thus be sent to a file. Writing error messages to `stderr` can be done by

```
fprintf(stderr,"Unable to open for writing");
```

This ensures that normal output will be redirected, but error messages will still appear on the screen. Observe the following program.

```
#include <stdlib.h>
#include <stdio.h>
int main()
```

```
{
    int i;
    printf("Input an integer:");
    /* read an integer from the standard input stream */
    if(fscanf(stdin,"%d", &i))
        printf("The integer read was: %i\n", i);
    else
    {
        fprintf(stderr,"Error in reading from stdin.\n");
        exit(1);
    }
    return 0;
}
```

Note

- One special case, where the null character is not automatically appended to the array, is when the array size is explicitly specified and the number of initializers completely fills the array size.
- printf() with the width and precision modifiers in the %s conversion specifier may be used to display a string.
- The %s format does not require the ampersand before the string name in scanf().
- If fewer input characters are provided, scanf() hangs until it gets enough input characters.
- scanf() only recognizes a sequence of characters delimited by white space characters as an external string.
- While using scanset with scanf(), dangling characters must be 'absorbed away' by a subsequent call to scanf() with %c or to getchar().

11.3.5 Character Manipulation in the String

In working with a string, one important point to remember is that it must be terminated with NUL (\0). The following program removes all the blank spaces in the character string.

```
#include <stdio.h>
#include <string.h>
int main()
{
    char a[80],t[80];
    int i,j;
    printf("\n enter the text\n");
    gets(a);
    for(i=0,j=0; a[i]!='\0';++i)
        if(a[i]!= ' ')
                t[j++]=a[i];
    t[j]='\0';
    printf("\n the text without blank spaces\n");
```

```
    puts(t);
    return 0;
}
```

Table 11.2 lists the character-handling functions of the header file. Notice that except for the toupper() and tolower() functions, all these functions return values indicating true or false. It may be recalled that in C, true is any non-zero number and false is zero. The character is seemingly typed as an integer in these functions. This is because the character functions are really looking at the ASCII values of the characters, which are integers.

Table 11.2 Character functions in <ctype.h> where c is the character argument

Function	Description
ialnum(c)	Returns a non-zero if c is alphabetic or numeric
isalpha(c)	Returns a non-zero if c is alphabetic
scntrl(c)	Returns a non-zero if c is a control character
isdigit(c)	Returns a non-zero if c is a digit, 0 – 9
isgraph(c)	Returns a non-zero if c is a non-blank but printing character
islower(c)	Returns a non-zero if c is a lowercase alphabetic character, i.e., a – z
isprint(c)	Returns a non-zero if c is printable, non-blanks and white space included
ispunct(c)	Returns a non-zero if c is a printable character, but not alpha, numeric, or blank
isspace(c)	Returns a non-zero for blanks and these escape sequences: '\f', '\n', '\r', '\t', and '\v'
isupper(c)	Returns a non-zero if c is a capital letter, i.e., A – Z
isxdigit(c)	Returns a non-zero if c is a hexadecimal character: 0 – 9, a – f, or A – F
tolower(c)	Returns the lowercase version if c is a capital letter; otherwise returns c
toupper(c)	Returns the capital letter version if c is a lowercase character; otherwise returns c

To see the actual effect of some of these character manipulation functions, write and run the following program on the computer. This program counts the number of words in a string.

```
#include <stdio.h>
#include <ctype.h>
int main()
{
    char s[30];
    int i=0,count=0;
    printf("\n enter the string\n");
    scanf("%[^\n]",s);
    while(s[i]!='\0')
    {
        while(isspace(s[i]))
```

```
i++;
if(s[i]!='\0')
{
  ++count;
  while(!isspace(s[i]) && s[i] != '\0')
  i++;
}
}
printf("\n NO. of words in the string is %d:", count);
return 0;
}
```

Here is a short program which illustrates the effect of the `tolower()` and `toupper()` functions. Notice that if a character is not lower case, the `toupper()` function does not change the character; the effect is similar if a character is not a capital letter. The following program converts a given text into a capital letter using `toupper()` function.

```
#include <stdio.h>
#include <string.h>
int main()
{
  char a[30];
  int i=0;
  printf("\n enter the string\n");
  gets(a);
  while(a[i]!='\0')
  {
    a[i]=toupper(a[i]);
    i++;
  }
  a[i]='\0';
  puts(a);
  return 0;
}
```

It should be remembered that there is a difference between characters and integers. If the character '1' is treated as an integer, perhaps by writing

```
int i = '1';
```

it will probably not get the value 1 in i; it will produce the value of the character '1' in the machine's character set. In ASCII, it is 49. When the numeric value of a digit character has to be found (or to put it in another way, to get the digit character with a particular value), it is useful to remember that in any character set used by C, the values for the digit characters, whatever they are, are contiguous. In other words, no matter what values '0' and '1' have, '1' - '0' will be 1 (and, obviously, '0' - '0' will be 0). So, for a variable c holding some digit character, the expression

```
c - '0'
```

gives its value. Similarly, for an integer value i, i + '0' gives us the corresponding digit character, as long as 0 <= i <= 9.

Just as the character '1' is not the integer 1, the string '123' is not the integer 123. When a string of digits is available, it can be converted to the corresponding integer by calling the standard function `atoi`.

```
char string[] ="123";
int i = atoi(string);
int j = atoi("456");
```

11.3.6 String Manipulation

C has the weakest character string capability of any general-purpose programming language. Strictly speaking, there are no character strings in C, just arrays of single characters that are really small integers. If `s1` and `s2` are such 'strings', a program cannot

- assign one to the other: `s1 = s2;`
- compare them for collating sequence: `s1 < s2`
- concatenate them to form a single longer string: `s1 + s2`
- return a string as the result of a function

A set of standard C library functions that are contained in `<string.h>` provides limited support for the first three. By convention, the end of a string is delimited by the non-printable null character (0 value), but there is no indication of the amount of memory allocated. Consequently, both user code and standard library functions can overwrite memory outside the space allocated for the array of characters.

The string header, `string.h`, provides many functions useful for manipulating strings or character arrays. Some of these are mentioned in Table 11.3.

Table 11.3 String manipulation functions available in `string.h`

Function	Description
`strcpy(s1,s2)`	Copies `s2` into `s1`
`strcat(s1,s2)`	Concatenates `s2` to `s1`. That is, it appends the string contained by `s2` to the end of the string pointed to by `s1`. The terminating null character of `s1` is overwritten. Copying stops once the terminating null character of `s2` is copied.
`strncat(s1,s2,n)`	Appends the string pointed to by `s2` to the end of the string pointed to by `s1` up to n characters long. The terminating null character of `s1` is overwritten. Copying stops once n characters are copied or the terminating null character of `s2` is copied. A terminating null character is always appended to `s1`.
`strlen(s1)`	Returns the length of `s1`. That is, it returns the number of characters in the string without the terminating null character.
`strcmp(s1,s2)`	Returns 0 if `s1` and `s2` are the same. Returns less than 0 if `s1<s2`. Returns greater than 0 if `s1>s2`.
`strchr(s1,ch)`	Returns pointer to first occurrence ch in `s1`.
`strstr(s1,s2)`	Returns pointer to first occurrence `s2` in `s1`.

Counting number of characters in a string

The first of these, `strlen()`, is particularly straightforward. Its single parameter is the address of the start of the string and its value is the number of characters in the string excluding the terminating NUL.

To demonstrate the use of `strlen()`, here is a simple program that reads in a string and prints it out reversed, a useful thing to do. The repeated operation of this program is terminated by the user by entering a string of length zero, i.e., by hitting the <**Return**> key immediately after the program prompt.

```
#include <stdio.h>
#include <string.h>
int main()
{
  char s[100];
  int    len;    /* holds length of string */
  while(1)
  {
    printf("Enter a string");
    gets(s);
    len = strlen(s);   /* find length */
    if(len == 0) break; /* termination condition */
    while(len > 0)
    {
      len--;
      printf("%c",s[len]);
    }
    printf("\n");
  }
  return 0;
}
```

The program operates by printing the characters one by one, starting with the last non-NUL character of the string. Notice that 'len' will have been decremented before the output of the character. This is correct since the length returned by `strlen()` is the length excluding the NUL but the actual characters are aggregate members, 0, ..., length–1. The outputs of this program for different sample runs are

(a) Enter a string 1234
    4321
(b) Enter a string   manas
    Sanam
(c) Enter a string abc def ghi
    ihg fed cba

Look at the following program that reads a line of text, stores it in a string, and prints its length (excluding the new line at the end).

```
#include <stdio.h>
int main()
{
  int n, c;
  char line[100];
  n = 0;
  while((c=getchar()) != '\n')
  {
```

```
    if(n < 100)
    line[n] = c;
    n++;
  }
  line[n]='\0';
  printf("length = %d\n", n);
  return 0;
}
```

Lastly, here is another version of `strlen()`.

```
int mystrlen(char str[])
{
  int i;
  for(i = 0; str[i] != '\0'; i++)
  {}
  return 0;
}
```

In this case, all one has to do is find the `\0` that terminates the string. It turns out that the three control expressions of the `for` loop do all the work; there is nothing left to do in the body. Therefore, an empty pair of braces `{}` are used as the loop body. Equivalently, a null statement could be used, which is simply a semicolon as shown.

```
for(i = 0; str[i] != '\0'; i++);
```

Empty loop bodies can be a bit startling at first, but they are not unheard of.

Copying a string into another

Since C never lets entire arrays to be assigned, the `strcpy()` function can be used to copy one string to another. `strcpy()` copies the string pointed to by the second parameter into the space pointed to by the first parameter. The entire string, including the terminating NUL, is copied and there is no check that the space indicated by the first parameter is big enough. The given code shows the use of the `strcpy()` function.

```
#include <string.h>
int main()
{
  char s1[] ="Hello, world!";
  char s2[20];
  strcpy(s2, s1);
  puts (s2);
  return 0;
}
```

The destination string is `strcpy`'s first argument, so that a call to `strcpy` mimics an assignment expression, with the destination on the left-hand side. Note that `string s2` must be allocated sufficient memory so that it can hold the string that would be copied to it. Also, at the top of any source file, the following line must be included

```
#include <string.h>
```

that contains external declarations for these functions.

Since a string is just an array of characters, all string-handling functions can be written quite simply, using no technique more complicated than the ones that are already known. In fact, it is quite instructive to look at how these functions might be implemented. Here is a version of strcpy.

```c
#include <stdio.h>
#include <string.h>
int main()
{
  char src[30], dest[30];
  int i = 0;
  printf("\n Enter the source string: ");
  scanf("%[^\n]",src);
  while(src[i] != '\0')
  {
    dest[i] = src[i];
    i++;
  }
  dest[i] = '\0';
  printf("\n Source string is :%s\n", src);
  printf("\n Destination string is : %s\n", dest);
  return 0;
}
```

Its operation is simple. It looks at characters in the src string one at a time, and as long as they are not \0, assigns them, one by one, to the corresponding positions in the dest string. On completion, it terminates the dest string by appending a \0. After exiting the while loop, i is guaranteed to have a value one greater than the subscript of the last character in src. For comparison, here is a way of writing the same code, using a for loop instead of while loop.

```c
for(i = 0; src[i] != '\0'; i++)
  dest[i] = src[i];
dest[i] = '\0';
```

The above statements can be rewritten using the following expression:

```c
for(i=0;(dest[i] = src[i]) != '\0';i++);
```

This is actually the same type of combined operation.

Comparing strings

Another function, strcmp(), takes the start addresses of two strings as parameters and returns the value zero if the strings are equal. If the strings are unequal, it returns a negative or positive value. The returned value is positive if the first string is greater than the second string and negative if the first string is lesser than the second string. In this context, the relative value of strings refers to their relative values as determined by the host computer character set (or collating sequence).

It is important to realize that two strings cannot be compared by simply comparing their start addresses although this would be syntactically valid. The following program illustrates the comparison of two strings:

```c
#include <stdio.h>
#include <string.h>
int main()
```

```c
{
  char x[50],y[]="a programming example";
  strcpy(x,"A Programming Example");
  if(strcmp(x,"A Programming Example") == 0)
    printf("Equal \n");
  else
    printf("Unequal \n");
  if( strcmp(y,x) == 0)
    printf("Equal \n");
  else
    printf("Unequal \n");
  return 0;
}
```

It produces the following output:
```
Equal
Unequal
```

Putting strings together

Arithmetic addition cannot be applied for joining of two or more strings in the manner

```c
string1 = string2 + string3; or
string1 = string2 +"RAJA";
```

For this, the standard library function, strcat(), that concatenates strings is needed. It does not concatenate two strings together and give a third, new string. What it really does is append one string at the end of another. Here is an example.

```c
#include <stdio.h>
#include <string.h>
int main()
{
  char s[30] ="Hello,";
  char str[] ="world!";
  printf("%s\n", s);
  strcat(s, str);
  printf("%s\n", s);
  return 0;
}
```

The first call to printf prints "Hello,", and the second one prints "Hello,world!", indicating that the contents of str have been appended to the end of s. Notice that s was declared with extra space, to make room for the appended characters.

Note that in arithmetic, char variables can usually be treated like int variables. Arithmetic on characters is quite legal, and often makes sense.

```c
c = c + 'A' - 'a';
```

converts a single, lower-case ASCII character stored in c to a capital letter, making use of the fact that corresponding ASCII letters are a fixed distance apart. The rule governing this arithmetic is that all chars are converted to int before the arithmetic is done. Be aware that conversion may involve a sign-extension; if the leftmost bit of a character is

1, the resulting integer might be negative.

Therefore, to convert a text into lower case, the following program can be used:

```c
#include <stdio.h>
int main()
{
    char c;
    while((c=getchar()) != '\n')
    if('A'<=c && c<='Z')
            putchar(c+'a'-'A');
            /* equivalent statement in putchar(C+32);*/
    else
            putchar(c);
    return 0;
}
```

Sample run:

```
TIMES OF INDIA
times of india
```

The following program will demonstrate the `strncat()` library function:

```c
#include <string.h>
#include <stdio.h>
int main()
{
    char aString1[80] ="RCC Institute of Information
            Technology" ,
    aString2[80] ="Oxford University Press";
    printf("\n Before the copy...\n");
    puts(aString1);
    puts(aString2);
    strncat(aString1, aString2, 6);
    printf("\n After the copy...\n");
    puts(aString1);
    puts(aString2);
    return 0;
}
```

Output

```
Before the copy...
RCC Institute of Information Technology
Oxford University Press
After the copy...
RCC Institute of Information Technology Oxford
Oxford University Press
```

> **Note**
>
> - Since C never lets entire arrays to be assigned, the `strcpy()` function can be used to copy one string to another.
> - Strings can be compared with the help of `strcmp()` function.
> - The arithmetic addition cannot be applied for joining two or more strings; this can be done by using the standard library function, `strcat()`.

Some sample programs

One interesting thing: This program tries to prove that a string is really an array of characters. Note the explicit placement of the string terminator at the end of the string. Note the term `&str[2]`. Remember that `str[2]` is the third character, so `&str[2]` is the address of the third character. Since `str` is the address of the first character, `&str[2]` effectively is `str` but with the first two characters removed. Try replacing `&str[2]` with `str+2`. Does this work? Lastly, notice the use of the `strcpy` (string copy) function from the `string.h` library.

```c
#include <stdio.h>
#include <string.h>
int main()
{
    char str[30];
    str[0]='M';
    str[1]='A';
    str[2]='D';
    str[3]='A';
    str[4]='M';
    str[5]= '\0'; /* terminate string with a null */
    printf("String is %s\n",str);
    printf("Part of string is %s\n",&str[2]);
    strcpy(str,"SIR");
    printf("String is %s\n",str);
    return(0);
}
```

Sample run:

```
String is MADAM
Part of string is DAM
String is SIR
```

To make sure that what is going on is understood, consider the following table:

Code	Output
`printf("%s?", str);`	MADAM
`printf("%s?", str[1]);`	Error
`printf("%s?", &str[1]);`	ADAM
`printf("%s?", &str);`	MADAM

Some of the following programs will illustrate the manipulation of strings. The following program toggles the case of every character in the input string.

```c
#include <stdio.h>
#include <string.h>
int main()
{
    char istr[128];  /* input buffer */
    char tstr[128];  /* translated string here */
    int i;
    int slen;        /* string length */
    while(1)
    {
```

```
printf("Enter a string");
gets(istr);
if((slen=strlen(istr))==0)
break;          /* terminate */
strcpy(tstr,istr);               /* make a copy */
i = 0;
while(i < slen)            /* translate loop */
{
  if(tstr[i] >= 'A' && tstr[i] <= 'Z')
                                 /* upper case */
      tstr[i] += 'a'-'A';
  else if(tstr[i] >= 'a' && tstr[i] <= 'z')
                                 /* lower case */
      tstr[i] += 'A'-'a';
  i++;                     /* to next character */
}
printf("Original string = %s\n",istr);
printf("Transformed string = %s\n",tstr);
}
  return 0;
}
```

Output

```
Enter string aBDefgXYZ
Original string = aBDefgXYZ
Transformed string = AbdEFGxyz
Enter string ab   CD   123
Original string = ab   CD   123
Transformed string = AB   cd   123
```

This program can also be written as follows where '\0' character is used as a tool.

```
#include <stdio.h>
#include <string.h>
int main()
{
  char istr[128]; /* input buffer */
  char tstr[128]; /* translated string here */
  int i;
                  /* string length */
  while(1)
  {
  printf("Enter a string");
  gets(istr);
  if(strlen(istr)==0) break; /* terminate */
  strcpy(tstr,istr);          /* make a copy */
  i = 0;
  while(tstr[i]!='\0')      /* translate loop */
  {
    if(tstr[i] >= 'A' && tstr[i] <= 'Z')
                                 /* upper case */
            tstr[i] += 'a'-'A';
    else if(tstr[i] >= 'a' && tstr[i] <= 'z')
                                 /* lower case */
            tstr[i] += 'A'-'a';
    i++;                     /* to next character */
  }
```

```
printf("Original string = %s\n",istr);
printf("Transformed string = %s\n",tstr);
}
  return 0;
}
```

The following program checks whether a string given by the user is a palindrome or not. In this program, the first character s[0] and the last character s[n-1] are compared. Then the second character s[1] and the last but one character s[n-2] are compared, and so on. This process will be continued up to half the length of the string. If characters are found to be different during any comparison, then the string is not a palindrome. Else it is a palindrome.

```
#include <stdio.h>
#include <string.h>
int main()
{
  int n,i,j,chk=1;
  char s[30];
  printf("\n Enter the string:");
  scanf("%[^\n]",s);
  n=strlen(s)-1;
  for(i=0,j=n;i<n/2;i++,j--)
  if(s[i]!=s[j])
    {chk=0;
    break;}
  if(chk==1)
    printf("String is Palindrome");
  else
    printf("String is not Palindrome");
  return 0;
}
```

Here, the variable chk is used to check the result of the comparison. Alternatively, the preceding program can be implemented as follows:

```
#include <stdio.h>
#include <string.h>
int main()
{
  int n,i,j;
  char s[30],t[30];
  printf("\n Enter the string:");
  scanf("%[^\n]",s);
  n=strlen(s)-1;
  for(i=0,j=n;j>=0;i++,j--)
  t[i]=s[j];
  t[i]='\0';
  if(strcmp(s,t)==0)
      printf("String is Palindrome");
  else
      printf("String is not Palindrome");
  return 0;
}
```

In the above example, the string given by the user is reversed and is stored in another array. Then using the `strcmp()` library function, two strings are compared to test whether they are equal or not. If the outcome of `strcmp()` is 0, then the string entered by the user is a palindrome.

Sample runs:

```
(a) Enter the string : madam
    String is Palindrome
(b) Enter the string: india
    String is not Palindrome
```

The following program deletes a word of a sentence. Here, the logic used is that each word is extracted from the sentence into the string `w`. The words are separated by a space except the last word, which is terminated by the NUL character. Each word is compared with the word to be deleted. If there is a match, then that word will not be concatenated at the target string `t`, else it is.

```c
#include <stdio.h>
#include <string.h>
int main()
{
  char s[50],w[20],t[50],d[20];
  int i,j;
  printf("\n Enter the sentence: \n");
  gets(s);
  printf("\n Enter the word to be deleted:");
  scanf("%s",d);
  i=0;
  while(s[i]!='\0')
  {
    j=0;
    while(1)
    {
      if(s[i]==' '||s[i]=='\0')
      break;
      w[j++]=s[i++];
    }
    w[j]='\0';
    if(strcmp(w,d)!=0)
    {
      strcat(t,w);
      strcat(t," ");
    }
    if(s[i]!='\0')
      i++;
  }
  printf("\n After deletion the sentence is as
          follows...\n");
  puts(t);
  return 0;
}
```

Sample run:

```
Enter the sentence: Ram is a good boy
Enter the word to be deleted:good
After deletion the sentence is as follows...
Ram is a boy
```

The following program takes the name of a person as input and prints the first letters of the first name and middle name (if any), and the title as it is. For example, printing Raj Kumar Santoshi as R.K. Santoshi.

```c
#include <stdio.h>
#include <string.h>
int main()
{
  char s[50],w[20],d[20];
  int i,j;
  printf("\n Enter the full name :");
  gets(s);
  i=0;
  while(s[i]!='\0')
  {
    j=0;
    while(1)
    {
      if(s[i]==' '||s[i]=='\0')
      break;
      w[j++]=s[i++];
    }
    w[j]='\0';
    if(s[i]==' ')
    {
      printf("%c",w[0]);
      printf("%c",'.');
    }
    if(s[i]=='\0')
      printf("%s",w);
    if(s[i]!='\0')
      i++;
  }
  return 0;
}
```

The logic as applied in the previous program is used here too. Each word is extracted and the first letter of the word `w[0]` is printed. If '\0' is encountered, that word must be the title and it is printed as it is.

Check Your Progress

1. What is the index of the element 'A' in the array below?
   ```c
   char myArray[] = {'m', 'y', 'A', 'r', 'r', 'a', 'y'};
   ```
   Output 2

2. What will be the output of the following programs?
   ```c
   (a) #include <stdio.h>
       int main()
       {
         char s1[]="Oxford";
         char s2[]="University";
   ```

```c
    s1=s2;
    printf("%s",s1);
    return 0;
}
```

Output There is a compilation error that states "it cannot be a modifiable 'lvalue'" or "Incompatible types in assignment"

(b)
```c
#include <stdio.h>
#include <string.h>
int main()
{
    char p[]="string";
    char t;
    int i,j;
    for(i=0,j=strlen(p);i<j;i++)
    {
        t=p[i];
        p[i]=p[j-i];
        p[j-i]=t;
    }
    printf("%s",p);
    return 0;
}
```

Output No output

(c)
```c
#include <stdio.h>
int main()
{
    char names[5][20]={"pascal","ada","cobol","f
       ortran","perl"};
    int i;
    char *t;
    t=names[3];
    names[3]=names[4];
    names[4]=t;
    for(i=0;i<=4;i++)
    printf("%s",names[i]);
    return 0;
}
```

Output Compiler error:"Lvalue required"
                    Or
    "Incompatible types in assignment"

(d)
```c
#include <stdio.h>
int main()
{
    int i;
    char a[]="\0";
    if(printf("%s\n",a))
       printf("Ok here \n");
    else
       printf("Forget it\n");
    return 0;
}
```

Output Ok here

(e)
```c
#include <stdio.h>
int main()
{
    char p[ ]="%d\n";
    p[1] = 'c';
    printf(p,65);
    return 0;
}
```

Output A

(f)
```c
#include <stdio.h>
#include <string.h>
int main()
{
    char str1[] = {'s','o','m','e'};
    char str2[] = {'s','o','m','e','\0'};
    while(strcmp(str1,str2))
    printf("Strings are not equal\n");
    return 0;
}
```

Output
    "Strings are not equal"
    "Strings are not equal"
       . . .

(g)
```c
#include <stdio.h>
#include <ctype.h>
int main()
{
    char p[]="The Matrix Reloaded";
    int i=0;
    while(p[i])
    {
        if( !isupper(p[i]++) )
        ++i;
    }
    printf("%d", i);
    return 0;
}
```

Output 19

11.4 MULTIDIMENSIONAL ARRAYS

Arrays with more than one dimension are called multidimensional arrays. Although humans cannot easily visualize objects with more than three dimensions, representing multidimensional arrays presents no problem to computers.

11.4.1 Declaration of a Two-dimensional Array

An array of two dimensions can be declared as follows:

```c
data_type array_name[size1][size2];
```

Here, `data_type` is the name of some type of data, such as `int`. Also, `size1` and `size2` are the sizes of the array's first and second dimensions, respectively.

Here is an example of defining an eight-by-eight array of integers, similar to a chessboard. Remember, because C arrays are zero-based, the indices on each side of the chessboard array run from zero through seven, rather than one through eight. The effect is the same. However, it is a two-dimensional array of 64 elements which has the following declaration statement.

```
int arr[8][8];
```

11.4.2 Declaration of a Three-dimensional Array

A three-dimensional array, such as a cube, can be declared as follows:

```
data_type array_name[size1][size2][size3]
```

Arrays do not have to be shaped like squares and cubes; each dimension of the array can be given a different size, as follows:

```
int non_cube[2][6][8];
```

Three-dimensional arrays, and higher, are stored in the same basic way as are two-dimensional ones. They are kept in computer memory as a linear sequence of variables, and the last index is always the one that varies the fastest (then the next-to-last, and so on).

11.4.3 Initialization of a Multidimensional Array

The number of subscripts determines the *dimensionality* of an array. For example, x[i] refers to an element of a one-dimensional array, x. Similarly, y[i][j] refers to an element of a two-dimensional array, y, and so on.

Multidimensional arrays are initialized in the same way as are single-dimension arrays. For example,

```
(a) int a[6][2] = {
                    1,1,
                    2,4,
                    3,9,
                    4,16,
                    5,25,
                    6,36
                  };
(b) int b[3][5] = {{1,2,3,4,5},
                   {6,7,8,9,10},
                   {11,12,13,14,15}
                  };
```

The same effect is achieved by

```
int b[3][5]={1,2,3,4,5,6,7,8,9,10,11,12,13,14,15};
```

Although the commas in the initialization braces are always required, the inner braces can be omitted. Thus, the initialization of an array val may be written as

```
int val[3][4] = {8, 16, 9, 52,
                 3, 15, 27, 6,
                 14, 25, 2, 10};
```

The separation of initial values into rows in the declaration statement is not necessary since the compiler assigns values beginning with the [0][0] element and proceeds row by row to fill in the remaining values. Thus, the initialization

```
int val [3][4] = {8, 16, 9, 52, 3, 15, 27, 6, 14, 25,
                  2, 10};
```

is equally valid but does not clearly illustrate to another programmer where one row ends and another begins.

As illustrated in Fig. 11.3, the initialization of a two-dimensional array is done in row order. First the elements in the first row are initialized, then the elements in the second row are initialized, and so on, until the initializations are completed. This row ordering is also the same as the ordering used to store two-dimensional arrays. That is, array element [0][0] is stored first, followed by element [0][1], followed by element [0][2], and so on. Following the first row's elements is the second row's elements, and so on for all the rows in the array.

Using the following rules, braces can be omitted when initializing the members of multidimensional arrays.

• When initializing arrays, the outermost pair of braces cannot be omitted.

• If the initializer list includes all the initializers for the object being initialized, the inner braces can be omitted.

Consider the following example.

```
int x[4][2] = {
               { 1, 2 },
               { 3, 4 },
               { 5, 6 }
              };
```

Initialization starts with this element

```
val[0][0] = 8 → val[0][1] = 16 → val[0][2] = 9 → val[0][3] = 52

val[1][0] = 3 → val[1][1] = 15 → val[1][2] = 27 → val[1][3] = 6

val[2][0] = 14 → val[2][1] = 25 → val[2][2] = 2 → val[2][3] = 10
```

Fig. 11.3 Storage and initialization of the val[] array

In this example, 1 and 2 initialize the first row of the array x, and the following two lines initialize the second and third rows, respectively. The initialization ends before the fourth row is initialized, so the members of the fourth row default to 0 or garbage depending on the compiler. Here is the result.

```
x[0][0] = 1;
x[0][1] = 2;
x[1][0] = 3;
x[1][1] = 4;
x[2][0] = 5;
x[2][1] = 6;
x[3][0] = 0;
x[3][1] = 0;
```

The following declaration achieves the same result.

```
int x[4][2] = { 1, 2, 3, 4, 5, 6 };
```

Here, the compiler fills the array row by row with the available initial values. The compiler places 1 and 2 in the first row (x[0]), 3 and 4 in the second row (x[1]), and 5 and 6 in the third row (x[2]). The remaining members of the array are initialized to zero or garbage value.

11.4.4 Unsized Array Initializations

If unsized arrays are declared, the C compiler automatically creates an array big enough to hold all the initializers. This is called an unsized array. The following are examples of declarations with initialization.

(a) `char e1[] ="read error\n";`

(b) `char e2[] ="write error\n";`

(c) `int sgrs[][2] =`
```
{
  1,1,
  2,4,
  3,9,
  4,16,
};
```

11.4.5 Accessing Multidimensional Arrays

The elements of a multidimensional array are stored contiguously in a block of computer memory. In scanning this block from its start to its end, the order of storage is such that the last subscript of the array varies most rapidly whereas the first varies least rapidly. For instance, the elements of the two-dimensional array x[2][2] are stored in the order: x[0][0], x[0][1], x[1][0], x[1][1]. Take a look at the following code.

```
#include <stdio.h>
int main()
{
  int i,j;
  int a[3][2] = {{4,7},{1,0},{6,2}};
  for(i = 0; i < 3; i++)
  {
    for(j = 0; j < 2; j++)
    {
      printf("%d", a[i][j]);
```

```
    }
    printf("\n");
  }
  return 0;
}
```

Since computer memory is essentially one-dimensional with memory locations running straight from 0 up through the highest, a multidimensional array cannot be stored in memory as a grid. Instead, the array is dissected and stored in rows. Consider the following two-dimensional array.

Row 0	1	2	3
Row 1	4	5	6
Row 2	7	8	9

Note that the numbers inside the boxes are not the actual indices of the array, which is two-dimensional and has two indices for each element, but only arbitrary placeholders to enable the reader to see which elements correspond in the following example. The row numbers correspond to the first index of the array, so they are numbered from 0 to 2 rather than 1 to 3.

In the computer, the above array actually 'looks' like this.

1	2	3	4	5	6	7	8	9
row 0			row 1			row 2		

Another way of saying that arrays are stored by rows and that the second index varies fastest, a two-dimensional array is always thought of as follows:

```
array_name[row][column]
```

Every row stored will contain elements of many columns. The column index runs from 0 to [size - 1] inside every row in the one-dimensional representation where size is the number of columns in the array. So the column index changes faster than the row index as the one-dimensional representation of the array inside the computer is traversed.

To illustrate the use of multidimensional arrays, the elements of the array a2 might be filled in or initialized using this piece of code.

```
int i, j;
for(i = 0; i < 5; i = i + 1)
{
  for(j = 0; j < 7; j = j + 1)
    a2[i][j] = 10 * i + j;
}
```

This pair of nested loops sets a[1][2] to 12, a[4][1] to 41, etc. Since the first dimension of a2 is 5, the first subscripting index variable, i, runs from 0 to 4. Similarly, the second subscript varies from 0 to 6.

The array a2 could be printed out in a two-dimensional way suggesting its structure, with a similar pair of nested loops.

```
for(i = 0; i < 5; i = i + 1)
{
  for(j = 0; j < 7; j = j + 1)
  printf("%d\t", a2[i][j]);
  printf("\n");
}
```

The character \t in the printf() string is the tab character, which is itself an escape sequence or control code. To understand this more clearly, the 'row' and 'column' subscripts could be made explicit by printing them too. So, the following code could be used.

```
for(j = 0; j < 7; j = j + 1)
  printf("\t%d:", j);
printf("\n");
for(i = 0; i < 5; i = i + 1)
{
  printf("%d:", i);
  for(j = 0; j < 7; j = j + 1)
        printf("\t%d", a2[i][j]);
  printf("\n");
}
```

This last fragment would print

```
      0:   1:   2:   3:   4:   5:   6:
0:    0    1    2    3    4    5    6
1:   10   11   12   13   14   15   16
2:   20   21   22   23   24   25   26
3:   30   31   32   33   34   35   36
4:   40   41   42   43   44   45   46
```

Finally, there is no reason to loop over the rows first and the columns second; depending on what the user wanted to do, the two loops could be interchanged, as follows.

```
for(j = 0; j < 7; j = j + 1)
{
  for(i = 0; i < 5; i = i + 1)
        printf("%d\t", a2[i][j]);
  printf("\n");
}
```

Notice that i is still the first subscript and it still runs from 0 to 4, and j is still the second subscript and it still runs from 0 to 6.

It will be found that the program still runs without any problems. This is because a multidimensional array is implemented as a big, single-dimensional array. When an element of the array is referenced, the two indices used are modified into a single index for the array.

11.4.6 Working with Two-dimensional Arrays

The most important application of the two-dimensional array is with a matrix. A matrix is defined as an ordered rectangular array of numbers. They can be used to represent systems of linear equations.

Transpose of a matrix

The transpose of a matrix is found by exchanging rows for columns, i.e., for

$$\text{Matrix } A = (a_{ij})$$

the transpose of A is $A^T=(a_{ji})$, where i is the row number and j is the column number.

For example, the transpose of a matrix A would be given by

$$A = \begin{pmatrix} 5 & 2 & 3 \\ 4 & 7 & 1 \\ 8 & 9 & 9 \end{pmatrix} \quad A^T = \begin{pmatrix} 5 & 4 & 8 \\ 2 & 7 & 9 \\ 3 & 1 & 9 \end{pmatrix}$$

In the case of a square matrix ($m = n$), the transpose can be used to check if a matrix is symmetric. For a symmetric matrix, $A = A^T$.

$$A = \begin{pmatrix} 1 & 2 \\ 2 & 3 \end{pmatrix} \quad A^T = \begin{pmatrix} 1 & 2 \\ 2 & 3 \end{pmatrix} = A$$

The following program finds the transpose of a matrix.

```
#include <stdio.h>
int main()
{
  int row,col;
  int i, j, value;
  int mat[10][10], transp[10][10];
  printf("\n Input the number of rows:");
  scanf("%d", &row);
  printf("Input number of cols:");
  scanf("%d", &col);
  for(i = 0 ; i < row; i++)
    for(j = 0 ; j < col; j++)
    {
      printf("Input Value for : %d: %d:", i+1,j+1);
      scanf("%d", &value);
      mat[i][j] = value;
    }
  printf("\n Entered Matrix is as follows:\n");
  for(i = 0; i < row; i++)
  {
    for(j = 0; j < col; j++)
        printf("%d", mat[i][j]);
    printf("\n");
  }
  for(i = 0; i< row; i++)
  {
    for(j = 0; j < col; j++)
    {
      transp[i][j]= mat[j][i];
```

```
      }
   }
   printf("\n Transpose of the matrix is as\
         follows:\n");
   for(i = 0; i < col; i++)
   {
      for(j = 0; j < row; j++)
      {
         printf("%d", transp[i][j]);
      }
      printf("\n");
   }
   return 0;
}
```

In the above example, it should be remembered that the number of both rows and columns must be less than or equal to 10.

Matrix addition and subtraction

Two matrices A and B can be added or subtracted if and only if their dimensions are the same, i.e., both matrices have an identical amount of rows and columns. Take the matrices,

$$A = \begin{pmatrix} 1 & 2 & 3 \\ 1 & 0 & 2 \end{pmatrix} \quad B = \begin{pmatrix} 2 & 1 & 2 \\ 1 & 0 & 3 \end{pmatrix}$$

Addition If A and B above are matrices of the same type, then their sum is found by adding the corresponding elements $a_{ij} + b_{ij}$.

Here is an example of adding A and B together.

$$A + B = \begin{pmatrix} 1 & 2 & 3 \\ 1 & 0 & 2 \end{pmatrix} + \begin{pmatrix} 2 & 1 & 2 \\ 1 & 0 & 3 \end{pmatrix} = \begin{pmatrix} 3 & 3 & 5 \\ 2 & 0 & 5 \end{pmatrix}$$

Subtraction If A and B are matrices of the same type, then their difference is found by subtracting the corresponding elements $a_{ij} - b_{ij}$.

Here is an example of subtracting matrices.

$$A - B = \begin{pmatrix} 1 & 2 & 3 \\ 1 & 0 & 2 \end{pmatrix} - \begin{pmatrix} 2 & 1 & 2 \\ 1 & 0 & 3 \end{pmatrix} = \begin{pmatrix} -1 & 1 & 1 \\ 0 & 0 & -1 \end{pmatrix}$$

The following program pertains to matrix addition.

```
#include <stdio.h>
#include <stdlib.h>
#define row 10
#define col 10
int main()
{
   int row1, col1;
   int row2, col2;
   int i,j;
   float mat1[row][col];
   float mat2[row][col];
   float mat_res[row][col];
```

```
   printf("\n Input the row of the matrix->1:");
   scanf("%d", &row1);
   printf("\n Input the col of the matrix->1:");
   scanf("%d", &col1);
   printf("\n Input data for matrix-> 1\n");
   for(i = 0; i< row1; i++)
   {
      for(j = 0; j<col1; j++)
      {
         printf("Input Value for: %d: %d:", i+1, j+1);
         scanf("%f", &mat1[i][j]);
      }
   }
   printf("\n Input the row of the matrix ->2:");
   scanf("%d", &row2);
   printf("\n Input the col of the matrix->2:");
   scanf("%d", &col2);
   printf("\n Input data for matrix-> 2\n");
   for(i = 0; i< row2; i++)
   {
      for(j = 0; j<col2; j++)
      {
         printf("Input Value for: %d: %d:", i+1, j+1);
         scanf("%f", &mat2[i][j]);
      }
   }
   printf("\n Entered Matrix First is:\n");
   for(i = 0; i < row1; i++)
   {
      for(j = 0; j < col1; j++)
      {
         printf("%f", mat1[i][j]);
      }
      printf("\n");
   }
   printf("\n Entered Matrix Two is:\n");
   for(i = 0; i < row2; i++)
   {
      for(j = 0; j < col2; j++)
         printf("%f", mat2[i][j]);
      printf("\n");
   }
   if((row1 == row2) && (col1 == col2))
   {
      printf("\n Addition is possible and");
      printf("the result is: \n");
      for(i = 0; i<row1; i++)
      for(j = 0; j<col1; j++)
      mat_res[i][j] = mat1[i][j]+mat2[i][j];
      for( i = 0; i < row1; i++)
      {
         for( j = 0; j < col1; j++)
            printf("%f", mat_res[i][j]);
```

```
        printf("\n");
    }
}
else
printf("\n Addition is not possible");
return 0;
}
```

Matrix subtraction can be implemented in a similar way.

Matrix multiplication

When the number of columns of the first matrix is the same as the number of rows in the second matrix, then matrix multiplication can be performed.

Here is an example of matrix multiplication for two 2×2 matrices.

$$\begin{pmatrix} a & b \\ c & d \end{pmatrix} \begin{pmatrix} e & f \\ g & h \end{pmatrix} = \begin{pmatrix} (ae+bg) & (af+bh) \\ (ce+dg) & (ef+dh) \end{pmatrix}$$

Here is an example of matrix multiplication for a 3×3 matrix.

$$\begin{pmatrix} a & b & c \\ d & e & f \\ g & h & i \end{pmatrix} \begin{pmatrix} j & k & l \\ m & n & o \\ p & q & r \end{pmatrix}$$

$$= \begin{pmatrix} (aj+bm+cp) & (ak+bn+cq) & (al+bo+cr) \\ (dj+em+fp) & (dk+en+fq) & (dl+eo+fr) \\ (gj+hm+ip) & (gk+hn+iq) & (gl+ho+ir) \end{pmatrix}$$

Now let us look at the $n \times n$ matrix case, where A has dimensions $m \times n$ and B has dimensions $n \times p$. The product of A and B is the matrix C, which has dimensions $m \times p$. The ijth element of matrix C is found by multiplying the entries of the ith row of A with the corresponding entries in the jth column of B and summing the n terms. The elements of matrix C are

$$c_{11} = a_{11}b_{11} + a_{12}b_{21} + \ldots + a_{1n}b_{n1}$$
$$c_{12} = a_{11}b_{12} + a_{12}b_{22} + \ldots + a_{1n}b_{n2}$$
$$c_{mp} = a_{m1}b_{1p} + a_{m2}b_{2p} + \ldots + a_{mn}b_{np}$$

Note $A \times B$ is not the same as $B \times A$.

```c
#include <stdio.h>
#include <stdlib.h>
#define row 10
#define col 10
int main()
{
    int row1, col1;
    int row2, col2;
    int i,j,k;
    float mat1[row][col];
    float mat2[row][col];
    float mat_res[row][col];
```

```c
    printf("\n Input the row of the matrix->1:");
    scanf("%d", &row1);
    printf("\n Input the col of the matrix->1:");
    scanf("%d", &col1);
    printf("\n Input data for matrix-> 1\n");
    for(i = 0 ; i< row1; i++)
    {
        for(j = 0 ; j<col1; j++)
        {
            printf("Input Value for: %d: %d:", i+1, j+1);
            scanf("%f", &mat1[i][j]);
        }
    }
    printf("\n Input the row  of the matrix->2:");
    scanf("%d", &row2);
    printf("\n Input the col of the matrix ->2:");
    scanf("%d", &col2);
    printf("\n Input data for matrix-> 2\n");
    for(i = 0 ; i< row2; i++)
    {
        for(j = 0 ; j<col2; j++)
        {
            printf("Input Value for: %d: %d:", i+1, j+1);
            scanf("%f", &mat2[i][j]);
        }
    }
    printf("\n Entered Matrix First is:\n");
    for(i = 0; i < row1; i++)
    {
        for(j = 0; j < col1; j++)
            printf("%f", mat1[i][j]);
        printf("\n");
    }
    printf("\n Entered Matrix Two is: \n");
    for(i = 0; i < row2; i++)
    {
        for(j = 0; j < col2; j++)
            printf("%f", mat2[i][j]);
        printf("\n");
    }
    if(col1 == row2)
    {
        printf("\n Multiplication is possible and the
                Result is as follows\n");
        for(i=0; i<row1; i++)
        for(j=0; j<col2; j++)
        {
            mat_res[i][j] = 0;
            for(k = 0; k < col1; k++)
                mat_res[i][j] += mat1[i][k] * mat2[k][j];
        }
```

```
    for(i = 0; i < row1; i++)
    {
        for(j = 0; j < col2; j++)
                printf("%f", mat_res[i][j]);
        printf("\n");
    }
}
else
printf("\n Multiplication is not possible");
return 0;
}
```

Finding norm of a matrix

The norm of a matrix is defined as the square root of the sum of the squares of the elements of a matrix.

```
#include <stdio.h>
#include <math.h>
#define row 10
#define col 10
int main()
{
    float mat[row][col], s;
    int i,j,r,c;
    printf("\n Input number of rows:");
    scanf("%d", &r);
    printf("\n Input number of cols:");
    scanf("%d", &c);
    for(i = 0 ; i< r; i++)
        for(j = 0 ;j<c; j++)
        {
            printf("\nInput Value for: %d: %d:", i+1, j+1);
            scanf("%f", &mat[i][j]);
        }
    printf("\n Entered 2D array is as follows:\n");
    for(i = 0; i < r; i++)
    {
        for(j = 0; j < c; j++)
        {
            printf("%f", mat[i][j]);
        }
        printf("\n");
    }
    s = 0.0;
    for(i = 0; i < r; i++)
    {
        for(j = 0; j < c; j++)
        {
            s += mat[i][j] * mat[i][j];
        }
    }
    printf("\n Norm of above matrix is: %f", sqrt(s));
    return 0;
}
```

Note

- Multidimensional arrays are kept in computer memory as a linear sequence of variables.
- The elements of a multidimensional array are stored contiguously in a block of computer memory.
- The number of subscripts determines the *dimensionality* of an array.
- The separation of initial values into rows in the declaration statement is not necessary.
- If unsized arrays are declared, the C compiler automatically creates an array big enough to hold all the initializers.

11.5 ARRAY OF STRINGS: TWO-DIMENSIONAL CHARACTER ARRAY

A two-dimensional array of strings can be declared as follows:

```
<data_type> <string_array_name>[<row_size>]
        [<columns_size>];
```

Consider the following example on declaration of a two-dimensional array of strings.

```
char s[5][30];
```

11.5.1 Initialization

Two-dimensional string arrays can be initialized as shown

```
char s[5][10] ={"Cow","Goat","Ram","Dog","Cat"};
```

which is equivalent to

s[0]	C	o	w	\0					
S[1]	G	o	a	t	\0				
S[2]	R	a	m	\0					
S[3]	D	o	g	\0					
S[4]	C	a	t	\0					

Here every row is a string. This mean that, s[i] is a string. Note that the following declarations are invalid.

```
char s[5][] ={"Cow","Goat","Ram","Dog","Cat"};
char s[][] ={"Cow","Goat","Ram","Dog","Cat"};
```

11.5.2 Manipulating String Arrays

The following program demonstrates how an individual string of an array of strings can be used to take input from the user. As mentioned before, each row (i.e., s[i], if 's' is the array of strings) of an array of strings is a string.

```
#include <stdio.h>
int main()
```

```
{
  int i;
  char s[10][30], t[30];
  for(i=0;i<10;i++)
    scanf("%s",s[i]);
    for(i=0;i<10;i++)
      printf("\n%s",s[i]);
  return 0;
}
```

The following codes show how arrays of strings may be manipulated. This program checks whether a number is odd or even without using any control statement.

```
#include <stdio.h>
int main()
{
  char s[2][5]={"EVEN","ODD"};
  int n;
  printf("\n enter the number:");
  scanf("%d",&n);
  printf("\n The number is %s",s[n%2]);
  return 0;
}
```

The following program accepts one line of text and prints the words in reverse order. For example, if input is 'Today is Tuesday', then output will be 'Tuesday is Today'.

```
#include <stdio.h>
#include <string.h>
int main()
{
  char st[25][30],s[80],w[20],d[20];
  int i,j, k=0;
  printf("\n Enter the Sentence :");
  gets(s);
  i=0;
  while(s[i]!='\0')
  {
    j=0;
    while(1)
    {
      if(s[i]==' '||s[i]=='\0')
```

```
      break;
      w[j++]=s[i++];
    }
    w[j]='\0';
    strcpy(st[k],w);
    k++;
    if(s[i]!='\0')
    i++;
  }
  for(k--;k>=0;k--)
  printf("%s",st[k]);
  return 0;
}
```

The following program sorts an array of strings using bubble sort. Note here that strcmp() is used to compare the string. strcpy() is used for interchanging the strings.

```
#include <stdio.h>
#include <string.h>
int main()
{
  char s[10][30], t[30];
  int i,j,n;
  printf("\n how many strings:");
  scanf("%d",&n);
  printf("\n enter the strings:\n");
  for(i=0;i<n;i++)
    scanf("%s",s[i]);
  printf("\n **starting comparing and sorting**");
  for(i=0;i<n-1;i++)
    for(j=i+1; j<n; ++j)
      if(strcmp(s[i],s[j])>0)
      {
        strcpy(t,s[i]);
        strcpy(s[i],s[j]);
        strcpy(s[j],t);
      }
  printf("\n **sorted array**\n");
  for(i=0;i<n;i++)
    printf("\n%s",s[i]);
  return 0;
}
```

SUMMARY

An array is a collection of individual data elements that are *ordered, fixed in size,* and *homogeneous*. When defining an array in a program, three things need to be specified: the *kind of data* it can hold, *the number of values* it can hold, and its *name*.

A one-dimensional array declaration is a *type* followed by an *array name* with a bracketed constant integral expression. The value of the expression, which must be positive, is the *size* of the array. It specifies the number of elements in the array.

The array subscripts (index) can range from 0 to (*size*–1). The lower bound of the array subscripts is 0 and the upper bound is (*size* –1). An element can be referenced by the array name and index. At the time of declaration, the size of the array has to be given; it is mandatory. Otherwise the compiler generates an error. No variables are allowed as the size of the array.

C never checks whether the array index is valid—either at compile time or when the program is running. Array elements are initialized using the assignment operator, braces, and commas. Single operations, which involve entire arrays, are not permitted in C.

Strings are an array of characters terminated by '\0'. Character arrays or strings allow a shorthand initialization. Although C does not have a string data type, it allows string constants. There are a set of input and output functions in C suitable for handling strings. The manipulation of strings can be carried out with the help of several functions provided in the `string.h` file. Arrays can also be formed with strings. These are categorized as two-dimensional arrays.

Arrays with more than one dimension are called multidimensional arrays. An array of two dimensions can be declared by specifying the data type, array name, and the size of the rows and columns.

KEY TERMS

Aggregate data type   It is an agglomeration of data, of any data type, that is identified with a single name and can be decomposed and related by some defined structure.

Array identifier   It is the name assigned to an array.

Array initialization   It is the procedure of assigning value to each element of an array.

Array of strings   It is an array that contains strings as its elements.

Array   It is a collection of individual data elements that is ordered, fixed in size, and homogeneous.

Concatenation of strings   It is a kind of string manipulation where one string is appended to another string.

Homogeneous data   Data of same kind or same data type is called homogeneous data.

Index of an array   It is an integer constant or variable ranging from 0 to (size − 1).

Library functions   Pre-written functions, provided with the C compiler, which can be attached to user written programs to carry out some task are called library functions.

Multidimensional array   It is an array that is represented by a name and more than one index or subscript.

One-dimensional array   It is an array that is represented by a name and a single index or subscript.

Scalar variable   It is a single variable whose stored value is an atomic data type.

Scanset   It is a conversion specifier that allows the programmer to specify the set of characters that are (or are not) acceptable as part of the string.

Size of array   It is the number of elements in an array.

Stderr   The side stream of output characters for errors is called standard-error.

stdin   It is standard input stream that is used to receive and hold input data from standard input device.

Stdout   It is standard output stream that is used to hold and transfer output data to standard output device.

String compare   A kind of string manipulation where two strings are compared to primarily find out whether they are similar or not.

String copy   A kind of string manipulation where one string is copied into another.

String manipulation   Carrying out various operations like comparing, appending, copying, etc. among strings is called string manipulation.

String   It is a one-dimensional array of characters that contain a NUL at the end.

FREQUENTLY ASKED QUESTIONS

1. Why is it necessary to give the size of an array in an array declaration?

When an array is declared, the compiler allocates contiguous memory for all the elements of the array. The size must be known to allocate the required space at compile time. Thus, the size must be specified.

2. Why do array subscripts start at 0 instead of 1?

It can make array subscripting somewhat faster. Two facts are known about an array. First, an array name say `arr` always designates the base address of the array. Second, address of ith element of `arr` is given by `&arr[i]`, which is eventually `(arr + i)`. The base address is the address of the first element which is the address of the first element `&a[0]`. This means that both `arr` and `&a[0]` hold the same value which is the address of the first element of the array. To carry the expression `(arr+i)`, same equivalence for all the elements of the array, the subscript of the first element must be 0. Having the subscript to start at 0 simplifies scaling a bit for the compiler.

3. Why do we have a null character ('\0' or NUL) at the end of a string?

A string is not a data type but a data structure. This means that its implementation is logical not physical. The physical data structure is the array in which string is stored. Since string, by definition, is a variable length structure, it is needed to identify the logical end of the data within the physical structure.

4. If a string `str` contains a string literal "Oxford University Press", then is it legal to print the string using the statement `printf(str);`?

Yes. It prints Oxford University Press on the screen.

EXERCISES

1. What is an array? What type and range must an array subscript have?
2. What does the array name signify?
3. Can array indexes be negative?
4. Illustrate the initialization of one-dimensional arrays, two-dimensional arrays, and strings.
5. Demonstrate the storage of two-dimensional arrays in memory with the help of a diagram.
6. Write a program to find the inverse of a square matrix.
7. Write a program to find the determinant of a matrix.
8. What is null character?
9. What is the difference between `strcat()` and `strncat()`?
10. Write the characteristics of array in C.
11. In what way does an array differ from an ordinary variable?
12. Take input from the user in a two-dimensional array and print the row-wise and column-wise sum of numbers stored in a two-dimensional array.
13. What is the difference between `scanf()` with `%s` and `gets()`?
14. What is the difference between character array and string?
15. Write C programs for the following.
    (a) Store a list of integer numbers in an array and print the following:
        (i) the maximum value
        (ii) the minimum value
        (iii) the range
            Hint: This is computed as maximum-minimum.
        (iv) the average value
            Hint: To compute this, add all the numbers together into Sum and count them all in Count. The average is Sum/Count.
    (b) Swap the kth and (k+1)th elements in an integer array. k is given by the user.
    (c) Find the binary equivalent of an integer number using array.
    (d) Find similar elements in an array and compute the number of times they occur.
    (e) Find the intersection of two sets of numbers.
    (f) Enter *n* numbers and store in an array and rearrange the array in the reverse order.
    (g) Sort the numbers stored in an array in descending order.
    (h) Arrange the numbers stored in an array in such a way that the array will have the odd numbers followed by the even numbers.
    (i) Find the frequency of digits in a set of numbers.
    (j) Remove duplicates from an array.
    (k) Merge two sorted arrays into another array in a sorted order.
    (l) Compare two arrays containing two sets of numbers.
    (m) Rearrange an array in reverse order without using a second array.

16. Write a C program to read a text and count all the occurrences of a particular letter given by the user.
17. Write a C program that will capitalize all the letters of a string.
18. Write a C program to check whether a string given by the user is a palindrome or not.
19. Write a C program that counts the total numbers of vowels and their frequency.
20. Write a C program to remove the white spaces (blank spaces) from a string.
21. Write a C program to print a sub-string within a string.
22. Write a C program that will read a word and rewrite it in alphabetical order.
23. Write a C program that deletes a word from a sentence. Note that the word may appear any number of times.
24. Write a C program that will analyze a line of text and will print the number of words, the number of consonants, and the number of vowels in the text.
25. Write a C program to find a string within a sentence and replace it with another string.
26. Write a C program that will insert a word before a particular word of a sentence.
27. Write a C program that takes the name of a person as input and prints the name in an abbreviated form, e.g., Manas Ghosh as M.G.
28. Write a C program that reads in a string such as '20C' or '15F' and outputs the temperature to the nearest degree using the other scale.
29. Write a C program that takes the name of a person as input and prints the first letter of the first name and middle name (if any), and the title as it is, e.g., Raj Kumar Santoshi as R.K. Santoshi.
30. Write a C program that reads a line of text and counts all occurrences of a particular word.
31. Write a program to convert each character of a string into the next alphabet and print the string.
32. Write a program that accepts a word from the user and prints it in the following way.

    For example, if the word is COMPUTER, the program will print it as

    C
    C O
    C O M
    C O M P
    C O M P U
    C O M P U T
    C O M P U T E
    C O M P U T E R

PROJECT QUESTIONS

1. Write a program that performs the following. The user inputs a number and then enters a series of numbers from 1 to that number. Your program should determine which number (or numbers) is missing or duplicated in the series, if any. For example, if the user entered 5 as the initial number and then entered the following sequences, the results should be as shown.

```
Input Sequence      Output
-----------------   ---------------
  1 2 3 4 5         Nothing bad
```

However, if 7 were the highest number, the user would see the results on the right for the following number entries:

```
Input Sequence      Output
-----------------   ---------------
  1 3 2 4 5         Missing 6
                    Missing 7
```

If 10 were the highest number and the user entered the numbers shown on the left, note the list of missing and duplicate numbers:

```
Input Sequence              Output
---------------------       ---------------
1 2 4 7 4 4 5 10 8 2 6     Duplicate 2 (2 times)
                           Missing 3
                           Duplicate 4 (3 times)
                           Missing 9
```

The program should check the highest number that the user inputs to ensure that it does not exceed the size of any array you might be using for storage.

2. Given an array of integers, find the subarray with the largest sum.

Functions

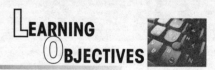

LEARNING
OBJECTIVES

After studying this chapter, the readers will be able to

- discuss a function and how its use benefits a program
- explain how a function declaration, function call, and function definition are constructed
- discuss how variables and arrays are passed to functions
- explain what scope rules mean in functions and blocks

- and learn about global and local variables
- discuss about storage class specifiers for variables
- highlight the basic concepts of recursion and discuss the technique of constructing recursive functions

12.1 INTRODUCTION

Software engineering is a discipline that is concerned with the construction of robust and reliable computer programs. Just as civil engineers use tried and tested methods for the construction of buildings, software engineers use accepted methods for analysing a problem to be solved, a blueprint or plan for the design of the solution and a construction method that minimises the risk of error. The discipline has evolved as the use of computers has spread. In particular, it has tackled issues that have arisen as a result of some catastrophic failures of software projects involving teams of programmers writing thousands of lines of program code. Just as civil engineers have learnt from their failures, so have software engineers.

One of the most important barriers to the development of better computer software is the limited ability of human

beings to understand the programs that they write. To design a program, we often use some method of software engineering. Each approach to software engineering divides the required task into sub-tasks, modules, sub-systems or processes of various types. Functions are a natural way of implementing such designs in C.

A particular method or family of methods that a software engineer might use to solve a problem is known as *methodology*. During the 1970s and the 80s, the primary software engineering methodology was *structured programming*. Dijkstra introduced the term structured programming to refer to a set of principles (e.g. sequence, selection or branching, iteration or looping etc.) for writing well-organized programs that could be more easily shown to be correct. Structured programming is a style of programming designed to make programs more comprehensible and programming errors less frequent. Other computer scientists added further principles, such as *modularization* (breaking down a program into separate procedures, such as for data input, different stages of processing, and output or printing). Modularization makes it easier to figure out which part of a program may be causing a problem, and to fix part of a problem without affecting other parts. It enables programmers to break problems into small and easily understood components that eventually will comprise a complete system.

The structured programming approach to program design was based on the following methods:

- Solving a large problem, by breaking it into several pieces and working on each piece separately
- Solving each piece by treating it as a new problem that can itself be broken down into smaller problems
- Repeating the process with each new piece until each can be solved directly, without further decomposition

Structured programming also encourages stepwise refinement, a program design process described by Niklaus Wirth, creator of Pascal. This is a *top-down approach* in which the stages of processing are first described in high-level terms (like pseudocode), and then gradually elaborated in their details. That is, the planning activities of problem solving are carried out in the direction from general to specific. Structured programming refers to the implementation of the resulting design. It requires planning and organization, but a good design will often save much time when it comes to actual implementation, and the resulting code will be more elegant and readable. Functions form an important part of top-down design and structured programming. Using functions removes the need to repeat identical groups of statements within programs when the same task must be performed several times. Also, the use of functions allows libraries of frequently used software to be built up and re-used in different programs thus allowing the creation of compact and efficient programs.

12.2 CONCEPT OF FUNCTION

A *function* is a self-contained block of program statements that performs a particular task. It is often defined as a section of a program performing a specific job. In fact, the concept of functions, which were originally a subset of a concept called subroutine, came up because of the following deliberation.

Imagine a program wherein a set of operations has to be repeated often, though not continuously, *n* times or so. If they had to be repeated continuously, loops could be used. Instead of inserting the program statements for these operations at so many places, write a separate program segment and compile it separately. As many times as it is needed, keep 'calling' the segment to get the result. The separate program segment

is called a function and the program that calls it is called the 'main program'.

C went one step further; it divided the entire concept of programming to a combination of functions. C has no procedures, only functions. scanf(), printf(), main(), etc. that have been used in programs so far, are all functions. C provides a lot of library functions; in addition, the programmers can write their own functions and use them. The special function called main() is where program execution begins. When a function is called upon, with or without handing over of some input data, it returns information to the main program or calling function from where it was called.

12.2.1 Why are Functions Needed?

The use of functions provides several benefits.

- First, it makes programs significantly easier to understand and maintain by breaking up a program into easily manageable chunks. Even without software engineering, functions allow the structure of the program to reflect the structure of its application.
- Second, the main program can consist of a series of function calls rather than countless lines of code. It can be executed as many times as necessary from different points in the main program. Without the ability to package a block of code into a function, programs would end up being much larger, since one would typically need to replicate the same code at various points in them.
- The third benefit is that well-written functions may be reused in multiple programs. The C standard library is an example of the reuse of functions. This enables code sharing.
- Fourth, functions can be used to protect data. This is related with the concept of local data. Local data is the data described within a function. They are available only within a function when the function is being executed.
- Fifth, by using functions different programmers working on one large project can divide the workload by writing different functions.

12.3 USING FUNCTIONS

Referring back to the Introduction, all C programs contain at least one function, called main() where execution starts. Returning from this function, the program execution terminates and the returned value is treated as an indication of success or failure of program execution.

When a function is called, the code contained in that function is executed, and when the function has finished executing, control returns to the point at which that function was called. The program steps through the statements in sequence in the normal way until it comes across a call to a particular function. At that point, execution moves to the start of that function—

that is, the first statement in the body of the function. Execution of the program continues through the function statements until it hits a return statement or reaches the closing brace marking the end of the function body. This signals that execution should go back to the point immediately after where the function was originally called.

Functions are used by *calling* them from other functions. When a function is used, it is referred to as the '*called function*'. Such functions often use data that is passed to them from the calling function. Parameters provide the means by which you pass information from the calling function into the called function. Only after the called function successfully receives the data, can the data be manipulated to produce a useful result.

12.3.1 Function Prototype Declaration

All the header files contain declarations for a range of functions, as well as definitions for various constants. In a C program, a user-written function should normally be declared prior to its use to allow the compiler to perform type checking on the arguments used in its call statement or calling construct. The general form of this function declaration statement is as follows:

```
return_data_type function_name (data_type variable1,
...);
```
or
```
return_data_type function_name (data_type_list);
```

There are three basic parts in this declaration.

function_name This is the name given to the function and it follows the same naming rules as that for any valid variable in C.

return_data_type This specifies the type of data given back to the calling construct by the function after it executes its specific task.

data_type_list This list specifies the data type of each of the variables, the values of which are expected to be transmitted by the calling construct to the function.

The following are some examples of declaration statements.

(a) `float FtoC(float faren);`

(b) `double power(double, int);`

(c) `int isPrime(int);`

(d) `void printMessage(void);`

(e) `void fibo_series(int);`

A function has a name that both identifies it and is used to call it for execution in a program. The name of a function is global. Functions which perform different actions should generally have different names. The names are generally created to indicate the particular job that the function does, as is seen in examples (a) to (e).

There are two ways for prototyping functions. The most common method is simply to write the function declaration with the arguments typed, with or without identifiers for each, such as example (a) can be written as either of the following:

```
float FtoC(float);
float FtoC(float faren);
```

The ANSI standard does not require variable names for the prototype declaration parameters. In fact, readability and understandability are improved if names are used.

In modern properly written C programs, all functions must be declared before they are used. This is normally accomplished using a function prototype. Function prototypes were not part of the original C language, but were added by C89. Although prototypes are not technically required, their use is strongly encouraged.

If there are no parameters to a function, you can specify the parameter list as void, as you have been doing in the case of the main() function. Actually, when a function takes no parameters, the inclusion of the word void inside the parentheses is optional, since it is the default. When a function returns no value, however, it is required to include void as the function type, since the default is int. If you are writing a function that returns an int, technically speaking you could leave out the type and you should always include it.

> **Note**
> - The name of a function is global.
> - It should not be forgotten that a semicolon is required at the end of a function prototype. Without it, the compiler will give an error message. Moreover, no function can be defined in another function body.
> - If the number of arguments does not agree with the number of parameters specified in the prototype, the behavior is undefined.
> - The function return type cannot be an array or a function type. These two cases must be handled by returning pointers to the array or function.

12.3.2 Function Definition

The collection of program statements in C that describes the specific task done by the function is called a function definition. It consists of the *function header* and a *function body*, which is a block of code enclosed in parentheses. The definition creates the actual function in memory. The general form of the function definition is as follows:

```
return_data_type function name(data_type variable1,
data_type variable2,……)
{
    /* Function Body */
}
```

The *function header* in this definition is

```
return_data_type function name(data_type variable1,
data_type variable2,……)
```

and the portion of program code within the braces is the *function body*. Notice that the function header is similar to the function declaration, but does not require the semicolon at the end. The list of variables in the function header is also referred to as the *formal parameters*.

One point to be noted here is that the names do not need to be the same in the prototype declaration and the function definition. If the types are not the same then the compiler will generate an error. The compiler checks the types in the prototype statements with the types in the call to ensure that they are the same or at least compatible.

A value of the indicated data type is returned to the calling function when the function is executed. The return data type can be of any legal type. If the function does not return a value, the return type is specified by the keyword void. The keyword void is also used to indicate the absence of parameters. So, a function that has no parameters and does not return a value would have the following header.

```
void function_name(void)
```

A function with a return type specified as void should not be used in an expression in the calling function. Since it does not return a value, it cannot sensibly be part of an expression. Therefore, using it in this way will cause the compiler to generate an error message.

There is no standard guideline about the number of parameters that a function can have. Every ANSI C compliant compiler is required to support at least 31 parameters in a function. However, it is considered bad programming style if a function contains an inordinately high (eight or more) number of parameters. The number of parameters a function has also directly affects the speed at which it is called—the more parameters, the slower the function call. Therefore, if possible, one should minimize the number of parameters to be used in a function.

The statements in the function body, following the function header, perform the desired computation in a function. To understand this, consider the following examples.

EXAMPLE

1. Write a function that computes x^n, where x is any valid number and n an integer value.

```
/***********************************************/
/* Function to compute integral powers of any valid
number. First argument is any valid number, second
argument is power index.*/
/***********************************************/

double power(double x, int n)
                              /* function header */
{
                  /* function body starts here... */
    double result = 1.0;
            /* declaration of variable result */
    for(int i = 1; i<=n; i++)
                                    /* computing x^n */
        result *= x;
                        /*       :       */
    return result;
              /* return value in 'result' to
                              calling function*/
}
              /* function body ends here...      */
```

In Example 1, the first statement in the function body declares a variable result that is initialized with the value 1.0. The variable result is local to the function, as are all automatic variables declared within a function body. This means that the variable result ceases to exist after the function has completed execution.

The calculation is performed in the for loop. A loop control variable i is declared in the for loop which will assume successive values from 1 to n. The variable result is multiplied by x once for each loop iteration. Thus, this occurs n times to generate the required value. If n is 0, the statement in the loop will not be executed at all because the loop continuation condition will immediately fail, and so result will be 1.0.

EXAMPLE

2. Function for converting a temperature from Fahrenheit scale to Celsius scale.

```
float FtoC(float faren) /*function header */
{              /* function body starts here…….*/
    float factor = 5.0/9.0;
    float freezing = 32.0;
    float celsius;
    celsius = factor *(faren - freezing);
    return celsius;
}           /* function body ends here……. */
```

Again, refer to Example 2. Here, several variables have been declared within the function FtoC().They are declared just like any other variable. They are called automatic local variables, because: first, they are local: their effect is limited to the function and second, they are automatic since they are automatically created whenever the function is called. Also, their value can be accessed only inside the function, not from any other function; some authors also use "auto" to indicate that they are automatically created.

The scope of variables declared within a function is limited to its use in the function only. Any change made to these variables, internally in the function, is made only to the local copies of the variables. Such variables are created at the point at which they are defined and cease to exist at the end of the block containing them. There is one type of variables that is an exception to this—those declared as static. Static variables will be discussed later in this chapter.

return statement

The general form of the return statement is as follows:

```
return expression;
```

or

```
return(expression);
```

where expression must evaluate to a value of the type specified in the function header for the return value. The expression can be any desired expression as long as it ends up with a value of the required type. In Example 1, the return statement returns the value of result to the point where the function was called. What might strike immediately is that the variable result, as stated earlier, ceases to exist on completing the execution of the function. So how is it returned? The answer is that a copy of the value being returned is made automatically, and this copy is available to the return point in the program.

The expression can also include function calls, if those functions return a numeric value! The following is a valid calling statement:

```
x = power(power(2, 5), 2);
```

The inner call to power returns 32, which is then used as an argument for the outer call to power. This call to power passes 32 and 2, and power will return the value 1024 which would get assigned to x.

If a function returns a value, usually it has to be assigned to some variable since a value is being returned. If there is no assignment specified, then is it a valid statement in C? The answer is yes but may fire a warning message. It is allowed as the returned value is simply discarded. Let us consider the following example.

— **EXAMPLE** —

3. ```
#include <stdio.h>
int sum(int, int);
int main()
{
    int a=5, b=10;
    sum(a,b);
    return 0;
}
int sum(int x, int y)
{
    return x+y;
}
```

The statement is valid but may elicit warning message.

The following statement may be used instead of the statement sum(a,b) to avoid the warning message.

```
(void)sum(a,b)
```

Thus the returned value is purposely discarded in this manner.

If the type of return value has been specified as void, there must be no expression appearing in the return statement. It must be written simply as

```
return;
```

For such a case the return statement may be omitted, if desired. Also, note that when a function does not return a value, the return statement is not followed by an expression, just a semicolon right away. Normally, if there is no return statement at the end of a function, and execution gets to the end of the function, a return statement is assumed and control goes back to the caller.

A function can only return one value. A function with return type void does not return any value. There may be more than one return statement in a function, but only one return statement will be executed per call to the function. As an illustration, the following function definition checks whether a given year is a leap year or not. The year is passed to that function as an argument. It returns 1 if the year is a leap year, otherwise it returns 0.

— **EXAMPLE** —

4. Function definition to check whether a given year is a leap year or not.

```
void leap_yr(int yr)
{
    if((yr%4==0)&&(yr%100!=0)||yr%400 ==0)
        return 1;
    else
        return 0;
}
```

Note

- If a program is compiled that contains a function defined with a void return type and tries to return a value, an error message will occur.
- An error message will be fired by the compiler if a bare return is used in a function, where the return type was specified to be other than void.

Standard C permits main to be defined with zero or two parameters as demonstrated below:

(a) ```
int main(void)
{
    ....
    return 0;
}
```

(b) ```
int main()
{
    ....
    return 0;
}
```

(c) ```
int main(int argc, char *argv[])
{
    ................
    return 0;
}
```

The value returned by the function `main()`, after the program instructions in its body are executed, is 0. Prior to C99, the return type of `main` was often omitted, defaulting to `int`. This is no longer used. In Microsoft based compiler, C programs use `void main(void)`. Most of the C compilers like Borland and GCC always recommend `main()` properly returning an `int`.

According to the newly ratified update to the C standard in 1999, `main()` should be defined with a return type of `int`. The practical reason to return an `int` from `main()` is that on many operating systems, the value returned by `main()` is used to return an exit status to the environment. On Unix, MS-DOS, and Windows systems, the low eight bits of the value returned by `main()` is passed to the command shell or calling program. This is often used to change the course of a program, batch file, or shell script.

12.3.3 Function Calling

It may be concluded that a function will carry out its expected action whenever it is invoked (i.e. whenever the function is called) from some portion of a program. This means that the program control passes to that of the called function. Once the function completes its task, the program control is returned back to the calling function. Generally, a function will process information passed to it from the calling statement of a program and return a single value. A function with returned type `void` does not return any value. It only returns the control from called function to calling function. The general form of the function call statement (or construct) is

```
function_name(variable1, variable2,…);
```

or

```
variable_name = function_name(variable1,
    variable2,…);
```

If there are no arguments to be passed in the function, i.e., the argument is `void`, then the calling statement would be

```
function_name();
```

or

```
variable_name = function_name();
```

Information will be passed to the function via special identifiers or expression called *arguments* or *actual parameters* and returned via the return statement.

> **Note**
> - One thing to notice here is that even when there are no parameters, you need to include left and right parentheses after the name of the function when you call it. If you leave them out, the code will still compile, but the function never actually gets called. What happens is that C interprets a function name without parentheses as the memory address where the func-tion is stored, and it is actually legal to have a number by itself as a statement. The statement is useless, but valid.

There are certain rules for parameters which must be keep in mind while writing a C program which uses one or more functions. These are listed below.

- The number of parameters in the actual and formal parameter lists must be consistent.
- Parameter association in C is *positional*. This means that the first actual parameter corresponds to the first formal parameter, the second matches the second, and so on.
- Actual parameters and formal parameters must be of compatible data types.
- Actual (input) parameters may be a variable, constant, or any expression matching the type of the corresponding formal parameter.

Concepts described above have been taken together in the following complete program.

--- **EXAMPLE** ---

5. Write a C program that uses a function to convert temperature from Fahrenheit scale to Celsius scale.

```
#include <stdio.h>
float FtoC(float);          Function prototype
                            declaration
int main(void)
{
  float tempInF;
  float tempInC;
  printf("\n Temperature in Fahrenheit scale: ");
  scanf("%f", &tempInF);
  tempInC = FtoC(tempInF);    Function calling
  printf("%f Fahrenheit equals %f Celsius \n",
      tempInF,tempInC);
  return 0;
}
/* FUNCTION DEFINITION */
float FtoC(float faren)     Function header
{
  float factor = 5.0/9.0;
  float freezing = 32.0;    Function
  float celsius;            body
  celsius = factor *(faren - freezing);
  return celsius;
}
```

> **Note**
> - The values passed to a function are referred to as *arguments*. The *parameters* of the called function can be thought of as declared local variables that get initialized with the values of the arguments. Some textbooks use the terms formal parameters and actual parameters instead of parameters and arguments.

Finally, there are some points which are very relevant as well as crucial here. When function prototypes are used:

- The number and types of arguments must match the declared types, otherwise the program causes an error message.
- The arguments are converted as if by assignment, to the declared types of the formal parameters. The argument is converted according to the following default argument promotions.
- Type float is converted to double.
- Array and function names are converted to corresponding pointers.
- When using traditional C, types unsigned short and unsigned char are converted to unsigned int, and types signed short and signed char are converted to signed int.
- When using ANSI C, types short and char, whether signed or unsigned, are converted to int.

12.4 CALL BY VALUE MECHANISM

The technique used to pass data to a function is known as parameter passing. Data is passed to a function using one of the two techniques: *pass by value* or *call by value* and *pass by reference* or *call by reference*.

In call by value, a copy of the data is made and the copy is sent to the function. The copies of the value held by the arguments are passed by the function call. Since only copies of values held in the arguments are passed by the function call to the formal parameters of the called function, the value in the arguments remains unchanged. In other words, as only copies of the values held in the arguments are sent to the formal parameters, the function cannot directly modify the arguments passed. This can be demonstrated by deliberately trying to do so in the following example.

EXAMPLE

```
6. #include <stdio.h>
   int mul_by_10(int num); /* function prototype */
   int main(void)
   {
     int result,num = 3;
     printf("\n num = %d before function call.", num);
     result = mul_by_10(num);
     printf("\n result = %d after return from\
         function", result);
     printf("\n num = %d", num);
     return 0;
   }
   /* function definition follows */
   int mul_by_10(int num)
   {
     num *= 10;
     return num;
   }
```

Output

```
num = 3, before function call.
result = 30, after return from function.
num = 3
```

The sample result obtained from this program shows that the attempt to modify the arguments of the function has failed. This confirms that the original value of num remains untouched. The multiplication occurred on the copy of num that was generated, and was eventually discarded on exiting from the function. Some more examples have been furnished on function calls and the passing of arguments using the 'pass by value' or 'call by value' technique.

The second technique, *pass by reference*, sends the address of the data rather than a copy. In this case, the called function can change the original data in the calling function. Unfortunately, C does not support pass by reference. Whenever the data in the calling function has to be changed, one must pass the variable's address and use it to change the value. Here, the values are passed by handing over the addresses of arguments to the called function, it is possible to change the values held within these arguments by executing the function. This appears as if multiple values are returned by the called function. Details on call by reference will be presented in the chapter on pointers.

Note

- C supports only call by value mechanism which means the values of the actual arguments are conceptually copied to the formal parameters. If it is required to alter the actual arguments in the called function, the addresses of the arguments must be passed explicitly.

12.5 WORKING WITH FUNCTIONS

Functions can be used in a program in various ways:

(a) Functions can perform operations on their parameters and return a value.
(b) Functions can manipulate information on their parameters and return a value that simply indicates the success or failure of that manipulation.
(c) Functions can have no return type that is strictly procedural.

Functions that perform operations on their parameters and return a value Functions in this category can be classified into two types.

1. A function with fixed number of parameters.
2. A function with variable number of parameters such as printf(). Writing a function with variable arguments will be discussed in Chapter 11.

The following example may be cited as an illustration of a function with fixed number of parameters.

EXAMPLE

7. Write a function that uses a function to find the greatest common divisor (GCD) of two integers.

To find the GCD using a function, two integers should be passed as parameters. Let them be x and y. It is needed to check whether k (for k = 2, 3, 4, and so on) is a common divisor for x and y until k is greater than x or y. The common divisor is to be stored in a variable named result. Initially result is 1. Whenever a new common divisor is found, the value of result is updated with the new common divisor. When all the possible common divisors from 2 up to x or y are checked, the value in the variable result is the greatest common divisor and it is returned to the calling function. Here is the implementation.

```
#include <stdio.h>
int GCD(int,int);
int main(void)
{
  int nOne, nTwo, n;
  printf("\n Enter two numbers: ");
  scanf("%d %d", &nOne, &nTwo);
  n=GCD(nOne,nTwo);
  printf("\n GCD of %d and %d is %d \n",
         nOne,nTwo,n);
  return 0;
}
int GCD(int x,int y)
{
  int result=1, k=2;
  while(k<=x && k<=y)
  {
    if(x%k==0 && y%k == 0)
      result=k;
    k++;
  }
  return result;
}
```

Functions that manipulate information on their parameters and return a value that simply indicates the success or failure of that manipulation For example, using function we can determine whether a number is a prime number or not. If it is a prime number then the function returns 1; otherwise it returns 0. Definition of the function may be implemented as follows:

```
int isPrime(int x)
{
  int d;
  for(d=2;d<=x/2;++d)
    if(x%d==0)
      return 0;
  return 1;
}
```

In a C99 compliant compiler, the above function can be rewritten using the standard header file stdbool.h. The return type of the function is bool.

```
bool isPrime(int x)
{
  int d;
  for(d=2;d<=x/2;++d)
    if(x%d==0)
      return false;
  return true;
}
```

Using the above function, it is possible to solve the following problem.

EXAMPLE

8. Print the prime factors of a given number using a function.

A number can always be divided by 1 and the number itself. The logic behind this program is that we have to divide the number starting from 2 to n/2 where n is the given number. In any case if the number becomes divisible by any number in the range 2 to n/2, then that is considered to be a factor of the number. If that factor is a prime number then the factor is a prime factor. We can use the function isPrime() to determine whether the factor is a prime factor or not.

```
#include <stdio.h>
#include <stdbool.h>
bool isPrime(int);
int main(void)
{
  int n, d=2;
  printf("\n Enter the Number: ");
  scanf("%d",&n);
  printf("\n Prime factors of %d is....\n",n);
  for(d=2;d<=n/2;++d)
    if(n%d==0 && isPrime(d))
      printf("%d ",d);
  return 0;
}
bool isPrime(int x)
{
  int d;
  for(d=2;d<=x/2;++d)
    if(x%d==0)
      return false;
  return true;
}
```
Sample run:
```
Enter the Number:  51
Prime factors of 51 is....
3  17
```

Function having no return type that is strictly procedural
The function may or may not have parameters. Unlike some

other languages, C makes no distinction between subroutines (procedures) and functions. In C, there is only the function, which can optionally return a value. A function with void as return type simulates the procedure in C.

We have seen that when we pass the value of a typical variable to a function, a copy of that value gets assigned to the parameter. Changing the value of the parameter within the called function does not affect the value of the local variable in the calling function. Things are different when an array is passed to a function. What we are actually passing is the memory address of the array (this may seem more clear after we learn about pointers), and if the called function changes specific entries in the array, these entries remain changed when control gets back to the calling function. So when arrays or strings are passed to a function, call by value mechanism is not followed. Thus any modification made in the array or string parameter within the called function will be reflected in the original array or string in the calling function that was passed to the function. This concept will be understood more clearly in Chapter 13. As a result in most of the cases, it is not required to return anything. Here is an example:

--------- **EXAMPLE** ---------

```
9. #include <stdio.h>
   void change(int []);
   int main(void)
   {
     int arr[3] = {1, 2, 3};
     change(arr);
     printf("Elements are %d, %d, and %d.\n", arr[0],
         arr[1], arr[2]);
     return 0;
   }
   void change(int my_array[])
   {
     my_array[0] = 10;
     my_array[2] = 20;
     return;
   }
```

This program will print "Elements are 10, 2, and 20." to the screen.

As a further illustration, Example 10 sorts a set of numbers stored in an array using a function.

--------- **EXAMPLE** ---------

10. Write a C program that uses a function to sort an array of integers using bubble sort algorithm.

Sorting an array in ascending order means that rearranging the values in the array so that the elements progressively increase in

value from the smallest to the largest. By the end of such a sort, the minimum value is contained in the first location of the array, whereas the maximum value is found in the last location of the array, with values that progressively increase in between.

This example implements the bubble sort algorithm, which has already been discussed in the previous chapter. A function called sort, takes two arguments: the array to be sorted and the number of elements in the array.

```
#include <stdio.h>
void sort (int [], int);
int main (void)
{
  int i;
  int arr[10] = {3,2,7,0,6,4,9,8,1,5};
  printf ("The array before the sort:\n");
  for (i = 0; i < 10; ++i)
    printf ("%i", arr[i]);
  sort (array, 10);
  printf ("\n\nThe array after the sort:\n");
  for (i = 0; i < 10; ++i)
    printf ("%i", arr[i]);
  return 0;
}
void sort (int a[], int n)
{
  int i, j, temp;
  for(i = 0; i < n-1; ++i)
  for(j = 0; j < n-i-1; ++j)
  if (a[j] > a[j+1])
  {
    temp = a[j];
    a[j] = a[j+1];
    a[j+1] = temp;
  }
}
```

Output
```
The array before the sort:
3 2 7 0 6 4 9 8 1 5
The array after the sort:
0 1 2 3 4 5 6 7 8 9
```

12.6 PASSING ARRAYS TO FUNCTIONS

Arrays can also be arguments of functions. When an array is passed to a function, the address of the array is passed and not the copy of the complete array. Therefore, when a function is called with the name of the array as the argument, address to the first element in the array is handed over to the function. Hence when an array is a function argument, only the address of the array is passed to the function called. This implies that during its execution the function has the ability to modify the contents of the array that is specified as the function argument. Therefore, the array is not passed to a function by value. This is an exception to the rule of passing the function arguments by value. Consider the following example.

EXAMPLE

```
11. #include <stdio.h>
    void doubleThem(int [], int);
                       /* declaration of function */
    int main(void)
    {
      int myInts[10] = {1,2,3,4,5,6,7,8,9,10};
      int size=10;
      printf("\n\n The given numbers are :");
      for (i = 0; i < size; i++)
        printf("%d,",myInts[i]);
      doubleThem(myInts,size);   /* function call */
      printf("\n\n The double numbers are : ");
      for (i = 0; i < size; i++)
        printf("%d,",myInts [i]);
      return 0;
    }
    /******* function definition *******/
    void doubleThem(int a[], int size)
    {
      int i;
      for(i = 0; i < size; i++)
      {
          a[i] = 2 * a[i];
      }
    }
```

Output
```
The given numbers are :1, 2, 3, 4, 5, 6, 7, 8, 9,
10,
The double numbers are : 2, 4, 6, 8, 10, 12, 14,
16, 18, 20,
```

It is to be noted that the value of the variable is initialized with 10 as there are 10 values in the array myInts. The value of the variable can also be determined by the expression

```
sizeof(myInts)/sizeof(myInts[0])
```

That is,

```
size=sizeof(myInts)/sizeof(myInts [0]);
```

EXAMPLES
---

12. Write a program that uses a function to find the average age of students of a class chosen for a junior quiz competition.

```
#include <stdio.h>
#define SIZE 50
```

```
float avg_age(int [],int);
int main(void)
{
  int i,b[SIZE],n;
  float average;
  printf("\n How many students? \n%");
  scanf("%d",&n);
  printf("\n Enter the age of students \n");
  for(i=0;i<n;i++)
    scanf("%d",&b[i]);
  average=avg_age(b,n);
  printf("\n the average age of students =%f",
      average);
  return 0;
}
float avg_age(int a[], int n)
{
  int j;
  float sum=0.0;
  for(j=0;j<n;j++)
    sum=sum+a[j];
  return sum/n;
}
```

13. Write a program that uses a function to find the maximum value in an array.

Solution
```
#include <stdio.h>
int maximum(int [],int); /* function prototype */
int main(void)
{
  int values[5], i, max;
  printf("Enter 5 numbers\n");
  for(i = 0; i < 5; ++i)
    scanf("%d", &values[i]);
  max = maximum(values,5); /* function call */
  printf("\nMaximum value is %d\n", max);
  return 0;
}
/**** function definition ****/
int maximum(int values[], int n)
{
  int max_value, i;
  max_value = values[0];
  for(i = 1; i < n; ++i)
    if(values[i] > max_value)
      max_value = values[i];
  return max_value;
}
```

Output
```
Enter 5 numbers
11 15 8 21 7
Maximum value is 21
```

When an array is passed to a function, the address of the first element (called the base address of an array) is passed which is nothing but passing arguments by address. In general, when a one-dimensional array is passed to a function, it degenerates to a pointer. This will be explained in the chapter on pointers.

A local variable max_value is set to the first element of values, and a for loop is executed which cycles through each element in values and assigns the maximum item to max_value. This number is then passed back by the return statement, and assigned to max in the main() function.

However, it has to be noted that an array name with an index number as a function argument will only pass that particular array element's value, like all other variables, to the function called.

Strings are passed to functions in the same way as are one-dimensional arrays. By implementing string functions, it will be shown how strings are passed into and out of functions. Some examples involving strings as function arguments follow.

EXAMPLE
---

14. Write a program that uses a function to copy one string into another without using the strcpy() function available in the standard library of C.

Solution
```c
#include <stdio.h>
void string_copy(char [], char []);
                        /* function prototype */
int main()
{
  char a[100]; /*** source string ***/
  char b[100]; /*** destination string ***/
  printf("\n Input source string :");
  scanf("%[^\n]",a); /* read input source string */
  string_copy(b,a); /* function call */
  printf("\n Destination string : %s\n",b);
  return 0;
}
/*** function definition ***/
void string_copy(char d[], char s[])
{
  int i = 0;
  printf("\n Source string : %s\n",s);
                        /* copying the string */
  for (i = 0; s[i] != '\0'; i++)
```

```c
    d[i] = s[i]; /* Copy NUL character to
                        destination string */
}
```

Multidimensional arrays can also be passed as arguments to functions. The simplest type of such an array is the two-dimensional array. It may be recalled here that when a two-dimensional array is initialized, the number of rows need not be specified. A similar technique is adopted while specifying the two-dimensional array as a formal parameter in a function header. The first dimension value can be omitted when a multidimensional array is used as a formal parameter in a function.

Of course, the function will need some way of knowing the extent of the first dimension. For example, the function header could be written as follows:

```c
double yield(double arr[][4], int index);
```

Here, the second parameter, index, would provide the necessary information about the first dimension of the array. The function can operate with a two-dimensional array with any value for the first dimension, but with the second dimension fixed at 4.

EXAMPLE
---

15. Write a program that uses a function to perform addition and subtraction of two matrices having integer numbers.

The computation that is carried out in the function is simply a nested for loop with the inner loop summing elements of a single row and the outer loop repeating this for every row.

```c
#include <stdio.h>
#define row 2
#define col 3
void mat_arith(int [][col], int [][col]);
                        /* function prototype */
int main()
{
  int a[row][col], b[row][col],i,j;
  printf("\n Enter elements of the first matrix.\n");
  for(i=0; i<row; i++)
            /** Read first matrix elements **/
    for(j=0; j<col; j++)
      scanf("%d",&a[i][j]);
        printf("\n Enter elements of the second
                matrix.\n");
  for(i=0; i<row; i++)
            /** Read second matrix elements **/
    for(j=0; j<col; j++)
      scanf("%d",&b[i][j]);
  mat_arith(a,b);          /** function call **/
}
```

```
void mat_arith(int a[][col], int b[][col])
{
  int c[row][col],i,j,choice;
  printf("\n For addition enter: 1 \n")
  printf("For subtraction enter: 2\n");
  printf("\nEnter your choice:");
  scanf("%d",&choice);
  for(i=0; i<row; i++)
  for(j=0; j<col; j++)
  {
    if(choice==1)
      c[i][j]= a[i][j] + b[i][j];
    else if(choice==2)
      c[i][j]= a[i][j] - b[i][j];
    else
    {
      printf("\n Invalid choice. Task not done.");
      return;
    }
  }
  printf("\n The resulting matrix is:\n");
  for(i=0; i<row; i++)
  {
    for(j=0; j<col; j++)
    printf("%d", c[i][j]);
    printf("\n\n");
  }
  return;
}
```

Output

```
Enter elements of the second matrix.
1 3 5 7 9 11
For addition enter: 1
For subtraction enter: 2
Enter your choice: 1
The resulting matrix is:
3  7  11
14 17 21
```

Till now, the function definition was always placed after the main program. In fact, C allows the function definition to be placed ahead of the main program. In such a case, the function prototype is not required.

12.7 SCOPE AND EXTENT

The region of the program over which the declaration of an identifier is visible is called the *scope* of the identifier. The scope relates to the accessibility, the period of existence, and the boundary of usage of variables declared in a statement block or a function. These features in turn define whether a variable is local or global in nature.

12.7.1 Concept of Global and Local Variables

There are two common terms related to the visibility or accessibility of a variable. They are global and local variables. Global and local are the terms related with lifetime. *Lifetime* is the period during execution of a program in which a variable or function exists. It will be discussed in detail later in this section.

Variables declared within the function body are called *local variables*. They have local scope. Local variables are automatically created at the point of their declaration within the function body and are usable inside the function body. These variables exist only inside the specific function that creates them. They are unknown to other functions and to the main program. The existence of the local variables ends when the function completes its specific task and returns to the calling point. They are recreated each time a function is executed or called.

Variables declared outside of all the functions of a program and accessible by any of these functions are called *global variables*. The existence and region of usage of these variables are not confined to any specific function body. They are implemented by associating memory locations with variable names. Global variables are created at the beginning of program execution and remain in existence all through the period of execution of the program. These variables are known to all functions in the program and can be used by these functions as many times as may be required. They do not get recreated if the function is recalled. Global variables do not cease to exist when control is transferred from a function. Their value is retained and is available to any other function that accesses them.

All global variables are declared outside of all the functions. There is no general rule for where outside the functions these should be declared, but declaring them on top of the code is normally recommended for reasons of scope, as explained through the given examples. If a variable of the same name is declared both within a function and outside of it, the function will use the variable that is declared within it and ignore the global one. If not initialized, a global variable is initialized to zero by default. As a matter of style, it is best to avoid variable names that conceal names in an outer scope; the potential for confusion and error is too great. Moreover, the use of global variables should be as few as possible. Consider the following example.

--- **EXAMPLE** ---

16. Write a program that uses a function to swap values stored in two integer variables to understand the concept of local and global variables.

```
#include <stdio.h>
void exchange(int, int);
```

```
int main()
{ /* main() program body starts here...*/
  int a, b;            /* local variables */
  a = 5;
  b = 7;
  printf(" In main: a = %d, b = %d\n", a, b);
  exchange(a, b);
  printf("\n Back in main:");
  printf("a = %d, b = %d\n", a, b);
  return 0;
} /* main() program body ends here... */
void exchange(int a, int b)
{ /* function body starts here...*/
  int temp; /* local variable */
  printf("\n In function exchange() before\ change:
        just  received  from  main...  a=%d\  and
        b=%d",a,b);
  temp = a;
  a = b;
  b = temp; /* interchange over */
  printf("\n In function exchange() after change:");
  printf("a = %d, b = %d\n", a, b);
} /* function body ends here...*/
```

Output

```
In main: a = 5, b = 7
In function exchange() before change: just received
from main... a=5 and b=7
In function exchange() after change: a = 7, b = 5
Back in main: a = 5, b = 7
```

The results depict that the above program code failed to exchange the numbers between the variables in the function main(). This happened because, first, the variables a and b in main() and that within the function exchange() are not the same. The variables a and b within exchange() are local variables and are created when the function is invoked. This means program control is taken over by the function, and the variables are killed the moment program control returns to the main() program. While calling the exchange() function from main(), copies of the values held by a and b, which are local to main(), are handed over to separate variables a and b that are local to the function exchange(). Within this exchange() function, the task of exchanging the values between its local variables a and b is carried out successfully, as is evident from the messages displayed when the program is run. This in no way affects the values in variables a and b in the main(). Moreover, this exchanged copy of values in the variables is not passed back from the function exchange() to the variables in main(). Hence, the values in the variables a and b within main() remained untouched and unchanged. This demonstrates

the difference in the scope of the local variables in main() and the function exchange(). One way to affect an interchange could be by declaring the variables that are to be exchanged, that is a and b, as global variables only. This is demonstrated by the following example program code.

EXAMPLE

```
17. #include <stdio.h>
   void exchange(void);
   int a, b;    /* declaration of global variables */
   int main()
   { /* main program starts here...*/
     a = 5;
     b = 7;
     printf(" In main: a = %d, b = %d\n", a, b);
     exchange();   /* function call, no parameters are
                 passed */
     printf("\n Back in main:");
     printf("a = %d, b = %d\n", a, b);
     return 0;
   } /* main program ends here */
   void exchange(void)
   { /* function body starts here...*/
     int temp; /* decl. of local variable in function*/
     printf("\n In function exchange() before\ change:
         just received from\
     main... a=%d and b=%d",a,b);
     temp = a;
     a = b;
     b = temp; /* interchange over */
     printf("\n In function exchange() after change:");
     printf("a = %d, b = %d\n", a, b);
   } /* function body ends here*/
```

Output

```
In main: a = 5, b = 7
In function exchange() before change: just received
from main... a=5 and b=7
In function exchange() after change: a = 7, b = 5
Back in main: a = 7, b = 5
```

The example shows that for global variables the interchange is possible by following the scope rules. By using pointers in functions, the same job can be done more effectively and the function call technique is known as call by reference, more strictly, call by address. This will be discussed in Chapter 13.

Note

- Rather than passing variables to a function as arguments, it is possible to make all variables global. But it is not recommended, as global variables break the normal safeguards provided by functions. Using parameter passing mechanism and declaring local variables as needed, C offers provision for making functions independent and insulated from each other, including the necessity of carefully designating the type of arguments needed by a function, the variables used in the function, and the value returned. Using only global variables can be especially disastrous in larger programs that have many user-defined functions. Since a global variable can be accessed and changed by any function following the global declaration, it is a time-consuming and frustrating task to locate the origin of an erroneous value.

- But it is not the case that use of global variables is always disadvantageous. There are certain instances where use of global variables is advocated. Global variables, however, are extremely useful in creating array of data and constants that must be shared between many functions. If many functions require access to a group of arrays, global variables allow the functions to make efficient changes to the same array without the need for multiple arrays passing.

12.7.2 Scope Rules

The region of the program over which the declaration of an identifier is accessible is called the *scope* of the identifier. The scope relates to the accessibility, the period of existence, and the boundary of usage of variables declared in a program. Scopes can be of four types.

- block
- file
- function
- function prototype

The following sections describe the scope associated with variables.

Block scope

This means that the identifier can only be used in the block in which it is declared. These variables are created at the point of their declaration inside the *block* and cease to exist outside it. Outside the block, these variables are unknown and non-existent. For blocks within blocks, termed as nested blocks, variables declared outside the inner blocks are accessible to the *nested blocks*, provided these variables are not redeclared within the inner block. The redeclaration of variables within the blocks bearing the same names as those in the outer block, masks the outer block variables while executing the inner blocks.

In general, it is always better to use different names for variables not common to outer and inner blocks to avoid unforced errors. The following are some examples illustrating the scope rules in blocks.

18. Write a program that illustrates the scope rules in blocks.

```c
#include <stdio.h>
int main()
{
    int x= 3;      /* variable declaration in outer
                                    block */
    printf("\n in outer block x = %d before\ executing
        inner block", x);
    {
        int x= 45; /* variable declaration in inner
                                    block */
        printf("\n in inner block x = %d", x);
    }
    printf("\n in outer block x = %d after executing\
        inner block", x);
    return 0;
}
```

Output
```
in outer block x = 3 before executing inner block
in inner block x = 45
in outer block x = 3 after executing inner block
```

This program shows that because the variable x has been redeclared as 45 in the inner block, a local variable gets created in the inner block. This variable is only accessible and known to the inner block.

Functions are considered as named block. Variables declared within a function block can be used anywhere within the function in which they are defined. The variable x declared in outer block has the block scope. Like blocks, functions can either be defined in parallel, where they are placed one after the other and a function can be called from any other function. But C does not allow functions to be nested, i.e. a function cannot be defined within another function definition.

Function scope

This applies only to labels. Normally labels are used with goto statement. It simply means that labels can be used anywhere within the function in which they are defined. This includes use before definition.

File scope

This means that the identifier can be used anywhere in the current file after the declaration of the identifier. This applies to functions and all variables declared outside functions. File scope variable is also known as global variable. The illustration involving global or file scope variables has already been discussed in Section 12.7.1. File scope identifiers may be hidden by the block scope declarations having same name.

Function prototype scope

In order to improve readability and understandabilty, function prototypes are usually written with 'dummy' variable names. For example

```
double max(double x, double y);
```

The identifiers 'x' and 'y' have function prototype scope, which terminates at the end of the prototype. This allows any dummy parameter names appearing in a function prototype to disappear at the end of the prototype. Consider the following program:

```
#include <stdio.h>
int main(void)
{
  void show(int x);
  int x=10;
  show(x);
  return 0;
}
void show(int x)
{
  printf("\n %d",x);
}
```

The int variable name does not conflict with the parameter name because the parameter went out of scope at the end of the prototype. However, the prototype is still in scope.

> **Note**
>
> - In standard C, formal parameters in the function definition have the same scope as variables declared at the beginning of the block that forms the function body and therefore they cannot be hidden or redeclared by declarations in the body. The following function definition, if used, will give error message at compile time.
>
> ```
> int sum(int x, int y)
> {
>     int x=5;
>     return x+y;
> }
> ```
>
> - Compilation error message displayed
>   ```
>   In function 'sum':
>   error: 'x' redeclared as different kind of symbol
>   note: previous definition of 'x' was here
>   ```

How long memory will be associated with identifiers is known as *extent* or *lifetime* of a data object. The storage duration of the identifier determines its lifetime, either *static duration* (global lifetime) or *automatic duration* (local lifetime). The *duration* of an object describes whether its storage is allocated only once, at program start-up, or is more transient in its nature, being allocated and freed as necessary. Static duration means that the object has its storage allocated permanently, i.e. storage is allocated at or before

the beginning of program execution and the storage remain allocated until program termination. Automatic duration means that the storage is allocated and freed as necessary.

The following rules specify whether an identifier has global (static) or local (automatic) lifetime:

Global lifetime All functions have global lifetime, as do the identifiers declared at the top level (that is, outside all blocks in the program at the same level of function definitions).

Local lifetime An object (unless it is declared as static) is said to have local lifetime when it is created on entry to a block or function and destroyed on exit from the block or function. Formal parameters and variables declared at the beginning of the block may have local lifetime depending on the place of declaration.

The data object created with the use of special library functions such as malloc() or calloc() have *dynamic duration* and the storage remains allocated from the time of creation at run time until program termination or until a call to special library function free().

12.8 STORAGE CLASSES

12.8.1 Storage Class Specifiers for Variables

In C, the variables are declared by the type of data they can hold. The name of a variable is associated with a memory location within the computer where the value assigned to the variable is stored in the form of bits. During the execution of the program, these variables may be stored in the CPU registers or the primary memory of the computer. To indicate where the variables would be stored, how long they would exist, what would be their region of existence, and what would be the default values, C provides four storage class specifiers that can be used along with the data type specifiers in the declaration statement of a variable. These four storage class specifiers are *automatic, external, register, and static*.

The storage class specifier precedes the declaration statement for a variable. The general form of the variable declaration statement that includes the storage class specifier is given as follows:

```
storage_class_specifier  data_type  variable_name;
```

The storage class – auto

By default, all variables declared within the body of any function are automatic. The keyword auto is used in the declaration of a variable to explicitly specify its storage class. For example, the following declaration statement within a function body

```
auto char any_alpha;
```

specifies that any_alpha is a variable that can hold a character and its storage class is automatic. Even if the variable declaration statement in the function body does not include the keyword auto, such declared variables are implicitly specified as belonging to the automatic storage class. In fact, all local variables in a function, by default, belong to automatic storage class. Their region of use is limited within the function body and vanishes when the function completes its specific task and returns to the main program from where the function was invoked. These variables are stored in the primary memory of the computer.

Local variables declared within nested blocks in a function belong by default to the automatic storage class.

EXAMPLE
---

19. Write a C program that demonstrates the use of the automatic storage class variable.

```
#include <stdio.h>
int main(void)
{
  auto int a =5;
  printf("\n a = %d",a);
  {
    int a = 10;
    printf("\n a = %d",a);
    printf("\n i = %d",i);
  }
  printf("\n a = %d",a);
  return 0;
}
```

Output
```
a = 5
a = 10
i = 4199232
a = 5
```

Notice that the variable *a* in the outer block is declared as auto but the variable *a* in the inner block is declared without auto keyword. The variable *a* in the inner block also has auto storage class by default. Since this local variable i is not initialized within the inner block, the value held by it is unpredictable and thus garbage. This is printed as 4199232. When inner block ends, the existence of both the variables a and i ends. So, outside the inner block, the value of a is printed as 5. Any attempt to access the variable i outside the inner block causes a compiler error. This example demonstrates the accessibility, existence, effect of initialization, and garbage default value of the automatic storage class or the local variable.

The storage class – register

Values stored in registers of the CPU are accessed in much lesser time than those stored in the primary memory. To allow the fastest access time for variables, the register storage class specifier is used. The keyword for this storage class is register. The variables thus specified are stored in

some register of the CPU. In most C compilers, the register specifier can only be applied to int and char type variables; however, ANSI C has broadened its scope. Arrays cannot be stored in a register but they may still receive preferential treatment by the compiler depending on C compiler and the operating system under which it is running.

The existence of the variables with the storage class specifier register is restricted within the region of a function or a block where it has been declared and exists as long as the function or block remains active. The default value within this variable is unknown, which is interpreted as garbage. Storage class of a global variable cannot be specified as register.

> **Note**
> - Global variables with register storage class are not allowed.
> - In C, it is not possible to obtain the address of a register variable by using '&' operator.
> - In addition, the only storage class specifier that can be used in a parameter declaration is register.

The storage class – static

Two types of variables are allowed to be specified as static variables: local variables and global variables. The local variables are also referred to as *internal static variables* whereas the global variables are also known as *external static variables*. The default value of a static variable is zero.

To specify a local variable as static, the keyword static precedes its declaration statement.

A *static local variable* is allotted a permanent storage location in the primary memory. This variable is usable within functions or blocks where it is declared and preserves its previous value held by it between function calls or between block re-entries. However, once a function is invoked, the static local variable retains the value in it and exists as long as the main program is in execution.

The *external static variables* in a program file are declared like global variables with the keyword static preceding its declaration statement. These static variables are accessible by all functions in the program file where these variables exist and are declared. The external static variables are not available to functions defined earlier in the same file or not accessible to functions defined in other files although these may use the extern keyword. These variables exist throughout the period of the main program execution. Such variables get stored in the primary memory.

EXAMPLE
---

20. Write a C program that illustrates the use of local static variables and functions.

```
#include <stdio.h>
int main()
{
```

```
void show(void);
printf("\n First Call of show()");
show();
printf("\n Second Call of show()");
show();
printf("\n Third Call of show()");
show();
return 0;
}
void show(void)
{
  static int i;
  printf("\n i=%d",i);
  i++;
}
```

Output

```
First Call of show()
i=0
Second Call of show()
i=1
Third Call of show()
i=2
```

The storage class – extern

A program in C, particularly when it is large, can be broken down into smaller programs. After compiling, each program file can be joined together to form the large program. These small program modules that combine together may need some variables that are used by all of them. In C, such a provision can be made by specifying these variables, accessible to all the small program modules, as an external storage class variable. These variables are global to all the small program modules that are formed as separate files. The keyword for declaring such global variables is extern. Such global variables are declared like any other variable in one of the program modules while the declaration of these variables is preceded with the keyword extern in all other combining program modules. The program modules may also be a function or a block. These variables remain in existence as long as the program is in execution and their existence does not terminate upon the exit of a function or a block or a program module from its state of execution. These variables are stored in the primary memory and their default value is zero. Table 12.1 provides a summary of the salient features of storage class specifiers. The following programs illustrate the use of the external storage class variable.

—————————————— EXAMPLE ——————————————

21.
```
/**********************************************/
/*          Program file: pgm1.c              */
/**********************************************/
#include <stdio.h>
#include "pgm2.c" /*** link program pgm2.c ***/
int i;           /*** external/global decl.**/
void show(void);   /*** function prototype ***/
int main()
{
  i=10;
  show(); /* call to function in program file
                            pgm2.c */
  printf("\n Value of i in pgm1.c=%d ",i);
  return 0;
```

Table 12.1 Summary of salient features of storage class specifiers

Storage class specifier	Place of storage	Scope	Lifetime	Default value
auto	Primary memory	Within the block or function where it is declared.	Exists from the time of entry in the function or block to its return to the calling function or to the end of block.	garbage
register	Register of CPU	Within the block or function where it is declared.	Exists from the time of entry in the function or block to its return to the calling function or to the end of block.	garbage
static	Primary memory	*For local* Within the block or function where it is declared. *For global* Accessible within the combination of program modules/files that form the full program.	*For local* Retains the value of the variable from one entry of the block or function to the next or next call. *For global* Preserves value in the program file.	0
extern	Primary memory	Accessible within the combination of program modules/files that form the full program.	Exists as long as the program is in execution.	0

```
}           /***** pgm1.c file ends **********/
/**********************************************/
/*      Program file: pgm2.c            */
/**********************************************/
extern int i;
/***** function definition of show()*********/
void show()           /*** function header ***/
{   /*** fn. body starts..**/
  printf("\n Value of i in pgm2.c=%d",i);
}                   /*** fn. body ends.. **/
```

Output

```
Value of i in pgm2.c=10
Value of i in pgm1.c=10
```

Here is another example where the global variable i is assigned a value in the program file in which the basic declaration statement and main() are absent. There is a minor difference between this example and the previous one.

EXAMPLE

```
22. /**********************************************/
    /*          Program file: pgm1.c            */
    /**********************************************/
    #include <stdio.h>
    #include "pgm2.c" /*** link program pgm2.c ***/
    int i; /*** external/global decl.**/
    void show(void);   /*** function prototype ***/
    int main()
    {
      show(); /* call to function in program file pgm2.c */
      printf("\n Value of i in pgm1.c=%d",i);
      return 0;
    } /******* pgm1.c file ends**********/
    /**********************************************/
    /*          Program file: pgm2.c          */
    /**********************************************/
    extern int i;
    /******* function definition of show() ********/
    void show()           /*** function header ***/
    {                 /*** fn. body starts..**/
      i = 20;
      printf("\n Value of i in pgm2.c=%d",i);
    }                 /*** fn. body ends.. **/
```

Output

```
Value of i in pgm2.c=20
Value of i in pgm1.c=20
```

12.8.2 Storage Class Specifiers for Functions

The only storage class specifiers that may be assigned with functions are extern and static. Extern signifies that the function can be referenced from other files, that is, the function name is exported to the linker. Static signifies that the function cannot be referenced from other files, that is, the function name is *not* exported to the linker. If no storage class appears in a function definition, extern is presumed.

12.8.3 Linkage

An identifier's *linkage* determines which of the references to that identifier refers to the same object. An identifier's linkage is determined by whether it appears inside or outside a function, whether it appears in a declaration of a function (as opposed to an object), its storage-class specifier, and the linkage of any previous declarations of the same identifier that have file scope. C defines three types of linkages – external, internal, and no linkage. In general,

- Functions and global variables have external linkage. This means they are available to all files that constitute a program.
- Identifiers with file scope declared as static have internal linkage. These are known only within the file in which they are declared.
- Local identifiers have no linkage and are therefore known only within their own block.

Two declarations of the same identifier in a single file that have the same linkage, either internal or external, refer to the same object. The same identifier cannot appear in a file with both internal and external linkage.

> **Note**
> - It is not always necessary to specify both the storage class and the type of identifiers in a declaration. Storage class specifiers appearing in declarations outside of functions are assumed to be extern. In a declaration inside a function, if a type but no storage class is indicated, the identifier is assumed to be auto. An exception to the latter rule is made for functions because functions with storage class auto do not exist; it is implicitly declared to be extern.

12.9 THE INLINE FUNCTION

C99 has added the keyword *inline*, which applies to functions. By preceding a function declaration with *inline*, the compiler is instructed to optimize calls to the function. Typically, this means that the function's code will be expanded in line, rather than called. Below is a definition of such inline function.

```
inline int sum(int x, int y)
{
  return x+y;
}
```

The inline designation is only a hint to the compiler, suggesting that calls to the inline function should be as fast as possible. The name comes from a compiler optimization called *inline expansion*, whereby a call to a function is replaced by a copy of the function body. This eliminates the overhead of the function call. There is no guarantee in general that the compiler will take note of a function being declared as *inline*. It is free to ignore the request.

12.10 RECURSION

The formal definition is given below.

A recursive function is one that calls itself directly or indirectly to solve a smaller version of its task until a final call which does not require a self-call.

Recursion is like a top–down approach to problem solving; it divides the problem into pieces or selects one key step, postponing the rest. On the other hand, iteration is more of a bottom–up approach; it begins with what is known and then constructs the solution step by step.

12.10.1 What is needed for implementing recursion?

- The problem should be decomposed into smaller problems of same type.
- Recursive calls must diminish problem size.
- A base case is needed.
- Base case must be reached. A recursive function acts as a terminating condition. Without an explicitly defined base case, a recursive function would call itself indefinitely.
- It is the building block to the complete solution. In a sense, a recursive function determines its solution from the base case(s) it reaches.

Note

- **What is a base case?** An instance of a problem the solution of which requires no further recursive calls is known as a base case. It is a special case whose solution is known. Every recursive algorithm requires at least one base case in order to be valid. A base case has two purposes.

The recursive algorithms will generally consist of an `if` statement with the following form:

```
if(this is a base case) then
   solve it directly
else
   redefine the problem using recursion.
```

Four questions can arise for constructing a recursive solution. They are as follows.

- How can the problem be defined in terms of one or more smaller problems of the same type?
- What instance(s) of the problem can serve as the base case(s)?

- As the problem size diminishes, will this/these base case(s) be reached?
- How is/are the solution(s) from the smaller problem(s) used to build a correct solution to the current larger problem?

It is not always necessary or even desirable to ask the above questions in strict order. For example, sometimes the solution to a problem is easier to imagine if it is first asked what instance(s) can serve as the base case(s) and then define the problem in terms of one or more smaller problems of the same type which are closer to the base case(s).

The following sections discuss some popular problems where recursive functions are constructed and used keeping in mind the above approach.

The Fibonacci sequence

The Fibonacci numbers are a sequence of numbers that have varied uses. They were originally intended to model the growth of a rabbit colony. The sequence is as follows:

```
1, 1, 2, 3, 5, 8, 13, 21, 34, 55, 89, 144, ...
```

The third term of the sequence is the sum of the first and second terms. The fourth term is the sum of the second and third terms, and so on. The problem is to compute the value of the nth term recursively.

Let `fib(n)` denote the nth term of the Fibonacci sequence. Four questions arise.

- How can the problem be defined in terms of one or more smaller problems of the same type?

```
fib(n) = fib(n-2) + fib(n-1) for n>2
```

This recursive relation introduces a new point. In some cases, one solves a problem by solving more than one smaller problem of the same type.

- What instance of the problem can serve as the base case?

One must be careful when selecting the base case in this situation. For example, if one simply says that `fib(1)` is the base case, what happens if `fib(2)` is called?

```
fib(2) is fib(0) + fib(1) but fib(0) is undefined.
```

That makes `fib(2)` undefined. Therefore, it is necessary to give `fib(2)` an explicit definition, i.e., to make it also a base case.

```
fib(1) = 1 for n = 1
fib(2) = 1 for n = 2
```

Two base cases are necessary because there are two smaller problems.

- As the problem size diminishes, will one reach these base cases?

As n is a non-negative integer and each call to the function will reduce the parameter n by 1 or 2, the base cases `n = 1`, `n = 2` will be reached.

- How are the solutions from the smaller problems used to build a correct solution to the current larger problem?

The recursive step adds the results from the two smaller problems fib(n-2) and fib(n-1) to obtain the solution to the current fib(n) problem. This function uses what is known as 'non-linear' recursion.

In this context, brief definitions of linear, non-linear, and mutual recursions are given as follows.

Linear recursion   This term is used to describe a recursive function where at most one recursive call is carried out as part of the execution of a single recursive process.

Non-linear recursion   This term is used to describe a recursive function where more than one recursion can be carried out as part of the execution of a single recursive process.

Mutual recursion   In order to check and compile a function call, a compiler must know the type of the function, the number of parameters, and so on. In direct recursion the function header, which contains this information, is seen before any call within the function body or later. In mutual recursion, the functions must be defined in some order. This means that a call of at least one function must be compiled before its definition is seen. Different programming languages approach this problem in various ways. Some use separate *forward* definitions of function headers to give sufficient information to compile a call and *body* definitions to contain those calls.

Coming back to the Fibonacci sequence problem, any number in the sequence can be determined by the following definition.

$$Fibo(n) = \begin{cases} 1 & \text{if } n \leq 2 \\ Fibo(n+1) + Fibo(n-2) & \text{otherwise} \end{cases}$$

Considering the definition, the following code may be used in a recursive function to generate the numbers in the Fibonacci sequence.

```
int fib(int val)
{
  if(val <= 2)
    return 1;
  else
    return(fib(val - 1) + fib(val - 2));
}
```

The following example illustrates the use of the preceding recursive function for generating the Fibonacci numbers.

EXAMPLE

```
23. /**********************************************/
    /* Program for computing the Fibonacci number
    sequence using recursion. */
    /**********************************************/
    #include <stdio.h>
    #include <stdlib.h>
    int fib(int); /* function prototype */
```

```
int main()
{
  int i,j;
  printf("\n Enter the number of terms: ");
  scanf("%d",&i);
  if(i < 0)
  {
    printf("\n Error - Number of terms cannot be\
        negative\n");
    exit(1);
  }
  printf("\n Fibonacci sequence for %d terms is:",i);
  for( j=1; j<=i; ++j)
  printf(" %d",fib(j)); /* function call to return
                        jth Fibonacci term*/
  return 0;
}
/**********************************************/
/*          Recursive function fib()          */
/**********************************************/
int fib(int val)
{
  if(val <= 2)
    return 1;
  else
    return(fib(val - 1) + fib(val - 2));
}
```

Output
```
(a)  Enter the number of terms: 6
     Fibonacci sequence for 6 terms is: 1 1 2 3 5 8
(b)  Enter the number of terms: 4
     Fibonacci sequence for 4 terms is: 1 1 2 3
```

The *non-recursive version* of the Fibonacci function discussed above is as follows.

```
int fib(int val)
{
  int current = 1;
  int old = 1;
  int older = 1;
  val -=2;
  while(val > 0)
  {
    current = old + older;
    older = old;
    old = current;
    --val;
  }
  return current;
}
```

Greatest common divisor

The greatest common divisor of two integers is the largest integer that divides them both. The problem is to calculate the GCD of two non-negative integers *m* and *n* recursively.

If *n* divides *m*, then by the definition of GCD, *gcd*(*m*, *n*) = *n*. *n* divides *m* if and only if (*m* % *n*) = 0. So, the base case is when (*m* % *n*) = 0. If *m* > *n* at the start, then *gcd*(*n*, *m* % *n*) is a smaller problem than *gcd*(*m*, *n*). If *m* < *n* at the start then (*m* % *n*) = *m* and the first recursive step *gcd*(*n*, *m* mod *n*) is equivalent to *gcd*(*n*, *m*). This has the effect of exchanging the parameter values *m* and *n*. So after the first call, it is back to the situation where the first parameter is greater than the second.

In this function, the result from the smaller problem gcd(*n*, *m* % *n*) is the solution to the current larger problem gcd(*m*, *n*). All the algorithm has to do is find the solution to the base case and return it unchanged until it reaches the original problem.

Using the definition given for gcd(), the following code may be used in a *recursive function* to find the GCD of two integers.

EXAMPLE
---

24. Write a C program to find the Greatest Common Divisor using recursion.

```
#include <stdio.h>
int gcd(int, int);      /* function prototype */
int main()
{
  int i,j;
  printf("\n Enter the numbers :");
  scanf("%d% d",&i,&j);
  printf("\n The GCD of %d and %d is\
      %d",i,j,gcd(i,j)); /* function call */
  return 0;
}
/********************************************/
/* Recursive function gcd() */
/********************************************/
int gcd(int a,int b)
{
  int remainder;
  remainder = a % b;
  if(remainder == 0)
    return b;
  else
    return gcd(b, remainder);
}
```

Output
```
Enter the numbers: 48 18
The GCD of 48 and 18 is 6
```

The Towers of Hanoi

The Towers of Hanoi problem is a classic case study in recursion. It involves moving a specified number of disks from one tower to another using a third as an auxiliary tower. Legend has it that at the time of the creation of the world, the priests of the Temple of Brahma were given the problem with 64 disks and told that when they had completed the task, the world would come to an end.

Move *n* disks from peg *A* to peg *C*, using peg *B* as needed. The following conditions apply.

- Only one disk may be moved at a time.
- This disk must be the top disk on a peg.
- A larger disk can never be placed on top of a smaller disk.

The solution should be in the form of a printed list of disk moves. For example, if *n* = 3, then the pegs would look as shown in Fig. 12.1.

Fig. 12.1 Moving of disks from and to different pegs

The key to the problem is not to focus on the first step (which must be to move the disk 1 from *A* to somewhere) but on the hardest step, i.e., moving the bottom disk to peg *C*. There is no way to reach the bottom disk until the top *n*–1 disks have moved. Further, they must be moved to peg *B* to allow the movement of the bottom disk to peg *C*. Now *n*–1 disks are on peg *B* that must be moved to peg *C* (using peg *A*). There is no reason why the *n*–1 remaining disks cannot be moved in the same manner; in fact, it must be done in the same manner since there is again a bottom disk that must be moved last. Therefore,

- Move *n*–1 disks from peg *A* to peg *B* using peg *C*.
- Move the *n*th disk from peg *A* to peg *C*.
- Move *n*–1 disks from peg *B* to peg *C* using peg *A*.

Notice that the size of the Towers of Hanoi problem is determined by the number of disks involved. This implies that the problem has been redefined in terms of three smaller problems of the same type.

- What instance(s) of the problem can serve as the base case(s)?

  If $n = 1$, then the problem consists of moving one disk from peg A to peg C, which can be clearly solved immediately.

- As the problem size diminishes, will the base case be reached?

  Since each call to the function will reduce the parameter n by 1, and n is non-negative, the base case $n = 1$ will always be reached.

- How is the solution from the smaller problem used to build a correct solution to the current larger problem?

As seen in the first question, when each of the three smaller problems are solved, then the solution to the current problem is completed. The following is a summary of the algorithm described earlier.

Algorithm

```
FUNCTION MoveTower(disk, from, to, using):
IF(n is 1) THEN
  move disk 1 from the "from" peg to the "to" peg
ELSE IF(n > 1) THEN
  move n-1 disks from the "from" peg to the "using"
      peg using the "to" peg
  move the n'th disk from the "from" peg to the "to"
      peg
  move n-1 disks from the "using" peg to the "to" peg
      using the "from" peg
ENDIF
```

If in the body of a function, a recursive call is placed in such a way that its execution is *never* followed by the execution of another instruction of the function; the call is known as *a tail recursive call*. The execution of such a call terminates the execution of the body of the function. A function may have more than one tail recursive call.

A non-tail recursive function can often be converted to a tail-recursive function by means of an 'auxiliary' parameter. This parameter is used to form the result. The idea is to attempt to incorporate the pending operation into the auxiliary parameter in such a way that the recursive call no longer has a pending operation. The technique is usually used in conjunction with an 'auxiliary' function. This is simply to keep the syntax clean and to hide the fact that auxiliary parameters are needed.

For example, a tail-recursive Fibonacci function can be implemented by using two auxiliary parameters for accumulating results. It should not be surprising that the tree-recursive fib function requires two auxiliary parameters to collect results; there are two recursive calls. To compute fib(n), call fib_aux(n 1 0)

```
int fib_aux(int n, int next, int result) {
  if (n == 0)
```

```
    return result;
  else
      return fib_aux(n - 1, next + result, next);
}
```

A tail recursive call can be eliminated by changing the values of the calling parameters to those specified in the recursive call, and repeating the whole function. Consider, for example, the function used to solve the Towers of Hanoi problem.

```
void MoveTower(int n, char from, char to, char using)
{
  if(n == 1)
  printf("\n Move disk 1 from peg %c to ped %c",
         from, to);
  else if(n > 1) {
  MoveTower( n-1, from, using, to);
  printf("\n Move disk %d from peg %c to ped %c",
         n, from, to);
  MoveTower(n-1, using, to, from);
  }
}
```

By removing *tail recursion,* the function can be rewritten as

```
void MoveTower(int n, char from, char to, char using)
{
  char temp;
  if(n > 1) {
  MoveTower( n-1, from, using, to);
  printf("\n Move disk %d from peg %c to ped %c", n,
         from, to);
  n = n - 1;
  temp = from;
  from = using;
  using = temp;
  }
  if(n == 1) then
  printf("\n Move disk 1 from peg %c to ped %c",
         from, to);
}
```

The recursive call, MoveTower(n-1, from, using, to);, is not a tail recursive call because its execution is followed by the execution of other instructions in the function, namely a printf() statement, various assignment statements, and if n == 1 is true, another printf() statement.

In general, any recursive call placed within a looping statement is not *tail recursive* because when control returns from the recursive call, there may be one or more cycles of the loop yet to be executed.

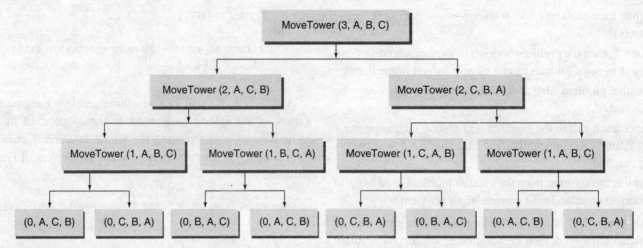

Fig. 12.2   Recursion tree for MoveTower (3,a,b,c)

Elimination of *tail recursion* is simple and can shorten the execution time quite considerably. It is not a necessary stage in the elimination of all recursive calls. In particular, compilers do not normally deal with removal of *tail recursions* separately, and this explains the gain in efficiency mentioned above.

A key tool for analyzing recursive algorithms is the recursion tree, which portrays the life history of a recursive process (or, equivalently, the life history of the runtime stack). A *recursion tree* can be built according to the following rules.

- Every tree must have a main root from which all branches originate. This principle root will represent the initial call to the function.
- The tree consists of nodes (vertices), each of which represents a particular call to the recursive function.
- A branch of the tree (solid line) represents a call-return path between any two instances of the function.

Figure 12.2 shows a call tree for `MoveTower(3,A,B,C)`.

12.10.2 How is Recursion Implemented?

The run-time stack   For the moment, let it be left to recursion to consider what steps are needed to call any function in a single processor computer system.

Fig. 12.3   The sequence of events that takes place when a stack is used with function calls

Modern languages are usually implemented in a manner such that storage for program code and storage for data items are allocated separately. The area of store set aside to hold the data items used in the call of a function is called its *data area* or *activation record*.

This data area essentially consists of calling parameters, local variables, and certain system information such as the address of the instruction that must be returned to on leaving the function.

The storage mechanism that most modern languages use is called *stack storage management*. Using this mechanism, storage for the main program's data area is allocated at load time, while storage for a function's data area is only allocated when the function is called. On exit from the function, this storage is de-allocated. This mechanism results in a stack of data areas called the *run-time stack*. When a function is called, space for its data area is allocated and placed on top of the run-time stack. On exit from the function, its data area is de-allocated and removed from the top of the run-time stack. Basically, the principle it follows is Last In First Out (LIFO) (Fig. 12.3).

Stack storage management is capable of dealing with recursive functions. In the recursive case, two recursive calls are regarded as being different so that the data areas for one call do not overlap with the other; just like one would not mix the data areas for different sub-functions, one called from within the other. This implies that several data areas may exist simultaneously, one for each recursive call.

In the stack implementation of recursion, the local variables of the function will be pushed onto the stack as the recursive call is initiated. When the recursive call terminates, these local variables will be popped from the stack and thereby restored to their former values.

But doing so is pointless because the recursive call is the last action of the function and so the function now terminates. The just-restored local variables are discarded. It is thus pointless to use the recursion stack, since no local variables need to be preserved. All that is needed is to set the calling parameters to their new values and branch to the beginning of the function.

Note

- It may not terminate if the stopping case is not correct or is incomplete (stack overflow: run-time error)
- Make sure that each recursive step leads to a situation that is closer to a stopping case.

12.10.3 Comparing Recursion and Iteration

Recursion is a very powerful tool for solving complex problems, particularly when the underlying problem or data to be treated is already defined in recursive terms. For such problems, recursion can lead to solutions that are much clearer and easier to modify than their iterative counterparts.

However, such recursive definitions do not guarantee that a recursive algorithm is the best way to solve a problem. Depending on the implementation available and the algorithm being used, recursion can require a substantial amount of runtime overhead. Thus, the use of recursion illustrates the classic trade-off between time spent in constructing and maintaining a program and the cost in time and memory of execution of that program.

The following two factors contribute to the inefficiency of some recursive solutions.

- The overhead associated with function calls
- The inefficient utilization of memory

With most implementations of modern programming languages, a function call incurs a booking overhead in the form of a runtime stack. Recursive functions magnify this bookkeeping overhead, because a single initial call to the function can generate a large number of recursive calls.

Recursion makes inefficient utilization of memory, as every time a new recursive call is made a new set of local variables is allocated to function. Moreover, it also slows down execution speed, as function calls require jumps, and saving the current state of the calling function onto stack before jump.

Recursion is of value when the return values of the recursive function are used in further processing within the calling version of the function (rather than being immediately passed back to an earlier version of the function). In this case it was *worth* saving the parameter and local variables on the stack because they are used later in some useful way.

If one problem can be solved in both ways (recursive or iterative), then choosing iterative version is a good idea since it is faster and does not consume a lot of memory.

Note

- In general, an iterative version of a program will execute more efficiently in terms of time and space than a recursive version. This is because the overhead involved in entering and exiting a function is avoided in iterative version. However, a recursive solution can be sometimes the most natural and logical way of solving a complex problem.

12.11 SEARCHING AND SORTING

12.11.1 Searching Algorithms

Searching an array of integers has already been discussed in Chapter 11. Among the searching algorithms, only two of them will be discussed here—sequential search and binary search.

Sequential or linear search algorithm

The idea behind sequential search is to compare the given number to each of the numbers in the array. If a number in the list matches the given key, we can return the index of that number. If we reach the end of the list, we can indicate that the key does not exist in the array by returning –1. Here is an implementation of this simple algorithm:

```
int  Lsearch(int ArrayElement[], int key,
                    int ArraySize)
{
  int i ;
  for (i = 0; i < ArraySize;  i++)
    if (ArrayElement[i] == Key)
                return (i) ;
  return (-1);
}
```

The function calling statement will be as follows:

```
p=Lsearch(a,k,n);
if(p = = -1)
  printf("\n KEY NOT FOUND");
else
  printf("\n KEY  FOUND AT POSITION %d", p);
```

Binary search algorithm

The precondition of binary search is that it requires sorted data to operate on. The basic technique is to compare the search element with the element which is in the middle of the search space and then to restrict further searching in the appropriate half of the search space (this can be done because the search space is sorted). Then at each step, the process is repeated (cutting the remaining search space in half at each step) until either the search element is found or we have run out of elements to compare and the element was not in the search space.

To implement binary search, variables beg and end keep track of the lower bound and upper bound of the array, respectively. We begin by examining the middle element of the array. If the key we are searching for is less than the middle element, then it must reside in the lower half of the array. Thus, we set end to (mid – 1). If the key we are searching for is greater than the middle element, then it must reside in the upper half of the array. Thus, we set beg to (mid + 1). This restricts our next iteration through the loop to the top half of the array. In this way, each iteration halves the size of the array to be searched. For example, the first iteration will leave three items to test. After the second iteration, there will be one item left to test. Therefore, it takes only three iterations to find any number.

To illustrate the algorithm, let us consider the following array:

3	10	15	20	35	40	60

Suppose we want to search the element "15".

1. We take beg = 0, end = 6 and compute the location of the middle element as

$$mid = \frac{(beg + end)}{2} = \frac{(0+6)}{2} = 3$$

2. We then compare the search key with mid, i.e. a[mid]==a[3] is not equal to 15. Since beg<end, we have to start the next iteration.

3. As a[mid]=20>15, therefore, we take end = mid−1 = 3 1 = 2 whereas beg remains the same.. Thus

$$min = \frac{(beg + end)}{2} = \frac{(0+2)}{2} = 1$$

4. Since a[mid], i.e. a[1]=10<15, therefore, we take beg=mid+1=1+1=2, while end remains the same.

5. Now beg=end. Compute the mid element:

$$min = \frac{(beg + end)}{2} = \frac{(2+2)}{2} = 2$$

Since a[mid], i.e. a[2]=15, the search terminates on success. The C code for binary search is given below.

```
#include <stdio.h>
int binarysearch(int a[], int n, int key)
{
    int beg,mid;
    beg=0; end=n-1;
    while(beg<=end)
    {
      mid=(beg+end)/2;
      if(key==a[mid])
            return mid;
        else if(key>a[mid])
                beg=mid+1;
        else
                end=mid-1;
    }
    return -1;
}
int main()
{
    int arr[50], n, key, index;
    printf("How many elements?");
    scanf("%d", &n);
```

```
    puts("Enter the array elements in ascending\
        order");
    for (index = 0; index < n; index++)
        scanf("%d", &arr[index]);
    printf("Enter the search key: ");
    scanf("%d", &key);
    index = binarysearch(arr, n, key);
    if (index == -1)
      puts("Sorry, the given key was not found");
    else
      printf("The given key was found at index:\
        %d\n", index);
    return 0;
}
```

Binary search in a recursive way

Binary search is often written using recursion, instead of iteration. This is because when the algorithm decides to search the right or left half of the array, it becomes a simpler version of the original problem. In the recursive Search function below, note how the parameters to the recursive calls are adjusted to specify either the right or left half of the array.

```
/* Given:x      Array of integers.
   Low         The low index of the range of integers
               to search.
   High        The top index of the range of integers
               to search.
   k           The integer for which to search.
   Task:       To do a recursive binary search for k in
               the specified range of Array.
   Return:     In the function name, return the index
               of where k was found or -1 if it was not
               found.
*/
int search(int x[ ], int k, int low, int high)
{
  int mid;
  if(low > high)
    return (-1);
  mid = (low + high) /2;
  return (k= =x[mid] ? mid : k < x[mid] ? search(x,
    k, low, mid - 1):search(x, k, mid+1, high));
}
```

12.11.2 Sorting Algorithms

Arranging elements of an array in a particular order is called sorting. The order of arrangement may be ascending or descending in nature. There are several methods of arranging or sorting arrays. Sorting algorithms are divided into two categories—internal and external sorts.

Internal sort Any sort algorithm, which uses main memory exclusively during the sort. This assumes high-speed random access to all memory.

External sort Any sort algorithm which uses external memory, such as tape or disk, during the sort.

A sort algorithm is said to be 'stable' if multiple items which compare as equal will stay in the same order they were in after a sort.

Some of the sorting methods include:

- Bubble sort
- Selection sort
- Insertion sort
- Merge sort
- Quick sort

The method of bubble sort has been explained with examples in Chapter 11. Hence, the discussion in the following section begins with selection sort.

Selection sort

Selection sort is a way of arranging the elements, of a supposedly unsorted array, in an ascending order. It works by finding the smallest element in the whole array and placing it at the first element position. It then finds the second smallest element in the array disregarding the first element and places it in the second position. Next, it finds the smallest element in the array disregarding the elements placed in position 1 and 2. This continues until the entire array has been sorted. The implementation algorithm for selection sort may be stated as follows:

1. Examine each element in the array or list to find the smallest.
2. Swap the element found in step 1 with the first element in the array or list.
3. Repeat steps 1 and 2, each time ignoring the element at the start of the last sort. Stop when only one element has to be sorted.

The selection sort is, therefore, a combination of searching and sorting. During each pass, the unsorted element with the smallest (or largest) value is moved to its proper position in the array. This sort also uses an incremental approach to sorting the array. The number of times the sort passes through the array depends on the size of the array. The algorithm makes one less pass than the number of elements in the array.

A function for the selection sort can be developed using two loops. An inner loop passes through the array and finds the next smallest (or largest) value, and an outer loop that places that value in its proper position. Selection sort is one of the easiest sorts to implement, but is among the least efficient. It provides no way to end a sort early even if it begins with an already sorted list. A function developed for implementing the selection sort technique for arranging a list of elements in ascending order is shown as follows:

```c
void selectsort(int numbers[], int array_size)
{
    int i, j;
    int min, temp;
    for (i = 0; i < array_size-1; i++)
    {
        min = i;
        for (j = i+1; j < array_size; j++)
        {
            if (numbers[j] < numbers[min])
                min = j;
        }
        temp = numbers[i];
        numbers[i] = numbers[min];
        numbers[min] = temp;
    }
}
```

An array formed with integers

Highlighted `for loop` finds the position of the smallest integer.

Highlighted statements interchange the position of the smallest integer with that at the first position.

For the above algorithm to work, it *must* ignore elements that have already been sorted. For instance, once the smallest element has been placed in its correct position, it must be ignored for the rest of the sort. In practice this means that to implement the algorithm, the already sorted elements have to be skipped, looking only for the smallest element that is not yet sorted. This can be implemented in the function `void selectsort()` by replacing the encircled portion of the program code with that shown within the box on the right.

```c
void selectsort(int numbers[], int array_size)
{
    int i, j;
    int min, temp;
    for (i = 0; i < array_size-1; i++)
    {
        min = i;
        for (j = i+1; j < array_size; j++)
        {
            if (numbers[j] < numbers[min])
                min = j;
        }
        temp = numbers[i];
        numbers[i] = numbers[min];
        numbers[min] = temp;
    }
}
```

```c
if(min != i)
{
    temp = numbers[i];
    numbers[i] = numbers[min];
    numbers[min] = temp;
}
```

Insertion sort

The primary idea in insertion sort is to pick up a data element from a list or an array and insert it into its proper place in the partial data list or array considered so far.

The process of insertion sort is started by considering the first element to belong to a sorted sub-array while the remaining array elements to another sub-array which is considered as unsorted. The first step then is to compare the first element of the unsorted array with the sorted array's element. If the sorting is for arranging the elements in ascending order, then the comparison is carried out to find whether the first element of the unsorted array is smaller than that of the sorted array's element. If this is true, then the first element of the unsorted array is placed at the first position of the sorted array while the existing element in the sorted array is shifted right by one position. The sorted sub-array will now contain two sorted elements while the unsorted sub-array will contain N − 2 elements, where N denotes the size of the whole array. In the second step, again the first element of the unsorted sub-array is compared with the elements of the sorted sub-array and the resulting element is placed at the proper position while shifting the larger elements by one position to the right in the sorted sub-array.

The sorted sub-array now contains three elements arranged in order, while the rest of the elements form the unsorted sub-array. In the same way, the next step repeats the same procedure of comparison and placing the appropriate element at the proper position. This process continues till the last element in the array. Thus, in each pass, the first element of the unsorted portion is picked up, transferred to the sorted sub-list, and inserted at the appropriate place. A list of N elements will take at most N−1 passes to sort the data.

Figure 12.4 shows the insertion sort technique. This illustration demonstrates the sorting of array. Every time the first element, which is shown highlighted, is compared with the elements of the sorted sub-array and interposed at the proper position in sorted sub-array by suitably shifting the larger value elements.

A function prepared for implementing the insertion sort algorithm for sorting an array in ascending order is given below Fig. 12.4.

Fig. 12.4 Insertion sort

```
void insertSort(int A[], int arr_size)
{
  int i, j,temp;
  for (i=1; i < arr_size; i++)
    {
      temp = A[i];
      j = i;
      while ((j > 0) && (A[j-1] >temp))
        {
          A[j] = A[j-1];
          j = j - 1;
        }
      A[j] = temp;
    }
}
```

An alternate function that can also do insertion sorting is shown below.

```
void insort(int A[], int size)
{
  int i, j, temp;
  for (i = 1 ; i < size; i++)
  {
    temp = A[i];
    for (j = i - 1; j >= 0 && temp < A[j] ; j--)
      A[ j + 1] = A[ j ];
    A[ j + 1] = temp;
  }
}
```

An advantage of this procedure is that it sorts the array only when it is really necessary. If the array is already in order, no moves for sorting are performed. However, it overlooks the fact that the elements may already be in their proper positions. When an element has to be inserted, all elements greater than this have to be shifted. There may be a large number of redundant shifts, as an element, which is properly located, may be shifted but later brought back to its position.

The best case is when the data is already in order. Only one comparison is made for each position and the data movement is 2N – 1, where N is the size of the array. The worst case is when the data is in reverse order. Each data element is to be moved to a new position and for that each of the other elements have to be shifted. When the elements are in random order, it turns out that both number of comparisons and movements turn out to be closer to the worst case.

Merge sort

The merge sort splits a data list to be sorted into two equal halves, and places them in separate arrays. This sorting method uses the divide-and-conquer paradigm. It separates the list into two halves and then sorts the two half data sets recursively. Finally, these are merged to obtain the complete sorted list.

To be more specific, the merge sort breaks an array down into smaller and smaller pieces until the individual pieces are just one item in size. Since a single item is always considered to be sorted, two contiguous items can be merged. The merge sort algorithm therefore breaks the array down into smaller chunks on the way down the recursion tree. On the way back up, it merges these smaller pieces of the array into larger pieces. One could say that the sorting is done on the way back up the tree.

Figure 12.5 shows a typical example of the merge sort algorithm for an unsorted array A of size 8 that contains the following data elements— 32, 45, 26, 15, 25, 91, 30, 73.

Fig. 12.5 Merge sort

In this example, the original array is split continuously in two halves till it reduces to an array of one element. These are then merged in the following steps:

1. Elements 32 and 45 are compared and merged to form the array [32 45] .

2. Elements 26 and 15 are compared and merged to form the array [15 26].

3. Next, sub-arrays [32 45] and [15 26] are compared and merged to form the array [15 26 32 45].

4. Elements 25 and 91 are compared and merged to form the array [25 91].

5. Elements 30 and 73 are compared and merged to form the array [30 73].

6. Next, sub-arrays [25 91] and [30 73] are compared and merged to form the array [25 30 73 91].

7. Finally, the sorted and merged sub-arrays in steps 3 and 6 are sorted and merged to form the array [15 25 26 30 32 45 73 91].

A function that implements the merge sort algorithm discussed above is given as follows:

```
void mergesort(int array[], int n)
{
    int j,n1,n2,arr1[n],arr2[n];
        if (n<=1)return;
    n1=n/2;
    n2 = n - n1;
    for(j = 0; j<n1; j++)
        arr1[j]= array[j];
    for(j = 0; j<n2; j++)
        arr2[j]= array[j+n1];
    mergesort(arr1, n1);
    mergesort(arr2, n2);
    merge(array, arr1, n1, arr2, n2);
}
void merge (int array[], int arr1[], int n1,
                    int arr2[], int n2)
{
    int j, p=0, p1=0,p2=0;
    printf("\n After merging [");
    for(j=0; j<n1; j++)
    printf("%d ",arr1[j]);
        printf("] [");
    for(j=0; j<n2; j++)
        printf("%d",arr2[j]);
    printf("]");
    while (p1 < n1 && p2 < n2)
    {
        if(arr1[p1] < arr2[p2])
            array [p++] = arr1[p1++];
        else
            array[p++] = arr2[p2++];
    }
```

```
while (p1 < n1)
    array [p++] = arr1[p1++];
while (p2 < n2)
    array[p++] = arr2[p2++];
printf("merged array is [");
for(j=0; j<n1+n2; j++)
    printf("%d", array[j]);
printf("]\n");
}
```

Quick sort

Quick sort is a recursively defined procedure for rearranging the values stored in an array in the ascending or descending order. Suppose, an array a of 11 integers is given as shown in Fig.12.6(a).

The idea is to use a process that separates the list into two parts, using a distinguished value in the list called a *pivot*. At the end of the process, one part will contain only values

(a) Array of 11 elements containing integers

(b) Separation of elements with values less or more than the pivot, 8

(c) Choosing the index of the pivot

(d) Moving the right_arrow to the left until 'value <= pivot'

(e) Swapping of the values in the a[left_arrow] and a[right_arrow] elements

(f) Position of the right_arrow after a[right_arrow] <=pivot condition becomes true as the right_arrow is moved left

(g) Position of left_arrow after a[left_arrow]>=pivot condition becomes true as the left_arrow is moved right

(h) Exchanging a[left_arrow] and a[right_arrow]

(i) Moving right_arrow to the Left till a[right_arrow]<=pivot

(j) Moving left_arrow right till a[left_arrow]>= pivot

(k) Exchanging pivot with right_arrow content

(l) The right_arrow is moved left and the left_arrow is moved right

Fig. 12.6 Step-by-step depiction of how quick sort works less than or equal to the pivot, and the other will contain only values greater than or equal to the pivot. So, if 8 is picked as the pivot, Fig. 12.6(b) shows the result at the end of the process.

The same process can then be reapplied exactly to the left-hand and right-hand parts separately. This reapplication of the same procedure leads to a recursive definition. The detail of the rearranging procedure is as follows. The index of the pivot value is chosen simply by evaluating

```
(first + last) / 2
```

where `first` and `last` are the indices of the initial and final elements in the array representing the list. A `left_arrow` and a `right_arrow` are then identified on the far left and the far right respectively. This can be seen in Fig. 12.6(c), where `left_arrow` and `right_arrow` initially represent the lowest and highest indices of the array components. Starting from the right, the `right_arrow` is moved left until a value less than or equal to the pivot is encountered. See Fig. 12.6(d).

Similarly, the `left_arrow` is moved right until a value greater than or equal to the pivot is encountered. Now, the contents of the two array components are swapped as can be seen in Fig. 12.6(e).

Now, continuing the movement of the `right_arrow` left till `a[right_arrow]<=pivot`, the position of the `right_arrow` is as shown in Fig. 12.6(f).

Having reached the status shown in Fig. 12.6(g), the contents of the `a[left_arrow]` and `a[right_arrow]` are interchanged. After this interchange, the contents of the elements are shown in Fig. 12.6(h).

The process of movement of the `left_arrow` and `right_arrow` stops only when the condition `left_arrow > right_arrow` becomes true. Since in Fig. 12.6(h), this condition is still False, move `right_arrow` left again as shown in Fig. 12.6(i).

Having reached the status shown in Fig. 12.6(k), the contents of the `a[left_arrow]` and `a[right_arrow]` are interchanged. It is acceptable to exchange the pivot because pivot is the value itself, not the index. As before, the `right_arrow` is moved left and the `left_arrow` is moved right as shown in Fig. 12.6(l).

The procedure's terminating condition `left_arrow > right_arrow` is now true, and the first subdivision of the list (i.e., array) is now complete.

Here, the quick sort procedure is coded as a recursive C function. This can be shown as follows.

```c
void quick_sort(int list[], int left, int right)
{
    int pivot, left_arrow, right_arrow;
    left_arrow = left;
    right_arrow = right;
```

```c
    pivot = list[(left + right)/2];
    do
    {
        while(list[right_arrow] > pivot)
            right_arrow--;
        while(list[left_arrow] < pivot)
            left_arrow++;
        if(left_arrow <= right_arrow)
        {
            swap(list[left_arrow], list[right_arrow]);
            left_arrow++;
            right_arrow--;
        }
    }
    while(right_arrow >= left_arrow);
    if(left < right_arrow)
        quick_sort(list, left, right_arrow);
    if(left_arrow < right)
        quick_sort(list, left_arrow, right);
}
```

12.12 ANALYSIS OF ALGORITHMS

One significant factor considered while designing algorithms is the algorithm's efficiency. The efficiency of an algorithm is determined by the amount of time it takes to run the program and the memory space the program requires. In analyzing an algorithm, rather than a piece of code, the number of times 'the principle activity' of that algorithm is performed, should be predicted. For example, if one is analyzing a sorting algorithm, one might count the number of comparisons performed, and if it is an algorithm to find an optimal solution, one might count the number of times it evaluates a solution.

Complexity of an algorithm is a measure of the amount of time and/or memory space required by an algorithm for a given input. It is a function describing the efficiency of the algorithm in terms of the amount of data the algorithm must process. Usually, there are natural units for the domain and range of this function. The factor or parameters or fields whose values affect the number of operations performed is called the *problem size* or the *input size*. The following are the two main complexity measures of the efficiency of an algorithm:

Time complexity   It is a function that describes the amount of time an algorithm takes with respect to the amount of input provided to the algorithm. 'Time' can mean the number of memory accesses performed, the number of comparisons between integers, the number of times some inner loop is executed, or some other natural unit related to the amount of real time the algorithm will take. It is denoted as $T(n)$ where n is the size of the input.

Space complexity   It is a function that describes the amount of memory (space) an algorithm takes with respect to the amount of input provided to the algorithm. Space complexity is sometimes ignored because the space used is minimal and/

or obvious, but sometimes it becomes as important an issue as time. It is denoted as $S(n)$, where n is the size of the input.

Complexity analysis

Complexity analysis attempts to characterize the relationship between the number of data elements and the resource usage (time or space) with a simple formula approximation. Using the RAM model of computation, one can count the number of steps required for an algorithm for executing a program based on the input provided. However, to really understand how good or bad an algorithm is, one must know how it works over all instances. There are three terms to describe these situations:

- The **worst-case complexity** of the algorithm is the function defined by the maximum number of steps taken on any instance of input size n.
- The **best-case complexity** of the algorithm is the function defined by the minimum number of steps taken on any instance of input size n.
- Finally, the **average-case complexity** of the algorithm is the function defined by the average number of steps taken on any instance of input size n.

Every input instance can be represented as a point on a graph, where the x-axis is the size of the problem (for sorting, the number of items to sort) and the y-axis is the number of steps taken by the algorithm on this instance. Worst-case complexity is represented by the curve passing through the highest point of each column. The curve passing through the lowest point of each column represents the best case complexity.

The average case is probably the most important, but it is problematic. One has to make some assumptions about the probabilities, and the analysis will only be as accurate as the validity of the assumptions. In simple cases, the average complexity is established by considering possible inputs to an algorithm, for each input, adding the number of steps for all the inputs and dividing by the number of inputs. Here, it is assumed that the possibility of the occurrence of each input is the same, which will not always be the case. To consider the probability explicitly, the average complexity is defined as the average over the number of steps executed when processing each input weighted by the probability of occurrence of this input.

If a function is linear, that is, if it contains no loops, then its efficiency is a function of the number of instructions it contains. In this case, its efficiency is dependent on the speed of the computer. On the other hand, functions that contain loops will vary widely in their efficiency. The study of algorithm efficiency is, therefore, largely devoted to the study of loops. The efficiency of an algorithm can be expressed as a function of the number of elements or inputs to be processed. The general format is

```
f(n) = efficiency
```

Loops can be of various types. Let us discuss these in detail.

Linear loops Consider the following simple loop.

```
for(i=1;i<=n;++i)    for(i=0;i<n;++i)
{                    {
  stmTs                stmTs
}                    }
```

The body of the loop will be repeated for n times. In the following loop,

```
for(i=1;i<=n; i=i+2)
{
  stmTs
}
```

the body of the loop will be executed $n/2$ times. In all of the above cases, the number of iterations is directly proportional to a factor. The higher the factor, the higher will be the number of iterations. If either of these loops was plotted, one would get a straight line. Hence such loops are known as linear loops. Because the efficiency is proportional to the number of iterations, it is

```
f(n) = n
```

Logarithmic loops Now, the following loops are to be considered in which the controlling variable is multiplied or divided in each iteration.

```
Multiply loop           Divide loop
for(i=1; i<n; i=i*2)    for(i=n; i>=1; i=i/2)
{                       {
  stmTs                   stmTs
}                       }
```

Let $n = 10$; the number of iterations in both cases is 4. The reason is that in each iteration the value of i doubles for the multiply loop and is cut in half for the divide loop. The number of iterations is a function of the multiplier or divisor. The loop continues till the following condition is true.

For the multiply loop, $2^{iteration} < n$
For the divide loop, $n/2^{iteration} >= 1$
Generalizing the analysis, $f(n) = [\log_2 n]$

Nested loop For the nested loop, the total number of iterations would be the product of the number of iterations for the inner loop and the number of iterations for the outer loop. There are various types of nested loops, namely quadratic, dependent quadratic, linear logarithmic, etc.

Quadratic loop Here, each of the loops iterates the same number of times as shown in the following code.

```
for(i=1;i<=n;i++)
  for(j=1;j<=n;j++)
  {
    stmTs
  }
```

For each iteration of the outer loop, the inner loop will be executed *n* times. The outer loop will be executed *n* times. Therefore,

```
f(n) = n²
```

Dependent quadratic   Consider the following nested loop:

```
for(i=1;i<=n;i++)
  for(j=1;j<=i;j++)
  {
    stmTs
  }
```

Here, the inner loop is dependent on the outer loop for one of its factors. It is executed only once for the first iteration, twice for the second iteration, thrice for the third, and so on. The number of iterations for the inner loop is

```
1+2+3+4+………n = n(n+1)/2
```

The average of this loop is $(n+1)/2$. Multiplying the inner loop by the number of times the outer loop is executed, gives the following formula for a dependent quadratic loop.

```
f(n) = n(n+1)/2
```

Linear logarithmic   Consider the following nested loop in which the outer loop is linear and the inner loop is logarithmic.

```
for(i=1;i<=n;i++)
  for(j=1;j<=n;j=j*2)
  {
    stmTs
  }
```

Therefore, the number of iterations in the inner loop is $[\log_2 n]$. The outer loop will be executed *n* times. So,

```
f(n) = [nlog₂ n]
```

It has been shown that the number of statements executed in the function for *n* elements of data is a function of the number of elements, expressed as f(n). There is a dominant factor in the equation that determines the 'order of magnitude' of the result. Therefore, it is not needed to determine the complete measure of efficiency, but only the factor that determines the magnitude. This factor is the Big-O.

12.12.1 Asymptotic notation

Asymptotic notation is a way of describing functions without having to deal with distracting details. In many ways, asymptotic notation can seem very imprecise and intuitive, but it should be precisely defined; it is also crucial to understand exactly what it means.

Big-O notation

The most well-known symbol in asymptotic notation is the *big-O* (historically, the Greek letter omicron). It is used to give an *upper limit* to the *asymptotic growth* of a function. order notation, or big-O notation, is a measure of the running time of an algorithm, as it relates to the size of the input to

that algorithm. It is intended not to measure the performance of the machine on which the algorithm is run, but rather to strictly measure the performance of the algorithm itself.

Big-O notation can be defined as follows:

If f(n) and g(n) are functions defined for positive integers, then f(n) = O(g(n)), if there exists a c such that |f(n)|<=c|g(n)| for all sufficiently large positive integers n.

```
f(n) = O(g(n)) is true if
lim f(n)/g(n) is a constant.
n → a
```

It is to be noted that the big-O notation says 'some constant multiple of' without saying what the constant is. This leaves out some information that is sometimes important, but it allows specifying time without reference to the speed of the computer and without measuring exactly how many instructions are in a certain block of code. The properties of the big-O notation are as follows.

1. O(k*f(n)) = O(f(n)), therefore, constants can be ignored.

2. O(f(n)*g(n)) = O(f(n)) * O(g(n)), i.e., if a function is a product then its order is the product of the orders of the factors.

3. O(f(n)/g(n)) = O(f(n)) / O(g(n)), i.e., the order is the same for a function that is a quotient.

4. O(f(n)) > O(g(n)), if and only if, f dominates g.

5. O(f(n)+g(n)) = Max[O(f(n)), O(g(n))], i.e., terms of lower degree can be ignored.

6. One should be careful with functions that have subtraction:

   If f(n) = O(h(n)) and g(n) = O(h(n)) then

   f(n)-g(n) is not equal to O(h(n)) – O(h(n)) = 0

7. Big O is transitive, that is, if f(n) = O(g(n)) and g(n) is O(h(n)), then f(n) = O(h(n)).

8. The powers of *n* are ordered according to the exponent $n^a = O(n^b)$ iff a <= b.

9. The order of log *n* is independent of the base taken $\log_a n = O(\log_b n)$ for all a, b > 1.

10. Logarithms grow more slowly than any power of n log. $n = O(n^a)$ for any a>0 but $n^a \neq O(\log n)$

11. na = O(bn), for all a, b > 1 but $b^n \neq O(n^a)$ for b > 1.

The big-O notation can be derived from f(n) using the following steps:

1. In each term, set the coefficient of the term to one.

2. Keep the largest term in the function and discard the others. Terms are ranked from lowest to highest as follows:

   ```
   log n, n, nlog n, n², n³, …, nᵏ, 2ⁿ, n!, …
   ```

For example, to calculate the big-O notation for

$$f(n) = n(n+1)/2 + 5n^3 = n^2/2 + n/2 + 5n^3$$

we first remove the coefficients. This gives us n2 + n + n3. The largest factor is n3. Therefore, the big-O notation is stated as

$$O(f(n)) = O(n^3)$$

Certain big-O expressions occur so frequently that they are given names. An algorithm is

- constant, if f(n) is O(1).
- logarithmic, if f(n) is O(log n).
- linear, if f(n) is O(n).
- quadratic, if f(n) is O(n²).
- polynomial, if f(n) is O(n^k), where k is a constant.
- exponential, if f(n) is O(n^k), where k is a constant.

Let us now discuss these in detail.

Constant O(1) An algorithm with the running time O(1) is said to have a 'constant' running time. Basically, this means that the algorithm always takes the same amount of time, regardless of the size of the input. To state it technically, if an algorithm never performs more than a certain number of steps, no matter how large the input is, then that algorithm is considered to have a constant running time.

Linear O(n) An algorithm which runs in O(n) is said to have a 'linear' running time. This means that the amount of time to run the algorithm is proportional to the size of the input. Alternatively, an algorithm which never performs more than a certain number of steps for each element in the input has a linear running time.

Quadratic O(n²) This means that whenever one increases the size of the input by a factor of n, the running time increases by a factor of n^2.

Logarithm O(log n) This means that as the size of the input increases by a factor of n, the running time increases by a factor of the logarithm of n. For example, if one increases the input size of O(logn) algorithm by a factor of 1024, the running time will increase by a factor of 10. This running time is better than O(n), but not as good as O(1). As the input size becomes larger, however, the behaviour becomes comparable to O(1) in many circumstances.

Linear logarithmic O(n log n) An algorithm which when given an input of size n never performs more than cn log n steps (for some c which is always the same regardless of the value of n) has a running time of O(n log n). This running time is better than O(n²).

Exponential O(2ⁿ) This means that its running time will double every time you add another element to the input. An algorithm with this running time is generally considered to be too slow to be useful for anything but the smallest of problems.

Lower bounds and tight bounds

Big O only gives an upper bound on a function, i.e., if the constant factors are ignored and n gets big enough, it is obvious that some function will never exceed some other function. But this can give too much freedom. For instance, the time for selection sort is easily O(n³), because n² is O(n³). But we know that O(n²) is a more meaningful upper bound. What is required is to be able to describe a *lower bound*, a function that always grows more slowly than f(n), and a *tight bound*, a function that grows at about the same rate as f(n). There is a symmetrical definition of the lower bound in the definition of big-Ω (omega):

The function f(n) is Ω (g(n)), if there exist positive numbers c and N such that f(n) > cg(n) for all n > N. In other words, cg(n) is a lower bound on the size of f(n) or in the long run f grows at least at the rate of g.

There is an interconnection between these two notations expressed by the equivalence.

f(n) is Ω (g(n)) iff g(n) is O(f(n)).

There is a common ground between big-O and big-Ω notations indicated by the equalities in the definition of these notations. Big-O is defined in terms of ≤ and big-Ω in terms of >; = is included in both inequalities. This restriction can be accomplished by the following definition of θ (theta) notation:

The function f(n) is θ(g(n)), if there exist positive numbers c1, c2, and N such that c1g(n) < f(n) < c2g(n) for all n > N.

12.12.2 Efficiency of Linear Search

Linear or sequential search has already been discussed in the Chapter 11 on arrays and strings. For the linear search algorithm, the number of steps depends on whether the key is in the list, and if so, where in the list or array, as well as on the length of the list (number of elements in the list or array).

For search algorithms, the main steps are the comparisons of values of array elements with the key value. Counting these for data models representing the *best case*, the worst case, and the *average case* produces the following table. For each case, the number of steps is expressed in terms of n, the number of elements in the array.

Table 12.2 Number of comparisons in linear search algorithm in least, worst, and average-case situations

Case	Comparisons as a function of n
Best case (fewest comparisons)	1
Worst case (most comparisons)	n
Average-case (average number of comparisons)	$n/2$

The best case for sequential search is that it does only one comparison. In the worst case, sequential search does n comparisons, and either matches the last element in the array or does not match anything.

The average case is harder to do. It is known that the number of comparisons depends on the position of the key in the array. But what is the typical position of the key? One reasonable assumption is that if the key is in the array, it is equally likely to be any position. So probability of occurences of position = $1/n$. Therefore, average number of comparisons

$$= \sum_{i=1}^{n} (1/n) \times i$$

$$= 1/n \sum_{i=1}^{n} i$$

$$= n(n+1)/2n$$

$$= (n+1)/2$$

But if key is not in the list, the number of comparisons is always n. Suppose for an array, any permutation of the list is equally likely. Then, we can average over all possible permutations. Therefore, average number of comparisons

$$= \sum_{i=1}^{n!} \frac{1}{n!} \cdot \text{(position of key in permutation i)}$$

$$= \sum_{p=1}^{n} \frac{1}{n!} \cdot p \cdot \text{(number of permutations with key in position p)}$$

$$= \sum_{p=1}^{n} \frac{1}{n!} \cdot p \cdot (n-1)!$$

$$= \sum_{p=1}^{n} \frac{1}{n!} \cdot p$$

$$= (n+1)/2$$

Hence, this assumption gives the same analysis. A second point to be made about average case analysis is that sometimes it makes sense to analyse different cases separately. The above analysis assumes that the key is always in the array; if the key is not in the array, it requires n comparisons. One could make up a probability p that x is in or out of the array and combine the two numbers above to get a total average number of comparisons equal to `pn + (1-p)(n+1)/2` but it makes more sense to just mention both numbers separately.

The best-case analysis on an average has no significance. If the first element checked happens to be the target, any algorithm will take only one comparison. The worst- and average-case analyses give a better indication of algorithm efficiency.

Notice that if the array grows in size, the number of comparisons required to find a key item in both worst and average cases grows *linearly*. In general, for an array of length n, the worst case is n comparisons. The algorithm is called *linear search* because its complexity/efficiency can be expressed as a linear function. The number of comparisons to find a target increases linearly as the size of the array. Therefore, `T(n) = O(n)`.

12.12.3 Binary Search Analysis

To evaluate binary search, count the number of comparisons in the best case and worst case. This analysis omits the average case, which is a bit more difficult, and ignores any differences between algorithms in the amount of computation corresponding to each comparison.

The best case occurs if the middle item happens to be the target. Then only one comparison is needed to find it. As before, the best-case analysis does not reveal much. When does the worst case occur? If the target is not in the array, then the process of dividing the list in half continues until there is only one item left to check. Figure 12.7 shows a pattern of the number of comparisons done after each division, given the simplifying assumption of an initial array length that is an even power of two which gives an exact division in half on each iteration. Consider an array in which the following elements are stored: 1, 2, 3, 4, 5, 6, 7, 8, and 9.

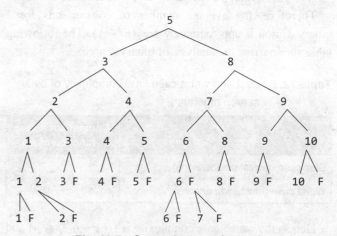

Fig. 12.7 Comparison tree for *n*=10

Every search ends at a leaf, whether successful or unsuccessful, denoted by F. To find the average number of comparisons for a successful search, one has to find the total comparisons for successful searches and divide by the number of searches (=n). That is, it is needed to a count number of branches leading from root to each leaf that terminates a successful search. From the comparison tree, the following observations can be made:

1. Height of tree = maximum number of key comparisons possible (height = number of levels below root).

2. Height of tree is at most one more than the average number of key comparisons because the levels of leaves can only differ by one, as size of lists when divided by algorithm can only differ by zero or one.

3. The number of leaves in a tree expands by a power of two (Fig. 12.8).

Fig. 12.8 Number of leaves in a tree expands by a power of two

Number of leaves = 2^h where h is the height of the tree. Therefore, if the tree has leaves on the same level then 2^h = 2n. If the tree has leaves on two levels, then 2^h > 2n (where h is smallest integer that matches the inequality). Generally, one can say that 2^h >= 2n. Taking logs of both sides (base 2) (i.e., given a^y = x, we get $\log_a x$ = y).

If 2^h >= 2n then h >= 1 + $\log_2 n$ {as log(2*n) becomes log(2) + log(n) and $\log_2 2$ = 1}.

As n gets larger, the inequality 2^h >= 2n tends to 2^h = 2n.

Therefore, the average number of comparisons for a binary search is approximately $\log_2(n + 1)$. The following table summarizes the analysis of binary search.

Table 12.3 Best and worst-case time complexity of binary search algorithm

Case	Comparisons as a function of *n*
Best case (fewest comparisons)	1
Worst case (most comparisons)	$\log_2 n$

Hence, the worse-case complexity is T(n) = O($\log_2$ n) and the best-case complexity is T(n) = O(1).

12.12.4 Analysis of Bubble Sort

To analyse bubble sort, it is needed to compare the first and second elements of an array and exchange, if necessary, so that the smaller is in the first position. This is repeated for the second and third pairs, third and fourth pairs, etc. until a pass through all adjacent pairs has been made. At the end of this first pass, the last item will be in its proper place (i.e., it will be the largest).

A second pass is performed on the first (*n*-1) items, after which the last two elements will be in place. (*n*-1) passes will be required to sort an array containing n elements. At the end of the ith pass, the last i elements will be ordered. If the pass is made in which no exchanges are required, then the array is in order, even if less than (*n*-1) passes have been made.

For a list containing *n* items, the number of swaps required for each location in the first half of the array can be shown as follows:

Location	1	2	3	..	..	n/2-2	n/2-1	n/2
Swaps	n-1 +	n-3 +	n-5 +	.. +	..+	5 +	3 +	1

Each swap is experienced by two elements and the number of swaps is counted, and it is experienced by half the elements. Every swap always moves the elements towards their eventual location and the sum of this series will be the total number of swaps required. Consider the following table.

Table 12.4 Number of comparisons, swaps, and moves in each pass of bubble sort algorithm

Pass	Comparisons	Swaps	Moves
First	(n-1)	(n-1)/2 swaps (average)	3(n-1)/2
Second	(n-2)	(n-1)/2 swaps(average)	3(n-2)/2
All passes	= (n-1)+(n-2)...+ 1 = n(n-1)/2 = ~ n2/2	= n(n-1)/4 =~ n2/4 (average)	~3n2/4 moves

Therefore,

$$T(n) = n + (n - 1) + (n - 2) + (n - 3) + (n - 4) \ldots (2) + (1)$$
$$= n(n(n-1)/2) = n^2/2$$

Hence, the time complexity of bubble sort is O(n^2). The average case behaviour of the bubble sort algorithm can be shown to be approximately equal to the worst-case behaviour. It can be assumed that for the worst-case situation, every element is approximately half the list away from its eventual location in the sorted list. This will require each element to experience a minimum of n/2-1 swaps. It cannot be assumed that the other element participating in the swap will benefit from the swap by being moved towards its desired location. It can be assumed that the swaps in the average-case situation are only 50 per cent as effective as the swaps in the worst-case situation. This leads to the conclusion that each element has to experience approximately *n* swaps and as each swap moves two elements, the total number of swaps is approximately $n^2/2$. This is the same number of swaps as required in the worst-case situation and will need at least as many iterations of the inner loop.

Therefore, the worst-case complexity is T(n) = O(n^2) and the average-case complexity is also T(n) = O(n^2).

12.12.5 Analysis of Quick Sort

In quick sort, each recursive call could have a different sized set of numbers to sort. Here are the three analyses that must be performed:

- Best case
- Average case
- Worst case

In the best case, a perfect partition is to be set every time. If we let $T(n)$ be the running time of quick sorting n elements, then $T(n) = 2T(n/2) + O(n)$, since partition runs in $O(n)$ time.

Now, consider how bad quick sort would be if the partition element was always the greatest value of the one remaining to be sorted. In this situation, one has to run partition $n-1$ times, the first time comparing $n-1$ values, then $n-2$, followed by $n-3$, etc. This points to the sum $1+2+3+...+(n-1)$ which is $(n-1)n/2$. Thus, the worst case running time is $O(n^2)$.

Now, lets us calculate the average-case running time. This is certainly difficult to ascertain because one cannot get any sort of partition. It is assumed that each possible partition (0 and $n-1$, 1 and $n-2$, 2 and $n-3$, etc.) is equally likely. One way to work out the mathematics is as follows. Assume that you run quick sort n times. In doing so, since there are n possible partitions, each equally likely, on average, each partition occurs once. So, the following recurrence relation is found:

```
nT(n) = T(0)+T(n-1)+T(1)+T(n-2)+...+T(n-1)+T(0) + n*n
      = 2[T(1)+T(2)+...T(n-1)] + n²        (12.1)
```

Now, putting $n-1$ in Eqn (12.1),

```
(n-1)T(n-1) = 2[T(1)+T(2)+...T(n-2)] + (n-1)²   (12.2)
```

Subtracting Eqn (12.2) from Eqn (12.1), gives

```
nT(n) - (n-1)T(n-1) = 2T(n-1) + 2n - 1 nT(n)
                    = (n+1)T(n-1) + (2n - 1)
T(n) = [(n+1)/n]T(n-1) + (2n - 1)/n        (12.3)
```

Since it is an approximate analysis, the –1 is dropped at the end of this equation. Dividing Eqn (12.3) by $n+1$, yields

```
T(n)/(n+1) = T(n-1)/n + 2/(n+1)        (12.4)
```

Now, substituting different values of n into this recurrence to form several equations, it evaluates to

```
T(n)/(n+1) = T(n-1)/n + 2/(n+1)T(n-1)/(n)
           = T(n-2)/(n-1) + 2/(n)
T(n-2)/(n-1) = T(n-3)/(n-2) + 2/(n-1)
```

```
T(2)/3 = T(1)/2 + 2/1
```

Now, summing up as the equations above reveal many identical terms on both sides. In fact, after cancelling identical terms, we are left with

```
T(n)/(n+1) = T(1)/2 + 2[1/1 + 1/2 + 1/3 + ... + 1/(n+1)]
```

The sum on the right hand side of the equation is a harmonic number. The nth harmonic number (H_n) is defined as

```
1 + 1/2 + 1/3 + ... 1/n.
```

Through calculus, it can be shown that $H_n \sim \ln n$ (ln is the natural log with the base e; e ~ 2.718282). Now,

```
T(n)/(n+1) ~ 1/2 + 2ln n
T(n) ~ n(ln n)  (simplifying a bit)
```

Thus, even in the average case for quick sort, it is found that $T(n) = O(n \log n)$.

Note, in order analysis, any function of the form logbn = $O(\log cn)$, for all positive constants b and c, is greater than 1.

Let us look at the best-case complexity. The best case occurs when the pivot is the median value; thus the two recursive calls are problems with approximately half the size of the original problem. This recurrence is given by

```
T(n) = 2T(n / 2) + O(n) = O(n log n)
```

Weiss derives the best-case performance figure to be

```
c * n * log n + n
```

where c represents the constant pivot selection time.

The main consideration is quick sort's average performance. This has been shown (see Kruse et al.) to be $1.39 * n * \log n + c * n$.

For quick sort, best case is $T(n) = O(n \log n)$, worse case is $T(n) = O(n^2)$, and average case is $T(n) = O(n \log n)$.

12.12.6 Disadvantages of Complexity Analysis

Complexity analysis can be very useful, but there are problems with it too. The disadvantages of complexity analysis are as follows.

- Many algorithms are simply too hard to analyse mathematically.
- The average case is unknown. There may not be sufficient information to know what the most important 'average' case really is, therefore analysis is impossible.
- Big-O analysis only specifies how it grows with the size of the problem, not how efficient it is.
- If there are no large amounts of data, algorithm efficiency may not be important.

SUMMARY

A function is a self-contained block of program statements that perform some particular task. Programs should be built with a large number of small compact functions rather than with a small number of large functions. The use of functions in programs makes it more manageable and easy to understand. They may be called as many times as the main program needs to use them. Functions are reusable and can therefore be used in multiple programs.

The linkage with the user-made functions and the main() program is established through three components associated with the user function. These three components are

- the *declaration* statement
- the *function* definition
- the *calling* statement

When a function is called, parameters are passed by value. Depending on its return type specified by its declaration, a function either does not return any value or returns some value of the type mentioned in its prototype. Another method of passing parameters to a function is known as call by reference more strictly 'call by address'.

Scope rules related to statement blocks and functions basically describe the existence, accessibility, and default values of variables called *local variables*, declared within the function body and those called *global variables*, declared outside all functions.

To indicate where the variables would be stored, how long they would exist, what would be their region of existence, and what would be the default values, C provides four *storage class* specifiers that can be used along with the data type specifiers in the declaration statement of a variable. These four *storage class* specifiers are as follows:

- automatic
- external
- register
- static

Recursion in programming is a technique for defining a problem in terms of one or more smaller versions of the same problem. A function that calls itself directly or indirectly to solve a smaller version of its task until a final call which does not require a self-call is a recursive function. The following are necessary for implementing recursion:

- The problem should be decomposed into smaller problems of same type.
- Recursive calls must diminish problem size.
- A base case is required.
- Base case must be reached.

An instance of the problem whose solution requires no further recursive calls is known as a base case. It is a special case whose solution is known. Every recursive algorithm requires at least one base case in order to be valid.

Some popular problems where the recursive functions can be used have been discussed in this chapter. While developing user-defined functions, the common errors encountered by programmers, ideas on how to choose test data, and the way these can be tracked have also been presented in detail.

KEY TERMS

Actual parameters Information is passed to a function via special identifiers or expression called *arguments or actual parameters.*

Average-case complexity The average-case complexity of an algorithm is the function defined by the average number of steps taken on any instance of input size.

Base case It is an instance of a problem the solution of which requires no further recursive calls.

Best-case complexity The best-case complexity of an algorithm is the function defined by the minimum number of steps taken on any instance of input size.

Big-O notation It is a measure of the running time of an algorithm, as it relates to the size of the input to that algorithm. It is intended not to measure the performance of the machine on which the algorithm is run, but rather to strictly measure the performance of the algorithm itself.

Call by value It means the values of the actual arguments are conceptually copied to the formal parameters.

Extent How long memory will be associated with identifiers is known as *extent.*

Formal parameters The list of variables in the function header is also referred to as the formal parameters.

Recursion It is a technique by which a function calls itself.

Scope The region of the program over which the declaration of an identifier is accessible is called the scope of the identifier.

Space complexity It is a function describing the amount of memory (space) an algorithm takes with respect to the amount of input provided to the algorithm.

Storage class It specifies where the variables would be stored, how long they would exist, what would be their region of existence, and what would be the default values.

Structured programming It refers to a set of principles for writing well-organized programs that could be more easily shown to be correct.

Time complexity It is a function describing the amount of time an algorithm takes with respect to the amount of input provided to the algorithm.

Worst-case complexity The worst-case complexity of the algorithm is the function defined by the maximum number of steps taken on any instance of input size.

FREQUENTLY ASKED QUESTIONS

1. Why is a function prototype required?

A function prototype tells the compiler what kind of arguments a function receives and what kind of value a function is going to give back to the calling function. Function prototype helps the compiler ensure that calls to a function are made correctly and that no erroneous type conversions take place. If the compiler finds any difference between the prototype and the calls to the function or the definition of the function, an error or a warning may be caused.

2. Why is scope important?

In structured programming approach, the program is divided into independent functions that perform a specific task. The key word here is *independent*. For true independence, it is necessary for each function's variables to be isolated from interference caused by other functions. Only by isolating each function's data can you make sure that the function performs its intended task without affecting or being affected by some other part of the program. It is also true that in some situation complete data isolation between functions is not always desirable. By specifying the scope of variables, a programmer may attain control over the degree of data isolation.

3. If global variables can be used anywhere in the program, why not make all variables global?

When the program becomes complex and large, it may be needed to declare more and more variables. Variables declared as global take up memory for the entire time during which the program runs; however, local variables do not. A local variable takes up memory only while the function to which it is local is active. Additionally, global variables are subject to unintentional alteration by other functions. If this occurs, the variables might not contain the values one expects when they are used in the functions for which they were created.

4. What is the advantage of using register storage class? What are the restrictions with register storage class?

The register identifier is used for the compiler to place the data value in a CPU register so that the data can be accessed fast. However, the compiler is free to treat a register declaration as an auto declaration because it is only a hint and not a directive.

There are some restrictions with register storage class. They include the following:

The variable must be of a type that can be held in the CPU's register. This usually means a single value of a size less than or equal to the size of an integer. Some machines have registers that can hold floating-point numbers as well.

An array should not be declared with register storage class; doing so is an undefined behaviour.

Address-of operator (&) cannot be applied to an identifier with register storage class. An attempt to do so would cause an error by the compiler.

Register storage class can only be applied to local variables and to the formal parameters in function. Global register variables are not allowed. That is, the register storage class should not occur in an external declaration.

5. What is linkage?

An identifier's linkage determines which of the references to that identifier refer to the same object. An identifier's linkage is determined by whether it appears inside or outside a function, whether it appears in a declaration of a function (as opposed to an object), its storage-class, and the linkage of any previous declarations of the same identifier that have file scope.

6. What is the use of linkage?

Linkage is used to determine what makes the same name declared in different scopes refer to the same thing. An object has one name, but in many cases we would like to refer to the same object from different scopes.

7. What are the different types of linkages?

C defines three types of linkages – external, internal, and no linkage. In general,

Functions and global variables have external linkage. This means they are available to all files that constitute a program.

Identifiers with file scope declared as static have internal linkage. These are known only within the file in which they are declared.

Local identifiers have no linkage and are therefore known only within their own block.

Two declarations of the same identifier in a single file that have the same linkage, either internal or external, refer to the same object. The same identifier cannot appear in a file with both internal and external linkages.

8. Differentiate between an internal static and external static variable.

An internal static variable is declared inside a block with static storage class whereas an external static variable is declared outside all the blocks in a file. An internal static variable has persistent storage, block scope, and no linkage. An external static variable has permanent storage, file scope, and internal linkage

9. What does extern mean in a function declaration?

Using `extern` in a function declaration means the function can be used outside the file in which it is defined.

10. Compare recursion and iteration.

Recursion is a top-down approach to problem solving; it divides the problem into pieces or selects one key step, postponing the rest. On the other hand, iteration is more of a bottom-up approach; it begins with what is known and from this constructs the solution step by step.

Depending on the implementation available and the algorithm being used, recursion can require a substantial amount of runtime overhead. Thus, the use of recursion illustrates the classic trade-off between time spent in constructing and maintaining a program and the cost in time and memory of execution of that program. For that reason, it is often the case that an iterative version of a solution is considerably more efficient than a recursive one.

11. Can `main()` be called recursively?

It is perfectly right to call `main()` recursively if properly written as follows:

```c
#include <stdio.h>
int main()
{
  static int c=5;
  if(c-->0)
  {
    printf("\t %d", c);
    return main();
  }
```

```
    else
        return 0;
}
```

Output

```
4 3 2 1 0
```

If the recursive call does not have base case as the following program; then this will go on till a point where runtime error occurs due to stack. overflow.

```
#include <stdio.h>
int main()
{
    main();
    return 0;
}
```

EXERCISES

1. A function that returns an integer value and takes a single integer as an argument can be prototyped as
   (a) `int myFun();`
   (b) `void myFun( int);`
   (c) `int myFun(void);`
   (d) `int myFun(int);`

2. If called by the statement
   ```
   n = myFun(9);
   ```
   what value will `myFun(9)` return for assignment to n?
   ```
   int myFun(int val) {
       return(val * (val + 1))/2;
   }
   ```

3. Which among the function prototypes below have no errors?
   (a) `void myFun1(int)`
   (b) `int myFun2(void);`
   (c) `float myFun3(a, b, c);`
   (d) `double myFun(void a, int b);`
   (e) `int myFun5(int var1, int );`

4. A function is defined that calculates and returns the hypotenuse of a right triangle with sides a and b. The function prototype is
   ```
   double hypot(double a, double b);
   ```
   Which among the statements below are correct uses of (calls to) this function (assume x, y, and z are double variables and that x and x have been initialized properly)?
   (a) `z = hypot(4.0, 4.5);`
   (b) `z = hypot(double x, double y);`
   (c) `hypot(x, y);`
   (d) `printf("%f", hypot(x, y));`
   (e) `z = x + y + hypot(x, y);`

5. A function, sumN, is defined that takes an integer *n* as argument and returns the sum of the integers from 1 through *n*. What is the value of the expression shown below?
   ```
   sumN(3456) - sumN(3455);
   ```

6. Choose all the correct ways of calling a function with prototype
   ```
   int f1(int, double);
   ```
   given the variables below and that the math library was included.
   ```
   int val1 = 5, retVal;
   double val2 = 9.8;
   ```
   (a) `retVal = f1(4, 3.5);`
   (b) `retVal = f1(int val1, float val2);`
   (c) `retVal = f1(1000, val2);`
   (d) `retVal = f1(2*val1, val2/3.5);`
   (e) `retVal = f1( val1, sqrt(val2));`

7. Given the function definition shown for `f1()` below, what will be printed?

```
int f1(void);
int main(void) {
    printf("%d", f1());
    printf("%d", f1());
    printf("%d", f1());
    return 0;
}
int f1(void) {
    int val = 1;
    return val++;
}
```

8. Given the function definition shown for `f1()` below, what will be printed?
```
int f1(void);
int main(void) {
    printf("%d", f1());
    printf("%d", f1());
    printf("%d", f1());
    return 0;
}
int f1(void) {
static int val = 1;
    return val++;
}
```

9. What will be printed by the following code?
```
void f1(void);
int val = 6;
int main(void) {
    f1();
    printf("%d", val);
    f1();
    printf("%d", val);
    return 0;
}
void f1(void) {
    ++val;
}
```

10. What will be printed by the following code?
```
void f1(int);
int val = 6;
int main(void) {
    f1(val);
    printf("%d", val);
    f1(val);
    printf("%d", val);
    return 0;
}
void f1(int val) {
    ++val;
}
```

11. Given the following array declaration and function prototype, choose all the correct ways of calling the function from `main()` and giving it a reference to `myarray[]`.

```
void myFun(int a[]);
int main() {
int myArray[] =
  {10,20,30,40,50,60,70,80};
/* function call here */
```

(a) `myFun(myArray);`

(b) `myFun(myArray[]);`

(c) `myFun(&myArray[0]);`

(d) `myFun(myArray[0]);`

(e) `myFun(myArray[8]);`

12. What will be the output of the following program?

```
#define swap(a,b) temp=a; a=b; b=temp;
int main()
{
  static int a=5,b=6,temp;
  if(a > b)
    swap(a,b);
  printf("a=%d b=%d",a,b);
  return 0;
}
```

(a) `a=5 b=6`   (b) `a=6 b=5`

(c) `a=6 b=0`   (d) None of these

13. The following code is not well written. What is the output?

```
int main()
{
  int a=1,b=2;
  printf("%d",add(a,b));
  return 0;
}
int add(int a,int b)
{
return(a+b);
}
```

(a) Run-time error   (b) Compile-time error

(c) `3`   (d) None of these

14. What will be the output of the following program?

```
int add(int a,int b)
{
  int c=a+b;
}
int main()
{
  int a=10,b=20;
  printf("%d %d %d",a,b,add(a,b));
  return 0;
}
```

(a) `10 20 0`   (b) Compile-time error

(c) `10 20 30`   (d) None of these

15. What will be the output of the following program?

```
int add(int a,int b)
{
  int c=a+b;
  return;
}
 int main()
{
  int a=10,b=20;
  printf("%d %d %d",a,b,add(a,b));
  return 0;
}
```

(a) `10 20 0`   (b) Compile-time error

(c) `10 20 30`   (d) None of these

16. What will be the output of the following program?

```
int main()
{
  int add(int,int);
  int a=7,b=13;
  printf("%d",add(add(a,b),
    add(a,b)));
  return 0;
}
int add(a,b)
int a,b;
{
  return(a+b);
}
```

(a) Compile-time error   (b) `20`

(c) `40`   (d) None of these

17. What will be the output of the following program?

```
int add(a,b)
{
  int c=a+b;
  return c;
}
int main()
{
  int a=10,b=20;
  printf("%d",add(a,b));
  return 0;
}
```

(a) `30`   (b) Compile-time error

(c) `0`   (d) None of these

18. What will be the output of the following program?

```
int funct2(int b)
{
  if(b == 0)
    return b;
  else
    funct1(b--);
}
int funct1(int a)
{
  if(a == 0)
    return a;
  else
    funct2(a--);
}
int main()
{
  int a=7;
  printf("%d",funct1(a));
  return 0;
}
```

(a) `0`   (b) Compile-time error

(c) Infinite loop   (d) `7`

19. What will be the output of the following program?

```
int funct1(int a)
{{;}{{;}return a;}}
int main()
{
  int a=17;
  printf("%d",funct1(a));
  return 0;
}
```

(a) `0`   (b) Compile-time error

(c) 17   (d) None of these

20. What will be the output of the following program?

```
int funct1(int a)
{
  if(a)
    return funct1(--a)+a;
  else
    return 0;
}
int main()
{
  int a=7;
  printf("%d",funct1(a));
  return 0;
}
```

(a) 7   (b) 21
(c) 28   (d) None of these

21. What will be the output of the following program?

```
int compute(int a,int b)
int c;
{
  c=a+b;
  return c;
}
int main()
{
  int a=7,b=9;
  printf("%d",compute(a,b));
  return 0;
}
```

(a) Compile-time error   (b) 16
(c) None of these

22. What will be the output of the following program?

```
int a=10;
void compute(int a)
{
  a=a;
}
int main()
{
  int a=100;
  printf("%d",a);
  compute(a);
  printf("%d",a);
  return 0;
}
```

(a) 10 10   (b) Compile-time error
(c) 100 100   (d) 100 10

23. What will be the output of the following program?

```
int funct(char ch)
{
  ch=ch+1;
  return ch;
}
int main()
{
  int a=127;
  printf("%d %d",a,funct(a));
  return 0;
}
```

(a) Compile-time error   (b) 127 128

(c) 127-128   (d) None of these

24. What will be the output of the following program?

```
char funct(int val)
{
  char ch=val;
  return ch;
}
int main()
{
  float a=256.25;
  printf("%d",funct(a));
  return 0;
}
```

(a) 0   (b) 256.25
(c) 256   (d) None of these

25. What will be the output of the following program?

```
auto int a;
void changeval(int x)
{
  a=x;
}
int main()
{
  a=15;
  printf("%d",a);
  changeval(75);
  printf("%d",a);
  return 0;
}
```

(a) Compile-time error   (b) 15 75
(c) 15 15   (d) None of these

26. What will be the output of the following program?

```
int val;
static int funct()
{
  return val*val;
}
int main()
{
  val=5;
  funct();
  val++;
  printf("%d",funct());
  return 0;
}
```

(a) Compile-time error   (b) 25
(c) 36   (d) None of these

27. What will be the output of the following program?

```
static int funct(int val)
{
  static int sum;
  sum+=val;
  return sum;
}
int main()
{
  int i,n=9;
  for(i=1; i<n-; i++)
    funct(i*2);
  printf("%d",funct(0));
  return 0;
}
```

(a) 20   (b) 0
(c) 30   (d) None of these

28. What will be the output of the following program?
```
void print(int a[],...)
{
while(*a != -1)
  printf("%d",*a++);
}
int main()
{
  int a[]={1,2,3,4,5,-1};
  print(a,5,6,7,8,9,-1);
  return 0;
}
```
(a) Compile-time error (b) Run-time error
(c) 12345 (d) 56789

29. What will be the output of the following program?
```
int main()
{
  int a=19,b=4;
  float c;
  c=a/b;
  printf("%f",c);
  return 0;
}
```
(a) 4.75 (b) 4
(c) 4.750000 (d) 4.000000

30. What will be the output of the following program?
```
int main()
{
  int _;
  _=70;
  printf("%d",_);
  return 0;
}
```
(a) Compile-time error (b) Run-time error
(c) 70 (d) None of these

31. What will be the output of the following program?
```
#define func(x,y) { func(x,y) }
int main()
{
  int a=5,b=6;
  c=func(x,y);
  printf("%d %d %d",c);
  return 0;
}
```
(a) Compile-time error (b) Linker error
(c) 5 6 11 (d) Infinite loop

32. What will be the output of the following program?
```
#define big(a,b) a > b ? a : b
#define swap(a,b) temp=a; a=b; b=temp;
int main()
{
```
```
    int a=3,b=5,temp;
    if((3+big(a,b)) > b)
      swap(a,b);
    printf("%d %d",a,b);
    return 0;
}
```
(a) 3 0 (b) 5 3
(c) 3 5 (d) 5 0

33. Write a function to find the sum of digits of a given number.
34. Write a program that uses a function to search a number within an array.
35. Write a function that takes a decimal number and base as argument and returns the equivalent number of the given base.
36. Write a function that will scan a string that is passed as an argument and convert all characters to capital letters.
37. Write a program that uses a function to add a string to the end of another string without using any library function.
38. Write a function to sort an array of integers in ascending order.
39. Write a function to reverse a given string and use it to check whether the given string is a palindrome or not.
40. Write a program to perform addition, subtraction, and multiplication on two matrices depending upon the user's choice.
41. Write a program to print the transpose of that matrix.
42. Write a program that sorts the words of a sentence in alphabetical order.
43. Write a function that will print the longest word written in a line.
44. Write a program to sort the numbers stored in a matrix.
45. Read two integers, representing a rate of pay (pence per hour) and a number of hours. Print out the total pay, with hours up to 40 being paid at basic rate, from 40 to 60 at rate- and-a-half, above 60 at double-rate. Print the pay as pounds to two decimal places.
Hints Construct a loop. Terminate the loop when a zero rate is encountered. At the end of the loop, print out the total pay. The code for computing the pay from the rate and hours is to be written as a function.
The recommended output format is
```
Pay at 200 pence/hr for 38 hours is 76.00 pounds
Pay at 220 pence/hr for 48 hours is 114.40 pounds
Pay at 240 pence/hr for 68 hours is 206.40 pounds
Pay at 260 pence/hr for 48 hours is 135.20 pounds
Pay at 280 pence/hr for 68 hours is 240.80 pounds
Pay at 300 pence/hr for 48 hours is 156.00 pounds
Total pay is 928.80 pounds
```
The 'program features' check that explicit values such as 40 and 60 appear only once, as a #define or an initialized variable value.

46. Write functions to convert feet to inches, convert inches to centimetres, and convert centimetres to metres. Write a program that prompts a user for a measurement in feet and converts and outputs this value in metres. Facts to use: 1 ft = 12 inches, 1 inch = 2.54 cm, 100 cm = 1 metre

Project Question

1. Write a menu-based program in C that uses a set of functions to perform the following operations
(a) reading a complex number
(b) writing a complex number
(c) addition of two complex numbers
(d) subtraction of two complex numbers
(e) multiplication of two complex numbers

Pointers in C

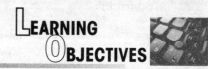

LEARNING **O**BJECTIVES

After studying this chapter, the readers will be able to

- list memory addresses
- discuss the concept of pointers
- use pointer variables and understand call-by-value and call-by-address
- analyse the use of dereferencing
- study equivalence among arrays and pointers—treating pointers as arrays
- explain pointer arithmetic
- explain the concept and construction of array of pointers and pointer to array

- discuss pointers and functions—parameter passing techniques, pointers as function parameters
- discuss pointers to functions—functions as arguments to another function
- explain dynamic memory allocation using pointers
- discuss memory leak, memory corruption, and garbage collection
- decipher (long) pointer declarations

13.1 INTRODUCTION

In programming with C, there are far too many things that can only be done with pointers. In many cases, C programmers use pointers because they make the code more efficient. But at the same time, pointers seem to make the code harder to understand. However, with increased power, pointers bring increased responsibility. Pointers allow new and ugly types of bugs, and pointer bugs can crash in random ways making them more difficult to debug. Nonetheless, even with their problems, pointers are a powerful programming construct.

The only peculiarity of C, compared to other languages is its heavy reliance on pointers and the relatively permissive view of how they can be used.

Before going on to discuss the concept of pointers, it is necessary to understand the use of memory in a C program.

Note

- Pointers allow new and ugly types of bugs.
- Pointer bugs can crash in random ways, which makes them more difficult to debug.

13.2 UNDERSTANDING MEMORY ADDRESSES

All computers have *primary memory*, also known as RAM or *random access memory*. For example, a computer may have 16, 32, 64, 128, 256, or 512 MB of RAM installed. RAM holds the programs that the computer is currently running along with the data they are currently manipulating (their variables and data structures). All the variables used in a program (and indeed, the program itself) reside in the memory when the program is executed. The organization of the memory is rather straightforward. It is a sequence of a large number of memory locations (cells), each of which has an address. Each memory location is capable of storing a small number (0 to 256), which is known as a byte. A char data is one byte in size and hence needs one memory location of the memory. Both integer and float need four bytes each, or four locations in a 32-bit machine. The size needed for a particular data type varies with the platform in which the program is run. Even if an int/float number is small, it will still occupy four locations. When a program in C is written and compiled, the compiler will allocate the memory necessary to run the program. This is one reason why declaring variables is very important. For example,

```
int x;
x=1000;
```

will first convey to the C compiler that x is an integer before assigning a value of 1000 to it. The declaration statement informs the compiler to allocate enough memory to store an integer and assign an address to that space in memory. Since an integer requires two or four bytes of memory, the compiler searches for two or four free bytes memory and holds them until a value is assigned to x. It then puts that value in the memory location and stores it there until x is redefined as something else. The same goes for other data types in C. Declaring variables first always allows the compiler to set aside space in memory which can then be filled up with useful numbers. Figure 13.1 represents these facts.

Fig. 13.1 The computer memory (16-bit system)

Variables can be stored in several places in the memory, depending on their lifetime. Variables that are defined outside any function (whether of global or file static scope), and variables that are defined inside a function as static variables, exist for the lifetime of the program's execution. These variables are stored in the *data segment*. The *data segment* is a fixed-size area in memory set aside for these variables. It is subdivided into two parts, one for initialized variables and the other for uninitialized variables.

There may be several global variables declared in the program, but they will not be stored contiguously, since the compiler is not compelled to store them in any order convenient to the programmer. They are randomly stored throughout the available global memory even though every C compiler will probably assign them in some contiguous manner.

There are virtual memory, cache memory, registers, and other types of memory that make the system run a little faster or appear to have more memory. The blocks returned to the program from the heap have additional housekeeping memory associated with them and there are byte alignment considerations for both the heap and the stack. Global memory also has some byte alignment considerations. For example, the compiler may require that all float and double type variables start on an even numbered byte boundary, or on a byte boundary that is modulo four. This may require some bytes added as padding to get to the boundary when one of these is encountered. The compiler/linker will take care of these details.

Variables that are defined inside a function as auto variables (that are not defined with the keyword static) come into existence when the program begins executing the block of code (delimited by curly braces {}) containing them, and they cease to exist when the program leaves that block of code. Variables that are the arguments to functions exist only during the call to that function. These variables are stored on the *stack*. *Stack* is an area of memory that starts out small and grows automatically up to some predefined limit. It has three major functions:

(i) Stack provides the storage area for local variables declared within the function.

(ii) It stores housekeeping information involved when function call is made.

(iii) It is needed for recursive call.

Once a variable is stored on the stack, it can be referred to by the code that puts it on the stack, so that it is a variable available for use in much the same manner as global variables are available. However, when the program has finished using the data on the stack, it can be discarded to allow the stack to be used for other data when needed. This is probably unclear at this point, but it will make more sense when one gets to the actual usage. It is to be noted that stack would not be needed except for recursive calls. If not, for these a fixed amount of space for local variables, parameters, and return addresses would be known at compile time and could be allocated in BSS.

In DOS and other systems without virtual memory, the limit is set either when the program is compiled or when it begins executing. In UNIX and other systems with virtual memory, the limit is set by the system, and it is usually so large that the programmer can ignore it.

The third and final area does not actually store variables, but can be used to store data pointed to by variables.

Pointer variables that are assigned to the result of a call to the malloc() function contain the address of a dynamically allocated area of memory. This memory is in an area called the *heap*. When the program requests a block of data, the dynamic allocation scheme carves out a block from the heap and assigns it to the user by returning a pointer to the beginning of the block. When the system has finished using the block, it returns the block to the heap where it is returned to the pool of available memory called the free list. This is called de-allocation. The heap can share a memory segment with either the data segment or the stack, or it can have its own segment. It all depends on the compiler options and operating system. The heap, like the stack, has a limit on how much it can grow, and the same rules apply as to how that limit is determined.

Since readers are interested only in the logical assignment of memory, they can ignore all of these extra considerations, and still write efficient, robust programs. Compiler writers must keep track of all of these entities in order to make the programmer's job easier. C uses pointers in three main ways.

(i) Pointers in C provide an alternative means of accessing information stored in arrays, which is especially valuable when working with strings. There is an intimate link between arrays and pointers in C.

(ii) C uses pointers to handle *variable parameters* passed to functions.

(iii) They are used to create *dynamic data structures*, that are built up from blocks of memory allocated from the heap at run time. This is only visible through the use of pointers.

Table 13.1 describes the memory layout of the memory elements of a C program.

Table 13.1 Memory layout summary

Memory Section Name	Description
Text (or the code segment)	This is the area of memory that contains the machine instructions corresponding to the compiled program. This area is READ ONLY and is shared by multiple instances of a running program.
Data	This area in the memory image of a running program contains storage for *initialized global* variables. This area is separate for each running instance of a program.

(Contd)

Table 13.1 Contd

BSS	This is the memory area that contains storage for *uninitialized global* variables. It is also separate for each running instance of a program.
Stack	This region of the memory image of a running program contains storage for the automatic (local) variables of the program. It also stores context-specific information before a function call, e.g., the value of the instruction pointer (program counter) register before a function call is made. On most architectures, the stack grows from *higher memory to lower memory addresses*.
Heap	This memory region is reserved for dynamically allocating memory for variables at run time. Dynamic memory allocation is done by using the malloc or calloc functions.
Shared libraries	This region contains the executable image of shared libraries being used by the program.

13.3 ADDRESS OF OPERATOR (&)

Readers might have noticed that when we call certain functions in C the & sign is used. For example,

```
scanf("%d", &n);
```

takes the input from the terminal and stores it in integer format in the variable named n. The & sign indicates the address in memory of the integer n, which must be previously declared using

```
int n;
```

where the function stores the inputted data. Just like a house address in a town, the memory address is an integer specifying the location where something resides. scanf needs to know this in order to redirect the data. If one forgets and types n instead, the scanf function interprets the actual integer value of n as an address and tries to send its output there. This address may not exist, it may be used by the operating system or otherwise blocked, or it may be impossible to find again. It is likely to get a

```
segmentation fault
```

error when one compiles, and certainly get nonsense values if the program runs.

To recap, the compiler considers n as the value of n (which will be junk if it has not been assigned yet) and &n as n's address. At the moment when the variable is declared, it must be stored in a concrete location in the succession of cells in the memory. The programs do not decide where the variable is to be placed. It is done automatically by the compiler and the operating system at run time. But once the operating system has assigned an address there may be cases where it may be of interest to know the location of the variable.

This can be done by preceding the variable identifier by an *ampersand* (&), which literally means 'address of'.

Now, the above ideas are illustrated with some more details. Consider the declaration,

```
int i = 3;
```

This declaration tells the C compiler to

- reserve space in memory to hold the integer value
- associate the name i with this memory location
- store the value 3 at this location

i's location in the memory may be logically represented with the memory map shown in Fig. 13.2.

i

```
3
```

2147478276

Fig. 13.2 Memory map

The computer has selected memory location 2147478276 as the place to store the value 3. This location number 2147478276 is not a number to be relied upon, because at some other time the computer may choose a different location for storing the value 3. This address can be printed using the following statement:

```
printf("\n Address of i = %u", &i);
```

The output will be: 2147478276. Look at the printf() statement carefully. The '&' used in this statement is C's address operator. The expression &i returns the address of the variable i, which in this case happens to be 2147478276.

The address is printed using %u control string as it is of type unsigned int. %X can also be used. Actually %p should be used because it prints the input argument as a memory address.

The following statement

```
printf("\n Address of i = %x", &i);
```

will print FFDC in hexadecimal as the address of variable 'i'.

Why an unassigned pointer should not be used?

According to an elementary school verse, "I shot an arrow into the air, where it lands, I don't care." It may rhyme, but its message is really not appropriate for little ones. However, when a pointer is declared and then used without first assigning it a value, it does the programming equivalent of the verse.

The following program declares a pointer and then attempts to output its value without first assigning it a value.

```
#include <stdio.h>
int main()
```

```
{
    int *ptr;
    printf("\n The value of ptr is %u", ptr);
    return 0;
}
```

The result, depending on the compiler and operating system, may be a compiler error, a run-time error, or a computer that locks up. Regardless, attempting to use a declared pointer without first assigning it a value is not a good idea.

It may be recalled from previous chapters that when a variable is declared and then an attempt is made to output its value without first assigning it a value, the result is a so-called *garbage value* that makes little sense. The reason for this result is that the computer attempts to interpret whatever value is left over from previous programs at the address of the variable.

When the variable is a pointer, that leftover value is interpreted as another memory address, which the pointer then tries to access when we attempt to use it. There are a number of memory address ranges that are not permitted to access programmatically, such as those reserved for use by the operating system. If the leftover value is interpreted as one of those prohibited addresses, the result is an error.

> **Note**
> - After declaring a variable, where the variable is to be located is decided by the compiler and the operating system at run time.
> - After declaring a variable, if an attempt is made to output its value without assigning a value, the result is a garbage value.

13.4 POINTER

A pointer provides a way of accessing a variable without referring to the variable directly. The mechanism used for this is the address of the variable. A program statement can refer to a variable indirectly using the address of the variable.

A pointer variable holds the memory address of another variable. Put another way, the pointer does not hold a value in the traditional sense; instead, it holds the address of another variable. They are called pointers for the simple reason that by storing an address, they 'point' to a particular point in memory. A pointer points to that variable by holding a copy of its address. Because a pointer holds an address rather than a value, it has two parts. The pointer itself holds the address. The address points to a value.

Pointers can be used to:

- call by address, thereby facilitating the changes made to a variable in the called function to become permanently available in the function from where the function is called

- return more than one value from a function indirectly

- pass arrays and strings more conveniently from one function to another

- manipulate arrays more easily by moving pointers to them (or to parts of them) instead of moving the arrays themselves

- create complex data structures, such as linked lists and binary trees, where one data structure must contain references to other data structures

- communicate information about memory, as in the function malloc() which returns the location of free memory by using a pointer

- compile faster, more efficient code than other derived data types such as arrays

Therefore, a pointer variable is a variable that stores the address of another variable. In C, there is an additional restriction on pointers—they are *not* allowed to store *any* memory address, but they can only store addresses of variables of a given type.

13.4.1 Declaring a Pointer

Just as any other variable in a program, a pointer has to be declared; it will have a value, a scope, a lifetime, a name; and it will occupy a certain number of memory locations. The pointer operator available in C is '*', called *value at address* operator. It returns the value stored at a particular address. The value at address operator is also called *indirection* operator. A pointer variable is declared by preceding its name with an asterisk. The syntax for declaring a pointer variable is

```
datatype * pointer_variable;
```

where *datatype* is the type of data that the pointer is allowed to hold the address of (that is, the type of data that the pointer is allowed to point to) and *pointer_variable* is the pointer variable name that is used to refer to the address of a variable of type datatype.

An example of a pointer declaration would be

```
char *ptr;
```

The above declaration should be evaluated as: ptr is a pointer to char type data. char is not the data type of ptr. ptr is an identifier of type pointer and char is a data specifier that is used to indicate the type of data at the memory address that ptr is holding. Pointers are variables that hold memory addresses. At the memory address, which is held in a pointer, a value is stored; this value may be of primitive or user-defined data type. In declaring a pointer variable, the programmer is actually declaring a variable that holds a memory address that points to a specific type of data value. Consider the following declaration.

```
int *a;
```

This declaration indicates that a is a pointer type variable that points to int type data. That is, the int indicates that the pointer variable is intended to store the address of an integer variable. Such a pointer is said to 'point to' an integer.

```
float *t;
```

The above declaration represents the fact that t is a pointer type variable that points to float type data. Some declarations are listed in Table 13.2.

Table 13.2 Meaning of some pointer type variable declarations

Declaration	What it means
int p	p is an integer
int *p	p is a pointer to an integer
char p	p is a character
char *p	p is a pointer to a character
long p	p is a long integer
long *p	p is a pointer to a long integer
unsigned char p	p is an unsigned character
unsigned char *p	p is a pointer to an unsigned character

Consider the following program.

```c
#include <stdio.h>
int main()
{
    int *p;
    float *q;
    double *r;
    printf("\n the size of integer pointer is %d",
        sizeof(p));
    printf("\n the size of float pointer is %d",
        sizeof(q));
    printf("\n the size of double pointer is %d",
        sizeof(r));
    printf("\n the size of character pointer is %d",
        sizeof(char *));
    return 0;
}
```

Output

In Turbo C
```
the size of integer pointer is 2
the size of float pointer is 2
the size of double pointer is 2
the size of character pointer is 2
```

In GCC
```
the size of integer pointer is 4
the size of float pointer is 4
the size of double pointer is 4
the size of character pointer is 4
```

The output shows that all the pointer type variables (p, q, and r) take up the same storage space. Depending upon the machine architecture, the size of a pointer will range from being a 16-bit field on the IBM PC class of machines, to a 64-bit field on a Cray supercomputer.

Why should pointers have data types?

Let it be assumed that an address in a hypothetical machine is 32-bits long. The addressing of a byte or word will, therefore, require a 32-bit address. This suggests that a pointer (as pointers store addresses) should be capable of storing at least, a 32-bit value irrespective of whether it is an integer or a character. This brings in a question. Why should pointers have data types when their size is always four bytes (in a 32-bit machine) irrespective of the target they are pointing to?

Before discussing why pointers should have data types, it would be beneficial to understand the following points about C.

- C has data types of different size, i.e., objects of different types will have different memory requirements.

- It supports uniformity of arithmetic operations across different (pointer) types.

- It does not maintain data type information in the object or executable image.

When objects of a given data type are stored consecutively in the memory (that is, an array), each object is placed at a certain offset from the previous object, if any, depending on its size. A compiler that generates a code for a pointer, which accesses these objects using pointer arithmetic, requires information on generating offset. The data type of the pointer provides this information. This explains the first point.

The second point is reasonable enough to suggest that pointers should have data types. Sizes of various data types are basically decided by the machine architecture and/or the implementation. Moreover, if arithmetic operations were not uniform, then the responsibility of generating proper offset for accessing array elements would completely rest on the programmer. This has the following drawbacks.

- A programmer is likely to commit mistakes such as typographical mistakes and providing wrong offsets.

- Porting the code to other implementations would require changes, if data type sizes differ. This would lead to portability issues.

> **Note**
>
> - Pointers have data types but the size of a pointer variable is always four bytes (in a 32-bit machine) whatever the data type used in declaring it.

Where is a pointer stored?

A pointer can be stored in any location like any other variable, but is generally not stored on the heap. It can be defined and stored globally, or it can be defined local to a function and stored on the stack. The size of the pointer depends on the implementation and for 32-bit operating systems, it generally requires four bytes of storage space. This is, however, not a requirement. A compiler writer can use any number of bytes desired to store a pointer.

Keep in mind, that a pointer is like any other variable in the sense that it requires storage space somewhere in the computer's memory, but it is not like most variables because it contains no data, only an address. Since it is an address, it actually contains a number referring to some memory location. Dynamically allocated arrays can also be expanded during the execution of the program.

13.4.2 Initializing Pointers

It should be noted that, unlike a simple variable that stores a value, a pointer must be initialized with a specified address prior to its use. One of the most common causes of errors in programming by novices and professionals alike is uninitialized pointers. These errors can be very difficult to debug because the effect of the errors is often delayed until later in the program execution. Consider the following program.

```
#include <stdio.h>
int main()
{
    int *p;            /* a pointer to an integer */
    printf("%d\n",*p);
    return 0;
}
```

This code conveys to the compiler to print the value that p points to. However, p has not been initialized yet; it contains the address 0 or some random address. A pointer must not be used until it is assigned a meaningful address. To use a pointer that has not been initialized properly will cause unpredictable results. When a program starts execution, an uninitialized pointer will have some unknown memory addresses in it. More precisely, it will have an unknown value that will be interpreted as memory addresses. To use a pointer that has not been initialized properly will cause unpredictable results. In most cases, a segmentation fault (or some other run-time error) results, which means that the pointer variable used points to an invalid area of memory. Sometimes the program will appear to run correctly but when the program terminates, the message 'Null Pointer Assignment' will be displayed. This message notifies the programmer that the program is using an uninitialized pointer. In other cases, the use of an uninitialized pointer will result in a 'Bus Error' or a 'Memory Fault' run-time error. No matter what, the use of an uninitialized pointer is extremely dangerous, especially on PC type systems, and difficult to track down.

Note

• A pointer should be initialized with another variable's memory address, with 0, or with the keyword NULL prior to its use; otherwise the result may be a compiler error or a run-time error.

Now, back to the new pointer variable p declared earlier. Suppose, p stores the address of the integer variable i that contains the value 3. To store the address of 'i' in 'p', the unary & address operator is to be used. This is shown as follows:

```
p = &i;
```

The & operator retrieves the lvalue (address) of i, even though i is on the right-hand side of the assignment operator '=', and copies that onto the contents of the pointer ptr. Now, ptr is said to 'point to' i. The & operator applies only to objects in memory, that is, variables and array elements. It cannot be applied to expressions, constants, or register variables.

The following program shows how to use the address operator to assign the address of a variable to a pointer. This program also demonstrates that the value of a pointer is the same as the address to which the pointer points.

```
#include <stdio.h>
int main()
{
  int i = 5;
  int *ptr = &i;
  printf("\nThe address of i using &num is %p", &i);
  printf("\nThe address of i using Ptr is %p", ptr);
  return 0;
}
```

The output (the following addresses might be different on different computers) is

```
The address of i using &num is 0012FED4
The address of i using Ptr is 0012FED4
```

Figure 13.3 shows how the pointer points to the integer variable.

```
     i              p
 ┌───────┐      ┌──────────┐
 │   5   │◄─────│ 0012FED4 │
 └───────┘      └──────────┘
 0012FED4        0012FEE4
```

Fig. 13.3 Pointer pointing to an integer variable

Another point to remember is that a *pointer variable is always bound to a specific data type (except void pointer)*. This means that the type of the pointer and the variable whose address is contained in the pointer must be of the same type. The following pointer initializations are invalid.

```
int a=3, *ip;
float *p;
char ch='A';
p=&a; ─────── INVALID
ip=&ch; ─────── INVALID
```

Any number of pointers can point to the same address. For example, we could declare p, q, and r as integer pointers and set all of them to point to i as shown here.

```
int i=3;
int *p, *q, *r;
p = &i;
q = &i;
r = p;
```

Note that in this code, r points to the same address that p points to, which is the address of i. We can assign pointers to one another, and the address is copied from the right-hand side to the left-hand side during the assignment. The pictorial representation is given in Fig. 13.4.

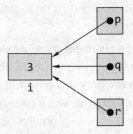

Fig. 13.4 Three pointers pointing to the same variable

The variable i can be accessed through i, *p, *q, and *r. There is no limit on the number of pointers that can hold, and therefore point to the same address.

Note

• A pointer is bound to a specific data type (except pointer to void). A pointer to an int cannot hold the address of a character variable in which case a compiler error would result.

Printing pointer value

A pointer variable contains a memory address that points to another variable. To print the memory address stored in pointers and non-pointer variables using the %p conversion specifier and to learn the use of the %p conversion specifier, study the following program.

```
#include <stdio.h>
int main(void)
```

```
{
    int a=10, *p;
    p=&a;
    printf("\n p = %p", p);
    return 0;
}
```

Output

```
p = 0022FF2C
```

On most systems %p produces a hexadecimal number. On ANSI C systems, the %p is preferred. Instead of %p, %x can be used giving the same output. If %u is used, the address will be printed in decimal form. Compare the output with the previous program.

```
#include <stdio.h>
int main(void)
{
    int a=10, *p;
    p=&a;
    printf("\n p = %u", p);
    return 0;
}
```

Output

```
p = 2293548
```

Note

- Addresses must always be printed using %u or %p or %x. If %p is used, the address will be printed in hexadecimal form. If %u is used, the address will be printed in decimal form.

Is it possible to assign a constant to a pointer variable?

Consider the following code:

```
int *pi;
pi= (int*)1000;
*pi = 5;
```

Location 1000 might contain the program. Since it is a read only, the operating system will throw up a segmentation fault.

What about *pi = 5? Again, it will most likely cause a segmentation fault because lower memory addresses are typically used for program code. This area is only read. It should be known in advance where this constant is located in the memory. This construction is useful when writing an operating system or device driver that communicates with the device using memory.

For example, in older PCs, the screen could be updated by directly accessing an array in memory (the address probably started at 0x10000). The array was of integers that were two bytes. The first byte held the ASCII character code and the second byte stored the character attributes. Once again, if one did not know what one were doing, the computer could crash.

Note

- A pointer is a variable that holds the address of a memory location that is, pointers are variables that *point* to memory locations.
- In C, pointers are not allowed to store any arbitrary memory address, but they can only store addresses of variables of a given type.

13.4.3 Indirection Operator and Dereferencing

The primary use of a pointer is to access and if appropriate, change the value of the variable that the pointer is pointing to. The other pointer operator available in C is '*', called the 'value at address' operator. It returns the value stored at a particular address. The value at address operator is also called indirection operator or dereference operator.

In the following program, the value of the integer variable num is changed twice.

```
#include <stdio.h>
int main()
{
    int num = 5;
    int *iPtr = &num;
    printf("\n The value of num is %d", num);
    num = 10;
    printf("\n The value of num after num = 10 is\ %d",
        num);
    *iPtr = 15;
    printf("\n The value of num after *iPtr = 15 is\
        %d", num);
    return 0;
}
```

Output

```
The value of num is 5
The value of num after num = 10 is 10
The value of num after *iPtr = 15 is 15
```

The second change should be familiar by the direct assignment of a value to num, such as num = 10. However, the third change is accomplished in a new way, by using the indirection operator.

```
*iPtr = 15;
```

The indirection operator is an asterisk, the same asterisk that is used to declare the pointer or to perform multiplication. However, in this statement the asterisk is not being used in a declaration or to perform multiplication. Therefore, in this context it is being used as an indirection operator. Observe the following statements carefully.

```
int i=5;
int *p;
p = &i;
printf("\nValue of i = %d", i);
```

```
printf("\nValue of * (&i) = %d", *(&i));
```
Output
```
value of i = 5
value of * (&i) = 5
```

Note that printing the value of *(&i) is same as printing the value of i. * always implies value at address. *(&i) is identical to i. The unary operators & and * bind more tightly than arithmetic operators; they associate right to left, hence *&i is equivalent to *(&i).

The placement of the indirection operator before a pointer is said to *dereference the pointer*. The value of a dereferenced pointer is not an address, but rather the value at that address—that is, the value of the variable that the pointer points to.

For example, in the preceding program, iPtr's value is the address of num. However, the value of iPtr dereferenced is the value of num. Thus, the following two statements have the same effect, both changing the value of num.

```
num = 25;
*iPtr = 25;
```

Similarly, a dereferenced pointer can be used in arithmetic expressions in the same fashion as the variable to which it points. Thus, the following two statements have the same effect.

```
num *= 2;
*iPtr *= 2;
```

In these examples, changing a variable's value using the indirection operator rather than through a straightforward assignment seems like an unnecessary complication. However, there are instances (discussed later in this chapter), such as looping through an array using a pointer, or using dynamic memory allocation, in which using the indirection operator is helpful or even necessary.

Note

- Address of operator (&): It is used as a variable prefix and can be translated as 'address of'. Thus, &variable can be read as .address of variable.
- Dereference operator (*): It can be translated by .value pointed by or 'value at address'. *ptr can be read as 'value pointed by ptr'. It indicates that what has to be evaluated is the content pointed by the expression considered as an address.

The following example shows how pointers can be used to add numbers given by the user through the use of pointers without using the variable directly.

```
#include <stdio.h>
int main()
{
  int a,b,c;
  int *pa,*pb,*pc;
  pa=&a;
  pb=&b;
```

```
pc=&c;
printf("\n ENTER THE FIRST NUMBER:");
scanf("%d",pa);
printf("\n ENTER THE SECOND NUMBER:");
scanf("%d",pb);
*pc=*pa+*pb;
printf("\n SUM IS %d",*pc);
return 0;
}
```
Output
```
ENTER THE FIRST NUMBER 5
ENTER THE SECOND NUMBER 6
SUM IS 11
```
The following statements are also valid.
```
*ptr = *ptr + 10;
```
increments *ptr by 10. The unary operators * and & bind more tightly than arithmetic operators, so the assignment
```
y = *ptr + 1
```
takes whatever ptr points at, adds 1, and assigns the result to y, while
```
*ip += 1
```
increments what ptr points to. A pointer variable does not always points to a particular variable throughout the program. It can point to any variable; the only precondition is that its type must be same because the pointer variable is bound to specific data type. The following program illustrates this fact.
```
#include <stdio.h>
int main()
{
  int a=5, b=10;
  int *p;
  p = &a;
  printf("\na=%d b=%d *p=%d", a, b,*p);
  p=&b;
  printf("\na=%d b=%d *p=%d", a, b,*p);
  return 0;
}
```
Output
```
a=5 b=10 *p=5
a=5 b=10 *p=10
```

13.5 VOID POINTER

A void pointer is a special type of pointer. It can point to any data type, from an integer value or a float to a string of characters. Its sole limitation is that the pointed data cannot be referenced directly (the asterisk * operator cannot be used on them) since its length is always undetermined. Therefore, *type casting* or assignment must be used to turn the void pointer to a pointer of a concrete data type to which we can refer. Take a look at the following example.

```
#include <stdio.h>
int main()
```

```
{
   int a=5,
   double b=3.1415;
   void *vp;
   vp=&a;
   printf("\n a= %d", *((int *)vp));
   vp=&b;
   printf("\n a= %d", *((double *)vp));
   return 0;
}
```

Output

```
a= 5
b= 3.141500
```

Note

- Void pointer can point to a variable of any data type, from an integer value or a float to a string of characters.
- The type casting or assignment must be used to turn the void pointer to a pointer of a concrete data type to which we can refer.

13.6 NULL POINTER

Suppose a variable, e.g., a, is declared without initialization.

```
int a;
```

If this is made outside of any function, ANSI-compliant compilers will initialize it to zero. Similarly, an uninitialized pointer variable is initialized to a value guaranteed in such a way that it is certain not to point to any C object or function. A pointer initialized in this manner is called a *null* pointer.

A null pointer is a special pointer that points nowhere. This means that no other valid pointer to any other variable or array cell or anything else will ever be equal to a null pointer.

The most straightforward way to get a null pointer in the program is by using the predefined constant NULL, which is defined by several standard header files, including <stdio.h>, <stdlib.h>, and <string.h>. To initialize a pointer to a null pointer, code such as the following can be used.

```
#include <stdio.h>
int *ip = NULL;
```

To test it for a null pointer before inspecting the value pointed to, code such as the following can be used.

```
if(ip != NULL)
   printf("%d\n", *ip);
```

It is also possible to refer to the null pointer using a constant 0, and to set null pointers by simply saying

```
int *ip = 0;
```

If it is too early in the code to know which address to assign to the pointer, then the pointer can be assigned to NULL,

which is a constant with a value of zero defined in several standard libraries, including stdio.h. The following program does so.

```
#include <stdio.h>
int main()
{
   int *p;
   p = NULL;
   printf("\n The value of p is %u", p);
   return 0;
}
```

Output

```
The value of p is 0
```

On most operating systems, programs are not permitted to access memory at address 0 because that memory is reserved by the operating system. It is not the case that the pointer points to a memory address that is reserved by the operating system. However, the memory address 0 has special significance; it signals that the pointer is not intended to point to an accessible memory location. Thus, if it is too early in the code to know which address to assign to a pointer, the pointer should first be assigned to NULL, which then makes it safe to access the value of a pointer before it is assigned a 'real' value such as the address of another variable or constant.

Furthermore, since the definition of 'true' in C is a value that is not equal to 0, the following statement tests for non-null pointers with abbreviated code such as

```
if(ip)
   printf("%d\n", *ip);
```

This has the same meaning as our previous example; if(ip) is equivalent to if(ip != 0) and to if(ip != NULL). The value 0 can be used to represent a null pointer in

- assignment and initialization
- comparison

All of these uses are correct, although the use of the constant NULL is recommended for clarity.

Note

- NULL is a constant that is defined in the standard library and is the equivalent of zero for a pointer. NULL is a value that is guaranteed not to point to any location in memory.

Consider the following code segment:

```
#include <stdio.h>
int main(void)
{
   char *p=NULL;
   printf("%s",p);
   return 0;
}
```

The C standard lays down that the argument for a %s specifier shall be a pointer to an array of characters. Since NULL is not an array of characters, the statement "printf("%s",p);" shows an undefined behaviour resulting in unpredictable or compiler defined output.

13.7 USE OF POINTERS

Call by address

One of the typical applications of pointers is to support call by reference. However, C does not support call by reference as do other programming languages such as PASCAL and FORTRAN. Typically, a function call is made to communicate some arguments to the function. C makes use of only one mechanism to communicate arguments to a function: *call by value*. This means that when a function is called, a copy of the values of the arguments is created and given to the function. For example,

```
#include <stdio.h>
void swap(int a, int b)
{
    int temp;
    temp=a;
    a=b;
    b=temp;
}
int main()
{
    int x=5,y=10;
    void swap(1nt,int);
    printf("%d %d\n",x,y);
    swap(x,y);
    printf("%d %d\n",x,y);
    return 0;
}
```

Output

```
5 10
5 10
```

No swapping takes place. Now when the function swap is called, the system automatically creates two new variables (called a and b in this case). These will contain a copy of the values that are specified in the function call (i.e., the value of x and the value of y). All the operations performed by the function operate on the copies of the values (a, b), and will not affect the original values (x, y).

Of course, in this particular example, the function will probably not accomplish what is needed. The function swap is used to exchange the content of two variables, but when the call is made, the function will receive and operate on the copies of the variables, leaving the original variables (x, y) untouched. So at the end of the function the effect of the changes done by swap is lost (the copies created when

the function is called are destroyed when the function is completed).

This is a common situation in C. Each function always receives copies of values and the function does not have any way of modifying the value of variables that exist outside the function (e.g., x, y in the example).

The way to obtain the desired effect is *call by reference*. This means that when the function is called, we do not create copies of values but the function is allowed to access the original values. This also means that if the function modifies such values, then the modification will affect the original value and will persist once the function execution is finished.

Call by reference does not exist in C, but it can be simulated through the use of pointers. To make a function be able to modify a certain variable, the function must be provided with information about the location of the variable in memory (i.e., its address). If the function knows where the variable is in memory, it will be able to access that area of memory by using pointers and change its content. This is known as *call by address*.

The way to obtain the desired effect is for the calling program to pass pointers to the values to be changed. For example,

```
swap(&x, &y);
```

Since the operator & produces the address of a variable, &x is a pointer to x. In swap itself, this will arrive to the function in the form of a pointer. That is, the parameters are declared as pointers, and the operands are accessed indirectly through them. Now, the preceding program is rewritten using call by address.

```
#include <stdio.h>
void swap(int *a, int *b)
{
    int temp;
    temp = *a;
    *a = *b;
    *b = temp;
}
int main()
{
    int x=5,y=10;
    void swap(int *,int *);
    printf("%d %d\n",x,y);
    swap(&x, &y);
    printf("%d %d\n",x,y);
    return 0;
}
```

Output

```
5 10
10 5
```

The values have been exchanged by the function `swap()`. Within the `main()` function, the `&` operator causes the address of arguments x and y to be passed in the call to `swap()`. In the `swap()` function header, the addresses being passed from the calling function are received in pointer type variables (`int *a, int *b`). Within the `swap()` function body, the `*` operator is used to retrieve values held at the addresses that were passed. The following example attempts to demonstrate how identifiers or variables are assigned locations in memory and how values are stored in those locations. All addressing in the following example is assumed arbitrarily.

	Variable name	Memory address	Value
`int main()`			
`{`			
`void swap(int *, int *);`			
`int`			
`  x = 5,`	x	2000	5
`  y = 10`	y	2002	10
`  ;`			
`  /* pass addresses */`			
`  swap(&x, &y);`			
`  return 0;`			
`}`			
`void`			
`swap(int *a, int *b)`	a	3000	2000
	b	3002	2002
`{`			
`  int temp;`	temp	4000	0/garbage
`  temp = *a;`	temp	4000	5
`  *a = *b;`	*a	2000	10
`  *b = temp;`	*b	2002	5
`}`			

In the above code, the addresses of x and y are passed to the function `swap()`. The parameters of the `swap()` function, `int *a` and `int *b` are pointers to integer type data. These pointers receive the addresses of x and y respectively that are passed in the call to `swap()`. Within the function `swap()`, a local variable `temp` is declared. The pointer a is dereferenced, meaning that the value at the address held in a is retrieved. This value is stored into `temp`. Then the value at the address held in b is retrieved and assigned to the value at the address held in a, thus exchanging values. The final statement in the function completes the exchange of values. Notice that the function does not return a value because of the `void` return type. Figure 13.5 presents this diagrammatically.

Fig. 13.5 Call by address

Suppose one accidentally forgets the `&` when the `swap` function is called, and that the swap line accidentally looks like this:

```
swap(x, y);
```

This causes a segmentation fault. When the value of a is passed instead of its address, a points to an invalid location in memory and the system crashes when `*a` is used.

> **Note**
>
> - C supports only call by value. C does not support call by reference in true sense, but it can be simulated through the use of pointers known as *call by address*.

Returning more than one value from a function

Functions usually return only one value and when arguments are passed by value, the called function cannot alter the values passed and have those changes reflected in the calling function. Pointers allow the programmer to 'return' more than one value by allowing the arguments to be passed by address, which allows the function to alter the values pointed to, and thus 'return' more than one value from a function.

EXAMPLE

```
1. #include <stdio.h>
   int main()
   {
     float r, area, perimeter;
     float compute(float, float *);
     printf("\n enter the radius of the circle:");
     scanf("%f",&r);
     area=compute(r, &perimeter);
     printf("\n AREA = %f", area);
     printf("\n PERIMETER = %f", perimeter);
     return 0;
   }
   float compute(float r, float *p)
   {
     float a;
     a=(float)3.1415 * r * r;
     *p=(float)3.1415 * 2 * r;
     return a;
   }
```

It must keep the value available until execution reaches a *sequence point*, which in this case means the end of the statement. When the system is notified to assign the value to area, a copy of it is saved. Following that, the compiler writer may delete the memory used to return the value. If it was returned on the stack, it is imperative to remove it from the stack in preparation for the next operation. But that can be done because the value is stored in area and can be used in any way.

Returning pointer from a function

It is also possible to return a pointer from a function. When a pointer is returned from a function, it must point to data in the calling function or in the global variable. Consider the following program. In this program, a pointer would point an integer variable whichever is larger between two variables through a function which returns the address of the larger variable.

```c
#include <stdio.h>
int *pointMax(int *, int *);
int main(void)
{
  int a,b,*p;
  printf("\n a = ?");
  scanf("%d",&a);
  printf("\n b = ?");
  scanf("%d",&b);
  p=pointMax(&a,&b);
  printf("\n*p = %d", *p);
  return 0;
}
int *pointMax(int *x, int *y)
{
  if(*x>*y)
    return x;
  else
    return y;
}
```

Output

```
a = ?5
b = ?7
*p = 7
```

When the function pointMax() is called, the addresses of two integer variables are passed to it. In the function, the pointers x and y point to a and b respectively. If a is greater than b, then the function pointMax()returns the address of a; otherwise, it returns the address of b. When the control returns to the main(), p points either to a or b.

Returning a pointer to a local variable in the called function is not effectual as illustrated in the following code segment. Because when the function terminates the address of the local variable becomes invalid. Some compilers issue a warning that 'function returns address of local variable'.

```c
int *pointMax(void)
{
  int a,b;
  :
  :
  :
  if(a>b)
    return a;
  else
    return b;
}
```

> **WRONG!**
> Never return a pointer to an automatic local variable. In C99, a warning will be issued.

But it is correct to write a function that returns a pointer to an external variable or to a static variable that has been declared *static*.

```c
include <stdio.h>
int *pointMax(void);
int main(void)
{
  int *p;
  p=pointMax();
  printf("*p = %d", *p);
  return 0;
}
int *pointMax(void)
{
  static int a=5, b=10;
  if(a>b)
    return &a;
  else
    return &b;
}
```

When an array is passed as argument to a function, sometimes it may be useful to return a pointer to one of the elements of the array as shown in the following function.

```c
int *findMiddle(int x[], int n)
{
  return &x[n/2];
}
```

13.8 ARRAYS AND POINTERS

Pointers and arrays are inseparably related, but they are not synonymous.

13.8.1 One-dimensional Arrays and Pointers

An array is a non-empty set of sequentially indexed elements having the same type of data. Each element of an array has a unique identifying index number. Changes made to one element of an array does not affect the other elements. An array occupies a contiguous block of memory. The array a is laid out in memory as a contiguous block, as shown in Fig. 13.6.

```c
int a[]={10, 20, 30, 40, 50};
```

a[0]	a[1]	a[2]	a[3]	a[4]
10	20	30	40	50

2147478270 2147478274 2147478278 2147478282 2147478286

Fig. 13.6 Memory layout for an integer array

Elements of array are stored in the successive increasing locations of memory. For example, if the array starts at memory location 2147478270 (considering a 32-bit machine), then with the assumed size of an integer as four bytes, the first element is stored at location 2147478270, the second element at location 2147478274, and so on. Here, the locations are taken as arbitrary.

Array notation is a form of pointer notation. The name of an array is the beginning address of the array, called the base address of the array., that is, the base address of an array is the address of the zeroth element of the array. The array name is referred to as an *address constant*. Mentioning the name of the array fetches its base address. Consider the following program.

EXAMPLE

```
2. (a) #include <stdio.h>
       int main()
       {
         int array[]={10, 20, 30, 40, 50};
         printf("%u %u", array, &array[0]);
         return 0;
       }
```

Output

```
2147478270 2147478270
```

Again, consider the following program.

```
(b) #include <stdio.h>
    int main()
    {
      int array[]={10, 20, 30, 40, 50};
      printf("%u %u", array, &array);
      return 0;
    }
```

Output
```
2147478270 2147478270
```

Both array and &array would give the base address of the array. Though both array and &array give the same address, there is a small difference between them. Under ANSI/ISO Standard C, &array yields a pointer, of type pointer-to-array-of-T, where T is the data type to the entire array. Under pre-ANSI C, the & in &array generally elicited a warning, and was generally ignored. Under all C compilers, an unadorned reference to an array yields a pointer, of type pointer-to-T, to the array's first element.

> **Note**
> - Array name is a *pointer constant*. It cannot be used as *lvalue*, that, is array names cannot be used as variables on the left of an assignment operator.
> - Both array and &array would give the base address of the array, but the only difference is under ANSI/ISO Standard C, &array yields a pointer, of type pointer-to-array of-the data type to the entire array.

An array can be subscripted to get to individual cells of data. With the name of the array actually being a constant that represents a memory address, the name of the array can be used as a pointer and an integer value can be used to represent an offset from the base address. This alternate method can be used to get to individual cells of an array. An element of the

array a is addressed as a[i] and the address of the ith element of the array a is given by &a[i]=a+i* size of the type pointed to by a.

The expression a + i (with integer i) means the address of the ith element beyond the one a points to. This is not measured in number of bytes, but in number of sizeof(*type*) bytes. This is known as *scaling*.

The compiler automatically scales a subscript to the size of the object pointed at. The compiler takes care of scaling before adding to the base address. This is the reason why pointers are always type-constrained to point to objects for only one type, so that the compiler knows how many bytes to retrieve on pointer dereference and it knows by how much to scale a subscript.

As indirection operator '*' implies value at address, a[i] is equivalent to *(a+i). Consider the following two versions of the same program.

EXAMPLE

```
3.(a) #include <stdio.h>
      int main()
      {
        int a[]={10, 20, 30, 40, 50};
        int i;
        for(i=0;i<5;++i)
          printf("\n%d", a[i]);
        return 0;
      }
```

Output
```
10
20
30
40
50
```

```
(b) #include <stdio.h>
    int main()
    {
      int a[]={10, 20, 30, 40, 50};
      int i;
      for(i=0;i<5;++i)
        printf("\n%d", *(a+i));
      return 0;
    }
```

Output
```
10
20
30
40
50
```

The integer identifier i is added to the base address of the array. The C compiler computes the resulting address that will be accessed by taking the value held in i multiplied by the size in bytes of the type of array a and adds the proper offset to a to give the correct memory address. Subscript notation is converted by the compiler into the pointer notation. Hence, pointer notation would work faster since conversion time can be saved by using it.

All the following four expressions are the same when their addresses are considered.

```
a[i]
*(a + i)
*(i + a)
i[a]
```

In the expression a[i], i must be an integer. The other may either be an array name or a pointer. For any one-dimensional array a and integer i, the following relationships are always true.

1. &a[0] == a

   The address of the first element of the array a is the value of a itself. In other words, a is a pointer; it points to the first element in the array.

2. &a[i] == a + i

   The address of the ith element of a is the value of a + i. This is one of the great truths (and a defining characteristic) of C. The first relationship is a special case of this more general relationship.

3. a[i] == *(a + i)

   This is basically the same as the previous relationship but this relationship still holds if both sides of the equality operator are dereferenced.

4. (&a[i] - &a[j]) == (i - j)

   This relationship defines the subtraction of pointers. The subtraction of two pointers of type t is the number of elements of type t that would fit between them.

A pointer variable (of the appropriate type) can also be used to initialize or point to the first element of the array. Then it can also be used as above.

```c
#include <stdio.h>
int main()
{
  int a[]={10, 20, 30, 40, 50};
  int i, *p;
  p=a; /* it can also be written as p=&a[0]; */
  for(i=0;i<5;++i)
    printf("\n%d", p[i]);

  return 0;
}
```

Output

```
10
20
30
40
50
```

```
printf ("\n%d", *(p+i));
         OR
printf ("\n%d", *(i+p));
         OR
printf ("\n%d", i[p]);
```

One can define a pointer of the same type as the elements of the array and can assign it the address of any element of the array and use it to access the array elements. In fact, one may add an integer value to it. Such a statement in the program uses the formula given earlier to do the assignment; so it also adjusts the count for the size of the element. Pointers and arrays are so closely related that their notation can be interchanged such that the following terms are identical if p contains the value of a.

```
a[i]
*(a + i)
*(p + i)
p[i]
where i=0,1,2,...(N-1). N is the size of the array.
```

The similarities between arrays and pointers end up being quite useful, and in fact C builds on the similarities, leading to what is called 'the equivalence of arrays and pointers in C'. This equivalence does not mean that arrays and pointers are the same (they are, in fact, quite different) but that they can be used in related ways, and that certain operations may be used between them. These operations are as follows.

- The first such operation is that it is possible to (apparently) assign an array to a pointer.

  ```c
  int a[10];
  int *p;
  p = a;
  ```

  C defines the result of this assignment to be that p receives a pointer to the first element of a. In other words,

  ```c
  p = &a[0];
  ```

- The second aspect of the equivalence is that the *array subscripting* notation [i] can be applied on pointers, too. p[3] can be written as *(p + 3).

So, a pointer that points to an array or a part of an array can be treated 'as if' it *was* an array, using the convenient [i] notation. In other words, at the beginning of this discussion, the expressions *p, *(p+1), *(p+2), and in general *(p+i), could have been written as p[0], p[1], p[2], and p[i]. This can be quite useful (or at least convenient).

The pointer to an array does not always point to the first element of the array. It can point to any element of the array. For example,

```c
int a[]={10,20,30,40,50};
int *p;
p = a + 3;
```

can also be written as follows

```c
p = &a[0] + 3;
```

which, in turn, gives the same result as

```c
p = &a[3];
```

Figure 13.7 depicts the equivalence among array notation and pointer notation.

a[0]	a[1]	a[2]	a[3]	a[4]
10	20	30	40	50

```
p = a              p = a+2            p = a+4
p = &a[0]          p = &a[2]          p = &a[4]
```

Fig. 13.7 Pointer notation of array elements

Is it possible to treat an array as if it were a 1-based array? Although this technique is attractive (and was used in old editions of the book *Numerical Recipes in C*), it does not conform to the C standards. Pointer arithmetic is defined only as long as the pointer points within the same allocated block of memory, or to the imaginary 'terminating' element one past it; otherwise, the behaviour is undefined *even if the pointer is not dereferenced.* The preceding code could fail if, while subtracting the offset, an illegal address was generated (perhaps because the address tried to 'wrap around' past the beginning of some memory segment). Here is a neat trick, the details of which will be discussed in Section 13.18.

```
int arr[10];
int *a = &arr[-1];
```

Note

For any one-dimensional array a and integer i, the following relationships are always true.

- a[i] ≡ *(a+i) ≡ *(i+a) ≡ i[a].

13.8.2 Passing an Array to a Function

An array may be passed to a function, and the elements of that array may be modified without having to worry about referencing and dereferencing. Since arrays may transform immediately into pointers, all the difficult stuff gets done automatically. A function that expects to be passed with an array can declare that formal parameter in one of the two ways.

```
int a[] or int *a
```

When passing an array name as argument to a function, the address of the zeroth element of the array is copied to the local pointer variable in the function. The values of the elements are *not* copied. The corresponding local variable is considered as a pointer variable, having all the properties of pointer arithmetic and dereferencing. It is *not* an address constant. This is illustrated with an example. The relevant function calls in main() and the corresponding function headers are shown as follows for easy reference.

```
#define MAX 50
int main()
{
    int arr[MAX],n;
```

```
    ...
    n = getdata(arr, MAX);
    show(arr, n);
    return 0;
}
int getdata(int a[], int n)
{
    ...
}
void show(int a[], int n)
{
    ...
}
```

When a formal parameter is declared in a function header as an array, it is interpreted as a pointer variable, *not* an array. Even if a size was specified in the formal parameter declaration, only a pointer cell is allocated for the variable, not the entire array. The type of the pointer variable is the specified type. In the preceding example, the formal parameter, a, is an integer pointer. It is initialized to the pointer value passed as an argument in the function call. The value passed from main() is arr, a pointer to the first element of the array, arr[].

Within the function, getdata(), it is now possible to access all the elements of the array indirectly. Since the variable a in getdata() points to the first element of the array arr[], it accesses the first element of the array. In addition, a + 1 points to the next element of the array, so it accesses the next element, i.e., arr[1]. In general, *(a + i) accesses the element arr[i]. To access elements of the array, we can either write *(a + i) or a[i], because dereferenced array pointers and indexed array elements are identical ways of writing expressions for array access.

The functions, getdata() and show() can be used to read objects into any integer array and to print element values of any integer array, respectively. The calling function must simply pass an appropriate array pointer and maximum number of elements as arguments. These functions may also be written explicitly in terms of indirect access. Such an example is as follows:

EXAMPLE

```
4. #include <stdio.h>
   #define MAX 50
   int main()
   {
       int arr[MAX],n;
       int getdata(int *, int);
       void show(int *, int);
       n = getdata(arr, MAX);
       show(arr, n);
       return 0;
   }
   /* Function reads scores in an array. */
   int getdata(int *a, int n)
   {
       int x, i = 0;
```

```
printf("\n Enter the array elements one by one\n");
while(i < n)
{
  scanf("%d", &x)
  *(a + i) = x;
  i++;
}
return i;
}
void show(int *a, int n)
{
int i;
for(i=0;i<n;++i)
  printf("\n %d", *(a+i));
}
```

Figure 13.8 illustrates the connection between the calling function main(), and the called functions.

```
int main()
{  int arr[MAX],n;
   ...
   n = getdata(arr, MAX);           a=arr;
  show(arr, n);
  return 0;
}
                              int getdata(int *a, int n)
 a=arr;                        {
                                ...
void show(int *a, int n)       }
{
  ...
}
```

Fig. 13.8 Passing array to a function

When an array is passed to a function, the C language allows the programmer to refer the formal parameter as either an array or as a pointer. The compiler knows that whenever a formal parameter is declared as an array, inside the function it will in fact always be dealing with a pointer to the first element of the array of unknown size. That is why the calling function must simply pass an appropriate array pointer and maximum number of elements as arguments.

Parts of an array, called a sub-array, may also be passed to a function. A pointer to a sub-array is also an array pointer; it simply specifies the base of the sub-array. In fact, as far as C is concerned, there is no difference between an entire array and any of its sub-arrays. For example, a function call can be made to print a sub-array by specifying the starting pointer of the sub-array and its size. Suppose we need to print the sub-array starting at arr[3] containing five elements; the expression, &arr[3] is a pointer to an array starting at arr[3]. The function call is,

```
show(&arr[3], 5);
```

Alternately, since arr + 3 points to arr[3], the function call can be

```
show(arr + 3, 5);
```

Note

- When an array is passed to a function, it degenerates to a pointer. All array names that are function parameters are always converted into pointers by the compiler. Because when passing an array to a function, the address of the zero-th element of the array is copied to the pointer variable which is the formal parameter of the function. However, arrays and pointers are processed differently by the compiler, represented differently at run time.

13.8.3 Differences between Array Name and Pointer

From the above discussion it seems that array name and pointer which points to the base address of the array, are equivalent. But it is not true. There are several differences between them. They are as follows.

- When memory is allocated for the array, the starting address is fixed, i.e., it cannot be changed during program execution. Therefore, array name is an address constant; the value contained in it should not be changed. To ensure that this pointer is not changed, in C, array names may not be used as variables on the left of an assignment statement, i.e., they may not be used as an lvalue. Instead, if necessary, separate pointer variables of the appropriate type may be declared and used as lvalues. Here is an example of a common error when an attempt to use an array as an lvalue is made.

```
#include <stdio.h>
int main()
{
  int i;
  float a[5];
  for(i = 0; i < 5; i++)
  {
    *a = 0.0;
    a++; /* BUG: a = a + 1; */
  }
  return 0;
}
```

In this example, a is fixed and cannot be used as an lvalue; the compiler will generate an error stating that an lvalue is required for the ++ operator. However, a pointer variable can be declared, which can point to the same type as the type of the array, and initialize it with the base address of array. This pointer variable can be used as an lvalue and no error message will be displayed. Here is the difference.

```
#include <stdio.h>
int main()
```

```
{
    int i;
    float *ptr, a[5];
    ptr = a;
    for(i = 0; i < 5; i++)
    {
        *ptr = 0.0; /* *ptr accesses a[i] */
        ptr++;
    }
    return 0;
}
```

Observe that the pointer variable, ptr, is type float *, because the array is of type float. It is initialized to the value of the fixed pointer, a (i.e., the initial value of ptr is set to the same as that of a, namely &a[0]), and may subsequently be modified in the loop to traverse the array. The first time through the loop, *ptr which points to (a[0]) is set to zero and ptr is incremented by one so that it points to the next element in the array. The process repeats and each element of the array is set to 0.0.

Following the same concept, an array cannot be assigned to another. The following code

```
int a[5]={1,2,3,4,5};
int b[5];
b = a;       /* WRONG */
```

is incorrect. To copy a into b, something like the following has to be entered.

```
for(i=0; i<5; i++)
    b[i]=a[i];
```

Or, to put it more succinctly,

```
for(i=0; i<5; b[i]=a[i], i++);
```

But two pointer variables can be assigned.

```
int *p1, *p2;
int a[5]={1,2,3,4,5};
p1 = &a[0];
p2 = p1;
```

Pointer assignment is straightforward; the pointer on the left is simply made to point wherever the pointer on the right does. The statement p1=p2 does not copy the data pointed to (there is still just one copy in the same place); it just makes two pointers point to the same location.

- The & (address of) operator normally returns the address of the operand. However, arrays are an exception. When applied to an array (which is an address), it has the same value as the array reference without the operator. This is not true of the equivalent pointers, which have an independent address. The following example shows this.

5. (a)
```
#include <stdio.h>
int main()
{
    int a[]={10, 20, 30, 40, 50};
    printf("%u %u %u", a, &a[0],&a);
    return 0;
}
```
Output
> 65506 65506 65506

(b)
```
#include <stdio.h>
int main()
{
    int a[]={10, 20, 30, 40, 50};
    int *ptr;
    ptr=a;
    printf("%u %u", &a[0],ptr,&ptr);
    return 0;
}
```
Output
> 65506 65506 65526

- The sizeof operator returns the size of the allocated space for arrays. In case of a pointer, the sizeof operator returns two or four or more bytes of storage (machine dependent).

6. (a)
```
#include <stdio.h>
int main()
{
    int a[]={10, 20, 30, 40, 50};
    printf("%d", sizeof (a));
    return 0;
}
```
Output
In Turbo C
> 10
In GCC
> 20

(b)
```
#include <stdio.h>
int main()
{
    int a[]={10, 20, 30, 40, 50};
    int *ptr;
    ptr=a;
    printf("%d", sizeof (ptr));
    return 0;
}
```
Output
In Turbo C

2

In GCC

4

Table 13.3 lists the differences between pointers and arrays.

Table 13.3 Differences between pointers and arrays

Arrays	Pointers
• It is a variable that can hold a set of homogeneous values.	• It is a variable which holds an address of another variable.
• It cannot be resized.	• It can be resized using `realloc()`.
• It cannot be reassigned.	• It can be reassigned.
• `sizeof(arrayname)` gives the number of bytes occupied by the array.	• `sizeof(p)` returns the number of bytes used to store the pointer variable p.

13.9 POINTERS AND STRINGS

Strings are one-dimensional arrays of type `char`. By convention, a string in C is terminated by the end-of-string sentinel \0, or null character. The null character is a byte with all bits off; hence, its decimal value is zero. It is useful to think of strings as having a variable length, delimited by \0, but with the maximum length determined by the size of the string. The size of a string *must* include the storage needed for the end-of-string sentinel. As with all arrays, it is the job of the programmer to make sure that string bounds are not overrun.

String constants are written between double quotes. For example, "abc" is a character array of size 4, with the last element being the null character \0. Note that string constants are different from character constants. For example, "a" and 'a' are not the same. The array "a" has two elements, the first with value 'a' and the second with value '\0'.

A string constant, like an array name by itself, is treated by the compiler as a pointer. Its value is the base address of the string. Like the numeric array, individual characters contained in a string can be printed.

```
#include <stdio.h>
int main()
{
  char s[]="Oxford";
  for(i=0;s[i]!='\0';++i)
  putchar(s[i]);
  return 0;
}
```

A string in C is a pointer itself. The following program proves the fact.

```
#include <stdio.h>
int main()
```

```
{
  for(i=0;*("I am a pointer" + i)!='\0';++i)
    printf("%c",*("I am a pointer" + i));
  return 0;
}
```

Output

```
I am a pointer
```

But this is not true for a numeric array. The following program gives an error.

```
#include <stdio.h>
int main()
{
  for(i=0;*({1,2,3,4,5} + i)!='\0';++i)
  putchar(*({1,2,3,4,5} + i));
  return 0;
}
```
Error

Consider the following code.

```
char *p = "abc";
printf("%s %s \n", p, p + 1);   /* abc bc is printed */
```

The variable p is assigned the base address of the character array "abc". When a pointer to char is printed in the format of a string, the pointed-at character and successive characters are printed until the end-of-string sentinel (that is, '\0') is reached. Thus, in the printf() statement, the expression p causes abc to be printed, and the expression p + 1, which points to the letter b in the string "abc", causes bc to be printed. Because a string constant such as "abc" is treated as a pointer, expressions such as

```
"abc"[1] and *("abc" + 2)
```

are possible. Such expressions are not used in serious code, but they help to emphasize that string constants are treated as pointers. It should be noted that arrays and pointers have similar uses. They also have differences. Let us consider two declarations

```
char *p = "abcde";
char s[] = "abcde";
```

In the first declaration, the compiler allocates space in the memory for p, puts the string constant "abcde" in memory somewhere else, and initializes p with the base address of the string constant. Now think of p as pointing to the string. The second declaration is equivalent to

```
char s[] = {'a', 'b', 'c', 'd', 'e', '\0'};
```

Because the brackets are empty, the compiler allocates six bytes of memory for the array s. The first byte is initialized with 'a', the second byte is initialized with 'b', and so on. Here is how these objects are stored in memory. (Fig. 13.9)

Fig. 13.9 Logical memory picture for p × s

A char is always stored in one byte, and on most machines a pointer is stored in a word. Thus, on the machine, p is stored in four bytes, and s is stored in six bytes of storage. For technical reasons, it is better not to print null characters. However, the printing of null strings is perfectly acceptable.

One question may arise—when an array is passed, how does the function know how many elements the array has?

For a string, the number of elements it has need not be passed because it has the terminating null character. For other types of arrays, the number of elements must be passed as well.

> **Note**
>
> - A string constant is treated by the compiler as a pointer.
> - For a string, the number of elements it has need not be passed to a function because it has the terminating null character.

13.10 POINTER ARITHMETIC

If p is declared as a pointer variable of any type and it has been initialized properly, then, just like a simple variable, any operation can be performed with *p. Because * implies value at address, working with *p means working with the variable whose address is currently held by p. Any expression, whether relational, arithmetic, or logical, can be written, which is valid for a simple value variable. But with only p, operations are restricted as in each case address arithmetic has to be performed. The only valid operations on pointers are as follows.

- Assignment of pointers to the same type of pointers: the assignment of pointers is done symbolically. Hence, no integer constant except 0 can be assigned to a pointer.
- Adding or subtracting a pointer and an integer.
- Subtracting or comparing two pointers (within array limits) that point to the elements of an array.
- Incrementing or decrementing the pointers (within array limits) that point to the elements of an array. When a pointer to an integer is incremented by one, the address is incremented by two (as two bytes are used for int). Such scaling factors necessary for the pointer arithmetic are taken care of automatically by the compiler.
- Assigning the value 0 to the pointer variable and comparing 0 with the pointer. The pointer with address 0 points to nowhere at all.

These valid address arithmetic are discussed below in detail. The following arithmetic operations on pointers are not feasible.

- Addition of two pointers
- Multiplying a pointer with a number
- Dividing a pointer with a number

13.10.1 Assignment

Pointers with the assignment operators can be used if the following conditions are met.

- The left-hand operand is a pointer and the right-hand operand is a null pointer constant.
- One operand is a pointer to an object of incompatible type and the other is a pointer to void.
- Both the operands are pointers to compatible types.

Some of the pointer assignment statements were discussed earlier. For the notion of incompatible types, including the use of void*, some complicated cases may be considered.

Pointers to void can be freely converted back and forth with pointers to any object or incomplete type. Converting a pointer to an object or an incomplete type to void* and then back gives a value which is equal to the original one.

EXAMPLE

```
7. #include <stdio.h>
   int main()
   {
     int i;
     int *ip;
     void *vp;
     ip = &i;
     vp = ip;
     ip = vp;
     if(ip != &i)
       printf("\n Compiler error\n");
     else
       printf("\n No Compiler error\n");
     return 0;
   }
```

Output

```
No Compiler error
```

Now, consider the revised version of the program in Example 7.

```
#include <stdio.h>
int main()
{
  int i=5;
  int *ip;
  void *vp;
  ip = &i;
  vp = ip;
  //printf("\n *vp= %d",*vp);      >ERROR<
  ip = vp;
  printf("\n *ip= %d",*ip);
  return 0;
}
```

This program gives an error in the first `printf` statement stating 'not an allowed type' because no type is associated with a `void` pointer. The `void` pointer can store the address of a variable of any type. But while using the `void` pointer, the right type has to be specified through type casting. The right version of this program is as follows.

```
#include <stdio.h>
int main()
{
    int i=5;
    int *ip;
    void *vp;
    ip = &i;
    vp = ip;
    printf("\n *vp= %d",*((int *)vp));
    ip = vp;
    printf("\n *ip= %d",*ip);
    return 0;
}
```

Output
```
*vp=5
*ip=5
```

The predefined constant NULL, which is defined by several standard header files, including `<stdio.h>`, `<stdlib.h>`, and `<string.h>` can be assigned.

```
int *p;
p = NULL;
```

It is also possible to refer to the null pointer by using a constant 0 by simply writing

```
int *ip = 0;
```

In fact, NULL is a preprocessor macro that typically has the value, 0.

The only values that can be assigned to pointers apart from 0 are the values of other pointers of the same type. However, one reason that makes C a useful replacement for assembly language is that it allows one to carryout operations that most other languages do not. Try this.

```
int *ip;
ip = (int *)6;
*ip = 0xFF;
```

Here, the pointer has been initialized to the value 6 (notice the type casting to turn an integer 6 into a pointer). This is a highly machine-specific operation, and the bit pattern that ends up in the pointer is quite possibly nothing like the machine representation of 6. After the initialization, a hexadecimal FF is written into wherever the pointer is pointing. The int at location 6 has had 0xFF written into it—subject to whatever 'location 6' means on this particular machine.

It may or may not make sense to do that sort of thing; C gives you the power to express it, it is up to the programmer to get it right. As always, it is possible to do things like this by accident, too, and to be very surprised by the output.

13.10.2 Addition or Subtraction with Integers

In a *closely related piece of syntax*, a '+' between a pointer and an integer does the same offset computation as explained earlier, but leaves the result as a pointer. The square bracket syntax gives the *n*th element while the '+' syntax gives a pointer to the *n*th element. So the expression (arr + 3) is a pointer to the integer arr[3].(arr + 3) is of type (int *) while arr[3] is of type int. The two expressions only differ in whether the pointer is dereferenced or not. So the expression (arr + 3) is equivalent to the expression (&(arr[3])). In fact those two probably compile to exactly the same code. They both represent a pointer to the element at index 3. Any [] expression can be written with the + syntax instead. It just needs the pointer dereference to be added in. So arr[3] is equivalent to *(arr + 3). For most purposes, the [] syntax is the easiest to use and the most readable as well. Every once in a while the + is convenient if one needs a pointer to the element instead of the element itself.

Therefore, expressions can add (or subtract, which is equivalent to adding negative values) integral values to the value of a pointer to any object type. The result has the type of the pointer and if *n* is added, then the result points *n* array elements away from the pointer. The most common use is to repeatedly add 1 to a pointer to step it from the start to the end of an array, but addition or subtraction of values other than 1 is possible. Consider the following two versions of the same program.

EXAMPLE
---

8. (a)
```
#include <stdio.h>
int main(void)
{
    int a[] = {10, 12, 6, 7, 2};
    int i;
    int sum = 0;
    for(i=0; i<5; i++)
    {
        sum += a[i];
    }
    printf("%d\n", sum);
    return 0;
}
```

(b)
```
#include <stdio.h>
int main(void)
{
    int a[] = {10, 12, 6, 7, 2};
    int i;
    int sum = 0;
    for(i=0; i<5; i++)
    {
        sum += *(a + i);
    }
    printf("%d\n", sum);
    return 0;
}
```

Note that if the pointer resulting from the addition points in front of the array or past the non-existent element just after the last element of the array, then it results in overflow or underflow and the result is undefined.

This is a typical string-processing function. Pointer arithmetic and dereferencing are used to search for various characters or patterns. Often, a character pointer is used to march along a string while parsing it or interpreting it in some way.

Table 13.4 Illustration of strlen(), strcpr() and strcat() functions

Declaration and initializations	
char s1[ ] = "India is a beautiful country"; s2[ ] = "C is sea";	
Expression	**Value**
strlen(s1)	28
strlen(s2 + 5)	3
Statements	**What gets printed**
printf("%s", s1 + 10); strcpy(s1 + 10, s2 + 8) strcat(s1, "great country"); printf("%s", s1);	beautiful country India is a great country

If p is a pointer to an element in an array, then (p+1) points to the next element in the array. The statement p++ can be used to step a pointer over the elements in an array. The program in Example 8 can be rewritten as follows.

```
#include <stdio.h>
int main(void)
{
  int a[] = {10, 12, 6, 7, 2};
  int i;
  int sum = 0;
  int *p;
  p = a;
  for(i=0; i<5; i++)
  {
    sum += *p;
    p++;
  }
  printf("%d\n", sum);
  return 0;
}
```

Similarly, since ++p and p++ are both equivalent to p=p + 1, incrementing a pointer using the unary ++ operator, either pre- or post-, increments the address it stores by the amount sizeof(type) where 'type' is the type of the object pointed to (i.e., 4 for an integer in a 32-bit machine).

Example 9 shows that pointers may be incremented and decremented. In either case, if the original pointer points to an object of a specific type, the new pointer points to the next or the previous object of the same type. Thus, pointers are incremented or decremented in steps of the object size that

the pointer points to. Hence, it is possible to traverse an array starting from a pointer to any element in the array. Consider the following program.

EXAMPLE

```
9. #include <stdio.h>
   #define N 5
   int main()
   {
     float arr[N], *ptr;
     int *iptr, a[N], i;
     /* initialize */
     for(i = 0; i < N; i++)
     {
       arr[i] = 0.3;
       a[i] = 1;
     }
     /* initialize ptr to point to element arr[3] */
     ptr = &arr[3];
     *ptr = 1.0;          /* arr[3] = 1.0 */
     *(ptr - 1) = 0.9;   /* arr[2] = .9 */
     *(ptr + 1) = 1.1;   /* arr[4] = 1.1 */
     /* initialize iptr in the same way */
     iptr = &a[3];
     *iptr = 0;
     *(iptr - 1) = -1;
     *(iptr + 1) = 2;
     for(i = 0; i < N; i++)
     {
       printf("arr[%d] = %f", i, *(arr + 1));
       printf("a[%d] = %d\n", i, a[i]);
       return 0;
     }
   }
```

The program is straightforward. It declares a float array of size 5, and an integer array of the same size. The float array elements are all initialized to 0.3, and the integer array elements to 1. The program also declares two pointer variables, one a float pointer and the other an integer pointer. Each pointer variable is initialized to point to the array element with index 3; for example, ptr is initialized to point to the float array element, arr[3]. Therefore, ptr - 1 points to arr[2], and ptr + 1 points to arr[4]. The value of *ptr is then modified, as is the value of *(ptr - 1) and *(ptr + 1). Similar changes are made in the integer array. Finally, the arrays are printed. Here is the output of the program.

```
arr[0] = 0.300000 a[0] = 1
arr[1] = 0.300000 a[1] = 1
arr[2] = 0.900000 a[2] = -1
arr[3] = 1.000000 a[3] = 0
arr[4] = 1.100000 a[4] = 2
```

Consider the following program.

```
int b[]={10,20,30,40,50};
```

```
int i,*p;
  p=&b[4]-4;
  for(i=0;i<5;++i)
   {
     printf("%d",*p);
     p++;
   }
```

The expression &b[4] gives the address of b[4]. Let the address of b[4] be 65540. Then the expression p = &b[4]-4 may give either 65536 or 65532 (considering a 16-bit machine). To explain this, consider the following statements assuming the previous array.

```
int *p;
p=&b[4]
p=p-4;
```

The statement p-4 gives the address of 65532 as p-4 evaluates as p-4* sizeof(int) i.e., 65540 – 8 (considering a 16-bit machine), that is, p points to the address of b[0] or &b[0]. The rest of the code is executed as usual.

Consider the following program where the elements of the array a are initialized, and then all elements in array a are copied into b, so that a and b are identical.

───────────────── **EXAMPLE** ─────────────────

```
10. #define MAX 10
    int main()
    {
      int a[MAX];
      int b[MAX];
      int i;
      for(i=0; i<MAX; i++)
          a[i]=i;
      b=a;        ◁ Error
      return 0;
    }
```

If it is compiled, there will be an error. Arrays in C are unusual in that variables a and b are not, technically, arrays themselves but permanent pointers to arrays. Thus, they point to blocks of memory that hold the arrays. They hold the addresses of the actual arrays, but since they are pointer constant or address constant, their addresses cannot be changed. The statement b=a;, therefore, does not work.

To copy array a into another array b, something like the following has to be entered.

```
for(i=0; i<MAX; i++)
  a[i]=b[i];
```

Or, to put it more succinctly,

```
for(i=0; i<MAX; a[i]=b[i], i++);
```

In the statement p++; if p points to an array, the compiler knows that p points to an integer. So this statement increments p by the appropriate number of bytes to move it to the next

element of the array. The array a can be copied into b using pointers as well. The following code can replace (for i=0; i<MAX; a[i]=b[i], i++); :

```
int *p *q;
p=a;
q=b;
for(i=0; i<MAX; i++)
{
  *q = *p;
  q++;
  p++;
}
```

This code can be abbreviated as follows.

```
p=a;
q=b;
for(i=0; i<MAX; i++)
  *q++ = *p++;
```

Further abbreviation leads to

```
for(p=a,q=b,i=0; i<MAX; *q++ = *p++, i++);
```

It is important to note that the unary operators ++ and -- have the same priority as *. All unary operators bind from right to left. Therefore, ++*p is equivalent to ++(*p); Notice the difference as shown in Table 13.5.

Table 13.5 Difference between (* ip) ++ and *ip++

	Equivalent:
(*ip)++;	int temp; (temp = *ip, *ip = *ip + 1)
*ip++;	Equivalent: *(ip++); int* temp; (temp = ip, ip = ip + 1)

Since * and ++ have the same precedence and associate from right to left, this is equivalent to *(ip++); the value of ip++ is ip, so this pointer will be dereferenced. After that the pointer ip is incremented by 1. Like always, it is recommended to use parentheses () in order to avoid unexpected results. Since ++ and -- are either prefix or postfix operators, other combinations of * and ++ and -- occur, although less frequently. For example,

```
*--p
```

decrements p before fetching the variable that p points to. Example 11 will clear these facts.

───────────────── **EXAMPLE** ─────────────────

```
11. #include <stdio.h>
    int main()
    {
      int A[] = {10, 20, 30, 40, 50};
      int *p, i;

      p = A;
```

```
printf("*p : %i\n\n", *p);
i = *(p++);
printf("i is: %i\n", i);
printf("*p is: %i\n\n", *p);
i = (*p)++;
printf("i is: %i\n", i);
printf("*p is: %i\n\n", *p);
i = *(++p);
printf("i is: %i\n", i);
printf("*p is: %i\n\n", *p);
i = ++(*p);
printf("i is: %i\n", i);
printf("*p is: %i\n\n", *p);
return 0;
}
```

Output

```
*p : 10
i is: 10
*p is: 20
i is: 20
*p is: 21
i is: 30
*p is: 30
i is: 31
*p is: 31
```

An integer can also be subtracted. This is illustrated in Example 12.

— **EXAMPLE** —

```
12. #include <stdio.h>
    int main(void)
    {
        int a[] = {10, 20, 30, 40, 50};
        int i, *p;
        p=a+4;
        for(i=4; i>=0; i--)
        printf("%d\n", *(p-i));
        return 0;
    }
```

Output

```
10
20
30
40
50
```

The above code may be replaced by the following code.

```
#include <stdio.h>
int main(void)
```

```
{
    int a[] = {10, 12, 6, 7, 2};
    int i, *p;
    p=a+4;
    for(i=4; i>=0; i--)
        printf("%d\n", p[-i]);
    return 0;
}
```

p[-i] is equivalent to *(p-i). Initially p points to the last element. At the beginning, i=4, p-i evaluates as p-i*sizeof(int)= p-16 (in a 32-bit machine) or =p-8(in a 16-bit machine). Now p-i gives the address of the first element of the array. p[-i], which is equivalent to, *(p-i), prints the first element of the array. Then i = 3, so p[-i] prints the second element, and so on. Look at Fig. 13.8.

a[0]	a[1]	a[2]	a[3]	a[4]
10	20	30	40	50
65004	65006	65008	65010	65012

Fig. 13.8 Subscripted notation value and address of elements of an array

Here a 16-bit machine is assumed. Initially p=65012, i=4. Therefore,

p[-i]=*(p-i)= value at address p-i*sizeof(int)
= value at address (p-8)
= value at address (65012-8) = value at address 65004 = 10.

When i=3, p[-i]=*(p-6)=*(65012-6)= value at address 65006 = 20 and so on. If i iterates from 0 to 4, then this code will print the elements of array in reverse order.

— **EXAMPLE** —

```
13. #include <stdio.h>
    int main(void)
    {
        int a[] = {10, 12, 6, 7, 2};
        int i, *p;
        p=a+4;
        for(i=0; i<5; i++)
            printf("%d\n", p[-i]);
        return 0;
    }
```

Output

```
50
40
30
20
10
```

The reason is very simple. Apply the same calculation as before. The study of strings is useful to further tie in the relationship between pointers and arrays. This discussion is also applicable to strings as strings are arrays of characters. Consider the following program that uses a pointer to shift to the next character of the string.

```
14. #include <stdio.h>
    int main()
    {
      char a[15] = "test string";
      char *pa;
      pa = a;
      while(*pa)
      {
        putchar(*pa);
        pa++;
      }
      printf("\n");
      return 0;
    }
```

Output

```
    test string
```

The while loop is equivalent to while(*pa!='\0'). More aspects of pointers and strings are illustrated here by studying versions of some useful functions adapted from the standard library string.h. The first function is strcpy(t,s), which copies the string s to the string t. It would be nice just to write t = s but this copies the pointer, not the characters. To copy the characters, a loop is needed. The array version is as follows.

```
15. #include <stdio.h>
    int main()
    {
      char a[50], b[50];
      void scopy(char *, char *);
      printf("\n Enter the string: ");
      gets(a);
      scopy(b,a);
      printf("\n %s",b);
      return 0;
    }
    /* scopy: copy s to t; array subscript version */
    void scopy(char *t, char *s)
    {
      int i;
      i = 0;
      while(s[i]!= '\0')
      {
        t[i] = s[i];
        i++;
      }
      t[i]='\0';
    }
```

An equivalent version of scopy() is given as follows.

```
    void scopy(char *t, char *s)
    {
      int i;
      i = 0;
      while((t[i] = s[i]) != '\0')
            i++;
    }
```

For contrast, here is a version of scopy() with pointers.

```
    /* scopy: copy s to t; pointer version */
    void scopy(char *t, char *s)
    {
      int i;
      i = 0;
      while((*t = *s) != '\0')
      {
        s++;
        t++;
      }
    }
```

Because arguments are passed by value, scopy can use the parameters b and a. Here they are conveniently initialized pointers, marching along the arrays one character at a time, until the '\0' that terminates s has been copied into t. Experienced C programmers would prefer the following version.

```
    /* scopy: copy s to t; pointer version 2 */
    void scopy(char *s, char *t)
    {
      while((*t++ = *s++) != '\0')
      ;
    }
```

This moves the increment of s and t into the test part of the loop. The value of *s++ is the character that s pointed to before t was incremented; the postfix ++ does not change s until after this character has been fetched. In the same way, the character is stored into the old t position before t is incremented. This character is also the value that is compared against '\0' to control the loop. The net effect is that characters are copied from s to t, up and including the terminating '\0'.

The C99 standards state that the strcpy() function must return a *copy* of its destination parameter. In both cases, we return a copy of the *destination* parameter—that is, we return *a pointer* as the function's value. Thus, the strcpy() in the standard library (<string.h>) returns the target string as its function value. It might look like

```
    char *strcopy(char *destination, char *source)
    {
      char *p = destination;
      while(*source != '\0')
      {
        *p++ = *source++;
      }
      *p = '\0';
      return destination;
    }
```

The following is the array subscript version of the strlen library function.

```
    int strlen(char s[])
    {
```

```
  int x;
  x=0;
  while(s[x] != '\0')
    x=x+1;
  return(x);
}
```

Using a pointer-based approach, this function can be rewritten as follows.

```
int strlen(char *s)
{
  int c=0;
  while(*s != '\0')
  {
    c++;
    s++;
  }
  return(c);
}
```

This code can be abbreviated as follows.

```
int strlen(char *s)
{
  int c=0;
  while(*s++)
    c++;
  return(x);
}
```

Now examine strcmp(s,t), which compares the character strings s and t, and returns negative, zero, or positive if s is lexicographically less than, equal to, or greater than t. The value is obtained by subtracting the characters at the first position where s and t disagree.

```
int stcmp(char *s, char *t)
{
  int i;
  for(i = 0; s[i] == t[i]; i++)
    if(s[i] == '\0')
      return 0;
  return s[i] - t[i];
}
```

The pointer version of stcmp is as follows:

```
int stcmp(char *s, char *t)
{
  for(; *s == *t; s++, t++)
  if(*s == '\0')
    return 0;
  return *s - *t;
}
```

To illustrate string processing, a function is written that counts the number of words in a string. It is assumed that words in the string are separated by white space. Here function will use the macro isspace(), which is defined in

the standard header file ctype.h. This macro is used to test whether a character is a blank, tab, new line, or some other white-space character. If the argument is a white-space character, then a non-zero (*true*) value is returned; otherwise, zero (*false*) is returned.

EXAMPLE

```
16. /* Count the number of words in a string. */
    #include <stdio.h>
    #include <ctype.h>
    int word_cnt(char *s)
    {
      int cnt = 0;
      while(*s != '\0')
      {
        while(isspace(*s))        /*skip white space */
          ++ s;
        if(*s != '\0')
        {                              /*found a word */
          ++cnt;
          while(!isspace(*s) && *s ! = '\0')
                                /* skip the word */
            ++s;
        }
      }
      return cnt;
    }
    int main()
    {
      char str [80]
      printf("\n ENTER THE SENTENCE");
      scanf("%[^\n]", str);
      printf("\n NO OF WORDS =% d", word_cnt(str));
      return 0;
    }
```

As an example, try to write a function that looks for one string within another, returning a pointer to the string if it can, or a null pointer if it cannot. Here is the function (using the obvious brute-force algorithm): at every character of the input string, the code checks for a match to the pattern string.

```
17. #include <stddef.h>
    #include <stdio.h>
    int main()
    {
    char a[50], b[30];
    char *mystrstr(char *, char *);
    printf("\n Enter the string:");
      gets(a);
    printf("\n Enter the substring to search:");
      gets(b);
    if(mystrstr(a,b) == NULL)
        printf("NOT FOUND\n");
```

```
   else
     printf("FOUND\n");
   return 0;
}
char *mystrstr(char *input, char *pat)
{
  char *start, *p1, *p2;
  for(start = &input[0]; *start != '\0'; start++)
  {  /* for each position in input string... */
    p1 = pat;  /* prepare to check for pattern
                              string there */
    p2 = start;
    while(*p1 != '\0')
    {
       if(*p1 != *p2)   /* characters differ */
         break;
       p1++;
       p2++;
    }
    if(*p1 == '\0')              /* match found*/
    return start;
  }
  return NULL;
}
```

The start pointer steps over each character position in the input string. At each character, the inner while loop checks for a match thereby using p1 to step over the pattern string (pat) and p2 to step over the input string (starting at start). The successive characters are compared until either the end of the pattern string (i.e. *p1 == '\0') is reached or two characters differ. When the end of the pattern string (i.e. *p1 == '\0') is reached it means that all preceding characters matched and a complete match is found for the pattern starting at start, so start is returned. Otherwise, the outer loop is executed again, to try another starting position. It no match is found, a null pointer is returned. Notice that the function is declared as returning (and does in fact return) a pointer-to-char.

mystrstr (or its standard library counterpart strstr) can be used to determine whether one string contains another. Hence, the code is as follows:

```
if(mystrstr(a,b) == NULL)
  printf("NOT FOUND\n");
else printf("FOUND\n");
```

In general, C does not initialize pointers to NULL, and it never tests pointers to see if they are null before using them. If one of the pointers in the programs points somewhere some of the time but not all the time, an excellent convention to use is to set it to a null pointer when it does not point to any valid location, and test to see if it is a null pointer before using it. But an explicit code must be used to set it to NULL, and to test it against NULL. (In other words, just setting an unused pointer variable to NULL does not guarantee safety; one also

has to check for the null value before using the pointer.) On the other hand, if it is known that a particular pointer variable is always valid, it is not required to test for NULL before using it.

13.10.3 Subtraction of Pointers

As has been seen, an integer can be added to a pointer to get a new pointer, pointing somewhere beyond the original (as long as it is in the same array). For example, one might write

```
p2 = p1 + 3;
```

Applying a little algebra,

```
p2 - p1 = 3
```

Here, both p1 and p2 are pointers pointing to the elements of the same array. From this it can be concluded that the two pointers are subtracted, as long as they point in the same array. The result is the number of elements separating them. One may also ask (again, as long as they point into the same array) whether one pointer is greater or less than another; one pointer is 'greater than' another if it points beyond where the other one points.

Therefore, pointer subtraction is also valid: Given two pointers p and q of the same type, the difference p – q is an integer k such that adding k to q yields p. The result is portable and useful only if the pointers to the elements of the same array. The difference k is the difference in the subscripts of the elements pointed by them. The following code illustrates this.

```
#include <stdio.h>
int main()
{
  double a[2],*p,*q;
  p=a;
  q=p+1;
  printf("%d\n",q - p);
  return 0;
}
```

Output

```
  1
```

To print the number of bytes resulting from q-p, each pointer may be typecast.

```
#include <stdio.h>
int main()
{
  double a[2],*p,*q;
  p=a;
  q=p+1;
  printf("%d\n",(int)q-(int)p);
  return 0;
}
```

Output

```
  8
```

It has been seen that two pointers to *compatible types* may be subtracted. Actually, the result is stored in the variable type `ptrdiff_t`, which is defined in the header file `<stddef.h>`. Both pointers must point into the same array, or one past the end of the array, otherwise the behavior is undefined. The value of the result is the number of array elements that separate the two pointers.

EXAMPLE

```
18. #include <stdio.h>
    int main()
    {
    int x[100];
    int *pi, *cpi = &x[99]; /* cpi points to the last
                                   element of x */
    pi = x;
    if((cpi - pi) != 99)
      printf("Error\n");
    pi = cpi;
    pi++;                    /* increment past end of x */
    if((pi - cpi) != 1)
      printf("Error\n");
    return 0;
    }
```

The execution of the above program prints nothing. Consider another version of the standard library function *strlen*.

```
    int stlen(char *s)
    {
      char *p = s;
      while(*p != '\0')
      p++;
      return p - s;
    }
```

In its declaration, s is initialized to s, that is, to point to the first character of the string. In the `while` loop, each character in turn is examined until the '\0' at the end is seen. Because p points to characters, p++ advances p to the next character each time, and p-s gives the number of characters advanced over, that is, the string length. The number of characters in the string could be too large to store in an `int`. The header `<stddef.h>` defines a variable type `ptrdiff_t` that is large enough to hold the signed difference of two pointer values. If we were being cautious, however, we would use `size_t` for the return value of `strlen` to match the standard library version. `size_t` is the unsigned integer type returned by the `sizeof` operator.

Note

- The += and -= operators can involve pointers as long as the left-hand side is a pointer to an object and the right-hand side is an integral expression.

13.10.4 Comparing Pointers

C allows pointers to be compared with each other. If two pointers compare equal to each other, then they point to the same thing, whether it is an object or the non-existent element of the end of an array (see arithmetic above). If two pointers point to the same thing, then they compare equal to each other. The relational operators such as >, <=, and so on, give the result that would be expected if the pointers point to the same array: if one pointer compares less than another, then it points nearer to the front of the array. Consider the following program.

EXAMPLE

```
19. #include <stdio.h>
    int main(void)
    {
       int a[] = {10, 20, 30, 40, 50};
       int i, *p;
       for(p=a; p<=a+4; p++)
           printf("%d\n", *p);
       return 0;
    }
```

Output
```
   10
   20
   30
   40
   50
```

Here, each time p is compared with the base address of the array.

One common use of pointer comparisons is for copying arrays using pointers. Here is a code fragment which copies 10 elements from `array1` to `array2`, using pointers. It uses an end pointer, `ep`, to keep track of when it should stop copying.

```
    int array1[10], array2[10];
    int *ip1, *ip2 = &array2[0];
    int *ep = &array1[10];
    for(ip1 = &array1[0]; ip1 < ep; ip1++)
      *ip2++ = *ip1;
```

As mentioned earlier, there is no element `array2[10]`, but it is legal to compute a pointer to this (non-existent) element as long as it is only used in pointer comparisons like this (that is, it is legal as long as no attempt is made to fetch or store the value that it points to).

The following program will print the line in reverse order. The program uses two pointers pointing to elements of the same array, illustrating the pointer comparison.

EXAMPLE

```
20. #include <stdio.h>
    #include <string.h>
```

```
int main()
{
  char a[50];
  void reverse(char *);
  printf("\n Enter the string:");
  gets(a);
  reverse(a);
  printf("\nAfter reversing the string is :\n");
  puts(a);
  return 0;
}
void reverse(char *string)
{
    char *lp = string;           /* left pointer */
    char *rp = &string[strlen(string)-1];
                                 /* right pointer */
    char tmp;
    while(lp < rp)
      {
        tmp = *lp;
        *lp = *rp;
        *rp = tmp;
        lp++;
        rp--;
      }
}
```

Output

```
Enter the string:manas
After reversing the string is:
sanam
```

A null pointer constant can be assigned to a pointer; that pointer will then compare equal to the null pointer constant. A null pointer constant or a null pointer will not compare equal to a pointer that points to anything which actually exists. This has already been discussed and illustrated earlier. A pointer arithmetic summary is given in Table 13.6.

13.11 POINTERS TO POINTERS

So far we have discussed about pointers that point directly to a variable that holds values. C allows the use of pointers that point to pointers, and these, in turn, point to data. For pointers to do that, we only need to add an asterisk (*) for each level of reference. Consider the following declaration.

```
int a=5;
int *p; ← pointer to an integer
int **q; ← pointer to a pointer to an integer
p=&a;
q=&p;
```

- To refer to a using pointer p, dereference it once, that is, *p.
- To refer to a using q, dereference it twice because there are two levels of indirection involved.
- If q is dereferenced once, actually p is referenced which is a pointer to an integer. It may be represented diagrammatically as follows.

So, *p and **q print 5 if they are printed with a printf statement.

```
#include <stdio.h>
int main()
{
    int a=5;
    int *p,**q;
    p=&a;
    q=&p;
    printf("\n *p=%d",*p);
    printf("\n **q=%d",**q);
    return 0;
}
```

Table 13.6 Pointer arithmetic summary

Operation	Condition	Example	Result
Assignment	Pointers must be of same type	int *p,*q ...	p points to whatever q points to.
Addition of an integer		p = q; int k,*p; ... p + k	Address of the kth object after the one p points to.
Subtraction of an integer		int k,*p; ... p - k	Address of the kth object before the one p points to.
Comparison of pointers	Pointers pointing to the members of the same array	int *p,*q; ... q < p	Returns true (1) if q points to an earlier element of the array than p does. Return type is int
Subtraction of pointers	Pointers to members of the same array and q < p	int *p,*q; ... p - q	Number of elements between p & q;

```
*p=5
**q=5
```

a   p   q

| 5 | ← | ● 65540 | ← | ● 65550 |

65540   65550   65558

In the preceding figure, the cells contain the content of the variable and its location is given below the cells. In this example, variable q can be described in three different ways; each one of them would correspond to a different value.

```
q is a variable of type (int **) with a value of
65550
*q is a variable of type (int *) with a value of
65540
**q is a variable of type (int) with a value of 5
```

Consider the following declarations.

```
int a;     /*integer variable */
int *p;    /*pointer to integer */
int **q;   /*pointer to pointer to integer */
a = 5;     /*assign value to a */
p = &a;    /*address of a is stored in p */
q = &p;    /*address of pa is stored in q */
```

Memory picture

Variable	Address	Value
a	65540	5
p	65550	65540
q	65558	65550

Consider introducing the following expression in the preceding memory picture.

```
*p = 7;
```

Variable	Address	Value
a	65540	5 7
p	65550	65540
q	65558	65550

As p is the address of int a, *p changes the value of a to 7. Now consider introducing the following expression in the same example.

```
**q = 10;
```

Variable	Address	Value
a	65540	5 7 10
p	65550	65540
q	65558	65550

Now, **q also refers to int a; it changes the value of a to 10. It is also possible to change the value of p using q because q points to p. Consider the following table.

Variable	Address	Value
a	65540	10
p	65550	65540
q	65558	65550
b	65512	

Now, *q = &b modifies the place where q is pointing, i.e., p. So we get the following table.

Variable	Address	Value
a	65540	10
p	65550	65512
q	65558	65550
b	65512	

The call by value and call by address mechanisms are also applicable to pointers. Consider the following program:

```
#include <stdio.h>
void change(int *);
int a,b;
int main(void)
{
    int *p;
    a=5;
    b=10;
    p=&a;
    change(p);
    printf("\n *p = %d", *p);
    return 0;
}
void change(int *q)
{
    q=&b;
}
```

Output

```
*p = 5
```

Both a and b are global variables. They can be accessible from all the functions of the program. The address of the variable a is assigned in the pointer p. Then, p is passed to the function change(). What is intended to be done here is that the address of the variable b is to be assigned to p through the function change(). But the output shows that though pointer is passed to a function, still it follows call by value mechanism. The address contained in p is passed to the function and stored in q through parameter passing. When the address of b is assigned to q, p still points to a because of call by value mechanism. Pointer is not an exception, it should be passed by address as in the following program.

```
#include <stdio.h>
void change(int **);
int a,b;
int main(void)
{
```

```
    int *p;
    a=5;
    b=10;
    p=&a;
    change(&p);
    printf("\n *p = %d", *p);
    return 0;
}
void change(int **q)
{
    *q=&b;
}
```

Output

```
*p = 10
```

As address of p is passed to a function, it follows call by address mechanism. The statement *q = &b is equivalent to p = &b; hence the value at address held by p is print 10.

The following program explores how pointer to a pointer to an integer and pointer to pointer to pointer can be used to read the value of the same variable.

EXAMPLE

```
21. #include <stdio.h>
    int main()
    {
        int a;
        int *p;
        int **dp;
        int ***tp;
        p=&a;
        dp=&p;
        tp=&dp;
        printf("\n ENTER THE VALUE OF a");
        scanf("%d",&a);
        printf("\n a=%d",a);
        printf("\n ENTER THE VALUE OF a");
        scanf("%d",p);
        printf("\n a=%d",a);
        printf("\n ENTER THE VALUE OF a");
        scanf("%d",*dp);
        printf("\n a=%d",a);
        printf("\n ENTER THE VALUE OF a");
        scanf("%d",**tp);
        printf("\n a=%d",a);
        return 0;
    }
```

Output

```
ENTER THE VALUE OF a 5
a=5
ENTER THE VALUE OF a 10
a=10
ENTER THE VALUE OF a 20
a=20
ENTER THE VALUE OF a 25
a=25
```

Now, how many levels of indirection can be used in a single declaration?

According to the ANSI C standard, all compilers must handle at least 12 levels. Generally, it depends on the compiler; some compilers might support more.

13.12 ARRAY OF POINTERS

An array of pointers can be declared very easily. It is done thus.

```
int *p[10];
```

This declares an array of 10 pointers, each of which points to an integer. The first pointer is called p[0], the second is p[1], and so on up to p[9]. These start off as uninitialized—they point to some unknown point in memory. We could make them point to integer variables in memory as follows.

```
int* p[10];
int a = 10, b = 20, c = 30;
p[0] = &a;
p[1] = &b;
p[2] = &c;
```

It can be seen from the diagram (Fig. 13.10) that there is no way of knowing in advance where the compiler will place these numbers in memory. They may not even be stored in order.

Fig. 13.10 Logical memory picture for array of pointers

The obvious thing to do is to sort the numbers in memory, not by moving the numbers themselves around but by altering the order of the pointers to them.

EXAMPLE

```
22. #include <stdio.h>
    /* the array of pointers is declared here so that the
    function display can access them */
    int *p[10];
    void display()
    {   int i;
        /* Displaying what each pointer in the array points
        to. */
        for(i = 0; i < 10; i++)
            printf("%d \n",*p[i]);
    }
    int main()
    { int a = 46, b = 109, c = 51, d = 66, e = 82, f = 47,
        g = 40, h = 36, k = 70, l = 79;
        int* temp;
```

```
    int i,j;
    p[0] = &a;
    p[1] = &b;
    p[2] = &c;
    p[3] = &d;
    p[4] = &e;
    p[5] = &f;
    p[6] = &g;
    p[7] = &h;
    p[8] = &k;
    p[9] = &l;
    display(); /* Displaying the values before
      sorting */
    for(i = 0; i < 10; i++)
      for(j = 0; j < 9-i; j++)
        if(*p[j] > *p[j+1])
          {
            temp = p[j];
            p[j] = p[j+1];
            p[j+1] = temp;
          }
    display();   /* Displaying after sorting */
  return 0;
}
```

This program is very clumsy. It can be rewritten. In the following program, an array of pointers contains the base address of three one-dimensional arrays.

```
{
  int a[]={1,2,3,4,5};
  int b[]={10,20,30,40,50};
  int c[]={100,200,300,400,500};
  int *ap[3]={a,b,c};
  int i;
  for(i=0;i<3;++i)
    printf("%d",*ap[i]);
}
```

In the `for` loop, `printf()` prints the values at the addresses stored in `ap[0]`, `ap[1]`, and `ap[2]`, which are 1, 10, and 100.

The above `for` loop can also be replaced by the following to get the same output.

```
{
  .
  .
  .
int *p; p=ap;
  for(i=0;i<3;++i)
  {
    printf("%d",**p);
    p++;
  }
}
```

Another illustration is as follows.

```
int main()
{
  int a[3][3]={1,2,3,4,5,6,7,8,9};
  int *ptr[3]={a[0],a[1],a[2]};
  int i;
  for(i=0;i<3;++i)
    printf("%d",*ptr[i]);
    printf("\n");
  for(i=0;i<3;++i)
    printf("%d",*a[i]);
    return 0;
}
```

Output
```
1 4 7
1 4 7
```

In the second `for` loop, the values of the base address stored in the array `a[]` are printed, which are again 1 4 7.

An array of character pointers that is pointed to the strings is declared as follows.

```
char *nameptr[MAX];
```

The array, `nameptr[]`, is an array of size `MAX`, and each element of the array is a character pointer. It is then possible to assign character pointer values to the elements of the array. For example,

```
nameptr[i] = "Oxford";
```

The string "Oxford" is placed somewhere in memory by the compiler and the pointer to the string constant is then assigned to `nameptr[i]`. It is also possible to assign the value of any string pointer to `nameptr[i]`. For example, if `s` is a string, then it is possible to assign the pointer value `s` to `nameptr[i]`.

```
nameptr[i] = s;
```

Again, for example,

```
char *name[] = {"Manas","Pradip","Altaf"};
/* Creates and initializes an array of 3 strings
name[0] is Manas, name[1] is Pradip and name[2] is
Altaf*/
```

Beginners are often confused about the difference between this example and a multidimensional array.

```
char name[3][10] = {"Manas","Pradip","Altaf"};
```

Both of these will behave the same way in most circumstances. The difference can only be seen if we look at the memory locations.

Fig. 13.11 (a)   Logical memory mapping for array of pointers to char (Array of strings)

This figure shows the first declaration `char *name[];name` contains an array of three pointers to `char`. The pointers to `char` are initialized to point to locations which may be anywhere in memory containing the strings "Manas", "Pradip" and "Altaf" (all correctly \0 terminated).

```
M a n a s \0 ? P r a d i P \0 ? A l t a f \0 ? ? ? ? ? ? ? ? ?
```

Fig. 13.11 (b) Physical memory mapping for arrary of pointers to char

This represents the second case—the \0 characters terminate the strings. The ? represents memory locations which are not initialized. `char *a[]` represents an array of pointers to `char`. This can be used to contain a number of strings.

Look at the following program, that uses an array of pointers.

EXAMPLES

23.
```c
char *rainbow[] = {"red", "orange", "yellow", "green",
"blue", "indigo", "violet" };
int main()
{
  int color;
  for(color = 0; color <= 6; color++)
  {
    printf("%s", rainbow[color]);
  }
  printf("\n");
  return 0;
}
```

Output

```
red
orange
yellow
green
blue
indigo
violet
```

The following program would clear the above facts.

24.
```c
#include <stdio.h>
char *getday(int);
int main()
{
  int iday;
  char *dayofWeek;
  printf("Enter a number from 1 to 7 for the day\
of the week:");
  scanf("%d",&iday);
  dayofWeek=getday(iday);
  if(dayofWeek!=NULL)
    printf("\n\nThat day of the week is %s", dayofWeek);
  else
    printf("Invalid entry for day!");
  return 0;
}
char *getday(int iNo)
{
  char *days[7];
  days[0]="Sunday";
  days[1]="Monday";
  days[2]="Tuesday";
  days[3]="Wednesday";
  days[4]="Thursday";
  days[5]="Friday";
  days[6]="Saturday";
  if(iNo >=1 && iNo<=7)
    return days[iNo-1];
  else
    return NULL;
}
```

In general, an array of pointers can be used to point to an array of data items, with each element of the pointer array pointing to an element of the data array. Data items can be accessed either directly in the data array, or indirectly by dereferencing the elements of the pointer array. The advantage of an array of pointers is that the pointers can be reordered in any manner without moving the data items. For example, the pointer array can be reordered so that the successive elements of the pointer array point to data items in a sorted order without moving the data items. Reordering pointers is relatively fast compared to reordering large data items such as data records or strings. This approach saves a lot of time, with the additional advantage that the data items remain available in the original order. The implementation of such a scheme is discussed here.

Sorting an array of strings requires swapping the strings; this can require copying a lot of data. For the sake of efficiency, it is better to avoid actual swapping of data whenever a data item is large, such as a string or an entire database record. In addition, arrays may be needed in more than one order; for example, an array of exam scores sorted by ID numbers and by weighted scores; or strings may be needed in both unsorted form and sorted form. In either of these cases, either two copies of the data, each sorted differently, must be kept, or a more efficient way to store the data structure must be found. The solution is to use pointers to elements of the array and swap pointers. Consider some examples.

```c
int data1, data2, *ptr1, *ptr2, *save;
  data1 = 100; data2 = 200;
  ptr1 = &data1; ptr2 = &data2;
```

The values of the data can be swapped and the swapped values stored in `data1` and `data2`. Or the values of the pointers can be exchanged.

```
temp = ptr1;
  ptr1 = ptr2;
  ptr2 = save;
```

Here, the values in data1 and data2 have not changed; but ptr1 now accesses data2 and ptr2 accesses data1. The pointer values have been swapped, so they point to objects in a different order. The same idea can be applied to strings.

```
char name1[] = "Oxford";
char name2[] = "University";
char *p1, *p2;
  p1 = name1;
  p2 = name2;
```

Pointers p1 and p2 point to strings name1 and name2. Now the pointer values can be swapped so that p1 and p2 point to name2 and name1, respectively. Given an array of strings, the following program uses pointers to order the strings in a sorted form, leaving the array unchanged.

EXAMPLE

```
25. #include <stdio.h>
  #include <stdlib.h>
  #include <string.h>
  #define COLS 50
  void sort_words(char *a[], int n)
  {
    int i,j;
    char *temp;
    for(i=0;i<n-1;++i)
      for(j=i+1;j<n;++j)
        if(strcmpi(a[i],a[j])>0)
          {
            temp=a[i];
            a[i]=a[j];
            a[j]=temp;
          }
  }
  int main()
  {
  char w[10][COLS];
  char *wdptr[10];
  int i;
  for(i=0; i<10; ++i)
  {
  gets(w[i]);
  wdptr[i]=w[i];
  }
  printf("\n Before sorting the strings\
          are.4......\n");
  for(i=0; i<10; ++i)
  puts(w[i]);
  sort_words(wdptr,10);
  printf("\n After sorting the strings are....\n");
  for(i=0; i<10; ++i)
```

```
    puts(wdptr[i]);
  return 0;
  }
```

When an array of pointers to strings is used, the strings can be initialized at the point where the array is declared, but the strings entered by the user cannot be received using scanf(). Consider the following program.

```
int main()
{
  char *name[5];
  int i;
  for(i=0;i<5;++i)
  {
    printf("\n ENTER NAME");
    scanf("%[^\n]",name[i]);
  }
    return 0;
}
```

The program may not work because when an array is declared it contains garbage value, and it would be wrong to send the garbage value to scanf() as address where the string received from the keyboard should be kept.

13.13 POINTER TO ARRAY

Suppose we have an array of unsigned long values called v. We can declare a pointer to a simple integer value and make it point to the array as is done normally.

```
int v[5] = {1004, 2201, 3000, 432, 500};
int *p = v;
printf("%d \n", *p);
```

This piece of code displays the number, which the pointer p points to, that is, the first number in the array, namely 1004.

C tends to treat arrays almost as though they were pointers, which is why we can set a pointer to an array straight rather than using the address of operator. The instruction p = v makes the pointer point to the address of the array. The number at this address is the first element of the array; so that is the value produced when we access *p.

p++ gives some extra arithmetic instructions that let us use the pointer to the array more flexibly.

```
    p++
```

This instruction increases the pointer so that it points to the next element of the array. If it is followed by the instruction `printf("%d \n", *p);` then it would display the number 2201, which is the content of element v[1] (i.e., the second element).

Similarly, we can use instructions such as `+=` and `-=` to refer to different elements in the array.

Reference can be made to the different array elements without having to alter the value of p. We have already used `*p` to refer to the first element of the array (or subsequent elements if p has been updated with `+=` or `-=`), but `*(p+1)` can be used to refer to the next element after `*p`, `*(p+2)` to refer to the one after that, etc.

Now it is time to turn to the problem of the two-dimensional array. As stated in Chapter 12, C interprets a two-dimensional array as an array of one-dimensional arrays. That being the case, the first element of a two-dimensional array of integers is a one-dimensional array of integers. Moreover, a pointer to a two-dimensional array of integers must be a pointer to that data type. One way of accomplishing this is through the use of the keyword 'typedef'. typedef assigns a new name to a specified data type.
For example,

```
typedef unsigned char byte;
```

causes the name *byte* to mean type `unsigned char`. Hence,

```
byte b[10];
```

would be an array of unsigned characters.

Note that in the `typedef` declaration, the word *byte* has replaced what would normally be the name of `unsigned char`, that is, the rule for using `typedef` is that the new name for the data type is the name used in the definition of the data type. Thus, in

```
typedef int Array[10];
```

Array becomes a data type for an array of 10 integers. This means that, `"Array my_arr";` declares `my_arr` as an array of 10 integers and `Array arr2d[5];` makes `arr2d` an array of five arrays of 10 integers each.

Also note that `Array *ptr2arr;` makes `ptr2arr` a pointer to an array of 10 integers. Because `*ptr2arr` points to the same type as `arr2d`, assigning the address of the two-dimensional array `arr2d` to `ptr2arr`, the pointer to a one-dimensional array of 10 integers is acceptable. Thus, `ptr2arr = &arr2d[0];` or `ptr2arr = arr2d;` are both correct.

Since the data type of the pointer is an array of 10 integers, it is expected that incrementing `ptr2arr` by one would change its value by `10*sizeof(int)`, which it does. Hence, `sizeof(*ptr2arr)` is 20. It can be proved by writing and running a simple short program.

Now, using `typedef` need not necessarily make things clearer for the reader and easier on the programmer. What is needed is a way of declaring a pointer such as `ptr2arr` without using the `typedef` keyword. It turns out that this can be done and that

```
int(*ptr2arr)[10];
```

is the proper declaration, i.e., `ptr2arr` here is a pointer to an array of 10 integers just as it was under the declaration using the array type. Note that this is different from

```
int *ptr2arr[10];
```

which would make `ptr2arr` the name of an array of 10 pointers to type `int`.

The elements of a two-dimensional array can be printed using a pointer to an array. The following program illustrates this.

EXAMPLE

```
26. int main()
    {
        int a[2][3]={{3,4,5},{6,7,8}};
        int i; int(*pa)[3];
        pa=a;
        for(i=0;i<3;++i)
          printf("%d\t",(*pa)[i]);
        printf("\n");
        pa++;
          for(i=0;i<3;++i)
            printf("%d\t",(*pa)[i]);
          return 0;
    }
```

Output
```
3 4 5
6 7 8
```

Table 13.7 summarizes the differences between array of pointer and pointer to an array.

Table 13.7 Difference between an array of pointers and a pointer to an array

Array of Pointer	Pointer to an Array
Declaration	Declaration
`data_type *array_name[SIZE];`	`data_type(*array_name)[SIZE];`
Size represents the number of rows	Size represents the number of columns
The space for columns may be allotted	The space for rows may be dynamically allotted

13.14 TWO-DIMENSIONAL ARRAYS AND POINTERS

A two-dimensional array in C is treated as a one-dimensional array whose elements are one-dimensional arrays (the rows). For example, a 4 × 3 array of T (where 'T' is any data type supported by C) may be declared by 'T a[4][3]', and described by the following scheme.

Figure 13.12 is the logical layout of a two-dimensional array in memory, but it does not give a good picture of what is happening internally. The 'internal pseudo-memory map' works just to display what the two-dimensional array looks like within the system, and can be used to illustrate how it is actually implemented. Figure 13.13 is the graphical representation of a two-dimensional array. Keep in mind that this may not be an accurate picture of what is actually stored in memory, but it is accurate in terms of the concept of a two-dimensional array.

a[0] →	a[0][0]	a[0][1]	a[0][2]
a[1] →	a[1][0]	a[1][1]	a[1][2]
a[2] →	a[2][0]	a[2][1]	a[2][2]
a[3] →	a[3][0]	a[3][1]	a[3][2]

Fig. 13.12 Logical representation of a two-dimensional array

The first thing to be noticed is that there is still a single pointer that is the name of the entire array, but in this case it is a constant pointer to a constant pointer. It points to an array of pointers, each of which points somewhere inside of the array. Finally, there is the actual storage for the elements of the array. According to the definition of C, all elements of the array must be contiguous. The elements are drawn in the manner shown to emphasize this fact. One may guess, and properly so, that none of the pointers are necessarily real pointers, but are somehow bound up in the addressing logic of the code, or they may be stored in registers. On the other hand, they could actually all be pointers if the implementers decided to do so. There are no assumptions made about the underlying implementation.

The address arithmetic for the a[n] array of pointers can be used as done earlier, but it is a slightly different case this time. The following formula is used with size being the number of bytes used to store a pointer.

```
byte_address = a + i * size
```

It will, however, be correct to think of these pointers existing somewhere in memory conceptually in order to understand how a two-dimensional array is stored in the computer memory.

Pointer arithmetic can be performed within each row as is done with the one-dimensional array. The constant pointer named a[0] can be considered to be a constant pointer to the first element in the first row and the formula mentioned earlier can be used for pointer arithmetic just as if it were referring to a one-dimensional array. Therefore, the following two expressions,

```
*(a[0] + 3)
```

and

```
a[0][3]
```

are identical as far as the compiler is concerned.

It is possible to keep the first array index set to zero and vary the second array index from zero to eleven, thereby accessing all twelve elements by varying a single subscript. This is considered bad practice in some programming circles

Fig. 13.13 Physical representation of a two-dimensional array

and its use is not encouraged, but it does illustrate how the elements are actually stored.

```
for(i = 0; i < 12; i++)
  a[0][i] = i;
```

This trick is possible because C does not do run-time range checking of array subscripts. The following code is also valid for the two-dimensional array a[4][3] of integer type

```
for(i = 0; i < 12; ++i)
  scanf("%d", &a[0][i]);
```

Readers may have noticed that in C the rightmost subscript of a two-dimensional array varies faster than the leftmost (in fact, there are no multidimensional arrays in C, but array of arrays). This fact suggests that the array is stored in a 'row major addressing' format. So the array equation for element 'a[m][n]' of type T is as follows:

```
Address of (a[i][j]) = address of a[0][0] + (i * n
                                                + j)
```

The array equation is important. In C, it is hidden from the programmer; the compiler automatically computes the necessary code whenever an array reference is made. The obvious advantage is that the number of rows is not required in the array equation, the address of an element does not have to be computed. That is why, when a two-dimensional array is passed to a function, it is not always necessary to specify the first dimension of the corresponding formal parameter in the function header of the function definition. But for higher-dimensional arrays, the equation gets more and more complicated.

Brian Kernighan and Dennis Ritchie tried to create a unified treatment of arrays and pointers, one that would expose rather than hide the array equation in the compiler's code. It has been already discussed that a[i] = *(a + i). Therefore, following the same concept, a two-dimensional array can be expressed as follows:

```
a[i][j] = *(a[i]+ j) = (*(a + i))[j] = *(*(a + i) + j)
```

The array equation discussed above is a consequence of the aforesaid notations in the case of a two-dimensional array. The following program illustrates the facts just discussed.

─── **EXAMPLE** ───

```
27.#include <stdio.h>
   int main()
   {
     int a[2][3]={10,20,30, 40,50,60};
     int i,j;
     for(i=0;i<2;++i)
     {
       printf("\n");
       for(j=0;j<3;++j)
         printf("%d\t",*(*(a+i)+j));
     }
     return 0;
   }
```

Output

```
10 20 30
40 50 60
```

The same output will result if the statement

```
printf("%d\t",*(*(a+i)+j));
```

is replaced by the following equivalent statements.

```
printf("%d\t",*(a[i]+j));
printf("%d\t",(*(a+i))[j]);
printf("%d\t",*(&a[0][0]+i*3+j));
```

Thus, to evaluate either expression, a total of five values must be known.

- The address of the first element of the array, which is returned by the expression a, i.e., the name of the array
- The size of the type of the elements of the array, in this case sizeof(int)
- The second dimension of the array
- The specific index value for the first dimension, 2 in this case
- The specific index value for the second dimension, 3 in this case

13.14.1 Passing Two-dimensional Array to a Function

The following are several alternative ways in C to handle an array passed to a function. They differ in the formal parameter. For illustration, the following C statements are considered.

```
#define MAX_ROWS   10
#define MAX_COLS   10
int A[MAX_ROWS][MAX_COLS];
```

When data is accessed in our matrix using the notation

```
A[i][j]
```

the location for this data is computed using

```
&A[0][0] + MAX_COLS * i + j
```

Some interesting information about a two-dimensional array A[10][10] is as follows.

- &A[0][0] is the base address.
- A[0] is the base address.
- A is the base address.
- &A[0] is the base address.

But these are not interchangeable. For instance,

```
&A[0][0] +1  points to A[0][1].
A[0] + 1     points to A[0][1].
A + 1        points to A[1][0].
       (A + 1 is the same as A[1] and points to row 1.)
&A[0] + 1    points to A[1][0].
```

This means that, C stores a matrix linearly in rows. The values for the matrix elements are referenced as

```
A[i][j] = (*(A+i))[j] = *((*(A+i))+j) = *(A[i]+j)
```

Therefore,

```
A[0][0] = (*(A))[0] = *((*A)+0) = *(A[0]+0)
A[0][2] = (*(A))[2] = *((*A)+2) = *(A[0]+2)
A[1][2] = (*(A+1))[2] = *((*(A+1))+2) = *(A[1]+2)
```

Thus, address equalities will be

```
&A[i][j] = (A+i)[j] = *(A+i)+j = A[i]+j
```

So,

```
&A[0][0] = (A)[0] = *A+0 = A[0]+0
&A[0][2] = (A)[2] = *A+2 = A[0]+2
&A[1][2] = (A+1)[2] = (*A+1)+2 = A[1]+2
```

The following program illustrates the above facts.

```c
#include <stdio.h>
int main()
{
int A[2][3] = { {1, 2, 3},{4, 5, 6} };
printf("\nThe value of element A[0][0] is \n");
printf("%d  %d  %d  %d \n", A[0][0], (*(A+0))[0],
       *((*A)+0), *(A[0]+0));
printf("\nThe address of element A[0][0] is \n");
printf("%x   %x   %x   %x\n",&A[0][0],(A)[0],(*A+0),
       (A[0]+0));
return 0;
}
```

Traditional method which uses array notation as a formal parameter—an array with an empty first dimension

```c
#include <stdio.h>
int main()
{
  int a[2][3]={10,20,30, 40,50,60};
  void show(int [][3]);
  show(a);
  return 0;
}
void show(int b[][3])
{
  int i,j;
  for(i=0;i<2;++i)
  {
      printf("\n");
      for(j=0;j<3;++j)
        printf("%d\t",*(*(b+i)+j));
  }
}
```

Pointer to an array as a formal parameter

Here the second dimension is explicitly specified. A pointer to the array of 10 integers can be declared as follows.

```c
    int(*ptr)[10] = &a;
```

The following program shows the use of a pointer to an array as a formal parameter.

```c
#include <stdio.h>
int main()
{
    int a[2][3]={10,20,30,40,50,60};
    void show(int(*)[3]);
    show(a);
    return 0;
}
void show(int(*b)[3])
{
    int i,j;
    for(i=0;i<2;++i)
    {
      printf("\n");
      for(j=0;j<3;++j)
      printf("%d\t",*(*(b+i)+j));
    }
}
```

A double pointer cannot be used directly as a formal parameter for a two-dimensional array. Consider the following program.

EXAMPLE

```c
28. #include <stdio.h>
   int main()
   {
      int a[2][3]={10,20,30,40,50,60};
      void show(int **);
      show(a);
      return 0;
   }
   void show(int **b)
   {
      int i,j;
      for(i=0;i<2;++i)
      {
        printf("\n");
        for(j=0;j<3;++j)
        printf("%d\t",b[i][j]);
      }
   }
```

It gives the wrong output instead of printing 10,20,30, 40,50,60. The reason is as follows.

Although the compiler may not complain, it is wrong to declare int **b and then use b as a two-dimensional array. These are two very different data types and by using them you access different locations in memory.

The array decays into pointer when it is passed to a function. The famous *decay convention* is that an array is treated as a pointer that points to the first element of the array. This mistake is common because it is easy to forget that the decay convention must not be applied recursively (more than once) to the same array, so a two-dimensional array is *not* equivalent to a double pointer. A 'pointer to pointer of T' cannot serve as a 'two-dimensional array of T'. The two-dimensional array is equivalent to a 'pointer to row of T', and this is very different from 'pointer to pointer of T'.

When a double pointer that points to the first element of an array is used with subscript notation 'ptr[0][0]', it is fully dereferenced two times. After two full de-referencings, the resulting object will have an address equal to whatever value was found *inside* the first element of the array. Since the first element contains the data, we would have wild memory accesses.

The extra dereferencing could be taken care of by having an intermediary 'pointer to T'.

```
type a[m][n], *ptr1, **ptr2;
ptr2 = &ptr1;
ptr1 = (type *)a;
```

But that would not work either; the information on the array 'width' (n) is lost. A possible solution to make a double pointer work with a two-dimensional array notation is to have an auxiliary array of pointers, each of them pointing to a row of the original two-dimensional array.

```
type a[m][n], *aux[m], **ptr2;
ptr2 = (type **)aux;
for(i = 0; i < m; i++)
    aux[i] = (type *)a + i * n;
```

Of course, the auxiliary array could be dynamic.

> **Note**
> - C does not do run-time range checking of array subscripts.
> - In C, the rightmost subscript of a two-dimensional array varies faster than the leftmost.
> - Multidimensional array is stored in a 'row major addressing' format.
> - The following expressions are equivalent for a two-dimensional array
>   a[i][j]= *(a[i]+ j)
>   = (*(a + i))[j] = *(*(a + i) + j)

A single pointer as a formal parameter

With this method general-purpose functions can be created. The dimensions do not appear in any declaration, so they can be added to the formal argument list. The manual array indexing will probably slow down the execution.

```
#include <stdio.h>
int main()
{
    int a[2][3]={10,20,30,40,50,60};
    void show(int *);
    show(&a[0][0]);         Can be replaced by
    return 0;               show(*a);
}
void show(int *b)
{
    int i,j;
    for(i=0;i<2;++i)
    {
        printf("\n");
        for(j=0;j<3;++j)
        printf("%5.2d", *(b + 3*i + j));
    }
}
```

Passing matrices to a function can be tricky. For more clarity, here are some examples of passing a 3 × 4 matrix to functions. Notice each and every program carefully.

──────────── **EXAMPLES** ────────────

```
29. #include <stdio.h>
    #define ROWS 3
    #define COLS 4
    int main()
    {
        int i, j;
        int mat[ROWS][COLS];
        int *ptr;
        void show(int [][COLS], int, int);
        printf("\nThe matrix is %d x %d \n",ROWS,COLS);
        printf("The original values using array indices \n");
        for(i=0; i < ROWS; i++)
        {
            printf("%p",mat[i]);
            for(j=0; j < COLS; j++)
            {
                mat[i][j] = i+j;
                printf("%d", mat[i][j]);
            }
            printf("\n");
        }
        printf("\n The first call to show \n");
        show(mat, ROWS, COLS);
        printf("\n The second call to show \n");
        show(&mat[0], ROWS, COLS);
```

```
printf("\nThe original values using a pointer. \n");
ptr = &mat[0][0];
for(i=0; i < ROWS; i++)
{
printf("%p",ptr);
for(j=0; j < COLS; j++)
{
  *ptr = i+j;
  printf("%d", *(ptr++));
}
printf("\n");
}
printf("\n The first call to show\n");
show(mat, ROWS, COLS);
printf("\n The second call to show\n");
show(&mat[0], ROWS, COLS);
return 0;
}
void show(int array[][COLS], int rows, int cols)
{
  int i,j;
  for(i=0; i < rows; i++)
  {
      printf("%p",array[i]);
      for(j=0; j < cols; j++)
      printf("%d", array[i][j]);
      printf("\n");
  }
}
```

Output
```
The matrix is 3 x 4
The original values using array indices
FFDC 0 1 2 3
FFE4 1 2 3 4
FFEC 2 3 4 5
The first call to show
FFDC 0 1 2 3
FFE4 1 2 3 4
FFEC 2 3 4 5
The second call to show
FFDC 0 1 2 3
FFE4 1 2 3 4
FFEC 2 3 4 5
The original values using a pointer
FFDC 0 1 2 3
FFE4 1 2 3 4
FFEC 2 3 4 5
The first call to show
FFDC 0 1 2 3
```

```
FFE4 1 2 3 4
FFEC 2 3 4 5
The second call to show
FFDC 0 1 2 3
FFE4 1 2 3 4
FFEC 2 3 4 5
```

In the first call to show( ) function, the base address is passed implicitly in function.

In the second call, the base address of the element in the first row is passed explicitly. This will run faster because there is no need to compute the location using &mat[0][0] + 4*i + j. A two-dimensional array is actually a one-dimensional array that maps to the storage map for mat; that is why we do not need the first index size.

In the following illustration, the function display() takes pointer to array of four integers. Here a pointer to an array of integers is used and only one index is used.

```
30. #include <stdio.h>
    #define ROWS 3
    #define COLS 4
    int main()
    {
      int i, j;
      int mat[ROWS][COLS];
      int * ptr;
      void display(int(*)[COLS], int, int);
      printf("\nThe matrix is %d x %d \n",ROWS, COLS);
      printf("The original values for mat and display \n");
      for(i=0; i < ROWS; i++)
      {
          printf("%p",mat[i]);
          for(j=0; j < COLS; j++)
          {
            mat[i][j] = i+j;
            printf("%d", mat[i][j]);
          }
          printf("\n");
      }
      printf("\n The first call to display\n");
      display(mat, ROWS, COLS);
      printf("\n The second call to display\n");
      display(&mat[0], ROWS, COLS);
      printf("\nThe original values using a pointer. \n");
      ptr = &mat[0][0];
      for(i=0; i < ROWS; i++)
      {
        printf("%p",ptr);
        for(j=0; j < COLS; j++)
        {
```

```
    *ptr = i+j;
    printf("%d", *(ptr++));
    }
    printf("\n");
    }
    printf("\n The first call to display\n");
    display(mat, ROWS, COLS);
    printf("\n The second call to display\n");
    display(&mat[0], ROWS, COLS);
    return 0;
}
void display(int (*array)[COLS], int rows, int cols)
{
    int i,j;
    for(i=0; i < rows; i++)
    {
        printf("%p", array);
        for(j=0; j < cols; j++)
        printf("%d",(*array)[j]);
        array++;
        printf("\n");
    }
}
```

Output

```
    Our matrix is 3 x 4
    The original values for mat and display
    FFDC 0 1 2 3
    FFE4 1 2 3 4
    FFEC 2 3 4 5
    The first call to display
    FFDC 0 1 2 3
    FFE4 1 2 3 4
    FFEC 2 3 4 5
    The second call to display
    FFDC 0 1 2 3
    FFE4 1 2 3 4
    FFEC 2 3 4 5
    The original values using a pointer
    FFDC 0 1 2 3
    FFE4 1 2 3 4
    FFEC 2 3 4 5
    The first call to display
    FFDC 0 1 2 3
    FFE4 1 2 3 4
    FFEC 2 3 4 5
    The second call to display
    FFDC 0 1 2 3
    FFE4 1 2 3 4
    FFEC 2 3 4 5
```

Now let us pass these values to print_mat() function. This will run faster than show and display. pt-array is a pointer that points to the elements in the matrix. This is convenient because C stores two-dimensional arrays in rows.

```
31. #include <stdio.h>
    #define ROWS 3
    #define COLS 4
    int main()
    {
        int i, j;
        int mat[ROWS][COLS];
        int *ptr;
        void print_mat(int *, int, int);
        printf("\n The matrix is %d x %d \n",ROWS, COLS);
        printf("The original values for the matrix \n");
        for(i=0; i < ROWS; i++)
        {
            printf("%p",mat[i]);
            for(j=0; j < COLS; j++)
            {
                mat[i][j] = i+j;
                printf("%d", mat[i][j]);
            }
            printf("\n");
        }
        printf("\n The first call to print_mat\n");
        print_mat(mat[0], ROWS, COLS);
        printf("\n The second call to print_mat\n");
        print_mat(&mat[0][0], ROWS, COLS);
        printf("\n The third call to print_mat\n");
        print_mat(*mat, ROWS, COLS);
            /* This will run faster as will print_mat.*/
        printf("\nThe original values for print_mat \n");
        ptr = &mat[0][0];
        for(i=0; i < ROWS; i++)
        {
            printf("%p",ptr);
            for(j=0; j < COLS; j++)
            {
                *ptr = i+j;
                printf("%d", *(ptr++));
            }
        printf("\n");
    }

        printf("\n The first call to print_mat\n");
        print_mat(mat[0], ROWS, COLS);
        printf("\n The second call to print_mat\n");
        print_mat(&mat[0][0], ROWS, COLS);
        printf("\n The third call to print_mat\n");
        print_mat(*mat, ROWS, COLS);
        return 0;
    }
```

```
void print_mat(int *pt_array, int rows, int cols)
{
  int i,j;
  for(i=0; i < rows; i++)
  {
    printf("%p",pt_array);
    for(j=0; j < cols; j++)
      printf(" %d", *(pt_array++));
    printf("\n");
  }
}
```

Output

```
The matrix is 3 x 4
The original values for the matrix
FFDC 0 1 2 3
FFE4 1 2 3 4
FFEC 2 3 4 5
The first call to print_mat
FFDC 0 1 2 3
FFE4 1 2 3 4
FFEC 2 3 4 5
The second call to print_mat
FFDC 0 1 2 3
FFE4 1 2 3 4
FFEC 2 3 4 5
The third call to print_mat
FFDC 0 1 2 3
FFE4 1 2 3 4
FFEC 2 3 4 5
The original values for print_mat
FFDC 0 1 2 3
FFE4 1 2 3 4
FFEC 2 3 4 5
The first call to print_mat
FFDC 0 1 2 3
FFE4 1 2 3 4
FFEC 2 3 4 5
The second call to print_mat
FFDC 0 1 2 3
FFE4 1 2 3 4
FFEC 2 3 4 5
The third call to print_mat
FFDC 0 1 2 3
FFE4 1 2 3 4
FFEC 2 3 4 5
```

In the above illustrations, the address of the corresponding rows is printed on the first column.

Consider the problem of date conversion, from day of the month to day of the year and vice versa. For example, March 1st is the 60th day of a non-leap year, and the 61st day of a leap year. Let us define two functions to do the conversions.

day_of_year converts the month and day into the day of the year and month_day converts the day of the year into the month and day. Since this latter function computes two values, the month and day arguments will be pointers.

month_day(1988, 60, &m, &d) sets m to 2 and d to 29 (February 29th).

Both these functions need the same information, a table of the number of days in each month. Since the number of days per month differs for leap years and non-leap years, it is easier to separate them into two rows of a two-dimensional array than to keep track of what happens to February during computation. The array and the functions for performing the transformations are as follows.

```
static char daytab[2][13] = {
  {0, 31, 28, 31, 30, 31, 30, 31, 31, 30, 31, 30, 31},
  {0, 31, 29, 31, 30, 31, 30, 31, 31, 30, 31, 30, 31}
};
/* day_of_year: set day of year from month & day */
int day_of_year(int year, int month, int day)
{
  int i, leap;
  leap = year%4 == 0 && year%100 != 0
            || year%400 == 0;
  for(i = 1; i < month; i++)
    day += daytab[leap][i];
  return day;
}
/* month_day: set month, day from day of year */
void month_day(int year, int yearday,
int *pmonth, int *pday)
{
  int i, leap;
  leap = year%4 == 0 && year%100 != 0
            || year%400 == 0;
  for(i = 1; yearday > daytab[leap][i]; i++)
    yearday -= daytab[leap][i];
  *pmonth = i;
  *pday = yearday;
}
```

Recall that the arithmetic value of a logical expression, such as the one for leap, is either zero (false) or one (true), so it can be used as a subscript of the array daytab. The array daytab has to be external to both day_of_year and month_day, so they can both use it. It is made as char to illustrate a legitimate use of char for storing small non-character integers.

In C, a two-dimensional array is really a one-dimensional array, each of whose elements is an array. Hence, subscripts are written as

```
daytab[i][j]
```

and elements are stored by rows. So the rightmost subscript, or column, varies fastest as elements are accessed in storage order.

Here, the array daytab is started with a column of zero, so that month numbers can run from the natural 1 to 12 instead of 0 to 11. Since space is not at a premium here, this is clearer than adjusting the indices.

Ragged arrays

It is required to contrast a two-dimensional array of type char with a one-dimensional array of pointers to char. Similarities and differences exist between these two constructs.

--- EXAMPLE ---

```
32. #include<stdio.h>
    int main(void)
    {
      char a[2][15]= {"abc:", "a is for apple"};
      char *p[2]= {"abc:", "a is for apple"};
      printf("%c %c %c %s %s \n", a[0][0],a[0][1],
    a[0][2], a[0], a[1]);
      printf("%c %c %c %s %s \n", p[0][0],p[0][1],p[0]
    [2],p[0],p[1]);
      return 0;
    }
```

Output

```
    abc abc: a is for apple
    abc abc: a is for apple
```

The program and its output illustrate similarities in how the two constructs are used. The identifier a is a two-dimensional array, and its declaration causes 30 chars to be allocated. The two-dimensional initializer is equivalent to

{{'a', 'b', 'c', ':', '\0'}, {'a', ' ', 'i', 's', ...}}

The identifier a is an array, each of whose elements is an array of 15 chars. Thus, a[0] and a[1] are arrays of 15 chars. Because arrays of characters are strings, a[0] and a[1] are strings. The array a[0] is initialized to

{'a', 'b', 'c', ':', '\0'}

and because only five elements are specified, the rest are initialized to zero (the null character). Even though not all elements are used in this program, space has been allocated for them. The compiler uses a storage mapping function to access a[i][j]. Each access requires one multiplication and one addition.

The identifier p is a one-dimensional array of pointers to char. Its declaration causes space for two pointers to be allocated (four bytes for each pointer on the 32-bit machine). The element p[0] is initialized to point at "abc:", a string that requires space for five chars. The element p[1] is initialized to point at "a is ...", a string that requires space for 15 chars, including the null character \0 at the end of the string. Thus, p works in less space than a. Moreover, the compiler does not generate code for a storage mapping function to access p[i][j], which means that p works faster than a. Note

that a[0][14] is a valid expression, but that p[0][14] is not. The expression p[0][14] overruns the bounds of the string pointed to by p[0]. Of course, a[0][14] overruns the string currently stored in a[0], but it does not overrun the array a[0]. Hence, the expression a[0][14] is acceptable.

Another difference is that the strings pointed to by p[0] and p[1] are constant strings, and hence, cannot be changed. In contrast to this, the strings pointed to by a[0] and a[1] are modifiable.

An array of pointers whose elements are used to point to arrays of varying sizes is called a *ragged array*. Because, in the preceding program, the rows of p have different lengths, it is an example of a ragged array. If we think of the elements p[i][j] arranged as a 'rectangular' collection of elements in rows and columns, the disparate row lengths give the 'rectangle' a ragged look. Hence, the name ragged array.

The following is a depiction of a ragged array.

Fig. 13.14 Representation of a ragged array

13.15 THREE-DIMENSIONAL ARRAYS

Arrays of dimension higher than two work in a similar fashion. Let us describe how three-dimensional arrays work. If the following is declared

```
int a[7][9][2];
```

then a compiler such as a[i][j][k] is used in a program. The compiler uses the storage-mapping function to generate the object code to access the correct array element in memory.

Initialization Consider the following initialization.

```
int a[2][2][3] = {
  {{1, 1, 0}, {2, 0, 0}},
  {{3, 0, 0}, {4, 4, 0}}
  };
```

C uses two implementations of arrays depending on the declaration. They are the same for one dimension, but different for more dimensions. For example, if an array is declared as

```
int array[10][20][30];
```

then there are exactly 6000 ints of storage allocated, and a reference of the form array[i][j][k] will be translated to

```
*(array + i*20*30 + j*30 + k)
```

which calculates the correct offset from the pointer 'array', and then does an indirection on it. To pass an array of this type to a function, the formal parameter must be declared as

```
int arg[][20][30];
```

Here is a function that will sum the elements of the array. Note carefully that all the sizes except the first must be specified.

```
int sum(int a[ ][9][2])
{
   int i, j, k, sum = 0;
   for(i = 0; i < 7; ++i)
     for(j = 0; j < 9; ++j)
       for(k = 0; k < 2; ++k)
         sum + = a[i][j][k];
   return sum;

}
```

In the header of the function definition, the following three declarations are equivalent.

```
int a[ ][9][2]  int a[7][9][2]  int(*a)[9][2]
```

In the second declaration, the constant 7 acts as a reminder to human readers of the code, but the compiler disregards it. The other two constants are needed by the compiler to generate the correct storage-mapping function.

> **Note**
> • In case of multidimensional arrays all sizes except the first must be specified.

Caution These three declarations are equivalent only in a header to a function definition.

If a three-dimensional array is declared as

```
int ***array;
```

(and it is assumed for the moment that it has been allocated space for a 10*20*30 array), then there is an array of 10 pointers to pointers to ints, 10 arrays of 20 pointers to ints, and 6000 ints. The 200 elements of the 10 arrays each point to a block of 30 ints, and the 10 elements of the one array each point to one of the 10 arrays. The array variable points to the head of the array with 10 elements.

In short, array points to a pointer to a pointer to an integer, *array points to a pointer to an integer, '**array' points to an integer, and '***array' is an integer.

In this case, an expression of the form array[i][j][k] is equivalent to the expression of the form

```
*(*(*(array+i) + j) + k)
```

This means take a pointer to the main array, add i to offset to the pointer to the correct second dimension array, and indirect to it. Now, there is a pointer to one of the arrays of 20 pointers, and j is added to get the offset to the next dimension, and an indirection is done on that. Now, a pointer to an array of 30 integers is obtained, and k is added to get a pointer to the desired integer, and an indirection is done to have the integer.

13.16 POINTERS TO FUNCTIONS

One of the power features of C is to define pointers to functions. Function pointers are pointers, i.e., variables, which point to the address of a function. A running program is allocated a certain space in the main memory. The executable compiled program code and the used variables are both put inside this memory. Thus a function in the program code has an address. Like other pointer variables, function pointers can be declared, assigned values, and then used to access the functions they point to.

13.16.1 Declaration of a Pointer to a Function

Function pointers are declared as follows:

```
Return_type(*function_pointer_name
           (argument_type1, argument_type2, ...);
```

In the following example, a function pointer named fp is declared. It points to functions that take one float and two char and return an int.

```
int(*fp)(float, char, char);
```

Some examples include the following.

```
int(*fp)();
  double(*fptr)();
```

Here, fp is declared as a pointer to a function that returns int type, and fptr is a pointer to a function that returns double. The interpretation is as follows for the first declaration: the dereferenced value of fp, i.e., (*fp) followed by () indicates a function that returns integer type. The parentheses are essential in the declarations. The declaration without the parentheses

```
int *fp();
```

declares a function fp that returns an integer pointer.

13.16.2 Initialization of Function Pointers

Like other pointer variables, function pointers must be initialized prior to use. It is quite easy to assign the address of a function to a function pointer. One simply uses the name of a function. It is optional to use the address operator & in front of the function's name. For example, if add() and sub() are declared as follows

```
int add(int, int);
```

and

```
int sub(int, int);
```

The names of these functions, add and sum, are pointers to those functions. These can be assigned to pointer variables.

```
fpointer = add;
fpointer = sub;
```

13.16.3 Calling a Function using a Function Pointer

In C, there are two ways of calling a function using a function pointer: use the name of the function pointer instead of the name of the function or explicitly dereference it.

```
    result1 = fpointer(4, 5);
    result2 = fpointer(6, 2);
```

The following program illustrates the above facts.

EXAMPLE

33.
```
int(*fpointer)(int, int);
                /* Define a pointer to a function */
int add(int, int);    /* Define a few functions. */
int sub(int, int);
int main()
{
  fpointer = add;
        /* Put the address of 'add' in 'fpointer' */
  printf("%d \n", fpointer(4, 5));
            /* Execute 'add' and print results */
  fpointer = sub;         /* Repeat for 'sub' */
  printf("%d \n", fpointer(6, 2));
  return 0;
}
int add(int a, int b)
{
  return(a + b);
}
int sub(int a, int b)
{
  return(a - b);
}
```

13.16.4 Passing a Function to another Function

A function pointer can be passed as a function's calling argument. The following code shows how to pass a pointer to a function, which returns a double and takes two double arguments. Suppose, a computation can be performed with different functions. Consider

$$\sum_{k=m}^{n} f(K)$$

where, in one instance $f(K) = x^K/K!$ and in another instance $f(K) = 1/x^K$.

$f(K) = x^K/K!$ can be implemented as follows.

```
double exp_term(double b, double x)
{
  return(pow(x,b)/fact(b));
}
double fact(double a)
  {
    double f=1.0;
    for(;a>0;a--)
      f*=a;
    return f;
  }
```

$f(K) = 1/x^K$ can be implemented as follows.

```
double by_term(double b, double x)
```

```
{
  return(1/pow(x,b));
}
```

Now, the summation function can be implemented as follows.

```
double sum(double f(double,double), int m, int n)
{
  int K;
  double s = 0.0;
  double x;
  printf("\n ENTER THE VALUE OF x");
  scanf("%lf",&x);
  for(K=m; K<=n;++K)
    s+=f(K,x);
  return s;
}
```

> May be treated as pointer to a function

When a function appears as an argument, the compiler interprets it as a pointer. The following is an equivalent header to the function.

```
double sum(double(*f)(double), int m, int n)
{
  ... same as above
}
```

Here, `double(*f)(double)` is a pointer to a function that takes an argument of type double and returns a value of type double.

Parentheses are very important as `()` bind more tightly than `*`. If the argument is written as `double f(double)` instead of `double(f)(double)`, then it implies that `f` is a function that takes an argument of type double and returns a pointer to a double.

In the body of the sum function, the statement

```
s+ = f(K)
```

can be replaced by

```
s+ = (*f)(K)
```

where the pointer to the function is explicitly dereferenced. Here,

`f` implies the pointer to a function.

`*f` implies the function itself.

`(*f)(K)` is the call to the function.

Figure 13.15 depicts the meaning of each part in a function pointer notation.

Fig. 13.15 Meaning of function pointer notation

Now, what should be the prototype of the functions? The prototypes of the corresponding functions used here are given by

```
double by_term(double);            (i)
double exp_term(double);           (ii)
double fact(double);               (iii)
double sum(double(*f)(double), int, int);  (iv)
```

There are several equivalent prototype declarations for the function prototype (iv) that shows a function as a formal parameter.

```
double sum(double(*)(double), int, int);
double sum(doublef(double), int, int);
double sum(doublef(double x), int m, int n);
```

Now, consider the calling statement of the sum() function.

```
int main()
{
printf("\n SUM OF COMPUTATION 1: %lf:",
      sum(exp_term,0,3));
printf("\n SUM OF COMPUTATION 2: %lf",
      sum(by_term,0,4));
return 0;
}
```

sum(exp_term, 0, 4) computes the sum of the following series.

$$s = \frac{x^0}{0!} + \frac{x^1}{1!} + \frac{x^2}{2!} + \frac{x^3}{3!} + \frac{x^4}{4!}$$

$$= 1 + x + \frac{x^2}{2!} + \frac{x^3}{3!} + \frac{x^4}{4!}$$

sum(by_term, 0, 4) computes the sum of the following series.

$$s = \frac{1}{x^0} + \frac{1}{x^1} + \frac{1}{x^2} + \frac{1}{x^3} + \frac{1}{x^4}$$

$$= 1 + \frac{1}{x} + \frac{1}{x^2} + \frac{1}{x^3} + \frac{1}{x^4}$$

The following is the complete program.

─────────── **EXAMPLE** ───────────

```
34. #include <stdio.h>
    #include <math.h>
    double fact(double a)
    {
      double f=1.0;
      for(;a>0;a--)
        f*=a;
      return f;
    }
    double exp_term(double b, double x)
    {
    return(pow(x,b)/fact(b));
    }
```

```
double by_term(double b, double x)
{
return(1/pow(x,b));
}
double sum(double f(double,double), int m, int n)
{
int K;
double s = 0.0;
double x;
printf("\n ENTER THE VALUE OF x ");
scanf("%lf",&x);
for(K=m; K<=n;++K)
s+=f(K,x);
return s;
}
int main()
{
    printf("\n SUM OF COMPUTATION 1: %lf:",
                    sum(exp_term,0,3));
    printf("\n SUM OF COMPUTATION 2: %lf",
                    sum(by_term,0,4));
    return 0;
}
```

Output

```
ENTER THE VALUE OF x 2
SUM OF COMPUTATION 1:6.333333
ENTER THE VALUE OF x 2
SUM OF COMPUTATION 2:1.937500
```

13.16.5 How to Return a Function Pointer

To return a function pointer is a little bit tricky but a function pointer can be a function's return value. In the following example, there are two solutions of how to return a pointer to a function that takes two float arguments and returns a float. If anyone wants to return a pointer to a function, all that needs to be done is to change the definitions/declarations of all function pointers.

```
float Add(float a, float b) { return a+b; }
float Sub(float a, float b) { return a-b; }
```

Add and Sub have been defined. They return a float and take two float values. The function takes a char and returns a pointer to a function that takes two floats and returns a float. <opCode> specifies which function to return.

```
float(*GetPtr1(char opCode))(float, float)
{
  if(opCode == '+') return &Add;
  if(opCode == '-') return &Sub;
}
```

A solution using a typedef defines a pointer to a function that takes two float values and returns a float.

```
typedef float(*ptr2Func)(float, float);
```

The function takes a `char` and returns a function pointer that is defined as a type above. `<opCode>` specifies which function to return.

```
ptr2Func GetPtr2(char opCode)
{
    if(opCode == '+') return &Add;
    if(opCode == '-') return &Sub;
}
void Return_A_Function_Pointer()
{
    printf("Executing Return_A_Function_Pointer\n");
    float(*fptr)(float, float);
                            /* define a function pointer*/
    fptr=GetPtr1('+');/* get function pointer from
                        function 'GetPtr1' */
    printf("%f \n",fptr(2, 4));
                /* call function using the pointer */
    fptr=GetPtr2('-');/*get function pointer from
                        function 'GetPtr2'*/
    printf("%f \n",fptr(2, 4));
                /* call function using the pointer */
}
```

13.16.6 Arrays of Function Pointers

As has been seen, there are arrays of pointers to an `int`, `float`, `string`, and `structure`. Similarly, an array of pointers to a function can also be used. Operating with arrays of function pointers is very interesting. It offers the possibility of selecting a function using an index. It is illustrated in the following program.

──────────── **EXAMPLE** ────────────

```
35. #include <stdio.h> int main()
{
    void(*p[3])(int, int);
    int i;
    void Add(int, int);
    void Sub(int, int);
    void Mul(int, int);
    p[0] = Add;
    p[1] = Sub;
    p[2] = Mul;
    for(i = 0; i <= 2; i++)
    (*p[i])(10, 5);
    return 0;
}
void Add(int a, int b)
{
printf("\n Result of Addition = %d",a+b);
}
void Sub(int a, int b)
{
    printf("\n Result of Subtraction = %d",a-b);
}
void Mul(int a, int b)
{
    printf("\n Result of Multiplication = %d",a*b);
}
```

13.17 DYNAMIC MEMORY ALLOCATION

A problem with many simple programs, such as those written so far is that they tend to use fixed-size arrays, which may or may not be big enough. There are more problems of using arrays. First there is the possibility of overflow since C does not check array bounds. Second there is wastage of space—if an array of 100 elements is declared and a few are used, it leads to wastage of memory space.

How can the restrictions of fixed-size arrays be avoided? The answer is dynamic memory allocation. It is the required memory that is allocated at run time (at the time of execution). Where fixed arrays are used, static memory allocation, or memory allocated at compile time, is used. Dynamic memory allocation is a way to defer the decision of how much memory is necessary until the program is actually running, or give back memory that the program no longer needs.

The area from where the application gets dynamic memory is called heap. The heap starts at the end of the data segment and grows against the bottom of the stack. If both meet, the program is in trouble and will be terminated by the operating system. Thus, C gives programmers the standard sort of facilities to allocate and de-allocate dynamic heap memory. These will be discussed here.

Static memory allocation The compiler allocates the required memory space for a declared variable. By using the address of operator, the reserved address is obtained that may be assigned to a pointer variable. Since most declared variables have static memory, this way of assigning pointer value to a pointer variable is known as static memory allocation.

Dynamic memory allocation A dynamic memory allocation uses functions such as `malloc()` or `calloc()` to get memory dynamically. If these functions are used to get memory dynamically and the values returned by these functions are assigned to pointer variables, such assignments are known as dynamic memory allocation. Memory is assigned during run-time.

C provides access to the heap features through library functions that any C code can call. The prototypes for these functions are in the file `<stdlib.h>`. So any code, which wants to call these, must #include that header file. The four functions of interest are as follows:

(i) `void* malloc(size_t size)` Request a contiguous block of memory of the given size in the heap. `malloc()` returns a pointer to the heap block or `NULL` if the request is not satisfied. The type `size_t` is essentially an `unsigned long` that indicates how large a block the caller would like measured in bytes. Because the block pointer returned by `malloc()` is a `void *` (i.e., it makes no claim about the type of its pointer), a cast will probably be required when storing the `void` pointer into a regular typed pointer.

(ii) `calloc()` Works like `malloc`, but initializes the memory to zero if possible. The prototype is

   void * calloc(size_t count, size_t eltsize)

This function allocates a block long enough to contain an array of `count` elements, each of size `eltsize`. Its contents are cleared to zero before `calloc` returns.

(iii) `void free(void* block)` `free()` takes a pointer to a heap block earlier allocated by `malloc()` and returns that block to the heap for reuse. After the `free()`, the client should not access any part of the block or assume that the block is valid memory. The block should not be freed a second time.

(iv) `void* realloc(void* block, size_t size)` Takes an existing heap block and tries to reallocate it to a heap block of the given size which may be larger or smaller than the original size of the block. It returns a pointer to the new block, or `NULL` if the reallocation was unsuccessful. Remember to catch and examine the return value of `realloc()`. It is a common error to continue to use the old block pointer. `realloc()` takes care of moving the bytes from the old block to the new block. `realloc()` exists because it can be implemented using low-level features that make it more efficient than the C code a programmer could write.

To use these functions, either `stdlib.h` or `alloc.h` must be included as these functions are declared in these header files.

> **Note**
>
> - All of a program's memory is de-allocated automatically when it exits. So, a program only needs to use `free()` during execution if it is important for the program to recycle its memory while it runs, typically because it uses a lot of memory or because it runs for a long time. The pointer passed to `free()` must be the same pointer that was originally returned by `malloc()` or `realloc()`, not just a pointer into somewhere within the heap block.

Let us discuss the functions and their use in detail. Note that if sufficient memory is not available, the `malloc` returns a `NULL`. Because `malloc` can return `NULL` instead of a usable pointer, the code should *always* check the return value of `malloc` to see whether it was successful. If it was not, and the program dereferences the resulting `NULL` pointer, the program will crash. A call to `malloc`, with an error check, typically looks something like this.

```
int *ip;
*ip =(int *) malloc(sizeof(int));
if(ip == NULL)
{
  printf("out of memory\n");
  exit(0);          /* 'return' may be used*/
}
```

About exit() In the previous example, there was a case in which we could not allocate memory. In such cases, it is often best to write an error message, and exit the program. The

exit() function will stop the program, clean up any memory used, and will close any files that were open at the time.

```
#include <stdlib.h>
void exit(int status);
```

Note that we need to include `stdlib.h` to use this function.

When memory is allocated, the allocating function (such as `malloc()` and `calloc()`) returns a pointer. The type of this pointer depends on whether one uses an older K&R compiler or the newer ANSI type compiler. With the older compiler, the type of the returned pointer is char; with the ANSI compiler it is void.

`malloc()` returns a void pointer (because it does not matter to `malloc` what type this memory will be used for) that needs to be cast to one of the appropriate types. The expression (`int*`) in front of `malloc` is called a 'cast expression'.
Although this is not mandatory in ANSI/ISO C, but it is recommended for portability of the code. Because many compilers are yet to be fully compliant with the standard. The following program illustrates `malloc()` in action.

─── **EXAMPLE** ───

```
36. #include <stdlib.h>
    #include <stdio.h>
    int main()
    {
      int * ip;
      double * dp;
      float.* fp1;
      float * fp2;
      ip = (int *) malloc(sizeof(int));
      if(ip == NULL)
      {
        printf("out of memory\n");
        exit(-1);
      }
      dp =(double *) malloc(sizeof(double));
      if(dp == NULL)
      {
        printf("out of memory\n");
        exit(-1);
      }
      fp1 =(float *) malloc(sizeof(float));
      if(fp1 == NULL)
      {
        printf("out of memory\n");
        exit(-1);
      }
      fp2 = (float *) malloc(sizeof(float));
      if(fp2 == NULL)
      {
        printf("out of memory\n");
        exit(-1);
      }
```

```
   *ip = 42;
   *dp = 3.1415926;
   *fp1 = -1.2;
   *fp2 = 0.34;
   printf("ip: address %d; contents %d\n", (int)ip, *ip);
   printf("dp: address %d; contents %f\n", (int)dp, *dp);
   printf("fp1: address %d; contents %f\n", (int)fp1,
         *fp1);
   printf("fp2: address %d; contents %f\n", (int fp2,
         *fp2);
   return 0;
   }
```

Output

```
   ip: address 133792; contents 42
   dp: address 133808; contents 3.141593
   fp1: address 133824; contents -1.200000
   fp2: address 133840; contents 0.340000
```

This program declares a number of pointer variables, calls malloc to allocate memory for their contents, stores values into them, and then prints out the addresses that were allocated and the values that were stored there. The size of the memory to be allocated must be specified in bytes as an argument to malloc(). Since the memory required for different objects is implementation-dependent, the best way to specify the size is to use the sizeof operator. Recall that the sizeof operator returns the size of the operand in bytes.

The above example is useless because in each case enough memory is allocated for exactly one object with each call to malloc(). Dynamic memory allocation is really needed when the amount of memory to be allocated will not be known until the program is run. For example, it will be determined on the basis of responses from a user of the program.

malloc() has one potential error. If malloc() is called with zero size, the result is unpredictable. It may return a NULL pointer or it may return some other implementationdependent value. We should never call malloc() with zero size.

> **Note**
>
> - In dynamic memory allocation, memory is allocated at run time from heap.
> - According to ANSI compiler, the block pointer returned by allocating function is a void pointer.
> - If sufficient memory is not available, the malloc()and calloc() returns a NULL.
> - According to ANSI compiler, a cast on the void pointer returned by malloc() is not required.
> - calloc() initializes all the bits in the allocated space set to zero, whereas malloc() does not do this. A call to calloc() is equivalent to a call to malloc() followed by one to memset(). calloc(m, n) is essentially equivalent to p = malloc(m * n); memset(p, 0, m * n);
> - When dynamically allocated, arrays are no longer needed, it is recommended to free them immediately.

13.17.1 Dynamic Allocation of Arrays

To allocate a one-dimensional array of length N of some particular type where N is given by the user, simply use malloc() to allocate enough memory to hold N elements of the particular type, and then use the resulting pointer as if it were an array. The following program will create an array of N elements, where the value of N is given by the user, and then print the sum of all the elements of the array.

--- EXAMPLE ---

```
37. #include <stdio.h>
    #include <stdlib.h>
    int main()
    {
    int N,*a,i,s=0;
    printf("\n enter no. of elements of the array:");
    scanf("%d",&N);
    a=(int *)malloc(N*sizeof(int));
    if(a==NULL)
    {
      printf("\n memory allocation unsuccessful...");
      exit(0);
    }
    printf("\n enter the array elements one by one");
    for(i=0; i<N;++i)
    {
      scanf("%d",&a[i])); /* equivalent statement
                            scanf("%d",(a+i));*/
      s+=a[i];
    }
    printf("\n sum is %d ",s);
    return 0;
    }
```

Here is a function that allocates memory and then prints out the values that happen to be stored there without initializing them.

```
   void show()
   {
     float *fp;
     int i;
     fp = (float *) malloc(10 * sizeof(float));
     if(fp == NULL)
     {
       printf("\nout of memory\n");
       exit(0);
     }
     for(i = 0; i < 10; i++)
     printf("%f\n", fp[i]);
   }
```

Upon being run, this program gives different results at different times depending on who else is using the computer and how much memory is being used. Usually it just prints out all zeroes, but every once in a while it prints something like the following.

```
433412852487419789416576.000000
0.000000
184955782229502459904.000000
178825664917759772545563649152.000000
768233769452934741562518226686208.000000
757781365851288653266944.000000
735638711504485109754090309550008.000000
756535199813913309525846266176.000000
7122070539941883803516396416.000000
4258569508226778963902464.000000
```

What happened was that there were non-zero values in the memory that were allocated, and the `printf` function tried to interpret those values as floating point numbers. Maybe they were floating point numbers, but they could have been characters, integers, pointers, or anything else.

It is a good idea to initialize the memory returned by `malloc()`. The reason is that the memory may not be 'clean'—it may have been recently used by some other program, and the values stored there might or might not make sense if interpreted as the type of object we expect to be there (in this case, as floating point numbers). Sometimes, there will be zeroes. Sometimes, odd values. Sometimes, the values will be so weird that the processor will detect what is called a 'bus error', and will dump core. If the memory is initialized to contain legitimate values of the appropriate type, this will not happen.

Here is a useful program that creates an array that can hold floating point numbers.

```
float * make_float_array(int size)
{
  int i;
  float *fa;
  fa = (float *) malloc(size * sizeof(float));
  if(fa == NULL)
  {
    printf("out of memory\n");
    exit(0);
  }
  for(i = 0; i < size; i++)
  fa[i] = 0.0;
  return(fa);
}
```

Another way is to use `calloc()` that allocates memory and clears it to zero. It is declared in `stdlib.h`.

```
void * calloc(size_t count, size_t eltsize)
```

This function allocates a block long enough to contain a vector of `count` elements, each of size `eltsize`. Its contents are cleared to zero before `calloc` returns. The sum of all `N` elements of an array that uses dynamic memory allocation through `malloc()` function can be written as follows.

EXAMPLE

```
38. #include <stdlib.h>
    #include <stdlib.h>
    int main()
    {
      int N,*a,i,s=0;
      printf("\n enter the number of elements of the
              array:");
      scanf("%d",&N);
      a=(int *)calloc(N,sizeof(int));
      if(a==NULL)
      {
        printf("\n memory allocation unsuccessful...");
        exit(0);
      }
      printf("\n enter the array elements one by one");
      for(i=0; i<N;++i)
        {
          scanf("%d",(a+i));
          s+=a[i];
        }
      printf("\n sum is %d ",s);
      return 0;
    }
```

`calloc()` can be defined using `malloc()` as follows.

```
void * calloc(size_t count, size_t eltsize)
{
  size_t size = count * eltsize;
  void *value = malloc(size);
  if(value != 0)
    memset(value, 0, size);
  return value;
}
```

But in general, it is not necessary that `calloc()` calls `malloc()` internally. `memset` sets n bytes of s to byte c where its prototype is given by

```
void *memset(void *s, int c, size_t n);
```

`memset` also sets the first n bytes of the array s to the character c. The following program illustrates the use of the `memset` function.

EXAMPLE

```
39. #include <string.h>
    #include <stdio.h>
    #include <mem.h>
    int main(void)
    {
      char b[] = "Hello world\n";
      printf("b before memset: %s\n", b);
      memset(b, '*', strlen(b) - 1);
```

```
printf("b after memset: %s\n", b);
return 0;
}
```

Output

```
b before memset: Hello world
b after memset: ***********
```

The `malloc()` function has one potential error. If `malloc()` is called with a zero size, the results are unpredictable. It may return some other pointer or it may return some other implementation-dependent value. It is recommended that `malloc()` never be called with a size zero.

Some programmers like to replace `malloc()` as follows.

```
#include <stdlib.h>
void *safe_malloc(size_t, char *);
```

Now, the function definition would be as follows.

```
/* Error checking malloc function*/
void *safe_malloc(size_t size, char *location)
{
    void *ptr;
    ptr= malloc(size);
    if(ptr == NULL) {
    fprintf(stderr,"Out of memory at function:\
        %s\n",location);
    exit(-1);
    }
    return ptr;
}
```

This function can then be called like a normal `malloc()` but will automatically check memory as follows.

```
void get_n_ints(int n)
{
    int *array;
    array= (int *) safe_malloc (n * sizeof(int),
        "get_n_ints()");
    ⋮
}
```

Note

- Regarding `size_t` type in the declaration of `safe_malloc`, it is a type declared in `stdlib.h` that holds memory sizes used by memory allocation functions. It is the type returned by the `sizeof` operation.

A final point worth mentioning related to `safe_malloc()` is the special variables `__LINE__` and `__FILE__` that are used to indicate a line number and a file name. They are put in by the pre-processor and are replaced by, respectively, an int that is the line number where the `__LINE__` tag occurs and a string which is the name of the file. A commonly used version is as follows.

```
#include <stdlib.h>
void *safe_malloc(size_t);
/* Error trapping malloc wrapper */
void *safe_malloc(size_t size)
/* Allocate memory or print an error and exit */
{
    void *ptr;
    ptr= malloc(size);
    if(ptr == NULL) {
    fprintf(stderr, "Out of memory at line %d file\
        %s\n", __LINE__, __FILE__);
    exit(-1);
    }
    return ptr;
}
```

Note

- `malloc()` requires two parameters, the first for the number of elements to be allocated and the second for the size of each element, whereas `calloc()` requires one parameter.
- `calloc()` initializes all the bits in the allocated space set to zero whereas `malloc()` does not do this. A call to `calloc()` is equivalent to a call to `malloc()` followed by one to `memset()`.
- `calloc(m, n)` is essentially equivalent to p = `malloc(m * n)`; `memset(p, 0, m * n)`;
- If `malloc()` is called with a zero size, the results are unpredictable. It may return some other pointer or it may return some other implementation-dependent value.

How much amount of memory that the compiler's implementation of `malloc()` can allocate at one time? The argument to `malloc()` is of type `size_t` so the integer type that corresponds to `size_t` will limit the number of bytes you can specify. If `size_t` corresponds to a 4-byte unsigned integer, you will be able to allocate up to 4,294,967,295 bytes at one time.

13.17.2 Freeing Memory

Memory allocated with `malloc()` does not automatically get de-allocated when a function returns, as automatic-duration variables do, but it does not have to remain for the entire duration of the program, either.

In fact, many programs such as the preceding one use memory on a transient basis. They allocate some memory, use it for a while, but then reach a point where they do not need that particular piece any more (when function or `main()` finishes). Because memory is not inexhaustible, it is a good idea to de-allocate (that is, release or *free*) memory that is no longer being used.

Dynamically allocated memory is de-allocated with the `free` function. If p contains a pointer previously returned by `malloc()`, a call such as

```
free(p);
```

will 'give the memory back' to the stock of memory (sometimes called the 'arena' or 'pool') from which malloc requests are satisfied. When the allocated memory is de-allocated with the free() function, it returns the memory block to the 'free list' within the heap.

When thinking about malloc, free, and dynamically-allocated memory in general, remember again the distinction between a pointer and what it points to. If we call malloc() to allocate some memory, and store the pointer which malloc gives us in a local pointer variable, what happens when the function containing the local pointer variable returns? If the local pointer variable has *automatic duration* (which is the default, unless the variable is declared static), it will disappear when the function returns. But for the pointer variable to disappear says nothing about the memory pointed to. That memory still exists and, as far as malloc() and free() are concerned, is still allocated. The only thing that has disappeared is the pointer variable we had which pointed at the allocated memory. Furthermore, if it contained the only copy of the pointer we had, once it disappears, we will have no way of freeing the memory, and no way of using it, either. Using memory and freeing memory both require that we have at least one pointer to the memory.

Look at the following program that is similar to the programs written earlier, but differs only in the use of free().

```
#include <stdio.h>
#include <stdlib.h>
int main(void)
{
  int *array;
  int size = 1;
  int i;
  printf("Enter the number of values:");
  scanf("%d", &size);
  array = (int *)calloc(size, sizeof(int));
  for(i=0; i<size; i++) {
  printf("Please enter value #%d: ", i+1);
  scanf("%d", array+i);
  }
 for(i=0; i<size; i++) {
     printf("Value #%d is: %d\n", i+1, array[i]);
  }
 free(array);
 return 0;
}
```

Naturally, once some memory has been freed, it must not be used any more. After calling

```
free(p);
```

it is probably the case that p still points at the same memory. However, since it has been given back, it is now available, and a later call to malloc() might give that memory to some other part of the program. If the variable p is a global variable

or will otherwise stick around for a while, one good way to record the fact that it is not to be used any more would be to set it to a null pointer.

```
free(p);
p = NULL;
```

Now, why should NULL be assigned to the pointer after freeing it? This has to be dealt in this manner based on long experience. After a pointer has been freed, the pointed-to data can no longer be used. The pointer is said to be a *dangling pointer*; it does not point at anything useful. If a pointer is 'NULL out' or 'zero out' immediately after freeing it, the program can no longer get in trouble by using that pointer. Also, there still might be copies of the pointer that refer to the memory that has been de-allocated; that is the nature of C. Zeroing out pointers after freeing them will not solve all problems.

malloc() and calloc() can also be used in a similar way with strings.

```
include <stdio.h>
#include <alloc.h>
#include <string.h>
int main(void)
{
  char *str = NULL;
  /* allocate memory for string */
  str = (char *)calloc(10, sizeof(char));
  /* copy "Hello" into string */
  strcpy(str, "Hello");
  /* display string */
  printf("String is %s\n", str);
  /* free memory */
  free(str);
  str=NULL;
  return 0;
}
```

How malloc() and free() work   Some steps from a typical malloc() call will show how much work is performed here.

- A program requests memory from the heap with

```
int* ptr = (int*) malloc(1024 * sizeof(int));
```

It expects a pointer back that points to a newly allocated area on the heap that is at least big enough to hold 1024 integer values, no matter how big an integer on this platform is. If the program would ask for (1024 * 2) bytes, it would assume 16-bit integer values and would not be portable to other hardware.

- The malloc() function is part of the C run-time library. It will now check the current status of free memory on the heap. It needs to find a piece of memory big enough for 1024 integers. Once it finds it, it will be returned to the application. What could be simpler?

The reason for malloc() being a very expensive call has many facets. First, finding the proper area needs a clever memory organization by malloc() so that it will find those pieces fast. Remember, malloc() does not know how much memory will be requested. The next problem appears when the current heap size becomes too small. The operating system allocates physical memory and maps it into the process address space that belongs to the heap. Frequent allocations are expensive if done in small sizes, but how should malloc() know? Moreover, when the memory is returned, malloc() has to try to reduce fragmentation of memory space. Otherwise, it will not find a piece of memory big enough to satisfy a request even though enough small pieces would be available.

13.17.3 Reallocating Memory Blocks

Sometimes, it is not known at first how much memory is needed. For example, if a series of items entered by the user has to be stored, the only way to know how many they are totally depends on the user input. Here, malloc() will not work. It is the realloc() function that is required. For example, to point ip variable from an earlier example in Section 13.17 at 200 ints instead of 100, try calling

```
ip = realloc(ip, 200 * sizeof(int));
```

Since each block of dynamically allocated memory needs to be contiguous (so that one can treat it as if it were an array), it may be a case where realloc cannot make the old block of memory bigger 'in place', but has to reallocate it elsewhere to find enough contiguous space for the new requested size. realloc() does this by returning a new pointer. If realloc() was able to make the old block of memory bigger, it returns the same pointer. If realloc() has to go elsewhere to get enough contiguous memory, it returns a pointer to the new memory after copying the old data there. (In this case, after it makes the copy, it frees the old block.) Finally, if realloc() cannot find enough memory to satisfy the new request at all, it returns a NULL. Therefore, usually the old pointer is not overwritten with realloc()'s return value until it has been tested to make sure it is not a null pointer.

```
int *np;
np = (int *)realloc(ip, 200 * sizeof(int));
if(np != NULL)
   ip = np;
else {
   printf("out of memory\n");
   exit(0);
}
```

If realloc() returns something other than a null pointer, then memory reallocation has succeeded and ip might be set to what it returned. If realloc() returns a null pointer; however, the old pointer ip still points at the original 100 values.

Putting all this together, here is a program that reads a series of numbers from the user and stores each integer in a dynamically allocated array and prints the sum.

EXAMPLE

```
40. #include <stdio.h>
    #include <stdlib.h>
    int main()
    {
     int N,*a,*np,i,s=0;
     char ans='Y';
     printf("\n Enter no. of elements of the array:");
     scanf("%d",&N);
     a=(int *)malloc(N*sizeof(int));
     if(a==NULL)
     {
       printf("\n memory allocation unsuccessful");
       exit(0);
     }
     i=0;
     while(toupper(ans)=='Y')
     {
     if(i >= N)
       {  /* increase allocation */
       N *=2;
       np =(int *)realloc(a,N*sizeof(int));
       if(np == NULL)
        {
        printf("out of memory\n");
        exit(1);
        }
       a = np;
       }
       printf("\n Enter the number ...");
       scanf("%d",&a[i]);
       s+=a[i];
       i++;
     printf("\n Do U 12 Continue(y/n)?...");
     fflush(stdin);
     scanf("%c", &ans)
     }
     N=i;
     printf("\n THE NUMBERS ARE:...\n");
     for(i=0;i<N;++i)
       printf("\n%d",a[i]);
     printf("\n Sum is %d",s);
     return 0;
    }
```

Two different variables are used here to keep track of the 'array' pointed to by a. N represents how many elements have been allocated, and i how many of them are in use. Whenever another item is about to be stored in the array, if i>=N, the old array is full, and it is time to call realloc() to make it bigger.

13.17.4 Implementing Multidimensional Arrays using Pointers

It is usually best to allocate an array of pointers, and then initialize each pointer to a dynamically allocated 'row'. Here is an example.

EXAMPLE

```c
41. #include <stdlib.h>
    #include <stdio.h>
    #define ROW 5
    #define COL 5
    int main()
    {
     int **arr,i,j;
     arr=(int **)malloc(ROW*sizeof(int *));
     if(!arr)
     {
         printf("out of memory\n");
         exit(EXIT_FAILURE);
     }
     for(i=0;i<ROW;i++)
     {
       arr[i]=(int *)malloc(sizeof(int)*COL);
       if(!arr[i])
       {
         printf("out of memory\n");
         exit(EXIT_FAILURE);
       }
     }
     printf("\n Enter the Elements of the matrix\n");
     for(i=0;i<ROW;++i)
       for(j=0;j<COL;++j)
       scanf("%d",&arr[i][j]);
     printf("\n The matrix Is as follows...\n");
     for(i=0;i<ROW;++i)
     {
     printf("\n");
     for(j=0;j<COL;++j)
       printf("%d\t",arr[i][j]);
     }
     return 0;
    }
```

With exit(), status is provided for the calling process as the exit status of the process.

Typically, a value of 0 indicates a normal exit and a non-zero value indicates some error.

The following exit status shown in Tanle 13.8 can be used.

Table 13.8 exit() status

Status	Indicates
EXIT_SUCCESS	Normal program termination.
EXIT_FAILURE	Abnormal program termination. Signal to operating system that program has terminated with an error.

arr is a pointer-to-pointer-to-int. At the first level, it points to a block of pointers, one for each row. The first-level pointer is the first one that is allocated; it has row elements, with each element big enough to hold a pointer-to-int, or int *. If it is successfully allocated, then the pointers (all row of them) are filled in with a pointer (obtained from malloc) to col number of ints, the storage for that row of the array. If this is not quite making sense the figure 13.16 should make everything clear:

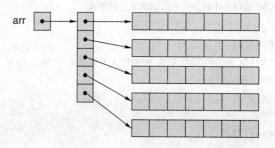

Fig. 13.16 Two-dimentional array implementation using malloc()

If the double indirection implied by the above schemes is for some reason unacceptable, a two-dimensional array with a single, dynamically allocated one-dimensional array can be simulated.

```c
int *arr = (int *)malloc(nrows * ncolumns * sizeof(int));
```

An appropriate block of memory is first allocated for the two-dimensional array size desired. Since array storage in C is in row major form, the block is treated as a sequence of rows with the desired number of columns. The pointer to the allocated block is a pointer to the base type of the array; therefore, it must be incremented to access the next column in a given row. It must also be incremented to move from the last column of a row to the first column of the next row.

The following program asks the user to specify the number of rows and columns for a two-dimensional array. It then dynamically allocates a block of memory to accommodate the array. The block is then treated as a two-dimensional array with the specified rows and columns. Data is read into the array, and then the array is printed.

EXAMPLE

```c
42. #include <stdlib.h>
    #include <stdio.h>
    void getdata(int *,int, int);
    void showdata(int *,int,int);
```

```c
int main()
{
int row, col;
int *a;
printf("\n ENTER THE NUMBER OF ROWS:");
scanf("%d",&row);
printf("\n ENTER THE NUMBER OF COLUMNS:");
scanf("%d",&col);
a=(int *)malloc(row*col*sizeof(int));
getdata(a,row,col);
showdata(a,row,col);
free(a);
a=NULL:
return 0;
}
void getdata(int *p,int r, int c)
{
int i,j;
printf("\n Enter the Numbers one by one....\n");
for(i=0;i<r;++i)
for(j=0;j<c;++j)
{
scanf("%d",p);
p++;
}
}
void showdata(int *p,int r,int c)
{
int i,j;
printf("\n the MATRIX is as follows....\n");
for(i=0;i<r;++i)
{
printf("\n");
for(j=0;j<c;++j)
{
printf("\t %d",*p);
p++;
}
}
}
```

The array's contents can be kept contiguous with the explicit pointer arithmetic.

```c
int **arr = (int **)malloc(nrows * sizeof(int *));
arr[0] = (int *)malloc(nrows * ncolumns * sizeof(int));
for(i = 1; i < nrows; i++)
  arr[i] = arr[0] + i * ncolumns;
```

In either case, the elements of the dynamic array can be accessed with normal-looking array subscripts: arr[i][j] (for 0 <= i < nrows and 0 <= j < ncolumns). Here is the program.

EXAMPLE

```c
43. #include <stdlib.h>
    #include <stdio.h>
    #define ROW 5
    #define COL 5
    int main()
    {
      int **arr;
      arr= (int **) malloc(ROW * sizeof(int *));
      if(!arr)
      {
      printf("out of memory\n");
      exit(EXIT_FAILURE);
      }
      arr[0] = (int *)malloc(ROW *COL* sizeof(int));
      if(!arr[0])
      {
      printf("out of memory\n");
      exit(EXIT_FAILURE);
      }
      for(int i=1; i < ROW; i++)
      arr[i] = arr[0] + i * COL;
      return 0;
    }
```

One way of dealing with the problem is through the use of the typedef keyword. Consider the following program.

```c
#include <stdio.h>
#include <stdlib.h>
#define COLS 5
typedef int RowArray[COLS];
RowArray *rptr;
int main(void)
{
  int nrows = 10;
  int r, c;
  rptr = malloc(nrows * COLS * sizeof(int));
  for(r = 0; r < nrows; r++)
  {
  for(c = 0; c < COLS; c++)
  {
  rptr[r][c] = 0;
  }
  }
  return 0;
}
```

Here, it has been assumed that an ANSI compiler has been used, so a cast on the void pointer returned by malloc() is not required. If an older K&R compiler is being used, it will have to cast using

```c
rptr = (RowArray *)malloc(...);
```

Using this approach, `rptr` has all the characteristics of an array name, (except that `rptr` is modifiable), and array notation may be used throughout the rest of the program. This also means that a function has to be written to modify the array contents, `COLS` must be used as a part of the formal parameter in that function, as was done when discussing the passing of two-dimensional arrays to a function.

In the above method, `rptr` turned out to be a pointer to type 'one-dimensional array of `COLS` integers'. It turns out that there is a syntax that can be used for this type without the need of `typedef`. If the following is written

```
int(*ptr)[COLS];
```

the variable `ptr` will have the same characteristics as the variable `rptr` in the method above, and it is not necessary to use the `typedef` keyword. Here, `ptr` is a pointer to an array of integers and the size of that array is given by the `#defined` `COLS`. The parentheses placement makes the pointer notation predominate, even though the array notation has higher precedence. Thus, if it is written as

```
int *ptr[COLS];
```

it implies that `ptr` is an array of pointers holding the number of pointers equal to that `#defined` by `COLS`. That is not the same thing at all. However, arrays of pointers have their use in the dynamic allocation of two-dimensional arrays. Consider the following program, which creates an array of strings through dynamic memory allocation and sorts the strings alphabetically and also uses pointer to a pointer in swapping by the bubble sort method. Here, instead of swapping the strings, their base addresses are exchanged.

EXAMPLE

```
44. #include <stdio.h>
    #include <stdlib.h>
    #define COLS 25
    int main()
    {
    char word[50];
    char *w[cols];
    for(i=0; i<COLS; ++i)
    {
    scanf("%s",word);
    w[i]=(char *)calloc(strlen(word)+1, sizeof(char));
    strcpy(w[i],word);
    }
    n=i;
    sort_words(w,n);
    return 0;
    }
    void sort_words(char *a[], int n)
    {
      int i,j;
```

```
for(i=0;i<n-1;++i)
  for(j=i+1;j<n;++j)
    if(strcmpi(a[i],a[j])>0)
      swap(&a[i],&a[j]);
}
void swap(char **p, char**q)
{
  char *tmp;
  tmp=*p;
  *p=*q;
  *q=tmp;
}
```

In the `swap()` function, the formal parameters are pointer, to a pointer. So, it is called with addresses of the successive strings.

With all of these techniques, it is necessary to remember to free the arrays which may take several steps as follows; when they are no longer needed, and one cannot necessarily intermix dynamically allocated arrays with conventional, statically allocated ones, it is recommended to free them immediately.

```
int i, **a;
  for(i=m;i>=0;++i)
    free(a[i]);
free(a);
```

Here, `m` is the number of rows of the dynamically allocated two-dimensional array.

All of the above techniques can also be extended to three or more dimensions. As before, it is assumed that the variable is defined as

```
int ***array;
```

and we want the dimensions to be 10*20*30. All of the following subscripts could be done for an arbitrary `i,j,k`, which is closer to what is needed.

First, we need an array of 10 int **s, so we use the following.

```
array = (int ***) malloc(10 * sizeof(int **));
```

The `sizeof` function returns an integer indicating how many bytes are needed by something of type `int**`, and we need 10 of them. The (`int***`) is a cast which changes the pointer type from `char *` to `int ***` to keep the types correct. Do not forget that after this call to `malloc`, one should check to see if `array==NULL`.

Now that there are 10 pointers, the next level of pointers can be obtained with the following code:

```
for(i = 0; i < 10; ++i) {
  array[i] = (int **) malloc(20 * sizeof(int *));
}
```

Finally, each of these pointers can be filled with an array

of 30 integers.

```
for(i = 0; i < 10; ++i) {
  for(j = 0; j < 20; ++j) {
    array[i][j] = (int *) malloc(30 * sizeof(int));
  }
}
```

Again, remember that each call to `malloc()` must check the result. Also note that the preceding two steps can be put together, filling each set of 20 pointers. It is much more efficient to combine all similar allocations and divide the memory after getting it.

Arrays of buffers can also be allocated from the heap. This allows for a dynamically allocated two-dimensional array.

EXAMPLE

```
45. #include <stdio.h>
    #include <stdlib.h>
    int main()
    {
    char **buf;
    int height, width, i, j;
      printf("\nEnter number of lines:");
      scanf("%d", &height);
      fflush(stdin);
      printf("\nEnter width of lines:");
      scanf("%d", &width);
      fflush(stdin);
      buf = (char **)malloc(height * sizeof(char *));
      if(buf == (char **)NULL)
      {
      fprintf(stderr, "\nCannot Allocate a Space\n");
      return 1;
      }
      for(i = 0; i < height; ++i)
      {
        buf[i] = (char *)malloc(width);
        if(buf[i] == (char *)NULL)
        {
        fprintf(stderr,"\nCannot allocate text space.\n");
        --i;
        while(i >= 0)
        {
          free(buf[i]);
          --i;
        }
        free(buf);
        return 1;
        }
      }
      for(i = 0; i < height; ++i)
      {
        printf("\nEnter text:");
```

```
      gets(buf[i]);
      }
      printf("\n\n\n\n\n");
      for(i = 0; i < height; ++i)
        printf("%s\n",buf[i]);
      for(i = 0; i < height; ++i)
      free(buf[i]);
        free(buf);
      return 0;
    }
```

13.18 OFFSETTING A POINTER

In mathematics, the subscript for vectors and matrices starts at 1 instead of 0. There are several ways to achieve it.

In vector (one-dimensional array), the following may be done.

```
double *allot_space(int n)
{
  double *v;
  v=(double *)(n, sizeof(double));
  return(v-1);
}
main()
{
  int n;
  double *a;
  a=allot_space(n);
  ...
  ...
  ...
}
```

Actually, what is done here is that the following code segment replaces the function `allot_space()`.

```
v=(double*)calloc(n, sizeof(double));
--v;
```

The following memory diagram may clarify the preceding program statements.

Here, a[0] should not be accessed, neither written to nor read. For de-allocating the memory space, the following statement should be used.

```
free(a+1);
```

For matrix, i.e., a two-dimensional array,

```
double **get_matrix_space(int m, int n)
{
  int i;
  double **a;
  a=(double **)calloc(m, sizeof(double*));
```

```
  --a;
  for(i=1;i<=m;++i)
  {
    a[i]=(double *)calloc(n, sizeof(double));
    --a[i];
  }
  return a;
}
```

The `main()` function will be as follows.

```
int main()
{
  int **v;
  int r,c;
  ...
  ...
  ...
  v=get_matrix_space(r,c);
  ...
  ...
  ...
  release_space(v,r);
  return 0;
}
```

De-allocating of memory space for the above matrix should be through the `release_space()` function that takes one parameter number of rows.

```
void release_space(double **a, int m)
{
  int i;
  for(i=1;i<=m;++i)
    free(a[i]+1);
  free(a+1);
}
```

There is another way to achieve the above by allocating all the memory at once. Here, the pointer that is used to allocate memory would have to be offset. The `get_matrix_space()` function can be rewritten as follows.

```
double **get_matrix_space(int m, int n)
{
  int i;
  double *p;
  double **a;
  p=(double *)malloc(m*n*sizeof(double));
  a=(double **)malloc(m*sizeof(double *));
  --a;                /*offset the pointer*/
}
```

```
void release_space(double **a)
{
  double *p;
  p=(double *)a[1]+1;
  free(p);
}
```

13.19 MEMORY LEAK AND MEMORY CORRUPTION

A *memory leak* occurs when a dynamically allocated area of memory is not released or when no longer needed. In C, there are two common coding errors that can cause memory leaks.

First, an area can be allocated, but under certain circumstances, the control path bypasses the code that frees the area. This is particularly likely to occur if the allocation and release are handled in different functions or even in different source files.

Second, the address of an area can be stored in a variable (of pointer data type) and then the address of another area stored in the same variable without releasing the area referred to the first time. The original address has now been overwritten and is completely lost. In a reasonably well-structured program, the second type is usually the harder to find. In some programming languages and environments, special facilities known as *garbage collectors* are available to track down and release unreferenced dynamically allocated blocks. But it should be noted that automatic garbage collection is not available in C. It is the programmer's responsibility to deallocate the memory that was allocated through the use of `malloc()` or `calloc()`. The following sample codes will cause memory leak.

```
...
char *oldString = "Old String";
char newString;
strcpy(newString, oldString);
...
free(newString);
```

Memory leaks are another undesirable result when a function is written as follows.

```
void my_function(void)
{
  int *a;
  a=(int *)malloc(100*sizeof(int));
  /* Do something with a*/
  /* forgot to free a */
}
```

This function is tested and it will do everything it is meant to. The only problem is that every time this function is called, it allocates a small bit of memory and never gives it back. If this function is called a few times, all will be fine and the difference will not be noticed. On the other hand, if it is called often, then it will gradually use all the memory in the computer. Even if this routine is only called rarely but the program runs for a long time, it will eventually crash the computer. This can also be an extremely frustrating problem to debug.

Dangling pointer   In C, a pointer may be used to hold the address of dynamically allocated memory. After this memory is freed with the free() function (in C), the pointer itself will still contain the address of the released block. This is referred to as a dangling pointer. Using the pointer in this state is a serious programming error. Pointers should be assigned 0, or NULL in C after freeing memory to avoid this bug.

If the pointer is reassigned a new value before being freed, it will lead to a 'dangling pointer' and memory leak. Consider the following example.

```
char *a = malloc(128*sizeof(char));
char *b = malloc(128*sizeof(char));
b = a;
free(a);
free(b);      /* will not free the pointer to the
              original allocated memory.*/
```

In a programming language such as C, which is weakly typed, garbage collection is not a serious option and the programmer must avoid leaks or take the consequences. Debugging leaky code can be tricky without some assistance. This assistance usually takes the form of variants of the memory allocation and release functions that keep a record of where they were called from (source file name and line number) and maintain a list of all allocated blocks. This list can be inspected or displayed periodically and usually gives a pretty good indication of the data area that is causing the difficulty.

A solution was found using the C pre-processor with declarations such as

```
#ifdef DEBUG
#define malloc(a) mymalloc((a),__LINE__,__FILE__)
#endif
```

The explanation of this code needs some expertise. This will be clear after reading Chapter 11.

Memory corruption   Memory when altered without an explicit assignment due to the inadvertent and unexpected altering of data held in memory or the altering of a pointer to a specific place in memory is known as memory corruption.

The following are some examples of the causes of memory corruption that may happen.

Buffer overflow   A case of overflow: Overwrite beyond allocated length

```
char *a = malloc(128*sizeof(char));
memcpy(a, data, dataLen);  /* Error if dataLen is
                           too long. */
```

A case of index of array out of bounds: (array index overflow—index too large/underflow—negative index)

```
Char *s="Oxford University";
ptr = (char *) malloc(strlen(s));
                    /* Should be (s + 1) to account */
                    /* for null termination.*/
strcpy(ptr, s);
    /* Copies memory from string s which is one byte
              longer than its destination ptr.*/
```
Overflow by one byte

Using an address before memory is allocated and set

```
int *ptr;
ptr=5;
```
In this case, the memory location is NULL or random.

Using a pointer which is already freed

```
char *a = (char *)malloc(128*sizeof(char));
...
...
free(a);
puts(a); /* This will probably work but dangerous. */
```

Freeing memory that has already been freed

Freeing a pointer twice:

```
char *a = malloc(128*sizeof(char));
free(a);
... Do Something ...
free(a);
/* A check for NULL would indicate nothing. This
memory space may be reallocated and thus one may
be freeing memory. It does not intend to free or
portions of another block of memory. The size of the
block of memory allocated is often held just before
the memory block itself..*/
```

Freeing memory which was not dynamically allocated

```
double a=6.12345, *ptr;
ptr = &a;
...
free(ptr);
```

13.20 POINTER AND CONST QUALIFIER

A declaration involving a pointer and const has several possible orderings.

13.20.1 Pointer to Constant

The const keyword can be used in the declaration of the pointer when a pointer is declared to indicate that the value pointed to must not be changed. If a pointer is declared as follows

```
int n = 10;
const int *ptr=&n;
```

The second declaration makes the object that it points at read-only and of course, both the object and what it points at might be constant. Because we have declared the value pointed to by ptr to be const, the compiler will check for any statements that attempt to modify the value pointed to by ptr and flag such statements as error. For example, the following statement will now result in an error message from the compiler:

```
*p = 100; /* ERROR */
```

As the declaration asserted that what ptr points to must not be changed. But the following assignment is valid.

```
n = 50;
```

The value pointed to has changed but here it was not tried to use the pointer to make the change. Of course, the pointer itself is not constant, so it is always possible to change what it points to:

```
int v = 100;

ptr = &v;  /* OK - changing the address in ptr */
```

This will change the address stored in ptr to point to the variable v.

It is to be noted that the following declarations are equivalent.

```
const int *ptr=&n;
int const *ptr=&n;
```

13.20.2 Constant Pointers

Constant pointers ensure that the address stored in a pointer cannot be changed. Consider the following statements:

```
int n = 10;
int *const ptr = &n; /* Defines a constant */
```

Here is how one could ensure that a pointer always points to the same object; the second statement declares and initializes ptr and indicates that the address stored must not be changed.

Any attempt to change what the pointer points to elsewhere in the program will result in an error message when you compile:

```
int v = 5;
ptr = &v; /* Error - attempt to change a constant
                                         pointer */
```

It is still legitimate to change the value that ptr points to using ptr though:

```
*ptr = 100;      /* OK - changes the value of v */
```

This statement alters the value stored in v through the pointer and changes its value to 100.

You can create a constant pointer that points to a value that is also constant:

```
int n = 25;
const int *const ptr = &n;
```

ptr is a constant pointer to a constant so everything is fixed. It is not legal to change the address stored in ptr as well as ptr cannot be used to modify what it points to.

13.20.3 Constant Parameters

Recall that arrays are passed to functions by address and it is also known that function implementations can alter the original array's contents. To prevent an array argument from being altered in a function, use the const qualifier as demonstrated in the following programs.

Version 1

```
#include <stdio.h>
void change(char *);
int main(void)
{
   char s[]="Siva";
   change(s);
   printf("\n The string after calling change():\
%s", s);
   return 0;
}
void change(char *t)
{
   *t= 'V';
}
```

Output

```
The string after calling change():Viva
```

Version 2

```
#include <stdio.h>
void change(const char *);
int main(void)
{
   char s[]="Oxford University";
   change(s);
   printf("\n The string after calling change():\
       %s", s);
   return 0;
}
void change(const char *t)
{
   *t='V';
}
```

Note the constant parameter

Output

```
Compiler error: Assignment of read-only location
```

The same error will occur when the following program is compiled.

```
#include <stdio.h>
void change(const int [], int);
```

```
int main(void)
{
    int a[]={1,2,3,4,5};
    int n,i;

    n=sizeof(a)/sizeof(a[0]);
    change(a,n);
    printf("\n The array elements after calling
            change()\n");
    for(i=0;i<n;++i)
        printf("\t%d",a[i]);
    return 0;
}
void change(const int b[],int n)
{
    int i;
    for(i=0;i<n;++i)
        b[i]+=10;
}
```

> The expression sizeof(a)/sizeof(a[0]) yields 5 as sizeof(a) returns 20 and sizeof(a[0]) returns 4.

In the above program, use of constant parameter protects the elements of the array from being modified within the function change() though arrays passed as arguments are passed by address automatically.

Check Your Progress

What will be the output of the following program?

1.
```
int main()
{
    int val = 5;
    int *ptr = &val;
    printf("%d %d", ++val, *ptr);
    return 0;
}
```
Output 6 5

2.
```
int main()
{
    int val = 5;
    int *ptr = &val;
    printf("%d %d", val, *ptr++);
    return 0;
}
```
Output 5 5

3.
```
int main()
{
    int val = 5;
    int *ptr = &val;
    printf("%d %d", val, ++*ptr);
    return 0;
}
```
Output 6 6

4.
```
int main()
{
    int a[] = {1,2,3,4,5,6};
    int *ptr = a + 2;
    printf("%d %d", *++a, --*ptr);
    return 0;
}
```
Output Error: Lvalue required

5.
```
int main()
{
    int a[] = {1,2,3,4,5,6};
    int *ptr = a + 2;
    printf("%d %d", --*ptr+1,1+*--ptr);
    return 0;
}
```
Output 2 3

6.
```
int main()
{
    char myArray[5], *p = myArray;
    int i;
    for(i = 4; i > 0; i--){
        *p++ = i * i; p++;}
    for (i = 4; i >= 0; i--)
        printf("%d", myArray[i]);
    return 0;
}
```
Output 0 1 4 9 16

7.
```
int main()
{
    int a = 555, *ptr = &a, b = *ptr;
    printf("%d %d %d", ++a, --b, *ptr++);
    return 0;
}
```
Output 556 554 555

8.
```
int main()
{
    int val = 5;
    int *ptr = &val;
    printf("%d %d", val,(*ptr)++);
    return 0;
}
```
Output 6 5

9.
```
int main()
{
    int a[100];
    int sum = 0;
    for(k = 0; k < 100; k++)
        *(a+k) = k;
    printf("%d", a[--k]);
    return 0;
}
```
Output 99

10.
```c
int main()
{
  void F(int *a, int n);
  int arr[5] = {5,4,3,2,1};
  F(arr,5);
  return 0;
}
void F(int *a, int n)
{
  int i;
  for(i = 0; i < n; i++)
  printf("&d", *(a++)+i);
}
```
   Output 55555

11.
```c
int main(void)
{
  int a[10];
  printf("%d", ((a + 9) + (a + 1)));
  return 0;
}
```
   Output Error

12.
```c
int main()
{
  char A[] = {'a','b','c','d','e','f','g','h'};
  char *p = A;
  ++p;
  while(*p != 'e')
  printf("%c", *p++);
  return 0;
}
```
   Output bcd

13.
```c
int main()
{
  char *p1 = "Name";
  char *p2;
  p2 = (char *) malloc(20);
  while(*p2++ = *p1++);
    printf("%s\n", p2);
    return 0;
}
```
   Output An empty string

14.
```c
int main()
{
  int a = 2, b = 3;
  printf("%d", a+++b);
  return 0;
}
```
   Output 5

15.
```c
int main()
{
  int a[] = {1,2,3,4,5,6,7};
  char c[] = {'a','x','h','o','k'};
```

```c
  printf("%d\t %d", (&a[3]-&a[0]),(&c[3]-&c[0]));
  return 0;
}
```
   Output 3 0

16.
```c
#include#<stdio.h>
int main()
{
  char s1[] = "Manas";
  char s2[] = "Ghosh";
  s1 = s2;
  printf("%s", s1);
  return 0;
}
```
   Output Error

17.
```c
int main()
{
  char *ptr = "Mira Sen";
  (*ptr)++;
  printf("%s\n", ptr);
  ptr++;
  printf("%s\n", ptr);
  return 0;
}
```
   Output Nira Sen
            ira Sen

18.
```c
int main()
{
  char *p = "The Matrix Reloaded";
  int i = 0;
  while(*p)
  {
    if(!isupper(*p++))
      ++i;
  }
  printf("%d", i);
  return 0;
}
```
   Output 16

19.
```c
int main()
{
  char str[] = "Test";
  if((printf("%s", str)) == 4)
    printf("Success");
  else
    printf("Failure");
    return 0;
}
```
   Output Test Success

20.
```c
int main()
{
  printf("Hi Friends"+3);
```

```
        return 0;
    }
```

Output Friends

21.
```c
int main()
{
    int a[] = {1,2,3,4,5,6};
    int *ptr = a + 2;
    printf("%d", *--ptr);
    return 0;
}
```

Output 2

22.
```c
int main()
{
    int i = 100, j = 20;
    i++ = j;
    i* = j;
    printf("%d\t %d\n", i,j);
    return 0;
}
```

Output Error lvalue required

23.
```c
int main()
{
    int a[5], *p;
    for(p = a; p < &a[5]; P++)
    {
        *p = p-a;
        printf("%d", *p);
    }
    return 0;
}
```

Output 2

24.
```c
int main()
{
    putchar(5["manas"]);
    return 0;
}
```

Output Nothing will be printed

25.
```c
int main()
{
    int a[] = {1,2,3,4,5};
    int i, s = 0;
    for(i = 0; i < 5; ++i)
        if((a[i]%2) == 0)
            s+ = a[i];
    printf("%d", s);
    return 0;
}
```

Output 6

26.
```c
int main()
{
```

```c
    int i;
    char s[] = "Oxford University Press";
    for(i = 0; s[i]!= '\0'; ++i)
        if((i%2) == 0)
            printf("%c %c", s[i], s[i]);
    return 0;
}
```

Output O Of fr r n nv vr ri iy yP Pe es s

27.
```c
int main()
{
    int i;
    char s[] = "Oxford University Press";
    for(i = 0; s[i]!= '\0'; ++i)
        if((i%2) == 0)
            putchar(s[i]);
    return 0;
}
```

Output Ofr nvriyPes

28.
```c
int main()
{
char s[3][6] = {"ZERO", ONE", TWO"};
    printf("%s", s[2]);
    printf("%c", s[2][0]);
    return 0;
}
```

Output TWOT

29.
```c
int main()
{
    int a[][3] = {0,1,2,3,4,5};
    printf("%d", sizeof(a));
    return 0;
}
```

Output 12

30.
```c
int main()
{
    int a[2][3] = {0,1,2,3,4,5};
    printf("%d", sizeof(a[2]));
    return 0;
}
```

Output 6 OR 12

31.
```c
int main()
{
    char *str = "This is my string";
    str[3] = 'B';
    puts(str);
    return 0;
}
```

Output ThiB is my string

```
32. int main()
    {
    int a[5]={1,3,6,7,0};
    int *b;
    b=&a[2];
    printf("%d", b[-1]);
    return 0;
    }
```

Output 3

```
33. int main()
    {
    register int x=5, *p;
    p=&x
    printf("%d",*p);
    return 0;
    }
```

Output Error

```
34. int main()
    {
    void x(void);
    x();
    return 0;
    }
    void x(void)
    {
    char a[]="HELLO";
    char *b="HELLO";
    char c[10]="HELLO";
    printf("%s %s %s\n", a, b, c);
    printf("%d %d %d\n",sizeof(a), sizeof(b), sizeof(c));
    }
```

Output HELLO   HELLO   HELLO
         6 4 10

`sizeof(b)` gives the bytes required for storing the pointer `b`. The other two are the array sizes.

SUMMARY

Think of memory as an array of *cells*. Each memory cell has a location/address/lvalue and contains a value/rvalue. There is a difference between the address and the contents of a memory cell. A pointer is a variable that contains the address in the memory of another variable. There can be a pointer to any variable type. The unary or monadic operator '&' gives the 'address of a variable'. The *indirection* or dereference operator '*' gives the 'contents of an object pointed to by a pointer'. A pointer to any variable type is an address in memory, which is an integer address. A pointer is definitely not an integer. When a pointer is declared, it does not point anywhere. It must be set to point somewhere before it can be used. Thus, an address must be assigned to the pointer by using an assignment statement or a function call prior to its use. A pointer is bound to a particular data type (void pointer is an exception). For instance, the address of a short int cannot be assigned to a long int. There is a special pointer which is defined to be zero. It is called the NULL pointer.

There are many cases when a passed argument in the function may need to be altered and the new value received back once the function has finished. Other languages do this. C uses pointers explicitly to do this. Other languages mask the fact that pointers also underpin the implementation of this. Pointers provide the solution: Pass the address of the variables to the functions and access address of function.

Pointers and arrays are very closely linked in C. When subscript notation is used, the C compiler generates an executable code that does the following.

- Determines the size of the elements in the array. Let us call that elemSize.
- Multiplies elemSize by the subscript value. Let us call that offset.
- Adds offset to the address that represents the beginning of the array. This is the address of the element that we want to access.

The address of ARRAY[i] is calculated each time by the compiler as follows.

```
address of ARRAY[i] = ARRAY+i*sizeof(int);
```

The equivalence of arrays and pointers must be understood. Assume that a is an array and i is an integer.

```
a[i] == *(a + i) == *(i + a) == i[a]
```

Although these are equivalent, it is recommended that i[a] never be written instead of a[i]. However, pointers and arrays are different.

- A pointer is a variable. We can do

```
pa = a and pa++
```

- An array *is not* a variable. a = pa and a++ are illegal.

When an array is passed to a function what is actually passed is its initial element's location in memory. Array decays into pointers when passed into function.

The following 'meaningful' arithmetic operations are allowed on pointers.

- Add or subtract integers to/from a pointer. The result is a pointer.
- Subtract two pointers to the same type. The result is an int.
- Assigning NULL or any pointer of same datatype.

Multiplying, adding two pointers, etc. does not make sense.

It is also possible to have arrays of pointers since pointers are variables. *Arrays of pointers* are a data representation that will cope efficiently and conveniently with variable length text lines. This eliminates

- complicated storage management
- high overheads of moving lines

Pointers, of course, can be 'pointed at' any type of data object, including arrays.

```
int(*p)[10];
```

is the proper declaration, i.e., p here is a pointer to an array of 10 integers just as it was under the declaration using the array type. Note that this is different from

```
int *p[10];
```

which would make p the name of an array of 10 pointers to type int.

A two-dimensional array is really a one-dimensional array, each of whose elements is itself an array. Array elements are stored row by row. When a two-dimensional array is passed to a function, the number of columns must be specified; the number of rows is irrelevant. The reason for this is pointers again. C needs to know the number of columns in order to jump from row to row in memory.

Consider int a[5][10] to be passed in a function.

It is possible to say

```
f(int a[][10]) {.....}
```

or even

```
f(int(*a)[10]) {.....}
```

It needs a parenthesis (*a) since [] have a higher precedence than *. So,

```
int(*a)[10]; declares a pointer to an array of 10 ints.

int *a[10]; declares an array of 10 pointers to ints.
```

Dynamic memory allocation is a way to defer the decision of how much memory is necessary until the program is actually running, get more if it runs out, or give back memory that the program no longer needs it. When memory is allocated, the allocating function (such as malloc() and calloc()) returns a pointer. The type of this pointer depends on the type of compiler, whether it is an older K&R compiler or the newer ANSI type compiler. With the older compiler the type of the returned pointer is char; with the ANSI compiler it is void. When the program finishes using whatever memory it dynamically allocates, it can use the free function to indicate to the system that the memory is available again.

The rules to be followed for deciphering pointer declarations are as follows. These are particularly important for function pointers.

- Start with the name that will identify the pointer, known as the identifier.
- Move to the right until you encounter a right-parenthesis ')' or reach the end. Do not stop if the () brackets are used to pass parameters to a function. Also do not stop on encountering brackets used with arrays: [].
- Now go left of the identifier to continue deciphering the declaration. Keep going left until you find a left-parenthesis '(' or reach the end. Do not stop if the brackets are used to pass parameters to a function.
- The whole interpretation should be a single long sentence.

KEY TERMS

Call by address It facilitates the changes made to a variable in the called function to become permanently available in the function from where the function is called.

Call-by-value A particular way of implementing a function call, in which the arguments are passed by their value (i.e., their copies).

Dangling pointer A pointer pointing to a previously meaningful location that is no longer meaningful; usually a result of a pointer pointing to an object that is deallocated without resetting the value of the pointer.

Dynamic data structures Those that are built up from blocks of memory allocated from the heap at run time.

Dynamic memory allocation It is the process of requesting and obtaining additional memory segments during the execution of a program.

Function pointer A function has a physical location in memory that can be assigned to a pointer. Thus, it is called function pointer. This address is the entry point of the function and it is the address used when the function is called.

Garbage collection If only implicit dynamic allocation is allowed then deallocation must also be done by implicit means, which is often called garbage collection.

Heap This memory region is reserved for dynamically allocating memory

for variables at run time. Dynamic memory allocation is done by using the malloc() or calloc() functions.

Memory leak A commonly used term indicating that a program is dynamically allocating memory but not properly deallocating it, which results in a gradual accumulation of unused memory by the program to the detriment of other programs, the operating system, and itself.

NULL A special C constant, defined as macro in stdio.h as or 0, or (void*) that can be used as the null value for pointers.

Null pointer A null pointer is a special pointer value that points nowhere. It is initialized with value 0 or NULL.

Pointer A value or a variable with two attributes: (i) an address and (ii) a data type of what should be found at that address.

Ragged array It is an array of pointers whose elements are used to point to arrays of varying sizes.

Stack A data structure resembling a deck of cards; a new item can only be put on top of the deck (the push operation) or removed from the top of the deck (the pop operation).

Static memory allocation It is memory layout for static data prepared by the compiler.

Void pointer It is a special type of pointer that can point to any data type.

FREQUENTLY ASKED QUESTIONS

1. What are the uses of pointers in C?

C uses pointers in three different ways:

(i)   Pointers allow different sections of code to share information easily. One can get the same effect by copying information back and forth, but pointers solve the problem better.

(ii)   In some cases, C programmers also use pointers because they make the code slightly more efficient. Pointers allow the creation of complex dynamic data structures like linked lists and binary trees.

(iii)   Pointers in C provide an alternative way to access information stored in arrays. Pointer techniques are especially valuable while working with strings. There is an intimate link between arrays and pointers in C.

Apart from these, C uses pointers to handle *variable parameters* passed to functions.

2. Why should pointers have data types when their size is always 4 bytes (in a 32-bit machine), irrespective of the variable they are pointing to?

Sizes of various data types are basically decided by the machine architecture and/or the implementation. Considering a 32-bit machine, the addressing of a byte or word will, therefore, require a 32-bit address. This suggests that a pointer (as pointers store addresses) should be capable enough to store, at least, a 32-bit value; no matter if it points to an integer or a character.

For an array, consecutive memory is allocated. Each element is placed at a certain offset from the previous element, if any, depending on its size. The compiler that generates code for a pointer, which accesses these elements using the pointer arithmetic, requires the number of bytes to retrieve on pointer dereference and it knows how much to scale a subscript. The data type of the pointer provides this information. The compiler automatically scales a subscript to the size of the variable pointed at. The compiler takes care of scaling before adding the base address.

3. What is wrong with the following code segment?

```
int *p;
*p=10;
```

The pointer p is an uninitialized pointer which may have some unknown memory address in it. More precisely, it may have an unknown value that will be interpreted as a memory location. Most likely, the value will not be valid for the computer system that is using or if it is, will not be valid for the memory that has been allocated. If the address does not exist, one may get immediate run time errors.

4. Does C have 'pass by reference' feature?

Not really. Strictly speaking, C always uses pass by value. One can simulate pass by reference by defining functions which accept pointers as formal parameters and then using the & operator when calling the function. The compiler will essentially simulate it when an array to a function is passed (by passing a pointer instead). But truly C has no equivalent to the formal pass by reference feature as C++ provides.

5. What is wild pointer in C?

A pointer in C which has not been initialized, is known as wild pointer.

6. Is a null pointer same as an uninitialized pointer?

A null pointer is conceptually different from an uninitialized pointer. An uninitialized pointer may point to anywhere, whereas a null pointer does not point to any object or function. Null pointer points to the base address of a segment while wild pointer does not point to any specific memory location.

7. What are the uses of null pointer?

The null pointer is used for three purposes:
- To stop indirection
- As an error value
- As a sentinel value

8. Is NULL always defined as 0?

NULL is defined as either 0 or (void*)0. These values are almost identical; either a literal zero or a void pointer is converted automatically to any kind of pointer, as necessary, whenever a pointer is needed (although the compiler cannot always tell when a pointer is needed).

9. What is the difference between NULL and NUL?

NULL is a macro defined in <stddef.h> for the null pointer. NUL is the name of the first character in the ASCII character set. It corresponds to a zero value. NULL can be defined as ((void*)0), whereas NUL is '\0'. Both can also be defined simply as 0.

10. Since 0 is used to represent the null pointer, can it be thought of as an address with all zero bits?

Each compiler interprets the null pointers differently and not all compilers use a zero address. For example, some compilers use a non-existent memory address for the null pointer; that way, attempting to access memory through a null pointer can be detected by the hardware. When NULL is assigned to a pointer, then 0 is converted to the proper internal form by the compiler.

11. What is the difference between arr and &arr where arr is an array name, though both display the base address of the array?

The array name arr is a pointer to the first element in the array whereas the &arr is a pointer to the array as a whole. Numerically, the values they display are same; however, their interpretation is not same.

12. When would you use a pointer to a function?

Pointers to functions are typically used when it is required to pass them to other functions. The called function takes function pointers as formal parameters. This is known as a 'callback'. It is frequently used in graphical-user interface libraries.

13. What are the uses of dynamic memory allocations?

Typical uses of dynamic memory allocation are:
- Creation of *dynamic arrays* – arrays whose sizes are chosen at run time;
- Creation of *dynamic data structures* – data collections that grow and shrink with the changing data storage needs of a program or module.

14. Why is it required to cast the values returned by malloc() to the pointer type being allocated?

Before ANSI/ISO Standard C introduced the `void *` generic pointer type, these casts were typically required to avoid warnings about assignment between incompatible pointer types. Under ANSI/ISO Standard C, these casts are no more required.

15. What happens if `malloc(0)` is called?

If `malloc()` is called with zero size, the result is unpredictable. Each compiler is free to define the behaviour of `malloc()` when the size is 0. It may either return `NULL` or it may return other implementation dependent value.

16. What is the difference between `calloc()` and `malloc()` ?

`malloc()` takes one argument, whereas `calloc()` takes two.

`calloc()` initializes all the bits in the allocated space set to zero, whereas `malloc()` does not do this.

A call to `calloc()` is equivalent to a call to `malloc()` followed by one to `memset()`.

```
calloc(m, n)
```

is essentially equivalent to

```
p = malloc(m * n);
memset(p, 0, m * n);
```

17. What is a dangling pointer?

A dangling pointer arises when you use the address of an object after its lifetime is over. This may occur in situations like returning addresses of the automatic variables from a function or using the address of the memory block after it is freed.

18. Why should NULL be assigned to the pointer after freeing it?

After a pointer has been freed, the pointer can no longer be used. After this memory is freed with the `free()` function, the pointer itself will still contain the address of the released block. Such a pointer is referred to as a dangling pointer; it does not point at anything useful. If the pointer is used without reinitializing it, it may or may not run; it merely produces a bug. Such a pointer must be assigned `NULL` after freeing memory to avoid this bug. The program can no longer get in trouble by using that pointer.

19. Is it correct to return a pointer to a local variable in the called function?

Absolutely not; it is an error to return a pointer to a local variable in the called function, because when the function terminates, its memory gets inaccessible.

20. What is memory leak?

When memory is allocated dynamically, it is the responsibility of the programmer to deallocate the dynamically allocated memory by calling `free()`. Freeing the memory returns it to the system, where it can be reassigned to another application when needed. When an application dynamically allocates memory, and does not free that memory when it has finished using it, that chunk of memory is still in use to the operating system. The memory is not being used by the application anymore, but it cannot be used by the system or any other program either. This is known as *memory leak*. Memory leaks add up over time, and if they are not cleaned up, the system eventually runs out of memory.

EXERCISES

1. What are pointers? Why are they important?

2. Explain the features of pointers.

3. Explain the pointer of any data type that requires four bytes.

4. Explain the use of (*) indirection operator.

5. What is a NULL pointer? Is it the same as an uninitialized pointer?

6. What is a NULL macro? What is the difference between a NULL pointer and a NULL macro?

7. What does the error 'Null Pointer Assignment' mean and what causes this error?

8. Explain the effect of ++ and −− operators with pointer of all types.

9. What is an array of pointer? How is it declared?

10. Explain the relation between an array and a pointer.

11. Why is the addition of two pointers impossible?

12. Which arithmetic operations are possible with pointers?

13. Explain the comparison of two pointers.

14. How does one pointer point to another pointer?

15. How will you recognize pointer to pointer? What does the number of '*'s indicate?

16. How are strings stored in the pointer variables? Is it essential to declare length?

17. What is base address? How is it accessed differently for one-dimensional and two-dimensional arrays?

18. Distinguish between the address stored in the pointer and the value at that address.

19. Why does the element counting of arrays always start from '0'?

20. Write a program to read and display a two-dimensional array of 5 by 2 numbers. Reduce the base address of an array by one and start element counting from one.

21. How is a pointer initialized?

22. Explain the effects of the following statements.

    (a) `int a, *b=&a;`

    (b) `int p, *p;`

    (c) `char *s;`

    (d) `a = (float*) &x;`

    (e) `double(*f)();`

23. Predict the output of each of the following programs (draw the memory diagram so that it will be easy to answer) where memory addresses are to be described. You can assume any six-digit number. Assume numbers starting from 333333.

    (a)
```
int a;
int *integer_pointer;
a=222;
integer_pointer=&a;
printf("The value of a is %d\n",a);
printf("The address of a is %d\n",&a);
```

```
    printf("The address of\
    integer_pointer %d\n", &integer_pointer);
    printf("Star integer_pointer\
    %d\n", *integer_pointer);
(b) char a;
    char *char_pointer;
    a='b';
    char_pointer=&a;
    printf("The value of a %d\n", a);
    printf("The address of a %d\n",&a);
    printf("The address of\
            char_pointer %d\n", &char_pointer);
    printf("Star char_pointer %d\n", *char_pointer);
(c) for float
    float a;
    float *float_pointer;
    a=22.25;
    float_pointer=&a;
    printf("The value of a %d\n", a);
    printf("The address of a %d\n", &a);
    printf("The address of\
    float_pointer %d\n", &float_pointer);
    printf("Star float_pointer %d\n", *float_
                pointer);
(d) int a, b
    int *ip1, *ip2;
    a=5;
    b=6;
    ip1=&a;
    ip2=ip1;
    printf("The value of a is %d\n", a);
    printf("The value of b is %d\n", b);
    printf("The address of a is %d\n",&a);
    printf("The address of b is %d \n"&b);
    printf("The address of ip1 is %d\n", &ip1);
    printf("The address of ip2 is %d\n", &ip2);
    printf("The value of ip1 is %d\n",ip1);
    printf("The value of ip2 is %d\n", ip2);
    printf("ip1 dereferenced %d\n",*ip1);
    printf("ip2 dereferenced %d\n", *ip2);
(e) int i, j, *ip;
    i=1;
    ip=&i;
    j=*ip;
    *ip=0;
    printf("The value of i %d\n", i);
    printf("The value of j %d\n", j);
```

```
(f) int x, y;
    int *ip1, *ip2;
    y=1;
    ip2=&y;
    ip1=ip2;
    x=*ip1+y;
    printf("The value of x %d\n", x);
    printf("The value of y %d\n",y);
```

24. Distinguish between `(*m)[5]` and `*m[5]`.

25. Explain the difference between 'call by reference' and 'call by value'.

26. Write a program using pointers to read an array of integers and print its elements in reverse order.

27. We know that the roots of a quadratic equation of the form

$$ax^2 + bx + c = 0$$

are given by the following equations:

$$x_1 = \frac{-b + \text{squareroot}\,(b^2 - 4ac)}{2a}$$

$$x_2 = \frac{-b - \text{squareroot}\,(b^2 - 4ac)}{2a}$$

Write a function to calculate the roots. The function must use two pointer parameters, one to receive the coefficients a, b, and c, and the other to send the roots to the calling function.

28. Does mentioning the array name give the base address in all contexts?

29. Write a C program to read through an array of any type using pointers. Write a C program to scan through this array to find a particular value.

30. Write a function using pointers to add two matrices and to return the resultant matrix to the calling function.

31. Using pointers, write a function that receives a character string and a character as argument and deletes all occurrences of this character in the string. The function should return the corrected string with no holes.

32. Write a function `day_name` that receives a number n and returns a pointer to a character string containing the name of the corresponding day. The day names should be kept in a static table of character strings local to the function.

33. Write a program to find the number of times that a given word (i.e., a short string) occurs in a sentence (i.e., a long string).

    Read data from standard input. The first line is a single word, which is followed by general text on the second line. Read both up to a new-line character, and insert a terminating null before processing. Typical output should be:

    > The word is "the".
    > The sentence is "the cat sat on the mat".
    > The word occurs 2 times.

34. Write a program to read in an array of names and to sort them in alphabetical order. Use sort function that receives pointers to the

functions `strcmp`, and `swap.sort` in turn should call these functions via the pointers.

35. Given an array of sorted list of integer numbers, write a function to search for a particular item using the method of *binary search*. Also show how this function may be used in a program. Use pointers and pointer arithmetic.

    Hint In binary search, the target value is compared with the array's middle element. Since the table is sorted, if the required value is smaller, we know that all values greater than the middle element can be ignored. That is, in one attempt, we eliminate one half of the list. This search can be applied recursively till the target value is found.

36. Differentiate between `p` and `*p`.

37. What is the equivalent pointer notation to the subscript notation `pt [0][2]`?

38. What is the difference between `*p++` and `p++`?

39. What is the result of adding an integer to a pointer?

40. What are the advantages of using pointers?

41. How do pointers differ from variables in C?

42. Explain the following declaration.

    ```
    int(*pf) (char *a, int *b);
    ```

43. What is the purpose of the `realloc()` function?

44. Differentiate between `calloc()` and `malloc()` functions in C.

45. For the version of C available on your computer, how many memory cells are required to store a single character–an integer quantity, a long integer, a floating-point quantity, a double-precisions quantity?

46. What is meant by the address of a memory cell? How are addresses usually numbered?

47. How is a variable's address determined?

48. What kind of information does a pointer variable represent?

49. What is the relationship between the address of a variable v and the corresponding pointer variable pv?

50. What is the purpose of the indirection operator? To what type of operand must the indirection operator be applied?

51. What is the relationship between the data item represented by a variable v and the corresponding pointer variable pv?

52. What precedence is assigned to the unary operators compared with the multiplication, division, and module operators? In what order are the unary operators evaluated?

53. Can the address operator act upon an arithmetic expression such as 2* (u + v)? Explain your answer.

54. Can an expression involving the indirection operator appear on the left side of an assignment statement? Explain.

55. What kinds of objects can be associated with pointer variables?

56. How is a pointer variable declared? What is the purpose of the data type included in the declaration?

57. In what way can the assignment of an initial value be included in the declaration of a pointer variable?

58. Are integer values ever assigned to pointer variables? Explain.

59. Why is it sometimes desirable to pass a pointer to a function as an argument?

60. Suppose a function receives a pointer as an argument. Explain how this function is declared within its calling function. In particular, explain how the data type of the pointer argument is represented.

61. Suppose a function receives a pointer as an argument. Explain how the pointer argument is declared within the function definition.

62. What is the relationship between an array name and a pointer? How is an array name interpreted when it appears as an argument to a function?

63. Suppose a formal argument within a function definition is an array. How can the array be declared within the function?

64. How can a portion of an array be passed to a function?

65. How can a function return a pointer to its calling routine?

66. Describe two different ways to specify the address of an array element.

67. Why is the value of an array subscript sometimes referred to as an offset when the subscript is a part of an expression indicating the address of an array element?

68. Describe two different ways to access an array element. Compare your answer to that of Question 62.

69. Can an address be assigned to an array name or an array element? Can an address be assigned to a pointer variable whose object is an array?

70. How is the library function `malloc` used to associate a block of memory with a pointer variable? How is the size of the memory block specified? What kind of information does the `malloc` function return?

71. Suppose a numerical array is defined in terms of a pointer variable. Can the individual array elements be initialized?

72. Suppose a character-type array is defined in terms of a pointer variable. Can the individual array elements be initialized? Compare your answer with that of the previous question.

73. Suppose an integer quantity is added to or subtracted from a pointer variable. How will this difference be interpreted?

74. Under what conditions can one pointer variable be subtracted from another? How will this difference be interpreted?

75. Under what conditions can two pointer variables be compared? Under what conditions are such comparisons useful?

76. How is a multidimensional array defined in terms of a pointer to a collection of contiguous array of lower dimensionality?

77. How can the indirection operator be used to access a multidimensional array element?

78. How is a multidimensional array defined in terms of an array of pointers? What does each pointer represent? How does this definition

differ from a pointer to a collection of contiguous array of lower dimensionality?

79. How can a one-dimensional array of pointers be used to represent a collection of strings?

80. If several strings are stored within a one-dimensional array of pointers, how can an individual string be accessed?

81. If several strings are stored within a one-dimensional array of pointers, what happens if the strings are reordered? Are the strings actually moved to different locations within the array?

82. Under what conditions can the elements of a multidimensional array be initialized if the array is defined in terms of an array of pointers?

83. What is the relationship between a function name and a pointer?

84. Suppose a formal argument within a function definition is a pointer to another function. How is the formal argument declared? Within the formal argument declaration, what does the data type refer to—deficient or abundant?

85. Define an integer pointer array of 10 integers. Initialize them to any integer values from the keyboard. Find the sum, average, minimum, and maximum of these 10 integers. Sort the 10 integers in descending order.

86. Write a program to display the starting day and ending day of the week for a project. The user is asked which day (0 to 6) is preferable to begin the project and the expected duration in number of days (a decimal number, e.g., 6.5 refers to 6.5 days) to complete the project. It then displays the starting and ending days as:

Project starts on Monday and ends on Wednesday—duration is 10.5 days (if the start day number is 1 and duration = 10.5 days). The program allows the user to continue until the start day number is entered as 9 to exit the program.

PROJECT QUESTION

Write a program that reads in up to 10 strings or to EOF by pressing Control +z, whichever comes first. The program should offer the user a menu with five choices: print the original list of strings, print the strings in alphabetical order, print the strings in order of increasing length, print the strings in order of the length of the first word in the string, and quit. The menu should recycle until the user enters the quit request. The program, of course, should actually perform the promised tasks.

User-defined Data Types and Variables

After studying this chapter, the readers will be able to

- learn about the user-defined data type called structure and its tag, members, and variables
- access, initialize, and copy structures and their members
- explain nesting of structures
- create and initialize arrays of structures

- discuss pointer to structures
- use structures as function arguments and return values
- learn about union data types
- list enumeration data types
- explain bitfields

14.1 INTRODUCTION

So far, fundamental data types have been used in the programs illustrated. However, C provides facilities to construct user-defined data types from the fundamental data types.

A user-defined data type may also be called a derived data type. The array type is a derived data type that contains only one kind of fundamental data type defined in C. This means that the array elements, represented by a single name, contain homogeneous data.

But what happens if the different elements in this cluster, known as array, are to be of different data types? Such non-homogeneous data cannot be grouped to form an array. To tackle this problem suitably, C provides features to pack heterogeneous data in one group, bearing a user-defined data type name, and forming a conglomerate data type. So, C provides facilities for the user to create a new data type called the 'structure' that can hold data of existing type.

14.2 STRUCTURES

Array is an example of a data structure. It takes basic data types such as int, char, or double and organizes them into a linear array of elements of the same data type. The array serves most, but not all of the needs of the typical C program. The restriction is that an array is composed of the same type of elements.

At first, this seems perfectly reasonable. After all, why would one want an array to be composed of twenty characters and two integers? Well, this sort of mixture of data types working together is one of the most familiar characteristics of data structures. Consider a record card which stores name, age, and salary. The name would have to be stored as a string, i.e., an array of characters terminated with an ASCII null character, and the age and salary would be integers. Hence, the only way one can work with this collection of data is as separate variables. This is not as convenient as a *single data structure* using a single name. Therefore, C provides a keyword `struct`, which is used to form a user-defined data type that can hold a collection of elements of different fundamental data types. This conglomerate of user-defined data type, is called a structure. At first, it is easier to think of this as a record, although it is a little more versatile than what it appears to be.

A structure is a collection of variables under a single name. These variables can be of different types, and each has a name which is used to select it from the structure. Therefore, a structure is a convenient way of grouping together several pieces of related information.

Thus, a structure can be defined as a new named type, thus extending the number of available data types. It can use other structures, arrays, or pointers as some of its members, though this can get complicated unless one is careful.

A structure provides a means of grouping variables under a single name for easier handling and identification. Complex hierarchies can be created by nesting structures.

Structures may be copied to and assigned. They are also useful in passing groups of logically related data into functions.

14.2.1 Declaring Structures and Structure Variables

A structure is declared by using the keyword `struct` followed by an optional structure tag followed by the body of the structure. The *variables* or *members* of the structure are declared within the body.

The general format of declaring a simple structure is given as follows.

```
struct <structure_tag_name >{
<data_type member_name1>;
<data_type member_name2>;
     :
} <structure_variable1>,<structure_variable2>,...;
```

The `structure_tag_name` is the name of the structure. The `structure_variables` are the list of variable names separated by commas. Each of these `structure_variable` names is a structure of type `structure_tag_name`. The `structure_variable` is also known as an instance variable of the structure. Each `member_name` declared within the braces is called a `member` or `structure element`.

Like all data types, structures must be declared and defined. There are three different ways to declare and/or define a structure. These are:

- Variable structure
- Tagged structure
- Type-defined structure

A variable structure may be defined as follows.

```
struct
{
member_list
}variable_identifier;
```

As an example the following statement is a definition of a variable structure:

```
struct
{
  int x;
  int y;
}a;
```

It does not offer any advantage over other declaration formats. A tagged structure has been described earlier. It has the following format:

```
struct tag_name
{
  member_list
}variable_identifier;
```

The preceding structure declaration may be expressed as a tagged structure as follows:

```
struct coordinate
{
  int x;
  int y;
}a;
```

This creates a structure variable named 'a' and has a separate instance of all members (x and y) in the structure `coordinate`. If one concludes the structure with a semicolon after the closing brace, no variable is defined. In this case, the structure is simply a type template with no associate storage. Once one has declared a tagged structure type, then the structure variable can be defined by specifying the following statement.

```
struct tag_name variable1, variable2, …;
```

Type-defined structures have been discussed later on (see Section 14.2.5).

The proper place for structure declarations is in the global area of the program before `main()`. This puts them within the scope of the entire program and is mandatory if the structure is to be shared by functions. If a declaration is placed inside a function, then its tag can be used only inside that function.

Here is an example of a structure that would be useful in representing the Cartesian coordinates of a point on a computer screen, that is, the pixel position.

```
struct point
{
    int x;
    int y;
};
```

The struct declaration is a user-defined data type. Here, the name of the structure is point. Variables of type point may be declared in the way variables of a built-in type are declared. For example,

```
struct point
{
    int x;
    int y;
} upper_right;
```

As mentioned earlier, the structure tag name provides a shorthand for declaring structures.
This is shown as follows.

```
struct point
{
    int x;
    int y;
};
struct point upper_left,lower_right;
struct point origin;
```

Here, upper_left, lower_right, and origin are the names of three structures of type point. The following are some examples of declaration of structures and structure variables.

─────────────── **EXAMPLE** ───────────────

```
1. struct personal_data
   {
       char name[100];
       char address[200];
       int year_of_birth;
       int month_of_birth;
       int day_of_birth;
   };
   struct personal_data monish, venkat, naresh;
```

The above statement is for defining a type of variable that holds a string of 100 characters called name, a string of 200 characters called address, and three integers called year_of_birth, month_of_birth, and day_of_birth. Any variable declared to be of type struct personal_data will contain these components, which are called members.

Different structures can have members with the same name, but the values of members of different structures are independent of one another. The name for a member same as for an ordinary variable in that program can also be used, but the computer will recognize them as different entities, with different values. This is similar to the naming convention for humans, where two different men may share the name 'Jogi Sharma', but are recognized as being different people.

In Fig. 14.1, the three structure variables declared are monish, venkat, and naresh. Each contains the member fields declared within the structure personal_data.

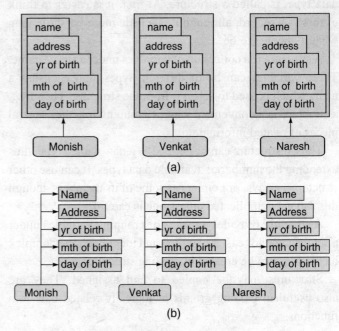

Fig. 14.1 Structure variables

─────────────── **EXAMPLES** ───────────────

```
2. struct country
   {
       char name[30];
       int population;
       char language[15];
   }Country;
```

Here, a structure variable Country has been declared to be of structure type country. This structure variable holds a string called name having 30 characters, an integer variable population and a string called language with 15 characters.

```
3. struct country
   {
       char name[30];
       int population;
       char language[15];
   }India, Japan, Indonesia;
```

This structure named country has three structure variables India, Japan, Indonesia. All three structure variables hold the same type of member elements, though with different values.

```
4. struct date                        /* the tag */
   {              /* start of struct date template */
     int day;                        /* a member */
     int month;                      /* a member */
     int year;                       /* a member */
     float sensex;                   /* a member */
   }dates, today, next;             /* instances */
```

This declaration has three structure variables `dates`, `today`, and `next`. These are also called *instances* and hold similar kind and number of variables, which may contain different values.

It has been seen that instances of structures can be declared at the same time the structure is defined. For example,

```
struct myStruct {
    int a;
    int b;
    int c;
} s1, s2;
```

would generate two instances of `myStruct`. `s1`, holding the first 12 bytes of the file (four bytes for each of the three integers) and `myStruct`. `s2`, holding the next 12 bytes of the file, considering a 32-bit machine. So, from the declaration of members, the compiler can determine the memory space needed and identify the different members in the structure.

Observe that the structure declaration construct is a template that conveys to the C compiler how the structure is mapped in memory and gives details of the member names. A (tagged) template does not reserve any instances of the structure; it only conveys to the compiler what it means. This is explained with the help of the following example.

```
struct date {
    int month;
    int day;
    int year;
};
```

This declares a new data type called `date`. The `date` structure consists of three basic data elements, all of type integer. It does not create any storage space and cannot be used as a variable. In essence, it is a new data type keyword, like `int` and `char`, and can now be used to create variables. Other data structures may be defined as consisting of the same composition as the `date` structure.

Structure type and variable declarations can be either local or global, depending on their placement in the code, just as any other declaration can be. Structures may be assigned, used as formal function parameters, and returned as functional values. Such operations cause the compiler to generate sequences of load and store instructions that might pose efficiency problems. C programmers particularly concerned about program speed will avoid such things and work exclusively with pointers to functions.

There are few actual operations that can be performed on structures as distinct from their members. The only operators that can be rightly associated with structures are '=' (simple assignment) and '&' (refers to the address). It is not possible to compare structures for equality using '==', nor is it possible to perform arithmetic on structures. Such operations need to be explicitly coded in terms of operations on the members of the structure.

Declaration of structure member conform to the same syntax as ordinary variable declarations. Structure member names should conform to the same syntax as ordinary variable names. However the same name can be used for a structure tag, an instance of the structure, and a member of the structure. Each structure defines a separate memory space as far as naming structure members is concerned.

The following rather bizarre and confusing codes are perfectly valid.

```
(a) struct a              (b) struct b
    {                         {
      int a;                    char b;
      int b;                    char a;
    } b;                      }a;
```

Structure members can be any valid data type, including other structures, aggregates, and pointers, including pointers to structures and pointers to functions. A structure may not, for obvious reasons, contain instances of itself but may contain pointers to instances of itself.

> **Note**
>
> - A structure can be defined as a user-defined data type that is capable of holding heterogeneous data of basic data type.
> - The structure is simply a type template with no associate storage.
> - The proper place for structure declaration is in the global area of the program before `main()`.
> - It is not possible to compare structures for equality using '==', nor is it possible to perform arithmetic on structures.

14.2.2 Accessing the Members of a Structure

The members of a structure can be accessed in three ways. One of the ways consists of using the '.', which is known as the 'dot operator'. The members are accessed by relating them to the structure variable with a dot operator. The general form of the statement for accessing a member of a structure is as follows.

```
< structure_variable >.< member_name > ;
```

The . (dot) operator selects a particular member from a structure. It has the same precedence as () and [], which is higher than that of any unary or binary operator. Like () and

[], it associates from left to right. For example, in

Conceptual view of memory allocated
for instances s1 & s2

```
struct myStruct
{
  int a;
  int b;
  int c;
} s1, s2;
```

the first member can be accessed by the construct

```
s1.a
```

For any other member of the structure, the construct for accessing it will be similar. Therefore, for assigning a value of 12, say, to the member b of the structure identified by the variable s2, the following statement is written

```
s2.b = 12;
```

To print this value assigned to the member on the screen, the following code is written.

```
printf("%d", s2.b);
```

Similarly, in the preceding example, member b of structure s2 will behave just like a normal variable of type int, although it is referred to as

```
s2.b
```

Now, consider the structure given as follows.

```
struct personal_data
{
  char name[100];
  char address[200];
  int year_of_birth;
  int month_of_birth;
  int day_of_birth;
};
```

and the declaration statement for the structure variables monish, venkat, and naresh is given by

```
struct personal_data monish, venkat, naresh;
```

To input the address of monish, the following code is used.

```
scanf("%s", monish.address);
```

The member address of structure personal_data will behave just like a normal array of char. However, it is referred to as monish.address.

In the following example, the year 1982 is assigned to the year_of_birth member of the structure variable monish, of type struct personal_data. Similarly, the month 5 is assigned to the month_of_birth member, and day 4 is assigned to the day_of_birth member. The following statements show the

assignment of the values to the member variables belonging to the structure variable monish.

```
monish.year_of_birth = 1982;
monish.month_of_birth = 5;
monish.day_of_birth = 4;
```

Hence, each member of a structure can be used just like a normal variable, but its name will be a bit longer. Therefore, the 'dot' is an operator that selects a member from a structure. This is just one of the ways of accessing any member in a structure. The other two ways will be described in the ensuing sections.

14.2.3 Initialization of Structures

A structure can be initialized in much the same way as any other data type. This consists of assigning some constants to the members of the structure. Structures that are not explicitly initialized by the programmer are, by default, initialized by the system. For integer and float data type members, the default value is zero. For char and string type members, the default value is '\0'.

The general construct for initializing a structure can be any of the two forms given as follows:

```
struct <structure_tag_name>
{
  <data_type member_name1>;
  <data_type member_name2>;
}<structure_variable1> = {constant1,constant2, . .};
```

or

```
struct <structure_tag_name> <structure_variable>
        = {constant1,constant2,..};
```

The following are some examples using both the forms for initialization.

EXAMPLE

5. Initialization of structure using the first construct.

```
#include <stdio.h>
struct tablets          Tag name
{
  int count;
  float average_weight;
                                        Members
  int m_date, m_month, m_year;

  int ex_date, ex_month, ex_year;
}batch1={2000,25.3,07,11,2004};
      Structure              Initialization
      variable               constants

int main()
{
```

```
printf("\n  count=%d,  av_wt=%f",batch1.count,\
    batch1.average_weight);
printf("\n mfg-date=%d/%d/%d", batch1.m_date,\
    batch1.m_month batch1.m_year);
printf("\n exp-date=%d/%d/%d", batch1.ex_date,\
    batch1.ex_month, batch1.ex_year);
return 0;
}
```

Output
```
count=2000, av_wt=25.299999
mfg-date=7/11/2004
exp-date= 0/0/0
```

In the preceding example, observe that after the '=' operator, the number of constants within the braces, that is, { and }, are not equal to the total number of members within the structure *tablets*. There are eight members in this structure whereas there are five initializing constants. Hence, the first five members are assigned the given constants and the remaining members are assigned the default value of zero. This is a case of *partial initialization* where always, the first few members are initialized and the remaining uninitialized members are assigned default values. Therefore, it is obvious that the *partial initialization* feature is supported in C.

It may, therefore, be stated that the initialization of all members in a structure is possible if the number of initializing constants placed within the braces is equal to the number of members. Otherwise, partial initialization will be done and the rule of assigning the default values to the rest of the members will be followed.

EXAMPLE

6. Initialization of structure using the second construct.
```
#include <stdio.h>
struct tablets
{
int count;
float average_weight;
int m_date, m_month, m_year;
int ex_date, ex_month, ex_year;
};
struct tablets batch1={2000,25.3,07,11,2004,06,10,2\
    007};
int main()
{
printf("\n count=%d, av_wt=%f mg.",batch1.count,\
    batch1.average_weight);
printf("\n  mfg-date=  %d/%d/%d",batch1.m_date,\
    batch1.m_month, batch1.m_year);
printf("\n  exp-date=  %d/%d/%d",batch1.ex_date,\
    batch1.ex_month, batch1.ex_year);
return 0;
}
```

Output
```
count=2000, av_wt=25.299999 mg.
mfg-date= 7/11/2004
exp-date= 6/10/2007
```

It must be noted that within the structure construct, no member is permitted to be initialized individually, which means the following initialization construct is wrong.

```
struct games_ticket
{
  int value = 500;
          /* wrong procedure of initialization */
  int seat_num = 52;
          /* wrong procedure of initialization */
  int date, month, year;
}fan1;
```

The initialization statements
```
int value = 500;
```
and `int seat_num = 52;`

placed within the `struct` construct are not permitted in C. The structure tag, `games_ticket`; is not a variable name. It is just a name given to the template of a structure. Thus, the statement, `games_ticket.value=500` will cause the compiler to generate an error. Note that `games_ticket` is a just a data type like `int` and not a variable. Just as `int=10` is invalid, `games_ticket.value=500`; is also invalid. The correct code allowed by C will be

```
struct games_ticket  /* structure tag */
{
  int value;                   /* member */
  int seat_num;                /* member */
  int date, month, year;       /* members */
} fan1={500, 52};      /* structure variable and */
                       /* initializing values */
```

Here, the members `value` and `seat_num` are initialized with the values 500 and 52 respectively.

The rules described upto this point, for the initialization of structures, is valid for the old C compilers that do not comply with C99 standards. The compilers that follow C99 standard allow the initialization of individual members of a `structure`. This method of initialization was forbidden in old compilers that are not C99 compliant. To demonstrate this kind of named initialization of a structure, look at the following examples.

EXAMPLES

7.
```
struct {
  float p, q,
  int r;
} k = { .p = 3.0, .q = 7.9, .r = 5};
```

The instance "k" of the above defined structure is initialized by assigning value to individual named members. Here, a "dot" is used with the member's name for assigning a value.

8.
```c
struct employee
{
    int emp_num;
    char designation[40];
    char kind_of_leave_applied[30];
    int number_of_days;
    int begin_date;
};
struct employee mangal_singh = {.kind_of_leave_
        applied = "Medical leave", .begin_date =
        230910, .emp_num = 0691};
```

The "struct employee" defines a template of a structure with tagname "employee". An instance of the structure is created by the statement "struct employee mangal_singh". This instance is initialized. But, it may be noted that only some of the members are initialized. In the C compilers not complying to C99, such initialization is not allowed. For such compilers, while initializing an instance of a structure, the members of the structure have to be assigned a value or a character, whichever is appropriate, in the order of their definition and members not assigned are given default value of 0 or \0, which has been mentioned earlier. But, C99 allows the members of a structure to be initialized by name, which is shown in the above example.

Further, note that the order of the initialization is different from that of the definition of the members in the structure. The member "kind_of_leave_applied" is placed first, the member "begin_date" is placed second and the member "emp_num" is placed third, while the other remaining members are not assigned anything. Members uninitialized are filled up with the default value of 0. It may be observed that this not only decouples the order of the definition from the order of the initialization, but it is more readable. This means, the programmer only needs to fill out the portions of the structure that are presently relevant and is able to initialize the elements of the structure using the set notation without feeling the need to remember the order of the elements of the structure. Also, if new elements to the structure are added in later versions, they get initialized to a known value.

Some examples using named initialization in structures are given below for getting more familiar with its applications.

9. Demonstration of named initialization in a structure.
```c
#include<stdio.h>
struct
{
    float x, y, z;
} s = { .y = 0.6, .x = 2.7, .z = 14.6};
int main()
{
    float p,q,r;
    p= s.x + s.y + s.z;
    q= s.z*s.x;
    r= s.z/s.x;
    printf("\n p = %5.2f",p);
```

```c
    printf("\n q = %5.2f",q);
    printf("\n r = %5.2f",r);
    return 0;
}
```

Output
```
p = 17.90
q = 39.42
r = 5.41
```

10. Another demonstration of named initialization in a structure.
```c
#include<stdio.h>
struct test
{
    float x, y, z;
}s;
int main()
{
    float p,q,r;
    struct test s= { .y = 1.24, .x = 3.8, .z = 11.7};
    p= s.x + s.y + s.z;
    q= s.z*s.x;
    r= s.z/s.x;
    printf("\n p = %5.2f",p);
    printf("\n q = %5.2f",q);
    printf("\n r = %5.2f",r);
    return 0;
}
```

Output
```
p = 16.74
q = 44.46
r = 3.08
```

11. One more demonstration of named initialization in a structure.
```c
#include<stdio.h>
struct test
{
    float x, y, z;
}s;
int main()
{
    float p,q,r;
    struct test s;
    s.y= 5.94;
    s.z= 19.45;
    s.x= 23.17;
    p= s.x + s.y + s.z;
    q= s.z*s.x;
    r= s.z/s.x;
    printf("\n p = %7.2f",p);
    printf("\n q = %7.2f",q);
```

```
    printf("\n r = %7.2f",r);
    return 0;
  }
```

Output

```
    p = 48.56
    q = 450.66
    r = 0
```

12. A railway ticket generation program that uses named initialization in a structure.

```
#include<stdio.h>
struct traveler
{
  int class;
  char train_num[40];
  char coach_num[6];
  int seat_num;
  char from[30];
  char to[30];
  char gender[10];
  int age;
  int dep_date[10];
  char name[80];
};
struct traveler passenger8 =
{
  .name = "JIT SINHA",
  .to = "Jaipur",
  .from = "Raigarh",
  .train_num = "superfast 154",
  .dep_date[0] = 30,
  .dep_date[1] = 8,
  .dep_date[2] = 2010,
  .gender = "M",
  .age = 28,
  .class = 1
};
int main()
{
  printf("\n enter coach number:");
  scanf("%s",&passenger8.coach_num);
  printf("\n enter seat number:");
  scanf("%d", &passenger8.seat_num);
  printf("\nxxxxxxxxxx Ticket xxxxxxxxx");
  printf("\n\n\n Name of Ticket holder : %s",\
       passenger8.name);
  printf("\n\n Train : %s:",passenger8.train_num);
```

```
  printf("\n\n From : %s, Date of Departure:",\
       passenger8.from);
  for(int i=0;i<3;i++)
  printf(": %d :",passenger8.dep_date[i]);
  printf("\n\n To: %s", passenger8.to);
  printf("\n\n Coach No.: %s Seat No.:%d",passenger8.\
       coach_num,passenger8.seat_num);
  printf("\n\n\nnxxxxxxxxxxxxxxxxxxxxxxxxxxxxxxx");
  return 0;
}
```

Output

```
enter coach number: S6
enter seat number: 41
xxxxxxxxxxxxxxxxxx Ticket xxxxxxxxxxxxxxxxxxxx
Name of Ticket holder : JIT SINHA
Train : Superfast 154:
From : Raigarh, Date of Departure : : 30 :: 8 :: 2010 :
To: Jaipur
Coach No.: S6  Seat No.: 41
```

14.2.4 Copying and Comparing Structures

A structure can be assigned to another structure of the same type. Here is an example of assigning one structure to another.

EXAMPLE

13. Copying one structure to another of the same type.

```
#include <stdio.h>
struct employee
{
  char grade;
  int basic;
  float allowance;
};
int main()
{
  struct employee ramesh={'b', 6500, 812.5};
                    /* member of employee */
  struct employee vivek;
                    /* member of employee */
  vivek = ramesh;   /* copy respective members of
                    ramesh to vivek */
  printf("\n vivek's grade is %c, basic is Rs %d, \
      allowance is Rs %f", vivek.grade,vivek.basic,\
      vivek.allowance);
  return 0;
}
```

Output

```
vivek's grade is b, basic is Rs 6500, allowance
is Rs 812.500000
```

This example illustrates that it is possible to copy the corresponding members of one *structure variable* to those of another *structure variable* provided they belong to the same structure type. It was mentioned earlier that the operator '=' can only be used on structure variables, as demonstrated in this example. The operator '&' can also be used on the structure variable. No other operators—arithmetic, logical, or relational—can be used with the structure variables.

Comparing one structure variable with another is not allowed in C. The components of a structure are stored in memory in the order they are declared. The first component has the same address as the entire structure. Padding is introduced between components to satisfy the alignment requirements of individual components. This can be explained in terms of *slack bytes*. Sometimes hardware requires that certain data such as integers and floating point members, be aligned on a word boundary in memory. When data in a structure are grouped, the arrangement of the data may require that *slack bytes* be inserted to maintain these boundary requirements. For example, consider the following structure.

```
struct test
{
    char c[25];
    long int l;
    char ch;
    int I;
};
```

On a byte-addressed machine, short of size two might be placed at even addresses and long int of size four at addresses that are multiples of four. In this structure, it is assumed that a long int is stored in a word that requires four bytes and must be on an address evenly divisible by four such as 20, 24, 28, or 32. It is also assumed that integers are stored in a two-byte word that requires an address evenly divisible by four. The 25-bytes string at the beginning of the structure forces slack bytes between the string and the long (see Fig. 14.2). Then, the character after the long forces slack byte to align with the integer at the end of the structure.

Fig. 14.2 Slack bytes in a structure

Since these extra bytes are beyond the control of the program, one cannot guarantee what their values will be. The gcc compiler aligns the structure fields on 4-byte boundaries. Considering the above structure, sizeof(test) will print 40 (25 bytes for char + 3 bytes padding + 4 bytes for long + 1 byte for char + 3 bytes padding + 4 bytes for int. Therefore, if two structures are compared and their first components are

equal, the inserted slack bytes could cause an erroneous result. C prevents this problem by not allowing selection statements with structures. Generally, it is good to group structure fields of the same type together to minimize the extra padding. Of course, when comparing two structures, one should compare the individual fields in the structure. To determine byte offset of a member within a structure, ANSI C defines offsetof macro in stdef.h. This can also be implemented as follows.

```
#define offsetof (type, mem) ((size_t) ((char *)
&((type *)0)->mem -\(char *) (type *)0))
```

To avoid wastage of space and to minimize the effects of padding, the members of a structure should be placed according to their sizes from the largest to the smallest. However, members of one structure can be compared with members of another on an individual basis. In fact, the members involved in the comparison will behave like any other variable. An example illustrating this feature is as follows.

EXAMPLE
---

14. Comparison of individual members of structures.

```
#include <stdio.h>
struct employee
{
    char grade;
    int basic;
    float allowance;
};
int main()
{
    struct employee ramesh = {'b', 5750, 818.75};
    struct employee vivek = {'b', 6500, 812.5};
    if(ramesh.grade!= vivek.grade)
        printf("Ramesh and Vivek are employed on\
            different grades");
    else if((ramesh.basic+ramesh.allowance)>(vivek.\
        basic+vivek.allowance))
        printf("Ramesh is senior and his total\
            remuneration is Rs%f",\
            (ramesh.basic+ramesh. allowance));
    else if((ramesh.basic+ramesh.allowance)==(vivek.\
        basic+vivek.allowance))
        printf("Ramesh and Vivek get the same total\
            remuneration of Rs%f",\
            (ramesh.basic+ramesh.allowance));
    else
        printf("Vivek is senior and his total\
            remuneration is Rs%f",\
            (vivek.basic+vivek.allowance));
    return 0;
}
```

Output
```
    Vivek is senior and his total remuneration is
Rs 7312.500000
```

Note

- Any member in a structure can be accessed by relating them to the structure variable with a dot operator.

- Structures that are not explicitly initialized by the programmer are, by default, initialized by the system. In most of the C compilers, for `integer` and `float` data type members, the default value is zero and for `char` and string type members, the default value is '\0'.

- Comparing one structure variable with another is not allowed in C. However, when comparing two structures, one can compare the individual fields in the structure.

14.2.5 Typedef and its Use in Structure Declarations

The `typedef` keyword allows the programmer to create a new data type name for an existing data type. No new data type is produced but an alternate name is given to a known data type. The general form of the declaration statement using the `typedef` keyword is given as follows.

```
typedef <existing data type> <new data type ,....>;
```

The `typedef` statement does not occupy storage; it simply defines a new type. `typedef` statements can be placed anywhere in a C program as long as they come prior to their first use in the code.

The following examples show the use of `typedef`.

```
typedef int id_number;
typedef float weight;
typedef char lower_case;
```

In the preceding example, `id_number` is the new data type name given to data type `int`, while `weight` is the new data type name given to data type `float` and `lower_case` is the new data type name given to data type `char`. Therefore, the following statements

```
id_number vinay, komal, jaspal;
weight apples, pears, mangoes;
lower_case a,b,c;
```

mean that `vinay`, `komal`, and `jaspal` are variable names that are declared to hold `int` data type. The new data type, `id_number`, suggests that the data content of the variable names `vinay`, `komal`, and `jaspal` are integers and that it gives their identification number. The two other examples shown also carry similar meanings. Therefore, by the `typedef` keyword, the suggested use of the type names can be understood easily. This is one of the benefits of using the `typedef` keyword. Moreover, `typedef` makes the code more portable.

Complex data type like structure can use the `typedef` keyword. For example,

```
typedef struct point
```

```
{
    int x;
    int y;
} Dot;
Dot left,right;
```

shows that `left` and `right` are the structure variables of structure type point.

When `typedef` is used to name a structure, the structure tag name is not necessary. Such an example follows.

```
typedef struct    /* no structure tag name used */
    {
    float real;
    float imaginary;
    } complex;        /* means complex number */
complex u,v;
```

The preceding example declares u and v as complex numbers having a real part and an imaginary part. The following are some examples involving structures and `typedef`.

EXAMPLES

15. Write a program that prints the weight of various sizes of fruits.

```c
#include <stdio.h>
typedef struct fruits
{
    float big;
    float medium;
    float small;
}weight;
int main()
{
    weight apples={200.75,145.5,100.25};
    weight pears={150.50,125,50};
    weight mangoes={1000, 567.25, 360.25};\
    printf("\n\n apples: big %7.2fkg, medium\
        %7.2fkg,small %7.2fkg",apples.big,apples.\
        medium, apples.small);
    printf("\n\n pears: big %7.2fkg, medium %7.2fkg,\
        small %7.2fkg",pears.big,pears.medium,\
        pears.small);
    printf("\n\n mangoes: big %7.2fkg, medium %7.2fkg,\
        small %7.2fkg", mangoes.big, mangoes.\
        medium, mangoes.small);
    return 0;
}
```

Output

```
apples: big 200.75kg, medium 145.50kg, small 100.25kg
pears: big 150.50kg, medium 125.00kg, small 50.00kg
mangoes: big 1000kg, medium 567.25kg, small 360.25kg
```

16. Write a program that prints the x–y coordinates of the two ends of a line.

```c
#include <stdio.h>
typedef struct                    /* no tag */
```

```
{
  int x;
  int y;
}Dot;                    /* a new type name */
Dot left,right;
                    /* declaring structures "left"
                                    and "right" */
int main()
{
printf("\n Enter x & y coordinates of left and\
     right:");
  scanf("%d %d %d %d",&left.x,&left.y,&right.x,\
     &right.y);
  printf("\n left: x=%d, y=%d, right: x=%d, y=%d",\
     left.x, left.y, right.x,right.y);
  return 0;
}
```

Output

```
Enter x & y coordinates of left and right:4 20 30 20
left: x=4, y=20, right: x=30, y=20
```

14.2.6 Nesting of Structures

A structure can be placed within another structure. In other words, structures can contain other structures as members. A structure within a structure means nesting of structures. In such cases, the dot operator in conjunction with the structure variables are used to access the members of the innermost as well as the outermost structures.

17. Write a program to demonstrate nesting of structures and accessing structure members.

```
#include <stdio.h>
struct outer   /* declaration of outer structure */
{
  int out1;      /* member of outer structure */
  float out2;    /* member of outer structure */
  struct inner /* declaration of inner structure */
  {
  int in1;       /* member of inner structure */
  float in2;     /* member of inner structure */
  }invar;
      /* structure_variable of inner structure*/
};
int main()
{
  struct outer outvar;
      /* declaring structure_variable of outer */
outvar.out1= 2;  /* assigning values to member */
outvar.out2= 10.57;
            /* assigning values to member */
outvar.invar.in1= 2* outvar.out1;
outvar.invar.in2= outvar.out2 + 3.65;
```

```
printf(" out1=%d, out2=%6.2f, in1=%d, in2=%6.2f",\
       outvar.out1, outvar.out2,outvar.invar.in1,\
       outvar.invar.in2);
  return 0;
}
```

Output

```
out1=2, out2= 10.57, in1=4, in2= 14.22
```

It must be noted that an innermost member in a nested structure can be accessed by chaining all the concerned structure variables, from outermost to innermost, with the member using the dot operator. This technique has been used in the previous example, where the innermost members in1 and in2, belonging to the structure inner, are assigned values.

What happens when the first structure type is declared outside and before the second structure type and is incorporated as a member of the second structure type? The following example depicts what happens in such a case. The structure members are accessed in the same way as was done in the earlier example.

18. Write a program to demonstrate nesting of structures, accessing structure members, and using structure type declaration different from that in the previous example.

```
#include <stdio.h>
struct first     /* declaration of first structure */
{
  int in1;              /* member of first */
  float in2;            /* member of first */
};
struct second  /* declaration of second structure */
{
  int out1;             /* member of second */
  float out2;           /* member of second */
  struct first inf;  /* structure_variable of first
                                    structure */
};
int main()
{
  struct second outs;   /* structure_variable of
                             second structure */
  outs.out1= 2;         /* assigning values to
                                    members */
  outs.out2= 10.57;     /* assigning values to
                                    members */
  outs.inf.in1= 2* outs.out1;
  outs.inf.in2= outs.out2 + 3.65;
  printf(" out1=%d, out2=%6.2f, in1=%d, in2=%6.2f",\
         outs.out1,  outs.out2,  outs.inf.in1,\
         outs.inf.in2);
  return 0;
}
```

Output
```
out1=2, out2= 10.57, in1=4, in2= 14.22
```

It must be understood that, in principle, structures can be nested indefinitely. Statements like the following are syntactically acceptable, but are bad style.

```
Outer_struct_variable.member1.member2.member3.
    member4.member5 = 3;
```

However, one may be curious to know what happens if a structure contains an instance of its own type. The following example may be examined in this context.

```
struct compute
{
  int int_member;
  struct compute self_member;
};
```

For the computer to compile a statement of this type, it would theoretically need an infinite amount of memory. In practice, however, the programmer will simply receive an error message along the following lines.

```
In function 'main':
field self_member has incomplete type
```

The compiler conveys to the programmer that 'self_member' has been declared before its data type 'compute' has been fully declared. Since the programmer declares 'self_member' in the middle of declaring its own data type, this is quite natural.

14.2.7 Arrays of Structures

Just as there can be arrays of basic types such as integers and floats, so also there can be *arrays of structures*. This means that the structure variable would be an array of objects, each of which contains the member elements declared within the structure construct. The general construct for declaration of an array of structure is given as follows.

```
struct <structure_tag_name >
{
  <data_type member_name1>;
  <data_type member_name2>;
    ⋮
}<structure_variable>[index];
```

or

```
struct <structure_tag_name> <structure_variable>[index];
```

Figure 14.3 depicts the arrays formed for the array objects declared to be of type structure_tag_name having structure_variable as its name. Here, the term 'index' specifies the number of array objects.

`<structure_variable>[0]`

`<structure_variable>[1]`   `<structure_variable>[N]`

Fig. 14.3   Array of structures

─────────── **EXAMPLE** ───────────

19. Write a program to illustrate the use of array of structures.
```c
#include <stdio.h>
struct test1
{
  char a;
  int i;
  float u;
}m[3];
int main()
{
  int n;
  for(n=0;n<=2;++n)
  {
    printf("\n Enter ch, in, fl:");
    fflush(stdin);        /* clear stdin stream */
                          /* input the values of array
                                     of structures */
    scanf("%c %d %f",&(m[n].a),&(m[n].i),&(m[n].u));
    fflush(stdout);       /* clear stdout stream */
                          /* output the values of array
                                     of structures */
    printf("\n a=%c, i=%d, u=%f", m[n].a, m[n].i, m[n].u);
  }
  return 0;
}
```

Output
```
Enter ch, in, fl:g 45 678.1956
a=g, i=45, u=678.195618
Enter ch, in, fl:j 76 345.5674
a=j, i=76, u=345.567413
Enter ch, in, fl:k 69 123.333547
a=k, i=69, u=123.333549
```

14.2.8 Initializing Arrays of Structures

Initializing arrays of structures is carried out in much the same way as arrays of standard data types. A typical construct for initializing an array of structures would appear as follows.

```
struct <structure_tag_name >
                        /* structure declaration */
{
  <data_type member_name_1>;
  <data_type member_name_2>;
    .
    .
  <data_type member_name_n>;
};
/* declaration of structure array and initialization */
struct <structure_tag_name> <structure_variable>[N]=
{
  {constant01,constant02,...................constant0n},
  {constant11,constant12,...................constant1n},
    .
    .
  {constantN1,constantN2,...constantNn}};
```

The following example shows how the initialization technique referred to above is implemented.

EXAMPLE
---

20. Write a program to print the tickets of the boarders of a boat using array of structures with initialization in the program.

```
#include <stdio.h>
struct boat     /** declaration of structure **/
{
  char name[20];
  int seatnum;
  float fare;
};
int main()
{
  int n;
  struct boat ticket[4]= {{"Vikram", 1,15.50},\
      {"Krishna", 2,15.50}, {"Ramu", 3,25.50},\
      {"Gouri", 4,25.50}};
                          /** initialization **/
  printf("\n Boarder Ticket num. Fare");
  for(n=0;n<=3;n++)
  printf("\n %s %d %f",ticket[n].name,ticket[n].\
      seatnum,ticket[n].fare);
  return 0;
}
```
Output
```
Boarder Ticket num. Fare
Vikram 1 15.500000
Krishna 2 15.500000
Ramu 3 25.500000
Gouri 4 25.500000
```

14.2.9 Arrays within the Structure

There can be arrays within a structure. In other words, any member within a structure can be an array. When arrays are used in a structure, they are accessed and initialized in a way similar to that illustrated in Example 20. In this example, name[20] is an array within the structure boat. Initialization of the structure means initialization of members: name[20], seatnum, and fare. The printf() statement within the for loop uses the dot operator to access the member name[20], an array, within the structure boat. Therefore, this example demonstrates how an array is used within a structure and also shows the way to initialize it.

> **Note**
> - By using typedef, no new data type is produced but an alternate name is given to a known data type.
> - typedef statements can be placed anywhere in a C program as long as they come prior to their first use in the code.
> - An innermost member in a nested structure can be accessed by chaining all the concerned structure variables, from outermost to innermost, with the member using the dot operator.

14.2.10 Structures and Pointers

At times, it is useful to assign pointers to structures. A pointer to a structure is not itself a structure, but merely a variable that holds the address of a structure. This pointer variable takes four bytes of memory just like any other pointer in a 32-bit machine. Declaring pointers to structures is basically the same as declaring a normal pointer. A typical construct for declaring a pointer to a structure will appear as follows.

```
struct <structure_tag_name >
                        /* structure declaration */
{
  <data_type member_name_1>;
  <data_type member_name_2>;
    .
    .
  <data_type member_name_n>;
}*ptr;
```
or
```
struct <structure_tag_name>
{
  <data_type member_name_1>;
  <data_type member_name_2>;
    .
    .
  <data_type member_name_n>;
};
struct <structure_tag_name> *ptr;
```

This pointer, *ptr, can be assigned to any other pointer of the same type, and can be used to access the members of its structure. To access the members within the structure, the dot operator is used with the pointer variable. For example, to enable the pointer variable to access the member member_name_1, the following construct is used.

```
(*ptr).member_name_1
```

The bracket is needed to avoid confusion about the '*' and '.' operators. If the bracket around *ptr is done away with, the code will not compile because the '.' operator has a higher precedence than the '*' operator. It gets tedious to type so many brackets when working with pointers to structures. Hence, C includes a shorthand notation that does exactly the same thing.

```
ptr-> member_name_1
```

This is less confusing and a better way to access a member in a structure through its pointer. The -> operator, an arrow made out of a minus sign and a greater than symbol, enables the programmer to access the members of a structure directly via its pointer. This statement means the same as the last line of the previous code example, but is considerably clearer. The -> operator will come in very handy when manipulating complex data structures.

For initializing the structure members through a pointer to the structure, any one of the following constructs is used.

```
(*ptr).member_name_x = constant;
```

or

```
ptr-> member_name_x = constant;
```

where x is 1 to N, and N is the total number of members in the structure. The following example uses pointer to structure.

--- **EXAMPLE** ---

21. Write a program using a pointer to structure illustrating the initialization of the members in the structure.

```
#include <stdio.h>
#include <conio.h>
struct test1
            /* declaration of structure "test" */
{
  char a;
  int i;
  float f;
};
int main()
{
  struct test1 *pt; /* declaring pointer to the
                                    structure */
  clrscr();
```

```
  pt->a='K';          /* initializing char a */
  pt->i=15;           /* initializing int i */
  pt->f=27.89;        /* initializing float f */
  printf("\n a=%c, i=%d, f=%f",pt->a,pt->i,pt->f);
  printf("\n Enter new char, int, float:");
  scanf("%c %d %f",&pt->a,&pt->i,&pt->f);
                         /* input for members */
  printf("\n a=%c, i=%d, f=%f",pt->a,pt->i,pt->f);
  return 0;
}
                      /* function to link-in floating
                                 point emulator */
void linkfloat()
{
  float a,*x;
  x=&a;
  a=*x;
}
```

Output

```
a=k, i=15, f=27.889999
Enter new char, int, float: d 45 67.53
a=d, i=45, f=67.529999
```

The function linkfloat() needs to be explained. If this function is not included, the following error is generated.

```
scanf: floating point format not linked
Abnormal program termination
```

A similar message saying "floating point not loaded" is printed by the Microsoft C run-time system when the software needs a numeric coprocessor but the computer does not have one installed. One may fix it by returning the program using the floating-point emulation library.

A floating-point emulator is used to manipulate floating point numbers in run-time library functions such as scanf() and atof(). When compiling the source program if the compiler encounters a reference to the address of a float, it sets a flag to have the linker link in the floating-point emulator. In some cases in which reference to float seems to guess wrongly when the program uses floating point formats in scanf() but does not call any other floating point routines. The function linkfloat() forces linking of the floating point emulator into an application. There is no need to call this function. Just include it anywhere in the program. This provides a solid clue to the Borland PC linker that the floating-point library is needed.

Another workaround is to define a function in a module that will be included in the link. The function is as follows:

```
static void forcefloat (float *p)
{
  float f=*p;
  forcefloat(&f);
}
```

The problem can also be solved by including the following code in the program instead of the functions such as `linkfloat()` or `forcefloat()`.

```
#include <math.h>
double dummy = sin(0.0);
```

This code forces the compiler to load the floating-point version of scanf().

EXAMPLES

22. Write a program using a pointer to structure illustrating the initialization of the members in the structure using a different technique to avoid the floating point error problem.

```
#include <stdio.h>
struct test1
{
  char a;
  int i;
  float f;
};
int main()
{
  float x;
  struct test1 *q,p;
  clrscr();
  printf("\n Enter char, int, float:");
  scanf("%c %d",&p.a,&p.i);
  scanf("%f",&x);
  p.f=x;
  q=&p;
  printf("\n a=%c, i=%d, f=%f",q->a,q->i,q->f);
  q=NULL;
  return 0;
}
```

Output

```
Enter char, int, float:g 32 87.64
a=g, i=32, f=87.639999
```

23. Write a program using a pointer to structure illustrating the initialization of the members in the structure using `malloc()`.

```
#include <stdio.h>
struct A
{
char ch;
int in;
float f;
};
int main()
{
  struct A *sp;
  int n,i;
  printf("\n How many members:");
  scanf("%d",&n);
  sp=(struct A *)malloc(n*sizeof(struct A));
```

```
if(sp==NULL)
{
  printf("\n Memory allocation unsuccessful");
  exit(0);
}
for(i=0;i<n;++i)
{
  printf("\n Enter ch, in and f:");
  fflush(stdin);
  scanf("%c %d %f",&sp[i].ch,&sp[i].in,&sp[i].f);
}
for(i=0;i<n;++i)
  printf("\n ch=%c in=%d f=%f",sp[i].ch,\
      sp[i].in, sp[i].f);
  return 0;
}
void linkfloat()
{
float a=0.0,*x;
x=&a;
a=*x;
}
```

Output

```
How many members:2
Enter ch, in and f: g 31 76.56
Enter ch, in and f: k 32 78.34
ch=g in=31 f=76.559998
ch=k in=32 f=78.339996
```

There are many reasons for using a pointer to a struct. One of them is to make two-way communication possible within functions. This aspect is explained with examples in the following section.

14.2.11 Structures and Functions

An entire structure can be passed as a function argument just like any other variable. When a structure is passed as an argument, each member of the structure is copied. In fact, each member is passed by value. In case the member is an array, a copy of this array is also passed. This can prove to be inefficient where structures are large or functions are called frequently. Passing and working with pointers to large structures may be more efficient in such cases. The general construct for passing a structure to a function and returning a structure is

```
struct structure_tag function_name(struct structure_
tag structure_variable);
```

Several variations in this construct are made while using this construct. In some cases, the function may receive a structure but may return void or some other data type. In another implementation, no parameters may be passed to a function but it may return a structure. Another option may be to pass a pointer to a structure and return any data type, including a user-defined structure. Hence, the preceding construct is formed based on the requirement. It must be noted that in any case the structure declaration and the definition of the structure variable should precede the function call construct stated above. The following are some examples involving structures with functions.

EXAMPLES

24. Write a program where a structure is passed to a function while it returns nothing.

```c
#include <stdio.h>
struct A
{
  char ch;
  int in;
  float f;
};
void show(struct A);
int main()
{
  struct A a;
  printf("\n Enter ch, in and f:");
  fflush(stdin);
  scanf("%c %d %f",&a.ch,&a.in,&a.f);
  show(a);
  return 0;
}
/*** function show() ***/
void show(struct A b)
{
  printf("\n ch=%c, in=%d, f=%f",b.ch,b.in,b.f);
}
/*** function linkfloat() ***/
void linkfloat()
{
  float a=0.0,*x;
  x=&a;
  a=*x;
}
```

Output

```
Enter ch, in and f:v 34 78.95
ch=v, in=34, f=78.949997
```

25. Write a program that passes a pointer to a structure and returns nothing.

```c
#include <stdio.h>
struct A
{
  char ch;
  int in;
  float f;
};
```

```c
void read(struct A *);
    /* function prototype with pointer to structure
            as a parameter and void as return */
void show(struct A);
          /* function prototype with structure as
              a parameter and void as return */
int main()
{
  struct A a;
          /* declaring "a" as structure variable */
  read(&a);      /* call to function read() */
  show(a);
                /* call to function show() */
  return 0;
}
/*** function read() ***/
void read(struct A *p)
{
  printf("\n Enter ch, in and f:");
              /* request for values to members */
  fflush(stdin);      /* clear input stream */
  scanf("%c %d %f",&p->ch,&p->in,&p->f);
                /* input values to members */
}
/*** function show() ***/
void show(struct A b)
{
  printf("\n ch=%c in=%d f=%f",b.ch,b.in,b.f);
}
/*** function linkfloat() ***/
void linkfloat()
{
  float a=0.0,*x;
  x=&a;
  a=*x;
}
```

Output

```
Enter ch, in and f:m 31 89.75
ch=m, in=31, f=89.75
```

26. Write a program using a function that does not require any parameter to be passed and returns a structure.

```c
#include <stdio.h>
struct A
{
  char ch;
  int in;
  float f;
};
struct A read(void);
void show(struct A);
int main()
```

```
{
    struct A a;
    a=read();
    show(a);
    return 0;
}
struct A read(void)
{
    struct A p;
    printf("\n Enter ch, in and f:");
    fflush(stdin);
    scanf("%c %d %f",&p.ch,&p.in,&p.f);
    return p;
}
/*** function show() ***/
void show(struct A b)
{

    printf("\n ch=%c, in=%d, f=%f",b.ch,b.in,b.f);

}
/*** function linkfloat() ***/
void linkfloat()
{
    float a=0.0,*x;
    x=&a;
    a=*x;
}
```

Output

```
Enter ch, in and f:g 30 92.55
ch=g, in=30, f=92.550003
```

From the preceding examples, it is evident that to modify the value of the members of the structure by a function, the programmer must pass a pointer to that structure to the function. This is just like passing a pointer to an int type argument whose value is to be changed.

If the programmer is only interested in one member of a structure, it is probably simpler to just pass that member to the function. This will make for a simpler function, which is easier to reuse. But, of course, if the value of that member has to be changed, a pointer to it should be passed to the function.

However, when a structure is passed as an argument to a function, each member of the structure is copied. This can prove expensive where structures are large or functions are called frequently. Passing and working with pointers to large structures may be more efficient in such cases.

Note

- A pointer to a structure is not itself a structure, but merely a variable that holds the address of a structure.
- Passing and working with pointers to large structures may be more efficient while passing structures to a function and working within it.

14.3 UNION

A union is a structure, the members of which share the same storage. The amount of storage allocated to a union is sufficient to hold its largest member. At any given time, only one member of the union may actually reside in that storage. The way in which a union's storage is accessed depends on the member name that is employed during the access. It is the programmer's responsibility to keep track of which member currently resides in a union.

A union is identified in C through the use of the keyword union in place of the keyword struct. Virtually, all other methods for declaring and accessing unions are identical to those for structures.

14.3.1 Declaring a Union and its Members

The general construct for declaring a union is given as follows.

```
union tag_name
    {
        member1;
        member2;
           .
           .
        memberN;
    }variable1,variable2,variable3,…,variableX;
```

Similar to structure, the union also has a tag name, members, and variable names. In the preceding declaration construct, the variable names, variable1, variable2, variable3,… ,variableX, are optional and therefore these may not be mentioned.

The general construct of declaring the individual union variables is

```
union tag_name variable1,variable2,…,variableX;
```

As an example, consider the following declarations for a union that has a tag named mixed.

```
union mixed
    {
        char letter;
        float radian;
        int  number;
    };
union mixed all;
```

The first declaration consists of a union of type *mixed*, which consists of a char, float, or int variable as a member. At a time only one member belonging to any one of the data types, that is, char, int, or float, can exist. This is due to the provision of a single memory address that is used to store the largest variable, unlike the arrangement used for structures. Figure 14.4 depicts the way the three members letter, radian, and number are stored in memory, for a 16-bit machine.

Fig. 14.4 Three members of a union sharing a memory location for a 16-bit machine

Therefore, the variable all can only be a character, a float, or an integer at any one time. C keeps track of what all actually is at any given moment, but does not provide a check to prevent the programmer accessing it incorrectly.

It is evident from the previous example that a union is similar to a structure except that all the members in it are stored at the same address in memory. Therefore, only one member can exist in a union at any instant of time. The union data type was created to prevent the computer from breaking its memory up into several inefficiently sized pieces, which is called *memory fragmentation*.

The union data type avoids fragmentation by creating a standard size for certain data. When the computer allocates memory for a program, it usually does so in one large block of bytes. Every variable allocated when the program runs, occupies a segment of that block. When a variable is freed, it leaves a 'hole' in the block allocated for the program. If this hole is of an unusual size, the computer may have difficulty allocating another variable to 'fill' the hole, thus leading to inefficient memory usage. However, since unions have a standard data size, any 'hole' left in memory by freeing a union can be filled by another instance of the same type of union. A union works because the space allocated for it is the space taken by its largest member; thus, the inefficiency of allocating small-scale memory space for the worst case leads to memory efficiency on a larger scale.

Unions can also be a member of a structure. The following is an example showing such a structure.

```
struct conditions
 {
  float temp;
  union feels_like {
```

```
   float wind_chill;
   float heat_index;
   }
 } today;
```

As is known, wind_chill is only calculated when it is 'cold' and heat_index when it is 'hot'. There is no need for both at the same time. So, when the today is specified, feels_like has only one value, either a float for wind_chill or a float for heat_index.

Within a union, data types can be of any kind; in fact, it may even be of struct type.

14.3.2 Accessing and Initializing the Members of a Union

Consider, the general declaration construct of a union.

```
union tag_name
{
  member1;
  member2;
    ⋮
  memberN;
  }variable1,variable2,variable3,…,variableX;
```

For accessing members of, say, variable1 to N of the union tag_name, the following constructs are used.

```
variable1.member1
variable2.member2
    ⋮
variableX.memberN
```

Only a member that exists at the particular instance in storage should be accessed. The general construct for individual initialization of a union member is

```
variableX.memberN = constant;
```

where X is any value 1 to X and N is any value 1 to N.

EXAMPLE
---

27. Write a program that illustrates the initialization of a member in a union.

```
#include <stdio.h>
#include <conio.h>
union test          /* declaration of union */
{
int i;              /* integer member */
char c;             /* character member */
}var;                   /* variable */
int main()
{
  var.i=65;    /* initializing integer member */
  printf("\n var.i=%d", var.i);
                    /* output integer member */
```

```
        printf("\n var.c=%c", var.c);
                        /* output character member */
        return 0;
    }
```
Output
```
    var.i=65
    var.c=A
```

Note See Fig. 14.5 for the storage location of union test.

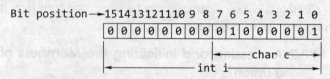

Fig. 14.5 The storage location of union test, for a 16-bit machine

Figure 14.5 shows the storage location of union test. The location has two bytes because the largest member in the union test is an integer named 'i'. The other member, 'c', being a character, occupies eight bits from bit 0 to bit 7. The integer member 'i' is assigned the value '65'. Hence, this value in binary form is stored in bits 0 to 15 as seen in the figure. So when printf() is executed, the value 65 for 'i' is printed on the screen. But the member 'c' has not been assigned any value. Therefore, the existing value of 65 in the referred storage location is taken when the printf() for the member 'char c' is executed. Referring to the ASCII table, the equivalent symbol for the decimal value 65 is 'A'. Thus, when the second printf() is executed, the output is 'A'.

It must be remembered that while accessing member variables, the user should make sure that they can access the member whose value is currently in storage. For example, considering the union in Example 27, the following statements
```
    var.i = 145;
    var.c = 273.85;
    printf("%d", var.i);
```
would produce an erroneous output. This results because the value assigned to var.c overlays the value assigned to var.i.

The initialization of only the first member of the union can be carried out during the declaration of the union variable. The initialization value must be of the same data type as the member. Again referring to Example 27, a declaration statement with initialization will appear as follows.
```
    union test var={65};
```
Here, the value used to initialize the member 'i' is of the same data type as that of 'i' in the previous case. But in this example, if the initialization value is a float data type, then the initialization will not be valid because the member 'i' is

an integer data type. Therefore, the following construct will be wrong and invalid with reference to Example 27.
```
    union test var={45.62};
```
A union is also employed as an important convenience for the programmer. For example, it is often useful to name a single cell to hold a type-independent value, say, one returned by any of the several functions or one returned by a macro whose arguments may have different types.

14.3.3 Structure versus Union

Memory allocation The amount of memory required to store a structure is the sum of the size of all the members in addition to the slack bytes or padding bytes that may be provided by the compiler. On the other hand, in case of a union, the amount of the memory required is same as that of the largest member. This can be proved by the following program.

```
#include <stdio.h>
#include <stdlib.h>
#include <string.h>
struct S
{
  int i;
  char ch;
  double d;
};
union U
{
  int i;
  char ch;
  double d;
};
int main()
{
printf("\n Size of the structure is %d", sizeof\
        (struct S));
printf("\n Size of the union is %d", sizeof(union U));
return 0;
}
```
Output
```
    Size of the structure is 16
    Size of the union is 8
```
Member access While all structure members can be accessed at any point of time, only one member of a union can be accessed at any given time. Because at a particular moment of time, only one union member will have a meaningful value. The other members have garbage values. It is the responsibility of the programmer to keep track of the active member. Consider the following program.

```
#include <stdio.h>
#include <stdlib.h>
#include <string.h>
struct S
```

```
{
    int i;
    char ch;
    double d;
};
union U
{
    int i;
    char ch;
    double d;
};
int main()
{
    struct S a={10,'A',3.1415};
    union U b={10};
    printf("\n a.i=%d a.ch=%c a.d=%lf",a.i,a.ch,a.d);
    printf("\n b.i=%d b.ch=%c b.d=%lf",b.i,b.ch,b.d);
    b.ch='B';
    printf("\n b.i=%d b.ch=%c b.d=%lf",b.i,b.ch,b.d);
    b.d=5.12345;
    printf("\n b.i=%d b.ch=%c b.d=%lf",b.i,b.ch,b.d);
    return 0;
}
```
Output
```
a.i=10 a.ch=A a.d=3.141500
b.i=10 b.ch=
b.d=0.000000
b.i=66 b.ch=B b.d=0.000000
b.i=-1388133430 b.ch=⊥ b.d=5.123450
```
Careful study reveals the aforesaid point.

Identifying active members   There is no way to find which of the members is active at any instant of time. The program must keep track of active members explicitly.

Do's and don'ts for unions

It is important to remember which union member is being used. If the user fills in a member of one type and then tries to use a different type, the results can be unpredictable. The following operations on union variables are valid.

- A union variable can be assigned to another union variable.
- A union variable can be passed to a function as a parameter.
- The address of a union variable can be extracted by using & operator.
- A function can accept and return a union or a pointer to a union.
- Do not try to initialize more than the one union member.
- Do not forget that the size of a union is equal to its largest member.
- Do not perform arithmetical or logical operations on union variables.

Note

- At any given time, only one member of the union may actually reside in the storage.
- In a union, the amount of memory required is same as that of the largest member.
- It is important to remember which union member is being used. If the user fills in a member of one type and then tries to use a different type, the results can be unpredictable.
- The following operations on union variables are valid:
  - A union variable can be assigned to another union variable.
  - A union variable can be passed to a function as a parameter.
  - The address of a union variable can be extracted by using & operator.
  - A function can accept and return a union or a pointer to a union.
- No attempt should be made to initialize more than one union member.
- Performing arithmetical or logical operations on union variables is not allowed.

14.4 ENUMERATION TYPES

Enumeration data types are data items whose values may be any member of a symbolically declared set of values. The symbolically declared members are integer constants. The keyword enum is used to declare an enumeration type. The general construct used to declare an enumeration type is

```
enum tag_name{member1, member2,…, memberN}
variable1,...,variableX;
```

In this declaration, either tag_name or variable name may be omitted or both may be present. But, at least one of them must exist in this declaration construct.

The enum tag_name specifies the user-defined type. The members are integer constants. By default, the first member, that is, member1, is given the value 0. The second member, member2, is given the value 1. Members within the braces may be initialized, in which case, the next member is given a value which is one more than the preceding member. So, each member is given the value of the previous member plus 1.

The general form of the construct for declaring variables of enum type separately is

```
enum tag_name variable1,...,variableX;
```

The variables can take on as values only the members in the member list. Therefore,

```
variable1 = member2;
```

assigns the value represented by member2 to variable1. A typical declaration would be

```
enum days {Mon, Tues, Wed, Thurs, Fri, Sat, Sun};
```

The above declaration means that the values 'Mon,...,Sun' may be assigned to a variable of type enum days. The actual values are 0,...,6 in this example and it is these values that must be associated with any input or output operations. The following example illustrates these features.

EXAMPLE
---

28. Write a program to illustrate the assignment of default values to the members of data type enum.

```
#include <stdio.h>
enum days{Mon, Tues, Wed, Thurs, Fri, Sat, Sun };
int main()
{
  enum days start, end;
  start= Tues;             /* means start=1 */
  end= Sat;                /* means end=5  */
  printf("\n start = %d, end = %d", start,end);
  start= 64;
  printf("\n start now is equal to %d", start);
  return 0;
}
```

Output

```
start = 1, end = 5
start now is equal to 64
```

It will be noticed that it is possible to assign a normal integer to an enum data type and no verification is carried out to find that an integer assigned to an enum data type is within range.

It is possible to associate numbers other than the sequence starting at zero with the names in the enum data type by including a specific initialization in the variable name list. This also affects the values associated with all the following variable names. For example, consider the following declaration construct.

```
enum coins{ p1=1, p2, p5=5, p10=10, p20=20, p50=50 };
```

Here, all the variables except p2 are initialized. Since p2 is next to p1, it will be assigned a value 2. Similar examples showing how the members in a enum data type are initialized are given below.

EXAMPLE
---

29. Illustrations of initialization of members in enum data type
    (a) enum fruit {mango=10, orange, apple=6, pear}fru;

    Here, since mango is initialized to 10, orange has a value of 11. For the same reasons, because apple is assigned a value of 6, pear has a value of 7. It may be observed that initialization of multiple values are allowed, but the member names must themselves be unique.

    (b) enum veg{tomato=15, beans=15, onions=15} veget1,veget2;

    Here, all the members are initialized with a value.

    (c) enum {teak,pine}tree;

    In this case, since no tag name has been specified, no other variable of type enum {teak,pine} can be declared.

    (d) enum veg{tomato,beans,onions}veg;

    The above example shows that a tag name can be reused as a variable name or as an enumerator. This is because the tag names have their own name space. Such usage, though valid, is not good programming practice.

    Few programmers use enum data types. The same effects can be achieved by use of #define although the scoping rules are different. The enum data types are rarely used in practice.

14.5 BITFIELDS

There are two ways to manipulate bits in C. One of the ways consists of using bitwise operators. The other way consists of using bitfields in which the definition and the access method are based on structure. The general format for declaring bitfields using a structure is given as follows.

```
struct bitfield_tag
  {
    unsigned int member1: bit_width1;
    unsigned int member2: bit_width2;
       .
       .
    unsigned int memberN: bit_widthN;
  };
```

In this construct, the declaration of variable name is optional. The construct for individually declaring the variables to this structure is given by

```
struct bitfield_tag variable_name;
```

Each bitfield, for example, 'unsigned int member1: bit_width1', is an integer that has a specified bit width. By this technique, the exact number of bits required by the bitfield is specified. This way a whole word is not required to hold a field. This helps in packing a number of bitfields in one word. The savings made possible by using bits within a word rather than whole words can be considerable. This idea directly motivates the concept of packed fields of bits and operations on individual bits. Consider the following example.

```
struct test
{
  unsigned tx : 2;
  unsigned rx: 2;
  unsigned chk_sum : 3;
  unsigned p : 1;
} status_byte;
```

This construct declares a structure that has a variable name, status_byte, containing four unsigned bitfields. The number following the colon is the field width. Field variables may be assigned values. However, the value assigned to a field must not be greater than its maximum storable value. Individual fields are referenced as though they are structure members. The assignment

```
chk_sum = 6;
```

sets the bits in the field `chk_sum` as 110. The signed or unsigned specification makes for portability; this is important because bitfields are extremely implementation-dependent. For example, C does not specify whether fields must be stored left to right within a word, or vice versa. Some compilers may not allow fields to cross a word boundary. Unnamed fields may be used as fillers. In declaring the following structure, a two-bit gap is forced between the fields `tx` and `rx`.

```
struct
{
  unsigned tx : 2;
         : 2;
  unsigned rx : 4;
}status;
```

The unnamed field of width 2 will cause the next field to begin in the following word instead of at the boundary of the last field. It should be noted that a field in a word has no address. Therefore, it is wrong to try and use the operator '&' with bitfields.

The use of bitfields may save some memory as against storing variables whose values are only 1or 0 in characters, but it should be remembered that extra instructions will be required to perform the necessary packing and unpacking. Bitfields are very rarely used in practice.

Here is an example of assigning a byte to memory and then examining each bit. The bitfields are used in a structure, and the structure is used in a union.

```
#include <stdio.h>
#include <stdlib.h>
struct cbits {
  unsigned b1 : 1;
  unsigned b2 : 1;
  unsigned b3 : 1;
  unsigned b4 : 1;
  unsigned b5 : 1;
  unsigned b6 : 1;
  unsigned b7 : 1;
  unsigned b8 : 1;
};
union U {
  char c;
  struct cbits cb;
};
```

```
int main()
{
  union U look;
  /* Assign a character to memory */
  look.c = 'A';
  /* Look at each bit */
  printf( "\nBIT 1 = %d\n", look.cb.b1 );
  printf( "BIT 2 = %d\n", look.cb.b2 );
  printf( "BIT 3 = %d\n", look.cb.b3 );
  printf( "BIT 4 = %d\n", look.cb.b4 );
  printf( "BIT 5 = %d\n", look.cb.b5 );
  printf( "BIT 6 = %d\n", look.cb.b6 );
  printf( "BIT 7 = %d\n", look.cb.b7 );
  printf( "BIT 8 = %d\n\n", look.cb.b8 );
  return 0;
}
```

This program returns the bits (in terms of unsigned `int`s 0 or 1) for the character A stored in memory at the address of character variable named `c`. The output looks like the following.

```
BIT 1 = 0
BIT 2 = 1
BIT 3 = 0
BIT 4 = 0
BIT 5 = 0
BIT 6 = 0
BIT 7 = 0
BIT 8 = 1
```

The output makes sense because 01000001 (binary) = 65 (decimal) = 101 (octal) = 41 (hexadecimal) which maps to an A in the ASCII character set. If one wants to do this with an integer, the size using the function `sizeof(int)` has to be first determined, then a structure is created with eight bit fields for each byte counted by `sizeof(int)`.

Note

- The members in an enumerator are integer constants.
- By default, the first member of a union is given the value 0.
- With reference to bitfields, it should be noted that a field in a word has no address.

SUMMARY

A structure is a collection of variables under a single name. These variables can be of different types, and each has a name that is used to select it from the structure. There can be structures within structures, which is known as nesting of structures. Arrays of structures can be formed and initialized as required. Pointers may also be used with structures. Structures may be passed as function arguments and they may also be returned by functions.

A union is a structure, all of whose members share the same storage. The amount of storage allocated to a union is sufficient to hold its largest member. Enumeration data types are data items whose values may be any member of a symbolically declared set of values. Bitfields are identifiers whose bit-width can be specified and used to form packed words containing different fields.

KEY TERMS

Accessing a structure member   It refers to the act of handling any member of a structure for the purpose of assigning a value or using the member in any expression.

Arrays of structures   It refers to that "structure variable" which is an array of objects, each of which contains the member elements declared within the structure construct.

Initialization of structure   It refers to assigning values to members of an instance variable.

Instance variable   It is one of the named pieces of data that make up a structure.

Non-homogeneous data   It includes data of different types such as integer, float, character, etc.

Structure   It is a collection of data grouped together and treated as a single object.

Type template   It is a document or file having a preset format, used as a starting point for a particular application so that the format does not have to be recreated each time it is used.

FREQUENTLY ASKED QUESTIONS

1. What is the difference between structure and union?

Memory allocation The amount of memory required to store a structure is greater or equal to the sum of the size of all the members in addition to the slack bytes or padding bytes that may be provided by the compiler. On the other hand, in case of a union, the amount of the memory required is same as that of the largest member.

Member access While all structure members can be accessed at any point of time, only one member of a union can be accessed at any given time. Because at a particular moment of time, only one union member will have a meaningful value. The other members have garbage values.

Identifying active members There is no way to find which of the members is active at any moment of time. The program must keep track of active members explicitly.

2. Why can't structures be compared?

There can be unused padding bytes with structures as needed by alignment requirements for a platform and how they are filled is not defined by the standard. Hence, a byte by byte comparison will also fail. This is because the comparison might stumble on random bits present in unused "holes" in the structure as padding is used to keep the alignment of the later fields correct. So, a `memcmp()` of the two structure will almost never work.

3. How can two structures be compared?

One way to compare two structures is comparing the individual fields in the structure.

4. Why do structures get padded?

Almost all modern processors support byte addressing, i.e. an address is the address of a byte. However, there is often a constraint that larger data items (integers and floating-point numbers) should start at locations whose address is a multiple of the size of the data item. This constraint called, an alignment constraint, much simplifies the handling of such data items. Structure padding occurs because the members of the structure must appear at the correct byte boundary. This enables the CPU to access the members faster. If they are not aligned to word boundaries, then accessing them might take up more time. So the padding results in faster access.

Additionally, the size of the structure must be such that in an array of the structures all the structures are correctly aligned in memory, so there may be padding bytes (also known as slack bytes) at the end of the structure too.

5. How can the effect of padding be minimized?

Structure padding definitely introduces unused holes. There is no standard method to control the padding of structure. One suggested way may be to arrange the members in the order of their largest to the smallest sizes.

6. While compiling a program the following error message "Floating point formats not linked is obtained". What is wrong with the program?

When parsing the source file, if the compiler encounters a reference to the address of a float, it sets a flag to have the linker link in the floating point emulator. A floating point emulator is used to manipulate floating point numbers in run time of library functions like `scanf()` and `atof()` etc.

There are some cases in which the reference to the float does not necessitate the compiler to involve the emulator. The most common case is the one which uses `scanf()` to read a float in an array of structures and does not call any other functions related with floating point manipulation. In such cases the run time error might be caused by giving the message "`Floating point formats not linked`".

The solution of this problem is that the emulator will be used in such a fashion that the compiler can accurately determine when to link in the emulator. To force the floating point emulator to be linked into an application, just include the following functions in your program.

```
void FloatLink()
{
  float a = 0 , *b = &a;
  a = *b;
}
```
Or
```
static void forcefloat (float *p)
{
  float f=*p;
  forcefloat(&f);
}
```

There is no need to call these functions; but it is necessary to include it anywhere in the program.

Another solution is to include the following statements at the beginning of the program.

```
#include <math.h>

double dummy = sin(0.0);
```

This code forces the compiler to load the floating-point version of `scanf()`.

EXERCISES

1. What is the difference between a structure and a union?

2. What is a member of a structure?

3. How is a structure different from an array?

4. What are member, tag, and variable name in a structure and what purpose do they serve?

5. What keyword is used in C to create a structure?

6. What is the difference between a structure tag and a structure instance?

7. What does the following code fragment do?

```
struct address {
    char name[31];
    char add1[31];
    char add2[31];
    char city[11];
    char state[3];
    char zip[11];
} myaddress = { "Barun Dasgupta",
        "Q_Software",
        "P.O. Box 1213",
        "Kolkata", "WB", "700 015"};
```

8. Assume that you have declared an array of structures and that `ptr` is a pointer to the first array element (that is, the first structure in the array). How would you change `ptr` to point to the second array element?

9. Write a code that defines a structure named time, which contains three `int` members.

10. Write a code that performs two tasks: defines a structure named `data` that contains one `int` type member and two `float` type members, and declare an instance of type `data` named `info`.

11. Continuing with Exercise 10, how would you assign the value `100` to the integer member of the structure `info`?

12. Write a code that declares and initializes a pointer to `info`.

13. Continuing with Exercise 12, show two ways of using pointer notation to assign the value `5.5` to the first float member of `info`.

14. Define a structure type named `data` that can hold a single string of up to 20 characters.

15. Create a structure containing five strings: `address1`, `address2`, `city`, `state`, and `zip`. Create a `typedef` called `RECORD` that can be used to create instances of this structure.

16. Using the `typedef` from Exercise 15, allocate and initialize an element called `myaddress`.

17. What is wrong with the following code?

```
struct {
    char zodiac_sign[21];
    int month;
} sign = "Leo", 8;
```

18. What is wrong with the following code?

```
/* setting up a union */
union data{
    char a_word[4];
    long a_number;
}generic_variable = {"WOW", 1000};
```

19. What will be the output of the following program?

```
struct {
    int i;
    float f;
}var;
int main()
{
    var.i=5;
    var.f=9.76723;
    printf("%d %.2f",var.i,var.f);
    return(0);
}
```

(a) Compile-time error

(b) 5 9.76723

(c) 5 9.76

(d) 5 9.77

20. What will be the output of the following program?

```
struct {
    int i;
    float f;
};
int main()
{
    int i=5;
    float f=9.76723;
    printf("%d %.2f",i,f);
    return(0);
}
```

(a) Compile-time error

(b) 5 9.76723

(c) 5 9.76

(d) 5 9.77

21. What will be the output of the following program?

```
struct values {
    int i;
    float f;
};
```

```
int main()
{
    struct values var={555,67.05501};
    printf("%2d %.2f",var.i,var.f);
    return(0);
}
```

(a) Compile-time error

(b) 55 67.05

(c) 555 67.06

(d) 555 67.05

22. What will be the output of the following program?

```
typedef struct {
    int i;
    float f;
    }values;
int main()
{
    static values var={555,67.05501};
    printf("%2d %.2f",var.i,var.f);
    return(0);
}
```

(a) Compile-time error

(b) 55 67.05

(c) 555 67.06

(d) 555 67.05

23. What will be the output of the following program?

```
struct my_struct {
    int i=7;
    float f=999.99;
    }var;
int main()
{
    var.i=5;
    printf("%d %.2f",var.i,var.f);
    return(0);
}
```

(a) Compile-time error

(b) 7 999.99

(c) 5 999.99

(d) None of these

24. What will be the output of the following program?

```
struct first {
    int a;
```

```
    float b;
    }s1={32760,12345.12345};
typedef struct {
    char a;
    int b;
    }second;
struct my_struct {
    float a;
    unsigned int b;
    };
typedef struct my_struct third;
int main()
{
    static second s2={'A',--4};
    third s3;
    s3.a=~(s1.a-32760);
    s3.b=-++s2.b;
    printf("%d%.2f\n%c%d\n%.\
        2f %u",(s1.a)--,\
        s1.b+0.005,s2.a+32,s2.b,\
        ++(s3.a),--s3.b);
    return(0);
}
```

(a) Compile-time error

(b) 32760 12345.12

A 4

1 -5

(c) 32760 12345.13

a -5

0.00 65531

(d) 32760 12345.13

a 5

0.00 65530

25. What will be the output of the following program?

```
struct {
    int i,val[25];
    }var={1,2,3,4,5,6,7,8,9};
        *vptr=&var;
int main()
{
    printf("%d %d %d\n",var.i,);\
            (vptr->i,(*vptr).i);\
    printf("%d %d %d %d %d %d",\
```

```
        var.val[4],*(var.val+4),vptr->val[4],\
        *(vptr->val+4),(*vptr).val[4],\
          *((*vptr).val+4));
    return(0);
    }
```

(a) Compile-time error

(b) `1 1 1`

    `6 6 6 6 6 6`

(c) `1 1 1`

    `5 5 5 5 5 5`

(d) None of these

26. What will be the output of the following program?

```
typedef struct {
    int i;
    float f;
    }temp;
void alter(temp *ptr,int x,float y)
{
    ptr->i=x;
    ptr->f=y;
}
int main()
{
    temp a={111,777.007};
    printf("%d %.2f\n",a.i,a.f);
    alter(&a,222,666.006);
    printf("%d %.2f",a.i,a.f);
    return(0);
}
```

(a) Compile-time error

(b) `111 777.007`

    `222 666.006`

(c) `111 777.01`

    `222 666.01`

(d) None of these

27. What will be the output of the following program?

```
union A {
    char ch;
    int i;
    float f;
    }tempA;
int main()
{
    tempA.ch='A';
    tempA.i=777;
    tempA.f=12345.12345;
    printf("%d",tempA.i);
    return(0);
}
```

(a) Compile-time error

(b) `12345`

(c) `Erroneous output`

(d) `777`

28. Write a program using enumerated types which when given today's date will print out tomorrow's date in the form 31st January.

29. Write a simple database program that will store a person's details such as age, date of birth, and address.

PROJECT QUESTIONS

1. Write a menu-based program in C that uses a set of functions to perform the following operations:

   (a) reading a complex number

   (b) writing a complex number

   (c) addition of two complex numbers

   (d) subtraction of two complex numbers

   (e) multiplication of two complex numbers

   Represent the complex number using a structure.

2. Declare a structure to store the following information of an employee:

   - Employee code
   - Employee name
   - Salary

   - Department number
   - Date of joining (it is itself a structure consisting of day, month, and year)

3. Write a C program to store the data of 'n' employees where n is given by the user (Use dynamic memory allocation). Include a menu that will allow user to select any of the following features:

   (a) Use a function to display the employee information while getting the maximum and minimum salary.

   (b) Use a function to display the employee records in ascending order according to their salary.

   (c) Use a function to display the employee records in ascending order according to their date of joining.

   (d) Use a function to display the department wise employe records.

Files in C

LEARNING OBJECTIVES

After studying this chapter, the readers will be able to

- analyse the concept of streams used in the C file system
- discuss text and binary files
- process text files as well as binary files using standard library functions
- explain the sequential and random access of data stored

- in a disk file using proper standard library functions
- discuss advanced file management system and low-level input and output

15.1 INTRODUCTION

A file is a repository of data that is stored in a permanent storage media, mainly in secondary memory. So far, data was entered into the programs through the computer's keyboard. This is somewhat laborious if there is a lot of data to process. The solution is to combine all the input data into a file and let the C program read the information from the file when it is required. Frequently, files are used for storing information that can be processed by the programs. Files are not only used for storing data, programs are also stored in files. The editor, which is used to write or edit programs and save, simply manipulates files for the programmer. The UNIX commands `cat`, `cp`, and `cmp` are all programs which process the files.

In order to use files one has to learn about *file I/O*, i.e., how to write information to a file, and how to read information from a file. It will be seen that file I/O is almost identical

to the terminal I/O that has been used so far. The primary difference between manipulating files and terminal I/O is that the programs must specify which files are to be used because there are many files on the disk. Specifying the file to use is referred to as *opening* the file. When one opens a file, what is to be done with the file must also be mentioned, i.e., read from the file, write to the file, or both.

A very important concept in C is the *stream*. The stream is a common, logical interface to the various devices that comprise the computer. In its most common form, a stream is a logical interface to a file. As defined by C, the term 'file' can refer to a disk file, the screen, the keyboard, a port, a file on tape, and so on. Although files differ in form and capabilities, all streams are the same. The stream provides a consistent interface to the programmer. Stream I/O uses some temporary storage area, called buffer, for reading from or writing data to a file. This is illustrated in Fig. 15.1.

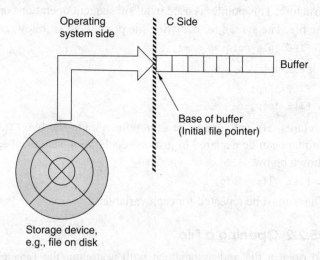

Operating
system side

C Side

Buffer

Base of buffer
(Initial file pointer)

Storage device,
e.g., file on disk

Fig. 15.1   Stream I/O model

The figure models an efficient I/O. When a stream linked to a disk file is created, a buffer is automatically created and associated with the stream. A buffer is a block of memory used for temporary storage of data being written to and read from the file. Buffers are needed because disk drives are block-oriented devices. This means that they operate most efficiently when data is read and written in blocks of a certain size. The size of the ideal block differs, depending on the specific hardware in use. It is typically of the order of a few hundred to a thousand bytes. However, it is not necessary to be concerned about the exact block size.

The buffer associated with a file stream serves as an interface between the stream (which is character-oriented) and the disk hardware (which is block-oriented). As the program writes data to the stream, the data is saved in the buffer until it is full, and then the entire contents of the buffer are written as a block to the disk. A similar process takes place when reading data from a disk file. The creation and operation of the buffer are handled by the operating system and are entirely automatic; the programmer does not have to be concerned with them. C does offer some functions for buffer manipulation. In practical terms, this buffer operation means that during program execution, data that the program wrote to the disk might still be in the buffer, and not on the disk. If the program hangs up, because of power failure, or in case of some other problem, the data that is still in the buffer might be lost, and the user will not know what is contained in the disk file. This is because data resides in the buffer until the buffer is flushed or written out into file. Any abnormal exit of code may cause problems.

A stream is linked to a file while using an open operation. A stream is disassociated from a file while using a close operation. The current location, also referred to as the current position, is the location in a file where the next file access will occur.

There are two types of streams—*text* and *binary*. A text file can be thought of as a stream of characters that can be processed sequentially. It can only be processed (logically) in the forward direction. For this reason, a text file is usually opened for only one kind of operation, that is, reading or writing or appending, at any given time. Similarly, since text files only process characters, they can only read or write one character at a time. Functions are provided that deal with lines of text, but these still essentially process one character at a time.

As text streams are associated with text files, they may contain a sequence of lines. Each line contains zero or more characters and ends with one or more characters that specify the end of the line. The maximum number of characters in each line is limited to 255 characters. It is important to remember that a 'line' is not a C string; there is no terminating NUL character ('\0'). When a text-mode stream is used, translation occurs between C's new-line character (\n) and whatever character(s) the operating system uses to mark end-of-line on disk files. On DOS systems, it is a carriage-return line feed (CR-LF) combination. When data is written to a text-mode file, each '\n' is translated to a CR-LF; when data is read from a disk file, each CR-LF is translated to a '\n'. On UNIX systems, no translation is done; new-line characters remain unchanged.

When text data files are used, there are two representations of data—*internal* and *external*. For example, a value of type int will usually be represented internally as two- or four-bytes (16- or 32-bit) of memory. Externally, though, that integer will be represented as a string of characters representing its decimal or hexadecimal value. Conversion between the internal and external representations is very easy. To convert from the internal representation to the external, printf or fprintf is used in almost all cases. For example, to convert an int, %d or %i format might be used. To convert from the external representation to the internal, scanf or fscanf can be used, or the characters are read and then functions such as atoi, strtol, or sscanf are used.

Binary file is a collection of bytes. In C, a byte and a character are equivalent. Hence, a binary file is also referred to as a character stream, but there are two essential differences.

First, the data that is written into and read from remain unchanged, with no separation between lines and no use of end-of-line characters. The NULL and end-of-line characters have no special significance and are treated like any other byte of data.

Second, the interpretation of the file is left to the programmer. C places no construct on the file, and it may be read from, or written to, in any manner chosen by the programmer.

In C, processing a file using random access techniques involves moving the current file position to an appropriate place in the file before reading or writing data. This indicates a second characteristic of binary files—they are generally processed using read and write operations simultaneously. For example, a database file will be created and processed as a binary file. A record update operation will involve locating the appropriate record, reading the record into memory, modifying it in some way, and finally writing the record back to disk at its appropriate location in the file. These kinds of operations are common to many binary files, but are rarely found in applications that process text files.

Some file input/output functions are restricted to one file mode, whereas other functions can use either mode.

Note

- When one opens a file, the operation that has to be carried on the file must also be specified, i.e., read from the file, write to the file, or both.
- C treats a disk file like a stream which can be opened either in text or in binary mode.
- The maximum number of characters in each line is limited to 255 characters.
- A 'line' of a text stream is not a C string; thus there is no terminating NULL character ('\0').
- In a binary file, the NULL and end-of-line characters have no special significance and are treated like any other byte of data.
- C places no construct on the binary file, and it may be read from, or written to, in any manner chosen by the programmer.

15.2 USING FILES IN C

To use a file, four essential actions should to be carried out. These are as follows:

- Declare a `file` pointer variable.
- Open a file using the `fopen()` function.
- Process the file using suitable functions.
- Close the file using the `fclose()` function.

For clarity, the above order is not maintained.

15.2.1 Declaration of File Pointer

Because a number of different files may be used in a program, when reading or writing, the type of file that is to be used must be specified. This is accomplished by using a variable called a file pointer, a pointer variable that points to a structure FILE. FILE is a structure declared in stdio.h. The members of the FILE structure are used by the program in various file access operations, but programmers do not need to be concerned about them. However, for each file that is to be opened, a pointer to type FILE must be declared.

When the function `fopen()` is called, that function creates an instance of the FILE structure and returns a pointer to that

structure. This pointer is used in all subsequent operations on the file. The syntax for declaring file pointers is as follows:

```
FILE *file_pointer_name,…;
```

For example,

```
FILE *ifp;
FILE *ofp;
```

declares `ifp` and `ofp` to be FILE pointers. Or, the two FILE pointers can be declared in just one declaration statement as shown below.

```
FILE *ifp, *ofp;
```

The `*` must be repeated for each variable.

15.2.2 Opening a File

To open a file and associate it with a stream, the `fopen()` function is used. Its prototype is as follows:

```
FILE *fopen(const char *fname, const char *mode);
```

File-handling functions are prototyped in <stdio.h>, which also includes other needed declarations. Naturally, this header must be included in all the programs that work with files. The name of the file to be opened is pointed to by `fname`, which must be a valid name. The string pointed at for `mode` determines how the file may be accessed.

Every disk file must have a name, and filenames must be used when dealing with disk files. The rules for acceptable filenames differ from one operating system to another. In DOS, a complete filename consists of a name that has one to eight characters, optionally followed by a period and an extension that has from one to three characters. In contrast, the Windows operating systems as well as most UNIX systems permit filenames with up to 256 characters.

Readers must be aware of the filename rules of the operating system they use. In Windows, for example, characters such as the following are not permitted: /, \, :, *, ?, ", <, >, and |.

A filename in a C program can also contain path information. The *path* specifies the drive and/or directory (or folder) where the file is located. If a filename is specified without a path, it will be assumed that the file is located wherever the operating system currently designates as the default. It is good programming practice to always specify path information as part of the filename. On PCs, the backslash character (\ ) is used to separate directory names in a path. For example, in DOS and Windows, the name

```
c:\examdata\marks.txt
```

refers to a file named `marks.txt` in the directory \examdata on drive C. It is to be remembered that the backslash character has a special meaning in C with respect to escape sequence when it is in a string. To represent the backslash character itself, one must precede it with another backslash. Thus, in a C program, the filename would be represented as follows.

```
"c:\\examdata\\list.txt";
```

However, if the filename is entered by the user through the keyboard, a single backslash has to be entered. Not all systems use the backslash as the directory separator. For example,

```
UNIX uses the forward slash (/).
```

File modes—What sort of open

Before a file can be used for reading or writing, it must be opened. This is done through the `fopen()` function. `fopen()` takes two string arguments. The first of these is the filename; the second is an option that conveys to C what processing is to be done with the file: read it, write to it, append to it, etc. Table 15.1 lists the options available with `fopen()`.

Table 15.1 File opening modes

Mode	Meaning
r	Open a text file for reading
w	Create a text file for writing
a	Append to a text file
rb	Open a binary file for reading
wb	Open a binary file for writing
ab	Append to a binary file
r+	Open a text file for read/write
w+	Create a text file for read/write
a+	Append or create a text file for read/write
r+b	Open a binary file for read/write
w+b	Create a binary file for read/write
a+b	Append a binary file for read/write

The following statements are used to create a text file with the name `data.dat` under current directory. It is opened in `w` mode as data is to be written into the file `data.dat`.

```
FILE *fp;
fp = fopen("data.dat","w");
```

`fopen()` requires two parameters—both are character strings. Either parameter could be a string variable. The following is an example where a file pointer " fp" is declared, the file name, which is declared to contain a maximum of 80 characters, is obtained from the keyboard and then the file is opened in the "write" mode.

```
char filename[80];
FILE *fp;
printf("Enter the filename to be opened");
gets(filename);
fp = fopen(filename,"w");
```

Checking the result of fopen( )

The `fopen()` function returns a `FILE *`, which is a pointer to structure `FILE`, that can then be used to access the file. When the file cannot be opened due to reasons described below, `fopen()` will return `NULL`. The reasons include the following.

- Use of an invalid filename
- Attempt to open a file on a disk that is not ready; for example, the drive door is not closed or the disk is not formatted
- Attempt to open a file in a non-existent directory or on a non-existent disk drive
- Attempt to open a non-existent file in mode `r`

One may check to see whether `fopen()` succeeds or fails by writing the following set of statements.

```
fp = fopen("data.dat","r");

if(fp == NULL)
{
    printf("Can not open data.dat\n");
    exit(1);
}
```

Attempts to open the file named "data.dat" in read mode

Alternatively, the above segment of code can be written as follows.

```
FILE *fp;
if((fp = fopen("data.dat", "r")) ==NULL)
{
    printf("Can not open data.dat\n");
    exit(1);
}
```

Whenever `fopen()` is used in a program, it is recommended to test for the result of an `fopen()` and check whether it is `NULL` or not. There is no way to find exactly which error has occurred, but one can display an error message to the user and try to open the file again, or end the program.

15.2.3 Closing and Flushing Files

After completing the processing on the file, the file must be closed using the `fclose()`function. Its prototype is

```
int fclose(FILE *fp);
```

The argument `fp` is the `FILE` pointer associated with the stream; `fclose()` returns `0` on success or `-1` on error. When a program terminates (either by reaching the end of `main()` or by executing the `exit()` function), all streams are automatically flushed and closed. Generally, in a simple program, it is not necessary to close the file because the system closes all open files before returning to the operating system. It would be a good programming practice to close all files.

When a file is closed, the file's buffer is flushed or written to the file. All open streams except the standard ones (stdin, stdout, stdprn, stderr, and stdaux) can also be closed by using the fcloseall() function. Its prototype is int fcloseall(void);

The above function also flushes any stream buffers and returns the number of streams closed. A stream's buffers can be flushed without closing it by using the fflush() or flushall() library functions. Use fflush() when a file's buffer is to be written to disk while still using the file. Use flushall() to flush the buffers of all open streams. The prototypes of these two functions are:

```
int fflush(FILE *fp);

int flushall(void);
```

The argument fp is the FILE pointer returned by fopen() when the file was opened. If a file was opened for writing, fflush() writes its buffer to disk. If the file was opened for reading, the buffer is cleared. The function fflush() returns 0 on success or EOF if an error occurred. The function flushall() returns the number of open streams.

> **Note**
> - The type of file that is to be used must be specified using a variable called a file pointer.
> - The Windows operating systems as well as most UNIX systems permit file names with up to 256 characters.
> - A filename in a C program can also contain path information.
> - If a filename is entered by the user through the keyboard, a single backslash or front slash has to be entered depending upon the system as the directory separator.
> - fclose() returns 0 on success or -1 on error.
> - The operating system closes all open files when the program execution finishes and before returning to the operating system.

15.3 WORKING WITH TEXT FILES

C provides four functions that can be used to read text files from the disk. These are

- fscanf()
- fgets()
- fgetc()
- fread()

C provides four functions that can be used to write text files into the disk. These are

- fprintf()
- fputs()
- fputc()
- fwrite()

15.3.1 Character Input and Output

When used with disk files, the term *character I/O* refers to single characters as well as lines of characters. This is because a line is a sequence of zero or more characters terminated by the new-line character. Character I/O is used with text-mode files. The following sections describe character input/output functions for files with suitable examples.

putc() function

The library function putc() writes a single character to a specified stream. Its prototype in stdio.h appears as follows:

```
int putc(int ch, FILE *fp);
```

The argument ch is the character to be outputted. As with other character functions, it is formally considered to be of type int, but only the lower-order byte is used. The argument fp is the pointer associated with the file, which is the pointer returned by fopen() when the file is opened. The function putc() returns the character just written if successful or EOF if an error occurs. The symbolic constant EOF is defined in stdio.h, and it has the value –1.

Because no 'real' character has that numeric value, EOF can be used as an error indicator with text-mode files only.

The following program illustrates how to write a single character at a time into a text file.

```
#include <stdio.h>
int main()              Declaring pointer to FILE
{
  FILE *fp;
  char text[80];        File name
  int i, c;
  fp = fopen("abc.txt", "w");
  printf("\n ENTER TEXT");
  scanf("%[^\n]", text);      Write mode
  for(c = 1; c <= 10; c++)
  {
    for(i = 0; text[i]; i++)
    putc(text[i], fp);
    putc('\n', fp);
  }
  fclose(fp);
  return 0;
}
```

To append more lines to the file abc.txt, the statement in bold font has to be replaced with the statement fp = fopen("abc.txt", "a");

The operating system close all open files when the program execution finishes and before returning to the operating system.

fputs( ) function

To write a line of characters to a stream, the library function fputs() is used. This function works just like the string library function puts(). The only difference is that with fputs() one can specify the output stream. Also, fputs() does not add a new line to the end of the string; to include '\n', it must be explicitly specified. Its prototype in stdio.h is

```
char fputs(char *str, FILE *fp);
```

The argument str is a pointer to the null-terminated string to be written, and fp is the pointer to type FILE returned by fopen() when the file was opened. The string pointed to by str is written to the file, ignoring its terminating\0. The function fputs() returns a non-negative value if successful or EOF on error.

> **Note**
> - With disk files, the term *character I/O* refers to single characters as well as lines of characters.
> - The function putc() returns the character just written if successful or EOF if an error occurs.
> - The symbolic constant EOF is defined in stdio.h, and it has the value −1.
> - fputs() does not add a "new line" to the end of the string written on to a file.
> - The function fputs() returns a non-negative value if successful or EOF on error.

15.3.2 End of File (EOF)

When reading from a file, how can the program detect that it has reached the end of the file? One way is to have a special marker at the end of the file. For instance,

- A # character on its own could be the last line.
- DOS uses **Ctrl-z** as the special character that ends a file. (It also knows how many characters are there in the file.) The use of **Ctrl-z** is historical and most people would want to do away with it.
- In UNIX, **Ctrl-d** is used as the end-of-file character. Using a special character is not satisfactory. It means that a file that contains these characters as real text behaves abnormally.

Detecting the end of a file

Sometimes, it is not known exactly how long a file is, but it is still possible to read data from the file, starting at the beginning and proceeding to the end. There are two ways to detect end-of-file.

When reading from a text-mode file character by character, one can look for the end-of-file character. The symbolic constant EOF is defined in stdio.h as -1, a value never used by a 'real' character. When a character input function reads

EOF from a text-mode stream, it ensures that it has reached the end of the file. For example, one could write the following.

```
while((c = fgetc(fp)) != EOF)
```

The variable returned from the getc() function is a character, so we can use a char variable for this purpose. However, there is a problem that could develop here if an unsigned char is used. This is because C returns a -1 for an EOF which an unsigned char type variable is not capable of containing. An unsigned char type variable can only have the values of 0 to 255, so it will return a 255 for a −1. The program can never find the EOF and will therefore never terminate the loop. This is easy to prevent. Always use a char type variable in returning an EOF.

There are three character input functions: getc() and fgetc() for single characters, and fgets() for lines.

getc( ) and fgetc( ) functions

The functions getc() and fgetc() are identical and can be used interchangeably. They input a single character from the specified stream. The following is the prototype of getc() in stdio.h.

```
int getc(FILE *fp);
```

The argument fp is the pointer returned by fopen() when the file is opened. The function returns the character that was input or it returns EOF on error.

If getc() and fgetc() return a single character, why are they prototyped to return a type int? The reason is that when reading files, one needs to be able to read in the end-of-file marker, which on some systems is not a type char but a type int.

fgets( ) function

fgets() is a *line*-oriented function. The ANSI prototype is

```
char *fgets(char *str, int n, FILE *fp);
```

The function reads from the stream pointed to by fp and places the output into the character array pointed to by str. It will stop reading when any of the following conditions are true.

- It has read n - 1 bytes (one character is reserved for the null-terminator).
- It encounters a new-line character (a line-feed in the compiler is placed here).
- It reaches the end of file.
- A read error occurs.

fgets() automatically appends a null-terminator to the data read. fgetc() gives the user more control than fgets(), but reading a file byte-by-byte from disk is rather inefficient. These functions are illustrated in the following programs. The following program displays the contents of a file on screen.

EXAMPLES

1.
```c
#include <stdio.h>
int main()
{
    FILE *fopen(), *fp;

    int ch;
    fp = fopen("a.txt", "r");
    if(fp == NULL)
    {
        printf("Cannot open the file a.txt \n");
        exit(1);
    }
    ch = getc(fp);
    while(ch != EOF)
    {
        putchar(ch);
        ch = getc(fp);
    }
    fclose(fp);
    return 0;
}
```

Alternatively, one could prompt the user to enter the filename again, and try to open it again.

2.
```c
#include <stdio.h>
#include <string.h>
int main()
{
    FILE *fopen(), *fp;
    int ch;
    char fname[30];
    printf("\n Enter the filename \n");

    fflush(stdin);

    scanf("%[^\n]",fname);
    fp = fopen(fname, "r");
    while(fp ==NULL || strcmp(fname, " ")!= 0)
    {
        printf("Cannot open the file %s for reading \n",
            fname);
        printf("\n Enter the filename \n");
        fflush(stdin);
        scanf("%[^\n]",fname);
        fp = fopen(fname, "r");
    }
    ch = getc(fp);
    while(ch != EOF)
    {
        putchar(ch);
        ch = getc(fp);
    }
}
```

```
    fclose(fp);
    return 0;
}
```

In this example, filenames are taken from the user until a valid existing filename is entered or the space bar followed by the **<Enter>** key is pressed. The following program illustrates that reading a line at a time from a file can be performed using `fgets()`.

3.
```c
#include <stdio.h>
int main()
{
    FILE *fp;
    char word[60];
    char *c;
    fp = fopen("abc.txt","r");
    do {
        c = fgets(word, 60,fp);
        if(c != NULL)
        printf("%s", word);
    }
    while(c != NULL);
    fclose(fp);
    return 0;
}
```

4. Write a C program that counts the number of characters and number of lines in a file.

```c
#include <stdio.h>
int main()
{
    FILE *fopen(), *fp;
    int ch, nc, nlines;
    char fname[30];
    nlines = 0;
    nc = 0;
    printf("Enter filename:");
    fflush(stdin);
    scanf("%s", fname);
    fp = fopen(fname, "r");
    if(fp == NULL)
    {
        printf("Cannot open the file %s for reading \n",
            fname);
        exit(0);
    }
    ch = getc(fp);
    while(ch != EOF)
    {
        if(ch == '\n')
            nlines++;
        nc++;
        ch = getc(fp);
```

```c
  }
  fclose(fp);
  if(nc != 0)
  {
    printf("There are %d characters in %s \n", nc,
        filename);
    printf("There are %d lines \n", nlines);
  }
  else
    printf("File: %s is empty \n", filename);
  return 0;
}
```

5. Write a program to display the contents of a file, 10 lines at a time.

```c
#include <stdio.h>
int main()
{
  FILE *fopen(), *fp;
  int ch,  nline;
  char fname[40], ans[40];
  printf("Enter filename:");
  scanf("%s", fname);
  fp = fopen(fname, "r");
                        /* open for reading */
  if(fp == NULL)
            /* check whether file exists or not */
  {
    printf("Cannot open the file %s  \n", fname);
    exit(0);
  }
  nline = 1;
  ans[0] = '\0';
  ch = getc(fp);
                  /* Read 1st character if any */
  while(ch != EOF &&  (ans[0] != 'Q' || ans[0] != 'q'))
  {
    putchar(ch);          /* Display character */
    if(ch  ==  '\n')
      nline++;
    if(nline == 10)
    {
      nline = 1;
      printf("[Press Return to continue, q to quit]");
      fflush(stdin);
      scanf("%s", ans);
    }
    ch = getc(fp);
  }
  fclose(fp);
  return 0;
}
```

The above program pauses after displaying 10 lines until the user presses either Q or q to quit or return to display the next 10 lines. The above program does the same as the UNIX command 'more'.

6. Write a program to compare two files specified by the user, displaying a message indicating whether the files are identical or different.

```c
#include <stdio.h>
int main()
{
  FILE *fp1, *fp2;
  int ca, cb;
  char fname1[40], fname2[40];
  printf("Enter first filename:");
  fflush(stdin);
  gets(fname1);
  printf("Enter second filename:");
  fflush(stdin);
  gets(fname2);
  fp1 = fopen(fname1,  "r");
                  /* open first file for reading */
  fp2 = fopen(fname2,  "r");
                  /* open second file for reading */
  if(fp1 == NULL)      /* check does file exist */
  {
    printf("Cannot open the file %s for reading \n",
        fname1);
    exit(1);              /* terminate program */
  }
  else if(fp2 == NULL)
  {
    printf("Cannot open %s for reading \n", fname2);
    exit(1);              /* terminate program */
  }
  else      /* both files opened successfully  */
  {
    ca  =  getc(fp1);
    cb  =  getc(fp2);
    while(ca! = EOF && cb != EOF && ca == cb)
    {
      ca  =  getc(fp1);
      cb  =  getc(fp2);
    }
    if(ca !== cb)
      printf("Files are identical \n");
    else if(ca!=cb)
      printf("Files differ \n");
    fclose(fp1);
    fclose(fp2);
  }
  return 0;
}
```

7. Write a file copy program in C that copies a file into another.

```c
#include <stdio.h>
int main()
{
  FILE *fp1, *fp2;
  int ch;
  char fname1[30], fname2[30];
  printf("Enter source file:");
  fflush(stdin);
  scanf("%s", fname1);
  printf("Enter destination file:");
  fflush(stdin);
  scanf("%s", fname2);
  fp1 = fopen(fname1, "r");
                        /* open for reading */
  fp2 = fopen(fname2, "w");
                        /* open for writing */
  if(fp1 == NULL)
            /* check whether file exists or not */
  {
    printf("Cannot open the file %s for reading \n",
        fname1);
    exit(1);            /* terminate program */
  }
  else if(fp2 == NULL)
  {
    printf("Cannot open the file %s for writing \n",
        fname2);
    exit(1);            /* terminate program */
  }
  else    /* both files has been opened successfully */
  {
    ch = getc(fp1);        /* read from source */
    while(ch! = EOF)
    {
      putc(ch, fp2);   /* copy to destination */
      ch = getc(fp1);
    }
    fclose(fp1);          /* Now close the files */
    fclose(fp2);
    printf("Files successfully copied \n");
  }
  return 0;
}
```

8. Write a C program that accepts the names of two files. It should copy the first file into the second line by line. Use the fgets() and fputs() functions.

```c
#include <stdio.h>
#include <stdlib.h>
int main()
{
  FILE *fp1, *fp2;
```

```c
  char fname1[30], fname2[30], t[60];
  printf("Enter source file:");
  fflush(stdin);
  gets(fname1);
  printf("Enter destination file:");
  fflush(stdin);
  gets(fname2);
  if((fp1 = fopen(fname1, "r")) == NULL)
  printf("Unable to open %s for reading \n", fname1);
  else if((file_2 = fopen(fname2, "w")) == NULL)
  printf("Unable to open %s for writing \n", fname2);
  else
  {
    while((fgets(t, sizeof(t), fp1)) ! = NULL)
        fputs(t, fp2);
    fclose(fp1);
    fclose(fp2);
  }
  return 0;
}
```

The other two file-handling functions to be covered are fprintf() and fscanf(). These functions operate exactly like printf() and scanf() except that they work with files. Their prototypes are

```c
int fprintf(FILE *fp, const char *control-string,
        ...);
int fscanf(FILE *fp, const char *control-string
        ...);
```

Instead of directing their I/O operations to the console, these functions operate on the file specified by fp. Otherwise, their operations are the same as their console-based relatives. The advantage of fprintf() and fscanf() is that they make it very easy to write a wide variety of data to a file using a text format. The components of the control string are the same as for scanf(). Finally, the ellipses (...) indicate one or more additional arguments such as the addresses of the variables where inputs are to be assigned. The following program illustrates how the function fscanf() can be used to write into a text file.

```c
9. #include <stdio.h>
int main()
  {
    FILE *fp;
    if((fp = fopen("afile.txt", "w")) != NULL)
    {
      fprintf(fp, "%s", "Introduction\n");
      fprintf(fp, "%s", "To\n");
      fprintf(fp, "%s", "Computing\n");
      fclose(fp);
    }
    else
      printf("Unable to open the file for writing");
      return 0;
  }
```

A file named 'afile.txt' is created in the current directory, the content of which is as follows:

```
Introduction
To
Computing
```

The next program reads five integer values from the keyboard and stores them in the data file num.dat. In this program the user-defined character is used, as end-of-file marker instead of standard EOF.

```c
10. #include <stdio.h>
    int main()
    {
      FILE *fp;
      int n[5],i;
      if((fp = fopen("num.dat", "w")) != NULL)
        {
          printf("Enter 5 numbers, to be stored in
              num.dat...");
          for(i = 0; i < 5; i++)
            {
              scanf("%d", &n[i]);
              fprintf(fp, "%d\n", n[i]);
            }
          fprintf(fp,"%d",9999);
          fclose(ptr);
        }
      else
        printf("Unable to open num.dat ...\n");
        return 0;
    }
```

Output

```
Enter 5 numbers, to be stored in num.dat ... 1 2 3
4 5
```

The file num.dat now contains the numbers arranged in the following format.

```
1
2
3
4
5
9999
```

Here, 9999 is used as end-of-file marker. It is not a member of the data set. While reading data from 'num.dat', the data is read until 9999 is found. The following program describes the usage where the numbers stored in the file 'num.dat' are summed up and displayed. Here fscanf() has to be used to read data from the file.

——————————— **EXAMPLE** ———————————

```c
11. #include <stdio.h>
    int main()
    {
```

```c
      FILE *fp;
      int n,s=0;
      if((fp = fopen("num.dat", "r")) != NULL)
      {
        fscanf(fp, "%d\n", &n);
        while(n!=9999)
        {
          s+=n;
          fscanf(fp, "%d\n", &n);
        }
        printf("Sum is %d",s);
        fclose(fp);
      }
      else
        printf("Unable to open num.dat ... \n");
        return 0;
    }
```

Output

```
Sum is 15
```

fscanf() is a *field*-oriented function and is *inappropriate* for use in a robust, general-purpose text file reader. It has two major drawbacks.

- The programmer must know the exact data layout of the input file in advance and rewrite the function call for every different layout.

- It is difficult to read text strings that contain spaces because fscanf() sees space characters as field delimiters.

Now, one might think that calls to fprinf() and fscanf() differ significantly from calls to printf() and scanf(), and that these latter functions do not seem to require file pointers. As a matter of fact they do. The file pointer associated with printf() is a constant pointer named stdout defined in <stdio.h>. Similarly, scanf() has an associated constant pointer named stdin. scanf() reads from stdin and printf() writes to stdout. This can be verified by executing the following program.

——————————— **EXAMPLE** ———————————

```c
12. #include < stdio.h>
    int main()
    {
      int a, b;
      fprintf(stdout, "Enter two numbers separated by a
      space:");
      fscanf(stdin, "%d %d", &a, &b);
      fprintf(stdout, "Their sum is: %d.\n", a + b);
      return 0;
    }
```

There is a third constant file pointer defined as `stderr`. This is associated with the standard error file. `stderr` has the following use: in some systems such as MSDOS and UNIX, the output of the programs can be redirected to files by using the redirection operator. In Dos, for example, if `abc.exe` is an executable file that writes to the monitor, then its output can be redirected to a disk file `abc.out` by the command

```
abc>abc.out<CR>
```

Output that would normally appear on the monitor can thus be sent to the file `abc.out`. On the other hand, while redirecting output, one would not want any error messages such as 'Unable to open abc.dat for writing' to be redirected; one wants them to appear on the screen. Writing error messages to `stderr`

```
fprintf(stderr, "Unable to open newfile.dat for writing");
```

ensures that normal output will be redirected, but error messages will still appear on the screen.

All three are, in fact, objects of type *pointer to FILE,* and they may be used in any file-handling function in just the same way as a pointer returned by `fopen()`. In fact, the macro `putchar(c)` is really nothing more than

```
putc(c,stdout)
```

It is sometimes useful to initialize a pointer to FILE to point to one of the standard items, to provide a 'standard input as default' type of operation.

```
FILE *ifp = stdin;
```

is a typical definition.

15.3.3 Detecting the End of a File Using the feof() Function

To detect end-of-file, there is library function `feof()`, which can be used for both binary- and text-mode files.

```
int feof(FILE *fp);
```

The argument `fp` is the FILE pointer returned by `fopen()` when the file was opened. The function `feof()` returns 0, if the end-of-file has not been reached, or a non-zero value, if end-of-file has been reached. The following program demonstrates the use of `feof()`. The program reads the file one line at a time, displaying each line on `stdout`, until `feof()` detects end-of-file.

--- EXAMPLE ---

```
13. #include <stdlib.h>
    #include <stdio.h>
    #define SIZE 100
    int main()
    {
      char temp[SIZE];
      char fname[60];
```

```
  FILE *fp;
  printf("Enter name of filename:");
  fflush(stdin);
  scanf("%s", fname);
  if((fp = fopen(fname, "r")) == NULL)
  {
    fprintf(stderr, "Error in opening file");
    exit(1);
  }
  while(!feof(fp))
  {
    fgets(temp, SIZE, fp);
    printf("%s",temp);
  }
  fclose(fp);
  return 0;
}
```

Output

```
Enter name of filename:
first.c
#include <stdio.h>
int main()
{
  printf("C is Sea");
  return 0;
}
```

Note

- DOS uses Ctrl-z as the special character that ends a file.
- In UNIX, Ctrl-d is used as the end-of-file character.
- `fgets()` automatically appends a null-terminator to the data read.
- `fgetc()` gives more control than `fgets()`, but reading a file byte-by-byte from disk is rather inefficient.
- `fscanf()` is a field-oriented function and is inappropriate for use in a robust, general-purpose text file reader.

15.4 WORKING WITH BINARY FILES

The operations performed on binary files are similar to text files since both types of files can essentially be considered as streams of bytes. In fact, the same functions are used to access files in C. When a file is opened, it must be designated as text or binary and usually this is the only indication of the type of file being processed. To illustrate a binary file, consider the following program containing a function, `filecopy()`, that is passed the names of the source and destination files and then performs the copy operation just as the outlined steps.

If there is an error in opening either file, the function does not attempt the copy operation and returns -1 to the calling program. When the copy operation is complete, the program closes both files and returns 0. The steps for copying a binary file into another are as follows.

(i) Open the source file for reading in binary mode.

(ii) Open the destination file for writing in binary mode.

(iii) Read a character from the source file. Remember, when a file is first opened, the pointer is automatically at the start of the file, so there is no need to position the file pointer.

(iv) If the function feof() indicates that the end of the source file has been reached, then close both files and return to the calling program.

(v) If end-of-file has not been reached, write the character to the destination file, and then go to step (iii).

EXAMPLE

```
14. #include <stdio.h>
    int filecopy(char *, char *);
    int main()
    {
      char source[80], destination[80];
      printf("\nEnter source file:");
      fflush(stdin);
      gets(source);
      printf("\nEnter destination file:");
      fflush(stdin);
      gets(destination);
      if(filecopy(source, destination) == 0)
        puts("\n Successfully copied");
      else
        fprintf(stderr, "Error in copying...");
      return 0;
    }
    int filecopy(char *s, char *d)
    {
      FILE *ofp, *nfp;
      int ch;
                  /* Open the source file for reading
                               in binary mode. */
      if((ofp = fopen(s, "rb")) == NULL)
        return -1;
                  /* Open the destination file for
                          writing in binary mode. */
      if((nfp = fopen(d, "wb")) == NULL)
      {
        fclose(ofp);
        return -1;
      }
      while(1)
```

```
      {
        ch = fgetc(ofp);
        if(!feof(ofp))
          fputc(ch, nfp);
        else
          break;
      }
      fclose(nfp);
      fclose(ofp);
      return 0;
    }
```

Output

```
Enter source file: a.txt
Enter destination file: b.txt
Successfully copied
```

Note

- At the time of file opening, it must be designated as text or binary for indicating the type of file being processed.
- The operations performed on binary files are similar to text files.

15.5 DIRECT FILE INPUT AND OUTPUT

Direct I/O is used only with binary-mode files. With direct output, blocks of data are written from memory to disk. Direct input reverses the process. A block of data is read from a disk file into memory. For cxample, a single direct-output function call can write an entire array of type double to disk, and a single direct-input function call can read the entire array from disk back into memory. The C file system includes two important functions for direct I/O: fread() and fwrite(). These functions can read and write any type of data, using any kind of representation. Their prototypes are

```
size_t fread(void *buffer, size_t size, size_t
       num,FILE *fp);
size_t fwrite(void *buffer, size_t size, size_t num,
       FILE *fp);
```

The fread() function reads from the file associated with fp, num number of objects, each object size in bytes, into buffer pointed to by buffer. It returns the number of objects actually read. If this value is 0, no objects have been read, and either end-of-file has been encountered or an error has occurred. One can use feof() or ferror() to find out whether end of file has been detected or an error has occurred. Their prototypes are

```
int feof(FILE *fp);
int ferror(FILE *fp);
```

The feof() function returns non-zero, if the file associated with fp has reached the end of file, otherwise it returns 0. This function works for both binary files and text files. The ferror() function returns non-zero if the file associated with fp has experienced an error, otherwise it returns 0.

The fwrite() function is the opposite of fread(). It writes to file associated with fp, num number of objects, each object size in bytes, from the buffer pointed to by buffer. It returns the number of objects written. This value will be less than num only if an output error has occurred. To check for errors, fwrite() is usually programmed as follows:

```
if((fwrite(buffer, size, num, fp)) != num)
    fprintf(stderr, "Error writing to file.");
```

The following program describes the use of fread() and fwrite() functions. The program initializes an array. Then, the fwrite() function is used to save the array to disk. After that, the fread() function is used to read the data into a different array. Finally, it displays both the arrays on screen to show that they now hold the same data.

EXAMPLE

```
15. #include <stdlib.h>
    #include <stdio.h>
    #define SIZE 10
    int main()
    {
      int i, a[SIZE], b[SIZE];
      FILE *fp;
      for(i = 0; i < SIZE; i++)
        a[i] = 2 * i;
      if((fp = fopen("dfile.txt", "wb")) == NULL)
      {
        fprintf(stderr, "Error opening file.");
        exit(1);
      }
      if(fwrite(a, sizeof(int), SIZE, fp) != SIZE)
      {
        fprintf(stderr, "Error writing to file.");
        exit(1);
      }
      fclose(fp);
      if((fp = fopen("dfile.txt", "rb")) == NULL)
      {
        fprintf(stderr, "Error in opening file.");
        exit(1);
      }
      if(fread(b, sizeof(int), SIZE, fp) != SIZE)
      {
        fprintf(stderr, "Error in reading file.");
        exit(1);
      }
      fclose(fp);
```

```
      for(i = 0; i < SIZE; i++)
        printf("%d\t%d\n", a[i], b[i]);
      return 0;
    }
```

Output

```
0    0
2    2
4    4
6    6
8    8
10   10
12   12
14   14
16   16
18   18
```

15.5.1 Sequential Versus Random File Access

Every open file has an associated file position indicator, which describes where read and write operations take place in the file. The position is always specified in bytes from the beginning of the file. When a new file is opened, the position indicator is always at the beginning of the file, i.e., at position 0. Because the file is new and has a length of 0, there is no other location to indicate. When an existing file is opened, the position indicator is at the end of the file if the file was opened in the append mode, or at the beginning of the file if the file was opened in any other mode.

The file I/O functions covered earlier in this chapter make use of the position indicator, although the manipulations go on behind the scenes. Writing and reading operations occur at the location of the position indicator and update the position indicator as well. Thus, if one wishes to read all the data in a file sequentially or write data to a file sequentially, it is not necessary to be concerned about the position indicator because the stream I/O functions take care of it automatically.

When more control is required, the C library functions that help determine and change the value of the file position indicator, have to be used. By controlling the position indicator, random access of a file can be made possible. Here, random means that data can be read from, or written to, any position in a file without reading or writing all the preceding data. This will be covered in the later sections of the chapter.

> **Note**
> - Direct I/O is used only with binary-mode files.
> - fread() and fwrite() functions can read and write any type of data, using any kind of representation.
> - There are two types of file accessing method—: sequential and random.
> - Every open file has an associated file position indicator. The position is always specified in bytes from the beginning of the file.

15.6 FILES OF RECORDS

Most C program files may be binary files, which can logically be divided into fixed-length records. Each record will consist of data that conforms to a previously defined structure. In C, this structure can be formed using a *struct* data type. The records are written into disk sequentially. This happens because as each record is written to disk, the file position indicator is moved to the byte immediately after the last byte in the record just written. Binary files can be written sequentially to the disk or in a random access manner.

15.6.1 Working with Files of Records

Using `fscanf()` and `fprintf()` The following structure records the code, name, and price of an item. Using this structure, a file of records can be processed. Here, 0 is used as end-of-file marker (logically) to indicate there are no records in the file.

—————————— **EXAMPLE** ——————————

```c
16. #include <stdio.h>
    struct item
    {
      int itemcode;
      char name[30];
      double price;
    };
    void append();
    void modify();
    void dispall();
    void dele();
    int main()
    {
      int ch;
      struct item it;
      FILE *fp;
      fp=fopen("item.dat","w");
      if(fp==NULL)
      {
        printf("\n ERROR IN OPENING FILE...");
        exit(0);
      }
      printf("\n ENTER ITEM CODE:");
      scanf("%d",&it.itemcode);
      printf("\n ENTER ITEM NAME:");
      fflush(stdin);
      scanf("%[^\n]",it.name);
      printf("\n ENTER PRICE:");
      scanf("%lf",&it.price);
      fprintf(fp,"%d \t%s\t%lf\n",it.itemcode,
            it.name,it.price);
      fprintf(fp,"%d",0);
      fclose(fp);
      while(1)
      {
        printf("\n \t 1.APPEND RECORD");
        printf("\n \t 2.DISPLAY ALL RECORD");
        printf("\n \t 3.EDIT RECORD");
        printf("\n \t 4.DELETE RECORD");
        printf("\n \t 5.EXIT");
        printf("\n \t ENTER UR CHOICE:");
        scanf("%d",&ch);
        switch(ch)
        {
            case 1:append(); break;
            case 2:dispall();break;
            case 3:modify(); break;
            case 4:dele();   break;
            case 5:exit(0);
        }
      }
      return 0;
    }
    void append()
    {
      FILE *fp;
      struct item it;
      fp=fopen("item.dat","a");
      if(fp==NULL)
      {
        printf("\n ERROR IN OPENING FILE...");
        exit(0);
      }
      printf("\n ENTER ITEM CODE:");
      scanf("%d",&it.itemcode);
      printf("\n ENTER ITEM NAME:");
      fflush(stdin);
      scanf("%[^\n]",it.name);
      printf("\n ENTER PRICE:");
      scanf("%lf",&it.price);
      fprintf(fp,"%d \t%s\t%lf\n",it.itemcode,
                  it.name,it.price);
      fprintf(fp,"%d",0);
      fclose(fp);
    }
    void dispall()
    {
      FILE *fp;
      struct item it;
```

```
fp=fopen("item.dat","r");
if(fp==NULL)
{
  printf("\n ERROR IN OPENING FILE...");
  exit(0);
}
while(1)
{
  fscanf(fp, "%d",&it.itemcode);
  if(it.itemcode==0)
    break;
  fscanf(fp,"%s",it.name);
  fscanf(fp,"%lf",&it.price);
  printf("\n \t %d\t%s\t%lf",it.itemcode,
                  it.name,it.price);
}
  fclose(fp);
}
void modify()
{
  FILE *fp,*fptr;
  struct item it;
  int icd,found=0;
  fp=fopen("item.dat","r");
  if(fp==NULL)
  {
    printf("\n ERROR IN OPENING FILE...");
    exit(0);
  }
  fptr=fopen("temp.dat","w");
  if(fptr==NULL)
  {
    printf("\n ERROR IN OPENING FILE...");
    exit(0);
  }
  printf("\n ENTER THE ITEM CODE TO EDIT");
  scanf("%d",&icd);
  while(1)
  {
    fscanf(fp,"%d",&it.itemcode);
    if(it.itemcode==0)
      break;
    if(it.itemcode==icd)
    {
      found=1;
      fscanf(fp,"%s",it.name);
      fscanf(fp,"%lf",&it.price);
      printf("\n EXISTING RECORD IS...\n");
      printf("\n \t %d\t%s\t%lf",it.itemcode,
```

```
                  it.name,it.price);
      printf("\n ENTER NEW ITEM NAME:");
      fflush(stdin);
      scanf("%[^\n]",it.name);
      printf("\n ENTER NEW PRICE:");
      scanf("%lf",&it.price);
      fprintf(fptr,"%d \t%s\t%lf\n",
      it.itemcode,it.name,it.price);
    }
    else
    {
      fscanf(fp,"%s",it.name);
      fscanf(fp,"%lf",&it.price);
      fprintf(fptr,"%d \t%s\t%lf\n",
      it.itemcode,it.name,it.price);
    }
  }
  fprintf(fptr,"%d",0);
  fclose(fptr);
  fclose(fp);
  if(found==0)
    printf("\nRECORD NOT FOUND...");
  else
  {
    fp=fopen("item.dat","w");
    if(fp==NULL)
    {
      printf("\n ERROR IN OPENING FILE...");
      exit(0);
    }
    fptr=fopen("temp.dat","r");
    if(fptr==NULL)
    {
      printf("\n ERROR IN OPENING FILE...");
      exit(0);
    }
  while(1)
  {
    fscanf(fptr,"%d",&it.itemcode);
    if(it.itemcode==0)
    break;
    fscanf(fptr,"%s",it.name);
    fscanf(fptr,"%lf",&it.price);
    fprintf(fp,"%d \t%s\t%lf\n",it.itemcode,
                  it.name,it.price);
  }
  fprintf(fp,"%d",0);
  fclose(fptr);
  fclose(fp);
}
```

```
}
void dele()
{
  FILE *fp,*fptr;
  struct item it;
  int icd,found=0;
  fp=fopen("item.dat","r");
  if(fp==NULL)
  {
    printf("\n ERROR IN OPENING FILE...");
    exit(0);
  }
  fptr=fopen("temp.dat","w");
  if(fptr==NULL)
  {
    printf("\n ERROR IN OPENING FILE...");
    exit(0);
  }
  printf("\n ENTER THE ITEM CODE TO DELETE");
  scanf("%d",&icd);
  while(1)
  {
    fscanf(fp,"%d",&it.itemcode);
    if(it.itemcode==0)
      break;
    if(it.itemcode==icd)
    {
      found=1;
      fscanf(fp,"%s",it.name);
      fscanf(fp,"%lf",&it.price);
    }
    else
    {
      fscanf(fp,"%s",it.name);
      fscanf(fp,"%lf",&it.price);
      fprintf(fptr,"%d \t%s\t%lf\n",
      it.itemcode,it.name,it.price);
    }
  }
  fprintf(fptr,"%d",0);
  fclose(fptr);
  fclose(fp);
  if(found==0)
    printf("\n RECORD NOT FOUND...");
  else
  {
    fp=fopen("item.dat","w");
    if(fp==NULL)
    {
```

```
      printf("\n ERROR IN OPENING FILE...");
      exit(0);
    }
    fptr=fopen("temp.dat","r");
    if(fptr==NULL)
    {
      printf("\n ERROR IN OPENING FILE...");
      exit(0);
    }
    while(1)
    {
      fscanf(fptr,"%d",&it.itemcode);
      if(it.itemcode==0)
        break;
      fscanf(fptr,"%s",it.name);
      fscanf(fptr,"%lf",&it.price);
      fprintf(fp, "%d \t%s\t%lf\n",it.itemcode,
                       it.name,it.price);
    }
    fprintf(fp,"%d",0);
    fclose(fptr);
    fclose(fp);
  }
}
```

Using fread() and fscanf() The following program demonstrates how the records stored in a binary file can be read sequentially from the disk. This program will work only if the structure of the record is identical to the record used in the previous example. Here, the file is opened using the fopen() function, with the file opening mode set to 'rb'. The file is read sequentially because after each read operation the file position is moved to point to the first byte of the very next record. It must be remembered that the feof() function does not indicate that the end of the file has been reached until after an attempt has been made to read past the end-of-file marker.

——————— EXAMPLE ———————

```
17. include <stdio.h>
    struct item
    {
      int itemcode;
      char name[30];
      double price;
    };
    void append();
    void modify();
    void dispall();
    void dele();
```

```
int main()
{
  int ch;
  struct item it;
  FILE *fp;
  fp=fopen("item.dat","wb");
  if(fp==NULL)
  {
    printf("\n ERROR IN OPENING FILE...");
    exit(0);
  }
  printf("\n ENTER ITEM CODE:");
  scanf("%d",&it.itemcode);
  printf("\n ENTER ITEM NAME:");
  fflush(stdin);
  scanf("%[^\n]",it.name);
  printf("\n ENTER PRICE:");
  scanf("%lf",&it.price);
  fwrite(&it,sizeof(it),1,fp);
  fclose(fp);
  dispall();
  while(1)
  {
    printf("\n \t 1.APPEND RECORD");
    printf("\n \t 2.DISPLAY ALL RECORD");
    printf("\n \t 3.EDIT RECORD");
    printf("\n \t 4.EXIT");
    printf("\n \t ENTER UR CHOICE:");
    scanf("%d",&ch);
    switch(ch)
    {
      case 1:append(); break;
      case 2:dispall();break;
      case 3:modify();break;
      case 4:exit(0);
    }
  }
  return 0;
}
void append()
{
  FILE *fp;
  struct item it;
  fp=fopen("item.dat","ab");
  if(fp==NULL)
  {
    printf("\n ERROR IN OPENING FILE...");
    exit(0);
  }
  printf("\n ENTER ITEM CODE:");
```

```
  scanf("%d",&it.itemcode);
  printf("\n ENTER ITEM NAME:");
  fflush(stdin);
  scanf("%[^\n]",it.name);
  printf("\n ENTER PRICE:");
  scanf("%lf",&it.price);
  fwrite(&it,sizeof(it),1,fp);
  fclose(fp);
}
void dispall()
{
  FILE *fp;
  struct item it;
  fp=fopen("item.dat","rb");
  if(fp==NULL)
  {
    printf("\n ERROR IN OPENING FILE...");
    exit(0);
  }
  while(1)
  {
    fread(&it,sizeof(it),1,fp);
    if(feof(fp))
    break;
    printf("\n %d \t %s \t %lf",it.itemcode,
                 it.name,it.price);
  }
  fclose(fp);
}
void modify()
{
  FILE *fp,*fptr;
  struct item it;
  int icd,found=0;
  fp=fopen("item.dat","rb");
  if(fp==NULL)
  {
    printf("\n ERROR IN OPENING FILE...");
    exit(0);
  }
  fptr=fopen("temp.dat","wb");
  if(fptr==NULL)
  {
    printf("\n ERROR IN OPENING FILE...");
    exit(0);
  }
  printf("\n ENTER THE ITEM CODE TO EDIT");
  scanf("%d",&icd);
  while(1)
  {
```

```
fread(&it,sizeof(it),1,fp);
if(feof(fp))
  break;
if(it.itemcode==icd)
{
  found=1;
  printf("\n EXISTING RECORD IS...\n");
  printf("\n \t %d\t%s\t%lf",it.itemcode,
                    it.name,it.price);
  printf("\n ENTER NEW ITEM NAME:");
  fflush(stdin);
  scanf("%[^\n]",it.name);
  printf("\n ENTER NEW PRICE:");
  scanf("%lf",&it.price);
  fwrite(&it,sizeof(it),1,fptr);
}
else
{
  fwrite(&it,sizeof(it),1,fptr);
}
}
fclose(fptr);
fclose(fp);
if(found==0)
  printf("\nRECORD NOT FOUND...");
else
{
  fp=fopen("item.dat","wb");
  if(fp==NULL)
  {
    printf("\n ERROR IN OPENING FILE...");
    exit(0);
  }
  fptr=fopen("temp.dat","rb");
  if(fptr==NULL)
  {
    printf("\n ERROR IN OPENING FILE...");
    exit(0);
  }
  while(1)
  {
    fread(&it,sizeof(it),1,fptr);
    if(feof(fptr))
      break;
    fwrite(&it,sizeof(it),1,fp);
  }
  fclose(fptr);
  fclose(fp);
}
}
```

Using `fgets()` and `fputc()`   It is not that only `fread()` and `fwrite()` or `fscanf()` and `fprintf()` are used for processing of files of records. `fgets()` and `fputc()` can also be used. The following program illustrates this. The program keeps the records of an item in a file `stock.dat`, uses a structure `item` and processes the file, and prints out all items where the quantity on hand is less than or equal to the reorder level.

EXAMPLE

```
18. #include <stdio.h>
    #include <stdlib.h>
    #include <ctype.h>
    #include <string.h>
    /* definition of a record of type item */
    struct item {
      char  name[20];
      float price;
      int   qty;
      int   reorder;
    };
    void show(struct item);
    int getrecord(struct item *);
    FILE *fp;                  /* input file pointer */
    void show(struct item rec)
    {
      printf("\nitem name\t%s\n", rec.name);
      printf("item price\t%.2f\n", rec.price);
      printf("item quantity\t%d\n", rec.qty);
      printf("item reorder level\t%d\n", rec.reorder);
    }
    int getrecord(struct item *p)
    {
      int i = 0, ch;
      char temp[40];
      ch = fgetc(fp);
      while((ch == '\n') || (ch == ' ') && (ch != EOF))
        ch = fgetc(fp);
      if(ch == EOF)
        return 0;
                              /* read item name */
      while((ch != '\n') && (ch != EOF)) {
        temp[i++] = ch;
        ch = fgetc(fp);
      }
      temp[i] = '\0';
      strcpy(p->name, temp);
      if(ch == EOF) return 0;
                  /* skip to start of next field */
      while((ch == '\n') || (ch == ' ') && (ch != EOF))
```

```
ch = fgetc(fp);
if(ch == EOF) return 0; /* read item price */
i = 0;
while((ch != '\n') && (ch != EOF))
{
  temp[i++] = ch;
  ch = fgetc(fp);
}
temp[i] = '\0';
p->price = atof(temp);
if(ch == EOF) return 0;
                /* skip to start of next field */
while((ch == '\n') || (ch == ' ') && (ch != EOF))
  ch = fgetc(fp);
if(ch == EOF) return 0;
                /* read item quantity */
i = 0;
while((ch != '\n') && (ch != EOF))
{
  temp[i++] = ch;
  ch = fgetc(fp);
}
temp[i] = '\0';
p->qty = atoi(temp);
if(ch == EOF) return 0;
                /* skip to start of next field */
while((ch == '\n') || (ch == ' ') && (ch != EOF))
  ch = fgetc(fp);
if(ch == EOF) return 0;
                /* read item reorder level */
i = 0;
while((ch != '\n') && (ch != EOF)) {
  temp[i++] = ch;
  ch = fgetc(fp);
}
temp[i] = '\0';
p->reorder = atoi(temp);
if(ch == EOF) return 0;
return 1;
                /* signify record has been
                   read successfully */
}
int main()
{
    struct item rec;
    fp = fopen("stock.dat", "r");
    if(fp == NULL) {
        printf("Unable to open the file %s\n", filename);
        if(fp != NULL)
        fclose(fp);
        exit(1);
    }
```

```
while(! feof(fp)) {
    if(getrecord(&rec) == 1) {
        if(rec.qty <= rec.reorder)
            show(rec);
    }
    else
    {
    if(fp != NULL)
      fclose(fp);
    exit(1);
    }
}

if(fp != NULL)
    fclose(fp);
exit(0);
    return 0;
}
```

Note

- Most C program files may be binary files, which can logically be divided into fixed-length records.
- The records in a file are written sequentially onto the disk.
- Binary files can be written sequentially to the disk or in a random access manner.
- With fread() and fscanf(), the file is read sequentially and after each read operation, the file position indicator is moved to the first byte of the next record.
- The feof() function does not indicate that the end of the file has been reached until after an attempt has been made to read past the end-of-file marker.

15.7 RANDOM ACCESS TO FILES OF RECORDS

For random access to files of records, the following functions are used.

- fseek()
- ftell()
- rewind()

By using fseek(), one can set the position indicator anywhere in the file. The function prototype in stdio.h is

    int fseek(FILE *fp, long offset, int origin);

The argument fp is the FILE pointer associated with the file. The distance that the position indicator is to be moved is given by offset in bytes. It is the number of bytes to move the file pointer. This is obtained from the formula: *the desired record number × the size of one record*. The argument origin specifies the position indicator's relative starting point. There can be three values for origin, with symbolic constants defined in stdio.h, as shown in Table 15.2.

Table 15.2 Possible origin values for fseek()

Constant	Value	Description
SEEK_SET	0	Moves the indicator offset bytes from the beginning of the file
SEEK_CUR	1	Moves the indicator offset bytes from its current position
SEEK_END	2	Moves the indicator offset bytes from the end of the file

The function fseek() returns 0, if the indicator is moved successfully or non-zero in case of an error. The following program uses fseek() for random file access. The program uses the previously created file item.dat and the structure item. It is assumed that there are four records in the file item.dat.

EXAMPLES

```c
19. #include <stdio.h>
    #include <string.h>
    struct item{
      int itemcode;
      char name[30];
      double  price;
        };
    typedef struct item product;
    FILE *fp;
    int main()
    {
      product it;
      int rec, result;
      fp = fopen("item.dat", "r+b");
      printf("Which record do you want [0-3]? Press\
    -1 to exit...");
      scanf("%d", &rec);
      while(rec >= 0)
      {
        fseek(fp, rec*sizeof(it), SEEK_SET);
        result = fread(&it, sizeof(it), 1, fp);
        if(result==1)
        {
          printf("\nRECORD %d\n", rec);
          printf("Item code........: %d\n",
          it.itemcode);
          printf("Item name.......: %s\n", it.name);
          printf("Price...: %8.2f\n\n", it.price);
        }
        else
        printf("\nRecord %d not found!\n\n", rec);
        printf("Which record do you want [0-3]? Press
    -1 to exit...");
        scanf("%d", &rec);
      }
```

```c
      fclose(fp);
      return 0;
    }
```

The following program will further clear the concept of fseek().

```c
20.#include <stdio.h>
   /* random record description—could be anything */
   struct rec
   {
     int x,y,z;
   };
   /* writes and then reads 10 arbitrary records from
           the file "junk". */
   int main()
   {
     int i,j;
     FILE *f;
     struct rec r;
     /* create the file of 10 records */
     f=fopen("junk","w");
     if(!f)
     {
       printf("File opening error for writing");
       exit(1);}
     for(i=1;i<=10; i++)
     {
       r.x=i;
       r.y=i*2;
       r.z=i*3;
       fwrite(&r,sizeof(struct rec),1,f);
     }
     fclose(f);
     /* read the 10 records */
     f=fopen("junk","r");
     if(!f) {
       printf("\n File opening error for reading");
       exit(1);}
     for(i=1;i<=10; i++)
     {
       fread(&r,sizeof(struct rec),1,f);
       printf("\n%d\t %d \t %d",r.x,r.y,r.z);
     }
     fclose(f);
     printf("\n");
                          /* use fseek to read the first 5
                             records in reverse order */
     f=fopen("junk","r");
     if(!f)
     {
       printf("\n File opening error for reading");
       exit(1);
```

```
}
for(i=4; i>=0; i--)
{
  fseek(f,sizeof(struct rec)*i,SEEK_SET);
  fread(&r,sizeof(struct rec),1,f);
  printf("\n%d\t %d \t %d",r.x,r.y,r.z);
}
fclose(f);
printf("\n");
/* use fseek to read every other record */
f=fopen("junk","r");
if(!f)
  {
  printf("File opening error for reading");
  exit(1);
  }
fseek(f,0,SEEK_SET);
for(i=0;i<5; i++)
{
  fread(&r,sizeof(struct rec),1,f);
  printf("\n%d\t %d \t %d",r.x,r.y,r.z);
  fseek(f,sizeof(struct rec),SEEK_CUR);
}
fclose(f);
printf("\n");
/* use fseek to read 4th record,
   change it, and write it back */
f=fopen("junk","r+");
if(!f)
  {
  printf("File opening error for reading and\
              writing");
  exit(1);}
fseek(f,sizeof(struct rec)*3,SEEK_SET);
fread(&r,sizeof(struct rec),1,f);
r.x=9;
r.y=99;
r.z=999;
fseek(f,sizeof(struct rec)*3,SEEK_SET);
fwrite(&r,sizeof(struct rec),1,f);
fclose(f);
printf("\n");
                    /* read the 10 records to ensure
                       4th record was changed */
f=fopen("junk","r");
if(!f)
  {
  printf("File opening error for reading and\
  writing");
  exit(1);
  }
```

```
for(i=1;i<=10; i++)
{
  fread(&r,sizeof(struct rec),1,f);
  printf("\n%d\t %d \t %d",r.x,r.y,r.z);
}
fclose(f);
return 0;
}
```

Output

1	2	3
2	4	6
3	6	9
4	8	12
5	10	15
6	12	18
7	14	21
8	16	24
9	18	27
10	20	30
5	10	15
4	8	12
3	6	9
2	4	6
1	2	3
1	2	3
3	6	9
5	10	15
7	14	21
9	18	27
1	2	3
2	4	6
3	6	9
9	99	999
5	10	15
6	12	18
7	14	21
8	16	24
9	18	27
10	20	30

To set the position indicator to the beginning of the file, use the library function rewind(). Its prototype in stdio.h is

```
void rewind(FILE *fp);
```

The argument fp is the FILE pointer associated with the stream. After rewind() is called, the file's position indicator is set to the beginning of the file (byte 0). Use rewind() to read some data from a file and to start reading from the beginning of the file again without closing and reopening the file.

To determine the value of a file's position indicator, use ftell(). The prototype of this function, located in stdio.h, reads

```
long ftell(FILE *fp);
```

The argument fp is the FILE pointer returned by fopen() when the file is opened. The function ftell() returns a type long that gives the current file position in bytes from the start of the file (the first byte is at position 0). In case of an error, ftell() returns -1L (a type long −1).

There are a number of interesting points here.

- The direct access functions always work with long integers and traditionally, associated variables are declared as being of type long int.
- The record numbering starts at zero and the file examination part of the program is terminated by a negative input. Strictly, the final parameter of fseek() ought to have been SEEK_SET, not zero.
- The value returned by ftell() is the byte position of the byte about to be read from the file. Therefore, when a new line is encountered, it is the start address of the next record.

The functions fsetpos() and fgetpos() do the same things as fseek() and ftell(), but they use parameters of type fpos_t rather than long int. This potentially allows for larger files to be handled. The use of these functions must be preferred.

> **Note**
>
> - By using fseek(), one can set the position indicator anywhere in the file.
> - The function fseek() returns 0 if the indicator is moved successfully or non-zero in case of an error.
> - To determine the value of a file's position indicator, use ftell().
> - The record numbering starts at zero and the file examination part of the program is terminated by a negative input.

15.8 OTHER FILE MANAGEMENT FUNCTIONS

The copy and delete operations are also associated with file management. Though one could write programs for them, the C standard library contains functions for deleting and renaming files.

15.8.1 Deleting a File

The library function remove() is used to delete a file. Its prototype in stdio.h is

```
int remove(const char *filename);
```

The variable *filename is a pointer to the name of the file to be deleted. The only precondition is that the specified file must not be open. If the file exists, it will be deleted and remove() returns 0. If the file does not exist or if it is read-only, if the programmer does not have sufficient access rights (for UNIX system), or in case of some other error, remove() returns -1.

The following program describes the use of the remove() function.

EXAMPLE

```c
21.#include <stdio.h>
   int main(void)
   {
     char file[80];
     /* prompt for filename to delete */
     printf("File to delete: ");
     gets(file);
     /* delete the file */
     if(remove(file) == 0)
       printf("Removed %s.\n",file);
     else
       perror("remove");
       return 0;
   }
```

In this program, a function perror() is used, the prototype for which is

```
void perror(const char *message);
```

perror() produces a message on standard error output, describing the last error encountered. The argument string message is printed first, then a colon and a blank, followed by the message and a new line. If the message is a NULL pointer or if it points to a null string, the colon is not printed.

15.8.2 Renaming a File

The rename() function changes the name of an existing disk file. The function prototype in stdio.h is as follows.

```
int rename(const char *oldname, const char *newname);
```

The filenames pointed to by oldname and newname follow the rules given earlier in this chapter. The only restriction is that both names must refer to the same disk drive; a file cannot be renamed on a different disk drive. The function rename() returns 0 on success, or -1 if an error occurs. Errors can be caused by the following conditions (among others).

- The file oldname does not exist.
- A file with the name newname already exists.
- One tries to rename on another disk.

Consider the following program.

EXAMPLE

```c
22.#include <stdio.h>
   int main(void)
   {
     char oldname[80], newname[80];
         /* prompt for file to rename and new name */
     printf("File to rename:");
     gets(oldname);
     printf("New name:");
```

```
    gets(newname);
                                /* Rename the file */
    if(rename(oldname, newname) == 0)
      printf("Renamed %s to %s.\n", oldname, newname);
    else
      perror("rename");
      return 0;
}
```

Note

- The copy and delete operations are also associated with file management.
- In case of remove() function, the only precondition is that the specified file must not be open.
- The only restriction in rename() function is that both names must refer to the same disk drive; a file cannot be renamed on a different disk drive.

15.9 LOW-LEVEL I/O

This form of I/O is unbuffered. This means that, each read or write request results in accessing the disk (or device) directly to fetch/put a specific number of bytes. There are no formatting facilities. Instead of file pointers, we use *low-level* file handles or file descriptors, which give a unique integer number to identify each file.

To open a file the following function is used.

```
int open(char *filename, int flag, int perms);
```

The above function returns a file descriptor or -1 for a failure. The flag controls the file access and has the following predefined in fcntl.h: O_APPEND, O_CREAT, O_EXCL, O_RDONLY, O_RDWR, O_WRONLY, and others. perms is best set to 0 for most of our applications.
The function

```
    creat(char *filename, int perms);
```
can also be used to create a file.

```
    int close(int handle);
```
can be used to close a file.

The following functions are used to read/write a specific number of bytes from/to a file stored or to be put in the memory location specified by buffer.

```
int read(int handle, char *buffer,unsigned length);
```

```
int write(int handle, char *buffer, unsigned length);
```

The sizeof() function is commonly used to specify the length. The read() and write() functions return the number of bytes read/written or -1 if they fail.

Note

- Low-level I/O has no formatting facilities.
- Instead of file pointers, low-level file handles or file descriptors, which give a unique integer number to identify each file, are used.

SUMMARY

Data can also be stored in disk files. C treats a disk file like a stream (a sequence of characters), just like the predefined streams stdin, stdout, and stderr. A stream associated with a disk file must be opened using the fopen() library function before it can be used, and it must be closed after use through the fclose() function. A disk file stream can be opened either in text or in binary mode.

After a disk file has been opened, data can be read from the file, written into the file, or both. Data can be accessed either in a sequential manner or in a random manner. Each open disk file has an associated file position indicator. This indicator specifies the position in the file, measured as the number of bytes from the start of the file, where subsequent read and write operations occur. With some cases, the position indicator is updated automatically by the system, and programmers do not have to be bothered with it. For random file access, the C standard library provides functions such as fseek(), ftell(), and rewind() for manipulating the position indicator.

Finally, C provides some rudimentary file management functions, allowing deletion and renaming of disk files. Low-level file handling functions that do not use formatting and file position indicators are also available.

KEY TERMS

Binary file   It is a collection of bytes or a character stream. The data that is written into and read from binary file remains unchanged, with no separation between lines and no use of end-of-line characters and the interpretation of the file is left to the programmer.

Buffer   It is a block of memory used for temporary storage of data being written to and read from the file. It serves as an interface between the stream (which is character-oriented) and the disk hardware (which is block-oriented).

File management   It refers to all operations related to creating, renaming, deleting, merging, reading, writing, etc. of any type of files.

Path   It specifies the drive and/or directory (or folder) where the file is located. On PCs, the backslash character is used to separate directory names in a path. Some systems like UNIX use the forward slash (/) as the directory separator.

Random file access   It means reading from or writing to any position in a file without reading or writing all the preceding data by controlling the position indicator.

Record   It consists of a collection of data fields that conforms to a previously defined structure that can be stored on or retrieved from a file.

Sequential file access   In case of sequential file access, data is read from or written to a file in a sequential manner while the position indicator automatically gets adjusted by the stream I/O functions.

Stream   It is a common, logical interface to the various devices that comprise the computer and is a logical interface to a file. Although files differ in form and capabilities, all streams are the same.

Text file   It is a stream of characters that can be processed sequentially and logically in the forward direction. The maximum number of characters in each line is limited to 255 characters.

FREQUENTLY ASKED QUESTIONS

1. What is a file?

A file is a collection of bytes stored on a secondary storage device, which is generally a disk of some kind. It is identified by a name, which is given at the time of its creation. It may be amended, moved from one storage device to another or removed completely when desired.

2. What is a stream?

In C, the stream is a common, logical interface to the various devices that form the computer. When the program executes, each stream is tied together to a specific device that is source or destination of data. The stream provides a consistent interface and to the programmer one hardware device will look much like another. In its most common form, a stream is a logical interface to a file. Stream I/O uses some temporary storage area, called buffer, for reading from or writing data to a file. A stream is linked to a file by using an open operation. A stream is disassociated from a file using a close operation.

The C language provides three "standard" streams that are always available to a C program. These are the following:

Name	Description	Example
stdin	Standard Input	Keyboard
stdout	Standard Output	Screen
stderr	Standard Error	Screen

3. What is a buffer? What is its purpose?

Buffer is a temporary storage area that holds data while it is being transferred to and from memory. Buffering is a scheme that prevents excessive access to a physical I/O device like a disk or a terminal. Its purpose is to synchronize the physical devices that the program needs. The buffer collects output data until there is enough to write efficiently. The buffering activities are taken care of by software called device drivers or access methods provided by the operating system.

4. How are buffers useful?

Buffers speed up input/output which can be a major bottleneck in execution times. Thus, it is less time-consuming to transmit several characters as a block than to send them one by one.

5. What is `FILE`?

`FILE` is a structure declared in `stdio.h`. The members of the `FILE` structure are used by the program in the various file access operations.

For each file that is to be opened, a pointer to type `FILE` must be declared. When the function `fopen()` is called, that function creates an instance of the `FILE` structure and returns a pointer to that structure. This pointer is used in all subsequent operations on the file. But programmers do not need to be concerned about the members of the structure `FILE`.

Because one may use a number of different files in the program, he or she must specify when reading or writing which file one wishes to use. This is accomplished by using a variable called a *file pointer*, a pointer variable that points to a structure `FILE`.

6. How many files can be opened simultaneously?

The number of files that can be opened simultaneously will be determined by the value of the constant FOPEN_MAX that is defined in `<stdio.h>`. FOPEN_MAX is an integer that specifies the maximum number of streams that can be opened at one time. The C language standard requires that the value of FOPEN_MAX be at least 8, including the standard streams stdin, stdout, and stderr. Thus, as a minimum, it is possible to work with up to five files simultaneously.

7. What happens if a file is not closed?

By default, the file should be closed when the program exits; however, one should never depend on this. A file must be closed as soon as the programmer has finished processing with it. This defends data loss which could occur if an error in another part of the program caused the execution to be stopped in an abnormal fashion. As a consequence, the contents of the output buffer might be lost, as the file would not be closed properly. It should be noted that one must also close a file before attempting to rename it or remove it.

8. What is the difference between `gets()` and `fgets()`?

gets()	fgets()
The function gets() is normally used to read a line of string from the keyboard.	The function fgets() is used to read a line of string from a file or keyboard.
It automatically replaces the '\n' by '\0'.	It does not automatically delete the trailing '\n'.
It takes one argument.	It takes three arguments.
It does not prevent overflow.	It prevents overflow.

EXERCISES

1. What are the primary advantages of using a data file?
2. What is `FILE`?
3. What is the purpose of the `fopen()` function?
4. What is the purpose of the `fclose()` function? Is it mandatory to use this in a program that processes a data file?
5. What is the difference between a text-mode stream and a binary-mode stream?
6. Describe different file opening modes used with the `fopen()` function.

7. What is a stream? Describe two different methods of creating a stream-oriented data file.

8. What are the three general methods of file access?

9. What is EOF? When is it used?

10. Describe the different methods for reading from and writing into a data file.

11. What is the difference between a binary file and a text file in C?

12. Compare `fscanf()` and `fread()` functions.

13. What is the purpose of the `feof()` function?

14. How do you detect the end of a file in text and binary modes? Write a code to close all file streams.

15. Indicate two different ways to reset the file position pointer to the beginning of the file.

16. Is anything wrong with the following program?

```
FILE *fp;
int c;
if((fp= fopen(oldname, "rb"))==NULL)
    return -1;
while((c = fgetc(fp)) != EOF)
    fprintf(stdout, "%c", c);
fclose(fp);
```

17. Write a program to copy one existing file into another named file.

18. Write a complete C program that can be used as a simple line-oriented text editor. The program must have the following capabilities.

   (i) Enter several lines of text and store them in a data file
   (ii) List the data file
   (iii) Retrieve and display a particular line

   (iv) Insert *n* lines
   (v) Delete *n* lines
   (vi) Save the new text and exit

   Carry out these tasks using different functions.

19. Write a program that opens a file and counts the number of characters. The program should print the number of characters when finished.

20. Write a program to compare two files and print out the lines where they differ.

21. Write an interactive C program that will maintain a list roll, name, and total marks of students. Consider the information associated with each roll to be a separate record. Represent each record as a structure. Include a menu that will allow the user to select any of the following.

   (i) Add a new record
   (ii) Delete a record
   (iii) Modify a record
   (iv) Retrieve and display an entire record for a given roll or name
   (v) Display all records
   (vi) End of computation

22. Write a program that opens an existing text file and copies it to a new text file with all lowercase letters changed to capital letters and all other characters unchanged.

23. Write a function that opens a new temporary file with a specified mode. All temporary files created by this function should automatically be closed and deleted when the program terminates.

24. Write a C code that will read a line of characters (terminated by a \n) from a text file into a character array called `buffer`. NULL terminates the buffer upon reading a \n.

Project Questions

1. Write a C program that takes the name of a file as a command-line argument, opens the file, reads through it to determine the number of words in each sentence, displays the total number of words and sentences, and computes the average number of words per sentence. The results should be printed in a table (as standard output), such as shown below:

```
This program counts the words and sentences in file
"comp.text".

        Sentence:   1      Words: 29
        Sentence:   2      Words: 41
        Sentence:   3      Words: 16
        Sentence:   4      Words: 22
        Sentence:   5      Words: 44
        Sentence:   6      Words: 14
        Sentence:   7      Words: 32
```

```
File "comp.text" contains 198 words words in
7 sentences for an average of 28.3 words per
sentence.
```

In this program, you should count a word as any contiguous sequence of letters, and apostrophes should be ignored. Thus, "O'Henry", "government's", and "friend's'" should each be considered as one word.

Also in the program, you should think of a sentence as any sequence of words that ends with a period, exclamation point, or question mark. A period after a single capital letter (e.g., an initial) or embedded within digits (e.g., a real number) should not be counted as being the end of a sentence. White space, digits, and other punctuation should be ignored.

2. Write a C program that removes all comment lines from a C source code.

Advanced C

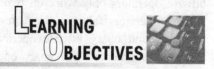

After studying this chapter, the readers will be able to

- explain bitwise operators and their uses
- discuss how command arguments can be passed and used
- discuss C preprocessor, its directives and predefined identifiers
- list the three data type qualifiers–const, volatile, and restrict

- use the data type qualifier restrict with pointers, functions, blocks, and structures
- comprehend variable length argument list and its uses
- discuss different memory models and their application

16.1 INTRODUCTION

This chapter deals with some of the topics that typically fall in the domain of advanced use of C. The features discussed in this chapter may not be required for general applications, but may be essential and extremely advantageous for certain specific cases.

Preprocessing is the first step in the C program compilation stage, which is an important feature of the C compiler. In C, all preprocessor directives begin with a #. It is used to define constants or any macro substitution.

It has been discussed in an earlier chapter that pointers provide control over low-level memory operations. There are many programs that operate at a low level when individual bytes are operated on. The combination of pointers and

bit-level operators makes C useful for many low-level applications and can almost replace assembly code. UNIX is mostly written in C.

Type qualifiers include the keywords const and volatile. The const qualifier places the assigned variable in the constant data area of memory which makes the particular variable unmodifiable. volatile is used less frequently and it indicates that the value can be modified outside the control of the program.

A function usually takes a number of arguments whose types are fixed when its code is compiled. But sometimes it is desirable to implement a function where the number of arguments is not constant or not known beforehand, when the function is written. For example, the printf function is a special type of routine that takes a variable number of arguments. The user-defined function may use variable-length argument list. The declaration requires a special syntax to indicate the fact that beyond a certain argument, the number and type of the parameters cannot be checked at compile time. Instead, the number and type of the parameters has to be computed at run time. Using ellipsis in the signature denotes a variable argument list.

16.2 BITWISE OPERATOR

Since a computer understands only machine language, data is represented as binary numbers that are various combinations of 0's and 1's. Readers are conversant with the binary number system and the binary arithmetic. Table 16.1 lists the bitwise operators that may be used to manipulate binary numbers.

Bitwise operators allow the user to read and manipulate bits in variables of certain types. It is to be remembered that bitwise operators only work on two types—int and char. Bitwise operators fall into two categories—binary bitwise operators and unary bitwise operators. Binary operators take two arguments while unary operators take only one. The ~ (bitwise NOT) is a unary bitwise operator as it acts on a single operand. The &, |, ^, and ~ are known as bitwise logical operators. The >> and << are termed as bitwise shift operators. Bitwise operators, like arithmetic operators, do not change the value of the operands. Instead, a temporary value is created. This can then be assigned to a variable.

Table 16.1 Bitwise operators used in C

Operator	Description
&	Bitwise AND
|	Bitwise OR
^	Bitwise Exclusive OR
~	Bitwise Complement
<<	Bitwise Shift Left
>>	Bitwise Shift Right

Arithmetic operators are used in conjunction with the assignment operator to form shorthand forms that do the desired operation as well as assignment. Such forms are +=, -=, *=, and so on. These shorthand forms can also be applied to bitwise operators. For example, |=, &=, and ^= are some of the shorthand forms with bitwise operators. Nearly all binary operators have a version with = after it. These operators do change the value of the operands.

Arithmetic operators have higher precedence than bitwise operators. The precedence and associativity of bitwise operators are given in Table 16.2.

Table 16.2 Precedence and associativity of bitwise operators and logical operators

Precedence	Associativity
<< >>	L → R
< <= > >=	L → R
== !=	L → R
&	L → R
^	L → R
|	L → R
&&	L → R
||	L → R
?:	R → L
= >>= <<= &= ^= |=	R → L

It is evident from the table that among bitwise operators, bitwise shift operators (<< and >>) have higher precedence than bitwise logical operators and bitwise compound operators (>>=, <<=, &=, ^=, and |=).

Uses of bitwise operations

- Bitwise operators can be used to set or clear any bit in an integer.
- They can be used to quickly multiply and divide integers.
- They are most often used in coding device and low-level applications as they can be used to mask off certain bits.

Assuming that unsigned ints use 32 bits of memory, two variables X and Y are defined for illustration as

$X = x_{31}x_{30}...x_0$
$Y = y_{31}y_{30}...y_0$

Each bit of X and Y is referred to by writing the variable name in lowercase with the appropriate subscript numbers.

16.2.1 Bitwise AND

The bitwise AND is true only if both the corresponding bits in the operands are set. The following chart defines the operation of '&' operator by applying ANDing on individual bits.

x_i	y_i	x_i & y_i
0	0	0
0	1	0
1	0	0
1	1	1

Result of logical ANDing between corresponding bit positions

However, here is an example of bitwise '&' operation applied on numbers represented by four bits.

Variable	Decimal equivalent	b_3	b_2	b_1	b_0
x	12	1	1	0	0
y	10	1	0	1	0
$z = x$ & y	8	1	0	0	0

The & operator can be used to check whether a number is a power of 2 or not. This can be achieved by using the `while` loop and the arithmetic operator % as follows.

EXAMPLE

```
1. #include <stdio.h>
   int main()
   {
   int n, r;
   printf("\n ENTER THE NUMBER :");
   scanf("%d",&n);
   while(n>1)
   {
       r=n%2;
       if(r==0)
       n=n/2;
       else
       break;
   }
   if(r!=0)
   printf("\n The number is not power of 2 ");
   else
   printf("\n The number is power of 2 ");
   return 0;
   }
```

r is assigned the value obtained as remainder from this expression.

Using bitwise AND, the program in Example 1 can be rewritten without using the loop or the arithmetic operators.

```
#include <stdio.h>
int main()
{
int n;
printf("\n ENTER THE NUMBER :");
scanf("%d",&n);
if((n & (n-1))==0)
printf("\n The number is power of 2 ");
else
  printf("\n The number is not power of 2 ");
return 0;
}
```

Bitwise operation

For illustration, let $n = 8$, n & $(n-1)$ evaluates to 0000. Here n is represented as four binary digits. Hence

n	1	0	0	0
$n-1$	0	1	1	1
n & $(n-1)$	0	0	0	0

So, the number 8 is a power of 2. But, when $n = 12$, then,

n	1	1	0	0
$n-1$	1	0	1	1
n & $(n-1)$	1	0	0	0

Thus, n & $(n-1)$ is not equal to 0. Therefore, it is not a power of 2, though it is divisible by 2.

Masking is a process by which a given bit pattern is converted into another bit pattern by means of a logical bitwise operator. One of the operands in the bitwise operation is the original bit pattern that is to be transformed. The other operand, called mask, is the selected bit pattern that yields the desired conversion. The bitwise AND operator, &, is often used to mask off some set of bits. The following segment of code uses a mask with the value 1 and prints an alternating sequence of 0's and 1's.

```
int i, mask=1;
for(i=0;i<16;++i)
    printf("%d",i & mask);
```

A mask value can be used to check if certain bits have been set. For example, to check whether bits 1 and 3 were set, the number should be masked with 10 and the result tested against the mask.

EXAMPLE

```
2. #include <stdio.h>
   int main()
   {
   int n, mask = 10;
   printf("Enter a number: ");
   scanf("%d", &n);
   if((n & mask) == mask)
       printf("Bits 1 and 3 are set");
   else
       printf("Bits 1 and 3 are not set");
   return 0;
   }
```

The above example is better understood with the following illustration:

Variable	Contents		Remarks
n	any decimal number	binary (16 bits) x x x x x x x x x x x x x x x x	x = 0 or 1 byte (most significant) byte (least significant)
mask	10	0 0 0 0 0 0 0 0 0 0 0 0 1 0 1 0	
n & mask		0 0 0 0 0 0 0 0 0 0 0 0 x 0 x 0 15... ... ... 8 7... ... 3 2 1 0	byte (most significant) byte (least significant) Bit number

In case the value of n & mask is equal to mask, that is, if the bits 1 and 3 marked as x are equal to 1, then the bits in 1 and 3 positions are set to 1.

Another important example of mask is 255; its binary equivalent is 0000 0000 1111 1111. As only the lower order bits are set to 1, the expression n & 255 produces a value having a bit pattern with all its most significant bytes 0 and its least significant byte the same as the least significant byte in n.

16.2.2 Bitwise OR

The | operator is used as bitwise OR. This operation returns a 1 if either of the two bits (but not both) is a 1. The following chart defines bitwise OR in individual bits which are represented by variables with subscript i.

x_i	y_i	$x_i \mid y_i$
0	0	0
0	1	1
1	0	1
1	1	1

Here is an example of bitwise | applied on four-bit numbers.

Variable	b_3	b_2	b_1	b_0
x	1	1	0	0
y	1	0	1	0
$z = x \mid y$	1	1	1	0

The bitwise OR operator | is used to turn bits on. In the following statement

```
n = n | mask;
```

the bits, which are set to 1 in mask, are set to 1 in n.

─── **EXAMPLE** ───

```
3. #include <stdio.h>
   int main()
   {
     int n, mask = 4;
     printf("\n Enter a number: ");
     scanf("%d", &n);
     num |= mask;
     printf("\n After ensuring bit 2 is set: %d\n", n);
     return 0;
   }
```

Output
```
Enter a number: 3
After ensuring bit 2 is set: 7
```

The binary equivalent of 3 represented in eight bits is 00000011. Here, the mask is 4, the binary equivalent of which is 00000100. The | operator sets the third bit of 3 from the right-hand side to 1. Thus, n becomes 7; its binary equivalent is 00000111.

One must distinguish the bitwise operators & and | from the logical operators && and ||, which imply left-to-right evaluation of a truth value. For example, if x is 1 and y is 2, then x & y is 0 while x && y is 1.

16.2.3 Bitwise Exclusive-OR

The ^ operator is known as the bitwise Exclusive OR (XOR). This operation returns a 1 if either of the two bits (but not both) is a 1. The following chart defines XOR applied on individual bits.

x_i	y_i	$x_i \verb|^| y_i$
0	0	0
0	1	1
1	0	1
1	1	0

The bitwise exclusive OR operator ^ sets a 1 in each bit position where its operands have different bits, and 0 where they are the same. However, the following chart is an example of bitwise ^ on four bit numbers.

Variable	b_3	b_2	b_1	b_0
x	1	1	0	0
y	1	0	1	0
$z = x \verb|^| y$	0	1	1	0

Using bitwise XOR operator, two integer variables can be swapped without using the third variable, as follows.

─── **EXAMPLE** ───

```
4. #include <stdio.h>
   int main()
   {
     int a, b;
     printf("\n Enter the value of a: ");
     scanf("%d", &a);
     printf("\n Enter the value of b: ");
     scanf("%d", &b);
     a^=b^=a^=b;
     printf("\n a = %d \t b = %d",a,b);
     return 0;
   }
```

Output
```
Enter the value of a:8
Enter the value of b:10
a = 10        b = 8
```

Initially, a = 8; its binary equivalent on an eight-bit machine is 00001000. b = 10; its binary equivalent is 00001010. The statement a^=b^=a^=b; can be split into three equivalent statements as it evaluates from right to left due to the associativity of the ^= operator.

(i) a ^= b

(ii) b ^= a

(iii) a ^= b

After the execution of (i), the values of a and b in binary equivalent will be 00000010 and 00001010 respectively. After the execution of (ii), the values of a and b in binary equivalent will be 00000010 and 00001000 respectively. After the execution of (iii), the values of a and b in binary equivalent will be 00001010 and 00001000 respectively. That is, a=10 and b=8.

The above logic may be applied to reverse a given string using a bitwise operator.

Variable	b_3	b_2	b_1	b_0
x	1	1	0	0
$z = \sim x$	0	0	1	1

EXAMPLE

5.
```c
#include <stdio.h>
#include <string.h>
void reverse(char *str)
{
int l,j;
l = strlen(str) -1;
if(l==l)
  return;              /* No need to reverse */
  for(j=0;j<l;j++,l--)
  {
    str[j]^=str[l]; /*triple xor will
    str[l]^=str[j]; /*replace c[j] with c[i]*/
    str[j]^=str[l]; /*without a temp var*/
  }
}
int main()
{
char s[80];
void reverse(char *);
printf("\n Enter the string : ");
fflush(stdin);
scanf("%[^\n]",s);
reverse(s);
printf("\n Reverse of the string is %s",s);
return 0;
}
```

16.2.4 Bitwise NOT

There is only one unary bitwise operator—bitwise NOT. It is also known as 1's complement operator. Bitwise NOT flips all the bits. This works on a single number and simply converts each 1 to 0 and each 0 to 1. Note that it is not the same operation as a unary minus.

The following is a chart that defines $\sim$ on an individual bit.

x_i	$\sim x_i$
0	1
1	0

The bitwise $\sim$ is easiest to demonstrate on four-bit numbers (although only two bits are necessary to show the concept).

EXAMPLES

6.
```c
#include <stdio.h>
int main()
{
  int num = 0xFFFF;
  printf("The complement of %X is %X\n", num, ~num);
  return 0;
}
```
Output

The complement of FFFF is 0

7.
```c
#include <stdio.h>
int main()
{
  int num = 0xABCD;
  printf("The complement of %X is %X\n", num, ~num);
  return 0;
}
```
Output

The complement of ABCD is 5432

16.2.5 Bitwise Shift Operator

The shift operators << and >> perform left and right shifts of their left operand by the number of bit positions given by the right operand, which must be non-negative.

Bitwise shift left

The bitwise shift left operator shifts the number left. The most significant bits are lost as the number moves left, and the vacated least significant bits are zero.

Suppose a is a number whose value is 7335. Its binary equivalent is 0001 1100 1010 0111. The expression b=a<<6 will shift all bits to the left. By shifting the bits to the left, the most significant bits are lost, and the number is padded with zeroes at the least significant bit. The following is the resulting number.

Bitwise shift right

The bitwise right shift operator causes all the bits in the first operand to be shifted to the right by the number of positions indicated by the second operand. The rightmost bits in the original bit pattern will be lost. The leftmost bit positions that become vacant will be padded with zeroes.

Taking the number stored in a, the expression b=a>>6 will shift all bits to the right.

Thus, x << 2 shifts the value of x by two positions, filling vacated bits with zero; this is equivalent to multiplication by 4. Right shifting an unsigned quantity always fits the vacated bits with zero. Right shifting a signed quantity will fill sign bit ('arithmetic shift') on some machines and 0 bits ('logical shift') on others. To divide an integer by 2^n, a right shift by n bit positions is applied. To multiply an integer by 2^n, a left shift by n positions is applied.

The following program uses the bitwise shift right and bitwise AND to display a number as a 16-bit binary number. The number is shifted right successively from 16 down to zero and bitwise ANDed with 1 to see if the bit is set. An alternative method would be to use successive masks with the bitwise OR operator.

EXAMPLES

8.
```c
#include <stdio.h>
int main()
{
    int counter, num;
    printf("Enter a number: ");
    scanf("%d", &num);
    printf("\n The binary Equivalent of %d is", num);
    for(counter=15; counter>=0; counter--)
        printf("%d",(num >> counter) & 1);
    putchar('\n');
    return 0;
}
```

Output
```
Enter a number: 7335
The binary Equivalent of 7335 is 0001 1100 1010 0111
```

9. A program to print the binary equivalent of an integer number using bitwise operator.

Solution
```c
#include <stdio.h>
int main()
{
    int n,i,k,m;
    printf("\n ENTER THE NUMBER :");
    scanf("%d",&n);
    for(i=15;i>=0; ++i)
    {
        m=1<<i;
        k=n&m;
        k==0? printf("0"):printf("1");
    }
    return 0;
}
```

A better version of the program in Example 9 that works on machines having either two- or four-byte words follows.
```c
#include <stdio.h>
#include <limits.h>
int main()
{
    int num,i,n,mask;
    printf("\n ENTER THE NUMBER :");
    scanf("%d",&num);
    printf(" \n BINARY EQUIVALENT IS :");
    n =sizeof(int) * CHAR_BIT;
    mask= 1 << (n-1);
    for(i=1;i<=n;++i)
    {
        putchar(((num & mask) ==0) ? '0': '1');
        num<<=1;
        if(i% CHAR_BIT == 0 && i<n)
            putchar(' ');
    }
    return 0;
}
```

Output
```
ENTER THE NUMBER :
BINARY EQUIVALENT IS : 00011100 10100111
```

In ANSI C, the symbolic constant CHAR_BIT is defined in limits.h whose value is 8, representing the number of bits in a char. Because a char takes 1 byte of storage space, the constant 1 contains only its LSB as 1. The expression 1 << (n-1) shifts that bit to the higher order end. Thus, the mask has all bits off except for its most significant bit, which is 1. If the high-order bit in num is 0, then the expression num & mask has all its bits set to 0 and the expression (num & mask)==0 evaluates to true. In the opposite case, if the high-order bit is set to 1, then the expression num & mask has all its bits set to 1 and the expression (num & mask) ==0) evaluates to false. Thus putchar() prints 0 if the most significant bit is 0 and prints 1 if the most significant bit is 1. After that, the expression num <<=1 evaluates the value of num with the same bit pattern except that the next bit is brought as the MSB. The following statement

```
if(i% CHAR_BIT == 0 && i<n)
    putchar(' ');
```

prints a blank space after each byte has been printed.

EXAMPLE

10. A program to rotate a given number called value, n number of times. If n is positive, rotate it left, otherwise right. It is to be noted that rotation means shifting each bit by one place and recovering the lost bit. For example, in a left shift, each bit is shifted one place to the left and the leftmost bit, which comes out is returned to the rightmost place.

Solution

```
/* Function to rotate an unsigned int left or right */
  unsigned int rotate (unsigned int value, int n)
  {
  unsigned int result, bits;
  if(n== 0|| n== -16 || n== 16)
  return(unsigned int)1;
  else if(n > 0)    /* left rotate */
  {
   n=-n;
  bits = value << (16 - n);
  result = value << n | bits;
  }
  else
  {
   n= -n;
  bits = value << (16 -n);
  result = value >> n | bits;
  }
  return(result);
  }
  int main()
  {
  unsigned int w1 = oxa1b5, w2 = 0xff22;
  printf("%x\n", rotate(w1, 4));
  printf("%x\n", rotate(w1, -4));
  printf("%x\n", rotate(w2, 8));
  printf("%x\n", rotate(w2, -2));
  printf("%x\n", rotate(w1, 0));
  return 0;
  }
```

Output

```
1b5a
5a1b
22ff
bfc8
a1b5
```

Note

- Arithmetic operators are used in conjunction with the assignment operator to form shorthand forms that do the desired operation as well as assignment. Such forms are +=, -=, *=, and so on.
- Shorthand forms can also be applied to bitwise operators. For example, |=, &=, and ^= are some of the shorthand forms with bitwise operators. Nearly all binary operators have a version with = after it. These operators do not change the value of the individual operands.
- Arithmetic operators have higher precedence than bitwise operators.

16.3 COMMAND-LINE ARGUMENTS

All C programs define a function main() that designates the entry point of the program and is invoked by the environment in which the program is executed. In the programs considered so far, main() did not take any arguments. However, main() can be defined with formal parameters so that the program may accept command-line arguments, that is, arguments that are specified when the program is executed. Thus, the program must be run from a command prompt. The following version of main() allows arguments to be passed from the command line.

```
int main(int argc, char *argv[])
```

This declaration states that

- main returns an integer value (used to determine if the program terminates successfully).
- argc is the number of command-line arguments including the command itself, i.e., argc must be at least 1.
- argv is an array of the command-line arguments.

The declaration of argv means that it is an array of pointers to strings. By the normal rules about arguments whose type is array, what actually gets passed to main is the address of the first element of the array. As a result, an equivalent (and widely used) declaration is

```
int main(int argc, char **argv)
```

When the program starts, the following conditions hold true.

- argc is greater than 0.
- argv[argc] is a null pointer.
- argv[0], argv[1], ..., argv[argc-1] are pointers to strings with implementation-defined meanings.

- argv[0] is a string that contains the program's name. The remaining members of argv are the program's arguments.

The following program echoes its arguments to the standard output. This program is essentially the UNIX or MSDOS echo command.

_____ **EXAMPLE** _____

```
11. #include <stdio.h>
    int main(int argc, char *argv[])
    {
      int i;
      for(i = 0; i < argc; i++)
      printf("%s \n", argv[i]);
        printf("\n");
    return 0;
    }
```

If the name of this program is prg.c, an example of its execution is as follows.

```
prg.c oxford pradip manas
```

Output

```
    prg.c
    oxford
    pradip
    manas
```

The following program is a version of the cat command in UNIX or type in MSDOS command that displays files specified as command-line parameters.

_____ **EXAMPLE** _____

```
12. #include <stdio.h>
    #include <stdlib.h>
    int main(int argc, char *argv[])
    {
      int i = 1;
      int c;
      int num_args = 0;
      FILE *fp;
      if(argc == 1)
      {
        fprintf(stderr, "No input files to display…\n");
      exit(1);
    }
    if(argc > 1)
      printf("%d files to be displayed\n", argc-1);
    num_args = argc - 1;
    while(num_args > 0)
    {
      printf("[Displaying file %s]\n", argv[i]);
      num_args--;
      fp = fopen(argv[i], "r");
      if(fp == NULL)
```

```
    {
      fprintf(stderr,"Cannot display %s \n", argv[i]);
        continue; /* Goto next file in list */
    }
    c = getc(fp);
    while(c!= EOF)
    {
      putchar(c);
      c = getc(fp);
    }
    fclose(fp);
    printf("\n[End of %s]\n————\n\n", argv[i]);
    i++;
  }
  return 0;
}
```

The following program named count.c is similar to the wc command in UNIX call. The output of the program, run on UNIX, is given here.

```
$ count prog.c
prog.c: 300 characters 20 lines
$ count -l prog.c
prog.c: 20 lines
$ count -w prog.c
prog.c: 300 characters
```

_____ **EXAMPLE** _____

```
13. /*count.c : Count lines and characters in a file */
    #include <stdio.h>
    #include <stdlib.h>
    int main(int argc, char *argv[])
    {
      int c, nc, nlines;
      char filename[120];
      FILE *fp, *fopen();
    if(argc == 1)
    {
      fprintf(stderr, "No input files\n");
      fprintf(stderr, "Usage: \% count [-l] [w] file\n");
      exit(1);
    }
    nlines = 0;
    nc = 0;
    if((strcmp("-l", argv[1]) == 0)||
                  (strcmp("-w", argv[1]) == 0))
        strcpy(filename, argv[2]);
    else
        strcpy(filename, argv[1]);
      fp = fopen(filename, "r");
    if(fp == NULL)
    {
        fprintf(stderr,"Cannot open %s\n", filename);
        exit(1);
```

```
    c = getc(fp);
    while(c!= EOF)
    {
        if(c == '\n')
        nlines++;
        nc++;
        c = getc(fp);
    }
    fclose(fp);
    if(strcmp(argv[1], "-w") == 0)
        printf("%s: %d characters \n", filename, nc);
    else if(strcmp(argv[1], "-l") == 0)
        printf("%s: %d lines \n", filename, nlines);
    else
        printf("%s: %d characters %d lines\n", filename,
                nc, nlines);
    return 0;
}
```

It should be noted that the preceding program crashes if it is run as

```
$ count -w
```

or

```
$ count -l
```

This is because, in this case, we failed to test if there was a third argument containing the filename to be processed. Here, trying to access this non-existent argument causes a memory violation. This gives rise to a so-called 'bus error' in a UNIX environment.

EXAMPLE

14. Write a cpy command to operate like the UNIX cp or MSDOS COPY command that takes its text files from the command line as follows.

```
cpy file newfile
```

Solution

```
#include <stdio.h>
int main(int argc, char **argv)
{
    FILE *in, *out;
    int key;
    if(argc < 3)
    {
        puts("The source must be an existing file");
        puts("If the destination file exists, it will be
            overwritten");
        return 0;
    }
    if((in = fopen(argv[1], "r")) == NULL)
    {
        puts("Unable to open the file to be copied");
        return 0;
    }
```

```
    if((out = fopen(argv[2], "w")) == NULL)
    {
        puts("Unable to open the output file");
        return 0;
    }
    while(!feof(in))
    {
        key = fgetc(in);
        if(!feof(in))
            fputc(key, out);
    }
    fclose(in);
    fclose(out);
    return 0;
}
```

main() may take the third command line argument env, though it is compiler dependent. The argument env is an array of pointers to the strings. Each pointer points to an environment variable from the list of environment variables. Consider the following program.

```
#include <stdio.h>
int main(int argc, char *argv[], char *env[])
{
    int i = 0;
    while (env[i])
    printf ("\n%s", env[i++]);
    return 0;
}
```

The above program produces a typical output when it was executed in Quincy which uses the MinGW port of the GCC compiler system.

```
ALLUSERSPROFILE=C:\ProgramData
APPDATA=C:\Users\Manas\AppData\Roaming
CommonProgramFiles=C:\Program Files\Common Files
COMPUTERNAME=MANAS-PC
ComSpec=C:\Windows\system32\cmd.exe
FLTK_DOCDIR=C:\Program Files\quincy\html\
programmerhelp\fltk\fltk1.1\
FP_NO_HOST_CHECK=NO
HOMEDRIVE=C:
HOMEPATH=\Users\Manas
LOCALAPPDATA=C:\Users\Manas\AppData\Local
LOGONSERVER=\\MANAS-PC
NUMBER_OF_PROCESSORS=2
OS=Windows_NT
Path=C:\Program  Files\quincy\mingw\bin\;C:\Program
        Files\quincy\bin\VistaBin;C:\Program Files\
        quincy\bin;C:\JavaFX\javafxsdk\bin;C:\
        JavaFX\javafxsdk\emulator\bin;C:\Windows\
        system32;C:\Windows;C:\Windows\System32\
```

```
        Wbem;C:\Windows\System32\WindowsPowerShell\
          v1.0\
    PATHEXT=.COM;.EXE;.BAT;.CMD;.VBS;.VBE;.JS;.JSE;
          .WSF;.WSH;.MSC
    PROCESSOR_ARCHITECTURE=x86
    PROCESSOR_IDENTIFIER=x86 Family 15 Model 6 Stepping
          5, GenuineIntel
    PROCESSOR_LEVEL=15
    PROCESSOR_REVISION=0605
    ProgramData=C:\ProgramData
    ProgramFiles=C:\Program Files
    PROMPT=$P$G
    PSModulePath=C:\Windows\system32\
    WindowsPowerShell\v1.0\Modules\
    PUBLIC=C:\Users\Public
    SESSIONNAME=Console
    SystemDrive=C:
    SystemRoot=C:\Windows
    TEMP=C:\Users\Manas\AppData\Local\Temp
    TMP=C:\Users\Manas\AppData\Local\Temp
    USERDOMAIN=Manas-PC
    USERNAME=Manas
    USERPROFILE=C:\Users\Manas
    windir=C:\Windows
```

16.4 THE C PREPROCESSOR

The C preprocessor is a program that processes any source program in C before compilation. Since it allows the user to define *macros*, the C preprocessor is also called a macro processor. A *macro* is defined as an open-ended subroutine. An open-ended subroutine is a set of program instructions, as in a function, that does not have a return statement.

The preprocessor provides its own language that can be a very powerful tool for the programmer. These tools are instructions to the preprocessor, and are called *directives*. The C preprocessor has several directives that are used to invoke it. A directive usually occupies a single line. The # symbol should be the first non-blank character on the line, which means that only spaces and tabs may appear before it. Blank symbols may also appear between the # and *directive*. A directive line may also contain a comment; these are simply ignored by the preprocessor. A # appearing in a line on its own is simply ignored. A line having only non-white space character in a # is termed as null directive in standard C and is treated the same as a blank line. Most directives are followed by one or more tokens. A token is anything other than a blank. A line with a directive whose last non-blank character is \, is assumed to continue in the line following it, thus making it possible to define multiple line directives.

Directives are generally placed at the beginning of a source program, which means that these are written before the main(). However, preprocessor directives can appear anywhere in a source file, but they apply only to the remainder of the source file. It is advantageous to use the preprocessor because it makes

- program development easier.
- programs easier to read.
- modification of programs easier.
- C code more transportable between different machine architectures.

16.4.1 The C Preprocessor Directives

The preprocessor directives can be classified into two categories: unconditional and conditional. Figure 16.1 depicts the two categories of directives.

Fig. 16.1 Types of preprocessor directives in C

The C preprocessor directives shown in Fig. 16.1 are given in Table 16.3 with brief explanations.

Table 16.3 The C preprocessor directives

Directive	Explanation
#define	Defines a macro
#undef	Undefines a macro
#include	Textually includes the contents of a file
#ifdef	Makes compilation of code conditional on a macro being defined
#ifndef	Makes compilation of code conditional on a macro not being defined
#endif	Marks the end of a conditional compilation block
#if	Makes compilation of code conditional on an expression being non-zero
#else	Specifies an else part for a #ifdef, #ifndef, or #if directive
#elif	Combination of #else and #if
#line	Change current line number and filename
#error	Outputs an error message
#pragma	Is implementation-specific

define

The general form for the define directive is

```
#define macro_name replacement_string
```

The #define directive is used to make substitutions throughout the program in which it is located. In other words, #define causes the compiler to go through the program, replacing every occurrence of macro_name with replacement_string. The replacement string stops at the end of the line. No semicolon is used at the end of the directive.

---------- EXAMPLES ----------

15. A typical illustration of the use of #define.

```
#include <stdio.h>
#define TRUE 1
#define FALSE 0
int main()
{
    int done=0;
    while(done=!TRUE)
        {
        printf("\n Here done is FALSE");
        done++;
        }
    printf("\n Now done is TRUE");
    return 0;
}
```

Output

```
    Now done is TRUE
```

Another feature of the #define directive is that it can take arguments, making it rather useful as a pseudo-function creator. Consider the following example.

16.
```
#include <stdio.h>
#define abs_value(a)((a<0)? -a : a)
int main()
{
    int a=-1;
```
Replaced by (a<0)? –a : a
```
    while(abs_value(a))
    {
      printf("\n Value of a=%d within while",a);
      a=0;
    }
    printf("\n Value of a=%d outside while",a);
    return 0;
}
```

Output

```
Value of a=-1 within while
Value of a=0 outside while
```

The next example shows how to use the #define directive to create a general-purpose incrementing for loop that prints out the integers 1 through 5.

17.
```
#include <stdio.h>
#define up_count(x,lo,hi)\
    for((x)=lo;(x)<=(hi);(x)++)
int main()
{
    int k;
```
Replaced by for (k = 1; k<=5; k++)
```
    up_count(k,1,5)
    {
        printf("\n k is %d",k);
    }
    printf("\n Test program ended");
    return 0;
}
```

Output

```
k is 1
k is 2
k is 3
k is 4
k is 5
Test program ended
```

It should be noted that a macro should be written in a single line, but it can be continued to more than one line by using the statement continuation character, \. One could write the following:

```
#define min(x, y) \
    ((x)<(y) ? (x) : (y))
```

Note

- Apart from parameterized macros, C99 adds a better way of creating function which expands in line.

#undef

The general form of this #undef directive is

```
#undef macro_name
```

This directive undefines a macro. A macro *must* be undefined before being redefined to a different value. For example,

```
#undef VALUE
#define VALUE 1024
#undef MAX
```

The use of #undef on an undefined identifier is harmless and has no effect. If a macro ceases to be useful, it may be *undefined* with the #undef directive. #undef takes a single argument, the name of the macro to be undefined. The bare macro name is used even if the macro is function-like. If anything appears on the line after the macro name, it is an error. Moreover, the #undef directive has no effect if the name is not a macro.

#include

The #include directive has two general forms

```
    #include <file_name>
```

and

```
#include "file_name"
```

The first form is used for referring to the standard system header files. It searches for a file named file_name in a standard header file library and inserts it at the current location. Header files contain details of functions and types used within the library. They must be included before the program can make use of the library functions. The angle brackets, < >, indicates the preprocessor to search for the header file in the standard location for library definitions.

The second form searches for a file in the current directory. This is used where multi-file programs are being written. Certain information is required at the beginning of each program file. This code in the file_name can be put into the current directory and included in each program file. Local header file names are usually enclosed by double quotes, " ". It is conventional to give header files a name that ends in '.h' to distinguish them from other types of files. Examples of both forms of #include have been given in earlier chapters.

In addition, each preprocessing directive must be on its own line. For example, the following will not work:

```
#include <stdio.h> #include <stdlib.h>
```

Include files can have #include directives in them. This is referred to as *nested includes*. The number of levels of nesting allowed varies between compilers. However, C89 stipulates that at least eight nested inclusions will be available. C99 specifies that at least 15 levels of nesting be supported.

#if, #else, #elif, and #endif

Here, #if is a conditional directive of the preprocessor. It has an expression that evaluates to an integer. The #else is also used with this directive if required. The #if and #else pair operates in a way similar to the if-else construct of C. The #endif is used to delimit the end of statement following the statement sequence.

The general form of #if with #endif and #else is

```
#if< constant_expression>
  <statement_sequence1>
#endif
```

or

```
#if< constant_expression>
  <statement_sequence1>
#else<statement_sequence2>
#endif
```

As an example, if a program has to run on an MSDOS machine and it is required to include file MSDOS.h, otherwise a default.h file, then the following code using #if can be used.

```
#if SYSTEM == MSDOS
  #include <msdos.h>
```

```
#else
  #include "default.h"
#endif
```

The general form for using #if with #elif, which is else-if, and #endif is

```
#if<constant_expression1>
  <statement_sequence1>
#elif<constant_expression2>
  <statement_sequence2>
  .
  .
  .
#elif<constant_expressionN>
  <statement_sequenceN>
#endif
```

Sometimes, it may be necessary to choose one of the different header files to be included into a program. For example, preprocessors might specify configuration parameters to be used on different types of operating systems. The programmer can do this using a series of conditional directives as shown in the following illustration.

```
#if SYSTEM1
#include "SYSTEM_1.h"
#elif SYSTEM2
#include "system_2.h"
#elif SYSTEM3
...
#endif
```

#ifdef and #ifndef

The #ifdef directive executes a statement sequence if the macro_name is defined. If the macro_name is not defined, the #ifndef directive executes a statement sequence. For both the directives, the end of statements is delimited by #endif. The general form of #ifdef is

```
#ifdef macro_name
  <statement_sequence>
#endif
```

and the general form of #ifndef is

```
#ifndef macro_name
  <statement_sequence>
#endif
```

These conditional directives are useful for checking if macros are defined or set, perhaps from different header files and program modules. For instance, to set integer size for a portable C program between Turbo C (on MSDOS) and LINUX (or other) operating systems, these directives can be used.

As an example, assume that if Turbo C is running, a macro TURBOC will be defined. So, the programmer just needs to check for this. Thus, the following code may be written.

```
#ifdef TURBOC
  #define INT_SIZE 16
```

```
#else
#define INT_SIZE 32
#endif
```

Another example of the use of #ifdef is given as follows.

--- **EXAMPLE** ---

```
18. #include <stdio.h>
    #define VAX 1
    #define SUN 0
    int main()
    {
    #ifdef VAX
      printf("This is a VAX\n");
    #endif
    #ifdef SUN
      printf("This is a SUN\n");
    #endif
      return 0;
    }
```

Output
```
This is a VAX
```

Note

- C89 states that #ifs and #elifs may be nested at least eight levels. C99 states that at least 63 levels of nesting be allowed.

The logical operators such as && or || can be used to test if multiple identifiers have been defined.

#error

The directive #error is used for reporting errors by the preprocessor. The general form is

```
#error error_message
```

When the preprocessor encounters this, it outputs the error_message and causes the compilation to be aborted. Therefore, it should be only used for reporting errors that make further compilation pointless or impossible. It is used primarily for debugging. For example,

```
#ifndef LINUX
#error This software requires the LINUX OS.
#endif
```

Another example of the use of #error is as follows:

```
#if A_SIZE < B_SIZE
#error "Incompatible sizes"
#endif
```

Here, the #error macro is used to enforce the consistency of two symbolic constants.

#line

The #line directive is used to change the value of the __LINE__ and __FILE__ variables. The filename is optional. The __FILE__ and the __LINE__ variables represent the current file and the line that is being read. The general form of this directive is

```
#line line_number <file _name>
```

The example,

```
#line 20 "program1.c"
```

changes the current line number to 20, and the current file to "program1.c".

#pragma

The #pragma directive allows the programmer the ability to convey to the compiler to do certain tasks. Since the #pragma directive is implementation-specific, uses vary from compiler to compiler. One option might be to trace program execution. Three forms of this directive (commonly known as *pragmas*) are specified by the 1999 C standard. A C compiler is free to attach any meaning it likes to other pragmas.

16.4.2 Predefined Macros

The preprocessor furnishes a small set of predefined macros that denote useful information. The standard macros are summarized in Table 16.4. Most implementations augment this list with many non-standard predefined identifiers.

Table 16.4 Standard predefined identifiers

Identifier	Denotes
__FILE__	Name of the file being processed
__LINE__	Current line number of the file being processed
__DATE__	Current date as a string (e.g., "16 Dec 2005")
__TIME__	Current time as a string (e.g., "10:15:30")

The predefined macros, also known as macros, can be used in programs just like program constants.

All predefined macros have two underscore characters more at the beginning and the other at the end. A demonstration of predefined identifiers is illustrated below:

```
#include <stdio.h>
int main()
{
printf("__DATE__ == %s\n",__DATE__);
printf("__FILE__ == %s\n",__FILE__);
printf("__LINE__ == %d\n",__LINE__);
printf("__TIME__ == %s\n",__TIME__);
printf("__STDC__ == %d\n",__STDC__);
return 0;
}
```
Output
```
__DATE__ == Dec 18 2010
__FILE__ == pred.c
```

```
__LINE__ == 11
__TIME__ == 17:25:09
__STDC__ == 1
```

The `__DATE__` macro provides a string representation of the date in the form `Mmm dd yyyy` where `Mmm` is the first three characters of the name of the month, `dd` is the day in the form of a pair of digits 1 to 31, where single-digit days are preceded by a blank and finally, `yyyy` is the year as four digits.

Similarly, `__TIME__`, provides a string containing the value of the time when it is invoked, in the form `hh:mm:ss`, which is evidently a string containing pairs of digits for hours, minutes, and seconds, separated by colons. Note that the time is when the compiler is executed, not when the program is run. Once the program containing this statement is compiled, the values that will be output by the `printf()` statement are fixed until it is compiled again. On subsequent executions of the program, the then current time and date will be output. Do not confuse these macros with the time function

C99 adds the following macros.

_ _STDC_HOSTED_ _	1 if an operating system is present
_ _STDC_VERSION_ _	199901L or greater; represents version of C
_ _STDC_IEC_559_ _	1 if IEC 60559 floating-point arithmetic is supported
__STDC_IEC_599_COMPLEX_ _	1 if IEC 60559 complex arithmetic is supported
_ _STDC_ISO_10646_ _	A value of the form *yyyymmL* that states the year and month of the ISO/IEC 10646 specification supported by the compiler

There are two special operators that can be used in macro. They are # and ##.

Stringizing operator

If the formal parameter associated with a macro is preceded by a "#" symbol in the replacement string, then a string complete with enclosing quotes and all relevant escapes is formed. This operation is known as *stringizing*. It is illustrated in the following program.

```
#include <stdio.h>
#define  SHOWX(x) printf(#x "= %d", (x));printf ("\n")
int main(void)
{
  int a = 5, b = 10;
  SHOWX(a);
  SHOWX(b);
  SHOWX(a+b);
  return 0;
}
```

Output

```
a = 5
b = 10
a+ b = 15
```

In this illustration, `SHOWX(a);` is expanded as

```
printf("a" "= %d",(a));printf("\n");
```

Similarly, `SHOWX(a+b);` is expanded as

```
printf("a+b" "= %d",(a+b));printf("\n");
```

Token pasting operator

The `##` operator within a macro expansion causes concatenation of the tokens on either side of it to form a new token. This is called **token pasting.** This means two tokens on either side of the `##` will be merged as if they were a single text token. The modified version of the above program is as follows:

```
#include <stdio.h>
#define  SHOWX(x) printf("%d",a##x);printf("\n")
int main(void)
{
  int a1 = 5, a2 = 10;
  SHOWX(1);
  SHOWX(2);
  return 0;
}
```

Output

```
5
10
```

When the preprocessor processed `SHOWX(1)`, it generated

```
printf("%d",a1);
```

The ## operator can be used to swap two variables of any data type as follows.

```
#include <stdio.h>
#define  SWAP(datatype, a,b) datatype a##b = a; \
              a = b; \
              b = a##b
int main(void)
{

  int x = 5, y = 10;
  float m = 1.23f, n = 4.56f;
  SWAP(int, x, y);
  printf("\n x = %d \t y = %d", x,y);
  SWAP(float, m, n);
  printf("\n m = %g \t n = %g", m,n);
  return 0;
}
```

Output

```
x = 5          y = 10
m = 1.23    n = 4.56
```

A formal parameter as an operand for `##` is not expanded before pasting. The actual parameter is substituted for the formal parameter; but the actual parameter is not expanded. For example,

```
#define a(n) aaa ## n
#define b 2
```

the expansion of `a(b)` is aaab, not aaa2 or aaan.

Note

- Command-line arguments are specified when a program is executed.
- Preprocessor directives can appear anywhere in a source program, but these are generally placed at the beginning of a source program.

16.5 TYPE QUALIFIER

A type is a fundamental concept in Standard C. When a variable is declared, it is associated with a data type. Each expression and sub-expression that is written has a type. This means that data type is a foundation attribute of a variable. Additional attributes include the following.

- Type specifier (`signed` or `unsigned`)
- Type qualifier (`const`, `volatile`, and/or `restrict`)
- Storage class (`auto`, `register`, `extern`, or `static`)

A type specifier affects the range of values that an object can have. It may either be signed or unsigned. Storage class has already been discussed in Chapter 12. Type qualifiers are used to provide greater control over optimization. Many important optimization methods are based on the principle of caching: under certain circumstances the compiler can remember the last value accessed (read or written) from a location, and use this stored value the next time that location is read. If this memory is a register of the machine, for example, the code can be smaller and faster using the register rather than accessing external memory.

There are two or three types of qualifiers—`const`, `volatile`, and/or `restrict`. The concepts of `const` and `volatile` are *completely independent*. A common misconception is to imagine that `const` is the opposite of `volatile` and vice versa. The C89 standards committee added two type qualifiers to C, `const` and `volatile`. The C99 committee added a third type qualifier with `restrict`. A discussion on the type qualifiers follows.

16.5.1 const Qualifier

`const` means something that is not modifiable. The `const` type qualifier is used to qualify an object whose value cannot be changed. Objects qualified by the `const` keyword cannot be modified. Using the `const` qualifier on an object protects it from the side effects caused by operations that alter storage.

The syntax and semantics of `const` were adapted from C++. Any variable that is declared with `const` as a part of its type specification must not be assigned to in the program. The following program clarifies the use of `const` in a C program.

――――――――――――― **EXAMPLES** ―――――――――――――

```
19.  #include <stdio.h>
     #include <stdlib.h>
     int main(){
     int i=10;
```

```
     const int c = 5;
     const int *cp;
     int *ncpi;
     cp = &c;
     ncpi = &i;

     cp = ncpi;
     printf("\n c=%d \t i=%d",c,i);
     printf("\n *cp=%d \t *ncpi=%d",*cp,*ncpi);
     exit(EXIT_SUCCESS);
     return 0;
     }
```

Output

```
     c=5 i= 10
     *cp=10 *ncpi=10
```

Now; if a statement `c=20;` is inserted in the program in Example 19, the compiler generates an error.

```
20.  #include <stdio.h>
     #include <stdlib.h>
     int main(){
     int i=10;
     const int c = 5;
     const int *cp;
     int *ncpi;
     cp = &c;
     ncpi = &i;
     cp = ncpi;
     printf("\n c=%d \t i=%d",c,i);
     printf("\n *cp=%d \t *ncpi=d",*cp,*ncpi);

     c=20;         ―――（ C compiler may give
                          an error here. ）

     printf("\n c=%d \t i=%d",c,i);
     printf("\n *cp=%d \t *ncpi=%d",*cp,*ncpi);
     *ncpi = 0;
     exit(EXIT_SUCCESS);
     return 0;
     }
```

Consider the following version of the program in Example 20.

```
21.  #include <stdio.h>
     #include <stdlib.h>
     int main()
     {
     int i=10;
     const int c = 5;
     const int *cp;
     int *ncpi;
     cp = &c;
     ncpi = &i;
     cp = ncpi;
     printf("\n c=%d \t i=%d",c,i);
     printf("\n *cp=%d \t *ncpi=%d",*cp,*ncpi);
     ncpi = (int *)cp;
       *ncpi=20;
```

```
printf("\n c=%d \t i=%d",c,i);
printf("\n *cp=%d \t *ncpi=%d",*cp,*ncpi);
exit(EXIT_SUCCESS);
return 0;
}
```

Output

```
c=5   i= 10
*cp=10 *ncpi=10
c=5   i= 20
*cp=20 *ncpi=20
```

The output obtained will be clear after reading the subsequent paragraphs. The following properties may be applied to the const type qualifier.

- The const qualifier can be used to qualify any data type, including a single member of a structure or union.

- If const is specified when declaring an aggregate type, all members of the aggregate type are treated as objects qualified with const. When const is used to qualify a member of an aggregate type, only that member is qualified.

For example,

```
const struct employee {
    char name[30];
    int age;
    int deptno;
    float salary;
} a, b;
```

Here, name, age, deptno, and salary are treated as though declared with const. Therefore, all members of a and b are const-qualified.

```
struct empl {
    char *name;
    const int age;
    int deptno;
    float salary;
} c, d;
```

Here, member age is qualified. All members in the previous structure are qualified with const. If the tag employee is used to specify another structure later in the program, the const qualifier does not apply to the new structure's members unless explicitly specified.

- The address of a non-const object can be assigned to a pointer to a const object (with an explicit const specifier), but that pointer cannot be used to alter the value of the object. For example,

```
const int i = 0;
int j = 1;
const int *p = &i;     Explicit const
                       specifier required.
int *q = &j;
```

```
*p = 1;
```

Error—attempt to modify a const-qualified object through a pointer.

```
*q = 1;     This is VALID.
```

- Attempting to modify a const object using a pointer to a non-const qualified type causes unpredictable behaviour.

There are two standards for const specifier. One, an object that is defined with 'const' may not be modified in any way by a strictly conforming program. Since the 'c' in Example 19 is const, it may not be modified; if it is modified, the behaviour is undefined. Two, an lvalue with the const-qualifier may not be assigned to. Note also that the following strictly conformant program must print '5, 7'.

EXAMPLE

```
22. #include <stdio.h>
    int v=5;
    int *p;
    void f(const int *);
    int main(void) {
        p = &v;
        f(&v);
        return 0;
    }
    void f(const int *vp) {
        int i, j;
        i = *vp;
        *p = 7;
        j = *vp;
        printf("%d, %d\n", i, j);
    }
```

The compiler cannot assume that i and j are equal, despite the fact that *vp is const-qualified, because vp can (and does) point to a modifiable lvalue and the assignment to *p can (and does) modify the lvalue to which the const-qualified vp pointer points. As this example illustrates, const does not mean constant.

Consider the following statements.

```
int c;
int *const p = &c;
```

Note, p is a pointer to an integer, which is exactly what it must be if the const were not there. The const means that the contents of p are not to be changed, although whatever it points to can be—the pointer is constant, not whatever it points to. The other way round is

```
const int *cp;
```

that indicates cp is now an ordinary, modifiable pointer, but what it points to must not be modified. So, depending on what one chooses to do, both the pointer and what it points to may be modifiable or not; just choose the appropriate declaration.

The `const` qualifier may be specified with the `volatile` qualifier. This is useful, for example, in a declaration of a data object that is immutable by the source process but can be changed by other processes, or as a model of a memory-mapped input port such as a real-time clock.

> **Note**
>
> - `const char *p` This is a pointer to a constant char. One cannot change the value pointed at by p, but can change the pointer p itself.
>
>   `*p = 'A';` is illegal.
>
>   `p = "Hello";` is legal.
>
> - `const * char p` This is a constant pointer to (non-const) char. One cannot change the pointer p, but can change the value pointed at by p.
>
>   `*p = 'A';` is legal.
>
>   `p = "Hello";` is illegal.
>
> - `const char * const p` This is a constant pointer to constant char! One cannot change the value pointed to by p, nor the pointer.
>
>   `*p = 'A';` is illegal.
>
>   `p = "Hello";` is also illegal.

16.5.2 volatile Qualifier

`volatile` is used to do away with the problems that are encountered in real time or embedded systems programming using C. A `volatile` value is one that might change unexpectedly. This situation generally occurs while accessing special hardware registers, usually when writing device drivers. The compiler should not assume that a `volatile`-qualified variable contains the last value that was written to it, or that reading it again would yield the same result that reading it the previous time did. The compiler should, therefore, avoid making any optimizations that would suppress seemingly redundant accesses to a `volatile`-qualified variable. Examples of `volatile` locations would be a clock register (which always gives an up-to-date time value each time you read it), or a device control/status register, which causes some peripheral device to perform an action each time the register is written to.

The `volatile` qualifier forces the compiler to allocate memory for the `volatile` object, and to always access the object from memory. This qualifier is often used to declare that an object can be accessed in some way not under the compiler's control. Therefore, an object qualified by the `volatile` keyword can be modified or accessed by other processes or hardware, and is especially vulnerable to side effects.

The following rules apply to the use of the `volatile` qualifier.

- The `volatile` qualifier can be used to qualify any data type, including a single member of a structure or union.

- Redundant use of the `volatile` keyword elicits a warning message. For example,

  ```
  volatile volatile int x;
  ```

When `volatile` is used with an aggregate type declaration, all members of the aggregate type are qualified with `volatile`. When `volatile` is used to qualify a member of an aggregate type, only that member is qualified. For example,

```
volatile struct employee {
  char name[30];
  int  age;
  int  deptno;
  float salary;
} a, b;

struct empl {
  char *name;
  volatile int age;
  int deptno;
  float salary;
} c, d;
```

If the tag `employee` is used to specify another structure later in the program, the `volatile` qualifier does not apply to the new structure's members unless explicitly specified.

The address of a non-volatile object can be assigned to a pointer that points to a `volatile` object. For example,

```
const int *intptr;

volatile int x;

intptr = &x;
```

Likewise, the address of a `volatile` object can be assigned to a pointer that points to a non-volatile object.

16.5.3 restrict Qualifier

The `restrict` qualifier is an invention of the C99 committee. The object that is accessed through the `restrict`-qualified pointer has a special relation with that pointer. Only pointer types can be `restrict`-qualified. A `restrict`-qualified pointer that is a function parameter, is the sole means of access to an object.

Some typical uses of the restrict qualifier

The typical uses are in

- file scope restricted pointers
- function parameters
- block scope

These uses are explained in the following sections.

File scope restricted pointers A file scope-restricted pointer is subject to very strong restrictions. It should point to a single array object for the duration of the program. That array object may not be referenced both through the restricted pointer and through either its declared name (if it has one) or another restricted pointer.

Note in the following example how a single block of storage is effectively subdivided into two disjoint objects.

```
float *restrict x, *restrict y;

void init(int n)

{
    float *t = malloc(2 * n * sizeof(float));

    x = t;      /* x refers to 1st half */

    y = t + n;  /* y refers to 2nd half */

}
```

Function parameters Restricted pointers are also very useful as pointer parameters of a function. A compiler can assume that a restrict-qualified pointer, that is, a function parameter, is at the beginning of each execution of the function, the sole means of access to an object. Note that this assumption expires with the end of each execution.

Block scope A block scope-restricted pointer makes an aliasing assertion that is limited to its block. This seems more natural than allowing the assertion to have function scope. It allows local assertions that apply only to key loops. In the following example, parameters x and y can be assumed to refer to disjoint array objects because both are restrict-qualified. This implies that each iteration of the loop is independent of the others, and hence the loop can be aggressively optimized.

```
void f1(int n, float * restrict x,
        const float * restrict y)

{
    int i;
    for(i = 0; i < n; i++)
        x[i] += y[i];
}
```

Members of structures

The restrict qualifier can be used in the declaration of a structure member. When an identifier of a structure type is declared, it provides a means of access to a member of that structure type. The compiler assumes that the identifier provides the sole initial means of access to a member of the type specified in the member declaration. The duration of the assumption depends on the scope of the identifier, not on the scope of the declaration of the structure. Thus, a compiler can assume that s1.x and s1.y below are used to refer to disjoint objects for the duration of the whole program, but that s2.x and s2.y are used to refer to disjoint objects only for the duration of each invocation of the f3 function.

```
struct t {
    int n;
```

```
    float * restrict x, * restrict y;
};

struct t s1;

void f3(struct t s2) { /* ... */ }
```

Note

- The const type qualifier is used to qualify an object value that cannot be changed.
- A volatile qualifed object is one that might change unexpectedly.
- The restrict-qualifier, used only with pointers, is used to access an object through a specially related pointer.

16.6 VARIABLE LENGTH ARGUMENT LIST

All the functions discussed so far accept a fixed number of arguments. But functions like printf() accept any number of parameters. How can a function with a variable number of arguments be written? To write such functions, macros defined in the header file stdarg.h have to be used. The presence of a variable-length argument list is indicated by an *ellipsis* (...) in the prototype. For example, the prototype for printf(), as found in <stdio.h>, looks something like this.

```
extern int printf(const char *, ...);
```

The three dots '...' allow the function to accept any number of parameters. Only the last parameters must be NULL and the function prototype must be as follows.

```
void function_name(const char *, ...);
```

The macros used are va_list, va_start(), va_arg(), and va_end(). va_list is an array or special 'pointer' type that is used in obtaining the arguments that come in place of the ellipsis. va_start() begins the processing of an argument list, va_arg() fetches argument values from it, and va_end() finishes processing. Therefore, va_list is a bit like the stdio FILE * type and va_start is a bit like fopen(). Consider the following program.

— **EXAMPLE** —

```
23. #include <stdarg.h>
    #include <stdio.h>
    void show(int n, ...)
    {
    va_list ap;
    va_start(ap, n);
    printf("count = %d:", n);
    while(n-- > 0)
    {
    int i = va_arg(ap, int);
    printf("%d", i);
    }
    printf("\n");
```

```
va_end(ap);
}
int main()
{
show(1, 1);
show(3, 1, 2, 3);
return 0;
}
```

The `show()` function declares a single parameter (n), followed by an ellipsis. The ellipsis specifies that a variable number of additional parameters are present. This means that a caller of `show()` can pass an arbitrary number of arguments in addition to the first int argument.

Output

```
count = 1: 1
count = 3: 1 2 3
```

There are some restrictions on functions with variable-length arguments.

- The first parameter must be present since its name has to be passed to `va_start()`.
- While calling the function, if the type of the variable passed does not match the type expected in the function, the results are unpredictable. The C variable argument mechanism is quite useful in certain contexts. But, the mechanism is error-prone because it defeats type checking.

For example, if the second `show()` call is changed to

```
show(3, 1, 2, 3.4);
```

the result is something like

```
count = 1: 1
count = 3: 1 2 858993459
```

The program assumes that an int argument has been passed, when in fact a double (3.4) is passed.

The macro `va_end()` performs clean-up operations. It releases any memory that might have been allocated when `va_start()` was called. Another function `vprintf()` is used to develop a function that outputs an error and exits.

```
void error(const char *fmt)
{
va_list ap;
va_start(ap, fmt);
vprintf(fmt, ap);
va_end(ap);
exit(0);
}
```

The use of the preceding function prompts the user to enter an integer greater than 0, failing which it outputs an error message and exits.

```
printf("\n enter an integer >0");
scanf("%d", &n);
if(n<=0)
```

```
error("value of n= %d it must be greater than 0
\n", i);
```

Notice that the function `error()` is called just like `printf()`.

Perhaps the most important change to the preprocessor is the ability to create macros that take a variable number of arguments. This is indicated by an ellipsis (. . .) in the definition of the macro.

The built-in preprocessing identifier `__VA_ARGS__` determines where the arguments will be substituted. For example, given the following definition,

```
#define Largest(. . .) max(__VA_ARGS__)
```

the statement,

```
Largest(a, b);
```

is transformed into,

```
max(a, b);
```

16.7 MEMORY MODELS AND POINTERS

The concept and use of pointers have been discussed in detail in Chapter 13. In C, each program is usually restricted to 64K of static data. In most C compilers, the programmer is able to select from a variety of *memory models* that control the way in which physical memory (RAM) is utilized by the program. It may be that the program needs to process large volumes of data in RAM or the applications (such as simulations) involve very large amounts of code. Most C compilers offer several memory models to achieve flexible ways of optimizing the use of available memory. Thus, choosing a memory model means making choices among meeting minimum system requirements, maximizing code efficiency, and gaining access to every available memory location. Modern compilers use the Win32 model. If the program's total size is under 640KB, one of the memory models in Table 16.5 should be chosen. These are the real mode memory models.

Table 16.5 Turbo C memory models

Memory model	Memory available	Pointers used
Tiny	64K code + data/stack	Near for code, Near for data
Small	64K code, 64K data/stack	Near for code, Near for data
Medium	1 M code, 64K data/stack	Far for code, Near for data
Compact	64K code, 1 M data/stack	Near for code, Far for data
Large	1 M code, 1 M data/stack	Far for code, Far for data
Huge	1 M code, 1 M data/stack	Far for code, Far for data (inc. static > 64K)

The important differences between the memory models are in the size of the data and code pointers, number of data and code segments, and the number and types of heaps available.

In all the 16-bit memory models, the compiler puts all static and global variables into a single data segment (called DGROUP) that can contain only 64KB. With far data, a particular data structure can be put into a data segment of its own. However, that data structure cannot be larger than 64KB. The major determinant of memory availability is the size of the *pointers* used to access memory locations.

If the pointer is declared globally, the value of its address will be 0000 in the case of a near pointer and 0000:0000 in the case of a far pointer. If the pointer is declared inside a function definition as an auto variable (default), then it is created on the stack and will have a default address of whatever value happened to be at that location on the stack when it was created. In either case; these default memory addresses are invalid. This is referred to as an uninitialized pointer and should never be dereferenced.

There are three types of pointers. They are *near, far,* and *huge.*

In Turbo C; almost all pointers are declared as *near* (16 bits per pointer by default) or *far* (32 bits per pointer). While *near pointers* simplify memory access in the segmented memory of Intel processors by allowing direct arithmetic on pointers, they limit accessible memory to 64 kilobytes (2^{16}). *Far pointers* can be used to access multiple code segments, each 64K, up to 1 megabyte (2^{32}), by using segment and offset addressing. The disadvantage is that the programmer cannot use the simple pointer arithmetic that is possible with near pointers.

The default model is small, which is effective for the majority of applications. The tiny model is specifically designed for the production of TSR (Terminate and Stay Resident) programs, which must fit into one code segment and be compiled as `.com` rather than `.exe` files. The remaining models are selectable in the compilation process through the IDE or in the make file.

GNU C does not have memory models because in this compiler all addresses are 32 bits wide. This is advantageous for the user, since it does not have the 64K limit. For DOS or Win16 compilers, a memory model must be selected.

Note

- The mechanism of using variable-length arguments with functions is error-prone because it defeats type checking.
- There are six types of memory models: tiny, small, medium, compact, large, and huge.
- The important differences between the memory models are in the size of the data and code pointers, number of data and code segments, and the number and type of heaps available.
- There are three types of pointers: near, far, and huge, which use different memory models and functions for memory allocation.

SUMMARY

There are several features in C that can be classified as advanced features. Among these are the bitwise operators. There are six bitwise operators, namely AND (&), OR (!), complement (~), XOR (^), left-shift (<<), and right-shift (>>). These operators act on the contents of bits individually when applied on bytes or words.

The function `main()` can be defined with formal parameters so that the program may accept command-line arguments. This means that arguments are specified to `main()` when the program is executed.

The C preprocessor is a program that processes any source program in C before compilation. Since it allows the user to define *macros*, the C preprocessor is also called a macro processor. The preprocessor provides its own instructions, called *directives*. There are several directives that are used to invoke it. A directive usually occupies a single line. The preprocessor also furnishes a small set of predefined identifiers that denote useful information.

There are two or three data type qualifiers—const, volatile, and/ or restrict—that have been introduced in C. The concepts of const and volatile are *completely independent*. A common misconception is to imagine that const is the opposite of volatile and vice versa.

The C89 standards committee added two type qualifiers to C, const and volatile and the C99 committee added a third type qualifier with restrict.

const means something that is not modifiable. The const type qualifier is used to qualify an object whose value cannot be changed. Objects qualified by the const keyword cannot be modified. On the other hand, a volatile value is one that might change unexpectedly. This situation generally occurs while accessing special hardware registers, usually when writing device drivers. The compiler should not assume that a volatile-qualified variable contains the last value that was written to it, or that reading it again would yield the same result that reading it the previous time did. An object qualified by the volatile keyword can be modified or accessed by other processes or hardware, and is especially vulnerable to side effects.

The restrict qualifier is an invention of the C99 committee. The object accessed through the restrict-qualified pointer has a special relation with that pointer. Only pointer types can be restrict-qualified. A restrict-qualified pointer that is a function parameter is the sole means of access to an object.

The functions discussed so far accepted a fixed number of arguments. But functions such as `printf()` can accept any number of parameters. How can a function with variable number of arguments be written? To write such functions, macros defined in the header file `stdarg.h` have to be used. The presence of a variable-length argument list is indicated by an *ellipsis* in the prototype.

There are six types of memory models: tiny, small, medium, compact, large, and huge. There are three types of pointers: near, far, and huge. They use different memory models and functions for memory allocation.

KEY TERMS

Bitwise operators These are Boolean operators that implement bit-to-bit operation between corresponding bit positions of two arguments.

Directives These are instructions that are given to the preprocessor.

Macro It is an open-ended subroutine, similar to a function, that does not have a return statement.

Masking It is a process by which a given bit pattern is converted into another bit pattern by means of a logical bitwise operator.

Predefined macros These are a set of identifiers that provide preset information.

Preprocessor It is a program that processes any macro in C before compilation of the main program.

Type qualifier It is an additional attribute attached to a data type that further specifies the implementation nature of the defined variable.

Type specifier It is an additional attribute attached to a data type specifying the signed or unsigned nature of a variable.

FREQUENTLY ASKED QUESTIONS

1. What is a translation unit?
A translation unit refers to a C program with all its header files. In a project involving different C source files to be compiled separately, each of them together with its header files forms a translation unit. Hence, there will be as many translation units as there are files to be compiled separately. The preprocessor produces this translation unit.

2. What is a preprocessor?
The C preprocessor is a program that processes any source program in C and prepares it for the translator. It can be an independent program or its functionality may be embedded in the compiler. The preprocessor is invoked as the first part of your compiler program's compilation step. It is usually hidden from the programmer because it is run automatically by the compiler.

While preparing code, it scans for special commands known as preprocessor directives. These directives instruct the preprocessor to look for special code libraries, make substitutions in the code and in other ways prepare the code for translation into machine language.

3. What facilities do a preprocessor provide to the programmer?
C preprocessor provides the following three main facilities to the programmers.
- file inclusion using #include directive
- macro replacement using #define directive
- conditional inclusion using directives like #if, #ifdef, etc.

The preprocessor reads in all the `include` files and the source code to be compiled and creates a preprocessed version of your source code. Macros get automatically substituted into the program by their corresponding code and value assignments. If the source code contains any conditional preprocessor directives (such as #if), the preprocessor evaluates the condition and modifies your source code accordingly.

4. Why should the preprocessor statements be used in the program?
The C preprocessor provides the tools that enable the programmer to develop programs that are easier to develop, read, modify, and to port to a different computer system. One should use the preprocessor statements in the program for the following basic demands of the software programming.

Improving readability and reliability of the program Macros can make the C program much more readable and reliable, because symbolic constants formed by non-parameterized macros aid documentation. They also aid reliability by restricting to one place the check on the actual representation of the constant.

Facilitating easier modifications Using a macro in one place and using it in potentially several places, one could modify all instances of the macro by changing it in one place rather than several places.

Providing portability The macros aid portability by allowing symbolic constants that may be system dependent to be altered once. Conditional compilation is often used to create one program that can be compiled to run on different computer systems.

Helping in debugging The C preprocessor can be used to insert debugging code into your program. By appropriate use of #ifdef statements, the debugging code can be enabled or disabled at your discretion. It is used to switch on or off various statements in the program, such as debugging statements that print out the values of various variables or trace the flow of program execution.

5. What is the difference between #include <file> and #include "file"?
Whether the filename is enclosed within quotes or by angle brackets determines how the search for the specified file is carried on.
#include <file> tells the preprocessor to look for the file in the predefined default location. This predefined default location is often an INCLUDE environment variable that denotes the path to the include files. #include

"file" instructs the preprocessor to look for the file in the current directory first, then in the predefined locations. In general, the location of the standard header files is system dependent. In UNIX, the standard header files are typically located in the directory /usr/include whereas in Borland C system they are found at \BC\INCLUDE. Integrated development environments (IDEs) also have a standard location or locations for the system header files.

The #include "file" method of file inclusion is often used to include non-standard header files created for use in the program. However, there is no hard and fast rule that demands this usage. The angle brackets surrounding the file name in #include instructs that the file being included is part of the C libraries on the system.

6. Why should one include header files?

Header files should be included because they have information that the compiler needs. The ANSI C standard groups the library functions into families, with each family having a specific header file for its function prototypes. Refer to the FAQs in Chapter 8.

7. Why should one create his or her own header file?

One can create his or her own header file to divide a program of larger size into several files and, of course, to manage the declarations for any library functions of his or her own. Using include files to centralize commonly used preprocessor definitions, structure definitions, prototype declarations, and global variable declarations is good programming practice.

8. Write a program which produces the source code.

```
#include <stdio.h>
int main(void)
{
    int c;
    FILE *f = fopen (__FILE__, "r");
    if (!f) return 1;
    for (c=fgetc(f); c!=EOF; c=fgetc(f))
    putchar (c);
    fclose (f);
    return 0;
}
```

9. What is the benefit of using const for declaring constants?

const has the advantage over #define while defining a constant. This is because a const variable can be of any type such as a struct or union, which cannot be represented by a #define constant. The compiler might be able to perform type checking as well as make optimizations based on the knowledge that the value of the variable will not change.

When an array or a string is passed to a function it degenerates into a pointer. As a consequence, any modifications on the corresponding formal parameters, in the called function, would affect the arguments in the calling function. The arguments can be made read-only inside the called function by declaring the parameter const in function prototype as well as in the formal parameter of the function definition. Also, because a const variable is a real variable, it is allocated in memory and has an address that can be used, if needed, with the aid of a pointer.

Apart from these, scope rules can be applied with the constants defined with const. The scope of a variable relates to parts of the program in which it is defined.

10. What can be put into a header file?

Basically, any code can be put in a header file but commonly used preprocessor definitions, structure definitions, prototype declarations, and global variable declarations are included in the header files. The following statements are recommended to be placed in a header file.

- Manifest constants defined with enum or #define.
- Function prototype declarations
- Parameterized macro definitions
- Declaration of external global variables
- Type definition with typedef and struct statements

It is to be noted here that header files are different from libraries. The standard library contains object code of functions that have already been compiled. The standard or user-defined header files do not contain compiled code.

11. Which is better to use: a macro or a function?

Macros are more efficient (and faster) than functions, because their corresponding code is inserted directly at the point where the macro is called. There is no overhead involved in using a macro, unlike function; in which case most C implementations impose a significant overhead for each function call. When a function is called, the processor maintains a data structure called a *stack,* which provides the storage area for "housekeeping" information involved when a function call is made, e.g. the return address from the function, the machine state on entry to the function, copies of the actual parameters and space for all the function's local variables. Maintaining the stack, each time when a function call is made, imposes system overhead. On the other hand, macro cannot handle large and complex coding constructs. A function is more suited for this type of situation. Thus, the answer depends on the situation in which one is writing the code for. To replace small, repeatable code sections, macro should be used and for larger code, which requires several lines of code, function should be employed.

12. What is argc and argv? What do argc and argv stand for? Can they be named other than argc and argv?

When main() is called by the run time system, two arguments are actually passed to the function. The first argument, which is called argc by convention (for *arg*ument *c*ount), is an integer value that specifies the number of arguments typed on the command line. The second argument in main is an array of character pointers, which is called argv by convention (for *arg*ument *v*ector). There are argc+1 character pointers contained in this array, where argc always has a minimum value of 0. The first entry in this array is a pointer to the name of the program that is executing or is a pointer to a null string if the program name is not available on the system. Subsequent entries in the array point to the values that were specified in the same line as the command that initiated execution of the program. The last pointer in the argv array, argv[argc], is defined to be NULL.

The names argc and argv are traditional but arbitrary. It is not mandatory to name these two parameters as argc and argv; any name maintaining the rules for identifier naming can be used.

13. How do I print the contents of environment variables?

The environment variables are available for all operating systems. Though it is compiler dependent, `main()` has the third command line argument `env`, which is used for these environment variables. `env` is an array of pointers to the strings. Each pointer points to an environment variable from the list of environment variables. The following program demonstrates the use of `env`.

```c
#include <stdio.h>
int main(int argc, char *argv[], char *env[ ])
{
    int i = 0 ;
    while (env[i])
        printf ("\n%s", env[i++]);
    return 0;
}
```

The last element in the array `env` is a null pointer. Therefore, `while(env[i])` can be used instead of `while(env[i])!= NULL)`. The typical output of the above code in Windows based GCC compiler (quincy v 1.3) is shown below.

```
ALLUSERSPROFILE=C:\Documents and Settings\All Users
APPDATA=C:\Documents and Settings\Owner\Application
    Data
CLIENTNAME=Console
CommonProgramFiles=C:\Program Files\Common Files
COMPUTERNAME=0DDB352EEEAB43E
ComSpec=C:\WINDOWS\system32\cmd.exe
FLTK_DOCDIR=C:\Program Files\quincy\html\
    programmerhelp\fltk\fltk1.1\
FP_NO_HOST_CHECK=NO
HOMEDRIVE=C:
HOMEPATH=\Documents and Settings\Owner
LOGONSERVER=\\0DDB352EEEAB43E
NUMBER_OF_PROCESSORS=2
=Windows_NT
Path=C:\Program Files\quincy\mingw\bin\;C:\Program
    Files\quincy\bin;C:\WINDOWS\system32;C:\
    WINDOWS;C:\WINDOWS\System32\Wbem;C:\Program
    Files\Panda Security\Panda Internet Security
    2011
PATHEXT=.COM;.EXE;.BAT;.CMD;.VBS;.VBE;.JS;.JSE;.
    WSF;.WSH
PROCESSOR_ARCHITECTURE=x86
PROCESSOR_IDENTIFIER=x86 Family 6 Model 28 Stepping
    2, GenuineIntel
PROCESSOR_LEVEL=6
PROCESSOR_REVISION=1c02
ProgramFiles=C:\Program Files
PROMPT=$P$G
SESSIONNAME=Console
SystemDrive=C:
SystemRoot=C:\WINDOWS
TEMP=C:\DOCUME~1\Owner\LOCALS~1\Temp
TMP=C:\DOCUME~1\Owner\LOCALS~1\Temp
USERDOMAIN=0DDB352EEEAB43E
USERNAME=Owner
USERPROFILE=C:\Documents and Settings\Owner
windir=C:\WINDOWS
```

14. What is #pragma?

The `#pragma` preprocessor directive allows each compiler to implement compiler-specific features. It provides a single well-defined implementation specific control and extensions such as source listing controls, structure packing, loop optimization, and warning suppressing.

15. What is the limitation of using bitwise operators?

Bit operations can be performed on any type of integer value in C—be it `short`, `long`, `long long`, and signed or unsigned—and on characters, but bitwise operators cannot be used with `float`, `double`, `long double`, `void`, or other more complex types. Consider the following program where bitwise AND is applied on a float variable.

```c
#include <stdio.h>
int main()
{
    float a, b=3.2;
    a=b&1;
        printf("a = %f\n", a);
    return 0;
}
```

The program would not compile and causes the following error message.

```
error: invalid operands to binary &
```

16. What are the uses of bitwise operators?

- The bitwise AND operator can be used to clear a bit. That is, if any bit is 0, in either operand, it causes the corresponding bit in the outcome to be set to 0.
- The bitwise OR operator, as the reverse of bitwise AND, can be used to set a bit. Any bit that is set to 1 in either operand causes the corresponding bit in the outcome to be set to 1.
- Bitwise shift operators can be used to quickly multiply and divide integers. A shift right effectively divides a number by 2 and a shift left multiplies it by 2. Bitwise shift operators can be used to pack four characters byte-by-byte into an integer on a machine with 32-bit words. There are several applications of bitwise operators in low-level programming.
- Bitwise operations are most often applied in coding device drivers such as modem programs, disk file routines, and printer routines because bitwise operations can be used to mask off certain bits.

- Bitwise-shift operations can be very useful in decoding input from an external device, such as a `digital-to-analog` converter, and reading status information.
- Bitwise operators are often used in cipher routines. To make a disk file appear unreadable, some bitwise manipulations can be applied on it.

17. What are the limitations or restrictions on using bitwise shift operators?

A right shift of a signed integer is generally not equivalent to division of power of two even if the implementation copies the sign into vacated bits. Thus, `-1>>1` is not equal to `0,` but `-1/2` produces `0` as result.

If a number being shifted is n-bits long, then the shift count must be greater than or equal to 0 and strictly less than n. Thus, it is not possible to shift all the bits (i.e., n bits) out of the value in a single operation, e.g. if an `int` occupies 32 bits and x is a variable of type int, then `x << 31` and `x << 0` are legal but `x << 32` or `x << -1` is illegal. The purpose of this restriction is to allow efficient implementation on hardware with the corresponding restriction.

18. What is masking?

Masking is an operation in which the desired bits of the binary number or bit pattern are set to 0. A *mask* is a variable or a constant, usually stored in a byte or in a short integer, that contains a bit configuration that is used for extracting or testing bits in bitwise operations. Bit masking is used in selecting only certain bits from byte(s) that might have many bits set.

To find the value of a particular bit in an expression, a mask 1 can be used in that position and 0 elsewhere, e.g. the expression `1 << 2` can be used to mask third bit counting from the right.

`(n & (1 << 2)) ? 1 : 0` has the value `1` or `0` depending on the third bit in n.

To set the bits of interest, the number is to be bitwise "ORed" with the bit mask. To clear the bits of interest, the number is to be bitwise ANDed with the one's complement of the bit mask.

19. How do you find whether the given number is a power of 2 using bitwise operator?

In a number which is an exact power of 2, only one bit is set and all others are zero. Let the position of this 1 bit be MSB. Mathematics rules for binary numbers tells us that if we subtract 1 from this number then the number that we would get would have all its bits starting from the bit position MSB+1 set to 1. For example, if the given number *num* is 8(00001000) then num-1 would be 7 (00000111). Now, we notice that these two bit patterns do not have a 1 in the same bit position. If num and (num –1) are bitwise ANDed, we get zero.

The following macro can be used.

`#define ISPOWOF2(n) (!((n) & (n-1))`

20. How do you find whether a given number is even or odd without using % (modulus) operator and using bitwise operators?

If the number is odd, then its least significant bit (LSB) is set i.e. it is 1. If it is even, then it is 0. When you *bitwise and* (&) this number with 1, the result would be either 1 if the number is odd or zero if it is even.

```
int isOdd(int num)
{
    return (num&1);
}
```

The returned value can be used to determine if the number is odd or not. If the value returned is 0, the number is even. It is odd otherwise.

21. There are null character, null statement, null pointer in C language. Is there any null directive?

A # on a line is a null directive and by itself does nothing. It can be used for spacing within conditional compilation blocks. Blank lines can also be used but the # helps the reader see the extent of the block.

22. What does the type qualifier volatile mean?

The `volatile` type qualifier is a directive to the compiler's optimizer that operations involving this variable should not be optimized in certain ways. A volatile variable is one that can change unexpectedly. While accessing special hardware like memory-mapped memory, interrupt-handler or shared memory, its value must be reloaded into a variable every time it is used instead of holding a copy in a register. The volatile qualifier forces the compiler to allocate memory for the volatile object and to access the object from memory.

23. What does the type qualifier restrict mean?

`restrict` qualifier was introduced by C99 committee. Only the pointer types can be restrict-qualified. The object which is accessed through the restrict-qualified pointer, that is a function parameter, is the sole means of access to an object at the beginning of each execution of the function. This assumption expires with the end of each execution.

Other than used as function parameter, the pointer with `restrict` qualifier can be used in file scope as well as in block scope.

A restricted pointer having file scope should point to an object for the duration of the program. That object may not be referenced both through the restricted pointer and through either its declared name (if it has one) or another restricted pointer.

A block scope restricted pointer makes an aliasing assertion that is limited to its block.

EXERCISES

1. What are bitwise operations?
2. What is the purpose of a complement operator? To what types of operands does it apply? What is the precedence and associativity of this operator? How can the 2's complement of a decimal number be found?
3. Describe the three logical bitwise operators. What is the purpose of each?

4. What is masking? Explain with an example.

5. How can a particular bit be toggled on and off repeatedly? Which logical bitwise operation is used for this?

6. What are precedence and associativity of bitwise shift operators?

7. What is a type qualifier?

8. Describe the use of the `const` type qualifier.

9. Compare `volatile` and `restrict` type qualifiers.

10. What is a memory model in C? Describe the different memory models used in C.

11. What is a far pointer? How does it differ from near and huge pointers?

12. Explain the use of `farmalloc()` with an example.

13. What are command-line arguments? What are their data types?

14. When a parameter is passed to a program from command line, how is the program execution initiated? Where do the parameters appear?

15. What useful purpose can be served by command-line arguments when executing a program involving the use of data files?

16. What is a macro?

17. Compare macros and functions.

18. How is a multiline macro defined?

19. What is meant by a preprocessor directive?

20. What is the difference between `#include <stdio.h>` and `#include "stdio.h"`?

21. What is the scope of a preprocessor directive?

22. Describe the preprocessor directives # and ##? What is the purpose of each?

23. What is meant by conditional compilation? How is conditional compilation carried out? What preprocessor directives are used for this purpose?

24. Define a mask and write C programs using masking to solve the following.

    (a) Copy the odd bits (bits 1, 3, 5, ..., 15) and place 0's in the even bit locations (bits 0, 2, 4, ..., 14) of a 16-bit unsigned integer number.

    (b) Toggle the values of bits 1 to 6 of a 16-bit integer while preserving all the remaining bits.

25. Write a function `setbits(x,p,n,y)` that returns x with the n bits that begin at position p set to the rightmost n bits of y, leaving the other bits unchanged.

26. Write a function `invert(x,p,n)` that returns x with the n bits that begin at position p inverted (i.e., 1 changed into 0 and vice versa), leaving the others unchanged.

27. Write a C program that will illustrate the equivalence between

    (a) Shifting a binary number to the left n bits and multiplying the binary number by 2^n

    (b) Shifting a binary number to the right n bits and dividing the binary number by 2^n

28. Write a function `rightrot(x,n)` that returns the value of the integer x rotated to the right by n positions.

29. Write a symbolic constant or macro definitions for each of the following.

    (a) Define a symbolic constant *PI* to represent the value 3.1415927.

    (b) Define a macro *AREA* that will calculate the area of a circle in terms of its radius. Use the *PI* defined above.

30. Write a multiline macro named 'interest' that will compute the compound interest formula

    $$F = P(1 + i)^n$$

    where F is the future amount of money that will accumulate after n years, P is the principal amount, and i is the rate of interest expressed as percentage.

31. Write a macro named *MAX* that uses the conditional operator (?:) to determine the largest number among three integer numbers.

32. Define a preprocessor macro `swap(t, x, y)` that will swap two arguments x and y of a given type t.

33. Define a preprocessor macro to select

    - the least significant bit from an `unsigned char`
    - the nth (assuming that the least significant is 0) bit from an `unsigned char`

34. Define plain macros for the following. An infinite loop structure called `forever`.

35. Define parameterized macros for the following.

    - Swapping two values
    - Finding the absolute value of a number
    - Finding the centre of a rectangle whose top-left and bottom-right coordinates are given (requires two macros)

36. Write directives for the following.

    - Defining `Small` as an unsigned char when the symbol `PC` is defined, and as unsigned short otherwise
    - Including the file `basics.h` in another file when the symbol `CPP` is not defined
    - Including the file `debug.h` in another file when release is 0, or `beta.h` when release is 1, or `final.h` when release is greater than 1

37. Write a macro named `When` which returns the current date and time as a string (e.g., "25 Sep 2005, 12:30:55"). Similarly, write a macro named `Where` which returns the current location in a file as a string (e.g., "file.h: line 25").

PROJECT QUESTIONS

Write a program that reads in employee data from two unsorted binary files (the format of these files is described below), merges the data from two files together in sorted order on employee name, and outputs the resulting sorted list of employee data to a binary file. Additionally, as the program reads each employee's information from an input file it should print it to standard output in tabular format, and before the program writes the resulting sorted merged data from the two input files, it should also print it to standard output in tabular format, and print out the total number of employees and the average salary . '\t' is the tab character that can

be used to get good tabular output. The three files used by the program (two input and one output) will be passed to the program via command line arguments.

The program will read employee data into a singly linked list. The employee list should be maintained and sorted alphabetically by employee name. Do not assume that the employee records in the input file are already in sorted order. However, the program should write the list to an output binary file in sorted order.

Bibliography and References

- A. L. Kelly and I. Pohl (1999), *A Book on C*, 4th edn, Pearson, Singapore.
- A. N. Kamthane (2002), *Programming ANSI and Turbo C*, 1st edn, Pearson, Singapore.
- A. Pandey (2003), *Programming in C*, 1st edn, Cybertech Publications, India.
- B. A. Forouzan and R. F. Gilberg (2001), *A Structured Programming Approach using C*, 2nd edn, Thomson Asia, Singapore.
- B. Kerninghan and D. Ritchie (1999), *C Programming Language*, 2nd edn, Prentice Hall, India.
- B. S. Gottfried (2000), *Programming with C*, 2nd edn, Tata Mcgraw-Hill, India.
- C. L. Tondo and S. E. Gimple (1989), *The C Answer Book*, 1st edn, Pearson, Singapore.
- Don Gookin (2004), C *Programming – 6 books in 1*, Willey Dreamtech Pvt Ltd
- E. Balaguruswamy (1998), *ANSI C*, 2nd edn, Tata McGraw-Hill, India.
- ftp://scitsc.wlv.ac.uk//pub/cprog/
- Gary J. Bronson (2001), *ANSI C*, 3rd edn, Thomson Asia, Singapore.
- Greg Perry (2000), *C by Example*, 1st edn, Prentice Hall, India.
- H. M. Deitel (2001), *C How to Program—Introducing C++ and Java*, 3rd edn, Pearson, India.
- H. Schildt (2000), *Complete Reference C*, 4th edn, Tata McGraw-Hill, India.
- Herbert Schildt (2000), *C: The Complete Reference*, 4th edn, Tata McGraw-Hill Education
- Ivor Horton (2006), *Beginning C-From Novice to Professional*, 4th edn, USA.

- Jeri R Hanly, Elliot B Koffman (2007), *Problem solving and Programming in C*, 5th edn, Pearson Education-Addison Wisley, USA
- K.N.King. *C Programming- A Modern Approach*, 2nd edn, W.W.Norton, NewYork, London
- Peter van der Linden (1994), *Expert C Programming: Deep C Secrets*, 1st edn, Prentice Hall, India.
- R. Heathfield et al. (2000), *C Unleashed*, 1st edn, Techmedia, India.
- R. Radcliffe (1992), *Encyclopedia C*, 1st edn, BPB Publications, India.
- S. Kaicker (1996), *The Complete ANSI C*, 1st edn, BPB Publications, India.
- S. Prata (1991), *C Primer Plus*, 3rd edn, Techmedia, India.
- S. Summit (2000), *C Programming FAQs*, 1st edn, Pearson, Singapore.
- Samuel P. Harbison III, Guy L. Steele Jr. (2007), *C: A Reference Manual*, 5th edn, Pearson Education, India
- Stephen G. Kochan (2005), *Programming in C*, 3rd edn, Pearson Education, India
- Stephen G. Kochan (2005), *Programming in C*, 3rd edn, Sams Publishing, Indiana
- Stephen Prata (1998), *C Primer Plus®*, 3rd edn, Sams Publishing, USA
- Y. Kanetkar (1991), *Let Us C*, 4th edn (revised), BPB Publications, India.
- Y. Kanetkar (2001), *Let Us C Solution*, 1st edn, BPB Publications, India.
- Y. Kanetkar (2001), *Understanding Pointers in C*, 3rd edn, BPB Publications, India.

- http://cplus.about.com
- http://cplus.about.com/mbiopage.htm
- http://en.wikipedia.org/wiki/C_syntax
- http://goforit.unk.edu/cprogram/default.htm
- http://mathbits.com/
- www.old.dkuug.dk/JTC1/SC22/WG14/docs/c9x/

- http://publications.gbdirect.co.uk/c_book
- http://students.cs.byu.edu/~cs130ta/index.html
- http://students.cs.byu.edu/~cs130ta/readings/readings.html
- http://users.evtek.fi/~jaanah/IntroC/DBeech/index.htm
- http://www.d.umn.edu/~gshute/C/statements.html

- http://www.netnam.vn/unescocourse/os/operatin.htm
- http://www.minich.com/education/psu/cplusplus/index.htm
- http://www.cs.utk.edu/~cs102/lectures/index.html
- http://www-ee.eng.hawaii.edu/Courses/EE150/Book/chap7/
- subsection2.1.3.1.html
- http://www.coronadoenterprises.com
- http://www.eskimo.com
- http://www.ics.uci.edu/~dan
- http://www.fredosaurus.com/notes-cpp/arrayptr/26arraysas
- pointers.html
- http://www.ibiblio.org/pub/languages/
- http://www.cs.cf.ac.uk/Dave/C/CE.html
- http://www.cplusplus.com/doc/tutorial/
- http://www.cs.mun.ca/~michael/c/problems.html
- http://www.comp.nus.edu.sg/~hchia/Teaching/cs1101c/
- tut10/tut10.html
- http://www.digitalmars.com/
- http://www.borland.com/
- http://www.function-pointer.org/
- http://www.juicystudio.com
- http://www.antioffline.com/h/c/
- http://www.coronadoenterprises.com/coders/index.html
- http://www.mrx.net/c/
- http://www.scit.wlv.ac.uk/cbook/
- http://www.cs.cmu.edu
- http://www-h.eng.cam.ac.uk/help/tpl/languages/C/
- teaching_C/node1.html
- http://www.its.strath.ac.uk/courses/c/tableofcontents3_1.
- html
- http://www.scit.wlv.ac.uk/~jphb/cbook/html/chap10.bit.
- fields.htm
- http://www.xploiter.com/mirrors/cprogram/default.htm
- http://yolinux.com/

Index

Related Titles

DATA STRUCTURES USING C [9780198065449]

Reema Thareja,

Assistant Professor, Shyama Prasad Mukherjee College for Women, University of Delhi

The book starts off with an overview of the concepts of C programming followed by pointers and functions, and then connects these concepts and applies them to the study of various data structures such as arrays, strings, linked lists, stacks, queues, trees, and graphs.

Key Features

- Provides a brush-up of C programming basics before delving into the analysis of data structures
- Includes a chapter on AVL trees, M-way search trees, B and B+ trees, red-black trees, and splay trees
- Makes use of numerous algorithms, programs, and illustrations to explain the concepts

DISCRETE MATHEMATICS [9780198065432]

S.K. Chakraborty, *Associate Professor, Department of Applied Mathematics, BIT, Ranchi;*

B.K. Sarkar, *Assistant Professor, Department of Information Technology and MCA, BIT, Ranchi*

The book begins with a detailed analysis of modern mathematical concepts like sets, relation and functions, and matrices, and then delves into core concepts of discrete mathematics like logic and truth tables, groups, order relation and lattices, Boolean algebra, trees, and graphs.

- Lays emphasis on the applicability of mathematical structures to computer science
- Includes separate chapters on combinatorics and automata theory

- Contains numerous solved examples and chapter-end exercises

OBJECT-ORIENTED PROGRAMMING WITH C++, 2/e (with CD) [9780198065302]

Sourav Sahay, *Lead Consultant, Capgemini, USA*

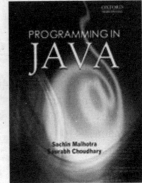

This second edition imparts a clear understanding of objects and the methods of modelling them in the object-oriented programming system.

Key Features

- New chapter on data structures containing new and original algorithms, especially an elegant and simple recursive algorithm for inserting nodes into trees
- New sections on explicit constructors, command-line arguments, and re-throwing exceptions
- Accompanied with a CD that contains the codes of all programs

PROGRAMMING IN JAVA [9780198063582]

Sachin Malhotra, *Chairperson, PGDM-IT, IMS Ghaziabad;*

Saurabh Choudhary, *Dean, Academics, IMS Ghaziabad*

The book provides a comprehensive discussion of the latest features of Java such as enumerations, generics, logging API, console class, StringBuilder class, Network Interface class, and assertions.

- Includes the concepts of object-oriented programming before discussing the fundamentals of Java
- Provides line-by-line explanations along with comments in the programs for an in-depth understanding of the programming examples
- Introduces advanced topics such as Java beans, servlets, and swings

Other Related Titles

- 9780198066231 Varsha H. Patil: *Data Structures Using C++*
- 9780198071068 Chander Kumar Nagpal: *Formal Language and Automata Theory*
- 9780198086390 Reema Thareja: *Introduction to C Programming*
- 9780198065289 Pradip Dey and Manas Ghosh: *Programming in C, 2e*
- 9780198083962 Bhushan Trivedi: *Programming with ANSI C++*

Visit us at www.oup.co.in and www.oupinheonline.com